Guide to
NetWare 5.0/5.1:
Network Administration
Enhanced Edition

David Doering
Ted Simpson

**COURSE
TECHNOLOGY**
——————★——————
™
THOMSON LEARNING

Australia • Canada • Mexico • Singapore • Spain • United Kingdom • United States

**COURSE
TECHNOLOGY**
™

THOMSON LEARNING

Guide to NetWare 5.0/5.1: Network Administration *Enhanced Edition* is published by Course Technology.

Associate Publisher: Kristen Duerr	**Production Editor:** Anne Valsangiacomo	**Text Designer:** GEX Publishing Services
Managing Editor: Stephen Solomon	**Development Editor:** Jim Markham	**Cover Designer:** Efrat Reis
Product Manager: Laura Hildebrand	**Quality Assurance Manager:** John Bosco	**Marketing Manager:** Toby Shelton
Associate Product Manager: Elizabeth Wessen	**Editorial Assistant:** Janet Eras	**Composition House:** GEX Publishing Services

BRIEF Contents

TABLE OF

Contents

CHAPTER FIVE
Planning the Network File System **201**

CHAPTER TEN
Managing Trustee Assignments and File Attributes 473

Preface

Our book—*Guide to NetWare 5.0/5.1: Network Administration Enhanced Edition*—is an in-depth study of configuring and managing networks using the Novell NetWare 5.0 and 5.1 network operating systems. Each chapter contains a thorough explanation of concepts, tools, and techniques, which build progressively from creating to administering a complete NetWare network.

We designed this book to provide you with the knowledge and skills you need to pass Novell's Certified Novell Administrator (CNA) exam for NetWare 5.1. This will let you take advantage of the many job opportunities in the rapidly growing field of network administration.

NetWare Versions

This book focuses on NetWare 5.0 and 5.1, the latest versions of the software. Earlier NetWare 4.x software shares many similarities with this latest release. However, NetWare 5.1 incorporates numerous changes in utilities and architecture—for example, it now includes native IP support for broad application in enterprise environments. The new Novell Client software offers a wider range of services through native Windows 95/98 utilities, making the administrator's tasks easier and more familiar.

Approach

We wrote this book for NetWare 5.0 and NetWare 5.1 networks with client workstations running Windows 95 or Windows 98 as well as the Novell Client that ships with NetWare 5.1 (the most up-to-date configuration at the time of the book). While workstations running earlier versions of the Client may log in to NetWare 5.1, they will not support the full set of functions in the administrator's tools and should be upgraded before starting the class.

We use a sample case—Cunningham, Burns, and Evans Laboratories (CBE Labs)—as our primary example in implementing NetWare 5.0. In Appendices B and C, the projects focus on installing and implementing NetWare 5.1. This example is reflected in the many illustrations in the book. Each chapter also includes a set of hands-on projects and case projects for additional practice with NetWare. Your instructor may also run a continuing project (Northwestern Technical College) in configuring and administering NetWare. When you complete this book, you will have the experience you need to actually administer a Novell network.

Features

To aid you in fully understanding NetWare 5.0 and 5.1 concepts, there are many features in this book designed to improve its pedagogical value.

- Two additional appendices that detail how to upgrade to NetWare 5.1 and use the new features of this version.

- **Chapter Objectives** Each chapter begins with a detailed list of the objectives. A glance at these objectives will give you an overview of the chapter and provide a review and study aid.

- **Illustrations and Tables** Numerous illustrations aid you in the visualization of common setup steps, theories, and concepts. In addition, many tables provide details and comparisons of both practical and theoretical information.

- **Chapter Summary** Each chapter contains a summary to review the primary concepts covered.

- **Command Summary** Each chapter contains a capsule summary of any command line utilities taught. The Command Summary provides you with a convenient resource for these commands.

- **Key Terms** Each chapter includes a list of any new terms introduced. All terms have definitions in the Glossary at the back of the book.

- **Review Questions** End-of-chapter assessment begins with a set of review questions that reinforce ideas introduced in each chapter.

- **Hands-on Projects** Each chapter provides numerous hands-on projects aimed at providing you with real-world implementation experience.

- **Case Projects** Located at the end of each chapter are case projects, which allow you to implement the skills and knowledge gained in the chapter using real-world scenarios.

Text and Graphic Conventions

Wherever appropriate, additional information and projects have been added to this book to help you better understand what is being discussed in the chapter. The icons used in this textbook to alert you to additional materials are described below.

The Note icon is used to present additional helpful material related to the subject being described.

Each Hands-on Project in this book is preceded by the Hands-on icon and a description of the project that follows.

The Tip icon presents a procedure or approach used by administrators in the field to more effectively handle a given task. The Tips help you perform with a greater level of competence by learning time-saving or effort-saving shortcuts.

The Caution icon indicates a common mistake or misunderstanding about working with NetWare 5.0. The Cautions help you avoid errors and the effort needed to correct them.

Case Project icons mark the running Case Project. These projects are more involved, scenario-based assignments. In this extensive case example, you are asked to implement independently what you have learned.

Instructor's Materials

The following teaching tools are available when this book is used in a classroom setting. All of the teaching tools available with this book are provided to the instructor on a single CD-ROM.

Electronic Instructor's Manual The Instructor's Manual that accompanies this textbook includes:

- Additional instructional material to assist in class preparation, including suggestions for lecture topics, suggested lab activities, tips on setting up a lab for the hands-on projects, and alternative lab setup ideas in situations where lab resources are limited.

- Solutions to all end-of-chapter materials, including the Hands-on and Case Projects.

ExamView Pro 3.0 This textbook is accompanied by ExamView®, a powerful testing software package that allows instructors to create and administer printed, computer (LAN-based), and Internet exams. ExamView includes hundreds of questions that correspond to the topics covered in this text, enabling students to generate detailed study guides that include page references for further review. The computer-based and Internet testing components allow students to take exams at their computers, and also save the instructor time by grading each exam automatically.

PowerPoint Presentations This book comes with Microsoft PowerPoint slides for each chapter. These slides are included as a teaching aid for classroom presentation, to make available to students on the network for review, or to be printed for classroom distribution. Instructors, please feel at liberty to add your own slides for additional topics.

ACKNOWLEDGMENTS

Creating a book of this magnitude is an incredibly complex process with many people involved in writing, editing, testing, and production. This version, along with its predecessors, benefits from hundreds of individuals who made it possible. We offer our thanks to them.

In particular, we thank the good people at Course Technology: Stephen Solomon, who got the ball rolling; David George and Laura Hildebrand, for shepherding the project; and especially Deb Kaufmann, Jim Markham, and Anne Valsangiacomo, for editing and overseeing the production.

Ted Simpson would like to thank his wife Mary, whose loving and patient help enabled him to complete this project. In addition, any success this book achieves is ultimately due to his parents, William and Rosemarie, who have made many sacrifices to provide a stable and motivating environment for learning and growing.

David Doering would like to thank his wife, Keri Lyn, who endured many nights patiently awaiting each chapter's completion. Her unfailing support made this possible. He would also like to thank his daughter Serena Noelle, born in the middle of the project, whose unending love made it worth doing. He also offers heartfelt thanks to his mother, Kim, who always encouraged writing. Finally, David would like to acknowledge the support of Edward Liebing of Novell Research for technical support and insights.

1

NETWORKING BASICS

In this chapter, you will learn:

♦ Explain the advantages of a local area network

♦ Identify and describe the hardware and software components that make up a local area network

♦ Develop a recommendation for implementing a local area network system

♦ Describe the responsibilities of a Certified Novell Administrator

The 1980s brought a major change in the way data was processed in organizations. Traditional centralized data processing on minicomputers and mainframe computers gave way to decentralized or distributed personalized applications and to productivity tools running on desktop and notebook-sized microcomputers. Along with the rapid development of microcomputer hardware and application software, our ability to connect these devices and applications to communicate and share resources has also developed. This rapid pace of development continues today, as the Internet ties local systems into a global network. In this chapter you will learn about the advantages of various computer network types and how to select the appropriate type for a given situation. You will learn how to use the NetWare network operating system to meet the requirements and challenges of integrating microcomputers into a network that can facilitate communications, share resources, and exchange data. You will also explore the role you will play as a network administrator and learn about the Certified Novell Administrator (CNA) program.

COMPUTER NETWORKS

When two or more computers are connected so they can communicate with each other, that setup is called a **computer network**. A computer network that exists in one location, such as a building, is called a **local area network (LAN)**. Tying two or more LANs in different geographic locations, such as cities, creates a **wide area network (WAN)**. Although this text focuses on LANs, the material covered applies to WANs as well. Figure 1-1 illustrates LANs and WANs.

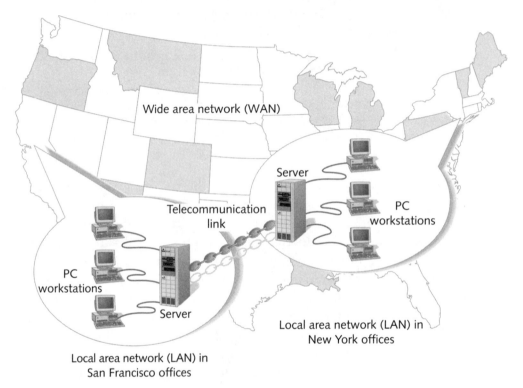

Figure 1-1   Local area and wide area networks

Do not confuse LANs and WANs with the global Internet or with corporate intranets. Although all are networks and link personal computers and servers, the **Internet** is a loose confederation of servers that share data among millions of users worldwide, using a common protocol, TCP/IP. LANs are tightly controlled, usually limited to one company (as are WANs), and may use protocols other than TCP/IP. **Intranets** are private networks that use the same protocol as the Internet to offer access to internal information. Intranets can be set up on both LANs and WANs, and who can access the network is usually controlled tightly.

The **network administrator** is the person responsible for the network. The role of network administrator is one of the most exciting, challenging, and important jobs in an organization's information systems department. However, it can also be one of the most frustrating jobs, because the field changes rapidly and the job involves many different responsibilities. These responsibilities range from hardware (e.g., computers and cables) to software (e.g., operating systems and applications) to working with people (e.g., users and vendors). Therefore, to be a successful network administrator, you will need to thoroughly understand the basic components of the network system. On this foundation you can build the skills you will need to perform your job. In this section you will learn about the basic components of a LAN. You will also learn about some options to consider when deciding how to construct a LAN.

A LAN is more completely defined as a high-speed communication system of cables and cards (hardware), along with instructions (software), that lets different types of computers and peripherals communicate and share resources over short distances, such as within a building or room. LANs differ significantly from older mainframe computers and mini-computers. With a **mainframe computer** or **minicomputer** system, the mainframe computer or minicomputer running the programs does all the processing. The user workstations are **terminals**, used simply as input and output devices for entering data and displaying results, without any computing power of their own. This type of setup is called **centralized processing**, because all the processing is done by the computer connected to the terminals.

A LAN uses **microcomputers** (also called **personal computers** or **PCs**) as workstations, each of which has its own computing ability. The processing is done at the microcomputer workstations instead of at the central computer, and the LAN ties the microcomputer workstations together as a high-speed communication system. The LAN is used primarily to give the workstations access to shared data files and other hardware devices such as printers. This type of processing is called **distributed processing**, because the processing is distributed to each of the workstations. In addition to the workstations, LANs also use servers. A **server** is a specialized computer that provides network resources for workstations. Several types of servers may be found on a network. Most common is a **network server**, commonly called simply a server, which provides shared data and application storage for users. A **print server** allows users to share printers. An **application server** is used with **client/server applications**, such as database systems, that split the processing between the server and the workstations. In this situation, the application server runs the server portion of the application, and the client portion runs on the users' workstations. A server that uses NetWare can perform all these functions and is called a **NetWare server**. Figure 1-2 shows the differences between centralized processing and distributed processing.

The term **NetWare file server** was used in NetWare 3.x documentation. In NetWare 4.1 and later versions, the term used is NetWare server.

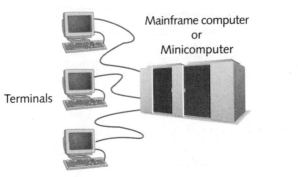
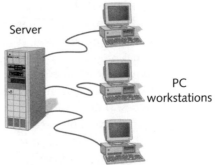

Centralized processing
- Terminals have no processing capability
- All processing done on Mainframe computer or minicomputer

Distributed processing
- PC workstations have their own processing capability
- Processing done on PC workstations

Figure 1-2   Centralized processing and distributed processing

Local Area Network Advantages

Although distributed processing can be performed by standalone computers not connected by a network, a LAN offers many advantages in sharing resources and improving communications. These advantages make distributed processing a strong competitor to traditional centralized minicomputer and mainframe computer systems, the traditional way to share resources and communicate. As a network administrator, to recommend a network system you need to be aware of the following LAN advantages.

Cost Savings

One important benefit of a LAN is cost savings, and management is always happy to hear how you can save money for the organization. A LAN provides the most direct cost savings from sharing and working with data in a group. For example, e-mail and work-flow software show significant cost savings over manually copying information. Costs can also be saved in hardware and software; for example, several workstations can share one high-quality printer, and an application package that requires 100 MB of disk space can be run from the server rather than installed on individual workstations.

Time Savings

A less tangible but perhaps even more important advantage of networks is the time saved by giving users access to shared data and communication capability. Without a LAN, users must resort to a "sneaker net," in which shared files are copied onto a floppy disk and physically transferred to another user's computer workstation by being carried on foot (wearing sneakers!) and copied to another hard drive.

Another time-saving benefit of LANs is that they allow the network administrator to install and maintain a software package on a server, a computer dedicated to storing commonly used program and data files, where it is accessible to all users. This is often preferable to installing the package on each user's workstation and then spending more time going to each workstation to configure that software or install an upgraded version.

Centralized Data

Without a network, certain crucial and often used data files, such as customer and inventory files, may need to be duplicated on several workstations, using too much data storage and requiring the difficult task of keeping all files current. Storing database files on the network server lets the information be kept current while also giving many users access to it. This ability to provide shared access to centralized database files makes the LAN a competitive alternative to centralized processing.

In addition to providing shared access to centralized data files, a network server used for centralized data storage makes regular backups of data easier. This backup ability helps establish a disaster recovery system for the organization. Data stored on users' workstations is rarely backed up, making it very difficult to recover lost data if a workstation crashes or the building or equipment is physically damaged. Keeping all of an organization's critical data on the network server lets you back up data every night. Each week you can store a backup tape offsite, to recover if the building is damaged. If a disaster occurs, you can restore the software and data onto a new server and get the organization up and running again very quickly. In contrast, the alternative requires you to back up the data on each workstation and restore each individual workstation's software and data after a disaster.

Security

At first glance, centralizing company data on a network server may seem to cause more security problems than it solves, because more users have potential access to the data. In the case of NetWare servers, however, data can be made more secure on the server than data stored on local workstations. The reason is that NetWare provides many security features such as requiring passwords to gain access to the network and restricting user access to network files. In addition, user accounts can be limited to specific times, such as normal working hours, and to specific workstations, making it difficult for an intruder to gain access to the system by logging in with a user's name and password after normal office hours. Compare those security advantages to the alternative of storing data on a local workstation. With data on an individual workstation, anyone with a little knowledge of PC operating systems and physical access to the office can sit down at the computer and access the applications and data.

Fault Tolerance

Storing data on individual workstations increases the chance of data loss due to operator error, software bugs, computer viruses, or hardware failure on the workstation. Data stored on the network servers can be placed on microcomputers specially designed and configured to protect against data loss caused by software or hardware problems. This is called **fault tolerance**. For example, with a NetWare server the data stored on a disk drive can be protected by a process called mirroring. **Mirroring** uses two identical disk drives linked so that all files on one disk drive are automatically duplicated on the second disk drive. If one drive fails, the data is still accessible on the second drive. **Duplexing** also involves two drives, except that the data goes through two controller boards rather than one, as with mirroring.

Communication

The high-speed communication a LAN provides between network computers creates opportunities for major changes in office management. For example, workgroup-oriented applications such as electronic mail and scheduling are commonly used on LANs. **Electronic mail (e-mail) applications** let users send messages and files directly to other users on the LAN. Many users feel that e-mail is quicker and more effective than voice mail, particularly in contrast to playing "phone tag" with hard-to-reach people. **Scheduling applications** let individuals and groups store their schedules on the server, where other users (with appropriate permission) can access them. This can save time by letting managers check the schedules of people and facilities quickly, to find free time in which to schedule meetings.

 Network communication systems are rapidly incorporating support for new applications that use both video and voice data. Video conferencing and computers integrated with telephone systems are just beginning to become popular in offices and may become widely used in the near future. This will enable members of a conference to see data being presented as well as see the reactions of other members.

Additional advantages and conveniences of LANs are too numerous to include in this chapter. Examining the major advantages, however, makes it clear why the use of LANs has been growing at such a fast pace.

Types of Network Operating Systems

The **network operating system (NOS)** is the software that controls network services. Depending on their design, NOSs can be defined as either peer-to-peer or client-server. **Peer-to-peer** NOSs enable workstations to communicate and share data with each other without the need for a dedicated server computer. **Client-server** NOSs use one computer as a dedicated server that acts as a central storage unit for client workstations.

NetWare is a client-server operating system, because its operation depends on a dedicated NetWare server. Figure 1-3 shows Peer-to-peer and client-server networks. In this section you will learn about the features of both client-server and peer-to-peer NOSs and how they compare to the NetWare operating system.

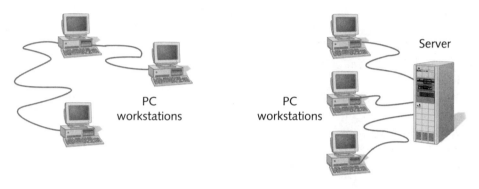

Server

PC
workstations

PC
workstations

Peer-to-peer network
•Data stored on PC workstations
•PC workstations *can* access data on
  other PC workstations

Client-server network
•Data stored on server
•PC workstations *cannot* access
  data on other PC workstations

Figure 1-3   Peer-to-peer and client-server networks

Peer-to-Peer Networks

In peer-to-peer networks, each computer can be both a server and a client workstation, allowing any computer to share files with other users on the network. Each computer can also function as a print server, enabling other users to share its printer. The main advantage of peer-to-peer NOSs is the ability to implement low-cost networks by saving the expense of dedicating a computer as a server. In addition, peer-to-peer systems let users in workgroups share data files and communicate easily with each other. In theory, this reduces the burden on the network administrator by placing more responsibility for data sharing in the hands of the users. However, large peer-to-peer networks can be very difficult to administer, because shared data can exist in several locations, making data more difficult to retrieve, secure, and back up. For example, if a workstation containing data needed by other users fails to boot its system or shuts down unexpectedly, other users may lose data or may not be able to access the information they need. In this section you will learn about several peer-to-peer NOSs as well as their advantages and disadvantages, compared to Novell NetWare.

LANtastic   LANtastic is a peer-to-peer NOS that is produced by Artisoft Corporation. Written for the Windows 95 environment, LANtastic is a great network system for sharing files and communicating among DOS-based as well as Windows-based computers. It is very popular for small networks in which all computers are attached to the same cable system. The primary advantages of LANtastic are low cost and ease of installation, making it an ideal choice for networks of fewer than 10 workstations. The major drawback of LANtastic as a peer-to-peer NOS is that it is not designed to support high-demand network workstations with file sizes over 1 MB.

Windows for Workgroups and Windows 95/98   Microsoft added peer-to-peer networking capabilities to its Windows software to create Windows for Workgroups (also called Windows 3.11). Microsoft again enhanced these networking capabilities in Windows 95 and Windows 98. These peer-to-peer networks are adequate for small systems of under five users. They eliminate the need to obtain, learn, and integrate another NOS. Windows 95/98 also provides each workstation with e-mail (through the Windows Exchange client). A scheduling client (Outlook) is included with Microsoft Office 97. However, any Windows 95 workstation running as a peer-to-peer server needs at least 16 MB of RAM (and preferably 32 MB). Otherwise a user of that system will note a significant slowdown when other users request data.

Windows NT Workstation   Windows NT represents a more powerful "big brother" of the Windows family of operating systems. Windows NT is a leading-edge operating system designed to support the advanced capabilities of Pentium- and multiprocessor-based computers and is a completely different operating system from Windows. Developed simultaneously with other Microsoft Windows products, Windows NT was written to take advantage of the 32-bit instruction set offered by Intel 80386 and later processors. (Windows, on the other hand, is based on the 16-bit instruction set of earlier Intel processors, and even Windows 95 retains some of the 16-bit heritage.) Windows NT provides additional levels of reliability, protection, and security not available in the other Windows products.

Windows NT comes in two variants: Windows NT Server and Windows NT Workstation. Windows NT Server is a full-featured NOS capable of administering large, client-server networks (preferably under 200 users). Like NetWare, Windows NT Server is tailored to provide a large number of users with file and print services, although real-world experience has shown that NT cannot handle as many users per server as NetWare. Windows NT Workstation can be used on clients to an NT Server, or on a server for a small peer-to-peer network. Although NT Workstation software is limited to 10 simultaneous connections, Windows NT Server can theoretically have hundreds. When used in peer-to-peer networks, the Windows NT Workstation operating system needs at least 32 MB of RAM.

Microsoft has announced that Windows 98 will be the last incarnation of that line. In the future, Windows NT will serve for both home and business use. For now, however, Microsoft is recommending Windows NT Workstation as the operating system for businesses and Windows 95/98 as the operating system for home computing.

Client-Server Networks

In a client-server network, servers running specialized software provide services to client workstation computers instead of having the workstations share data among themselves. As a result, client-server networks, such as those using NetWare, provide centralized data storage, reliability, and high performance not currently attainable with peer-to-peer networks. One reason for the increased performance and reliability of client-server networks, such as NetWare is that a server's hardware can be specialized to share files by providing multiple high-speed disk channels along with a large memory for file caching. In Chapter 2 you will learn about many hardware options that enable you to increase the performance and reliability of your servers. The rest of this section compares and contrasts the client-server NOSs currently available.

NetWare 3 and 4   Although NetWare 5.0 is now Novell's flagship NOS, Novell continues to sell and support NetWare 3 (currently at version 3.2) and version 4.11, the predecessor to version 5. Both NetWare 3.2 and NetWare 4.11 are widely installed and highly stable network platforms that network administrators depend on for consistent and stable performance.

The primary difference between NetWare 3 and NetWare 4 was the introduction of the Novell Directory Services or NDS (which continues in NetWare 5.0). NetWare 3 had a flat database, called the Bindery, that stored information about network files, volumes, users, and printers. This worked well when networks consisted of one or two servers and under 50 users. However, when networks began to include a dozen or more servers and hundreds of users, the Bindery became a bottleneck for administration.

NDS, in contrast, is immensely scalable and can support more than a million objects on the network. In essence, the NDS database is shared among all the servers so users logging in can do so from any workstation and be recognized. With the Bindery, users had to log into each server, because the Bindery database was not shared among the servers.

NetWare 3.x was **server-centric**, which means that the network was managed by each server individually. NetWare 5.0 is **network-centric**, which means that the network as a whole is managed through a centralized administration tool. Administration is through **Novell Directory Services (NDS)**, which uses a database to store information about the various network resources. NetWare has a set of NDS administration utilities to let the network administrator manage the resources in the NDS database. You will learn about NDS in Chapter 4, and you'll work with it in many other chapters as you add resources to the network.

NetWare 5   NetWare 5.0 is Novell's latest version of the NetWare NOS. It is a 32-bit dedicated NOS that is highly specialized to provide a variety of services to client workstations. It is the fastest and most scalable NOS available today.

This book focuses on NetWare 5.0. The term IntranetWare 4.11 refers to the most recently preceding version of NetWare. For marketing reasons, the name was changed from NetWare to IntranetWare for one year. All versions of NetWare will be referred to by their version number, which is how most users refer to them. In other words, IntranetWare 4.11 will be referred to as NetWare 4.11.

NetWare 5.0 incorporates enhancements to NetWare 4.11, and adds previously unavailable features. It continues the use of NDS from NetWare 4.x, with its own NDS enhancements, better graphical utilities, and improved file and printing services. NetWare 5.0 is readily adaptable by large firms that need to support multiple servers in multiple locations.

Enhancements released with Netware 4 include:

- Enhanced security
- Improved long filename support
- Increased directory entry volume capacity, from 2 million to 16 million
- NetWare Client 32 workstation client software
- NetWare Application Manager and NetWare Application Launcher network application management software
- Enhanced printer support for printers attached to workstations
- Various network operating system patches and updates
- Enhanced installation procedures, including a utility to plan the 5.0 network
- Major enhancements of the NetWare Administrator utility, which is the network administrator's main utility for managing the network; the enhancements include a Windows 95 version, a configurable toolbar, and the ability to simultaneously manage multiple networks
- Support for multiple microprocessors in the NetWare server
- Software licensing management capabilities
- Integrated support for NetWare IP, Novell's version of the Internet Protocol (IP)
- Enhanced backup abilities
- Novell's new network printing system, NetWare Distributed Print Services (NDPS)

Features introduced with NetWare 5.0 include:

- GUI installation tool
- NDPS now included in the installation process

- TCP/IP now the default protocol for communications
- NetWare Storage Services (greatly enhances volume and disk management)

These features are discussed in the main text of this book. Selected new features, such as NDPS, are covered in more detail in relevant chapters. Together, this coverage will introduce you to NetWare 5.0 and provide the skills to manage a network with it. The many improvements added to NetWare 5.0, its acknowledged stability, and the increased need for large multiserver networks in industry will lead many organizations to upgrade their NetWare servers to NetWare 5.0.

 The scope of the changes between these earlier versions of NetWare and NetWare 5 requires training and planning on the part of the network administrator before the conversion can take place.

Banyan Vines   A major strength of the Banyan Vines network is its "StreetTalk" protocol, which allows users to log in once to a multiserver network and then to access any server to which they have been granted access rights. This is the same network–centric approach found in NetWare's NDS. However, NDS follows the industry X.500 standard on an Intel platform, implementing a network global database, whereas Vines implements X.500 on a Unix platform. Despite this disadvantage, the Banyan Vines NOS, which existed several years before the release of NetWare 4.0, has maintained a respectable share of the client-server NOS market in the Unix world.

Windows NT Server   The Windows NT Server client-server operating system provides client workstations with centralized and highly fault-tolerant high-speed access to data. The advantages of Windows NT are that it provides centralized management of multiple servers through the familiar Windows environment and that it supports access to TCP/IP and NetWare servers as well as mainframe computers. A final advantage is its usefulness as an application server, a server that runs the server portion of client/server applications. Many vendors offer client/server applications designed to run on the Windows NT server.

 Many network administrators are using NetWare as their main network operating system for file and print services, and using Windows NT Server as application servers.

Network Components

As defined previously, a LAN is basically a system that enables computers of different types to communicate and share data. As a network administrator, you need to understand the hardware and software components that make up the network so that you can select and maintain a network system that will meet the communication needs of your organization. This chapter introduces you to a network system's hardware and software components and explains why NetWare is the most prevalent NOS in use today. Chapters 2 and 3 will give you an in-depth view of the microcomputer hardware components and network cable system as well as the options you will need to know about to select and maintain computers on the network.

Hardware Components

Hardware components are the most obvious parts of a network system to identify, because they can be easily seen. The hardware components of a typical network are shown in Figure 1-4.

Server The first stop on your tour of the network is the computer that is the network server, called a NetWare server in NetWare 5.0 networks. Many who are familiar with minicomputers and mainframe computers tend to think of the server in terms of network control. In a LAN, however, a server is actually a servant of the network, responding to the requests of workstations for access to the files and software stored on the server's disk system. With the exception of its disk system and typically large memory capacity, a server is similar to the client workstation computers on the network. Some servers are **nondedicated**, meaning that they can function as a user's workstation in addition to providing access to shared areas of the disk system. The server in Figure 1-4 is **dedicated**, meaning that it cannot be used as a workstation. This provides better performance and eliminates the possibility of a user shutting down or rebooting the server while other users are still accessing it. To prevent unauthorized access to the server's hardware and software, most network administrators keep servers in a separate room that can be secured.

1

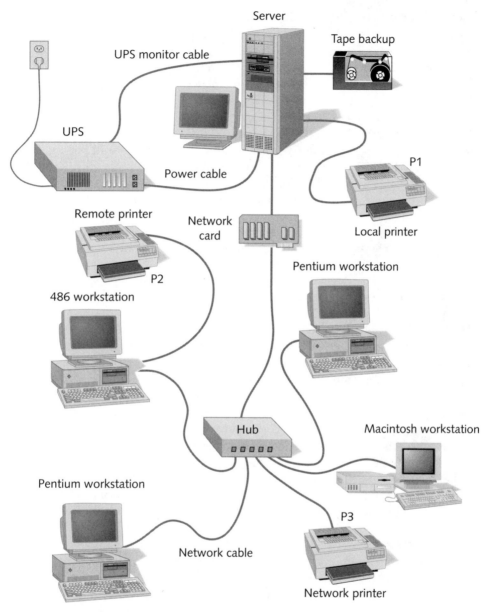

Figure 1-4   Sample network hardware components

The server shown in Figure 1-4 is a PC specifically designed to be a server (many vendors offer PCs designed for use as servers); it has an Intel 233 MHz Pentium processor with 96 MB of memory and two high-capacity 9 GB disk drives. The two disk drives are automatically synchronized (mirrored) so that if one drive fails, the server can continue to provide information services by using the data from the other drive.

Client Workstation   Generally, each computer attached to the network for running user applications is called a **client workstation**. The client workstation is where the actual processing of user software applications occurs. Placing more memory or a faster processor on the server does not directly increase speed of programs run on client workstations; to increase user application performance, you must upgrade the client workstation. The processing power of the client workstation often equals or exceeds the speed of the server computer. For example, in the sample network the server contains a 233 MHz Pentium processor with lots of memory and disk space and a low-resolution color monitor. The Windows-based workstations contain 200 MHz Pentium processors with 32 MB of memory, 1.2 GB of disk storage, and high-resolution color monitors. Because most files and software will be kept on the network server, the client workstations can focus on processing speed and graphics resolution rather than on high-capacity disk storage.

On networks needing file and print services, the server is specialized to provide high-speed disk access, whereas the client workstations require fast processors and high-resolution graphics. On networks using client/server applications, the server will need to run the server portion of the application and thus must be specialized to handle the application processing.

Network Interface Card   A **network interface card (NIC)** is installed in each computer attached to the network, including the servers. The NIC allows the computer to be attached to the network cable system and is responsible for transmitting and receiving data packets on the network. A **packet** consists of hundreds to several thousand bytes of formatted data that is framed with control bits identifying the address of the computer the packet is being sent to. When it is manufactured, each NIC is assigned a unique address or serial number. The NIC listens to the network and accepts any packets that contain its address. It then notifies its host computer that the NIC has received a packet, and if no errors are detected in the packet, it is sent to the operating system software for processing. When transmitting data, the network operating system will send a block of data to the NIC, which then waits for the network cable to become available. When no other computers are using the cable system, the NIC transmits the packet bit by bit.

Cable System   A network's cable system is the highway through which information travels from one computer to another. A **cable system** consists of the wiring that connects the computers in the network. Just as getting onto a highway requires obeying certain traffic laws, sending information through the network requires each computer to follow a set of access rules. And in the same way that gridlock can slow down or stop traffic on a highway, a network can also experience bottlenecks when the amount of information on the network exceeds the transmission capacity of the cable system. One responsibility you will have as a network administrator is monitoring the network cable system for errors or performance bottlenecks. The cable system in the sample network consists of twisted-pair cable similar to the cable that connects your telephone's handset to its base unit. In Chapter 3 you will learn about the different types of cable systems and access methods commonly used in LANs, along with some of the advantages and disadvantages of each system. In the sample network in Figure 1-4, twisted-pair cable runs from each computer in the network to a central connection box called a **hub** or **concentrator**, giving all computers equal access to the network system.

Uninterruptible Power Supply   The box to the left of the server in Figure 1-4 is the **uninterruptible power supply** (UPS). The UPS contains batteries that supply temporary power to the server if the local power system fails. The UPS is a very important piece of equipment for the server computer, because it prevents data loss in a power outage or brownout.

 Because a power outage that occurs while many users are accessing the server is likely to result in lost data, do not even consider running a server computer without a UPS. Power interruptions when a UPS unit is not attached to the server can necessitate restoring data from a backup tape in order to restart the server.

The UPS in Figure 1-4 contains an optional monitor cable that connects to a port on the server. This connection lets the server know when the UPS is using battery power. This connection is also important in an extended power outage because it allows the server to close all files and take itself off line automatically before exhausting the UPS batteries.

Tape Backup   The tape backup system in the network shown in Figure 1-4 consists of a digital audio tape (DAT) cartridge tape drive and uses Novell's Storage Management System (SMS) software to back up all data on the server automatically every night. At 1 a.m. each weekday morning, the tape software starts up and copies all data to the tape cartridge. The network administrator then places this tape in the organization's fireproof vault for safe storage. A rotation system using several tapes allows each backup to be kept for at least one week, and one day's backup tape (for example, the tape made on Fridays) is then stored off site in case of a disaster that wipes out the entire site. In Chapter 14 you will learn more about developing a backup and recovery system for your server environment.

Network Printers   Sharing printers on the network is often an important advantage of a LAN. Each client workstation can send output to any printer by first directing the printed output to the server, to be stored in a special directory called a **print queue**. After a workstation has completed printing, the server directs the printout to the selected printer by using special print server software. Printers can be attached and shared on the network in three different ways: as local printers, as remote printers, and as directly attached printers.

Notice that printer P1 in the network shown in Figure 1-4 is attached to the server. This makes it a **local printer**, because it is attached to the server's local printer port. Local printers have the advantages of working at high speeds and of reducing network traffic but have the disadvantage of limiting the locations in which the printers can be placed.

Printer P2 is attached to a user's workstation. It is controlled by the print server software, which allows users on any client workstation to send output through the server to printer P2. Printer P2 is referred to as a **remote printer**, because it is not directly attached to a printer port of the server. Remote printers have the advantage of being located anywhere on the network where there is a workstation. However, performance problems, as well as software conflicts for the workstation's user, can occur when large print jobs are processed.

The third network printer shown in Figure 1-4, P3, is a **directly attached printer**, which has its own network card and is connected directly to the network cable system. This direct connection offers the benefits of independence from a workstation without the loss of speed that is associated with a remote printer. Today, for the highest possible level of performance, most network administrators attach their high-speed printers directly to the network cable system.

You'll learn more about NetWare printing and the new NDPS print system in Chapter 12.

Software Components

The software components of the network are perhaps the most difficult to understand because they are not physical objects. In the network configuration shown in Figure 1-4, the network software components can be divided into four major categories: card drivers, protocol stacks, the network operating system, and client support. Figure 1-5 shows how these software components are combined to let workstations and servers communicate on the network. In this section you will learn what role each of these software components plays in a local area network.

Network Interface Card Drivers   Each server and client workstation must have a network interface card (NIC) to attach it to the cable system and to communicate on the network. A **network interface card driver** is software that contains instructions that let the processor on the computer control card functions and interface with the application software. Periodically, card manufacturers release new versions of driver software to fix bugs or offer compatibility with new applications. As a result, one responsibility of a network administrator involves updating application and system software. In a later chapter you will learn how to make this task more efficient by using the automatic software update utilities built into the NetWare operating system. In the sample network configuration, the workstations use the older but reliable MicroDyne NE2000 NICs, and an NE2000 driver program controls the network interface cards and provides an interface with the workstation operating system software.

Protocol Stacks   The **protocol stack** is the software used to format requests and information packets transmitted on the network. The protocol you use will depend on your server and client workstations. The default protocol for NetWare 5.0 is TCP/IP (Transmission Control Protocol/Internet Protocol) commonly used with the Unix operating system and the Internet. Previously, the most common protocol on NetWare networks was the Internetwork Packet eXchange (IPX) protocol. In addition, NetWare networks support other protocols, such as the AppleTalk protocol used with Macintosh computers.

NetWare 5.0 retains IPX as an option for those networks still using it. Both IP and IPX can run concurrently on the same NetWare 5.0 server.

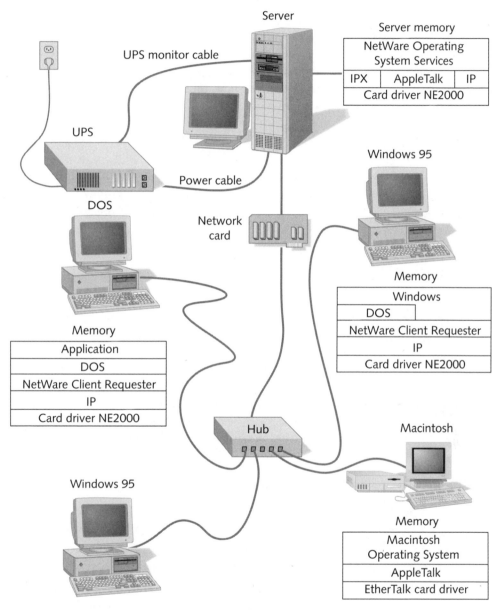

Figure 1-5   Network software components

The IPX protocol used by NetWare was first developed by Xerox in the late 1970s and later adopted by Novell for use in its networking products. It provided automatic addressing for network components rather than the manual addressing used by TCP/IP.

Network Operating System   As discussed, a network operating system is system software that provides network services. In a client-server network such as NetWare, the network operating system controls the server to provide services to the client workstations. Most of the NetWare operating system resides on the server computer, but the client workstations also need a requester program, such as the Novell Netware Client for Windows 95/98, to format and direct requests for network services to the server for processing. In Chapter 6 you will learn the steps for installing NetWare on both the server and the client workstations.

The NetWare network operating system was specifically designed to directly control the server hardware as well as provide a server environment to support file sharing and other network services. This makes NetWare an efficient network operating system because it enables a NetWare server to provide faster support with fewer hardware requirements.

The server in the network shown in Figure 1–5 runs NetWare 5.0 as its network operating system. It uses two protocols:

- The IP protocol to communicate with the DOS and Windows workstations

- The AppleTalk protocol to communicate with Apple Macintosh computers

This enables both DOS/Windows and Macintosh computers to access the NetWare server and share data and other resources.

The ability to provide faster support for workstations will become even more important as servers are increasingly used to store large documents, images, and multimedia files. Similarly, the increasing use of application servers to run the server portion of client/server applications is requiring more processing power from the server itself.

Client Software   Client workstations require the following components:

- Their own operating systems, such as DOS, OS/2, Windows 3.x, Windows 95/98, Windows NT, or Macintosh OS, to control local devices and run application software

- Client workstation driver software to control the network interface card

- Requester and protocol software programs to format and send requests for network file and print services to the server; the requester program works closely with the workstation's operating system (OS) to provide access to network services

The network in Figure 1-5 shows a DOS computer using the NetWare Client Requester to send IP-formatted requests via the NE2000 driver through the cable system to the NetWare server. The Macintosh computer shown has an EtherTalk driver so it can simultaneously use the same cable to send requests to the server by using the AppleTalk protocol. The ability to support different types of client operating systems is one strength of the NetWare server.

The NetWare Server

As explained earlier in this chapter, the main function of a server is to provide file and printer services to client workstations. As a result, the server can be enhanced with specialized hardware and software to improve performance, security, and reliability beyond what can be expected from a peer-to-peer network operating system. Although Microsoft Windows NT and Banyan Vines offer client-server network operating systems, NetWare still has the largest share of the client-server network operating system market for Intel processors. NetWare offers server-based software designed from the ground up to make maximum use of the server's hardware. It does this by including performance, fault tolerance, security, and client support features.

Performance The performance of a server is determined by how fast it can respond to requests for data from client workstations. Therefore, the major factors that affect the server's performance are its ability to keep frequently used information in memory, the speed of its disk system, and, if the first two are adequate, the speed of its processor unit. Some performance features of NetWare are discussed in Chapter 2.

Fault Tolerance Fault tolerance is the ability of a system to continue to operate satisfactorily in the event of errors or other problems. The NetWare server environment was designed with different levels of fault tolerance in its disk system, in order to continue server operations despite physical errors on the disk drives or controller cards. NetWare's fault tolerance system is discussed in Chapter 2.

Security (preventing unauthorized access to information on the server) is one of the most important responsibilities of a network administrator. The NetWare server provides security features that you can use to meet the security needs of your organization's users and data.

Login security requires all users of the server to provide a valid user name and optional password before being given access to the network. As a network administrator you can assign user names and passwords for each of your network users, thereby controlling use of the network. To further protect passwords, NetWare lets you require passwords of at least five characters and force users to change their passwords within a specified time limit. In addition, the optional intruder protection system locks out a user's account if someone exceeds the number of login attempts you have set. You will work with user accounts and login security in Chapter 9.

Trustee assignments let you assign privileges, called **trustee rights**, to NetWare users, to let them perform certain functions on the network. Trustee assignments form the basis for **NDS security**, which controls access to Novell Directory Services (NDS). NDS is Novell's system for managing network resources such as printers and servers. Trustee assignments are also the basis for **file system security**, which controls access to the network file system (the directory structure of the hard drive and the files in that directory structure). A new user has no rights to access any data stored on a NetWare server until you provide that user with rights to use certain parts of a file system on a NetWare server in your network. Trustee assignments, NDS security, and file system security are discussed in detail in Chapters 9 and 10.

Finally, NetWare provides **system console security** features. The **system console** is the keyboard and monitor connected to a NetWare server, which are used for many NetWare server- and network-related tasks. NetWare enables you to set the system console so that only authorized individuals can use it. You will work with the system console in Chapter 14.

Client Support   Because a NetWare server runs its own network operating system, it does not depend on a specific type of client environment (unlike peer-to-peer networks) and can support many types of workstations. As a result, a NetWare server can let you integrate diverse computing environments, enabling Apple Macintosh users to share files with DOS- and Windows-based computers. In some organizations, NetWare has provided a means for engineering departments operating Unix-based computers for computer-aided design (CAD) software (used by engineers to draw plans and diagrams) to make the design files available to DOS-based computers that control the machines that physically cut out engineered parts. Client support is discussed in Chapter 6.

Selecting a Network

Selecting a network system for an organization involves three steps:

1. Decide on the type of network operating system to use.

2. Determine the cable system that will best support the needs of the network.

3. Specify any computer hardware that will be needed to implement servers and attach workstations to the network.

In this section you will learn about the criteria you should consider when developing a recommendation for a network operating system. In Chapters 2 and 3 you will learn about computer hardware options and cable configurations that you will need to know when recommending and implementing a new network or maintaining an existing system.

1

Defining Network Needs

Before recommending or justifying a network operating system, you first need to analyze the processing needs of the organization and determine how they will be supported by the network. The processing needs of an organization that affect the type of network operating system to be selected include number of users, diversity of workstations, type of applications to be supported, and the need for centralized data.

Network Size An important consideration in determining whether to use a peer-to-peer or client-server network operating system is the number of workstations that will be attached to the network. As a general rule, the fewer users, the more likely a peer-to-peer network will meet the needs of the organization. You also need to look at the future growth of the organization and how this will affect the network system. If you think the organization will expand in the next few years to include more users requiring heavy-duty file and printer sharing to support such applications as desktop publishing and CAD, you might want to recommend a client-server network operating system.

Client Workstations The types of client workstations that will be attached to the network are another factor to consider in selecting the type of network operating system. Peer-to-peer networks are best used in networks in which all the attached clients are running the same type of operating system. For example, if all workstations will run Windows, the Windows 95/98 system could be an attractive alternative, provided it meets the other processing needs of the network. If the client workstations are running a combination of DOS and Windows, then LANtastic or a client-server operating system such as NetWare 5.0 may be the best choice, depending on the organization's other processing needs.

Network Use Certain common uses of networks, such as printer sharing and e-mail routing, have small disk storage needs and can run nicely on peer-to-peer networks. For example, if an organization plans to use its network to support workgroup-oriented software such as e-mail and scheduling with some sharing of files and printers within small workgroups, a peer-to-peer operating system that supports its workstation operating systems may be the best choice.

If an organization will be running applications that require fast access to large network data files such as desktop publishing, document imaging, and multimedia presentation packages, select a client-server network such as NetWare, to provide reliable, high-speed access to large disk systems consisting of gigabytes of data storage.

If the network is using a client/server application, then a client-server network with an applications server is necessary. The Windows NT Server environment provides a good platform for serving applications, because the operating system is designed to support application development.

 Database software such as Microsoft's SQL Server and Oracle Corporation's Oracle are designed to run on an application server to perform certain database functions for the workstations, reducing the load on the network and workstation. Database use is an increasingly important function of LANs.

Centralized Storage Another important consideration in selecting a network operating system is the network's need for centralized storage for files and documents. If an organization's employees use word processors and spreadsheet programs to access common documents and files, a client-server network system will give them consistent and reliable shared storage areas that can be routinely backed up, to allow for disaster recovery.

Client-server environments are also the best choice when users in an organization need access to large centralized databases containing inventory and customer information. These database files should be placed on a dedicated server or application server, to take advantage of the speed of file caching and the assurance of high reliability and fault tolerance gained by mirroring or duplexing the disk drives.

Selecting a Network Operating System

The flowchart in Figure 1-6 shows how to analyze the network processing needs of an organization to select a network operating system. As shown in the flowchart, the number of user workstations to be attached to the network is the first consideration. If there are fewer than 15 workstations, a peer-to-peer network is probably the best alternative. However, if several of these workstations will be using large files that must be shared on the network, such as those used by departments running computer-aided design applications, a client-server network operating system is preferable. The choice of the peer-to-peer network operating system will also depend on the type of operating systems used by client workstations.

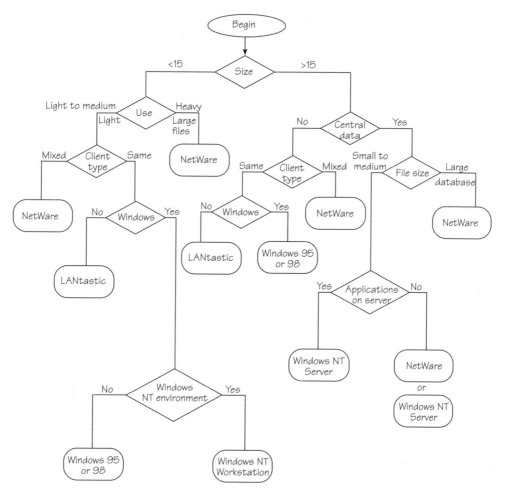

Figure 1-6 Selecting a network operating system

When the number of users exceeds 15, the need for centralized data typically becomes an important factor in choosing between a client-server and peer-to-peer system. If the network will be used mostly for sharing printers and personal communication, you need to consider the operating systems that the client workstations will be running. If client workstations will be running different types of operating systems, NetWare is usually the best operating system choice because it can be configured to support communications and file sharing between different client operating environments.

When centralized data storage is a major function of the network, a client-server system such as NetWare or Windows NT Server is the best choice because it provides a secure and efficient platform that helps make sure data will always be available. When large database or multimedia files crucial to an organization's operation must be accessed from a centralized server, NetWare 5.0 is generally the best choice, depending on the number of servers.

Wherever performance, security, and reliability are a must, NetWare is probably the best choice, because it has been used extensively for many years and its performance and compatibility with many applications are well established. Other client-server environments, such as Windows NT Server, are newer to the marketplace and should be considered and researched carefully to determine their performance and compatibility in the proposed network environment. Also, take care to properly calculate the added hardware requirements to support NT Server and its domain services.

Today many network administrators are gaining the best of both peer-to-peer and client-server networks by implementing combinations of network operating systems. For example, a NetWare client-server network can include clients running Windows 95 or 98, whereas Windows NT Server is used to provide access to certain Windows NT–based client/server applications. As these operating systems gain popularity, network administrators will be increasingly called on to implement network systems combining compatible products, to provide the services needed by the organization's LAN users.

Cunningham, Burns, and Evans Laboratories

Consider how what you've learned about networks can be used to select a new network for an organization. The organization you'll work with is Cunningham, Burns, and Evans Laboratories (CBE Labs).

The Organization

Located in Portland, Oregon, CBE Labs is a small, independent consulting firm specializing in testing and reporting on computer hardware and software. The firm's highly respected industry newsletter, *The C/B/E Networker*, has a reputation for impartial and detailed evaluations, and information system specialists often refer to it when deciding which hardware or software to purchase. Most, if not all, of the Fortune 500 companies and all major firms in the computer industry subscribe to *The C/B/E Networker*.

CBE Labs is organized into three departments: administration, laboratories, and publications. An organization chart for CBE Labs is shown in Figure 1-7.

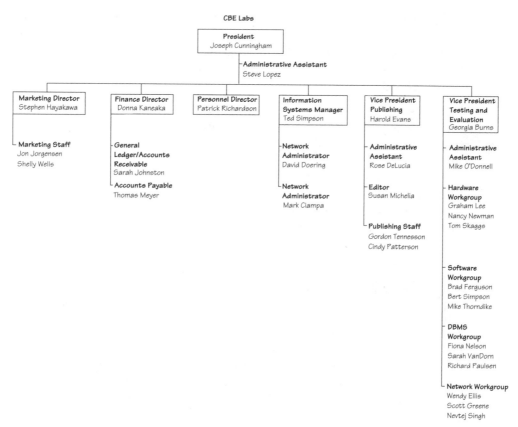

Figure 1-7   CBE Labs organization chart

Administration of CBE is overseen by President Joseph Cunningham and an administration assistant. Administration includes marketing, finance, personnel, and information systems. There are three people in marketing, three in finance, one in personnel, and three in information systems.

The CBE Labs testing labs are organized around four technology workgroups: hardware (workstation PCs and their components), software (workstation operating systems and application programs), database management systems (DBMSs), and networking (network server PCs and their components, network operating systems, and network applications). CBE Labs has three employees in each workgroup, along with Vice President for Testing and Evaluation Georgia Burns, and one administrative assistant. Hardware and software being tested are not considered part of CBE Labs' own equipment.

CBE Labs does use its own equipment to store the data resulting from testing and evaluations, to create *The C/B/E Networker*, and to run the business applications necessary to manage the organization. The publishing workgroup is managed by Vice President for Publishing Harold Evans, who oversees a staff of three plus one administrative assistant.

CBE Labs needs to update the company's LAN. Although CBE Labs could simply upgrade its existing software to newer versions, the administrators have decided they do not want to be locked into software simply because they already own a version of it. The purchasing decision will be a "zero-based" decision, in which all network operating systems will be evaluated.

The company expects to use three servers in the new network: one for lab data and reports, one for publishing *The C/B/E Networker*, and one for company administration. The company needs e-mail, fax capability, and Internet access in the network. All workstations will run Windows 95 or Windows 98 and need to access large databases stored on the servers. Some applications will be run from the servers, but most standardized user applications (word processing, spreadsheet, and presentation graphics software) will be loaded on the users' workstations. Finally, the company's existing network is a client-server network using a single-server NetWare 3.2. Management wouldn't mind if the new network could accommodate the existing server and NetWare license, but this is not a requirement.

Choosing the New Network

Apply the flowchart in Figure 1-6 to determine which network operating system CBE Labs should use. The number of users is greater than 15, so you initially branch to the right at the Size decision point. The organization will be storing centralized data on the servers, so you branch to the right at the Central Data decision point. At the File Size decision point, you have to consider whether large database files will be kept on the servers. The answer is yes, so you branch to the right and choose NetWare as the network operating system. This path through the flowchart is shown in Figure 1-8.

However, CBE Labs may also be using client/server applications. Windows NT Server is considered a better applications server NOS than NetWare. This doesn't mean that NetWare doesn't perform well as an applications server, only that Windows NT Server performs better in that task because it has a GUI interface familiar to users. (There are also many more applications available for NT than for NetWare.) You can still run client/server applications if necessary, so NetWare is your choice for the network operating system.

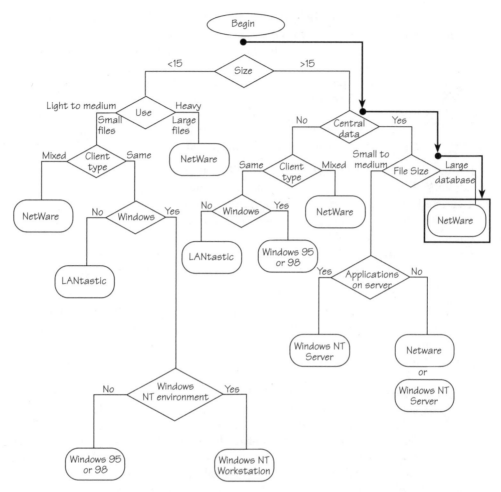

Figure 1-8　Selecting a NetWare operating system for CBE Labs

THE CERTIFIED NOVELL ADMINISTRATOR (CNA)

The microcomputer networking field is an exciting arena with new developments occurring on an almost daily basis. The rapid growth of this field has created the need for network professionals, trained individuals who can be trusted with the responsibilities of creating and maintaining LANs and WANs. Novell has created a means for a network administrator to demonstrate his or her competency at NetWare administration by passing a qualifying exam. Passing the exam earns the network administrator the designation of Certified Novell Administrator. A **Certified Novell Administrator (CNA)** is considered qualified to be the network administrator of an installed NetWare system. Originally called the Certified NetWare Administrator program, Novell developed the

CNA program in 1992 to help define the role of network administrators in a NetWare environment. The program provides a standard of knowledge and performance that organizations can use to help ensure the quality of network administration and support.

Although it is not a prerequisite for taking the CNA exam, Novell expects that all CNAs understand DOS and can use DOS commands. This is even true for the Windows 95/98 environment, because the DOS prompt is still available and DOS commands can still be run. For that reason, explanations of DOS operations will be included occasionally in this book.

Notice that by Novell's definition the CNA is ready to take care of an *already installed* network. The installation itself would be done by a Certified Novell Engineer. The **Certified Novell Engineer (CNE)** designation is awarded to people who earn 19 Novell credits by passing a series of exams about NetWare. (The CNA exam is actually one of the tests for CNE and is worth 4 CNE credits.) However, because as a network manager you must understand the NetWare installation and how to create the NDS and file system for the network, this text includes material on these topics.

CNA and CNE tests are available for a variety of Novell products, and the actual certification you receive depends on which test(s) you take. To become a CNA for NetWare 5.0, you must take Novell's Certified NetWare 5 Administrator exam. Tests are also available for certification on two earlier versions of NetWare and three products in Novell's GroupWare product line.

Current information on the CNA and CNE programs can be found on Novell Education's World Wide Web site at *http://education.novell.com*. A current list of test objectives for the CNA exam, as well as other CNA- and CNE-related information, can be obtained from the Novell website. The content of these programs and exams changes periodically, so it's a good idea to get the latest information from Novell before taking the CNA exam.

CNA was originally Certified *NetWare* Administrator, and CNE was Certified *NetWare* Engineer. Similarly, NDS was originally *NetWare* Directory Services. The name changes reflect a broadening of Novell's outlook and its product line. You can be certified on Novell products other than NetWare, and NDS is being developed to work with other network operating systems such as Unix and Windows NT.

As a CNA your job will be to direct your organization's networking services and support to meet the workgroup-oriented processing needs of microcomputer users. To develop the CNA program, Novell researched the job duties of thousands of NetWare network administrators around the world to determine the common tasks that network administrators needed to perform on a regular basis. The sections that follow summarize Novell's research. They will help you understand the typical duties of a network administrator as well as give an overview of the NetWare knowledge and skills you will need to become a CNA.

Understanding NetWare Components and Commands

A NetWare administrator needs a solid foundation in the components of a NetWare network and how they interoperate. When a problem—such as the message "File server not found"—occurs on a workstation attached to the network, the network administrator must be able to troubleshoot the network and isolate the cause of the error by drawing on his or her knowledge of the network components.

Just as a mechanic must learn how to use the tools necessary to maintain and repair an automobile, a CNA must learn how to use the many NetWare commands and utilities to be able to perform network maintenance and repair tasks such as creating users, granting access rights, listing directory information, and working with printers. Starting with this chapter and continuing throughout the book, you will be learning how to use the commands and utilities that are the CNA's essential tools.

Supporting Client Workstation Environments

The majority of computers attached to NetWare networks today run either the DOS or Windows operating system, and therefore as a CNA you need to know how to install and configure the client software used to attach DOS or Windows workstations to the network and establish communications. With the rapid advances in microcomputer technology that require organizations to add new computers and replace existing ones each year, one of your main CNA tasks will be to install and update client software regularly.

In addition to the DOS and Windows workstations, your organization may also need to provide network support for Apple Macintosh and Unix-based computers. Although Novell does not currently require a CNA to install client software on Macintosh and Unix operating systems, you will need to be able to identify how the NetWare software components allow Unix and Macintosh computers to attach to a NetWare network.

Managing Novell Directory Services

One of the most important features in NetWare 5.0 is Novell Directory Services (NDS). On a NetWare 5.0 network, a user connects to the network itself rather than to a server (or group of servers). This requires a comprehensive, logical network design, as well as tools for administering the resources (such as disk space and printers) for the entire network. Novell Directory Services (NDS) is the tool that you as a CNA will use to create, maintain, and administer the network design and resources. The logical network design is called the **NDS Directory tree**. NDS is actually a database of information about the network and is built on the X.500 standard for a network global database. You will learn about NDS in detail in Chapter 4.

Novell Directory Services is proving a useful network design and administration tool, and Novell is licensing NDS to other companies, such as Hewlett-Packard and SCO (Santra Cruz Operations), for use in their network operating systems and software products. Novell also has developed NDS for NT to run on the Windows NT Server NOS. These developments will make NDS a tool for managing a network with servers running a variety of network operating systems.

Managing the Network File System

A network file system uses a directory structure to define how the data storage of your server(s) is organized. You may already know how a good directory structure on your workstation's local hard disk makes it easier to run applications and access files. On a server, a good directory structure becomes even more important because many users share the same storage device. As a result, one of the most important tasks a CNA must undertake when installing a new server is planning and implementing an efficient directory structure to support the users' processing needs. In this book you will learn the essential NetWare file system components as well as the design techniques that will help you create and maintain a workable network directory structure.

Establishing and Maintaining Network Users and Security

NetWare has a very sophisticated security system that enables the network administrator to give users access to information while at the same time protecting special information from unauthorized access. To implement this security system, as a CNA you will need to create a user account for each person who will access the network and then assign the appropriate security restrictions such as passwords and other limitations you feel are necessary to protect user accounts from unauthorized access. In addition, to access files on the network, users need access rights to NDS objects and the directories and files they will be using. As a CNA, you will assign these rights. In Chapters 9 and 10 you will learn how to use NetWare utilities and commands to create users as well as assign the necessary rights to access NDS objects and the network file system. Because organizational structures continually change, an ongoing task you will have as a CNA is to add and delete users as well as to modify the rights assigned to users and groups.

Setting Up and Maintaining Network Printing

Perhaps one of the most complex and demanding tasks of a network administrator is creating and maintaining the network printing environment. Network printing has become an increasingly important issue on networks with sophisticated applications such as desktop publishing and WYSIWYG ("what you see is what you get") word processors and spreadsheets. These applications require expensive laser and ink-jet printers, which are often shared to control costs. As a CNA, you will find you need to continually upgrade your network printing environment to support faster and more sophisticated printers and applications as they become available. In this book you will learn how to use the NetWare printing components and tools that allow you to install and maintain a network printing environment to meet your users' needs.

Loading and Updating Application Software

An ongoing and important job of the network administrator is installing and upgrading application software packages that run on the client workstations. Whenever possible you will want to install applications on the server, so they can be shared and centrally maintained. However, some applications will not run from a server, or will run much more efficiently when installed on the workstation's local hard drive. As a CNA, you will need to be familiar with installing and configuring many different application software packages and know how to support these packages on either the server or local workstations. These functions are covered in Chapter 11.

The CNA must continually obtain and install software upgrades, as well as respond to user questions and problems. As a result, CNAs often find they need strong interpersonal skills to work with frustrated or angry users. Yet another responsibility is policing copyright licenses of application software to be sure your organization always has enough licenses to cover the number of users who are running the applications. This task is very important, because your company can be sued and fined if it is found in violation of copyright laws. To make the CNA's responsibility easier, some companies produce software that counts the number of users currently using a software package and does not allow more users than the number you have identified according to your software licenses.

Creating an Automated User Environment

For CNAs to set up and maintain an easy-to-use network environment, Novell requires them to know how to use NetWare utilities to create and maintain NetWare login script files. In Chapter 13 you will learn how to use NetWare login scripts to create a user-friendly network environment that will allow users on your network to log on to the server easily.

Developing and Implementing a Backup and Recovery System

Information is the lifeblood of an organization, and as a CNA you will be the guardian of the information stored on the local area network system. One of the worst nightmares a CNA can have is a server crash, losing all the network information stored on its hard drives. To prevent this catastrophe and let you sleep more easily, you need to be sure your server environment is as reliable as possible. You will also need a good backup system to restore all the programs and data on your server after a major system failure. In Chapter 2 you will learn about fail-safe measures that can be implemented on NetWare servers and how you can develop system specifications that will provide a reliable and fault-tolerant system. No matter how reliable or fault-tolerant a system is, however, you still need to be prepared for a worst case scenario, such as your building being destroyed or the equipment being damaged by an electrical failure or lightning. In Chapter 14 you will learn how to plan for disasters by implementing a backup and recovery system using the NetWare Storage System and utilities.

Managing the Server and Monitoring Network Performance

A NetWare server has its own operating system and console commands that enable a network administrator to control the server environment, as well as to run special software called **NetWare Loadable Modules (NLMs)** to perform certain tasks or add new services. Therefore a CNA will need to spend some time each week at the server console using console commands and utilities to monitor server activity as well as to add new services and modify or configure existing ones.

With the addition of users to the network, large printing loads, and the ever-increasing demands by the high-speed workstations for graphics applications, network performance can sometimes falter. As a CNA, you will regularly need to monitor your network system as well as the server to detect performance bottlenecks or problems and then to determine if additional hardware or configuration changes are necessary. In Chapter 14 you will learn about several common network problems caused by insufficient hardware, as well as how to configure your server and workstations to improve performance and avoid problems.

CHAPTER SUMMARY

❐ A computer network is formed when two or more computers are connected so they can communicate electronically with each other. Local area networks (LANs) are located in one site, whereas wide area networks (WANs) connect two or more LANs. The network administrator is responsible for running the network. Networks use servers, which are specialized computers that provide network services. Examples are network servers, print servers, and application servers.

❐ Networks are becoming widespread in many organizations because they cut costs by letting users share expensive hardware and software, save time by making it easier for users to work together, offer shared access to database and document files, provide a more secure environment to protect sensitive data from unauthorized access, provide a more reliable storage system to prevent loss of data and time, and offer a communication system that can be used for electronic mail and scheduling applications, as well as to access minicomputer and mainframe computer systems.

❐ Network operating systems (NOSs) can be classified into two types: peer-to-peer and client-server. Peer-to-peer operating systems do not require a dedicated server but instead can share data among the client workstations. Generally, peer-to-peer operating systems such as LANtastic, Windows 95/98, and Windows NT Workstation are best implemented for smaller workgroups that do not require frequent access to centralized data files. Because client-server operating systems such as NetWare and Windows NT Server have dedicated servers, they can be more efficient and reliable platforms for storage of centralized files.

❐ When selecting an operating system for your network, you need to consider such factors as number of users and workstations, type of operating systems and applications to be used by the client workstations, and need for high-speed centralized data storage. In most cases in which a client-server network is needed, NetWare equals or exceeds the capabilities of other systems such as Windows NT Server and Banyan Vines. Because each type of operating system has certain strengths, however, many organizations must be able to combine network operating systems and workstations to meet their network processing needs. Windows NT Server is often chosen as the operating system for an application server.

◻ To succeed as a network administrator, you will need a good understanding of the hardware and software components in a network system and how they interoperate. The basic hardware components of a network consist of the server, cable system, network cards, uninterruptible power supply (UPS), client workstations, and shared printers. Printers can be added to the network by attaching them to a local printer port on the server, attaching them remotely to a client workstation, or attaching them directly to the network cable. The software components of a network consist of the card driver program, which directly controls the network interface card (NIC); the protocol stack, which formats the data transmitted between computers; the DOS requester program, which provides an interface between applications and the network; and the network operating system, which runs on the server computer and provides the shared network services.

◻ Network administration is an exciting field with a great future, and a Certified Novell Administrator (CNA) will be in a position to grow with the industry. As a CNA, your responsibilities will include such activities as supporting client workstation applications, creating and maintaining the network directory structures, creating and maintaining the Novell Directory Services (NDS) database and Directory tree, establishing network users and security, setting up and maintaining the network printing environment, managing the server console, maintaining a user-friendly environment, and implementing a fail-safe backup and recovery system.

KEY TERMS

application server

centralized processing

Certified Novell Administrator (CNA)

Certified Novell Engineer (CNE)

client/server applications

client-server network operating system

client workstation

computer network

concentrator

cable system

dedicated

directly attached printer

distributed processing
duplexing
electronic mail (e-mail) applications
fault tolerance
file system security
hub
Internet
intranet
local area network (LAN)
local printer
login security
mainframe computer
microcomputer
minicomputer
mirroring
NDS Directory tree
NDS security
NetWare file server
NetWare Loadable Module (NLM)
NetWare server
network administrator
network-centric
network interface card (NIC)
network interface card driver
network operating system (NOS)
network server
nondedicated
Novell Directory Services (NDS)
packet
peer-to-peer
personal computer (PC)
protocol stack
print queue
print server
remote printer
scheduling applications
server
server-centric

1

system console
system console security
terminals
trustee assignments
trustee rights
wide area network (WAN)
uninterruptible power supply (UPS)

REVIEW QUESTIONS

1. Two or more computers connected so that they can communicate electronically with each other are known as _____.

2. Computer networks that exist in one location are called _____; computer networks that exist in two or more geographic locations are called

   _____.

3. The LAN supports _____ processing by allowing microcomputers to access centralized data and resources.

4. Define the following types of servers: network server, print server, application server.

5. List two advantages of using a LAN for centralized data storage.

6. Identify two areas in which a LAN can be used to save personnel time.

7. In many networks, sharing _____ will provide the most direct cost savings.

8. A network operating system that allows client computers to share files among themselves is called a _____.

9. A _____ network operating system requires a server.

10. List two advantages of peer-to-peer network operating systems.

11. List two advantages of client-server network operating systems.

12. A network in which a new user's account must be created on every server is _____; a network where the account must be created only once is

    _____.

13. List the seven network hardware components.

14. If a server can also be used as a client workstation, then it is a _____ server.

15. List three ways a printer can be attached to a network.

16. The _____ software component controls communications on the network cable.

17. The _____ software component formats the information being transmitted between computers.

18. The _____ software component provides access to shared files and other resources.

19. The _____ software component interfaces the network to DOS.

20. List four types of NetWare security.

21. Identify the CNA responsibility under which each of the following tasks belongs:

   a. Deciding where to place the quality control database in order to allow shared access by several users throughout an organization.

   b. Making a new printer available to the users in the sales department.

   c. Making it possible for the users in the sales department to easily select the new sales printer from their workstations.

   d. Determining why certain workstations cannot log in to the new server.

   e. Providing computers in the sales department with the ability to run the new PowerPoint presentation software.

   f. Determining how much memory the server computer is using for file caching.

   g. Getting a good night's sleep.

   h. Adding users to the e-mail system.

   i. Modifying the logical network design to accommodate the addition of a new server purchased for the use of the sales group.

HANDS-ON PROJECTS

Project 1-1: Recording Network Information

1. So that you can perform the exercises and project assignments in this book, your instructor has created a user account for you on the network. Your instructor will provide you with information about your user account. Record the information provided in the following space:

   NOS Directory tree name: _____

   Username: _____

   Last name: _____

   Full name: _____

   Student reference number: _____

   Context: _____

   Home directory location: _____

   Volume name: _____

   Home directory path and name: _____

2. Your instructor will take your class on a tour of your local area network. Use information presented during the tour to fill in the information in the following tables.

Network Server Information

Name	Operating System	Memory (MB)	Disk Capacity (MB/GB)	NIC & Protocol	UPS

Network Printer Information

Printer Name	Type	Location	Attachment Method

Your Client Workstation

Name (if any)	Operating System	Memory (MB)	Disk Capacity (MB/GB)	NIC & Protocol

Project 1-2: Logging in to the Network

1 Your instructor will explain how to log in to your network. Record the steps on a separatesheet of paper.

2. Using the instructions given by your instructor, log in to the network.

Project 1-3: Setting Your Password

You can assign a password to provide more security for your user name. Be sure to assign a password you can remember or you will suffer the embarrassment of having to ask your instructor or lab supervisor to reassign a new password for you. When you enter your password, it will display onscreen as asterisks.

1. If necessary, log in to the network by using your assigned user name.

2. In Windows 95/98, right-click the N (Novell) icon in the System Tray.

3. Click User Administration on the menu, then click Novell Password Administration.

4. Click Change Password. Type your old password, then your new password two times to confirm it. Click OK.

Project 1-4: Logging out of the Network

In this exercise you will learn how to log out of your Network.

1. Your instructor will explain how to log out of your network. Record the steps on a separate sheet of paper.

2. Using the instructions given by your instructor, log out of your network.

CASE PROJECTS

Case 1-1: Selecting a Network Operating System for the J.Q. Adams Corporation

The J. Q. Adams Corporation manufactures office equipment and supplies and then sells these products to companies that retail them. J. Q. Adams does not sell directly to the end user of their products. J. Q. Adams is a medium-sized company with more than 15 employees.

The company is planning to downsize its quality control system from a minicomputer to a LAN. Part of this system involves collecting information such as quantities produced and inspection results from the shop floor, and saving them in a central database. Product defects from returned goods will also be coded and stored in a separate database. These database files are expected to become quite large, and it is crucial that the collection process not be interrupted during daily operations. Other computers in the office will then have access to this data to be used in spreadsheet and database software, to produce reports and analyze production problems.

Along with this reorganization of the quality control system, the information systems manager at J. Q. Adams has decided to expand the LAN to include administrative operations. He plans to use two servers, one for administration and one for production, connected by the LAN. Administration users will use word processing, spreadsheet, database, and accounting software.

Given the preceding information, use the flowchart in Figure 1-6 to help select the best network operating system for the J. Q. Adams Corporation. Write a memo to your instructor documenting your decision. In the memo, explain your decision by diagramming your path through the flowchart and writing a brief paragraph justifying your selection.

Case 1-2: Selecting a Network Operating System for the Jefferson County Courthouse

Jefferson County is getting ready to install a network in the Jefferson County Courthouse. The network will connect 12 users in the social services department. The network will allow them to implement e-mail and group scheduling applications while sharing access to two laser printers. The 12 users include program administrator Janet Hinds, her assistant Tom Norihama, receptionist Lisa Walsh, department secretary Terry Smith, and eight social workers. Terry Smith is familiar with advanced features of the word processing package and often does final editing of the documents created by the social workers. As a result, social workers will need to pass documents periodically to Terry's computer so she can finalize them for printing.

1. Given the preceding information, use the flowchart in Figure 1-6 to help select the best network operating system for the Jefferson County Courthouse social services department. Write a memo to your instructor documenting your decision. In the memo, explain your decision by diagramming your path through the flowchart and writing a brief paragraph justifying your selection.

   The Jefferson County Courthouse also houses the county's courtroom facilities. There are three courtrooms that support the operations of four judges, four bailiffs, six court reporters, and 12 administrative staff. Each judge has his or her own office. The bailiffs share an office, but each has a separate desk. A similar situation applies to the court reporters. The administrative staff is in four offices, and each has a desk. If a network were installed, each employee would have a client workstation on his or her desk. In addition, the administration personnel would require four more workstations set up at windows where they deal with the public. A database of legal documents would be created and stored on the network, and this database is expected to grow very large over time. It is not clear whether a client/server database application would be used.

2. How would your decision change if Jefferson County also included the county court system in the network? What difference does it make if a client/server application is used for the database? Use the flowchart in Figure 1-6 to help select the best network operating system for the Jefferson County Courthouse with each database option. Write a memo to your instructor documenting your decision for each option. In the memo, explain your decision for each option by diagramming your path through the flowchart and writing a brief paragraph justifying your selection.

2

MICROCOMPUTER HARDWARE

After reading this chapter and completing the exercises you will be able to:

♦ Identify the hardware components that make up a microcomputer system

♦ Compare and contrast microprocessors used on workstations and NetWare servers

♦ Describe the purpose of and use of expansion buses, I/O ports, and interrupts in a microcomputer system

♦ Compare and contrast storage systems used on NetWare servers

♦ Apply knowledge of computer hardware components to developing NetWare server specifications

In the previous chapter you learned about networks and the basic components of a LAN. LANs support distributed processing on a variety of computer systems, so a network administrator must have a solid background in the fundamentals of microcomputer hardware and software components. Each new generation of software applications demands more processing power, and microcomputer systems are based on complex and evolving technologies. Components from many manufacturers are combined to build a microcomputer. To help you make sense of the many concepts and terms used in today's computer environments, this chapter provides a basic background in microcomputer terminology and concepts to keep you abreast of developments in microcomputer hardware and software. This knowledge will enable you to develop specifications for purchasing PC workstations and NetWare servers. In addition, the information in this chapter provides a basis for configuring network interface cards (NICs) and evaluating NetWare server performance, topics that are discussed in future chapters.

THE MICROCOMPUTER

The microcomputer is commonly called a **personal computer** or **PC**. The people who use them to get the job done are referred to as **end users** or just **users**. PCs used by users are often referred to as **PC workstations** or just **workstations**.

 The term workstation is sometimes also used to refer to microcomputers that are more powerful than the normal PC. These workstations generally run the Unix operating system and are often used for graphics-intensive work such as the engineering drawings produced by computer-aided design (CAD) systems. Often only the context of the discussion indicates which type of workstation is referred to.

The System Board

The **system board** (also called the *motherboard* or *mainboard*) is the most important component of a microcomputer because it links all the individual system components. The design of the system board directly affects the performance of a computer system. Figure 2-1 illustrates a system board and its major components. This section discusses how the system board components are linked by buses, and the following sections discuss the components themselves.

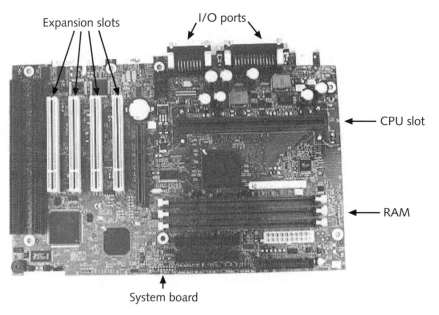

Figure 2-1   System board components

The System Board Buses

The system board circuits that connect components are called **buses**. Buses are the pathways for electronic communication between parts of the computer. They can be visualized as a set of wires running together (in "parallel") from component to component. In actuality, circuits etched into the system board are used instead of wires, but the idea is the same. Buses vary in size (number of "wires") and speed, and are usually referred to by names that reflect their purpose. In this section you will learn about the data bus, the address bus, the expansion bus, and the local bus. A typical bus structure is shown in Figure 2-2.

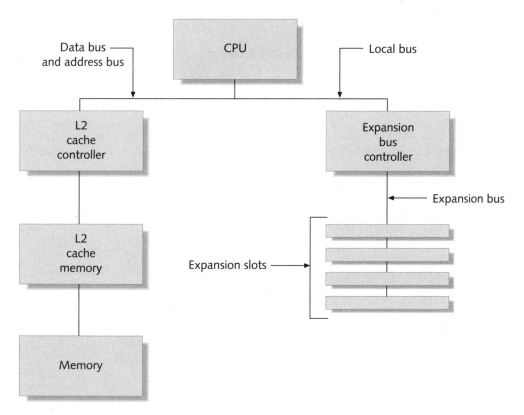

Figure 2-2 System board bus structure

The Local Bus. The system board circuits that connect the CPU to memory and other system board components are referred to as the **local bus** of the computer. The local bus is closely associated with the functions of the microprocessor chip and is designed to support the data and address bus of a specific microprocessor.

The Data Bus. As shown in Figure 2-3, the **data bus** is the highway that transfers data bits to and from the microprocessor registers where the microprocessor stores the data it uses. Just as the number of lanes on a highway determines the amount of traffic that can flow, the size of the data bus determines the number of bits that can be transferred into the microprocessor at one time.

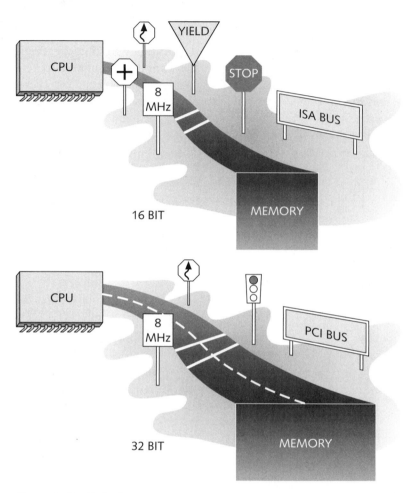

Figure 2-3 Data bus

The Address Bus. Just as each box in a post office is given a unique number to identify it, each byte in the computer's memory is identified by a binary number called an **address**. The microprocessor uses an address to identify the memory byte to or from which it is transferring data. The **address bus** carries the address of the memory byte from the microprocessor to the memory unit. When the memory unit receives the address along with a signal to read, it responds by placing the contents of that memory byte on the data bus. The number of bits in the address bus determines the maximum amount of memory the microprocessor can access directly. If an address bus consists of only two wires, for example, its maximum binary number is 11. A computer with this address bus is limited to a maximum of four byte addresses: 00, 01, 10, and 11. In the binary system, each additional bit on the address bus doubles the

2

amount of memory capacity, so a three-bit address bus has a maximum of eight byte addresses: 000, 001, 010, 011, 100, 101, 110, and 111. The 16-bit address bus commonly found on microprocessors before 1980 could access only 64 KB of RAM; the 20-bit address bus found on the 8088 can access up to 1 MB; the 24-bit address bus on the 80286 and 80386SX could access up to 16 MB; and the 32-bit address bus on the 80386DX, 80486, Pentium, and Pentium Pro can access up to 4 GB. The new 64-bit bus will handle 64 GB of memory.

The Expansion Bus. Some microcomputer components, such as video display controllers and network interface controllers, are not usually built into the system board. Instead these components are built on separate cards, called **expansion cards**, that can be attached to the system board by inserting them into an **expansion slot** on the system board. For example, network connections are commonly made using the network interface card (NIC) described in Chapter 1. The NIC is inserted into one of the expansion slots. The **expansion bus** is the bus that connects the expansion card slots to the components of the system board. The expansion bus connection is made through a specialized chip set on the system board that controls the operation of the expansion bus and the expansion cards attached to it. There are several types of expansion buses, which are discussed in the section on expansion slots later in this chapter.

Direct Memory Access. A **direct memory access (DMA) channel** is the part of the local bus that is used to automate the transfer of data between the computer's memory and external devices such as disk drives and NICs. DMA channels are assigned to specific devices. This means that when you are configuring a device such as a NIC, be sure to assign an unused DMA channel number.

Because local buses are designed to support a specific microprocessor, it is impossible to upgrade the microprocessor chip on the system board in older microcomputers. For example, if you want to upgrade a system from an Intel 80386SX to an Intel 80486 processor, you need to replace the system board. Newer system boards are designed for microprocessor upgrading. However, these system boards still have the original local bus built into them, which will limit the performance of the upgraded system. For example, Intel now sells a Pentium microprocessor to replace 80486 processors on properly designed system boards. But these boards were designed with a 32-bit data bus, whereas the Pentium is designed to work with a 64-bit data bus. Typically, the cost of both a new processor with system board is only slightly more than a processor alone, so replacing just the processor is only cost-effective for the latest models.

The Central Processing Unit (CPU)

The **central processing unit (CPU)**, also referred to as a **microprocessor**, is the brain of the microcomputer system. Built into the silicon of modern microprocessors are more than 3 million transistors that make up circuits to interpret and control the execution of program instructions and perform arithmetic and logical operations.

Experts say that etching all the circuit paths onto a microprocessor chip is comparable to mapping all the highways and streets of Los Angeles onto the head of a pin.

This section describes the different types of microprocessor chips and explains the limitations and capabilities of each. To compare microprocessors, you first need to understand the parameters that determine the performance and functionality of microprocessors: clock speed, word size, instruction set, data bus size, and address bus size.

Clock Speed.   If the microprocessor is the brain of the computer, then the clock is the heartbeat of the system unit, and its beats synchronize all the operations of the internal components. The microprocessor's **clock** is used to provide precisely timed signal pulses called **cycles**. Each clock cycle consists of an electronic pulse that is transmitted to each component of the system unit to trigger and synchronize processing within the computer system. Each clock pulse received by the microprocessor causes its circuits to perform part or all of an instruction.

Clock speed is measured in millions of cycles per second, called **megahertz (MHz)**. A **wait state** is a clock cycle during which the processor does not perform any operations; wait states were necessary to slow down high-speed processor chips and allow them to work with slower devices. (Contemporary hardware no longer requires wait states.) In general, higher clock rates mean faster processing speeds. The processing speed, when combined with the speed of a computer's disk storage and video card, determines its throughput performance.

Word Size.   A microprocessor chip holds instructions and data temporarily in storage areas called **registers**. Each processor chip has several registers for various purposes. A microprocessor's **word size** is the number of bits each register can hold. A larger word size enables a microprocessor to work on more data per clock cycle. Old processor chips, such as Intel's 8088 and 80286, had 16-bit registers. Newer processors, such as the Pentium, Pentium Pro, and Pentium II have 32-bit registers.

Instruction Set.   The **instruction set**, also called the **machine language**, is the group of commands that the microprocessor chip has been designed to process. All software must be converted to the microprocessor's machine language before it can be run. This is often accomplished with the aid of a special program called a **compiler**, which converts English-like commands to the binary language of the processor chip. DOS machine language programs use the filename extension .COM or .EXE. On a NetWare server, machine language programs have the extension .NLM.

A machine language program can be run only on the processor for which it was designed. Intel and Motorola processors, for example, have very different instruction sets, making it impossible for the Motorola chip to run a machine language program written for an Intel chip. The NetWare 3.2, 4.11, and 5.0 operating systems were written for the instruction set of an Intel 80386 microprocessor and therefore cannot be run on earlier Intel processors. Both NetWare 4.11 and 5.0 are Pentium-aware. If the software finds the system has a Pentium-class processor, it will take advantage of the faster Pentium instruction set as well. A Pentium is not *required* to run the NetWare server software; however, as a practical matter NetWare 5.0 will not run well on anything less.

Computers with Intel and most Motorola chips are classified as **complex instruction set computers (CISC)** because their instructions have a wide range of formats and because one instruction can require many clock cycles. The resultant speed of the microprocessor is often expressed in **millions of instructions per second (MIPS)**.

Companies such as Cyrix and Advanced Micro Devices produce Intel-compatible processor chips that are used in some IBM-compatible systems. These include the Cyrix MX-P233 and M-II P266 chips as well as the AMD K6 line. They perform just as well (and often better) but are much cheaper in price than comparable Intel chips. They provide an effective alternative for CPUs on NetWare servers and on desktops for general office applications.

To maximize speed, many engineering workstations running CAD applications (such as SUN workstations) are based on processors called **reduced instruction set computers (RISC)**. RISC processors are very fast and efficient because their instructions are all the same length, and each instruction performs a very specific process. There are also fewer instructions than on a CISC chip. The disadvantage of RISC processors is that the software development is more complex, requires sophisticated compilers to convert programs to the machine language format, and can perform slower with general office applications.

The biggest advantage of RISC- over CISC-based computers is the increased speed of floating-point math calculations. This speed advantage is the reason RISC-based processors are often used in workstations that run engineering, CAD, or scientific applications.

A **math coprocessor** is an extension of a chip's basic instruction set that allows the microprocessor to perform more complex arithmetic operations such as square root and trigonometric functions. Math coprocessors are built into the 80486DX, Pentium, Pentium Pro, and Pentium II processors. Math coprocessors can greatly increase the speed of spreadsheet programs and applications used for engineering and CAD, which typically perform many square root and trigonometric calculations.

Intel Microprocessors

The Intel family of microprocessor chips is probably the best known because of the wide acceptance of IBM-compatible computers based on this processor design. Knowing the capabilities and limitations of the processors can help you make the best use of existing systems on a network as well as select the correct processor chip when a new system needs to be purchased.

The Intel 8088 processor chip, included in the IBM PC, which was introduced in 1981, started the IBM PC-compatible industry. The 8088 has a 4 MHz clock speed, a 20-bit address bus that can access up to 1 MB of RAM, and a 16-bit register system. It allowed designers to create everything a PC user would need in the then-foreseeable future. Running the instruction set that comes with the original Intel 8088 microprocessor is referred to as operating in **real mode**. Real-mode instructions use 16-bit data registers and can directly access only 1 million bytes of memory. The DOS operating system—and the thousands of DOS software applications still in use—were designed specifically for the original 8088 microprocessor. This means that even if you have the latest and fastest Intel processor chip, your workstation computer is limited to 640 KB of RAM and 16-bit instructions when it runs DOS-based software in real mode.

The need for more powerful processor chips led to the development of the 80286 processor, which provided up to seven times the performance of the 8088 processor while providing compatibility for real-mode programs. Included in the IBM AT, which was introduced in 1984, the 80286 microprocessor added three new capabilities:

- The address bus was increased to 24 bits to allow for up to 16 MB of system RAM.

- The clock speed was increased to between 8 and 20 MHz.

- It can switch between real mode and protected mode.

Real-mode operation allows the microprocessor to act like a very fast 8088; **protected mode** allows it to run multiple programs more reliably by preventing one program from affecting the operation of another. For example, if you are using real mode to run a new program in your computer and the program attempts to write data into memory cells used by DOS, the computer can crash and interrupt all other applications. When the new program is run in protected mode, however, its attempt to write the data will be recognized as invalid and will be terminated, although other programs continue to operate normally.

The 80386 chip represented a significant advancement over earlier chips while still retaining compatibility with software written for the older processors. Although the design is now dated, it was popular, and you may still encounter a number of workstation computers based on the 80386 processor chip. Although the 80386 is capable of 32-bit processing (because of its 32-bit internal registers and data paths), most PC add-on boards and software were designed for older 8- or 16-bit processors and are therefore unable to make optimum use of the 80386's 32-bit capability. Other features of the 80386 include:

- The use of **virtual memory** to allow hard disk space to simulate a large amount of internal RAM. Although the use of virtual memory slows down the computer's throughput, it also allows you to run large programs that would not otherwise fit in the existing RAM

- The addition of **virtual real mode** enabling multiple real-mode programs to run simultaneously

- The ability to run at a variety of clock speeds ranging from 16 to 40 MHz

Beginning with NetWare 3.1x, the NetWare server required an 80836 or later processor because the network operating system (NOS) was written for the virtual real-mode instruction set.

2

All new Intel-based workstations and NetWare servers you install will be based on Pentium, Pentium Pro, or Pentium II microprocessors. The Pentium microprocessors all provide compatibility with software written for earlier processors but with the increased computing power needed for high-speed graphics-based software (such as for Windows). They can also support the powerful NetWare servers that accommodate multiple high-speed workstations as well as communications services.

The 80486 chip was a supercharged version of the 80386 chip that incorporated more than 1 million transistor components. Many workstations you may encounter as a network administrator will still contain this processor. The 80486 included the following features:

- Clock speeds were higher, ranging from 33 to 100 MHz

- An 8 KB high-speed memory cache (L1 cache) allowed the processor to access commonly used memory locations without going through the slower external data bus

- A math coprocessor was built in

There were two main versions of the 80486 chip. The 80486SX was a less expensive version of the 80486DX chip and did not include the math coprocessor.

Intel's Pentium chip represented a major leap ahead of earlier Intel chips by incorporating two 80486-type microprocessors on a single chip that can process two instructions simultaneously. The first Pentium chip operated at 75 MHz with 64-bit registers and more than 3 million transistors. The Pentium math coprocessor has been redesigned to achieve a 300% improvement in geometric computations over 80486 chips, allowing graphics-intensive applications to operate at much faster speeds.

Intel has usually tried to move users to each new microprocessor as quickly as possible. With the Pentium, however, Intel has continued developing the chip to extend its useful life span. The result is the Pentium MMX microprocessor, a version of the Pentium released in late 1996 that has been enhanced to speed up multimedia functions. In fact, software must be specifically written to take advantage of the MMX capability or there will be no performance enhancement at all. The need for multimedia processing is increasing as more software products are delivered on CD-ROM and as Internet content includes more audio, video, and 3D components.

The Intel Pentium Pro processor was designed for optimal performance with 32-bit software while maintaining compatibility with previous Intel processors. It still uses a 32-bit word, but its design includes 5.5 million transistors in the chip, and it operates at speeds up to 200 MHz. The Pentium Pro chip also includes a 256 KB L2 cache to accelerate data input. One of the Pentium Pro's main features is called dynamic execution. **Dynamic execution** combines three processing techniques: multiple branch prediction, dataflow analysis, and speculative execution. In multiple branch prediction, the Pentium Pro looks several programming steps ahead in the program and predicts which steps will be processed next. Dataflow analysis is then used to set up an optimized schedule for performing the program steps, which leads to speculative execution, which performs the steps as scheduled by the dataflow analysis. Table 2-1 lists the basic specifications of the Intel family of microprocessors for easy comparison.

Table 2-1   Microprocessor specifications

Processor	Word Size	Data Bus	Address Bus	Maximum Clock Speed	Math Coprocessor	Millions of Instructions per Second
8088	16	8	20	10 Mhz	No	0.33
80286	16	16	24	20 Mhz	No	3
80386SX	32	16	24	33 Mhz	No	5
80386DX	32	32	32	33 Mhz	No	11
80486SX	32	32	32	33 Mhz	No	41
80486DX	32	32	32	100 Mhz (DX4)	Yes	80
Pentium	32	64	32	200 Mhz	Yes	>100
Pentium MMX	32	64	32	233 Mhz	Yes	>100
Pentium Pro	32	64 (+8 ECC)	36	200 Mhz	Yes	>100
Pentium II	32	64 (+8 ECC) (effective 128 with DIMMS)	36	450 Mhz	Yes	>100

Note

The Pentium Pro runs best with a true 32-bit operating system such as Windows NT Workstation or OS/2. If Windows 95 is used as the operating system, performance suffers. That is because Windows 95 (despite its advertising) has a significant amount of 16-bit code. The Pentium Pro cannot handle 16-bit code directly, but has to emulate this ability. A Pentium system running Windows 95 therefore can actually outperform the Pentium Pro system when using older 16-bit user applications.

The Intel Pentium II processor is the most common processor offering on new systems and is quite similar to the Pentium Pro. It offers an enhanced L1 cache of 32 KB, plus 512 KB of L2 cache. This is double the cache in the Pentium Pro. Intel offers the chip in 233, 266, 300, 333, and 400 MHz versions, although they anticipate higher speeds in future releases.

For NetWare 5.0, the preference is to run a Pentium 233 or better. If more money is available in the budget, put it into additional RAM. NetWare performance can increase dramatically when RAM goes from 64 MB (the minimum on NetWare 5.0) to 128 or 264 MB.

Other Microprocessors

Some workstations you will encounter as a network administrator are not based on Intel or Intel-compatible microprocessors. Apple Macintosh computers are based on the Motorola 68000 line of microprocessors; Apple PowerMac computers are based on the PowerPC microprocessor. These processors are not covered in this book.

Interrupts and I/O Ports

To provide for input from and output to the computer system, you need to be able to attach such devices as keyboards, printers, monitors, network cards, and the mouse. These devices are commonly known as **peripherals** because they are added on to the system board. Each peripheral device attached to the system board—from the hard disk to the keyboard—must be controlled and monitored by the microprocessor. This monitoring is accomplished by interrupts and input/output (I/O) ports. To configure adapter cards correctly, you need to know how interrupts and I/O ports work. (Chapter 5 tells you how to configure network adapter cards and software when you install NetWare on both server and workstation computers.)

Common Interrupts. An **interrupt request (IRQ)** is a signal that a device or controller card sends to the processor to inform it that the device or controller needs attention. Your telephone is a good example of how an interrupt request works in a computer. When the phone rings, it means that someone is trying to contact you, and you normally try to answer it as soon as possible before you lose the opportunity to speak with the caller. On a network, when a packet arrives at the network card of the NetWare server, it signals the server by "ringing" its interrupt. When the NetWare server detects the interrupt signal of a packet arrival, it temporarily stops its work and spends a few microseconds putting the data packet from the network card into memory before returning to its work.

Each device in a computer system needs to have its own unique interrupt so that the processor will not misinterpret the source of the interrupt signal. If your doorbell is wired so that it also causes your telephone to ring, you cannot be sure which to answer when you hear them. A wrong guess results in the loss of information. In a similar way, two devices using the same interrupt number in a computer system cannot interact correctly with the processor, and your system performance will be sporadic at best.

Because of the limited number of system interrupt numbers, it is impossible to assign unique numbers to every category of computer peripheral. There are some general usage guidelines for system interrupts, however. Figure 2-4 shows interrupt numbers used on several of the most common system devices. Each manufacturer allows you to adjust the interrupt setting of its peripheral device, so you can choose an interrupt setting that does not conflict with other system devices.

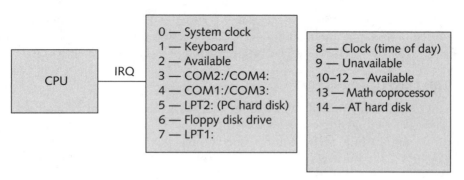

Figure 2-4 Common interrupt usage

Input/Output Ports. An **input/output (I/O) port** is a memory location that the processor uses to send control commands to a peripheral device and read back status information. To communicate with each device separately, each peripheral attached to the computer system needs a unique I/O port address range. Table 2-2 lists I/O port addresses for several common peripherals. To avoid conflicts with other devices in a computer, each peripheral controller card manufacturer provides a number of different I/O port address options. The network administrator's job includes assigning unique I/O port settings for network cards.

Table 2-2 Common device configurations

Device	Interrupt	I/O Address
COM1	4	3F8-3FFh
COM2	3	2F8-2FFh
COM3	4	3E8-3EF
LPT1	7	378-37Fh
LPT2	5	278-27Fh
Hard disk controller	14	1F0-1F8 170-177
Network interface card	3	300-31Fh

The **parallel port** connects the computer to a parallel cable, which transfers data from the computer to a peripheral device eight bits at a time on parallel wires. The parallel port is commonly referred to as the printer port because almost all printers use a standard parallel port interface. This makes it easy to plug almost any printer into the parallel port of a computer. The parallel cable attaches to a 25-pin connector on the back of the computer and a larger 36-pin card edge connector on the printer. The use of the parallel port for printers was standardized by the Centronics printer company. As a result of the early popularity of the Centronics standard, all IBM-compatible computer and printer manufacturers today include the Centronics parallel port on their systems.

In contrast to parallel ports, which transmit an entire byte at one time, the **serial port** on IBM-compatible computers sends only one bit of data at a time. One advantage of the serial port is its ability to send information between devices over long distances by using only a few wires in a twisted-pair cable. In addition, serial ports allow the attachment of devices, such as modems, that can translate bits into an analog signal compatible with telephone systems, thereby allowing a worldwide range of computer communications.

A new type of serial port, called the **Universal Serial Bus (USB)**, is now available on systems. This allows for multiple devices to be connected to the same port. Also, it is up to ten times faster in throughput (up to 12 Mbps) than the earlier specification. However, the hardware devices connected to it must be manufactured to support USB or they won't gain any advantage from using the port.

The speed of the serial signal is the **baud rate**. Standard serial port baud rates on a computer range from 300 up to 115,000 baud. For digital signals, such as those from the flashlight, the baud rate is equal to the number of **bits per second (bps)**. When a modem sends analog frequencies over the telephone, the bit pattern is represented by a change in frequency, which allows several bits to be transmitted for each baud. In this case, the rate of bits per second is often much faster than the baud rate.

Serial communication can be either synchronous or asynchronous. **Synchronous communication**, commonly used with LAN cards to send packets consisting of 1,500 or more bytes between computers, takes place at very high speeds ranging from 4 to more than 100 Mbps (megabits per second). Synchronous ports are generally quite expensive because they require special control and timing circuitry. Asynchronous communication is much simpler, sending only one character at a time. **Asynchronous communication** is often used by modems to transmit information between microcomputers, or between a microcomputer and the Internet or an on-line information service provider such as America Online or CompuServe.

In asynchronous communication, each character is transmitted separately and is encapsulated with a start and stop bit and an optional **parity bit** for error checking (see Figure 2-5). The parity bit is set to either odd (off) or even (on). Even parity means that the total number of one bits, including the parity bit, is even. In the case of the letter *C*, the parity bit is turned on by the transmitter to indicate an even number of one bits. If one of the bits is accidentally changed during transmission by a bad cable or a noise on the line, the receiving computer detects an error because the number of one bits is no longer even. Parity works well for single-bit errors, but its reliability falls off when more than one bit is changed.

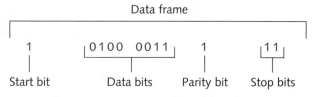

Figure 2-5 Asynchronous data frame

Most system board manufacturers build one or more asynchronous ports into their IBM-compatible systems. These ports are generally referred to as COM1 through COM4, have either 25-pin or 9-pin connectors, and are located on the back of the computer. Two types of serial port connectors, known as **RS232** connectors, were standardized by the Electronic Industry Association (EIA) in the early days of computing. **Data Terminal Equipment (DTE)** connectors are used on computers, and **Data Communications Equipment (DCE)** connectors are used on modems. This means that a simple connector-to-connector cable can connect a computer to a modem, as shown in Figure 2-6. Most of the 25-pin connections on the RS232 cable are not used by standard PC serial communications, allowing a 9-pin connector to consist of only the required pin connections. A special type of RS232 cable called a **null modem cable** is used to connect two DTE computers without the use of a modem. Note that the null modem cable pictured at the bottom of Figure 2-6 has certain wires crossed to allow the signals from the sending computer to go to the correct connectors on the receiving computer.

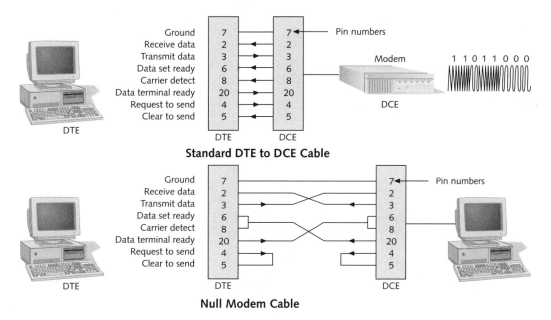

Figure 2-6 RS232 serial cables

Expansion Slots

As you learned earlier in this chapter, the expansion slots connect add-in cards, such as video cards and NICs, to the system board. They are connected to other components by the expansion bus. As the capabilities of microprocessors have improved, the demands placed on the expansion bus have grown. The architecture of the expansion bus has changed and improved over time. Part of the change in the expansion bus consists of changes in the connectors used in the expansion slot. This is illustrated in Figure 2-7, which shows various PC connector types. Notice that an expansion card designed for one expansion bus system cannot be used in another because of differences in the design of the expansion slot connectors.

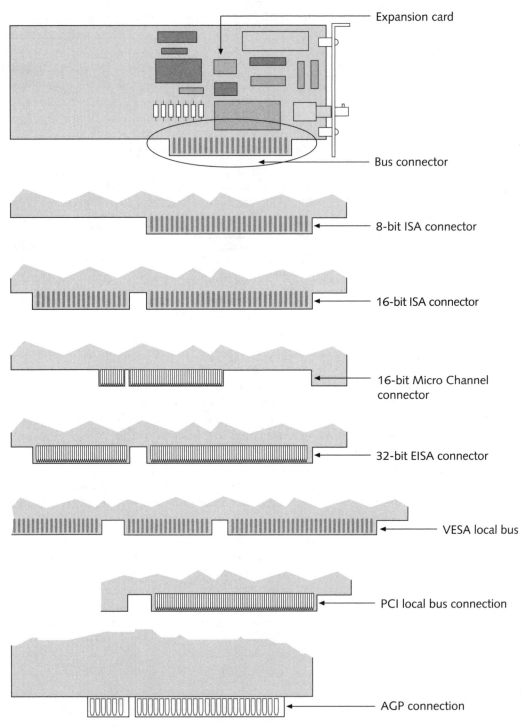

Figure 2-7   Common PC connector types

ISA Bus.   The **Industry Standard Architecture (ISA) bus** was introduced in 1984 with the IBM AT computer. It supported 16-bit data and 24-bit address buses running at 8 MHz. The system board also contained a local bus that supported up to 32-bit data and address paths at high clock speeds (such as 33 MHz) between the microprocessor and memory. Many lower-cost personal computers used the ISA bus because it provided satisfactory performance for many applications and low-end NetWare servers. (In fact, most systemboards sold still include one or more ISA slots for backward compatibility.) The main disadvantage of the ISA bus was seen in graphics applications that required high-speed video processing. Because a video card placed in an ISA expansion slot was limited to a 16-bit data bus and an 8 MHz clock speed, Windows or graphics-based applications ran slowly even on Pentium-based computers. To determine if a system has an ISA bus, you can check the system's manual or examine the system board. ISA slots on the system board have 16-bit card slots composed of two sockets placed together, one containing 31 pins and the other containing 18 pins.

Micro Channel Bus.   The **Micro Channel bus** architecture is owned by IBM and can support 32-bit expansion slots running at high clock speeds (such as 33 MHz). A major advantage of the Micro Channel architecture was that it kept card configuration information in **CMOS (Complementary Metal–Oxide Semiconductor) memory** on the system board, allowing software instead of hardware setting of card options and configurations. Because the CMOS memory is backed up by a small battery, these card settings are preserved when the computer is turned off.

Micro Channel was developed for IBM's PS/2 line, but lack of success with that line and with licensing the architecture forced IBM to discontinue using Micro Channel architecture in its PCs. (IBM now uses Intel's PCI bus in its products.) However, you may encounter a few older PCs with the Micro Channel bus still in use.

 ISA and PCI cards cannot be used in Micro Channel slots. Because the expansion slots are different, cards designed for the ISA bus cannot be used on a Micro Channel computer.

EISA Bus.   When IBM introduced its proprietary Micro Channel bus, other PC manufacturers who wanted to sell systems with the increased performance of IBM's 32-bit bus slots were required to pay IBM royalties as well as redesign their systems. As a counteraction, a number of IBM-compatible computer manufacturers cooperated on the design of an enhanced version of the ISA bus that would support 32-bit expansion cards and higher clock speeds. The result was the **Extended Industry Standard Architecture (EISA) bus**, which supported 32-bit data and address expansion slots that could support adapter cards at 8 MHz clock speeds. Because the EISA bus was an extension of the ISA bus, it included 16-bit expansion slots that accepted older ISA cards. Of course, ISA cards placed in these slots still used the limited ISA address and data bus sizes.

In the end, however, consumers responded to Intel's PCI bus initiative rather than EISA, in part because the various vendors in the EISA consortium, although agreeing on a standard, did not develop consistently compatible cards for the EISA bus. Users were continually frustrated that EISA cards would not work in an EISA system board. Although Intel suffered many of the same problems with the PCI bus, they were fewer. Users then began to migrate to the new PCI standard.

Bus mastering, a technique first used in EISA and Micro Channel bus systems and now included with the PCI bus, enables adapter cards to off-load such tasks as moving information into memory to improve overall system performance. Bus mastering is an important option to consider when selecting a NetWare server computer. Much of a NetWare server's processing involves moving information to and from memory. Bus mastering can greatly improve the performance of a NetWare server by making the system's CPU available more frequently.

VESA Bus. Not long after the 80486 chip was introduced, IBM-compatible system board manufacturers struggled to provide systems that would enable the video and hard-drive peripherals to match the increased speed of the latest microprocessors. The Video Electronics Standards Association (VESA) cooperated with Intel to design a new system bus architecture that would allow peripheral cards such as the video adapter to have direct access to the local bus of the system board at the same clock speed as the system board. With the advent of the Pentium chip, Intel's PCI bus became the commonly used expansion bus. You might encounter the VESA bus in PC workstations and NetWare servers that have an 80486 microprocessor. The **VESA bus** consisted of an extension to the 16-bit ISA slot, enabling the slot to be used for either a VESA-compatible device or a 16-bit adapter. This extension allowed a card placed in a VESA slot to become part of the local bus of the system board and achieve much faster data transmission. VESA slots can be included on 80486 system boards that have both ISA or EISA expansion slots. On PC workstations using graphics-intensive applications, a system's VESA slot was most often used for the video card, as this greatly increased the performance of graphics-based applications. On NetWare servers, which must be able to move many large blocks of data to and from the disk and the network cards, the VESA slot was often used for high-speed disk controllers and NICs.

PCI Bus. The latest local bus designed by Intel is called the **Peripheral Component Interface (PCI) bus**. The PCI bus improves on the older VESA bus design by avoiding the standard input/output bus and using the system bus to take full advantage of the Pentium chip's 64-bit data path. In addition, the PCI bus runs at the 60 or 66 MHz speed of the processor (compared with the 33 MHz maximum speed of the VESA bus). (It will soon have a 100 Mhz version as well.) The biggest limitation of the PCI bus is that it will support only three to four slots on a system board. However, new systems are being designed that will provide multiple PCI buses on the same system board, to provide eight or more PCI slots.

Intel will continue to develop the PCI bus, and it will be used as a standard expansion bus in new workstations and servers. Combination buses will be the normal configuration, as the PCI bus is usually combined with an ISA bus (on PC workstations) or the EISA bus (on servers).

Speedy as the PCI bus is, it still isn't fast enough for onscreen video. To further enhance the display of full-motion video, Intel introduced the **Accelerated (or Advanced) Graphics Port (AGP)** specification. System boards with AGP can support adapters tailored for the delivery of high-speed, high-resolution video data. (You can see an example of an AGP slot in Figure 2-1, just to the right of the white PCI slots in the middle of the board.)

Memory

The purpose of the computer's primary memory unit is to store software and data in a manner that allows the microprocessor unit to access each storage cell directly. Memory consists of millions of tiny switches built into silicon memory modules that can be turned on or off to represent a binary one or zero. The memory switches are arranged in groups of eight to form memory cells called bytes. Every byte is assigned a unique number or address that distinguishes it from other memory bytes. Each memory byte can then be used to store one character of data or part of an instruction. The microprocessor can access memory by sending the address number of the desired byte on the address bus and then receiving the contents of the memory cell(s) on the data bus. On a 32-bit data bus, four sequential memory bytes can be sent to or from the microprocessor with one memory access.

Memory Types.   Four primary types of memory are used in microcomputer systems: RAM, ROM, CMOS, and high-speed cache. Each of these memory types has a specific function in processing information in a computer system. In this section you will learn about each type of memory and its role in operating a computer system.

RAM. Random-access memory (RAM) is considered a volatile form of memory because it depends on constant power; when power is turned off, the contents of the RAM are erased. A computer's RAM is its primary workspace, where programs and data are stored during processing. More RAM in workstations allows the use of larger and more complex software applications. A NetWare server computer uses additional RAM for file and directory caching (file caching is the process of storing often-used disk information in memory and is discussed in detail later in this chapter). Because memory is more than 100 times faster than disk access time, the amount of memory available for file caching directly affects the performance of a NetWare server computer.

The most common RAM in new systems is **Extended Data Output (EDO) RAM.** This type of RAM is faster than older RAM and is now the standard RAM used in Pentium, Pentium Pro, and Pentium II microcomputers.

The latest development in RAM is **Synchronous Dynamic RAM** or **SDRAM**. It differs from earlier types of RAM in being able to support higher clock speeds (up to 100Mhz). It actually synchronizes with the CPU's bus, which makes it about twice as fast as EDO RAM.

A special type of RAM, Video RAM, or VRAM, is used on graphics cards

When adding RAM to a microcomputer, be sure you add the correct type of RAM for that microcomputer. Check the specifications in the user's guide that came with the PC. It should be both the same type (EDO RAM, SDRAM, VRAM) and the same speed (60 ns [nanoseconds], 70 ns, etc.)

Read-only memory (ROM), as its name suggests, cannot be changed. On most microcomputer systems, ROM is used to store boot instructions and control such basic hardware functions as inputting data from the keyboard or accessing the disk drive. Because they cannot be changed, instructions stored in ROM are referred to as firmware. Because ROM is slower than RAM, most 80386 and later microprocessors allow moving the contents of ROM into RAM during booting, a process known as RAM shadowing. **RAM shadowing** can significantly increase the speed of such hardware-oriented operations as accessing the screen and keyboard.

The original IBM PC bus contained switches that were used to set configuration options such as memory capacity, disk drives, and video. Today's system boards contain a built-in setup program that is used to store this configuration information in a special memory type called CMOS. **CMOS (Complementary Metal-Oxide Semiconductor)** memory uses very little power, and its contents can be maintained with a small on-board battery when the computer's power is off. The CMOS battery is recharged whenever the system is powered. If you add a new disk drive or more memory, you will need to run a setup program to update your computer's CMOS configuration. Many CMOS setup programs are built into the ROM of the system board and can be executed by pressing a special key sequence (such as the Escape key) while the computer system is initially booting. Some computers need to be booted with a special disk in order to change the CMOS configuration settings.

Be aware that the CMOS battery can completely discharge when a computer is turned off for an extended period of time, causing loss of configuration information. It can also die due to old age. In either case, it is extremely wise to write down the CMOS settings and keep them in a safe place. That way you can restore them when required.

Cache memory is very high-speed memory made of chips called **SRAM (static RAM).** Most RAM consists of relatively inexpensive chips called **DRAM (dynamic RAM).** Although inexpensive, DRAM bears a hidden cost; it needs a special clock cycle to maintain its memory contents. Because of this extra refresh cycle, DRAM is slower than SRAM because it requires wait states when used with processors running at speeds above 20 MHz. SRAM's speed advantage over DRAM makes it more suitable for caching the most recently used memory locations. It increases the speed of processing by allowing the processor to access data or instructions without using wait states. High-speed (33 MHz

2

and above) computers typically need and use 128–256 KB of cache memory to improve their performance. Intel 80486, Pentium, Pentium Pro, and Pentium II microprocessors use built-in cache. The 80486 has 8 or 16 KB of cache memory, the Pentium has 16 KB, and the Pentium Pro has 16 KB built into the microprocessor chip. This is known as the level 1 (L1) cache (primary cache). Additional cache, known as the level 2 (L2) cache (secondary cache), can often be installed on the system board to increase system performance. Typically, 128–256 KB of L2 cache is used with the 80486 and Pentium. The Pentium Pro uses a built-in L2 cache of 256–512 KB. The Pentium II has 512 KB.

Single In-Line Memory Modules (SIMMs). Most RAM is currently provided on small memory cards called **single in-line memory modules (SIMMs)**, shown in Figure 2-8. SIMMs are arranged on the system board in banks. A bank can contain from one to four SIMM sockets, and a computer's system board contains several memory banks. Memory is added in banks by filling all SIMM sockets in the bank with the same type of SIMM chip. The number of SIMM banks determines the maximum amount of memory that can be placed on the system board as well as the ease of memory expansion. If a memory board does not contain enough SIMM banks, you can replace existing SIMMs with SIMMs of higher capacity in order to expand the computer's memory.

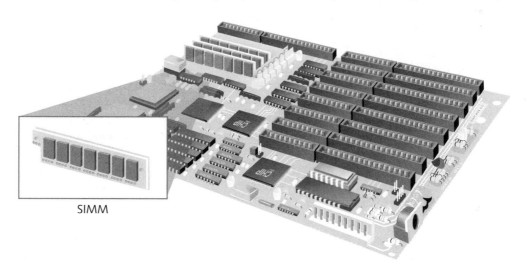

SIMM

Figure 2-8   Single in-line memory module (SIMM)

SIMMs most often contain 16, 32, or 64 MB of RAM and are supplied in 72-pin models; older 30-pin SIMMs are also found frequently. They supply 8 bits to the data bus per module; whereas the 72-pin SIMMs supply 32 bits per module. (The 30-pin SIMMs appeared in 80486 and earlier systemboards; the 72-pin appeared in later models.)

Various vendors offer special adapters to use 30-pin SIMMs in 72-pin slots. These are useful for expanding a system's RAM by salvaging SIMMs from older PCs.

As mentioned previously, each memory bank must be filled with the same type of SIMM, because SIMMs of different capacities cannot be mixed within a bank. (For example, a 4 MB SIMM cannot be mixed with a 16 MB SIMM.)

In addition to obtaining the correct capacity for the SIMMs, you need to make sure the SIMMs are the same speed (60 ns is typical, but many systems have 70 ns). The speed of most SIMMs ranges between 60 and 80 nanoseconds. When adding SIMMs to a computer, check the system's manual to verify the appropriate chip speeds. Some SIMMs are also marked with the speed.

Finally, you need to match the type of RAM used in the PC. If the PC was purchased with EDO RAM, use EDO RAM when you add memory.

The Pentium Pro and Pentium II also support dual in-line memory modules (DIMMs). This is a combination of two SIMMs, which are read alternatively in memory access cycles. This results in an effective data bus of 128 bits over the Pentium Pro's normal 64-bit data bus. These come as 168-pin modules, with a speed of 10ns.

Memory Usage.   Windows 95 for the most part automates memory management that you previously had to specify by statements in the CONFIG.SYS and AUTOEXEC.BAT files. The same memory models and terms, however, still apply, because Windows 95 must still support old DOS applications. DOS was designed to run on an 8088 processor in real mode and therefore is limited to managing 1 MB (1,024 KB) of RAM. As shown in Figure 2-9, the first 640 KB of this 1 MB memory area is referred to as **conventional memory** and is used by DOS to run software applications. The memory between 640 KB and 1 MB is called **upper memory** and is reserved for hardware use. For example, part of upper memory is used by your video card to store data displayed on the screen. The network administrator might need to use this memory area when configuring certain NICs. The memory above 1 MB is called **extended memory** and is available to microprocessors running in either protected or virtual mode. DOS requires an extended memory manager such as the HIMEM.SYS driver to take advantage of that memory. Operating systems that do not rely on DOS—Windows NT workstation, UNIX, OS/2, and NetWare—can access extended memory directly, without the need for special drivers.

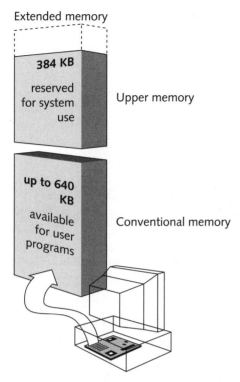

Figure 2-9   Memory map

Storage Systems

Advances in disk storage systems have been as important to the development of micro-computer systems as the improvements made to processors and memory. Instructions and data need to be retrieved from disks and placed in RAM before the processor chip can act on them. Therefore, both the speed and the capacity of disk storage are critical to the performance of a computer system. Consider a NetWare server's primary purpose for a moment. Its major function involves the shared use of its hard disk drives. The NetWare operating system is specifically designed to maximize the performance and reliability of its disk storage system. In this section you will learn about the basic terminology and concepts needed to understand and configure disk systems.

Magnetic Disk Drives

The magnetic disk drive is the component of the disk storage system in which data is stored by means of magnetic fields representing ones and zeros. The recording surface of the disk is coated with a metal oxide that retains magnetic fields. The polarity of each magnetic field is used to represent either a one or a zero. To perform record and play-back functions on the disk surfaces, recording heads containing electronic magnets are attached to a device called an **access arm** that allows the recording heads to move back and forth across the disk surface, as shown in Figure 2-10.

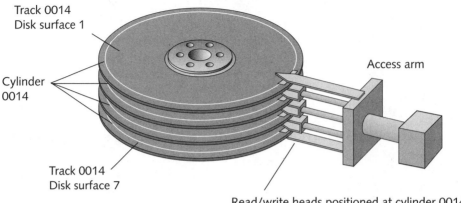

Figure 2-10   Disk drive components

The disk surface is divided into concentric circles called **tracks**. The set of recording tracks that can be accessed by the recording heads without the access arm being repositioned is referred to as a **cylinder**. A track, which can contain a large amount of data, is divided into smaller recording areas called **sectors**, as shown in Figure 2-11. Reading or recording information in sectors, which are small, specific areas, allows efficient access to the information.

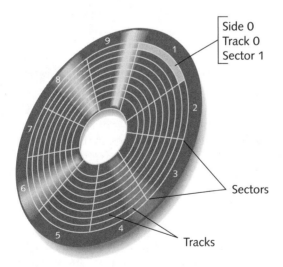

Figure 2-11   Tracks and sectors

2

Floppy Disk Drives

Microcomputer floppy disks used to be available in two sizes: 5¼ inches or 3½ inches. Although the 5¼-inch disks are obsolete, you still need to be familiar with their proper use and handling, because many files have been archived on 5¼-inch disks.

The 3½-inch floppy disk is today's standard because it provides higher densities, more reliability, and easier storage than the older 5¼-inch disk. Table 2-3 compares the storage capacities of 5¼-inch and 3½-inch floppy disks. However, even the venerable 3½-inch floppy is close to vanishing from newer PCs. Most software is now shipped using CD-ROM discs. Sharing files almost always requires more capacity than a 3½-inch disk can provide. For that reason, some vendors are offering Iomega's ZIP drives with 100 MB of capacity per disk in their systems. Others offer a new, higher-density disk with 120 MB of storage, called the LS-120 (or SuperDisk). Neither of these have gained enough market share to be called standards at the time of this writing.

Table 2-3   Floppy disk capacity

Size	Density	Number of tracks	Number of sectors	Capacity
5¼"	Double	40	9	360 KB
5¼"	High	80	15	1,200 KB or 1.2 MB
3½"	Double	80	9	720 KB
3½"	High	80	18	1,400 KB or 1.4 MB

Hard Disk Drives

A hard drive is so named because it contains one or more rigid aluminum platters coated with a metal oxide that holds magnetic fields. Each platter has a read/write head positioned above and below each disk surface. Rotating the disk surface at high speeds causes the read/write head to fly just above the disk surface. Because the recording head on hard drives does not touch the disk surface, hard drives do not wear out, as floppy disks do, and can last for several years.

You cannot assume that your data will always be safe even on a hard disk. Component failure, software bugs, and operator errors can and will eventually cause data loss, so it is critical that you establish a regular backup plan for data stored on hard disks.

For information to be recorded or retrieved on the hard disk, the recording head must first be positioned on the proper track. The time it takes to perform this operation is called the **seek time**. After it is positioned over the correct track, the read head begins looking for the requested sector. The time it takes for the sector to come into position is called the **rotational delay**. When the requested sector comes under the read head, it is read into a computer memory buffer. This is called the **transfer time**. The seek time plus the rotational delay plus the transfer time yields the **access time**. On hard disk drives, the access time is measured in milliseconds (ms). Most current hard disk drive access times range between 9 and 12 ms. The access time for floppy disks is close to 300 ms, making hard disk drives 10 to 25 times faster.

Once installed, a new hard disk needs to be partitioned for use by the operating system. With the exception of Windows, which uses a DOS partition, each operating system requires its own separate hard disk partition. **Partitioning** establishes boundaries within which an operating system formats and stores information on a hard disk. Several different operating system partitions can exist on the same hard disk. When you install NetWare on the NetWare server computer, for example, you need to create one partition for DOS and another for NetWare. Generally the DOS partition is very small— about 50 MB—because it is needed only to boot the computer and then load the NetWare operating system. The NetWare partition contains the storage areas used to store the data and software that will be available to the network. After the partition areas are established, each operating system needs to format its partition for its own use. In DOS this is done by the FORMAT program. The NetWare Install Wizard allows you to partition and format the disk drive for the NetWare server.

The directory area of the disk partition contains the names and locations of files and other information about each file stored in the partition. Storing an entire file can require many sectors scattered throughout the partition. DOS 6.22 and earlier operating systems used a **file allocation table (FAT)** to link all the sectors belonging to one file. Windows 95 (and the included DOS 7.0) uses a 32-bit **virtual file allocation table (VFAT)**, which is backward-compatible with the older FAT.

When you add information to an existing file, the new sectors can be located anywhere in the disk partition. The FAT or VFAT allows the computer to find all sectors for a file. When you load a file from the disk, the computer first reads the directory to determine the location of the first sector. It then reads each sector of the file as specified by the FAT or VFAT. The NetWare network operating system also uses a FAT, and the NetWare server keeps the entire FAT and the most frequently accessed directory sectors in memory.

Disk Interfaces

Disk interfaces, or **controller cards**, enable a system's microprocessor to control the hard and floppy disk drives in a computer and provide a path for data to be transferred between the disk and memory. The disk controller card plugs into one of the expansion bus slots in a computer's system board or may be built into the circuits of the system board. There are several types of disk controller cards. This section describes the most common ones: the IDE/EIDE/ATA controllers found in most workstations today, and the SCSI controller cards often used in NetWare servers and high-end workstations. To configure the NetWare operating system correctly, a network administrator must be able to distinguish among different controller cards.

2

Today there are two major types of **Integrated Drive Electronics (IDE)** hard disk controller cards on the market: IDE and enhanced IDE. IDE controller cards are often referred to as paddle cards because most of the control electronics are built into the disk drive itself. Because few circuits are required for the IDE disk controller, most IDE controller cards come with a floppy disk controller as well as serial, parallel, and game ports.

Standard IDE controllers can control up to two hard disk drives and support drive capacities between 40 and 528 MB, along with transfer speeds of 3.3 MB/sec and data access speeds of less than 18 ms. As a result of their low cost and high performance, IDE controllers became very popular and were used on most desktop computers. Although IDE controllers and drives are appropriate for small- to medium-sized NetWare servers having a total disk capacity of less than 528 MB, most NetWare servers use either SCSI or enhanced IDE controller cards.

Enhanced IDE (EIDE) controllers and drives offer **Logical Block Addressing (LBA)**, which allows them to provide up to 8.4 GB (billion bytes), well above the standard IDE limit of 528 MB. In addition, Enhanced IDE offers transfer rates of up to 13.3 MB/sec and access times of 8.5 ms. The Enhanced IDE speed improvements are achieved by increasing the disk drive rotational speed from 3,000 rpm to more than 10,000 rpm, by employing better read/write heads, and by using an advanced technology that allows the access arm to move from track to track in one-tenth the time required by standard IDE drives. To take advantage of the increased transfer speed, the Enhanced IDE card must be installed in a PCI expansion slot. In addition to increased capacity and drive speed, Enhanced IDE also provides for up to four devices, including nondisk peripherals such as CD-ROM or tape drives. The increased speed and capacity of the Enhanced IDE disk system, combined with the ability to connect up to four devices, make it a good choice for many NetWare server environments.

Ultra DMA or ATA-33 is a newer implementation of EIDE now appearing on the market. It offers a 33 MB/second transfer speed, but requires special drivers with Windows 95 to recognize the drive. There is even a proposed upgrade called ATA-66 with a 66 MB/sec speed possibly ready for delivery in the next year.

The **Small Computer System Interface (SCSI)** is a general-purpose interface card that can control hard disks, tape backup systems, CD-ROM drives, and floppy disks. As shown in Figure 2-12, up to seven SCSI devices can be chained together and attached to a single SCSI control card. The last device in each chain has a terminator enabled to properly end the cable segment. Multiple SCSI controllers can coexist in the same computer.

The SCSI standard theoretically supports a service priority using the highest numbers and on in descending order. However, in real-world usage this ranking does not produce any significant results. A better performance solution would be to load two SCSI buses with two devices each, rather than one board with four.

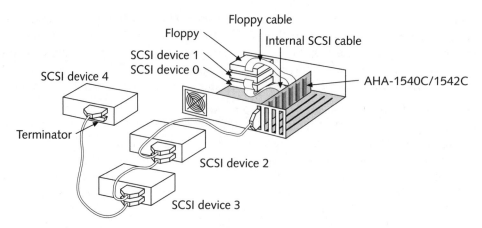

Figure 2-12   SCSI drive interface

SCSI hard disk capacities normally range from 2.1 GB to 18 GB or more. Because they are more complex, SCSI controller cards and drives are generally more expensive than comparable ATA drives. SCSI controllers use a parallel form of communication, sending eight or more bits to a drive at one time. This provides for higher transfer rates to and from the drive. Other controllers use serial communication, transferring only one bit at a time.

SCSI-2 is an upgrade to the original SCSI specifications that provided a more standard command set along with additional commands to access CD-ROM drives, tape drives, optical drives, and several other peripherals. A feature of SCSI-2 called **command queuing** allows a device to accept multiple commands and execute them in the order the device deems most efficient. This feature is particularly important for NetWare servers that could have several workstations making requests for information from the disk system at the same time. Another feature of the SCSI-2 controller is a high-speed transfer option called Fast SCSI-2, which, at 40 Mbps, is nearly twice as fast as previous SCSI transfer speeds. In addition to the Fast SCSI-2 option, the SCSI-2 controller can further increase transfer speeds by using a 16-bit data bus between the SCSI-2 controller card and devices called Wide SCSI-2. This 16-bit data bus allows for twice as much data to be transferred between the controller and disk drive as could be transferred using the original 8-bit data bus found on standard SCSI controllers.

Because SCSI-2 controller cards accommodate more devices and provide larger storage capacities, they are often the choice for NetWare server computers on medium to large networks requiring more than 10 GB of hard disk, along with support for CD-ROM drives and tape drives. SCSI-2 drives have the following advantages over Enhanced IDE drives for use in a NetWare server:

- SCSI-2 supports as many as seven devices chained to a single adapter; Enhanced IDE supports a maximum of four devices attached to two controller cards

- SCSI-2 provides multitasking via command queuing, which results in better performance when multiple disk requests are pending

- The variety of SCSI-2 storage peripherals is far greater than is afforded by Enhanced IDE, especially regarding special devices such as magneto-optical drives that are sometimes used for data archiving

 The SCSI-3 interface provides the ability to transfer data at a rate of 100 Mbps over a six-wire cable, compared to the 40 Mbps maximum of Fast Wide SCSI-2 over a 128-wire cable.

RAID Systems

A network administrator is concerned with data integrity because network downtime can result in significant loss of revenue for an organization. Thus, the NetWare server computer must be as reliable as possible. A popular way to increase the reliability of the NetWare server disk system is to use a **Redundant Array of Independent Disks (RAID)**. RAID provides protection from loss of data due to a bad disk drive. There are three levels of RAID systems in general use: 1, 3, and 5. RAID level 1 is the most common; it uses multiple disk drives and controllers along with software to provide basic disk mirroring and duplexing available with NetWare (these concepts are discussed later in the chapter). RAID level 3 is a hardware solution that takes each byte of data off several drives; one drive is used for parity checking and error correcting. If a drive fails in a level 3 RAID system, the parity drive can be used to reconstruct each data byte on the replacement drive.

A level-5 RAID system is more sophisticated. It takes data off the drives by sector. The parity information is embedded in the sectors, eliminating the use of a dedicated parity drive. Many RAID systems also support **hot-swapping**, which allows a drive to be replaced while the computer is running. With hot-swapping, the network administrator can replace a malfunctioning disk drive and have the system resynchronize the drive without interrupting network services. The hot-swapping feature can be well worth its extra cost when your NetWare server needs to support mission-critical applications that cannot be interrupted.

CD-ROM Drives

Compact disc read–only memory (CD-ROM) technology is different from that of magnetic disk drives in that it uses light from low-intensity laser beams to read binary ones and zeros from the disk platter rather than sensing magnetic fields contained on hard and floppy disk surfaces. Data is permanently recorded on a CD-ROM at the factory. The main benefit of a CD-ROM is its storage capacity. A standard CD-ROM can store more than 680 MB of data, which makes CD-ROMs a very good way to distribute and access large software applications, collections of programs, or other data-intensive files such as sound, graphic images, and video.

CD-ROMs store data using microscopic "pits" arranged in a single spiral track that winds continuously from the outside to the inside of the disk, much like the tracks on old vinyl phonograph records. There are about 2.8 billion pits on a single CD-ROM spiral track. When a CD-ROM is accessed, the drive uses a laser beam to measure the reflections off the pits in the spiral track. These reflections vary in intensity as the light reflects off the pits. The fluctuations in the reflected light are then converted into digital ones and zeros.

Many users need access to CD-ROMs on their workstation computers. This can be accomplished by installing CD-ROM drives on each workstation, by sharing CD-ROM drives from the network NetWare server, or by a combination of both strategies. CD-ROM drives are attached to a computer through either a SCSI or an IDE/EIDE bus interface controller card.

CD-ROM technology also includes two writable versions: CD-R and CD-RW. CD-R is a write-once medium. This means that once you record on the disc, you cannot erase that information. CD-RW is a rewritable system. This means you can erase data you record on the device. All CD-RW devices can record CD-Rs as well as CD-RW media.

 If you try to store information on a CD-ROM, you will receive a Write Protected error message because the device is read-only.

The main advantage of attaching one or more shared CD-ROM drives to a NetWare server rather than running the discs at each workstation is that it reduces the cost of multiple CD-ROM titles. When a shared CD-ROM drive is attached to the NetWare server, NetWare assigns a drive pointer to it. This allows the information to be accessed and shared across the network, just like any other data on the NetWare server's hard disks.

DVD-ROM Drives

The **Digital Versatile Disc (DVD)** is the successor to the CD-ROM. It represents the merging of three technologies: computer, audio, and video. DVDs come in two basic types: DVD-video, for home entertainment, and **DVD-ROM**, targeted for computer application. DVD technology uses the same-sized disc as CD-ROM (120MM) but stores 4.7 GB of data (8.5 GB double-sided).

 Although DVD-ROM drives may read DVD-video discs, your PC might not be capable of handling the video data stream fast enough to display it in real time on your monitor.

DVD-ROM also uses a new data format called **Universal Data Format (UDF)**. Windows 98 reads UDF discs without added drivers. Windows 95 and earlier devices however, require special software to read the contents of UDF discs.

When you purchase a system with DVD-ROM drives, look for the MultiRead logo. This tells you that the drive can read all other types of 120 MM optical media including CD-ROM, CD-R, and CD-RW. Look for the MultiRead logo on new CD-ROM systems as well. Otherwise there's no guarantee that the system will read CD-RW discs.

Video Monitors

A network administrator can be called on to make decisions regarding the types of monitors and adapter cards to be used in workstation computers. This section provides an overview of the video system information that you need to meet the requirements of Novell's network administrator exam.

The ability of a computer to display graphics depends on the video adapter and type of monitor connected. A **pixel** (or picture element) is a point on the screen that can be turned on or off. It is composed of three very small dots—one red, one green, and one blue. The dots are adjusted and combined to create the color and intensity of the pixel. The **resolution** of a video adapter is measured by the number of pixels on each line and on the number of lines. For example, a resolution of 320 × 200 indicates 320 pixels per line with 200 lines, for a total of 64,000 pixels.

Dot pitch is a measurement of how close together the dots that make up each pixel are placed. A smaller dot pitch results in a clearer and crisper display screen. A dot pitch of 0.28 or less is generally desirable for a video monitor.

Noninterlaced monitors are preferable to interlaced monitors. An interlaced monitor scans every other line on the screen, causing more eye strain. Noninterlaced monitors have a faster scanning system that scans each line from top to bottom to create a smoother screen image. Most monitors today are noninterlaced.

VGA

The **Video Graphics Array (VGA)** adapter and monitor is found routinely on older systems. VGA supported all previous video modes and both monochrome and color monitors. A monochrome monitor was often the best choice for an inexpensive monitor for a NetWare server computer, because it could be plugged directly into a standard VGA interface card and provided a good-quality text display. One big difference between VGA and previous video adapters was its use of analog signals rather than the digital RGB interface. The more expensive analog signal provides many more color variations over the same number of wires.

Super VGA (SVGA)

The **Super VGA (SVGA)** adapter is an enhanced version of the VGA adapter that allows better resolution and more color combinations. Additional memory is usually required on VGA adapters in order to provide the enhanced capabilities. Super VGA adapters can display 256 colors with a resolution of 800 × 600, or up to 1024 × 768 when used with 16 colors. Most monitors sold today are SVGA monitors.

XGA

The **eXtended Graphics Array** or **XGA** is the latest in monitor technology for laptops and notebook computers. It offers up to 1024 × 768 resolution, similar to the SVGA standard, but with additional colors (such as 65,536 versus 16 for SVGA at 640 × 480 resolution).

Graphics Accelerators

Because of the increasing graphics demands of programs, video card manufacturers started building video adapters with a microprocessor called a **graphics accelerator** to speed up graphics operations. Accelerators are now found on most graphics cards and are often built into the system board. Graphics adapters based on accelerators feature resolutions of 1024 × 768, 1280 × 1024, and 1600 × 1200, with up to 16.7 million colors.

To further enhance the display of onscreen video, systemboards with the new AGP specification mentioned earlier can support adapters tailored for delivering high-speed video data.

Power System

All system components depend on electricity to operate, so the last but most important part of any computer system is its power system. Power problems can often cause intermittent computer crashes and losses of data that cannot be tolerated on a NetWare server computer. A network administrator needs to be familiar with the components that make up a NetWare server's power system. In this section you will learn about the major power components and how you can use them to provide reliable power to a NetWare server.

Power Supply

A power supply that does not have enough amps or that does not filter out power irregularities can cause system errors or crashes. Because a NetWare server often has multiple high-capacity hard drives along with many other peripherals such as CD-ROM drives, tape drives, and NICs, the power supply must be able to support the amperage needed by all these devices. A NetWare server should have a switching power supply of at least 400 watts. A **switching power supply** will stop working if there is a serious component failure or short in the system. A built-in surge suppressor and a power filter are both good features that will help protect system components from damage by voltage spikes during electrical storms or if your computer is running on the same power line as other high-power electrical equipment such as motors and copy machines.

Power Line

The first rule in providing good power to a NetWare server computer is to have an electrician install a separate power line from the main fuse box to the server room. This power line should have no other equipment or computers attached to it. Especially avoid attaching laser printers or copy machines to the same power line used by the NetWare server, because these devices can create power fluctuations and electrical noise that harm the system.

Power Filters

The second line of defense in the power system is a good power filter that will remove any noise or power surges from the incoming line. It is a good idea to have your local power company or an electrician use a voltage monitor on your incoming power over a period of several days, to determine the extent of any electrical noise or power surges experienced in the NetWare server room. You can then use the voltage monitor information to buy the correct power filter to protect your server from unwanted electrical noise and surges.

Uninterruptible Power Supply

In addition to a high-quality power supply and filter, each NetWare server should be protected from brownouts and blackouts by an uninterruptible power supply (UPS). A UPS contains a battery that automatically provides power in the event of a commercial power failure. Depending on the capacity of its battery, a UPS unit can provide power to the server for up to 30 minutes after commercial power has failed. The capacity of most UPS systems is measured in volt-amps (VA). Volt-amps are calculated by multiplying the number of amps needed times the voltage. To determine the correct size of the UPS needed for a server, first list each piece of equipment to be protected (CPU, monitor, external drives, and so on). Include its nameplate-rated wattage or VA. Then total all wattage and VA to obtain the total wattage and total volt-amps necessary—this total must be less than or equal to the recommended output of the UPS.

Another important feature of a UPS is its ability to send a signal to the computer informing it that the system has switched to battery backup power. NetWare has a UPS monitoring feature that lets the NetWare server tell how much time the UPS battery will last and shut itself down before all power is drained from the UPS battery. Because a NetWare server keeps much information in RAM cache buffers, if a system's power is turned off before the NetWare server is shut down, important information can easily be lost. In many cases the NetWare server will not be able to mount its disk volumes after an unexpected crash, requiring the network administrator to take the extra step of performing a volume fix.

Use your UPS capacity wisely. Attach your server, monitor, and any disk subsystems to the unit, but don't attach a high-demand device such as a laser printer on the same unit. Remember, the UPS is there to provide you with a gentle way to handle a power failure or brownout, not to serve as a portable generator.

THE WORKSTATION

Now that microcomputers in general have been discussed, it's time to consider the user's workstation. Each user's workstation should provide that user with the ability to handle any job responsibilities and provide network connectivity. Although many operating systems exist that may be used on workstations—DOS, OS/2, Windows for Workgroups, Windows 95/98, Windows NT Workstation, Macintosh System 7.5/8—the focus will be on Windows 95/98 in this discussion. Windows 98 is the current version of the widely used Windows environment. It differs only modestly from its predecessor Windows 95, with a newer desktop design and many bug fixes. Both Windows 95 and Windows 98 incorporate the current version of DOS, DOS 7.0, but generally keep it hidden from the user.

Windows 95/98 Microprocessor Requirements

At one time Microsoft claimed that Windows 95 could be run on an Intel 80386 DX microprocessor. Practical experience quickly showed that even an 80486-100 was hard-pressed to handle the software. The practical minimum is commonly considered to be at least a Pentium 100 chip. As of this writing, most new PCs being sold have at least a 166 MHz Pentium CPU, so this minimum is easily met for new PC purchases. Network administrators typically purchase (or recommend for purchase if they don't have purchasing authority) an entry-level PC for most employees. An **entry-level PC** is the PC that a company commonly purchases as its standard microcomputer. The exact specifications of an entry-level PC differ from company to company, and they change over time as new hardware components push down the price of older components.

A good general rule is to set the price you want to pay for the workstation and then buy the hardware configuration closest to that amount. As prices of existing components will continually fall, you'll get nowhere waiting for the "best" system as new technology replaces the old.

Windows 95/98 Memory Requirements

As with the microprocessor requirements, Microsoft also fudged on the memory requirements for Windows 95/98. Although it says Windows can be run on 8 MB, the practical minimum is 16 MB. The preferred amount is 32 MB of RAM. This will let you run both Windows and several applications at the same time without undue delays.

Workstation Storage Requirements

The size of the hard drive needed in a workstation is determined by the number and size of applications programs and data files that will be stored on the workstation. At present, most new PCs are being shipped with at least 2 GB hard drives, and many have hard drives with a capacity of 6.4 GB or more. These hard drives give you plenty of room to install Windows 95/98 and application software and still have enough disk space for most users' current storage needs.

THE NETWARE SERVER

As explained in Chapter 1, the main function of NetWare is to provide network resources such as file and print services to client workstations. As a result, the NetWare server can be enhanced with specialized hardware and software to give better performance, security, and reliability than can be expected from a peer-to-peer NOS.

Microcomputer manufacturers often offer microcomputers labeled as LAN servers. These microcomputers offer features not found in microcomputers designed as user workstations, and should be purchased for NetWare servers whenever possible. They include more RAM, a larger hard drive, and a preinstalled NIC. Most significantly they have a larger case designed to incorporate additional hard drives, interface cards, supplemental power supplies, and larger fans for cooling.

NetWare Server Microprocessor Requirements

A NetWare 5.0 server requires at least a Pentium 75 microprocessor. However, performance will be slow, and a faster CPU is desirable. A NetWare server typically is used more for input and output operations (reading and writing files) than for computations. Therefore, server performance can often be better enhanced by adding more memory or a faster NIC than by using the fastest processor. However, some applications run on the server. For example, a client/server database such as Oracle will run part of the program (the server portion) on the NetWare server and other parts of the program (the client) on the user workstations. In this case, a faster processor may be important for reasonable application performance.

A good general rule is that when you are purchasing a new NetWare server, you should buy one with a microprocessor at least equivalent to the microprocessor in the standard PCs you are buying for your users. For example, if the standard PCs you buy use a Pentium 166 MHz CPU, then your NetWare server should have at least a Pentium 166 MHz chip. Because your network depends on the server, don't skimp on the processor in the server.

NetWare Server Memory Requirements

The NetWare server uses extended memory to run the NOS, to run the utility modules called NetWare Loadable Modules (NLMs), and to keep available in RAM information frequently accessed from the hard disk. Adding more memory to a NetWare server generally increases NetWare server performance because it allows more disk information to be kept in RAM, thereby reducing read and transmission time. Adding memory to a NetWare server will not enhance the performance of applications stored and used on the individual workstations, however, because each workstation's memory is managed by its own local operating system—the NetWare server provides only data and communication services.

To run NetWare 5.0, the NetWare server should contain at least 64 MB of RAM. This is an absolute minimum, and normally the NetWare Server will require more RAM than that.

If you plan to use the Java-based ConsoleOne (see Chapter 14), for example, Novell rec-ommends at least 128 MB of RAM. To calculate the approximate memory requirements for a NetWare server, you can use the simplified equation shown in Figure 2-13.

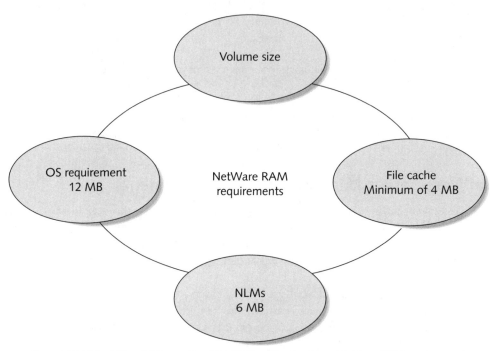

Server RAM in MB = (Volume Size X 0.008) + File Cache + NLMs + OS Requirement

Figure 2-13   Calculating NetWare server memory requirements

The equation for calculating server memory requirements has four variables: operating system requirements, volume-related requirements, disk caching, and NLM require-ments. You need to allow 12 MB for the operating system, and some large NLMs that are commonly used may require another 2 to 6 MB. For each hard disk volume, you'll need to calculate the space using the following formula:

Volume size/block size 2 volume size 2 0 .008 = FAT cache RAM requirements

Add a minimum of 4 MB for disk caching (you can add more if you want, and the addi-tional RAM will improve caching performance).

A sample calculation follows. If a NetWare server has an 18 GB disk capacity, the memory requirement is calculated as 12 MB for the operating system, plus the FAT cache calculation of 18,000 megabytes divided by 64 equals 281.25. (The default block size for NetWare 5.0 is 64K.) This saves you the most space on the system, so most administrators leave it set at 64.) Then, 281.25 multiplied by 18,000 equals 5,062,500; 5062500 multiplied by 0.008 equals 40,500,000 bytes or about 40 MB of RAM for effective caching. Now add 2 to 6 MB for

2

NLMs. Thus the memory requirement for this NetWare server is 54 MB of RAM. You can round this up to 64 MB, and use two 32 MB SIMMs.

Microcomputers designed as LAN servers are often available with a kind of RAM called **error checking and correcting (ECC) memory**. ECC memory employs algorithms that increase a server's ability to continue operating, despite a single-bit memory error, by actually correcting minor memory errors. If a company's NetWare server controls a mission-critical application, ECC memory can be worth its expense. A **mission-critical application** is one that an organization depends on for the day-to-day operation of its business. In a mail order business, for example, the order entry system is considered mission-critical because a system failure directly influences the company's profits.

 The Pentium Pro and Pentium II microprocessor's data bus supports ECC by adding 8 bits of ECC circuits beyond the 64 bits used for the data itself to support ECC.

NetWare Server Storage Requirements

When selecting a hard disk system for your NetWare server, you first need to determine the storage capacity required for your server. Allow at least 500 MB for the NetWare 5.0 operating system files and for print jobs. Next determine which software packages you want to store on the NetWare server and record how much storage space is required by each package. To determine how much data storage is required, identify each application and estimate the current storage requirement and future growth over the next three years. Determine how much space each user will be allowed for his or her personal data storage needs, along with any shared document storage areas, and add these to obtain the estimated total data requirements. After the storage requirements have been estimated, add at least 25 to 50% for expansion and overhead to obtain the total hard disk capacity needed.

 Novell offers a new storage system as an option in NetWare 5.0. Novell Storage Services (NSS) allows for volumes in the terabyte range using only nominal amounts of RAM (32 MB for a 100 million file directory, for example). As a new product, NSS currently has significant limitations such as no compression, no mirroring, and no support for the SYS volume. (It is most useful for database volumes.) For these reasons NSS won't be covered in this text.

Performance Features

The performance of a NetWare server is determined by how fast it can respond to requests for data from client workstations. Therefore the major factors that affect the server's performance are its ability to keep frequently used information in memory, the speed of its disk system, and, if the first two are adequate, the speed of its processor unit. NetWare is the best-performing network operating system in the industry because it was designed to operate on a NetWare server and therefore does not contain some of the additional overhead associated with general-purpose operating systems such as DOS, Unix, or Windows NT. Some of the performance features of NetWare are file caching, directory caching, and elevator seeking.

File Caching

File caching is the process by which NetWare increases the speed of response to requests for disk information. It does this by keeping the most frequently accessed disk blocks in memory. Because the computer's memory is about 100 times faster than the disk system, retrieving a block of data from the file cache greatly improves the performance of the server. As a general rule, at least 50% of the computer's memory should be allocated to file caching, resulting in more than 70% of the data requests being handled from the computer's memory rather than read directly from the disk.

Directory Caching

Directory caching is the process of keeping the directory entry table and file allocation table (FAT) for each disk volume in the memory of the computer. Like file caching, directory caching greatly increases the performance of the server by allowing it to find filenames 100 times faster than when the directory information is read directly from disk. In addition to directory caching, NetWare also uses a process called **directory hashing** to create a binary index system that improves file lookup time by as much as 30%. Figure 2-14 illustrates how requests from two different workstations to run the WP.EXE program would be handled by NetWare's caching system. In Step 1, the server initially loads the directory cache and FATs with directory information from the disk volume and then builds the hash table. In Step 2, the first request arrives from Workstation A for the file WP.EXE. The server looks up the WP.EXE file in the hash table and then uses the directory table and FAT to identify the necessary disk blocks. Because the cache buffers are empty, the server reads the necessary disk blocks into the cache and then sends the WP.EXE file to Workstation A. In Step 3, a second request, from Workstation B, is received for the WP.EXE program file. This time, after looking up the filename in the hash table, the server finds that the needed disk blocks are in the cache buffers. The server then immediately sends the data directly to Workstation B from the file cache, saving the time otherwise required to read the WP.EXE file from disk.

Elevator Seeking

Because the NetWare server environment is multitasking, at any given time it might be responding to several data requests from different client workstations. **Elevator seeking** is the process of minimizing the amount of disk drive head movement by accessing the information in the sequence of the head movement rather than in the order in which the requests were received. Elevator seeking gets its name from the way an elevator works when picking up people on different floors. Imagine that an elevator is at the top of a 10-story building when someone on floor 2 pushes the down button. As the elevator passes the eighth floor, another person on floor 5 also pushes the down button. The elevator will stop at floor 5 first and then floor 2 even though the person on floor 2 pushed the down button first. After picking up the person on floor 5, the elevator will finally move to floor 2 and pick up the person there.

Step 1. Loading directory and FAT buffers

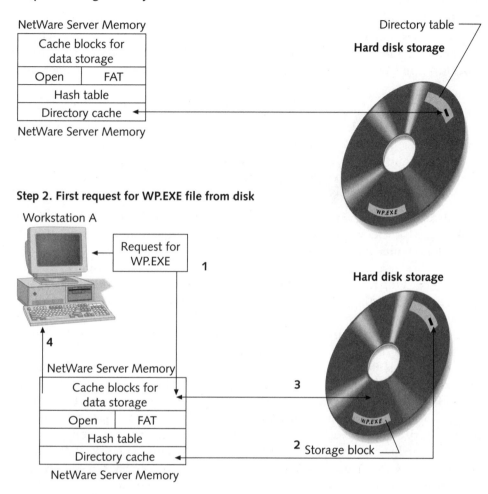

Step 2. First request for WP.EXE file from disk

Step 3. Second request for WP.EXE from cache

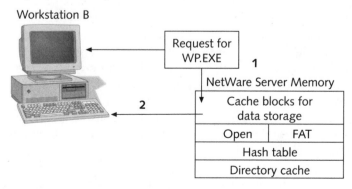

Figure 2-14   Cache memory

Fault Tolerance

Fault tolerance can be defined as the ability of a system to continue to operate satisfactorily despite errors or other problems. The NetWare server environment was designed with four levels of fault tolerance in its disk system in order to continue server operations in the event of physical errors on the disk drives or controller cards.

A hard disk's directory information is extremely important in enabling the server to locate information on the disk system. Therefore, NetWare's first level of fault tolerance is set by providing second copies of the directory entry table and FAT on different locations of the disk drive. If a storage block in one of the tables is damaged, NetWare automatically switches to the duplicate table to retrieve the requested directory information. The faulty sector is then listed in the disk's bad block table, and the data contained in the bad sector is stored in another disk location.

As a disk drive ages, certain recording sectors of the disk's surface can become unreliable. To make sure that data written to the disk is stored in a good storage sector, NetWare implements a read-after-write verification process. If data cannot be reliably written to a disk sector after three attempts, NetWare implements the second level of fault tolerance, referred to as "hot fix." **Hot fix** involves redirecting bad and unreliable disk storage sectors to a location elsewhere on the disk surface. When a new disk drive is first formatted by NetWare, a certain percentage of the disk capacity (2% by default) is reserved for the hot fix redirection area, allowing the disk drive to continue normal operation despite bad sectors that might develop on the disk surface. Step 1 in Figure 2-15 illustrates the NetWare server attempting to write a data buffer to disk block 201 and receiving a disk error when the data is read back by using the read-after-write verification process. In Step 2, the data in the cache memory buffer is written to the redirection area and the NetWare server remaps block 201 of the disk to point to the block in the redirection area. As mentioned in Chapter 1, one responsibility of a network administrator is to monitor the NetWare server to determine how many blocks have been redirected and thus when the disk drive should be replaced. In Chapter 14, you will learn how to use the NetWare MONITOR utility to track the condition of the redirection area and determine when a disk drive should be replaced.

The third level of fault tolerance is the continued operation of the NetWare server despite a complete failure of the disk system. NetWare protects a NetWare server in two ways from major failures of the disk storage system. The first method, called **mirroring**, involves attaching two drives to the same disk controller card and then mirroring the drives to synchronize the data on both disks. After the disks have been mirrored, NetWare automatically keeps the information updated on both drives so that in a failure of one disk drive, the server can continue normal operation by using the second drive. The network administrator can then replace the defective drive at a convenient time, and NetWare will resynchronize the data on the new drive without requiring the administrator to restore any information from the backup tape. Figure 2-16 illustrates the use of disk mirroring to protect your server against failure of a disk drive. Disk mirroring works well, but requires each block to be written twice by the controller card, which can slow the performance of the NetWare server. In addition, with disk mirroring a failure of the controller card will make data on both drives unusable.

Step 1. Data written to a bad disk block

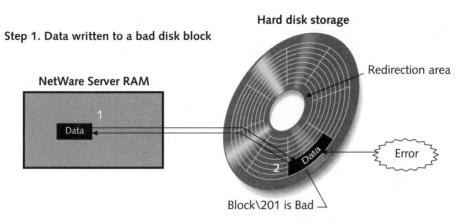

Hard disk storage

NetWare Server RAM

Redirection area

Error

Block\201 is Bad

Step 2. Hot fix redirection area used

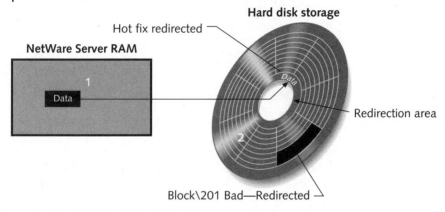

Hard disk storage

Hot fix redirected

NetWare Server RAM

Redirection area

Block\201 Bad—Redirected

Figure 2-15   NetWare's hot fix

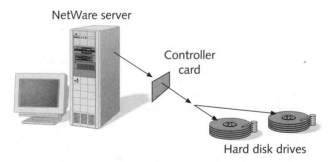

NetWare server

Controller card

Hard disk drives

Figure 2-16   Disk mirroring

With the second method, **disk duplexing**, NetWare provides fault tolerance for both the disk drive and controller card. Disk duplexing uses two disk drives and two controller cards, as illustrated in Figure 2-17. Disk duplexing also increases performance over disk mirroring in that one disk write operation can write data to both disk drives. An additional advantage of disk duplexing over a single-disk drive is that it actually improves a NetWare server's performance. Both controllers are requested to find data, and then the information from whichever drive is closest to the data location is read first. In a sense, implementing disk duplexing is like doubling the number of disk heads and thereby increasing disk read performance.

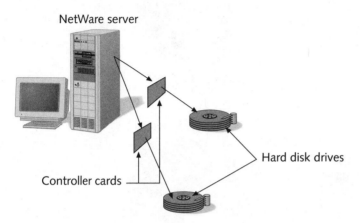

NetWare server

Hard disk drives

Controller cards

Figure 2-17   Disk duplexing

The fourth level of fault tolerance in NetWare is in essence **server duplexing**. Novell calls this SFT III (for System Fault Tolerance Level III). Here two NetWare servers on the network duplicate each other exactly. If one system fails, the other takes over instantly. Users never know there's been a problem. This feature is important for mission-critical applications on LANs and thus appeals to organizations that cannot afford any interruption in network services. However, NetWare 5.0 does not support SFT III. Novell promises a clustered solution in the next year.

File Compression

NetWare server disk storage capacity is always limited, no matter how much capacity you have. NetWare 5.0 provides a **file compression** capability so that files can be compressed to a smaller size. As network manager you can control how long a file stays inactive before it is compressed, and it will be automatically uncompressed whenever a user opens it again. The compression cycle can be scheduled to take place during server low-use hours.

NetWare provided file compression starting in NetWare 4.1. Several third-party vendors also provide similar functionality for NetWare 3.x systems.

Block Suballocation

NetWare 5.0 also helps conserve hard disk space by using block suballocation. On a hard disk, files are stored in blocks, where each block holds a set number of bytes. In NetWare 3.2, for example, the default block size was 4 KB. Thus a file must be stored in 4 KB blocks, which leads to a problem with small files: a file with only one character in it (1 byte) would take up one block of 4 KB of storage—wasting a lot of disk space. The problem gets worse with larger block sizes, and NetWare 5.0 uses different default block sizes depending on volume size, as shown in Table 2-4.

Table 2-4   Default block sizes

Volume Size	Default Block Size
1–31 MB	4 KB
32–149 MB	16 KB
150–499 MB	32 KB
500 or more MB	64 KB

NetWare 5.0 solves this problem with **block suballocation**, which allows large block sizes to be divided into 4 KB sub-blocks when necessary. For example, if the block size is 64 KB, and a file contains 65 KB, then the file will be stored in one 64 KB block and one 4 KB sub-block (a total of 68 KB) instead of in two 64 KB blocks (a total of 128 KB).

Although the problem of wasted disk space because of large block sizes also existed in NetWare 3.x, there were no tools to fix it. Beginning with **NetWare 4.1**, Novell added block suballocation to the network administrator's tools to provide a solution to the problem.

CHAPTER SUMMARY

❑ Microcomputer systems are like those of any other computer. They perform four basic processes: input, processing, storage, and output. Input devices take information and commands from the outside world and convert them into the binary one and zero system used in digital computers. The system unit of the computer, comprising several components, enables the computer to process input data and produce information. The system board of the computer ties all the system unit components together.

❑ The most important component on the system board is the brain of the system unit, the microprocessor chip, also known as the central processor unit (CPU). The CPU fetches instructions and data from memory and then performs the requested function. IBM-compatible computers are based on the Intel line of microprocessors.

❏ The power of a microprocessor chip is based on several factors including clock speed, word size, instruction set, and bus size. Most IBM–compatible computers today use the Pentium, Pentium Pro, or Pentium II microprocessor. The Pentium Pro and Pentium II offer a Dynamic Execution feature that improves performance.

❏ The system board components are tied together by a bus structure. The local bus supports the data and address buses, and the expansion bus supports the expansion slots, which attach peripheral controller cards. The ISA expansion bus was designed with 16-bit data and 24-bit address buses running at 8 MHz. The EISA bus was an enhanced version of the ISA bus that allowed 32-bit buses and higher clock speeds. IBM used a proprietary bus, called the Micro Channel, that also provided 32-bit bus access at high clock speeds and an automatic configuration utility that made installing cards much easier. PCI is called a local bus because it provides direct access to the CPU and memory at much higher speeds than either EISA or Micro Channel. Use the PCI bus slots for devices—such as video and disk controller cards—that require very high access speeds. If video performance is critical, look for systems with the Accelerated Graphics Port (AGP) support.

❏ The system board uses I/O ports and interrupts to communicate with peripheral devices such as keyboards, video monitors, modems, disk drives, and network cards. Parallel ports are most frequently used to connect printers, whereas serial ports provide longer-distance communication. When a device is added with an expansion card, it is attached to a controller card that must be assigned a unique interrupt and I/O port address. This is done by changing settings on the cards or using a setup program. After the cards have been installed, the card driver software must be configured to use the selected interrupt and I/O address settings.

❏ Memory is the primary storage area for the microcomputer system. All instructions and data must be stored in memory before they can be processed by the CPU. RAM is the computer's work area and is used primarily to contain instructions and data that are currently being processed. Workstations running Windows 95 or 98 should have at least 16 MB and preferably 32 MB of RAM to provide adequate performance.

❏ Hard disk storage consists of the controller card and drive. Hard drives are based on either IDE/EIDE/ATA or SCSI controller cards. IDE is a very popular controller for Windows workstations and small- to medium-sized NetWare servers. The EIDE or ATA controllers provide higher speed and increased storage capacity (up to 8.5 GB) and support up to four devices. SCSI-2 controller cards can be used to attach up to seven different types of devices, including disk drives, CD-ROM drives, and tape drives. They allow for higher capacity and faster drives than IDE and are used for larger NetWare servers requiring multiple devices and more than 10 GB of disk space.

❏ CD-ROMs allow 680 MB to be stored permanently on a removable disk. CD-ROMs are used to store a variety of data including sound, text, graphics, and video. Because so much material is available on CD-ROMs,

2

sharing them on a network has become an important function controlled by the network administrator. If the CD-ROM drives are attached to a NetWare server, special NetWare modules are used to make the information on the CD-ROM available to all networked workstations. DVD-ROM is an improvement of the CD-ROM technology. Functionally it is similar, but it holds up to 4.7 GB of data.

❑ The power system of the computer is critical to proper operation. Insufficient or faulty power supplies can cause computers to lock up or give parity error messages. Be sure the wattage of your computer's power supply provides the necessary amps for all attached devices. A UPS (uninterruptible power supply) uses a battery to provide continuous power to the computer for a short period of time after a commercial power failure. This gives the network administrator or the NetWare server computer time to save the contents of the computer's memory and properly shut down before full loss of power. All NetWare server computers need to be protected by a UPS and proper power filters.

❑ User workstations using Windows 95 or 98 need at least a Pentium 100 CPU and 16 MB of RAM. Hard drive storage of at least 850 MB is preferred if applications and data will be stored on the PC.

❑ Novell designed the NetWare network operating system specifically as a LAN server operating system, with performance features such as high-volume file caching, directory caching and hashing, and elevator seeking. In addition to high performance, NetWare includes such fault-tolerant features as hot fix, disk mirroring, disk duplexing, and server duplexing. To conserve disk space, NetWare also provides automatic file compression and block suballocation.

❑ NetWare 5.0 requires a Pentium 75 or better CPU. The NetWare server uses its RAM to run the operating system and cache information from the hard disk for faster access. Although a NetWare server with a small disk drive can run with as little as 64 MB of RAM, this is an absolute minimum and you will normally need more RAM. A large server using multiple protocols may need up to 2 GB of RAM. Although placing additional RAM in a NetWare server does not directly affect what applications can be run on the workstation, it does affect network performance. A shortage of memory in a NetWare server computer can cause it to crash or lock up the network.

KEY TERMS

access arm
access time
address
address bus
Advanced (or Accelerated) Graphics Port (AGP)

asynchronous communication
baud rate
bits per second (bps)
block suballocation
bus
bus mastering
cache memory
central processing unit (CPU)
clock
command queuing
compact disc read-only memory (CD-ROM)
compiler
Complementary Metal-Oxide Semiconductor (CMOS) memory
complex instruction set computer (CISC)
controller card
conventional memory
cycle
cylinder
data bus
Data Communications Equipment (DCE)
Data Terminal Equipment (DTE)
Digital Versatile Disc (DVD)
direct memory access (DMA) channel
directory caching
directory hashing
disk duplexing
dot pitch
DVD-ROM
dynamic execution
dynamic RAM (DRAM)
elevator seeking
end user
Enhanced IDE (EIDE)
entry-level PC
error checking and correcting (ECC) memory
expansion bus
expansion card
expansion slot
Extended Data Output (EDO) RAM

2

eXtended Graphics Array (XGA)
Extended Industry Standard Architecture (EISA) bus
extended memory
fault tolerance
file allocation table (FAT)
file caching
file compression
graphics accelerator
hot fix
hot-swapping
Industry Standard Architecture (ISA) bus
input/output (I/O) port
instruction set
Integrated Drive Electronics (IDE)
interrupt request (IRQ)
local bus
Logical Block Addressing (LBA)
machine language
math coprocessor
megahertz (MHz)
Micro Channel bus
microprocessor
millions of instructions per second (MIPS)
mirroring
mission-critical application
null modem cable
parallel port
parity bit
partitioning
PC workstation
Peripheral Component Interface (PCI) bus
peripherals
personal computer (PC)
pixel
protected mode
RAM shadowing
real mode
reduced instruction set computer (RISC)
Redundant Array of Independent Disks (RAID)

register
resolution
rotational delay
RS232
SCSI-2
sector
seek time
serial port
server duplexing
single in-line memory module (SIMM)
Small Computer System Interface (SCSI)
static RAM (SRAM)
Super VGA (SVGA)
switching power supply
synchronous communication
Synchronous Dynamic RAM (SDRAM)
system board
tracks
transfer time
uninterruptible power supply (UPS)
Universal Data Format (UDF)
Universal Serial Bus (USB)
upper memory
users
VESA bus
Video Graphics Array (VGA)
virtual file allocation table (VFAT)
virtual memory
virtual real mode
wait state
word size
workstation

REVIEW QUESTIONS

1. A(n) _____ is the amount of storage capacity needed to record one character of data in the computer's memory.

2. List the components found on the system board of a microcomputer system.

3. The _____ is the "brain" of a microcomputer system.

2

4. The _____ is used to provide precisely timed signals that synchronize the internal working of the system unit.

5. A microprocessor's word size is a measurement of the number of bits that can be stored in each _____.

6. The _____ is the part of the CPU that is responsible for performing calculations.

7. In addition to real and protected modes, the 80386 microprocessor added _____.

8. Which processing mode is used by 8088 microprocessor chips?

9. Which processing mode allows access to extended memory?

10. The _____ is the highway that transfers bits to and from the memory chips.

11. The size of the _____ limits the amount of memory the microprocessor can directly access.

12. Briefly explain a difference between the 80486SX and 80486DX microprocessors:

13. Briefly explain a difference between the Pentium and Pentium II microprocessors.

14. Briefly explain a difference between the Pentium and Pentium Pro microprocessors.

15. _____ is a very high speed form of memory that does not require refresh clock cycles.

16. The _____ memory area is used by NetWare and other workstation operating systems such as Windows NT Workstation and OS/2.

17. The _____ memory area is used by video cards, ROM, and expansion cards.

18. The _____ expansion bus provides 32-bit buses and is owned by IBM.

19. The _____ and _____ are two local bus specifications used with expansion slots that provide high-speed direct access to the CPU and memory.

20. The _____ bus provides the best high-speed direct access to a Pentium processor.

21. The _____ bus provides compatibility with older expansion cards while providing 32-bit slots running at 8 MHz for use with disk controllers and network cards.

22. _____ memory is used to store configuration information on the system board and is backed up by battery power.

23. What is the minimum amount of memory needed by a NetWare server that has 11GB of disk space?

24. To increase the performance of Pentium processors, from 64 to 256 KB of _____ memory is used because it does not require wait states and provides very high speed memory access, being composed of expensive SRAM chips.

25. After low-level formatting, a drive needs to be _____ for use by an operating system.

26. The _____ is used to link all disk sectors belonging to one file.

27. If mirrored 6 GB disks are used on a small- to medium-sized network, what type of disk controller would you recommend for the NetWare server computer?

28. List three types of data that can be stored on CD-ROMs.

29. _____ is measured by the number of pixels.

30. _____ is the measurement of the distance between pixels.

31. Which provides the higher-quality image, a monitor with 0.28-dot pitch or one with 0.35-dot pitch?

32. List two things to consider when you are purchasing a UPS for a NetWare server computer.

33. The _____ is used by a device to send a signal to the CPU.

34. Each device must have a unique _____ that is used to receive commands from the CPU.

35. A NetWare server uses _____ to keep the most frequently accessed blocks of data in memory.

36. A NetWare server uses _____ to keep the directory entry table and the FAT in memory.

37. List the four types of fault tolerance available in NetWare.

38. A NetWare server uses _____ to make more efficient use of hard disk space.

39. List the *minimum* processor and RAM requirements for a Windows 95/98 workstation.

40. List the *minimum* requirements for a NetWare 5.0 server for processor, RAM, and hard drive storage.

HANDS-ON PROJECTS

Project 2-1: Determining Workstation Hardware Configuration

Your instructor will explain how to use Windows commands and utilities or other hardware documenting programs (supplied by your instructor) to determine information about the hardware environment of your PC workstation. Fill out the worksheet in Figure 2-18 to document that workstation environment.

Computer Worksheet

Specification developed by: _____

SYSTEM INFORMATION

Computer make/model: _____

CPU: _____ **Clock speed:** _____ **Bus:** _____

Memory capacity: _____

DISK INFORMATION

Disk controller

Type: _____

Manufacturer/model : _____

Drive address	Type	Manufacturer	Cyl/Hd/Sec	Speed/Capacity	DOS Partition size
_____	___	_____	__/__/__	_____	_____

DEVICE INFORMATION

Device name	IRQ	I/O port
_____	_____	_____
_____	_____	_____
_____	_____	_____

Figure 2-18   Computer worksheet

CASE PROJECTS

Case 2-1: Calculating NetWare Server Memory Requirements for J. Q. Adams

The J. Q. Adams Corporation is planning to buy a dedicated NetWare server computer to support a 25-user network with a 4,000 MB (4 GB) hard disk drive. Using the memory formula in this chapter, calculate the amount of RAM you would recommend for this NetWare server. Write a memo to your instructor with your recommendations. Show your calculations.

Case 2-2: Developing Workstation Specifications for J. Q. Adams

1. The J. Q. Adams Corporation wants to develop a specification for an entry-level PC workstation for the company. As the network administrator for this company, you have been asked to develop this specification.

   New workstations will run the Microsoft Windows 98 operating system and will need to be able to run word processing applications and do basic spreadsheet calculations. The workstations will require about 2 GB of local disk storage for software and work files plus access to the network.

   Write a memo to your instructor containing the specification. Attach a copy of the worksheet shown in Figure 2-18.

2. Some new workstations are intended to be used for word processing and desktop publishing applications that need high-resolution graphics and a more powerful microprocessor. These workstations will require about 1.6 GB of local disk storage for software and work files. They will have access to the network so they can share data files and access network printers.

   Write a memo to your instructor containing the specification. Attach a copy of the worksheet shown in Figure 2-19.

Bid Specification Form

Specification developed by: _____

SYSTEM INFORMATION

Computer make/model: _____

CPU: _____ Clock speed: _____ Bus: _____

Memory capacity: _____

Estimated cost: _____

DISK INFORMATION

Disk controller

Type: _____

Manufacturer/model :_____

Drive Address	Type	Manufacturer	Cyl/Hd/Sec	Speed/Capacity	DOS Partition Size
_____	____	_____	__/__/__	_____	_____

NETWORK CARD INFORMATION

Network type	Manufacturer ID	I/O port	Interrupt
_____	_____	_____	_____

NON-NETWORK DEVICE INFORMATION

Device name	IRQ	I/O port
_____	_____	_____
_____	_____	_____
_____	_____	_____
_____	_____	_____

Figure 2-19   Bid specification form

Case 2-3: Determining NetWare Server Disk Requirements for J. Q. Adams

The J. Q. Adams Corporation wants to store catalog information on a NetWare server in order to give all computers access to the information. Currently the catalog comes on a CD-ROM, and copying it to the server's hard disk will require about 500 MB of disk storage. The company also wants to move a customer database, which currently takes up 250 MB of disk space, to the NetWare server, along with a word processing program.

1. What type of disk controller and disk system would you recommend for this application? Justify your choice. Write a memo to your instructor containing the specification. Discuss your decision in the memo by describing why you made the choices you did.

2. Given the NetWare server disk requirements you just recorded, calculate the amount of RAM that the J. Q. Adams NetWare server that stores this data will require. Write a memo to your instructor stating the requirements. Justify your decision in the memo by showing your calculations.

Case 2-4: Developing NetWare Server Specifications for J. Q. Adams

The J. Q. Adams Corporation wants to purchase a new NetWare server to replace its existing NetWare server and has budgeted $10,000 for the new computer. Its current NetWare server is an 80486DX computer with 16 MB of RAM and a 500 MB hard disk drive. The company's system is running out of storage space, and the NetWare server runs slowly when it performs network printing. In addition, the company recently experienced some disk errors on the NetWare server that required an employee to restore data from backups and then re-enter a day's worth of transactions. If possible, the company wants to avoid disk errors causing this type of problem in the future. As the company's network administrator, you have been asked to select a computer system that will meet these needs within the requested budget.

The new system will need to support at least 4 GB of usable hard drive space. Write a memo to your instructor containing the specification. Attach a copy of the worksheet shown in Figure 2-20.

If you think you need to spend more than $10,000 for the new server, develop two specifications: one for the system you think is necessary and one priced under $10,000. In your memo, explain why the better system is needed and why the system that stays within budget is inadequate.

2·

NetWare Server Worksheet

Specification developed by: _____

SYSTEM INFORMATION

Computer make/model: _____

CPU: _____ Clock speed: _____ Bus: _____

Memory capacity: _____

Estimated cost: _____

DISK INFORMATION

Disk controller

Type: _____

Manufacturer/model :_____

Drive Address	Type	Manufacturer	Cyl/Hd/Sec	Speed/Capacity	Partition Size DOS NetWare	Mirrored with Controller Drive
_____	__	_____	__/__/__	_____	__ __	_____

NETWORK CARD INFORMATION

Network type	Manufacturer ID	I/O port	Interrupt
_____	_____	_____	_____

NON-NETWORK DEVICE INFORMATION

Device name	IRQ	I/O port
_____	_____	_____
_____	_____	_____
_____	_____	_____

Figure 2-20   NetWare Server Worksheet

3

DESIGNING THE NETWORK

> **After reading this chapter and completing the exercises you will be able to:**
>
> ♦ Describe the process of transmitting data on a NetWare LAN
> ♦ Identify and describe the hardware and software that connect computers to the NetWare LAN
> ♦ Apply your knowledge of LAN systems to develop a recommendation for a network system

As a network administrator, you must understand the hardware and software components that make up a local area network. This knowledge will enable you to recommend and implement network systems. It will also help you troubleshoot problems on the network. Chapter 1 introduced you to the hardware and software components of a LAN. You also learned criteria for selecting a network operating system (NOS). In Chapter 2, you learned about the microcomputer hardware used in PC workstations and NetWare servers. In this chapter, you will learn about how computers exchange data. You will increase your understanding of LANs by studying network cabling systems, network topologies, and protocols. As a network administrator, you will probably be the main source of network information for your organization. You will help make important decisions about buying hardware and software when the LAN is implemented or expanded. You will therefore need a good background in how computers use LANs to communicate, as well as in the options and standards currently available for such communication.

LAN COMMUNICATIONS

Computers communicate over LANs by sending blocks of data called **packets**. Each packet contains the information to be transmitted, along with control information that the receiving computer uses to identify and process data in the packet. Reliable transmission of data packets over a network is a complex technical task performed by hardware and software, but the concepts can be broken down into basic steps or modules that are reasonably easy to understand.

For LAN communication to occur, standards must let products from different manufacturers work together. The term **interoperability** refers to the capability of different computers and applications to communicate and share resources on a network. Several organizations help set and control recognized standards that provide worldwide interoperability. Because many products you will need to implement your network system depend on standards these organizations have developed, you should become familiar with their basic functions. The two major organizations that govern LAN standards are the **International Standards Organization (ISO)**, which works on LAN communication software models, and the **Institute of Electrical and Electronic Engineers (IEEE)**, which works on physical cable and access method standards. In this chapter you will learn about LAN standards that these institutions maintain and how the standards affect network products you will work with as network administrator.

OSI Model

To recommend and implement a LAN successfully, you first need to understand the components of a network system and how they function together. Just as breaking a complex program into separate modules helps you write a computer program, breaking the LAN communication process into separate logical tasks or modules makes it easier to understand and work with. To help standardize network system implementation, the ISO introduced a seven-layer model in 1980 known as the **Open Systems Interconnect (OSI) model**. This model acts as a blueprint to help network designers and developers build reliable network systems that can interoperate. As a network administrator, you need to know the basic levels and functions of the OSI model to understand LAN communication and to select and configure hardware and software. In addition, a good understanding of the basic principles of network communication provided by the OSI model will help you troubleshoot and identify network problems.

As Table 3-1 shows, the seven layers of the OSI model range from the application software level to the physical hardware. The layers allow network software to be implemented in structured modules, giving the network administrator more flexibility in designing and configuring network systems.

Table 3-1   OSI model

OSI Layer	Action	Result
Application	Interaction with user	Application program executed
Presentation	Conversion of input to ASCII, data compression, and encryption	Syntax of input checked and message formatted. Message packet formed
Session	Make initial connection with receiving computer, maintain communication during session, and end session when complete. Control data flow by sequencing packets. Addition of packet sequence numbers	Packet sequence number added to message packet
Transport	Identification and acknowledgment fields added to the message	Segment package formed
Network	Determination of the best route to the destination computer and addition of network address to the packet	Datagram packet formed
Data Link	Addition of the physical address of the destination computer	Ethernet frame formed
Physical	Transmission of packet one bit at a time	Electronic signals representing bits appear on the cable system

 There is a simple phrase to help you remember the OSI layers, from the application layer to the physical layer: "All People Seem To Need Data Processing."

The application layer is where a user initiates a request for network services—such as a word processing program to access a shared document stored on the NetWare server. Starting with the application layer, each layer is responsible for performing certain network processing and control operations and then for passing the data packet on to the next lower layer. Each layer in the OSI model communicates with its peer layer on the receiving computer. For example, the transport layer on one computer includes control information in the network packet that the transport layer on the receiving computer can use to acknowledge receipt of the packet. At the bottom of the OSI model, the physical layer consists of the network cards and cables that actually carry the signals, representing ones and zeros, of the data packet from one machine to another.

The OSI functions can be compared to the familiar process of sending a letter via the postal system, as illustrated in the following sections.

Application Layer

The **application layer** consists of software that interacts with the users and lets them do their work without becoming involved with the full complexity of the computer or network systems. Examples of application software include word processors, spreadsheets, and other software products used in offices. Using the application layer is like using a word processor to write and print a letter. The word processor is the application program you use to format and type the letter.

Presentation Layer

The purpose of the **presentation layer** is to organize the data in machine-readable form. The desktop operating system of your computer is the software component that directly takes input from devices and converts it into a format the machine can process. The resulting block of information created by the presentation layer is called a **message packet**. The information in the message packet is then sent for processing to the presentation layer on the receiving computer.

 Presentation layer software can also compress information, to save space and transmission time. For increased security, the presentation layer can also encrypt data using a password, or key, to make it difficult for an intruder to capture and access the information. Banking companies often use special encrypting software to secure electronic fund transfers.

The presentation layer can be compared to the mechanics of the word processor that allow your keystrokes to be printed. The resulting piece of paper, on which your formatted letter is printed, and which you then put in an in-box on your assistant's desk, is like a message packet.

Session Layer

The purpose of the **session layer** is to initiate and maintain a communication session with the network system. The session layer lets you log in to the NetWare server by providing the server with a valid user name and password. On successfully completing the login, you are granted access to certain resources of the server.

The job of the session layer is much like your company's mail delivery schedule as arranged with the local post office. To use the mail service, your organization initially contacts the post office and sets up an address along with a schedule for delivery and pickup services. This process corresponds to the session layer initiating a login session with a NetWare server.

Transport Layer

The main function of the **transport layer** is reliably delivering information packets from source to destination. The transport layer accomplishes this on the sending computer, which provides proper address information. Then the transport layer on the receiving computer sends an acknowledgment of each packet it successfully receives from the network.

The transport layer creates a packet, called a **segment**, by surrounding the message packet with the necessary acknowledgment and identification fields. Then it sends the segment packet to the network layer to complete addressing requirements.

The transport layer on some multitasking computers can also put parts of several message packets from different applications in each segment. The process of putting pieces of multiple message packets in one segment is called **multiplexing**. Multiplexing can save communication costs by letting one cable connection carry information from several applications simultaneously.

The function of the transport layer is a bit like your assistant removing the letter from the in-box, checking to make sure it contains all the necessary address information, and then deciding the type of service your letter needs. If this letter is very urgent, your assistant will probably use overnight delivery service. If the message contains information that you must be certain is received, you can send the letter by registered mail, requiring the receiver to acknowledge delivery. After deciding on the type of service, your assistant fills out any necessary forms and puts the letter in the appropriate envelope.

Network Layer

The **network layer** provides the information necessary to route packets through the proper network paths to arrive at the destination address. To route packets to a destination computer efficiently, the network layer uses **network addresses** that identify each group of computers on your network system. The network layer then creates a **datagram packet** by encapsulating or wrapping the information in the segment packet with the necessary packet routing information. The datagram packet is then sent to the data link layer for delivery.

When designing a NetWare network system, you will need to establish a network address for each cable system used in your network.

In postal delivery, a ZIP code is necessary to route a letter through the system. The ZIP code identifies the destination post office location. Similarly, the network address identifies the destination location in a network. The network layer's task is comparable to looking up the correct ZIP code for the destination city and then correctly marking the ZIP code on the envelope along with the name and street address of the receiver. After the ZIP code information has been added to the letter, the envelope can be taken to the post office for delivery.

Data Link Layer

The **data link layer** is the delivery system of the computer network and is responsible for using the destination address to send the packet through the requested network cable system. Using the information provided by the network layer, the data link layer creates a packet, called a **frame**, that encapsulates the datagram packet with control information, including the source and destination physical addresses.

Physical addresses are unique NIC addresses that the manufacturer permanently assigns to each NIC. Each physical address is a hexadecimal number divided into two parts: the first part identifies the manufacturer, and the second part is a unique number to identify the card among all the cards that manufacturer has produced. For example, if the NIC has the hexadecimal physical address 0B00AA123456, then 0B00AA is a code assigned to the manufacturer, and 123456 is the unique number that the manufacturer assigns to the card.

The data link layer then transmits the frame to the physical layer. In our example, after the letter is placed in the mailbox, it is up to the postal system to deliver the letter. A postal employee or machine determines to which post office the letter gets sent, based on the ZIP code and address information. The letter is then placed in a delivery truck to be taken to that post office.

 The IEEE 802 committee, which is the IEEE group that works on network standards, divides the data link layer into two sublayers: the **logical link control (LLC) layer** and the **media access control (MAC) layer**. The LLC layer interfaces with the network layer, and the MAC layer provides compatibility with the NIC used by the physical layer.

Physical Layer

The **physical layer** consists of the network cable system and connectors that are responsible for sending the data frame packet out as a series of bits. The bits appear as electrical signals on the network cable system. In the postal system example, the physical level consists of aircraft, trucks, and trains that physically deliver the letter to the designated post office.

Sending a Message

Now that you have a better idea of the purpose and function of each OSI layer, you can apply that knowledge to understand how NetWare sends a message between two network users.

For example, Ted Simpson, the information systems manager of Cunningham, Burns, and Evans Laboratories, wants to send a message to another user on the network. To do this, he will use the NetWare Send Message utility. (Although the Send Message tool is available on NetWare networks, users typically communicate with each other using a messaging package such as GroupWise. You'll use Send Message here to demonstrate the underlying technology.) This Send Message tool enables a user to send messages to other users from the Windows desktop. Follow the steps Ted takes to send his message.

To send the message:

1. Log in.

2. Right-click the N icon in the System Tray of the Windows desktop. The NetWare Client displays a menu.

3. Choose Send Message. NetWare displays a list of available servers in your tree.

4. Select your server. NetWare displays a list of users who have logged into that server. (If you want to send to a group, click the Show Groups button.)

5. Highlight one or more users.

6. In the space provided, type the message "I need to see you as soon as possible." The command appears as shown in Figure 3-1.

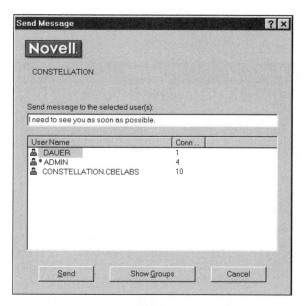

Figure 3-1   NetWare SEND command

7. Click Send to send the message.

On a NetWare network, all messages are first received by the NetWare server and then distributed to the users. This is similar to the way the post office receives mail and then distributes it to individual mailboxes. The following steps, summarized in Table 3-2, explain how the OSI model enables NetWare to send a message from one user to another.

The NetWare Send Message utility works with the presentation layer to convert the message to the proper ASCII format needed to form a message packet. The formatted message packet is then combined with the recipient's user name and passed to the session layer.

In a NetWare workstation, the session layer sets up and maintains a connection between Windows 95/98 and the NetWare operating system. A session is originally established when you boot your computer and run the NetWare software that attaches it to the NetWare server. When the session is established, the session layer maintains your workstation's connection to the network by responding to requests from the NetWare server. When the session layer receives the message packet, it checks the status of the network connection, adds any necessary control information needed by the NetWare software, and then sends the message to the transport layer. A major function of the transport layer is to guarantee delivery of the message packet to the recipient's computer. It does this by placing control information in the packet, much as you would fill out identifying information if you were sending a registered letter through the postal system. The control information uniquely identifies the packet and tells the receiving computer how to return an acknowledgment. The new packet containing the transport control information is called a segment. The transport layer on the recipient's computer processes the segment heading information to acknowledge that the segment packet has been received successfully. After adding its control information, the transport layer next passes the segment packet to the network layer.

Table 3-2   Sending a message

OSI Layer	Representation	Function
Application		The NetWare Send Message utility is a DOS command line utility that is the application layer in this example. The Send Message utility allows you to enter and send a message to another user. Other e-mail applications could serve the same purpose.
Presentation		Presentation layer converts input to binary ASCII code and creates the message packet.
Session		Session layer establishes communication session with receiving computer. Sequence number added to message packet.
Transport		Transport layer adds identification and acknowledgment fields to form segment packet. This provides "certified delivery."
Network		Network layer adds routing information to network containing destination computer. Network address added to segment packet to form datagram packet.
Data link		Data link layer adds physical address of destination computer to create Ethernet frame.
Physical		At the physical layer the NIC converts bits to electronic signals and transmits them on the cable system.

The network layer in the computer is responsible for determining the correct route for sending the packet. In a NetWare network, each cable system is assigned a unique network address similar in purpose to the ZIP codes used by the postal system. The network address allows the packets to be routed quickly and efficiently to the cable system containing the destination computer. The network layer in each computer keeps a table—similar to a ZIP code reference book—that contains the correct network address of all NetWare servers. In this example, the network layer looks up the address of the recipient's NetWare server and then creates a datagram packet by encapsulating the segment information with control information including the network address of the recipient's NetWare server.

The data link layer is responsible for delivering the datagram by first creating a unique **data frame packet** for the network cable system. The data link layer encapsulates the datagram packet received from the network layer with heading information, including the addresses for the destination and source computers, along with error-checking codes. The data link layer then sends the data frame to the NIC for transmission, working closely with the NIC to ensure the data frame transmits successfully. If an error occurs during transmission, the data frame is sent again. After several unsuccessful attempts, the data link layer reports an error back to the network layer, stating that it could not deliver the packet.

The physical layer of a computer network consists of hardware devices such as NICs, connectors, and cable systems that are responsible for transmitting the message bit by bit across the network system. The task of transmitting the frame can be compared to the job of a telegraph operator. Just as the telegraph operator must wait for the line to become available and then must translate the characters in a message into dots and dashes, so the physical layer must wait for the cable to become available and then must use the NIC to transmit the frame by encoding the binary digits into the correct electronic signals.

 The IEEE organization controls the standards controlling access on the physical network, as well as the electronic signals used. Later in this chapter you'll learn about the standards used on different network systems.

Receiving a Message

A packet of data received from the network goes up the OSI stack, reversing the steps used in transmission, starting with the physical layer and proceeding to the application layer. The following steps describe the process.

The physical layer sends the frame of information transmitted by the NIC throughout the network—all network cards read the address contained in the data frame. Because all messages must be received and then retransmitted by a NetWare server, the frame is actually addressed to be initially received by a NetWare server. When the network card in the specified NetWare server recognizes its address, it reads the data frame and passes the bits of data to the data link layer. In the mail delivery example, this is comparable to unloading the letter at the destination post office.

The data link layer then uses the error-checking codes to perform a **cyclic redundancy check (CRC)**, in which a mathematical algorithm compares bits received to the CRC code contained in the frame packet. If the calculated CRC matches the CRC contained in the data frame, the frame is assumed to be valid and the datagram packet is unpacked and passed to the network layer. If the CRCs do not match, the frame is considered bad, which causes an error to be logged with the NetWare server.

Next the network layer on the NetWare server checks the information contained in the datagram's heading. After confirming that the packet does not need to be sent to another server, it unpacks the segment packet and sends it to the transport layer. The transport layer then checks the control information contained in the segment packet heading, extracts the message packet, and—depending on the control information—creates and sends an acknowledgment packet segment to your computer. The analogy of this process is the recipient of a registered letter signing to confirm receipt of the letter. The transport layer on the sending computer is then informed that the packet has been successfully delivered. The transport layer extracts the message information and passes it to the correct NetWare session layer.

The NetWare server presentation and application layers next process the message information and retransmit the message to the recipient's computer, which receives and displays it in a dialog box on the screen. After reading the message, your friend can press the Ctrl + Enter key combination to remove the message from the screen and continue with the current application.

NETWORK COMPONENTS

You can apply your knowledge of how information flows from one computer to another to understanding the components and product options available at each level of the OSI model. Knowledge of the common network components and product options will allow you to make good decisions in selecting, maintaining, and troubleshooting network systems. In this section you will learn about the network components that make up each layer of the OSI model, what product options are commonly used today, and some trends that might affect network products in the near future.

Physical Layer Components

The physical layer components of a network system consist of the hardware that sends electrical signals from computer to computer. From time to time a network administrator must install cables between computers. So you will probably be involved in network hardware selection decisions and will need to be familiar with the different options available for connecting computers. Understanding the network cable system will also enable you to isolate network problems that result from a faulty cable component.

The two aspects of the physical network system are the **media**, the transmission systems used to send electronic signals, and the **topology**, the physical geometry of the network wiring. In this section you will learn about some common network media and topologies and their advantages and disadvantages.

Network Media

The network media consist of the communication systems used to transmit and receive bits of information. Most network media used today are in the form of cables or wires that run to each computer in the network. These types of media are often called **bounded media**, because the signals are contained in or "bounded" by a wire. Another medium type, which is much less common in LANs, involves beaming signals between computers with radio and light waves. These types of transmission media are called **unbounded media**. Although unbounded media are generally used in wide area network (WAN) systems and involve satellite and microwave links over hundreds or thousands of miles, certain specialized types of unbounded media, such as infrared, are gaining acceptance for specialized local area network (LAN) applications.

Consider three major factors when selecting a medium for your network system: bandwidth, resistance to electromagnetic interference, and cost. The **bandwidth** of a network medium is a measure of the medium's capacity in number of bits per second that can be transmitted. A general rule is that the higher the bandwidth, the more traffic and higher speed the network medium can support.

Electromagnetic interference (EMI) refers to a medium's susceptibility to interference from outside electrical or magnetic fields. Networks that operate near high levels of electrical and magnetic fields, such as given off by power plants or large pieces of electrical equipment, will need to install a medium with a high EMI resistance that can carry the network signals reliably without interference.

Cost of installation is another factor in selecting a medium. If more than one medium meet the bandwidth and EMI specifications of an organization, the final factor will depend on the cost of installing the system. Some media types—such as fiber-optics—are relatively expensive to install and maintain compared to other media types, so even though fiber has a very high bandwidth and virtually no EMI problems, it is not a common medium in most LANs.

To help you select the best medium for a network system, the following sections describe some of the most common network mediums and compare these systems in terms of bandwidth, EMI, and cost.

Twisted-Pair Cable

Twisted-pair cable is probably the most common form of bounded medium in use on LANs today. **Twisted-pair cable** can be unshielded or shielded and consists of pairs of single-strand wire twisted together, as shown in Figure 3-2.

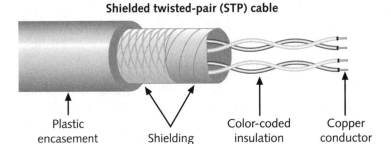

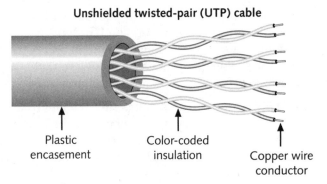

Figure 3-2   Twisted-pair cable

Twisting the wires together reduces the possibility of a signal in one wire affecting a signal in another wire. Normally if two wires run side by side, the electrical signal in one wire will create a magnetic field that can induce a small current in the nearby wire. This causes "noise" and results in errors on the network. Twisting the wires eliminates this noise by canceling out the magnetic field. Fifty or more pairs of twisted wire can be put together in one large cable called a **bundled pair**.

3

Twisted-pair cabling comes in various grades or categories:

- *Category 1*: Phone cable before 1983. Not used for data transfer.

- *Category 2*: A data-grade cable used in older networks with speeds up to 4 Mbps.

- *Category 3*: Another data-grade cable, this one useable with 10BaseT Ethernet but no faster.

- *Category 4*: A better grade of cable for data speeds up to 16 Mbps (the Token Ring network standard.)

- *Category 5 ("Cat 5")*: **Category 5 cable** is four-wire, 100-ohm cable useful for networks to 100 Mbps in Fast Ethernet. Efforts are being made to upgrade this speed to 1000 Mbps (GigEther). However, vendors are proposing a new standard, Cat 6, for this faster speed.

Today, the standard network cable is Cat 5.

Not all Cat 5 cabling is the same. If your cable is more than three years old, you will need to do some testing to ensure that your Cat 5 cable will support 100 Mbps or faster.

One problem of **unshielded twisted-pair (UTP) cable** is that external electrical voltages and magnetic fields can create noise inside the wire. The noise, or EMI, is unwanted current that can result when the twisted-pair cable lies close to a fluorescent light fixture or an electrical motor. To reduce EMI, **shielded twisted-pair (STP) cables** are surrounded by a metal foil that acts as a barrier to ground out the interference. For STP cable to work, it is important to connect the cable ground to the building's grounding system properly. Unfortunately, the shield of STP cable changes the electrical characteristics of the wire, reducing the distance and speed at which the network's signal can be transmitted.

Two types of connectors can be used on the ends of twisted-pair cable: RJ-45 plugs and IBM data connectors, shown in Figure 3-3. RJ-45 plugs are similar to the modular RJ-11 plugs commonly used to connect telephones to wall jacks and are generally preferred for unshielded cable because of their low cost and ease of installation. IBM engineered the data connector as a universal connector for use with STP cables. Although the data connector is rather large and difficult to install, it provides a very reliable connection for high-speed signals and has the advantage of being able to connect cables without needing special cable connectors.

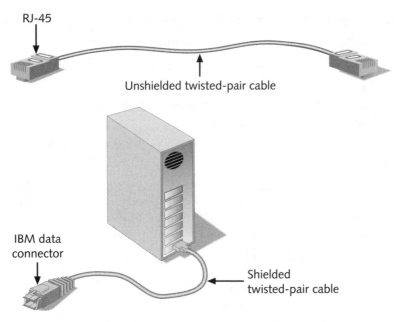

RJ-45

Unshielded twisted-pair cable

IBM data
connector

Shielded
twisted-pair cable

Figure 3-3 Connectors for twisted-pair cable

In general, UTP media are more common, less expensive, and more readily available than other bounded media. In addition to being shielded or unshielded, twisted–pair cable is available in different varieties that affect the speed at which signals can be sent over the cable. Signal speed is measured in millions of bits per second (Mbps).

Do not confuse mega*bits* with mega*bytes*. They are quite different. Although the rule is 8 bits to the byte, a handy rule of thumb for measuring data throughput is to make the calculation with 10 bits (to cover overhead) rather than 8 bits. This means that a 10 Mbps signal actually transmits about 1 MB (one million bytes) of data.

Table 3-3 lists the common types of twisted–pair cable, their associated transmission speeds, and typical usage.

Table 3-3 Twisted-pair cable specifications

Wire Type	Speed Range	Typical Use
1 and 2	Up to 4 Mbps	Voice and low-speed data
3	Up to 16 Mbps	Data
4	Up to 20 Mbps	Data
5	Up to 100 Mbps	High-speed data

Companies that install twisted-pair cable will normally provide you with the correct type of cable for your networking needs. If you are evaluating the existing wiring of a building for use in your network, however, you should first have the cable evaluated by a wire expert to determine if it will support the required network speeds.

The major disadvantages of twisted-pair cable, especially UTP, are its sensitivity to EMI and increased susceptibility to wiretapping by intruders. Wiretapping involves using special equipment, called a sniffer, to detect the signals on the cable by sensing the electrical fields. A wiretapper can also physically splice into the cable to access all network signals. If your organization is concerned about possible security violations due to wiretapping or if it needs to run network cable near electrical motors or generators, consider using STP cable or some other medium that is more secure and less vulnerable to EMI.

Coaxial Cable

Coaxial cable, commonly called "coax," is made of two conductors, as shown in Figure 3-4. The name *coaxial* derives from the fact that the two conductors in the cable share the same axis. At the center of the cable is a fairly stiff wire encased in insulating plastic. The plastic is surrounded by the second conductor, which is a wire mesh tube that also serves as a shield. A strong insulating plastic tube forms the cable's outer covering.

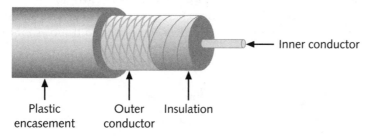

Figure 3-4   Coaxial cable

Coaxial cable is available in a variety of types and thicknesses for different purposes. Table 3-4 lists the varieties of coaxial cables, their electrical resistance, and their typical use. Generally, thicker cable is used to carry signals longer distances but is more expensive and less flexible. Compared to twisted-pair, coaxial cable supports higher data rates and is less susceptible to EMI and wiretapping. However, coaxial cable is generally more expensive, harder to install, and more susceptible to damage due to linking. In the past, many networks were wired with coaxial cable. Today, improvements in twisted-pair cable's bandwidth, along with its flexibility and lower cost, are influencing most organizations to select UTP as a medium for new network installations, rather than coaxial cable.

Table 3-4   Coaxial cable types

Cable Type	Resistance	Typical Usage
RG-8	50 ohms	Thick Ethernet networks
RG-58	50 ohms	Thin Ethernet networks
RG-59	75 ohms	Cable TV and IBM broadband networks
RG-62	93 ohms	ARCnet networks

Fiber-Optic Cable

As shown in Figure 3-5, **fiber–optic cable** looks similar to coaxial cable. It consists of light-conducting glass or plastic fibers at the center of a thick tube of protective cladding (wrapping) surrounded by a tough outer sheath. One or more fibers can be bounded in the center of the fiber-optic cable. Pulses of light are transmitted through the cable by either lasers or light-emitting diodes (LEDs) and received by photo detectors at the far end. Fiber-optic cables are much lighter and smaller than either coaxial or twisted-pair cables, and can support significantly higher data rates, from 100 million bits per second to more than 2 billion bits per second. Because light signals do not attenuate (lose strength) over distances as quickly as electrical signals, fiber-optic cables can carry high-speed signals over long distances. In addition, fiber-optic transmission is not susceptible to EMI and is very difficult to tap. The principal disadvantages of fiber-optic cable are relatively high cost, lack of mature standards, and difficulty of locating trained technicians to install and troubleshoot it.

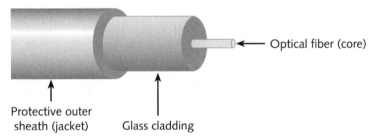

Optical fiber (core)

Protective outer
sheath (jacket)   Glass cladding

Figure 3-5   Fiber-optic cable

Fiber-optic cable comes in two varieties: single-mode and multimode. Single-mode (or single-index monomode) supports a single frequency of light. It therefore supports a far greater cable length than multimode. Multimode supports several frequencies of light. Thus it has a greater total carrying capacity with current technology than does single-mode. Most products today take advantage of multimode fiber.

Fiber-optic cable is used primarily to connect servers as a kind of backbone to share data at high speeds. Occasionally a workstation may be connected using fiber-optic to provide high-speed access to large data files. Finally, fiber-optic may be used when there is a need for maximum protection from EMI or wiretapping. Figure 3-6 shows a backbone connecting several high-volume NetWare servers or minicomputers to form a backbone network. A **backbone network** is a cable system used primarily to connect a host computer to NetWare servers, each of which can have its own local network. Fiber makes a good backbone network because it allows the NetWare servers to be spread out over long distances and still provides a high-speed communication system that is safe from EMI or differences in grounding among buildings. A backbone may also be used to connect networks among buildings such as on a campus or industrial park.

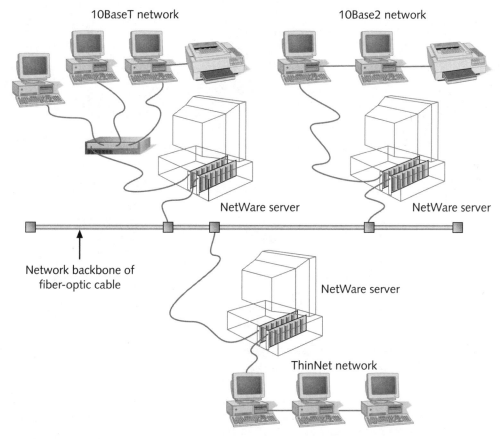

Figure 3-6   Backbone network

Infrared

Infrared is a wireless medium based on infrared light from LEDs. Infrared signals can be detected by direct line-of-sight receivers or by indirect receivers capturing signals reflected off walls or ceilings. Infrared signals, however, cannot penetrate walls or other opaque objects and are diluted by strong light sources. These limitations make infrared most useful for small, open, indoor environments such as a classroom or a small office area with cubicles.

Infrared transmission systems are very cost-efficient and capable of high bandwidths similar to those found in fiber-optic cables. As a result, an infrared medium can be a good way of connecting wireless LANs when computers are all located within a single room or office. Infrared eliminates the need for cables and allows computers to be easily moved as long as they can always be pointed toward the infrared transmitter/receiver, normally located near the ceiling, as shown in Figure 3-7.

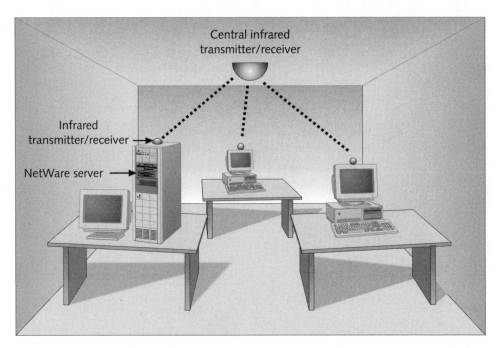

Figure 3-7 Infrared wireless network

 Although the high frequency of infrared waves can accommodate high data transfer rates, advances in infrared technology have been slow, primarily because of limitations in connecting computers separated by walls. Growth of infrared media is expected to accelerate as other radio frequencies become increasingly congested. A large pool of potential infrared installations exists in the networking of classroom computers and limited home or small business applications.

Comparing Network Media

Table 3-5 summarizes the various network media in terms of cost, ease of installation, transmission capacity, and immunity to EMI and tapping. The cost comparisons are based on costs of media and other required hardware. The numbers given for maximum transmission capacity may be deceiving, because they are based on the current use of the signaling technology and not on the media's raw bandwidth potential. In the case study exercises at the end of this chapter, you will have an opportunity to apply this information to selecting cable systems.

Table 3-5   Media summary

Medium	Cost	Installation	Capacity/Speed	Immunity from EMI and Tapping
Unshielded twisted-pair cable	Low	Simple	1–100 Mbps	Low
Shielded twisted-pair cable	Moderate	Simple to moderate	1–100 Mbps	Moderate
Coaxial cable	Moderate	Simple	10–1000 Mbps	Moderate
Fiber-optic cable	Moderate to high	Difficult	100–2000 Mbps	Very high
Infrared	Moderate	Simple	10–100 Mbps	Subject to interference from strong light sources

Network Topologies

An important aspect of a network system using bounded media is the method chosen to connect the networked computers. As mentioned previously, the physical geometry or cable layout used to connect computers in a LAN is the network topology, or just the topology. As a network administrator, you will need to be familiar with the topology of your network in order to attach new computers or isolate network problems to a faulty segment of the cable. As shown in Figure 3-8, the linear bus, ring, and star are the three major topologies used to connect computers in a LAN. In this section you will learn about each of these topologies and how they affect network systems in terms of cost, reliability, and expandability.

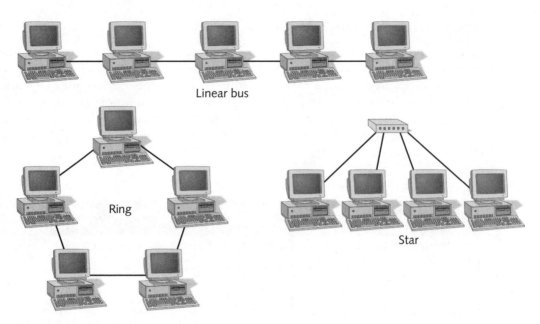

Figure 3-8 Topologies

Star Topology

The **star topology** derives its name from the fact that all cables on the network radiate from a central hub. The **hub** is a device that connects the network cables and passes the signals from one cable to the next. The type of hub you need will depend on the access system used by the network cards (described in the section on data link components). Although star topologies cost more because of the amount of wire needed, they are generally more reliable and easier to troubleshoot than other topologies. Because each cable in a star topology is a separate component, the failure of one cable does not affect the operation of the rest of the network. Troubleshooting for star topologies is easy because a network cable problem can be quickly isolated to the cable "run" on which a network device is experiencing errors. Another advantage of the star topology is the ease of adding or removing devices on the network without affecting the operation of other computers— using unallocated access ports on the hub, you simply plug or unplug cables.

 The star topology has become the most popular way to wire computers together, because of its exceptional flexibility and reliability.

Today star networks are usually wired with a **patch panel**, as shown in Figure 3-9. In a patch panel system, a wire runs from each potential computer location in the building through a drop cable to a central patch panel. A **patch cable** is then used to connect a device in any given location to the hub. A patch panel system makes it easy to move a computer to another location as well as to connect or disconnect computers from the network for troubleshooting.

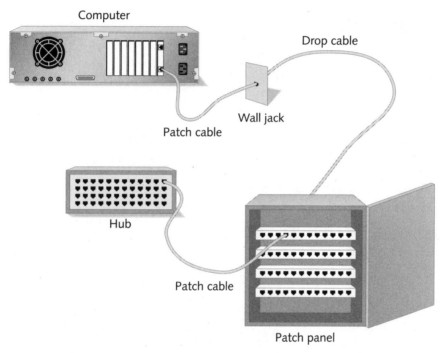

Figure 3-9 Patch panel system

Star topologies are generally implemented with twisted-pair cable rather than coaxial cable because of lower cable cost combined with the increased flexibility and smaller size of twisted-pair cable. RJ-45 connectors on twisted-pair cable allow easy connection of computers to wall outlets and between hubs and patch panels.

Linear Bus Topology

The **linear bus topology** connects computers in series by running a cable from one computer to the next. The method of attaching the computers to the "bus" depends on the network card and cable system. When coaxial cable is used, each computer is usually attached to the bus cable by means of a T-connector, as Figure 3-10 shows. When twisted-pair cable is used, each network card usually contains two RJ-45 female connectors that allow twisted-pair cable to be run from one computer to the next.

Each end of a linear bus network requires some sort of terminator or "wire-wrap" plug, to prevent echo signals from interfering with communication signals. The resistance and size of coaxial cable is an important factor and depends on the requirements of the network cards (described in the section on data link components).

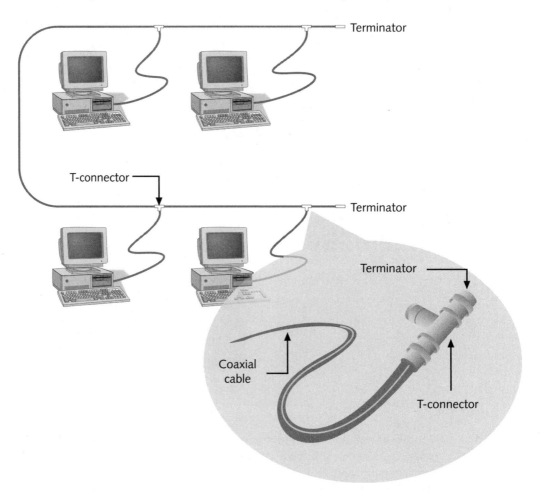

Figure 3-10   Coaxial cable network

The primary advantages of a linear bus topology are the small amount of cable needed and the ease of wiring computers clustered in locations such as a classroom or a computer lab. The two biggest disadvantages of a bus network are adding or removing computers and troubleshooting. Adding or removing a computer from a bus network often involves interrupting communication on the network segment. Troubleshooting the network is difficult because when the failure of a cable component causes a network error, it often disrupts communications on the entire network segment and requires special test equipment to locate the faulty network component. Therefore, linear bus networks are generally limited to smaller applications or are used when linking computers is particularly cost-effective.

 Linear bus networks are gradually being replaced by star networks in many organizations because star networks are easier to troubleshoot. A broken wire in a star network configuration affects only one workstation. In a linear bus network, in contrast, all computers on the cable segment fail when the cable is disconnected or broken anywhere in the network.

Ring Topology

A **ring topology** is similar to a linear bus topology, except that the ends of the cable are connected instead of terminated. As a result, signals on the ring topology travel around the network in one direction until they return to the device from which they originated. In a ring topology, each computer in the ring receives signals and then retransmits them to the next computer in the ring. Because the signals are regenerated at each device along the network, a ring topology lets its network signals travel longer distances as long as another computer is located within the distance limit of each network card's transmitter.

The disadvantage of a ring topology is the extra cable needed to complete the ring's circle when computers are spread out in a serial fashion. In addition, the ring has the same disadvantage as the linear bus in terms of interrupting network transmissions to add or remove workstations. An advantage of the ring topology over the linear bus topology is that rings are often easier to troubleshoot. Because each computer on the ring receives and then retransmits a signal, the troubleshooter can use software that quickly determines which computer is not receiving the signal. The damaged cable component can then be isolated to the cable segment between the computer that does not receive the signal and its "upstream" neighbor.

Comparing Topologies

Table 3-6 compares each of the three popular network topologies in terms of wiring needs, ease of expansion, fault tolerance, and troubleshooting. The type of topology and cable system you select is closely linked to the types of network cards supported on the network.

Table 3-6   Topology comparison

Topology	Wiring	Expansion	Fault Tolerance	Troubleshooting
Star	Requires the most wire because a cable must be led from each computer to a central hub	Easy to expand by using a patch panel to plug new computers into the hub	Highly fault-tolerant because a bad cable or connector will affect only one computer	Easiest to troubleshoot by removing suspect computers from the network
Linear bus	Usually requires the least amount of cable, because the cable is connected from one computer to the next	Difficult to expand unless a connector exists at the location of the new computer	Poor fault tolerance because a bad connector or cable will disrupt the entire network segment	The most difficult to troubleshoot, because all computers can be affected by one problem
Ring	Requires more wire than a linear bus because cable ends must be connected, but requires less than a star	Difficult to expand because the ring must be broken to insert a new computer	Poor fault tolerance because a bad connector or cable disrupts the entire network segment	Fairly easy to troubleshoot with software that can identify which computer cannot receive the signal

Data Link Layer Components

As mentioned in the previous section, the data link components actually control the way the network cable system transmits and receives signals. As a result, the components you select for the data link level of your network will determine what network topologies and cable types you can use on the network. Conversely, when you want to use an already existing cable system, you will want to select data link products that best support it. The data link layer components consist of the network interface cards and card driver programs.

Network Interface Card

The network interface card (NIC) acts as an interface between the network's data link and physical layers by converting the commands and data frames from the data link layer into the appropriate signals used by the connectors on the physical cable system.

Driver software is needed to control the network card and provide an interface between the data link layer and the network layer software. To provide this software interface, Novell has developed a set of driver specifications called the **Open Data**

3

Interface (ODI). ODI-compatible drivers allow the network card to be shared by multiple programs running on the workstation or on the NetWare server. For example, ODI drivers enable the NetWare server to communicate with both Apple Macintosh and IBM PCs attached to the same network.

Microsoft networks, in contrast, use a driver interface called **Network Driver Interface Specifications (NDIS)** to interface network card drivers to Microsoft's network operating system. NDIS-compatible drivers allow software developers to write programs for use on Windows 95/98 and Windows NT computers without requiring them to write instructions to control the network card—the NDIS drivers perform the hardware functions for them. Microsoft's approach results in fewer programming requirements for applications developers as well as in more standardized and reliable networking functionality in those applications.

Because there are two types of driver interfaces, ODI and NDIS, you will need to be sure the network cards you obtain for your network contain the correct driver for the type of NOS you will be supporting. Novell provides ODI-compatible driver programs for many popular network cards with NetWare 5.0, but some cards are not supported. The manufacturer of an unsupported card should supply a disk with the ODI-compatible driver program that will interface its NIC to a NetWare server or workstation. In Chapter 6 you will learn about the standard card drivers that are included with NetWare and how to install them on the server or workstation computers.

 Whenever possible, try to obtain NICs that work with the standard NetWare ODI drivers, to make it easier to install and maintain your network system. Avoid off-brand NICs despite their low cost, because their nonstandard drivers are difficult to maintain and troubleshoot.

So that network cards and drivers from different manufacturers can communicate with each other, certain data link standards need to be followed. These standards are controlled by committees within the IEEE. The two major committees that affect LANs today are the **IEEE 802.3** and **IEEE 802.5** committees.

In addition to controlling types of signals, data link standards control how each computer accesses the network. Because only one signal can be sent on the network cable at any one time, a **channel access method** is necessary to control when computers transmit, to reduce **collisions** that can occur when two or more computers try to transmit at the same time. Collisions cause network errors by distorting data signals, making them unreadable. Channel access methods used on today's LANs are either token passing or contention based.

The **token passing method** enables only one computer to transmit a message on the network at any given time. This access to the network is controlled by a **token**, which is a special packet passed from one computer to the next to determine which machine can use the network. When a computer needs to transmit data, it waits until it receives the token packet and then transmits its data frame packet on the network. After the transmission is complete, the transmitting computer releases the token. The next computer on the network can pick it up and then proceed to transmit. In actual implementation, the token passing system is very complex, involving token priorities, early release of tokens, and network monitoring and error detection functions. As a result, network cards based on the token passing method are generally more expensive.

 IBM originally developed the token passing technology, which has now been standardized by the IEEE 802.5 committee.

The **contention access method** allows a node to transmit a message whenever it detects that the channel is not in use. Think of the contention access method in terms of CB radio use. When no one is talking on a CB radio channel, you are free to transmit your message. When someone else is talking on the radio channel, however, you must wait for his or her transmission to end before you start your own transmission. The main problem with contention-based access arises when two or more computers sense an open channel and start transmitting at the same time. A collision results, and the colliding computers must wait a few microseconds before retransmitting their messages. On a computer network, this contention system is called **Carrier Sense Multiple Access with Collision Detection (CSMA/CD)** and has been standardized by the IEEE 802.3 committee into several different product types, based on speed and cable type. The three most popular IEEE 802.3 committee standards, 10BaseT, 100BaseT, and 10Base2, will be described later.

A contention system works very well when network traffic is light, but its performance can drop off quickly under heavy network transmission loads. Token-based systems perform better under heavy loads because the performance does not drop off as abruptly. The following sections describe the different types of NICs and data link standards in use today and compare the network topology, performance, and access methods of these products.

Token Ring Networks

IBM originally designed the token ring system for use in industrial environments that require reliable high-speed communications. Today, a token ring is widely considered to be the best network system in terms of overall performance and reliability. A token ring network is shown in Figure 3-11.

3

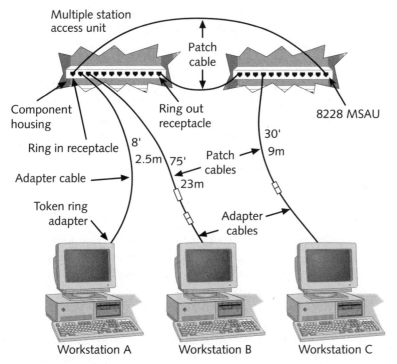

Figure 3-11 Token ring network

Standard token ring cards were originally transmitted at 4 Mbps. Today, however, most token ring cards use 16 Mbps transmission speeds. You cannot mix cards running at 4 Mbps with cards running at 16 Mbps on the same token ring network.

The token ring system shown in Figure 3-11 consists of workstations connected by twisted-pair cables to a central hub, called a **Multiple Station Access Unit (MSAU)**. Although this appears to be a star arrangement, the network signals actually travel in a ring, which is why it is often called a star ring. A signal originating from Workstation A in Figure 3-11, for example, is initially transmitted to the MSAU. The MSAU relays the signal to the cable for workstation B. After receiving the signal, Workstation B retransmits the signal and returns it to the MSAU. The MSAU then relays the signal to Workstation C, and Workstation C transmits the signal back to the MSAU from whence it is relayed back to its source, Workstation A. If the wire running from the MSAU to Workstation B is broken, or if Workstation B is shut down, a relay in the MSAU will automatically pass the signal on to Workstation C. Thus the token ring system is very resistant to breakdowns.

The IBM token ring network is often called a star ring because it combines the physical topology of a star with the logical topology of a ring.

The advantages of token ring systems are speed, expandability, and fault tolerance. In addition, token ring systems are usually easy to troubleshoot because bad connections or cable runs can be quickly isolated. The disadvantages include the extra wiring required by the star topology and the higher cost of most token ring cards over other types of network cards. This, added to the cost of an MSAU for every eight computers on your network, makes token ring networks quite expensive. For this reason, token ring is not gaining in market share over Ethernet.

Ethernet Networks

The term *Ethernet* originally applied to networks using a linear bus topology and CSMA/CD on coaxial cable. This system, discussed in detail in this section, is also known as 10Base2. However, several variants of the specification have been created, and now the term **Ethernet** is used as a general reference to the entire family of variations. The members of the Ethernet family discussed here are 10Base2, 10BaseT, and 100BaseT.

10Base2 Networks.   The **10Base2** system, shown in Figure 3-12, is based on the linear bus topology on coaxial cable and uses the CSMA/CD system standardized by the IEEE 802.3 committee. The term 10Base2 stands for 10 Mbps baseband using digital baseband signals over a maximum of two 100-meter coaxial cable segments. The term **baseband** describes a computer network that carries **digital signals**; a **broadband** system carries **analog signals**, like the signals used for television and radio transmissions. In 10Base2, thin RG-58 coaxial cable with T-connectors enables up to 30 machines to be attached to a single cable run, which is called a segment. According to the 10Base2 standards, a segment cannot exceed 607 feet in length, and no more than five segments can be joined by repeaters to form the entire network. In addition, a maximum of three of the five segments can have workstations attached. Network professionals often refer to 10Base2 as **ThinNet** because of its thin coaxial cable.

10Base2 cards use the same CSMA/CD system and 10 Mbps speed as 10BaseT cards (discussed next). Some manufacturers supply cards that can be configured for either the twisted-pair 10BaseT system or the RG-58 cable bus. Although both 10Base2 and 10BaseT provide excellent throughput under normal network loads, wiring 10Base2 is simpler and more cost-effective than 10BaseT in certain environments—those in which groups of computers are located in a small area, such as a computer lab, where one coaxial cable runs from machine to machine.

Thick coaxial cable is sometimes used instead of thin coaxial cables. Networks using thick coaxial cable are referred to as 10Base5, Thick Ethernet, or ThickNet. These, however, are not common.

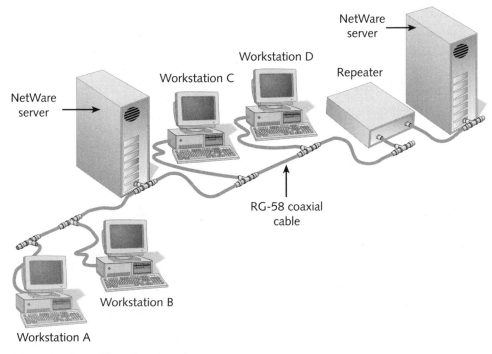

Figure 3-12   10Base2 network

10BaseT Networks.   The 10BaseT network system is very popular in business offices today because it combines the flexibility of the star topology with the lower cost of the CSMA/CD channel access method. The IEEE 802.3 designation of **10BaseT** stands for 10 Mbps baseband network using twisted-pair cable. A 10BaseT network is shown in Figure 3-13.

A 10BaseT network uses a device called a **concentrator** as a hub to connect all machines in a star topology with twisted-pair cable. Although the 10BaseT network uses the same star topology as a token ring network, the 10BaseT signals are not sent from one station to the next as in token ring. They are broadcast to all stations simultaneously by using the CSMA/CD method standardized by the IEEE 802.3 committee. In many instances a cable system designed for token ring can easily be converted to support 10BaseT simply by replacing the MSAUs with concentrators. The concentrator acts as a repeater, receiving signals on one cable port and then retransmitting those signals on all other ports. When two or more network stations attempt to transmit at the same instant, a collision occurs, and the stations must retransmit after waiting a random period of time.

Novell uses what it calls the 802.2 frame type on IPX networks. This 802.2 is actually the IEEE's 802.3 frame type. (Novell also had an 802.3 frame type which isn't the IEEE's in older versions.) NetWare 5.0's default frame type is Ethernet II, which is used by the IP protocol. NetWare 5.0 only loads the 802.3 frame type if you ask for IPX support during installation.

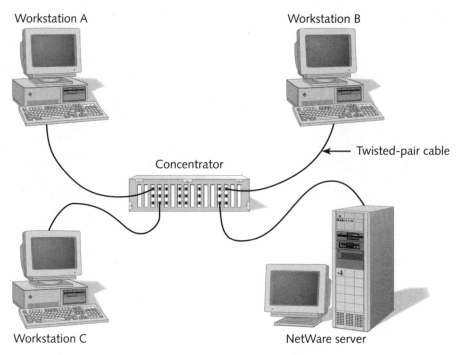

Figure 3-13   10BaseT network

The advantages of 10BaseT include high performance under light-to-medium network loads and low costs for network cards due to the relative simplicity of the CSMA/CD system. Although 10BaseT performance can be faster than token ring under light loads, it is more easily slowed due to collisions when many stations are transmitting on the network. Another disadvantage of the 10BaseT system is additional cost both for concentrators and for the star topology wiring.

100BaseT Networks.   The 100BaseT network systems are extensions of the 10BaseT system and are overseen by the IEEE 802.3 committee. They use the same star topology and the CSMA/CD channel access method. The designation of **100BaseT** indicates a 100 Mbps baseband network using twisted-pair cable or IBM STP cable. (The **100BaseFX** designation indicates a 100 Mbps baseband network using fiber-optic cable.) 100BaseT networks appear identical to 10BaseT networks. A concentrator is used as the hub to connect all machines in a star topology. The concentrator still acts as a repeater.

The advantages of 100BaseT include higher performance for networks needing fast data transmission, such as those using video. The disadvantages include shorter maximum cable run lengths in some cable systems, which is a tradeoff necessary to gain the extra speed, and a higher cost of hubs and NICs capable of handling the higher speed.

Comparing Network Systems

Selecting a network system is a complex task that depends on such variables as type and location of computers, existing wiring, and the amount of load expected on the network. In many organizations, multiple network systems are necessary to meet the needs of different departments. Such network systems can be connected with bridges and routers, described in the next section. Table 3-7 summarizes the major network systems.

Table 3-7   Network system comparison

Network System	Cable Types	Topology	Maximum Number of Nodes	IEEE Standard	Speed	Access Method	Distance
Token ring	UTP, STP, fiber	star	96	802.5	4–16 Mbps	token	150 feet (50 meters) per cable run
10Base2	coaxial	linear bus	30 per segment with maximum of 3 populated segments	802.3	10 Mbps	CSMA/CD	607 feet (185 meters) per segment
10BaseT	UTP	star	512	802.3	10 Mbps	CSMA/CD	300 feet (100 meters) per cable run on UTP Cat 3 & 4; 450 feet (150 meters) on UTP Cat 5
100BaseT	UTP, STP	star	512	802.3	100 Mbps	CSMA/CD	300 feet (100 meters) per cable run on UTP Cat 3 & 4; 300 feet (100 meters) on UTP Cat 5; 300 feet (100 meters) on STP type 1

If you decide to install new cable above a ceiling or in walls, be sure to obtain cable that meets your local building codes. Some cable is not allowed in suspended ceilings, whereas others are not permitted where heating/air-conditioning ducts are nearby. (You need what is called "plenum grade" for such cables.)

Repeaters, Bridges, and Routers

Each network system presented in this chapter has unique limitations. In some cases, you will want to take advantage of certain features found in two different products. For example, in a school environment you might want the Ethernet system in computer labs, to take advantage of the economical coaxial wiring arrangement. If other computers in the building are located many feet apart in completely separate areas, however, you will not want to connect them this way. You can solve this problem by creating two separate networks: Ethernet for the lab and token ring for the office. You then connect the networks so they share access to the same NetWare server. In other cases, it might be necessary to break a large network into two or more smaller networks to overcome performance problems or cabling distances, or to accommodate large numbers of users.

Within a network system, you use repeaters to maintain a strong, reliable signal throughout the network. To connect separate network systems, you use bridges or routers, and the resulting connected networks are called an **internetwork**. Repeaters, bridges, and routers are shown in Figure 3-14.

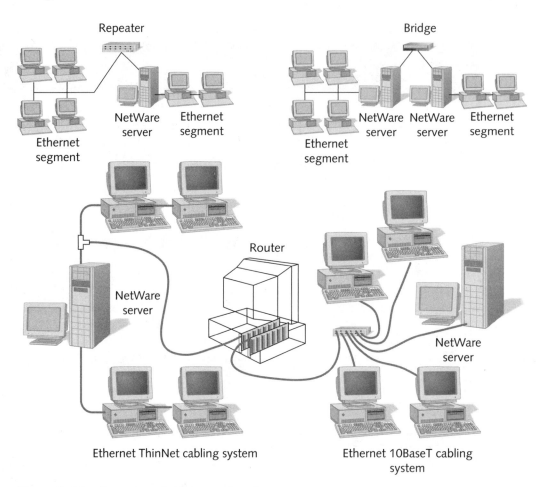

Figure 3-14   Repeaters, bridges, and routers

Repeaters

Network cable systems consist of one or more cable lengths, called segments, that have termination points on each end. **Repeaters** are hardware devices that let you link network segments. Repeaters work at the physical layer of the OSI model. This means that the repeater simply receives signals from one network segment and then retransmits them to the next segments. The hub of a star network topology, for example, can act as a repeater, receiving a signal from one computer cable and broadcasting it on the other cables. Each computer in a ring topology acts as a repeater, receiving the signal from the "upstream" computer and retransmitting it to the next computer on the ring. Repeaters can also connect two linear bus segments, as Figure 3-12 shows. This use of repeaters increases the fault tolerance of a linear bus network because a bad connector or cable on one segment does not prevent computers on other segments from communicating. As a network administrator, you should be aware of the role of repeaters on your network for easy maintenance and troubleshooting of network problems.

Bridges

A **bridge** operates at the data link layer of the OSI model. This means that the bridge sees only the packet's frame information, which consists of the addresses of the sender and receiver along with error-checking information. During network operation, the bridge watches packets on both networks and builds a table of workstation node addresses for each network. When it sees a packet on one network that has a destination address for a machine on the other network, the bridge reads the packet, builds new frame information, and sends the packet out on the other network. Because bridges work at the data link level, they are used to connect networks of the same type. For example, a bridge can connect two different token ring networks and allow more than 100 users to access the same NetWare server. Another use for a bridge might be to break a heavily loaded Ethernet or 10BaseT network into two separate networks, to reduce the number of collisions occurring on any one network system. A bridge is often contained in a separate black box, but can also consist of specialized software running on a microcomputer that simply contains two network cards.

Routers

Routers are needed to create more complex internetworks. A **router** operates at the network layer of the OSI model and therefore has access to the datagram information containing the logical network address along with control information. When a router is used, each network must be given a separate network address. Remember that a network address is similar in function to a ZIP code. Just as each postal area has a unique ZIP code, each network system must have a unique network address. The router information contained in the datagram packet lets a router find the correct path and, if necessary, break up a datagram for transmission on a different network system. Two disadvantages of routers are that they require a little more processing time than bridges and that network packets must use a datagram format that the router can interpret.

Networks with different network topologies generally are connected with routers, whereas networks of the same topology are connected with bridges. Novell uses routers in its NetWare servers to allow up to eight different network cards to be installed in a single NetWare server computer. This lets you use the NetWare server to connect networks of different types and topologies to form an internetwork.

Protocol Stacks

The network's **protocol stack** is responsible for formatting requests to access network services and transmit data. Whereas the delivery of the data packets throughout a network system is the responsibility of its data link and physical layer components, the functions of the network, transport, and session layers are built into a network operating system's protocol stack.

NetWare 5.0's default protocol is TCP/IP, or IP for short. Administrators need to know how to configure an IP-protocol network with NetWare. In the past, Novell's IPX/SPX protocol stack was commonly used to support clients on NetWare networks. You can install either IP or IPX or both on a NetWare LAN. Because today's networks often need to support protocol stacks of computers running other operating systems as well, the network administrator should also be familiar with the common protocol stacks used by such operating systems as Macintosh, UNIX, and Windows.

In this section you will learn about protocol stacks and some of their advantages and disadvantages, which will help you make informed recommendations on which protocol stacks should be supported on a network.

TCP/IP

As Table 3-8 shows, **TCP/IP (Transmission Control Protocol/Internet Protocol)** covers the network and transport OSI layers, as does IPX/SPX. Unlike IPX/SPX, however, TCP and IP don't overlap in the transport layer.

Table 3-8   TCP/IP protocol

OSI Model Layers

	Physical	Data Link	Network	Transport	Session	Presentation	Application
NCP					X	X	
SPX				X	X		
IPX			X	X			
Ethernet	X	X					
Token ring	X	X					
Others	X	X					

TCP/IP is responsible for formatting packets and then routing them between networks using IP (Internet Protocol). IP is more sophisticated than IPX in fragmenting packets and transmitting over wide area network links. When IP is used, each workstation is assigned a logical network and node address. IP allows packets to be sent out over different routers and then reassembled in the correct sequence at the receiving station. TCP (Transport Control Protocol) operates at the transport level and provides the guaranteed delivery of packets by

3

receiving acknowledgments. The acknowledgment system lets the sender and receiver establish a window for the number of packets to acknowledge. This allows for better performance than with WANs, because each packet need not be individually acknowledged before another packet is sent.

Today TCP/IP is commonly used on many LANs as well as the Internet. NetWare 5.0 servers use IP as the native protocol, rather than IPX. (NetWare 4.x can also use IP if the appropriate NLMs are loaded and configured.) NetWare uses the TCP/IP protocol to communicate with workstations, to provide Internet services, and to route TCP/IP packets between network cards. The need to implement TCP/IP on a NetWare network is growing rapidly, because of the exploding popularity of the Internet and the need for network administrators to provide a single protocol for all network services.

The primary drawback of TCP/IP has been the need to manually configure the address for each node on the network. If you don't plan on connecting your system to the Internet, you may want to use a default number such as 255.255.25.25 or something similar for your server, and then variations on that for each workstation.

IPX/SPX

The IPX/SPX protocol is Novell's proprietary system that implements the session, transport, and network OSI layers, as shown in Table 3-9. Notice that IPX/SPX is not a true implementation of the OSI model, because IPX and SPX functions overlap layers. This is true of many older protocol stacks that were developed before the OSI model was developed and standardized.

Table 3-9   Novell IPX/SPX and NCP protocols

OSI Model Layers

	Physical	Data Link	Network	Transport	Session	Presentation	Application
TCP				X			
IP			X				
Ethernet	X	X					
Token ring	X	X					
Others	X	X					

IPX (Internetwork Packet eXchange) is the NetWare protocol that manages packet routing and formatting at the network layer. To function, IPX must be loaded on each network workstation and on the NetWare server. In addition to IPX, each workstation and NetWare server must have loaded a network card driver to transmit the frames containing the packets. IPX software and the network card driver are brought together during the network installation process, which is described in Chapter 6. In addition to IPX, NetWare uses two protocols, SPX and NCP, to provide network services.

The key advantage to IPX (and the reason Novell developed it despite the ready availability of IP) is that it offers automatic addressing for network nodes. Despite improved IP address automation, administrators still have to manually configure addresses for one or more nodes on an IP network. With IPX, the addresses are done for you.

SPX (Sequential Packet eXchange) operates at the OSI transport level and guarantees delivery of packets by receiving an acknowledgment for each packet sent. **NCP (NetWare Core Protocol)** provides the session and presentation levels at the workstation through the Novell Client software. The client establishes and maintains network sessions as well as directs information and requests from the workstation and formats them for the NetWare server. On the NetWare server, NCP provides network services such as login, file sharing, printing, security, and administrative functions.

Novell has incorporated many improvements into its client software for DOS/Windows/Macintosh workstations. Unless there is a reason why older client software must be used at your site, you should upgrade all workstations to the newest client software. This will prevent potential error conditions. The software is available free from Novell's Web site at www.novell.com.

NetBEUI

The **NetBEUI** protocol is Microsoft's own protocol stack and is integrated into Windows for Workgroups, Windows 95/98, and Windows NT products. Of the three protocols described in this section, NetBEUI is the easiest to use. It has few features, however, and cannot be used in large internetwork environments because it does not support the network layer needed for routing packets between networks. As a result, the NetBEUI protocol is limited to only the most basic of networking, communicating with other computers attached to the same network cable system.

Avoid using NetBEUI except in peer-to-peer networking on small networks of under 10 to 15 workstations.

The NetBEUI protocol stack consists of **NetBIOS** and **service message blocks (SMBs)** at the session layer and **NetBIOS frames (NBF)** at the transport layer, as Table 3-10 shows. SMBs and NetBIOS offer a well-defined standard method for servers and workstations to communicate with each other. Many peer-to-peer applications have been written to interface with NetBIOS, allowing an application to span multiple computers. Because NetBIOS-based applications are popular, Novell has provided a NetBIOS interface to work with its IPX/SPX protocol. This allows workstations to run peer-to-peer applications while still accessing services from NetWare servers.

Table 3-10 NetBEUI protocol

OSI Model Layers

	Physical	Data Link	Network	Transport	Session	Presentation	Application
NetBIOS/SMB					X		
NBF or NBT			X	X			
Ethernet	X	X					
Token ring	X	X					
Others	X	X					

Because NetBEUI's NBF does not maintain routing tables, it is extremely small and fast, making it useful for networks ranging from 2 to 50 devices. Because the NBF does not support packet routing, however, the protocol is limited to communication among computers attached to a single network. The NetBEUI protocol allows the replacement of NBF with **NBT (NetBIOS over TCP/IP)**, which lets the protocol stack communicate directly over large TCP/IP-based networks.

AppleTalk

The **AppleTalk** protocol suite was originally developed to let Macintosh computers communicate in peer-to-peer networks. It currently provides connectivity for a variety of computer systems, including IBM PCs running MS-DOS, IBM mainframes, and various Unix-based computers. The AppleTalk protocol suite was developed after the OSI model was conceived and therefore can be mapped reasonably well to the OSI layers, as shown in Table 3-11.

Table 3-11 AppleTalk protocol

OSI Model Layers

	Physical	Data Link	Network	Transport	Session	Presentation	Application
Apple Filing Protocol (AFP)						X	
Apple Session Protocol (ASP)					X		
Apple Transition Protocol (ATP)				X			

Table 3-11   AppleTalk protocol (continued)

OSI Model Layers

	Physical	Data Link	Network	Transport	Session	Presentation	Application
Datagram Delivery Protocol (DDP)			X				
AARP (Apple Address Resolution Protocol)	X	X					
Local Talk	X	X					
Ethertalk (Ethernet)	X	X					
Token Talk (token ring)	X	X					

On the data link level, the **Apple Address Resolution Protocol (AARP)** connects the AppleTalk protocol stack to the Ethernet, 10BaseT, or token ring protocol. AppleTalk supports the routing of packets between networks by using the **Datagram Delivery Protocol (DDP)**. In addition, AppleTalk uses zones to organize the names of service providers logically on large internetworks. Zones limit the number of service providers presented at one time, which simplifies the user's choices.

Because the Macintosh and the AppleTalk protocol are so popular, Novell has included AppleTalk support with NetWare 5.0. Loading the AppleTalk protocol on a NetWare server allows Macintosh or other computers using AppleTalk to see the NetWare server as another AppleTalk service provider.

On NetWare 4.x and later versions, you can use any combination of PC and Macintosh clients. The total number of users who can simultaneously log in to the network is set by the NetWare license you purchase (for example, a 100-user NetWare license allows 100 simultaneous logins), but it doesn't matter whether the workstation is a PC or a Macintosh.

In the NetWare 5.0 environment, the Macintosh workstations can also log in to Novell Directory Services (NDS). However, the Mac workstations must load and run MacIPX, which lets the Macintoshes use the IPX protocol. For the Macintosh workstation to use NDS, IPX is required.

CHAPTER SUMMARY

3

❏ Network communication depends on packets of information being passed from one computer to another. Understanding how information packets flow through a network system means knowing the functions of the seven layers of the Open Systems Interconnect (OSI) model. The application layer software is responsible for interacting with the user and providing software tools to perform specific tasks. The presentation layer then translates data from the application layer into the appropriate ASCII and binary codes. The session layer initiates and maintains a communication session with the NetWare server computer, providing an interface between the local DOS and the network operating system. The transport layer is responsible for reliable delivery of data packets, called segments, and often requires the receiving computer to send acknowledgments confirming receipt of segment packets. The network layer places the segment packet in a datagram and routes datagrams to the correct computer. The data link and physical layers act as the delivery system by placing datagram packets in frames and sending them on the network cable system. Special committees of the Institute of Electronic and Electrical Engineers (IEEE) control the physical and data link standards for LAN network systems. The IEEE 802.3 committee controls the contention-based carrier sense multiple access with collision detection (CSMA/CD) system, and the IEEE 802.5 committee controls the token passing standard.

❏ Cable types used with today's LANs include shielded and unshielded twisted-pair cable, coaxial cable, and fiber-optic cable. Infrared is a special communication medium that uses light beams rather than cable to transmit information from each computer to a central device. The infrared system is a good alternative for a network in a single room where installing cable can be particularly difficult or expensive. The physical geometry of a bounded medium is called its topology. Major physical topologies include ring, linear bus, and star.

❏ Regardless of the type of topology used, only one machine can transmit on a network at any given instant, and with some, a method of access control must be used to avoid data collisions. Network access control methods can be either contention-based or token-based. Ethernet 10Base2, 10BaseT, and 100BaseT networks use a contention system in which computers attempt to transmit whenever they sense an open period on the network. On busy networks, however, when two or more machines sense an open period and try to transmit at the same time, a collision occurs. The machines then each wait a random time period before retrying their transmissions. This system is CSMA/CD.

❑ Token ring uses a deterministic system called token passing. A token is passed around the network when no data packet is being transmitted. A machine needing to transmit must wait for the token. When it receives the token, it can transmit its packet without any collisions. Collisions cause CSMA/CD systems to slow significantly under heavy network transmission loads, whereas token passing systems provide more uniform and predictable performance. A repeater works at the physical layer, connecting network segments and passing signals between them. An internetwork consists of two or more network topologies connected by a bridge or router. Working at the data link layer, bridges are very efficient, but they are limited to moving frames between networks of similar design. Routers are more sophisticated because they work at the network layer and have access to the datagram control information. Because of this access, routers can select the most efficient path for a packet and fragment packets into the correct size to send over the selected network.

❑ Protocols are the languages used to implement the OSI layers. Popular protocols you will probably encounter as a network administrator include Novell NetWare's IPX/SPX, the TCP/IP protocol used by Unix and the Internet; NetBEUI, used in Microsoft Windows-based networks; and the AppleTalk protocol used for Macintosh computers. NetWare 5.0 servers use the IP protocol by default. Earlier versions used IPX/SPX protocol by default, but could also be configured to handle TCP/IP and AppleTalk. TCP/IP is becoming a very popular protocol for use in Unix environments and international WANs such as the Internet. Both IP and IPX are network layer protocols that control the routing and flow of packets in the network system. TCP and SPX are similar in that they are both transport protocols that provide guaranteed delivery of packets.

KEY TERMS

10Base2
10BaseT
100BaseFX
100BaseT
analog signals
Apple Address Resolution Protocol (AARP)
AppleTalk
application layer
backbone network
bandwidth
baseband
bounded media
bridge
broadband

3

bundled pair
Category 5 cable
Carrier Sense Multiple Access with Collision Detection (CSMA/CD)
channel access method
coaxial cable
collision
concentrator
contention access method
cyclic redundancy check (CRC)
data frame packet
data link layer
Datagram Delivery Protocol (DDP)
datagram packet
digital signals
driver software
electromagnetic interference (EMI)
Ethernet
fiber-optic cable
frame
hub
IEEE 802.3
IEEE 802.5
Internetwork Packet eXchange (IPX)
infrared
Institute of Electrical and Electronic Engineers (IEEE)
International Standards Organization (ISO)
internetwork
interoperability
linear bus topology
logical link control (LLC) layer
media
media access control (MAC) layer
message packet
Multiple Station Access Unit (MSAU)
multiplexing
NetBEUI
NetBIOS
NetBIOS frames (NBF)

NetBIOS over TCP/IP (NBT)
NetWare Core Protocol (NCP)
network address
network layer
Network Driver Interface Specifications (NDIS)
Open Data Interface (ODI)
Open Systems Interconnect (OSI) model
packet
patch cable
patch panel
physical address
physical layer
presentation layer
protocol stack
repeater
ring topology
router
segment
service message block (SMB)
session layer
shielded twisted-pair (STP) cable
Sequential Packet eXchange (SPX)
star topology
ThinNet
token
token passing method
topology
transport layer
Transport Control Protocol/Internet Protocol (TCP/IP)
twisted-pair cable
unbounded media
unshielded twisted-pair (UTP) cable

REVIEW QUESTIONS

1. The _____ standards organization works on physical cable standards.

2. The _____ layer of the OSI model provides guaranteed delivery of segment packets.

3. The data link layer is responsible for _____.

4. Sequence the following OSI layers, starting from the hardware level, and match the following packet types with the OSI layers that use them:

Sequence layer   Packet type

_____ session   _____ a. frame

_____ application   _____ b. message

_____ presentation   _____ c. segment

_____ data link   _____ d. datagram

_____ physical   _____ e. bits

_____ network

_____ transport

5. The _____ unbounded medium would be well suited for use in a classroom.

6. _____ is the most common form of bounded medium.

7. _____ network cable is similar to the wire used to connect your telephone to the phone system.

8. What can be done to reduce EMI in electrical cables?

9. In a(n) _____ topology, a cable is run from each computer to a central device.

10. In a(n) _____ network, all computers are attached to the same cable segment.

11. An MSAU is used on a(n) _____ network system.

12. Under the _____ access method, only one node is given permission to transmit a message on the network at any given time.

13. The _____ access method performs best under heavy loads.

14. Match the IEEE standards to the following appropriate products:

_____ 10Base2   a. IEEE 802.3

_____ Token ring   b. IEEE 802.5

_____ 10BaseT   c. IEEE 802.12

_____ 100BaseT   d. no IEEE standard

15. A concentrator is used on a(n) _____ network system.

16. Identify which type of medium is commonly used by each of the following network systems:

10Base2 _____

10BaseT _____

100BaseT _____

token ring _____

17. A(n) _____ operates at the physical layer of the OSI model and relays messages from one segment to another.

18. A(n) _____ operates at the network layer of the OSI model and can be used to connect networks of different topologies.

19. A(n) _____ consists of two or more networks attached by a bridge or router.

20. A(n) _____ is a method of implementing the network, transport, and session layers of the OSI model in a network system.

21. The _____ protocol is commonly used by the Unix operating system.

22. The _____ protocol is commonly used with Windows NT and Windows 95/98 workstations.

23. _____ is a proprietary protocol used in NetWare networks.

24. _____ is the default protocol that provides NetWare network services in NetWare 5.0.

25. TCP operates at the _____ layer of the OSI model.

26. IPX operates at the _____ layer of the OSI model.

27. List one advantage and one disadvantage of the NetBEUI protocol.

HANDS-ON PROJECTS

This chapter focused on the various services provided in the OSI model. Unfortunately, it isn't possible to contact these services and test them directly. You can, however, test them indirectly using various utilities. In these exercises and projects, you will use some NetWare commands to demonstrate the OSI layers that attach your workstation to the network and access the NetWare server. You will then use NetWare commands on the server to view information about NetWare servers on your internetwork, log in to a selected NetWare server, view information about users attached to your NetWare server, send a message to another user, and log out from the network.

Each of the following projects asks you to write a memo to your instructor discussing the results of each exercise. Depending on which of the projects you complete, you may be able to combine these memos into one memo. Your instructor will tell you exactly how to report the results of your work.

Project 3-1: Attaching to the Network

You normally log in to the network from the Novell Client Login dialog box in Windows 95/98. When you do so, you are using the Novell Client for Windows 95/98. This project demonstrates steps that the normal login automates and hides from you. To demonstrate these steps, you will log in to the network using DOS commands, not through a Windows 95/98 utility. Ask your instructor for instructions on installing the DOS version of Client32.

This project also requires that the DOS client files be located in a separate directory from the Novell Client for Windows 95/98 directory. In the steps that follow, you will be using the Client for DOS files that are probably in the C:\Novell\Client32\C32DOS directory on your local drive. Please consult your instructor for information on installing the Novell Client for DOS/Windows 3.1.

For this project, your workstation must be booted in DOS (not Windows 95/98), but not attached to the NetWare server. There are many possible variations to this exercise, depending on how your workstation is configured. Your instructor will give you specific instructions on how to prepare your workstation for this exercise, and on how to log in.

When you are at the DOS prompt:

1. Type **CD C:\Novell\Client32\C32DOS** and then press **[Enter]** to make the C32DOS subdirectory the active directory.

2. Type **Set NWLANGUAGE=ENGLISH**, and then press **[Enter]**. Record any message obtained.

3. Type **NIOS.EXE**, and then press **[Enter]** to load the network input/output system driver. Record the message obtained from loading NIOS.

Do not be concerned about any error messages if and when they appear. You can reboot your system to recover.

4. Type **LOAD LSLC32.NLM**, and then press **[Enter]** to load the 32-bit link support layer driver. Record the message obtained from loading LSLC32.

5. Type **LOAD CMSM.NLM**, and then press **[Enter]** to load the 32-bit connection manager driver. Record the message obtained from loading CMSM.

6. Type **LOAD ETHERTSM.NLM**, and then press **[Enter]** to load the 32-bit Ethernet driver. Record the message obtained from loading ETHERTSM.

7. Your instructor will tell you the name of your NIC driver, as well as interrupt, port, and frame data. Use the driver name in place of the name *NICdriver* in the following command. Similarly, replace *INT#*, *PORT#,* and *FrameType* with the appropriate information. Type **LOAD *NICdriver* INT=*INT#* PORT=*PORT#* FRAME=*FrameType*** and then press **[Enter]** to load the NIC driver. Record the message obtained from loading the NIC driver.

8. Type **LOAD IPX.NLM**, and then press **[Enter]** to load IPX support. Record the message obtained from loading IPX.

9. Type **LOAD CLIENT32.NLM**, and then press **[Enter]** to load the Client 32 module for your network. Record the message obtained from loading Client 32.

The session layer of the Novell Client will try to make a connection with a NetWare server. If a preferred server is specified in a NetWare client configuration file named NET.CFG (which may be located in the Novell\NWClient directory), the workstation tries to attach to that NetWare server. If there is no preferred server, or if the preferred server is not available, the Novell Client sends out a special Get Nearest Server packet and the session is started with the first server to respond to this packet. Your instructor will tell you the name of your preferred server. Record that information here _____.

After establishing a server connection, the Novell Client maps the first available network drive letter to the LOGIN directory of the attached NetWare server. The first available network drive may be F: or G:, but other drives may be used (the first network drive may also be specified in the NET.CFG file). Your instructor will tell you which drive your workstation will use as the first network drive. Record that information here _____.

DOS then has access to load and run programs from the NetWare server by going through the first network drive. After the Novell Client files are loaded in memory, they work with the DOS presentation layer to redirect any requests for network file or print services to the NetWare server.

10. Type the drive letter of your first network drive followed by a colon (for example, **G:**), and then press **[Enter]** to change to the NetWare server's LOGIN directory.

11. Type **DIR** and then press **[Enter]** to list the files in the NetWare server's LOGIN directory.

12. Type **DIR >DIRLIST.TXT** and then press **[Enter]** to create a file containing a list of files in the NetWare server's LOGIN directory.

13. Write a memo to your instructor discussing the process of attaching to the network. Include each command you used and the result of that command, and attach the file containing the results of the DIR command.

Project 3-2: Viewing Network Information

One NetWare command you can test at the DOS prompt is the NLIST command. NLIST can be used to obtain network information about the network. You use the /? parameter to display information about the command and its parameters and options. The /? parameter is available with all NetWare command line commands.

1. Log in and from the DOS prompt type **NLIST /?** and then press **[Enter]** to display information about the NLIST command.

   An initial help screen listing options for viewing other help screens is displayed. The ALL option displays all help screens, one after another, so that you can scroll through them.

2. Type **NLIST /? ALL** and then press **[Enter]** to display all help screens. After you have read each screen, press **[Enter]** to see the next screen.

You can use the NetWare command NLIST /TREE to display a list of Directory trees on your internetwork. (Directory trees are introduced in Chapter 4.)

3. **NLIST /TREE** and then press **[Enter]** to display a list of directory trees.

4. Type **NLIST /TREE > C:\TREE.TXT** and then press **[Enter]** to create a file containing a list of servers.

5. Write a memo to your instructor discussing the NLIST command. In your discussion, include what you learned from using the help screens, describe the result of the NLIST /TREE command, and attach the file containing the results of the NLIST/ TREE command. Delete the TREE.TXT file after you send it to your instructor.

Project 3-3: Viewing User Information

You can also use the NLIST command to find out network information about users on your system. You use the /R and /S parameters with NLIST so it searches for all users on your system. (You will learn about how these work in NetWare's directory in Chapter 4.)

1. From the DOS prompt, type **NLIST USER /R /S** and then press **[Enter]** to list users in your directory tree.

2. Type **NLIST USER /R /S > C:\USERS.TXT** and then press **[Enter]** to create a copy of the list in a text file.

3. Write a memo to your instructor discussing the NLIST command. In your memo, describe the result of the NLIST USER /R /S command and attach the file containing the results of the NLIST USER /R /S command. Delete the USERS.TXT file once it is submitted to your instructor.

Project 3-4: Logging in to NetWare

One of the most sophisticated DOS commands you can use is the NetWare LOGIN command. It is used, obviously, to log into NetWare. If you enter the command LOGIN *fullusername*, the DOS requester will attempt to log in to NetWare. Your full user name is your user name preceded by a period (.), which your instructor will give you. For example, .TSIMPSON.FACULTY.NWTC identifies the user Ted Simpson. Your instructor will explain your login command. On the following line, write the command you will use to log into NetWare.

Login command: _____

1. Test this command and record the results.

2. At this point, you may want to type **NLIST USER /R /S** again and view the results. Compare them with the results you saw before you logged in.

3. Write a memo to your instructor discussing the result of the LOGIN command. Also describe any differences you may have seen using the NLIST USER command.

Project 3-5: Sending a Message to Another User

In this chapter, you learned how to use the NetWare Send Message utility from Windows to send a message to others on the network. In this exercise you use the DOS-based Send command to perform this function. You can use the NetWare NLIST USER /A /R /S command to create a list of users currently logged in to the network. You add the /A parameter this time to limit the search to currently logged-in users.

1. From the DOS prompt, type **NLIST USER /A /R /S** and then press **[Enter]** to list the users currently logged in to the network. Select the name of a classmate in the lab with you and write it down.

   Username: _____

2. Type **NLIST USER /A /R /S > C:\USERS.TXT** and then press **[Enter]** to create a file containing a list of logged-in users.

3. Create a message to send to your classmate. For example, you could use the message **"Hello, username, this is a test message."** Write down the message, including quotation marks (" "), that you want to send:

   _____

4. Return to the Windows 95/98 desktop. Right-click the **N** icon in the System Tray and choose **Send Message**. Choose **Constellation** as your server. Then choose the username you selected in Step 1. Type the message you created in Step 3 as "message." Then click **Send**.

5. When you receive a message, read it and then hold down the **[Ctrl]** key while pressing **[Enter]** to clear the message.

6. Write a memo to your instructor discussing the use of the NLIST USER /A /R /S and SEND commands. In your memo, include the user name and message you used and attach the file containing the results of the NLIST USER /A /R /S command.

Project 3-6: Logging Out of the Network

To log out of the network from the DOS prompt, use the NetWare command LOGOUT.

1. Type **LOGOUT** and then press **[Enter]**. Record the information provided by the logout process.

2. Write a memo to your instructor discussing the result of the LOGOUT command.

CASE PROJECTS

Case 3-1: The J. Q. Adams Network System

3

As described in Chapter 1, the J. Q. Adams Corporation would like to update its network system to collect quality-control information from the shop floor and save it on the central NetWare server for processing by other computer users. J. Q. Adams currently has 12 computer workstations located in the business office, two data collection workstations in production, and two data collection workstations in shipping/receiving. Two NetWare servers (one already owned by the company and one being purchased) are located in the wire and phone equipment room. One problem faced by the computers in the production shop is the increased level of electrical interference created by motors and other equipment. J. Q. Adams needs your help to recommend a topology and network system that will meet their requirements, and then draw the necessary cable runs on the floor plan shown in Figure 3-15.

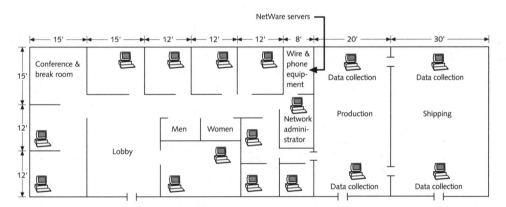

Figure 3-15   J.Q. Adams Corporation

Select the topology and network system. Draw a proposed network cable system based on the building layout shown in Figure 3-15. Write a memo to your instructor recommending a topology and network system. Discuss your justification for this selection. Attach your proposed network cable system.

Case 3-2: The Jefferson County Courthouse Network

As described in Chapter 1, the social workers in the Jefferson County Courthouse are planning a network system to let 12 users communicate and share files and printers. Plans are also being developed to add users in other departments to the network, to meet the communication needs of the entire courthouse. For this reason, the NetWare 5.0 network operating system has been chosen, and a new NetWare server has been ordered.

The floor plan for the first floor of the courthouse is shown in Figure 3-16. Given this floor plan, recommend a topology and network system that will best meet the current needs of the social workers and allow for easy network expansion in the future.

Select the topology and network system. Draw a proposed network cable system based on the building layout shown in Figure 3-16. Write a memo to your instructor recommending a topology and network system. Discuss your justification for this selection. Attach your proposed network cable system.

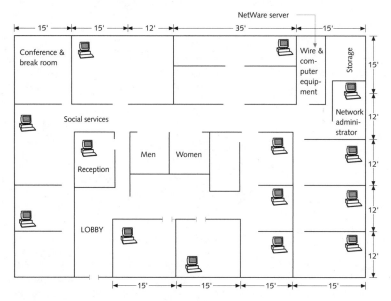

Figure 3-16   The Jefferson County Courthouse network

4

PLANNING THE NOVELL DIRECTORY SERVICES (NDS) DIRECTORY TREE

After reading this chapter and completing the exercises you will be able to:

♦ Describe the components of Novell Directory Services (NDS)

♦ Explain the use of each object in an NDS Directory tree

♦ Design an NDS Directory tree

♦ Use NetWare Administrator to create objects in an NDS Directory tree

♦ Plan the partitioning of an NDS Directory tree

In previous chapters you studied the hardware and software components of a LAN. You learned how microcomputers, both NetWare servers and PC workstations, function. You studied the hardware that ties the microcomputers together into a LAN. You were also introduced to the operating system software used by the servers and PC workstations, the network software protocols used for communication between microcomputers, and the software drivers used by the network interface cards to actually send messages across the network. Because, as a network administrator, you will be specifically concerned with administering NetWare network operating systems, you now need to go beyond a general knowledge of networks to a specific knowledge of NetWare.

In this chapter you will start learning about NetWare 5.0 in detail. For a network administrator, the heart of NetWare 5.0 is Novell Directory Services (NDS). NDS provides the network administrator with the tools needed to manage network resources such as NetWare servers and printers from an organizational perspective.

NOVELL DIRECTORY SERVICES (NDS)

Novell Directory Services (NDS) is a database that contains information about all network resources. It also refers to various tools for using that data. The database is properly referred to as the Novell Directory database, but this is often shortened to **Directory database** or just the Directory. All three terms refer to the same part of NDS, and in this book the term Directory database will be used consistently.

 The original name of NDS was NetWare Directory Services. Novell changed the name to Novell Directory Services in early 1996 to reflect the growing use of NDS on NOSs other than NetWare. You will still find references to NetWare Directory Services in many publications, including older Novell documentation.

Novell's earlier versions of NetWare also had a database, called the **bindery**. The bindery, however, contained the data about the resources on only one server and was therefore described as **server-centric**. For example, each NetWare 3.x server had its own bindery, and a network administrator could work with only one bindery at a time. NDS is **network-centric** and provides a central location for storing data about network resources such as users, printers, NetWare servers, and volumes. A network-centric system makes it easier for users to use the network and for network administrators to manage the network. For example, if you have three servers in your network, you can manage all three by using NDS, as shown in Figure 4-1.

When you upgrade a NetWare 3.x server to NetWare 5.0, most bindery data is automatically added to the Directory database. This saves you from having to re-create all the data about your users and groups, and makes upgrading a NetWare server a straightforward process.

NDS has some other important features. The Directory database is divided into sections called partitions. The partitions are distributed among the servers in the network so that if you lose a single server you don't lose the entire Directory database. In addition, the partitions are replicated, which means that a copy of one partition, called a replica, is stored on one or more additional servers. This creates backup copies of the partitions so that the network data is safe even if the server containing the original copy of the partition stops working. These concepts are discussed in more detail later in this chapter.

Even though replicas are stored on other servers, you still need to make tape backup copies of your server's hard drives. The other files (programs and data) on the server are *not* replicated and must be backed up. (The tape backup copies, of course, will also contain the NDS partition data.)

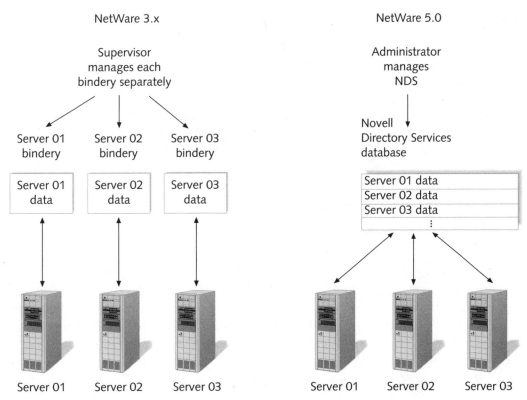

Figure 4-1   Managing binderies vs. managing NDS

Do not confuse NDS replicas with what Novell itself calls Novell Replication Services, which also uses the terms replication and replicas. Again, these are not the same as NDS replicas or replication. Rather, they refer to data replication from one storage device to another.

Logging into the Network

As discussed in Chapter 1, NDS is network-centric; when a user logs in, he or she logs into the *network*, not to an individual file server. In earlier versions of NetWare, each user initially logged into one specific server. As Figure 4–2 shows, the user then used the old NetWare ATTACH command to log into additional file servers and had access to resources, such as files, on all those servers.

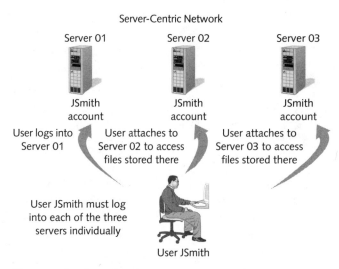

Figure 4-2   Logging into a server

In NetWare 5.0, the user logs into NDS and is then given access to whatever resources he or she has rights to. If those resources are files on three different file servers, then the user will have access to the servers where those resources are located, as Figure 4–3 shows.

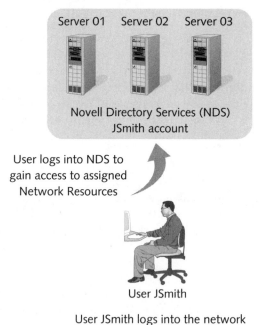

Figure 4-3   Logging into the network

Benefits of NDS

NDS provides the network administrator with several benefits beyond those found in Microsoft NT domain services or the bindery services found in NetWare 3.x:

- *Administration.* With NDS, you can work with all your network resources at once, using one administration tool: the MS Windows-based NetWare Administrator utility (NWAdmin).

- *Security.* NDS uses the RSA encryption algorithm, which enables a secure, encrypted single login to the network.

- *Reliability.* Because the Directory database is distributed and replicated, NDS provides fault tolerance for the network. For example, because information about users will be stored on at least two servers, a single server going down doesn't prevent users from logging into the network and accessing those resources still available to them.

- *Scalability.* **Scalability** gives you the capability to work with systems of different sizes. NDS works just as well with small networks with only one server as with global networks with hundreds of servers. If your network expands, NDS can easily handle the expansion. No matter how large or small the network, NDS can still be administered from one location.

NDS and the Network File System

As a network administrator, it is important that you understand that NDS is *not* a network file system. A **network file system** is used to organize file storage on the network. When you plan a network file system, you plan the set of volumes, directories, and subdirectories that will be created on the hard drives in your servers to store system, application, and data files. (In Chapter 5 you'll learn more about network file systems.) When working with NDS, on the other hand, you create a logical design for administering network resources.

 In this book, when Directory is spelled with a capital "D" it refers to the Directory database. When directory is spelled with a lowercase "d," it refers to part of the network file system. The directories in the network file system are discussed in Chapter 5.

NDS COMPONENTS

The visual and logical design that you create to organize data in the Directory database is called the **Directory tree**. In computer terminology, the word *tree* refers to a **hierarchical structure** used for organizing data or information. A tree starts at a single point, called the **[Root]**, and branches out from there. The tree usually is drawn inverted, which means that, unlike a real tree, the [Root] is at the *top* of the diagram. A familiar example of a tree structure is a family tree, as shown in Figure 4-4.

The root of the tree is usually shown in square brackets—[Root]—to match its onscreen appearance in Netware Administrator.

In the Burns family tree in Figure 4-4, the [Root] of the tree is the marriage of Franklin Burns and Dorothy Stevenson. Branches of the tree lead to their children, Michael and Susan. Additional branches lead to the children of Michael and his wife Mary Richards, and to the children of Susan and her husband, William Taylor. Because the [Root] of the tree is at the top of the diagram, this is an inverted tree.

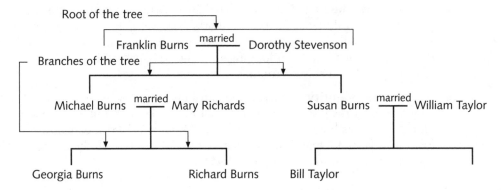

Figure 4-4   Burns family tree

NDS Directory Trees

The same inverted tree structure is seen in the Directory tree of F. D. Roosevelt Investments, Inc., as shown in Figure 4-5.

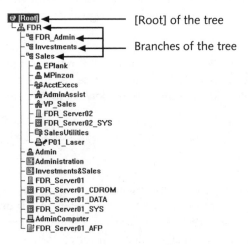

Figure 4-5   Directory tree of F. D. Roosevelt Investments, Inc.

The Directory tree starts at the [Root] at the top of the diagram and branches down from there. The Directory tree's hierarchical structure makes it easy for the network administrator to create a graphic representation of his or her organization and the location of network resources within the organization. For example, in Figure 4-5 the Directory tree begins at the [Root], and then branches to an object named FDR, which represents the F. D. Roosevelt Investments organization. From FDR, the tree branches to the three organizational subdivisions of FDR: FDR_Admin (Administration), Investments, and Sales. Other branches from FDR lead to network resources: the user named Admin (the NetWare administrator), a NetWare server (FDR_Server01), and three volumes on the server (FDR_Server01_CDROM, FDR_Server01_DATA, and FDR_Server01_SYS). Branches from Sales lead to additional network resources.

The Directory tree links NDS objects into an organized and understandable structure; the term **object** is a general term, referring to any network resource in your network. An object is *not* the network resource itself; it is an NDS representation of the resource, and is used to store data about the resource in the Directory database. Objects can be associated with **logical entities** or **physical entities**:

- *Physical entities*—things that have a physical existence such as users, NetWare servers, and printers.

- *Logical entities*—things that exist as a logical or mental creation, such as print queues, rather than a true physical entity. An important type of logical entity is the **organizational entity**, which represents a structural part of an organization, such as a group, an organizational unit, or the organization itself.

The term object comes from object-oriented programming languages, such as Smalltalk and C++. Many of the concepts developed for object-oriented programming languages have been carried into database management system development. A new type of database, the object-oriented database, is evolving based on these concepts. Other software, such as NDS, also uses the concept of objects, and you can expect to encounter objects in an increasing number of programs.

Objects are represented in the Directory tree by icons, symbols that help you visually recognize what an object represents. In Figure 4-5, object icons are included to represent the organization itself (FDR), subdivisions of the organization (FDR_Admin, Investments, and Sales), users (Admin, EPlank, and MPinzon), a group of users (AcctExecs), positions in the organization (VP_Sales and AdminAssist), a NetWare server used by FDR (FDR_Server01), and three volumes on the NetWare server (FDR_Server01_CDROM, FDR_Server01_DATA, and FDR_Server01_SYS).

The Directory tree is a graphic representation of the data in the Directory database. Data in the Directory database *must* be associated with an object in the Directory tree. In fact, you enter data into the Directory database by creating Directory tree objects and assigning the data to those objects. The Directory tree must be given a name, called the

Directory tree name, when you first create the tree. When you log in to NDS, you do so by logging into the Directory tree by name.

The NDS Directory tree was designed to be consistent with the CCITT X.500 specification (CCITT is the United Nations-chartered Comité Consultatif International Telegraphique et Téléphonique, which sets international telecommunications standards). The X.500 specification provides a basis for global directory services and is becoming an international standard. X.500 was developed to complement the CCITT X.400 e-mail specification, particularly to provide X.400-compatible name and address information to e-mail systems. The use of such standards becomes increasingly important as networks throughout the world communicate with one another. In addition, NDS is also LDAP-accessible. The Lightweight Directory Access Protocol (LDAP) is the Internet's directory information protocol. Many Internet tools and software support LDAP and so in turn also support NDS.

NDS Objects, Properties, and Property Values

An NDS object always represents some definable network element, either physical or logical, for which you can record data. For example, for a user, you can record the login name, last name, first name, and so on. For a printer, you can record the printer name and the printer agent that sends it print jobs. (Printer agents are covered later in this chapter.) For a group, you can record the names of the members of the group.

The types of data that you use objects to collect are called **properties**. The data itself is called the **property value**. For example, the vice president for sales of FDR is Edgar Plank. Because Edgar is a network user, the Directory tree for FDR has a User object for Edgar named EPlank (which is Edgar's login name). One property of a User object is the user's Login Name, and for Edgar the property value for Login Name is EPlank. As shown in Table 4-1, the Directory database stores the properties and property values for each object in the Directory tree.

Table 4-1   Objects, properties, and property values

Object:	User
Property	Property Value
Login Name	EPlank
Last Name	Plank
Full Name	Edgar Plank

Object:	User
Property	Property Value
Login Name	MPinzon
Last Name	Pinzon
Full Name	Maria Pinzon

Object:	NetWare Server
Property	Property Value
Server Name	FDR_Server01
Network Address	080009 3D45F8

Object:	Printer
Property	Property Value
Printer Name	P01_Laser
Network Address	080009 12CF89

There are two types of NDS objects: container objects and leaf objects. **Container objects**, as the name implies, contain or hold other objects. **Leaf objects** cannot contain any other objects—they are the "leaves" at the ends of the "tree branches." Figure 4-6 shows the FDR Directory tree with container and leaf objects marked.

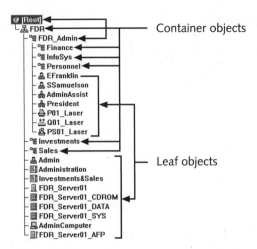

Figure 4-6 FDR Directory tree container and leaf objects

Container objects are used primarily to organize network resources (users, groups, NetWare servers, etc.), which are represented by the leaf objects. For example, in the FDR Directory tree Sales is a container object that enables the resources of the FDR Sales group to be grouped together for ease of administration. In Figure 4-6, all employees in Sales (Edgar Plank and Maria Pinzon) have their associated User objects located in the Sales container. The network administrator can easily keep track of all Sales personnel this way, and the same concept applies to other container objects and the leaf objects they contain.

Container Objects

There are four container objects that can be used in a Directory tree: [Root], Country, Organization, and Organizational Unit. The NDS container objects and their features are summarized in Table 4-2 and Figure 4-7.

Table 4-2 NDS container objects

Object Icon	Object	Required/Optional	Can Contain:
◎	[Root]	Required	Country, Organization, Alias (leaf object)
🖧	Country	Optional	Organization, Alias (leaf object)
🖧	Organization	Required	Organizational Unit, leaf objects
🖳	Organizational Unit	Optional	Organizational Unit, leaf objects

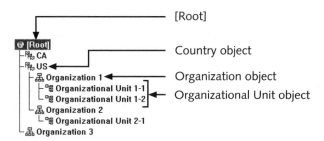

Figure 4-7   NDS Container objects in a Directory tree

4

 NDS actually has an unused fifth container object called Locality. The Locality object allows specification of geographical locations within a country. The Locality object is included in NDS for X.500 compliance but has not been implemented in NetWare 5.0. This means that although the object is coded into the operating system and discussed in the documentation, you cannot include it in a Directory tree at this time. Future versions of NetWare might implement the Locality object. If implemented, the Locality object would be optional, could be contained in [Root] and Organization objects, and could contain Organization and Organizational Unit objects. It could *not* contain leaf objects.

 [Root]

The **[Root] object** is always the first object in the Directory tree, and there is only one [Root] object in each Directory tree. The [Root] object has no properties—its function is to be the highest access point in the Directory tree. When you first create a Directory tree during NetWare 5.0 installation, you assign the Directory tree name and create the [Root] object. The [Root] object is used by all other NetWare 5.0 servers added to the tree. There *must* be a [Root] object in a Directory tree, and you cannot modify or delete the [Root] object once it is created. For example, the [Root] object is the first object in the FDR Directory tree shown in Figure 4-7. The [Root] object can contain Country objects, Organization objects, and Alias objects (the Alias object is a leaf object described later in this chapter).

 In network file systems, there is another root: the root directory. The root directory is the first directory on a hard disk or NetWare volume. For example, the root directory of the C: drive on a PC is C:\. Although both systems use the term *root*, they refer to two very different things.

Country

The **Country object** organizes the Directory tree for organizations that operate in more than one country. The Country object uses a unique two-letter code to designate each country. For example, in Figure 4-7 US is the United States. The Country object is optional, but if it is used, it must be used immediately after the [Root] object and before an Organization object. The Country object can contain Organization objects and Alias objects.

> Although Novell includes the Country object for X.500 compliance, it is generally not used. If you need to include countries in your Directory tree, you can use the Organization object or Organizational Unit object with a country name instead. This allows more flexibility, such as placing country designators below an Organization object. For example, you could have a Sales Organization unit that branches into two Organizational Unit objects named United States and Europe.

Organization

The **Organization object** is used to provide the first level of organizational structure to the Directory tree. You must use at least one Organization object in your Directory tree. There is usually only one Organization object in the Directory tree, representing the company or organization that built the network. For example, in Figure 4-6 there is only one Organization object, FDR. This, of course, represents the company F. D. Roosevelt Investments, the company that built and uses the network. You can, however, have more than one Organization object in your NDS tree if the organizational structure requires it. The Organization object can contain Organizational Unit objects and leaf objects.

Organizational Unit

The **Organizational Unit object** subdivides the organizational structure of the Directory tree. You are not required to use any Organizational Unit objects, as you did for the Organization object. However, the Organizational Unit object is very useful for creating organizational structure in Directory trees. You will probably use this object frequently. For example, in Figure 4-5 the Directory tree for F. D. Roosevelt Investments uses three Organizational Unit objects to subdivide the company into administration (FDR_Admin), investments (Investments), and sales (Sales), for ease of network administration. The Organizational Unit object can contain Organizational Unit objects and leaf objects. In fact, the Organizational Unit object's ability to contain other Organizational Unit objects makes it the main "building block" of a Directory tree.

Leaf Objects

Leaf objects represent network resources and are used to store data about those resources. You can use many types of leaf objects in Directory trees. To understand how to use leaf objects, it helps to group them according to their purpose. As Table 4-3 shows, Novell categorizes leaf objects as User-related, Server-related, Printer-related, Messaging-related, NetWare Application Manager-related, Informational, and Miscellaneous.

Table 4-3   Leaf object groups

Leaf Object Group	Purpose
User-Related	To manage network users
Server-Related	To manage NetWare servers and their associated volumes
Printer-Related	To manage printers and their associated queues and print servers
Messaging-Related	To manage electronic messaging services on the network
NetWare Application Manager-Related	To manage network applications used with the NetWare Application Manager
Informational	To store data about network resources that cannot be managed by NDS
Miscellaneous	Leaf objects that do not fit in the other groups

Leaf objects must be located in a container object, and they cannot contain any other objects. Before you create a leaf object, select the container object that will hold it, by clicking on that container object in the Directory tree. When a leaf object is created, it is always assigned to the active or selected container object.

 NDS lets software companies create additional leaf objects that are added into NDS when the new software is installed. The leaf objects listed here are the standard NetWare 5.0 objects, but as a network administrator you may have to become familiar with others associated with the software products you install.

User-Related Leaf Objects

User-related leaf objects have properties that enable you, as a network administrator, to manage the users on your network. User-related leaf objects include the User object, the Group object, the Organizational Role object, and the Profile object. See Table 4-4 and Figure 4-8.

Table 4-4   User-related leaf objects

Object Icon	Object	Purpose
☺	User	Represents a network user
☺☺	Group	Represents a group of users
☺	Organizational Role	Represents a position in an organization
📇	Profile	Provides a common login script for a group of users

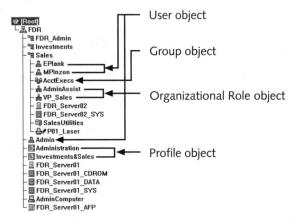

Figure 4-8   User-related leaf objects in a Directory tree

 User

The **User object** represents each network user. As a network administrator, you use the User object to record and manage data about each of your users. About 67 properties are associated with the User object. Two of these, Login Name and Last Name, are mandatory and must be specified when you create a user. As you create each user, a User object icon representing that user is added to the Directory tree.

To create users, you must be logged in to the network as a user. This requires that at least one user account be automatically created when NetWare 5.0 is installed. In fact, exactly one account is created, for a user named Admin, and the Admin User object is added to the Directory tree. Admin is the network administrator and is assigned the necessary rights to create and manage the Directory tree and the network file structure. You will use the Admin user account in later chapters to create the objects in the Directory tree.

Group

The **Group object** represents groups of related network users and is used to record and manage data about each designated group on your network. You must specify the Group Name when you create a group. No groups are automatically created during NetWare 5.0 installation.

Groups are useful when you want to assign some network resource to several users. For example, you could put into a group the users who need to use a certain printer, and give the group, rather than each individual user, the right to use the printer. Each group member then gets to use the printer because of his or her membership in the group, as Figure 4-9 shows.

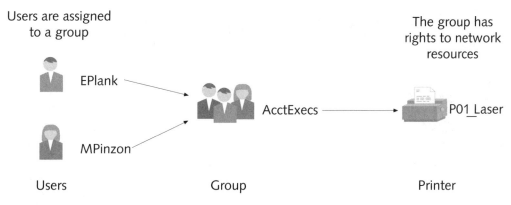

Figure 4-9   Using groups

Organizational Role

The **Organizational Role object** represents a position in an organizational structure such as president, chief financial officer (CFO), or sales manager. You use the Organizational Role object to record and manage data about each organizational role in your Directory tree. When you create the Organizational Role object, you must specify the Organizational Role name. No organizational roles are created automatically during NetWare 5.0 installation.

Organizational roles are useful when a position in the organization has certain rights and resources available to it regardless of the person in that position. You can easily assign a user to an organizational role, and that user then automatically gets all the rights of that role. For example, Edgar Plank is the vice president of sales for FDR. Rather than assigning the rights of the vice president of sales to the User object EPlank, the FDR network administrator has created an Organizational Role object named VP_Sales and assigned the rights to that object. The network administrator then assigns the user EPlank to the role of vice president, so EPlank can do whatever the vice president can do. This is illustrated in Figure 4-10. If Martha Truman becomes vice president of FDR, the network administrator can remove EPlank from the role of vice president and assign MTruman to the role. Then she will automatically have the associated rights.

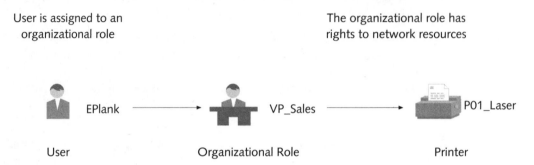

| User is assigned to an organizational role | | The organizational role has rights to network resources |

| User | Organizational Role | Printer |

Figure 4-10   Using organizational roles

 ## Profile

The **Profile object** is used to run login scripts and assign resources to groups of users. **Login scripts** are a series of NetWare commands that automatically run when the user logs in to the network. Although you can create login scripts for Organization objects, Organizational Unit objects, and User objects, you cannot create a login script for a Group object. The Profile object gives the network administrator a tool for creating login scripts for groups of users. You'll learn about login scripts in detail in Chapter 14. You must specify the Profile Name when you create a profile. No profiles are automatically created during NetWare 5.0 installation.

NetWare 5.0 creates a default login script that runs if no other login scripts have been created. The default login script provides access to the basic network resources that a user needs, and it is sufficient for user access during the initial development of the network.

Although the Profile object provides the network administrator with a useful tool, you might find yourself initially confusing the Group object and the Profile object. They are conceptually similar because both are used with "groups" of users. To understand the differences between these two objects, remember that:

- Users are assigned to groups as members of the group, and groups are used primarily to give those members access to network resources.

- Profiles are assigned to users (not groups), and profiles are used primarily to give users a login script. Although a profile may be shared by many users, there is no formal "membership" in a profile.

For example, in FDR's Directory tree, the Investments&Sales Profile object is used as the source of the login script for users in both the Investments and Sales organizational units because all these users can use a common login script. However, each of these organizational units has a Group object that is used to grant access to department-specific network resources to the users in that department: the InvestmentManagers Group object is Investments and the AcctExecs Group object is Sales. As shown in Figure 4-11, GSakharov and EPlank thus share a common login script through the Profile object but have their access to other network resources controlled by their departmental groups.

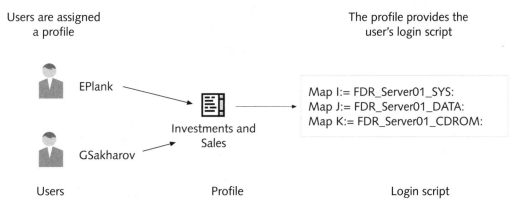

Figure 4-11   Using the Profile object

If Group objects could have login scripts, the same login requirements and resource assignments could have been provided by using just the InvestMngrs and AcctExecs groups. This would, of course, have required two separate copies of the same login script. But groups cannot have login scripts, so Profile objects are needed.

Server-Related Leaf Objects

Server-related leaf objects have properties that enable you to manage the NetWare servers on your network. Server-related leaf objects include the NetWare Server object, the Volume object, and the Directory Map object. Table 4-5 and Figure 4-12 show these objects.

Table 4-5   Server-related leaf objects

Object Icon	Object	Purpose
▯	NetWare Server	Represents a network NetWare server
▤	Volume	Represents a hard disk volume on a server
⊡	Directory Map	Represents a reference to a directory or subdirectory on a volume

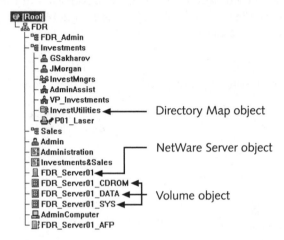

Figure 4-12   Server-related leaf objects in a Directory tree

NetWare Server

The **NetWare Server object** represents each server on the network that is running a version of NetWare. This object is also referred to as an **NCP Server object**, where NCP stands for NetWare Core Protocol. You must create and place the NetWare Server object in the Directory tree so that the server's volumes, directories, subdirectories, and files are available to users. The NetWare Server object is created for each NetWare 5.0 server during NetWare installation.

Whenever you create a NetWare Server object, you must specify the NetWare server name. For example, when FDR installs NetWare 5.0 on the NetWare server named FDR_Server01, the server name FDR_Server01 is used to create a NetWare Server object named FDR_Server01. During the installation process, NetWare prompts you for the server's location in the Directory tree. In this case, you would specify the location of FDR_Server01 as the Organization object FDR, as shown in Figure 4-12.

Volume

Volumes, which you will study in detail in Chapter 5, are the physical hard disk storage spaces in NetWare servers. The **Volume object** represents a volume in the Directory tree. Volumes and their associated Volume objects are created during NetWare 5.0 installation. When they are created, you must specify a volume name, and this same name is used to create the Volume object name. The name of the Volume object will always be the server's name, followed by an underscore character, followed by the volume name:

`ServerName_VolumeName`

For example, NetWare requires that a volume named SYS (short for system) be created during installation. Therefore, when FDR installs NetWare 5.0 on FDR_Server01, a Volume object named FDR_Server01_SYS is created. The Volume object is placed in the same Directory tree location as the server, which in this case is the Organization object FDR, as shown in Figure 4-12. You will learn about planning network file systems in Chapter 5 and managing file systems in Chapter 7.

Directory Map

The **Directory Map object** is used to reference a single directory in the network file system. This object is a useful management tool for creating and managing login scripts, and you'll learn more about it when you study login scripts in Chapter 13. Figure 4-12 shows an example of a Directory Map object. The network manager for FDR has created the Directory Map object named InvestUtilities to refer to the location of some utility programs used by the investment managers in the Investments Organizational unit.

Printing-Related Leaf Objects

Printing-related leaf objects let you manage network printing. When a user wants to print a document or a spreadsheet on a network printer using NetWare's **Novell Distributed Print Services (NDPS)**, the user begins by using the application's PRINT command. The application generates the print data, or the material to be printed. The print data is sent to a NetWare **printer agent**, the software component of NDPS that transfers output from the client and controls the physical printer. Printer agent software can be loaded on a NetWare server, or is embedded as firmware inside a network-attached printer itself. The printer agent sends the print data to the printer, and the output is printed. The print job thus flows as indicated by the arrows in in Figure 4-13.

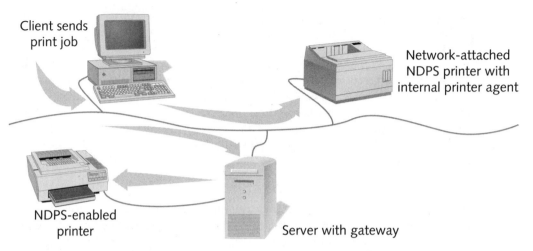

Figure 4-13 NetWare 5 NDPS printing

 NDPS is backward-compatible with software that requires the older Novell print queues and/or print servers. Also, it will support network printers that run directly attached to the network using print server software. (You can also create Print Server and Print Queue objects if you want to run the older style print services in NetWare 5.0.)

 Chapter 12 covers NetWare printing in detail. The examples used in this chapter are intended to help you learn about Directory tree objects, not all about possible details of setting up printing on a NetWare network.

 ## Printer

The **Printer object** is used to represent an actual printer. The Printer object must be created and placed in the Directory tree so that you can link a printer to a printer agent. You must name the printer when you create the Printer object.

For example, FDR has a laser printer used by the administration group that is referred to as P01_Laser (the "P" stands for printer, and "01" gives a number to the printer).

 ## Printer Agent

The **Printer Agent object** is used to represent a service that handles print jobs on NetWare. Each brand of printer requires a specific printer agent. For example, Hewlett–Packard (HP) offers a printer agent, as does Lexmark. NetWare also ships with a default printer agent for use with generic printers. You should name the Printer Agent object after the brand and class of printer it will support, such as HP4_Agent.

Application Manager-Related Leaf Objects

The Novell NetWare Client software includes the Novell Application Launcher. The **Novell Application Manager (NAM)** allows network managers to control which network users can use software applications that are stored on a NetWare server. The **Application Manager-related leaf objects**, shown in Table 4-6, have properties that enable you to manage the application software controlled by NAM. You'll study NAM in Chapter 11, as well as the Application Manager-related leaf objects.

Table 4-6   Application Manager-related leaf objects

Object Icon	Object	Purpose
DOS	DOS Application	Represents a DOS application that will be run from a network NetWare server
3.1	Windows 3.x Application	Represents a Windows 3.x application that will be run from a network NetWare server
95	Windows 95 Application	Represents a Windows 95 application that will be run from a network NetWare server
NT	Windows NT Application	Represents a Windows NT application that will be run from a network NetWare server

Informational Leaf Objects

Informational leaf objects let you store data about network resources that would otherwise not be represented in the Directory tree. These objects are created only to provide a place for data storage—their creation has no effect on the operation of the network. The Informational leaf objects include the Computer object and the AFP Server object, shown in Table 4-7 and Figure 4-14. To be truly useful, the Directory database must be able to store all needed data about network resources, and these objects help provide that capability.

Table 4-7   Informational leaf objects

Object Icon	Object	Purpose
🖥	Computer	Represents a user's computer
AFP	AFP Server	Represents a network AppleTalk File Protocol server

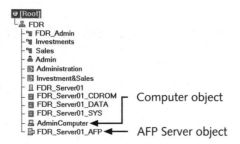

Figure 4-14   Informational leaf objects in a Directory tree

Computer

The **Computer object** represents any computer on the network that is not a server. You must specify a name for the Computer object when you create it. You can use it to store data such as the computer serial number and which user is using it. You can also add a description of the computer. Using a Computer object for each PC workstation on your network will provide you with a basic system for keeping an inventory of the PC workstations you manage. Or you can create a Computer object only for special-use PC workstations, such as Apple Macintosh workstations used in a PC workstation environment. For example, the FDR network manager has a Macintosh workstation that he uses to run graphics programs. A Computer object named AdminComputer has been created for this computer; it appears in Figure 4-14.

AFP Server

The **AFP Server object** is used to represent an **AppleTalk File Protocol (AFP) server**, a NetWare server that runs special modules that enable it to provide file and print services to Macintosh workstations. You can use this object to store data about the AFP server such as a description and network address. An AFP Server object in a Directory tree indicates that Apple Macintosh workstations are attached to the network, and the AFP server acts as a router connecting the Macintoshes to the rest of the network. FDR is running the AFP modules on the FDR_Server01 NetWare server to connect the Macintosh computer named AdminComputer to the network. As Figure 4-14 shows, an AFP Server object named FDR_Server01_AFP has been created to store data about the configuration of the AFP server.

Miscellaneous Leaf Objects

As their name implies, Miscellaneous leaf objects have various purposes. The Miscellaneous leaf objects include the Alias object, the Bindery object, the Bindery Queue object, and the Unknown object, shown in Table 4-8 and Figure 4-15.

Table 4-8   Miscellaneous leaf objects

Object Icon	Object	Purpose
🏷	Alias	Refers to another NDS object in another part of the Directory tree
Ⓑ	Bindery	Represents NetWare 3.1x bindery data unrecognized during an upgrade
±	Bindery Queue	Represents a NetWare 3.1x queue unrecognized during an upgrade
⓪	Unknown	Represents a corrupted object that cannot be recognized

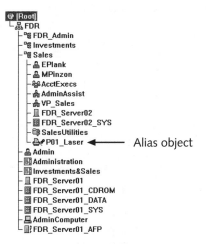

Figure 4-15   Miscellaneous leaf objects in a Directory tree

Alias

The **Alias object** refers to another object in a different part of the Directory tree. The Alias object is useful because of how NetWare tracks a user's current location or context in the Directory tree (context is discussed later in this chapter). Referring to an object *not* in the same location can be a complex procedure, but using an Alias object in the same location can be helpful. The Alias object contains the location reference to the original object, so the user has to refer only to the Alias object to access the original object. For example, the Investments workgroup unit at FDR also needs to use the laser printer. To simplify how the users in the Investments workgroup specify the location of the laser printer, the network administrator has created an Alias object named P01_Laser in the Investments organizational unit, as shown in Figure 4–15.

Bindery Object and Bindery Queue Object

When a NetWare 3.x server is updated to NetWare 5.0, there may be objects or queues in the NetWare 3.x bindery that NetWare 5.0 can't identify. Because there are network utilities that work with data stored in the bindery, a **Bindery object** or a **Bindery Queue object** will be created and placed in the Directory tree. This allows for backward compatibility with the network utilities that work with bindery data to use the NetWare 5.0 bindery emulation mode. **Bindery emulation mode** is a special connection feature that enables utilities designed to work with NetWare 3.x's bindery database to operate in the NetWare 5.0 environment. The Bindery object and the Bindery Queue object exist only to support bindery emulation mode. They are automatically created during an upgrade if needed—you will never create them yourself. If these objects appear in your Directory tree, you should determine what they represent and, if possible, create a replacement NDS object.

Unknown

If an NDS object becomes corrupted so that NDS can't recognize it, NDS will rename it and identify it as an **Unknown object**. As the network administrator, you will need to re-identify the object, delete the Unknown object, and re-create the proper object for the network resource.

Unknown objects may occur when using NetWare 4.11 utilities (such as NWAdmin) to view a NetWare 5.0 tree. This is because NetWare 4.11 does not know about the new object types in NetWare 5.0. Even though the object is valid, the older NWAdmin doesn't know how to recognize it. For this reason, it is recommended that you update any older utilities to the latest version when using NetWare 5.0.

NDS is extensible, which means that Novell and other vendors can add new objects to it. For example, a software vendor could create objects indicating that the software is installed on the network and provide software management capabilities. As a network administrator, you will need to be aware of any new objects that can be used in Directory trees.

Naming NDS Objects

Each object in a Directory tree has a name that uniquely identifies the object within the Directory tree. In this section, you will learn about object names and the naming conventions used in NDS.

4

Common Names

NDS uses a set of **name types**, which are descriptions of the type of object being named, and each name type has an abbreviation. The Country object, the Organization object, and the Organizational Unit object all have equivalent name types. The Country name type is abbreviated as C, the Organization name type is abbreviated as O, and the Organizational Unit name type is abbreviated as OU. There is no name type for the [Root] object, and all leaf objects are referred to by the **common name (CN)** name type, because each leaf object is the object name that appears in the Directory tree. For example, the common name for the EFranklin User object is EFranklin.

Context

The position or location of an object in the Directory tree is called the object's **context**. Context is specified as the path from the [Root] to the object. For example, consider the context of the User object EFranklin in the FDR Directory tree shown in Figure 4-16.

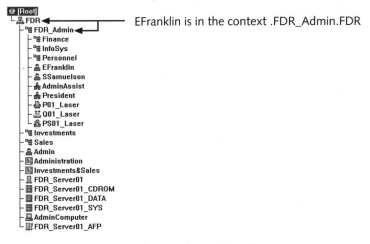

Figure 4-16 Context of user object EFranklin

Starting at EFranklin, we see that she is in the organizational unit FDR_Admin, which is in the organization FDR, which is directly below the [Root]. Her context is

     .FDR_Admin.FDR

The context of an object reads from left to right, starting at the lowest level of the tree, and works upward to the [Root]. Notice that [Root], however, is not included in the context. The **leading period** in the context, the period in front of FDR_Admin, indicates that the path begins at the [Root]. Periods are also used to separate object names. A period after an object name is called a **trailing period** and indicates a shift up one level in the Directory tree. For example, the FDR_Admin Organizational Unit object is one level lower down the Directory tree than the FDR Organization object; the period after FDR_Admin in the context shows the shift from one level to the next.

Although each object has a fixed context in the Directory tree, a network user will want to view different parts of the Directory tree while working on the network. The part of the Directory tree that the user is actively working with is called the user's **current context**. The context of an object never changes, but a user's current context does change as the user works with different parts of the Directory tree. This is why the leading period in a context is important—a context *with* a leading period is read starting at the [Root], regardless of the user's current context. A context *without* the leading period would be read starting at the user's current context.

Object Names

The complete name of any object is the object name plus the object's context. This is called the object's **distinguished name**, which specifies the path to the object starting at the [Root] object. As shown in Figure 4-17, EFranklin's distinguished name is

```
.EFranklin.FDR_Admin.FDR
```

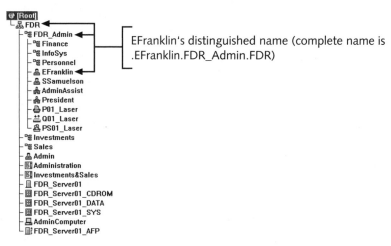

Figure 4-17   EFranklin's complete name

A name written with name type initials is called a **typeful name**. Without the initials, the name is a **typeless name**. Thus *.CN=EFranklin.OU=Admin.O=FDR* is a typeful name, and *.EFranklin.Admin.FDR* is a typeless name.

Whereas a distinguished name shows the path to an object from the [Root], a **relative distinguished name** specifies the path to an object from another object. For example, if the current context is .FDR, the relative distinguished name for Eleanor Franklin is *EFranklin.FDR_Admin* without a leading period (not a path from the [Root]) or a trailing period (no need to move up a Directory tree level).

Novell has developed a new function called **contextless login**. A user who wants to log into the network only has to type a valid user name to start the process, rather than a name and a context. If more than one user on the system has that name, then NetWare will offer the user a list to choose from. The user will still have to provide a valid password to complete the login process.

Object Names and Logging into the Network

4

Directory tree context and distinguished names have important uses in NetWare 5.0. When you log in to a NetWare 5.0 network, you log into an NDS Directory tree. For your login to succeed, you must use your **login name** (which is the same as the name of your User object in the tree) together with the correct context for your User object.

If Eleanor Franklin of F. D. Roosevelt Investments wants to log in to the FDR Directory tree from the DOS prompt, she would use her distinguished name. For example, she could use the following login command:

```
Login .EFranklin.FDR_Admin.FDR
```

If Eleanor has access to more than one NetWare 5.0 Directory tree, she can also specify the name of the Directory tree that she wants to log into by preceding her distinguished name with the Directory tree name and a slash (/):

```
Login FDR/.EFranklin.FDR_Admin.FDR
```

There are easy ways to designate the tree and context for login by modifying the user's Novell Client settings, which NetWare checks during the login process. You'll study Novell Client software settings in Chapter 6.

DESIGNING THE DIRECTORY TREE

One of the network administrator's main responsibilities when administrating a NetWare 5.0 network is designing the Directory tree. Now that you understand the components of Directory trees, you are ready to put these components together to create a Directory tree.

There are three important design principles to keep in mind when designing a Directory tree:

- Use agreed-on network standards such as naming conventions.

- Balance tree depth and tree width.

- Use a design approach that matches the Directory tree to the organization.

Defining Network Standards

As the size of the network increases, using network standards will minimize confusion as more servers are installed, more users are added, and new Directory tree objects appear in the Directory tree. **Network standards** are agreements about how to operate the network. For example, user names should be standardized. It's confusing if one network administrator creates user names based on the user's first initial and then last name, such as *EFranklin*, while another administrator creates user names based on the user's last name and then first initial, such *FranklinE*.

Naming Conventions

One of the most important areas for network standards is naming conventions. A consistent and meaningful way of assigning names to users, servers, printers, print queues, print servers, and other network resources can minimize confusion for the network administrator. Before naming conventions are discussed, however, you need to be aware of the rules for naming NDS objects.

First, because the complete or distinguished name of an object includes the context where the object is located, object names need be unique only in their container. For example, FDR could have two users named Eleanor Franklin with login EFranklin as long as they worked in different parts of the organization. An Eleanor Franklin in administration would be *.EFranklin.FDR_Admin.FDR*, while an Eleanor Franklin in Sales would be *.EFranklin.Sales.FDR*. But what happens if both of them end up in the same department? This would be a problem, so avoid it by using *unique* object names for each object. For example, an Admin User object in the FDR Directory tree has the distinguished name *.Admin.FDR*. If the FDR administration Organizational Unit object was named simply *Admin* instead of *FDR_Admin*, then its distinguished name would also be *.Admin.FDR*, which would create two objects with the same distinguished name. Because each NDS distinguished name must be unique, the problem is resolved by naming the organizational unit *FDR_Admin*, creating the name *.FDR_Admin.FDR*, which is unique.

Second, you can use up to 64 characters in the object name. NDS names can use both uppercase and lowercase letters, but NDS names are not case sensitive. For example, *EFRANKLIN*, *EFranklin*, and *efranklin* are identical as far as NDS is concerned.

Third, you can use some special characters, spaces, and underscores. However, underscores are displayed as spaces, so *Eleanor_Franklin* and *Eleanor Franklin* are identical as far as NDS is concerned.

NetWare 5.0 allows some network clients, such as standalone print servers, to connect to the network in bindery emulation mode, which means that they behave as though they were attached to a NetWare 3.x server, which only supports 47 characters in object names. In this case, NetWare 5.0 object names longer than 47 characters are truncated to 47 characters.

Similarly, NetWare does not allow the following characters in names:

/   (slash)

\   (backslash)

,   (comma)

;   (semicolon)

*   (asterisk)

?   (question mark)

For clients running in bindery emulation mode, spaces in names are converted to under-scores. You should not use the other characters for client names that will connect to the NetWare server in bindery emulation mode.

 If you use spaces in NetWare 5.0 object names, you must enclose the name in quotation marks when using command line utilities. This may be reason enough for not using spaces in object names. Using the underscore instead eliminates this problem and helps ensure compatibility for bindery emulation clients.

When using these rules, you should develop consistent ways of naming NDS objects. One important consideration is length. Remember that the user—or, for that matter, you as network administrator—may have to use the names you create in distinguished names. Therefore, shorter names are better than longer names. For example, it is easier to write *.EFranklin.FDR_Admin.FDR* than to write *.Eleanor_Franklin.FDR_Administration.FDRoosevelt_Investments.*

User Name Considerations

User login names should always be created in the same way. It is easier to locate the user if user names are consistent. For example, if all user names start with the first letter of the user's first name, you know you need to look for E to find Eleanor Franklin. If there is no consistency, you will not be sure which letter to look for. This can be done in various ways:

- Use just the user's last name: Franklin

- Use the user's first initial and last name: EFranklin

- Use the user's first and last names: Eleanor_Franklin

- Use the first three characters of the user's first name and the first three characters of the user's last name: EleFra

How you choose to create user names will depend on your and your users' preferences. It will also depend on how many users you are managing and how difficult it is to maintain uniqueness of the user name. For example, a small network may have only one John Smith, but a larger organization could easily have two or more employees named John Smith. There are many ways to create user names that will work—the important consideration is consistency.

Print System Considerations

When working with some object types, it's a good idea to include a code in the name that identifies the object type. NetWare printing is a good example. If you start printer names with the code "P," you can easily identify the object type from the object name. You also can include a number, a location, or a type in the name to help further identify the object.

For example, FDR can name a laser print P01_Laser, including a number and the type of printer. If this printer is going in Room 201 and is a Hewlett-Packard LaserJet IV, the name could be P01_Rm201_HPLJIV. The same ideas work with servers and other NDS objects that have a physical existence on the network.

Directory Tree Name Considerations

It's possible to have more than one NetWare NDS Directory tree visible to network users in a WAN. For example, a corporation might not have implemented a corporate-wide NetWare 5.0 network. Within the corporation, two divisions might each have a NetWare 5.0 LAN. If these LANs are connected to a corporate backbone to form a WAN, NetWare users will see both NDS Directory trees and may log into one or both LANs.

Directory tree names need to be unique if more than one exists on a WAN. The "shorter is better" idea also applies here—a user might need to specify the tree name during login. For example, FDR can use FDR as the tree name of its Directory tree.

Depth Versus Width

The term depth refers to the number of levels in a Directory tree. The term width refers to the number of branches at any level, but particularly at the first level of a Directory tree. When designing a Directory tree, you need to be careful not to create more levels (depth) than necessary, because each level adds another term to an object's distinguished name. If there are too many levels, the names become unwieldy. For example, what user wants a name like *.JMartin.QualityControl.Prod.Ops.Plant16.Region2.DivisionIII.EastCoast.JKHCompany*?

 Novell considers five to eight levels reasonable but notes that NDS can handle as many levels as necessary to reflect an organization's structure.

In contrast, using too few levels will create a very flat Directory tree (width) that probably won't clearly show the actual structure of most organizations. You're aiming for a Directory tree design that reflects the structure of the organization and at the same time balances the depth and width of the tree.

APPROACHES TO DIRECTORY TREE DESIGN

You can take several different approaches in designing the Directory tree. You can reflect the actual structure of the organization, you can build on the geographic locations of the organization, or you can use a combination of the two.

Organizational Structure

Because resources within an organization are allocated and accounted for according to the organization's organization chart, the actual structure of an organization provides one approach to designing the Directory tree. Two possible organizational structures focus on functional areas and workgroups.

Functional

Most businesses can be organized around the classic functional areas of business: operations, marketing, finance, and personnel. Although this list doesn't include every possible organizational unit (for example, executive administration and support units such as information systems are not included), it does cover most of them. Other organizational units can be added and the four main units broken down into other organizational units as necessary. For example, marketing includes sales, advertising, and market research; and receiving, production, and shipping are part of operations. Figure 4-18 shows a Directory tree for Wilson Manufacturing, a company that manufactures home furniture. The Directory tree is based on a functional structure.

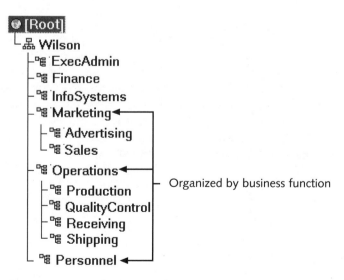

Figure 4-18   Wilson Manufacturing Directory tree

Workgroups

Some organizations prefer to focus on project workgroups composed of members from the functional areas. In this case, the Directory tree structure needs to show the resources assigned to each workgroup. Figure 4-19 shows a Directory tree for South Atlantic Coast Publishing, a book publisher that uses workgroups for different book topic areas. The Directory tree is based on a workgroup approach.

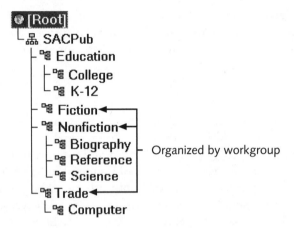

Figure 4-19   South Atlantic Coast Publishing Directory tree

Geographic

Some organizations create their primary organizational structure based on geographic location. In each location, the Directory tree might then reflect a functional or workgroup structure. This is one situation in which you may want to use the Country object, although it is not absolutely necessary. Figures 4-20 and 4-21 show Directory trees for International Metals, a company that produces a variety of metal products in several countries. The Directory tree in Figure 4-20 uses the Country object, whereas the Directory tree in Figure 4-21 uses the Organization object to represent the countries. When using the Country object, you are limited to a standardized two-letter code for that country.

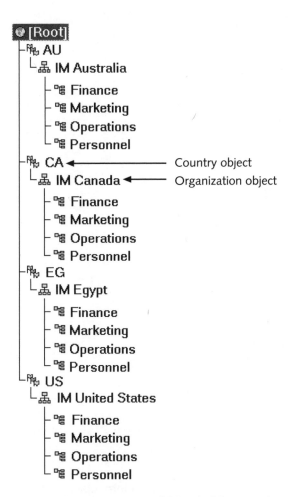

Figure 4-20   International Metals Directory tree with Country objects

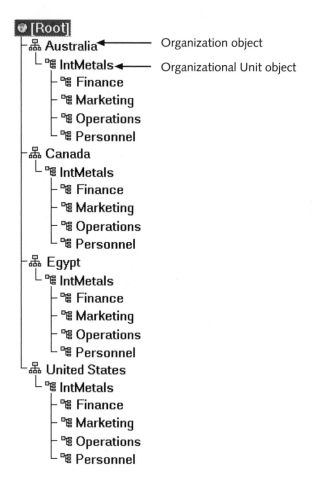

Figure 4-21   International Metals Directory tree without Country objects

Combinations

In some situations, you might find yourself needing to combine the functional area, workgroup, and geographical approaches. A company organized along functional lines might still have some special workgroups or units in other geographical locations that need to be appropriately represented in the Directory tree. For example, Wilson Manufacturing recently bought a lumber mill in Canada to ensure a steady supply of wood to the company. Although now part of the company (*not* a separate organization), this operation is entirely different from Wilson's main business. The network administrator decided to show the network resources for the Canadian operation using a geographical extension to Wilson's Directory tree, as shown in Figure 4-22.

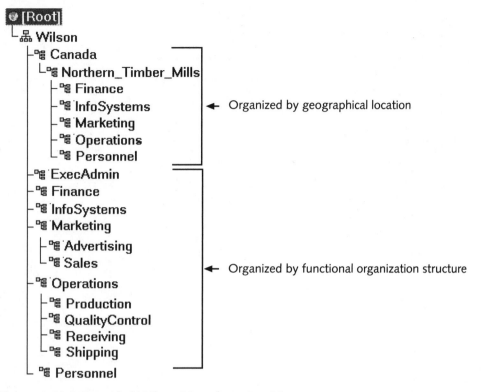

Figure 4-22   Extended Wilson Manufacturing Directory tree

THE CBE LABS TREE DESIGN PROCESS

This section describes the general process of designing a Directory tree. In Chapter 7, you will use NetWare Administrator to actually create this tree on your network.

To illustrate the use of objects in an NDS tree, you'll follow the process of designing a Directory tree model for Cunningham, Burns, and Evans Laboratories (CBE Labs). This small, independent consulting firm tests computer hardware and software and then reports the results in its publication, The *C/B/E Networker*. You observed CBE Lab's procedure for choosing a new NOS in Chapter 1, and more details about the company are discussed in that chapter. Figure 4-23 shows the organization chart for CBE Labs.

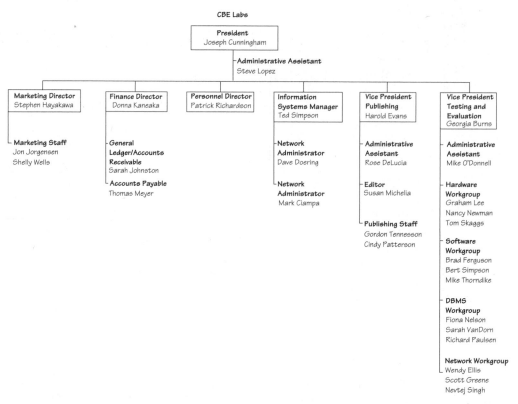

Figure 4-23   CBE Labs organization chart

Building a Directory Tree Model

After discussions among the CBE Labs information systems manager and the CBE Labs network administrators, a combination Directory tree structure has been selected for the CBE Labs Directory tree. The Directory tree will reflect the CBE Labs workgroup-oriented organization chart, while at the same time using traditional business function divisions within the administration workgroup. Using this structure, the CBE Labs organization chart shown in Figure 4-23 should provide the basis for building the Directory tree model.

Determining Container Objects

Construction of the Directory tree model begins with determining what the container objects will be. Using the organization chart in Figure 4-23, the container objects for CBE Labs were chosen by the network administrator, and are listed in Table 4-9.

Table 4-9   CBE Labs Directory tree container objects

Object Type	Object Name	Branch Of
Organization	CBE_Labs	[Root]
Organizational Unit	CBE_Labs_Admin	CBE_Labs
Organizational Unit	Pubs	CBE_Labs
Organizational Unit	Test&Eval	CBE_Labs
Organizational Unit	Marketing	CBE_Labs_Admin
Organizational Unit	Finance	CBE_Labs_Admin
Organizational Unit	Personnel	CBE_Labs_Admin
Organizational Unit	InfoSystems	CBE_Labs_Admin
Organizational Unit	Hardware	Test&Eval
Organizational Unit	Software	Test&Eval
Organizational Unit	DBMS	Test&Eval
Organizational Unit	Network	Test&Eval

In a Directory tree, the container tree levels below a designated or selected container are called the **children** of that container, and the designated or selected container object is called the **parent**. These terms are relational—the container above a container is its parent and the container object below it are its children. Thus, the CBE_Labs Organization object is the parent of the Organizational Unit objects listed in Table 4-9, and the Organizational Unit objects are children of CBE_Labs. A Directory tree with the container objects in Table 4-9 would look like Figure 4-24.

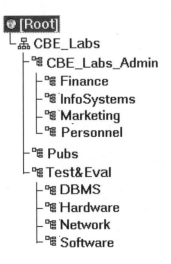

Figure 4-24   Container objects in CBE Labs Directory tree

Adding Leaf Objects

Once the structure of the Directory tree is established by creating the container objects, the leaf objects must be added. The CBE Labs tree will use the following types of leaf objects: Users, Groups, Organizational Roles, NetWare Servers, and Volumes.

Users   The first user to be added to the CBE Labs Directory tree will be the Admin user. NetWare 5.0 automatically creates this User object during the installation process. Although the Admin object can be placed anywhere in the Directory tree structure, it is usually located near the [Root] of the tree. The CBE Labs Admin object will be placed in the CBE_Labs Organization container.

Table 4-10 shows the CBE Labs user names to be included in the various Organizational Unit objects.

Table 4-10   CBE Labs Organizational Unit users

Organizational Unit Objects	User Objects
Administration	JCunningham
	SLopez
Finance	DKaneaka
	SJohnston
	TMeyer
InfoSystems	DDoering
	MCiampa
	TSimpson
Marketing	JJorgensen
	SHayakawa
	SWells
Personnel	PRichardson
Pubs	CPatterson
	GTennesson
	HEvans
	RDeLucia
	SMichelia
Test&Eval	GBurns
	MODonnell

Table 4-10   CBE Labs Organizational Unit users (continued)

Organizational Unit Objects	User Objects
DBMS	FNelson
	RPaulsen
	SVanDorn
Hardware	GLee
	NNewman
	TSkaggs
Network	NSingh
	SGreene
	WEllis
Software	BFerguson
	BSimpson
	MThorndike

Groups   The CBE Labs Directory tree will include the Group objects shown in Table 4-11 in its Organizational Unit objects.

Table 4-11   CBE Labs Organizational Unit groups

Organizational Unit Objects	Group Objects
Finance	Financers
InfoSystems	NetworkAdmins
Marketing	Marketers
Pubs	Publications
Test&Eval	Testing&Eval

Organizational Roles   Another object type you will use is the Organizational Role object. CBE Labs will use the Organizational Role objects shown in Table 4-12.

NetWare Servers   CBE Labs will use three NetWare servers. The first two NetWare servers use NetWare 5.0, and the third runs NetWare 3.2. The servers will be named after U.S. Navy aircraft carriers at the request of the president of the company, Joseph Cunningham, who served in the U.S. Navy. The first server will be named CONSTELLATION after the USS Constellation, the second SARATOGA after the USS Saratoga, and the NetWare 3.2 server is to be named RANGER after the USS Ranger. The CONSTELLATION server will be used by all the personnel at CBE Labs. For this reason, it is placed high in the Directory tree, in the CBE_Labs Organization object.

Table 4-12   CBE Labs Organizational Role objects

Organizational Unit Objects	Organizational Role Objects
CBE_Labs_Admin	AdminAssist
	President
Finance	Finance Director
InfoSystems	InfoSystems_Manager
	Network_Admin
Marketing	Marketing_Director
Personnel	Personnel_Director
Pubs	AdminAssist
	VP_Pubs
Test&Eval	AdminAssist
	VP_Test&Eval

Volumes   CONSTELLATION and SARATOGA each have three volumes—SYS, DATA, and CDROM—but RANGER has only a SYS volume. The system volume for CONSTELLATION, referred to as the SYS volume and with a common name of CONSTELLATION_SYS will be accessed by all personnel. The Volume object for the CONSTELLATION_SYS volume will be located with the CONSTELLATION object in the CBE_Labs Organization container.

CONSTELLATION and SARATOGA also have DATA and CDROM volumes that will be represented by DATA and CDROM Volume objects.

Figure 4-25 shows the CBE Labs Directory tree structure after adding the Users, Groups, Organizational Role, NetWare Server, and Volume objects. You will use NetWare Administrator to implement this tree in Chapter 7.

Figure 4-25   CBE Labs Directory tree

4

NDS AS A REPLICATED, DISTRIBUTED DATABASE

One of the main security concerns in the NetWare 5.0 environment is protecting the Directory database. Because the Directory database contains all the information necessary for users to log in to and use the network, losing this data would be catastrophic. Novell's solution assumes that there is more than one server in the network. With more than one NetWare server, the Directory database is broken into parts, and those parts are stored on different NetWare servers. For even better protection, copies of each part of the Directory database are stored on additional NetWare servers. The parts of the database are called *partitions*, and the copies are called *replicas*. A database that is stored in sections on different computers is called a **distributed database**. The Directory database is a replicated, distributed database. To maintain current data in each of the replicas, NetWare 5.0 updates all replicas using a process called *replica synchronization*.

Partitions

A **partition** is a logical division of the Directory database based on the Directory tree. A partition starts at some organization or organizational unit branch of the Directory tree and includes all leaf objects in that container plus all subsequent container and leaf objects in that branch of the tree. The data for each object is also included in the partition, but no data about the file system is included in a partition. Partitions cannot overlap, and an NDS object can be in only one partition. There should be at least one NetWare 5.0 server in each partition. For example, Figure 4-26 shows the partitioned Wilson Manufacturing Directory tree.

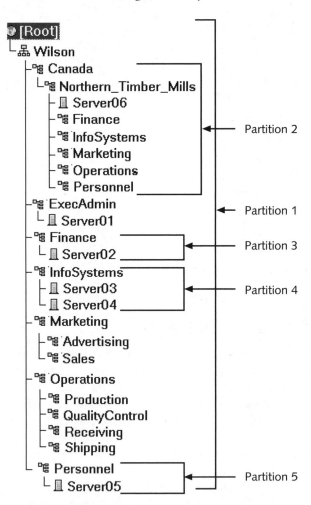

Figure 4-26   Partitioned Wilson Manufacturing Directory tree

There are five partitions in the Wilson Manufacturing Directory tree. The [Root] is included in the first partition, which is created when the first NetWare 5.0 server is installed. This partition is called the **[Root] partition**. Other partitions receive names based on the name of the container object in the partition closest to the [Root]. A partition is called a **child partition** if it is lower in the directory tree than another partition (**subordinate** to another partition), which is called the **parent partition**. In the Wilson Manufacturing Directory tree, the [Root] partition is the parent partition, and all the other partitions are child partitions.

The term *partition* is also used to mean a *physical subdivision of a hard drive.* Be careful not to confuse the two uses of the word *partition*.

Replicas

A **replica** is a copy of a partition. Replicas are stored on NetWare 5.0 servers to create NDS fault tolerance and faster access on a WAN. Fault tolerance is achieved because a user can log into the network even when the server containing the main copy of the user's data is not available. Faster access on a WAN is achieved when the main copy of a user's data is on a server physically close to the user. For example, if a WAN links offices in San Francisco and New York, a user in San Francisco will log into the network faster by accessing the replica on the San Francisco NetWare server. There are four types of replicas: master, read/write, read-only, and subordinate reference.

Master Replica

The **master replica** is the main copy of the partition. There can be only one master replica for each partition. The master replica can be read from and written to and is also the place where other partition operations occur, including creating a partition, merging a partition, moving a partition, repairing a partition, creating a replica, and deleting a replica.

Read/Write Replica

The **read/write replica** is a copy of the master replica that can be read from and modified. You can create as many read/write replicas as you want, but the actual number you create will be determined by the size of your network and the number of NetWare servers in the network. Read/write replicas can be used for authenticating user login, so you must have enough replicas to permit users to log into the network if NetWare servers become inaccessible.

Read-Only Replica

The **read-only replica** is a copy of the master replica that can only be read from; however, read-only replicas cannot be used for user login. You can create as many read-only replicas as you want, but these copies are not as useful as read/write replicas. Servers that are running bindery services cannot have a read-only replica—they must have a master or read/write replica.

 Because of the user login and bindery services limitations, it is usually more efficient to use a read/write replica than a read-only replica. Using the read/write replica lets users authenticate logins and permits the setting up of bindery services later if the need arises.

Subordinate Reference

The **subordinate reference replica** is based on the parent partition/child partition system. If a parent partition has a master, read/write, or read-only replica on a NetWare server and a child partition does not have a replica on that NetWare server, NetWare 5.0 will automatically add a nonmodifiable replica of the child partition. This replica is called a *subordinate reference replica*. If you later put a read/write or read-only replica of the child partition on the server, NetWare 5.0 will automatically remove the subordinate reference replica. This safety measure is built into NetWare 5.0 to make sure there are enough replicas of all the partitions.

Replica Synchronization

Changes to the Directory database can be made initially in either the master replica or a read/write replica of a partition. When someone changes an NDS object, a copy of the change is sent from the partition where the change was first recorded, to all other replicas of the partition. This update is necessary to ensure that the Directory database is **consistent**. However, because updating all the replicas takes some time, the Directory database is said to be **loosely consistent** at any given moment. This updating procedure is called **replica synchronization.**

Designing Partitions and Replica Distribution

The purpose of partitioning the Directory database is to achieve fault tolerance and faster access on a WAN. The number of partitions that must be created depends on what it takes to achieve those goals, but you should have at least two read/write replicas for every master replica if possible.

NetWare 5.0 will automatically create some partitions and replicas for you. A new partition is created during NetWare 5.0 installation if (1) you create a new Organization object or Organizational Unit object during the installation and (2) the NetWare Server object corresponding to the new NetWare 5.0 server is a leaf object in the new branch. The new partition starts in the new container object and includes all branches of that container object. A master replica for this partition is created and stored on the NetWare server. For example, when you install your first NetWare 5.0 server you must create an Organization object. When you do so, NetWare creates a partition based on that Organization object and places a master replica on the server.

When you install NetWare 5.0 on a server whose corresponding Server object is a leaf in an Organization or Organizational Unit object that is already in a partition, NetWare 5.0 creates a read/write replica of that partition on the new server. However, NetWare creates only three replicas of a partition automatically. If you install more than three servers in a partition, replicas will exist only on the first three. You can, however, add more if you want the added security of having extra copies of the partition of additional NetWare servers.

4

In a small LAN, partitioning gains little access time, and a single partition can be sufficient. If you have at least three servers, you can have a master replica and two read/write replicas, which gives you the necessary fault tolerance.

In larger LANs and in WANs, partitioning improves user access. To accomplish this, store the master replica containing the user's data on a server in the partition that contains the user's User object. Partitioning also can help create fault tolerance when you store read/write replicas in partitions other than the partition containing the master replica.

The master replica of a partition need not be stored on a server in that partition. A large organization may place *all* master replicas on one server. A tape backup of this server then backs up all the master replicas for the entire Directory database.

CHAPTER SUMMARY

- Novell Directory Services (NDS) is the main administrative tool of NetWare 5.0. NDS consists of the Directory database and administrative tools to use the data in the Directory database. Earlier versions of NetWare used a database called the *bindery*.

- NDS is network-centric; that is, it deals with the entire network. Users log into the network, not to an individual server. The benefits of this approach include easier network administration, more network security, higher reliability, and scalability (the ability to work with any size network).

- The logical design of NDS is the Directory tree, which is a hierarchical tree structure containing objects that represent the organizational structure of the network and all network resources. The Directory tree, which is given a Directory tree name during NetWare 5.0 installation, consists of NDS objects. Objects represent physical, logical, or organizational entities. Objects have properties, which are the types of data associated with each object. Each property can store one or more property values.

- The Directory tree consists of container objects and leaf objects. Container objects provide organizational structure to the Directory tree. They can contain other container objects or leaf objects. Leaf objects represent network resources such as users and printers. They cannot contain other objects.

❐ Container objects include the [Root] object, the Country object, the Organization object, and the Organizational Unit Object. These are abbreviated as [Root], C, O, and OU, respectively. Leaf objects can be classified by function for easier understanding. User-related leaf objects have properties that concern users and include the User object, the Group object, the Organizational Role object, and the Profile object. Server-related leaf objects have properties that concern the NetWare servers on your network, and include the NetWare Server object, the Volume object, and the Directory Map object. Printing-related leaf objects represent network printing components and include the Printer object and the Printer Agent object. The Application Manager-related objects help the network administrator control access to software programs run from the NetWare servers. The Informational leaf objects include the Computer object and the AFP Server object. The Miscellaneous leaf objects include the Alias object, the Bindery object, the Bindery Queue object, and the Unknown object.

❐ The location of an object in the Directory tree is the object's context. Context is the path from the [Root] to the object. Context is combined with an object's name to create the distinguished name, which is the complete name of the object. If object type abbreviations are included in the name, it is called a *typeful name*. Names without abbreviations are called *typeless names*.

❐ When designing a Directory tree, first establish naming conventions to provide a uniform method of naming network objects. Limit the depth of the Directory tree so that objects' distinguished names are not too long. You can base the Directory tree design on functional or geographic principles, or on a combination of the two. Functional design principles include an organizational approach and a workgroup approach.

❐ The Directory database can be divided into sections called *partitions*. The partitions can and should be copied to other servers to provide fault tolerance and faster network response times on a WAN. The copies are called *replicas*. There are four types of replicas: master, read/write, read-only, and subordinate reference. Partitions and replicas are created automatically when NetWare 5.0 is installed, but the network administrator can and should actively manage them to ensure good network performance and security.

KEY TERMS

AFP Server object
Alias object
AppleTalk File Protocol (AFP) server
Application Manager-related leaf objects
bindery
bindery emulation mode
Bindery object

4

Bindery Queue object
child partition
children
common name (CN)
Computer object
consistent
container object
context
contextless login
Country object
current context
depth
Directory database
Directory Map object
Directory tree
Directory tree name
distinguished name
distributed database
Group object
hierarchical structure
Informational leaf objects
leading period
leaf object
Lightweight Directory Access Protocol (LDAP)
logical entity
login name
login scripts
loosely consistent
master replica
name type
NCP Server object
NetWare Server object
network-centric
network file system
network standards
Novell Application Manager (NAM)

Novell Directory Services (NDS)
Novell Distributed Print Services (NDPS)
object
Organization object
organizational entity
Organizational Role object
Organizational Unit object
parent
parent partition
partition
physical entity
printer agent
Printer Agent object
Printer object
Printing-related leaf objects
Profile object
properties
property value
read-only replica
read/write replica
relative distinguished name
replica
replica synchronization
[Root]
[Root] object
[Root] partition
scalability
server-centric
Server-related leaf objects
subordinate
subordinate reference replica
trailing period
typeful name
typeless name
Unknown object
User object
User-related leaf objects
Volume object
width

REVIEW QUESTIONS

1. _____ is a database that concerns network resources, along with tools for using the data in the database.

2. The NetWare 5.0 NDS database is called the _____.

3. List four benefits of using NDS.

4. The logical design of NDS is called the _____.

5. The NDS database uses _____ to represent network resources. The types of data stored about each resource are called _____; the data itself is called the _____.

6. Briefly explain container objects.

7. Briefly explain leaf objects.

8. The container object created when the first NetWare 5.0 server is installed is the _____. This object is assigned the name of the Directory tree.

9. List the names of the four container objects.

10. List the names of the four User-related leaf objects.

11. List the names of the three Server-related leaf objects.

12. For each of the objects in the Objects column, give the letter from the Object Groups column indicating which object group the object belongs to.

Objects	Object Groups
Printer object	A. Printer-related leaf object
Unknown object	B. Informational leaf object
Computer object	C. Miscellaneous leaf object
Printer Agent object	
Alias object	
Bindery object	
AFP Server object	

13. NetWare includes _____, which adds the capability of using electronic messaging and e-mail to the network.

14. The location of an object in a Directory tree is called its _____.

15. For each object type listed next, list its associated abbreviation:

   Country _____

   Organization _____

   Organizational Unit _____

   All leaf objects _____

16. An object's complete name, which is the object's name together with its context, is called its _____.

17. The name *CN=GWashington.OU=WhiteHouse.O=USGovernment.C=US is* a(n) _____ name, whereas *GWashington.WhiteHouse.USGovernment.US* is a(n) _____ name.

18. For each of the following names, indicate whether it is an acceptable name in NetWare 5.0:

    Joan*Jones

    Joan_Jones

    Joan_with_a_very_very_very_very_very_very_very_long_name

    Joan*Jones

19. The Directory database can be divided into sections called _____. Copies of these are called _____ and can be stored on other servers to create fault tolerance in the network.

20. To accommodate devices that use the NetWare 3.x bindery, but not NetWare 5.0 NDS, NetWare 5.0 includes _____.

21. Briefly describe the steps in planning to implement NDS.

22. Washington Management Services (WMS) is a consulting company specializing in consulting work with government organizations and agencies. Figure 4-27 shows the Directory tree for WMS. In the Directory tree, identify and label:

    The [Root] object

    All container objects by type

    All leaf objects by type

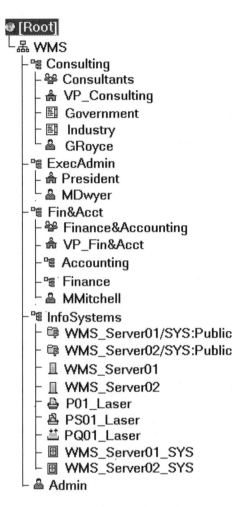

Figure 4-27   Washington Management Services Directory tree

HANDS-ON PROJECT

Project 4-1: Creating an NDS Directory Tree

In this exercise, you will examine an existing corporate structure to create an NDS tree. The company is F. D. Roosevelt Investments, Inc. (FDR). Figure 4-28 shows a copy of the FDR organizational chart. In these steps, you refer to the CBE Labs directory tree discussed in this chapter, and then create one for FDR. When designing your own models, remember that a directory tree is used for managing network resources and does not necessarily mirror a company's organizational chart.

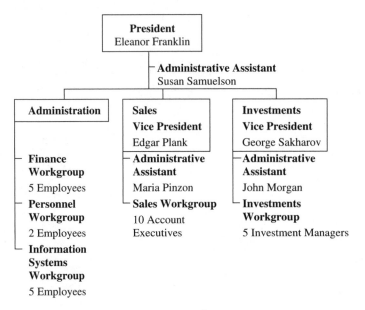

Figure 4-28   FDR organization chart

1. Designate a name for the directory tree.

2. Using the organizational chart shown in Figure 4-28, determine what, if any, container objects you will use in the tree.

3. Next identify the organizational units you will use.

4. List the leaf objects you will need to create for this tree.

5. Designate which User objects you will create and which Organizational Role objects.

6. Label and locate a NetWare Server object with appropriate volumes in the tree.

7. Label and locate appropriate Printer and Printer Agent objects.

8. Verify that your design complies with the guidelines outlined in the chapter for NDS trees.

9. Draw an appropriate partitioning scheme for FDR.

10. Write a short memo to your instructor discussing your design. Include a list of the objects you would create as well as the partitioning scheme diagram.

CASE PROJECTS

Case 4-1: Jefferson County Courthouse Network

The Jefferson County Courthouse network is proceeding according to plan. The network proposal is still for just the 12 users in the Social Services section, including program administrator Janet Hinds, her assistant Tom Norihama, receptionist Lisa Walsh, department secretary Terry Smith, and 8 social workers. The group will use one NetWare server. Because the network may be expanded later to include other courthouse functions, NetWare 5.0 was selected as the NOS for its scalability.

From discussions with Janet, the following decisions have been made:

1. The name of the Directory tree will be JCCH.

2. No Country or Locality objects will be used, and there will be only one Organization object: JCCH.

3. Because standalone print servers are used, the NetWare 5.0 server will need to have bindery services enabled.

Create a proposed NDS Directory tree for the project. When designing your model, remember that a Directory tree is used for managing network resources and does not necessarily mirror a company's organizational chart. In your proposal, discuss the following questions:

1. With only one server, there can be only one partition with a master replica. Because you don't have fault tolerance with read/write replicas on other servers, how will you protect the data in the Directory database?

2. What bindery context will be used to provide bindery services?

Turn in the proposal to your instructor in memo form.

Case 4-2: The J. Q. Adams Corporation Directory Tree

The J. Q. Adams Corporation is expanding its networking plans. Donna Hulbert, president of Adams, has decided to use two NetWare 5.0 servers in the network. One will be dedicated to administration tasks and the other to supporting production. After conferring with the appropriate people at J. Q. Adams, the following decisions have been made:

1. The name of the Directory tree will be ADAMS.

2. No Country or Locality objects will be used, and there will be only one Organization object: ADAMS.

3. There will be partitions of the Directory tree created for administration and production.

4. Because standalone print servers are used, both NetWare 5.0 servers will need to have bindery services enabled.

Figure 4-29 shows an organization chart for J. Q. Adams.

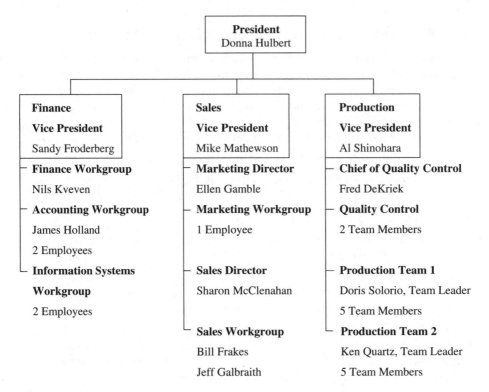

Figure 4-29   J. Q. Adams Corporation organization chart

Prepare your proposal for the NDS Directory tree. When designing your model, remember that a Directory tree is used for managing network resources and does not necessarily mirror a company's organizational chart. Include proposed partitions, replicas, and bindery contexts.

Turn in the proposal to your instructor in memo form.

5

PLANNING THE NETWORK FILE SYSTEM

> **After reading this chapter and completing the exercises you will be able to:**
>
> ◆ Describe the components of the NetWare file system
>
> ◆ Explain the purpose of each NetWare-created directory and Novell-suggested directory
>
> ◆ Write valid path statements to identify directories and files
>
> ◆ Apply directory design concepts to developing and documenting a directory structure for an organization
>
> ◆ Use NetWare commands and utilities to view volume and directory information

One of the network administrator's most important tasks is designing a network file system that will meet the special needs of the organization. The design must be completed before installing NetWare and setting up the network system. The file system must be designed to allow a smooth workflow for users. Also, it must not disrupt the information flow that existed before the network was implemented.

The NetWare file system offers several advantages:

- Centralized management of data and backups ensures that duplicate copies of data are always automatically available for restoring lost or damaged files.

- Improved security prevents users from modifying or accessing data they are not responsible for maintaining.

- Improved reliability and fault tolerance enable data to be backed up at regular intervals and allow recovery if data is lost or a NetWare server goes down.

- Shared and private storage areas facilitate the creation of workgroups by enabling users to share files or to transfer files from one user to another without having to carry disks between machines. Private storage areas let individuals save their own work in a secure area of the NetWare server.

- NetWare allows access to data by many different operating system platforms— it supports Apple Macintosh, Unix, and OS/2 file structures in addition to Windows Long File Name and standard 8.3 DOS syntax.

- The NetWare file system saves money by eliminating the need for separate servers to handle each operating system.

The NetWare file system can enable compatible applications running on Windows and Apple Macintosh platforms (for example, Microsoft Word) to share data files. As networks grow, a network administrator's skill in integrating the file formats of different operating systems in the network file system is becoming increasingly important.

Network administrators frequently use NetWare to integrate PC workstations using various desktop operating systems, including DOS, Windows, Macintosh System 8.0, OS/2, and Unix, to let people in an organization communicate and exchange data easily.

NDS COMPONENTS VERSUS NETWORK FILE SYSTEM COMPONENTS

In Chapter 4 you learned about Novell Directory Services (NDS) and the Directory tree. The Directory tree is a logical organizational view of the entire network. The Directory tree allows a network administrator to manage and control network resources. A **network file system**, in contrast, is a design for storing files on one or more hard disks in your NetWare servers. The term *network file system* refers to how file storage is structured across all NetWare servers in the network. The term *file system* refers to the file storage structure on an *individual* NetWare server. The network file system is the sum of *all* the NetWare server file systems.

The network file system enables a network administrator to manage and control system, application, and data files on the network. Each NetWare server file system is used to organize and secure the information stored on that server. A good network file system design is necessary to facilitate the setup, use, and growth of a network.

Directory Tree Components

As you learned in Chapter 4, a Directory tree consists of objects. Using container objects such as Organization objects and Organizational Unit objects, you can create the organizational structure of the Directory tree. Using leaf objects such as User objects and NetWare Server objects, you can represent network resources in the Directory tree.

Network File System Components

As Figure 5-1 shows, the four main components of the NetWare file system are the NetWare server, volumes, directories and subdirectories, and files.

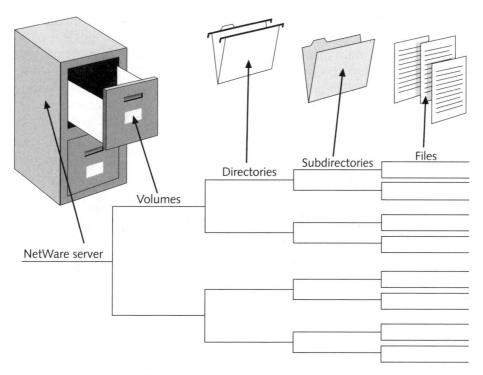

5

Figure 5-1 NetWare file system components

NetWare Server

The top level in the network file system structure is the NetWare server. As defined in Chapter 1, a NetWare server is a computer system dedicated to running the NetWare operating system. The function of a NetWare server in the network file system is like that of a file cabinet in an office, because it contains applications and data for access by users on the network. Just as an office needs many file cabinets to organize all its data in an accessible and secure form, an organization's network file system often consists of multiple NetWare servers. To provide access to its unique data, each NetWare server is given a name consisting of 2 to 47 characters.

 Server names cannot use any of the following special characters: = < > ? " * + , : ; \ / | [ ]

Volumes

Just as file cabinets have one or more drawers, the storage space on each NetWare server has one or more volumes. **Volumes** are the major divisions of NetWare server storage; all files are accessed through volumes, and each volume is associated with a specific

NetWare server. A NetWare volume is a physical amount of storage on one or more hard disk drives or other storage media, such as a CD-ROM. In DOS terms, a volume is equivalent to a partition of a hard disk drive on a local workstation. However, NetWare 5.0 volumes are more flexible than workstation hard disk drives because each volume can use or span multiple disk drives and occupy terabytes (TB) of data storage capacity. By allowing a volume to consist of up to 32 disk drives and a maximum capacity of 32 TB, NetWare provides for almost unlimited volume size. A NetWare 5.0 server can have a maximum of 64 volumes.

Each NetWare server is required to have at least one volume, named SYS (for *system*). During installation, NetWare 5.0 creates and stores its operating system files and utility programs in directories it creates in the SYS volume. Many network administrators create at least one additional volume in which to store the organization's data files separately from the NetWare operating system software. When multiple volumes are used, the SYS volume is typically reserved for the operating system files, print queues, and general-purpose application software such as spreadsheets and word processors. One or more data volumes are then created to store the organization's files. Placing the organization's data files and special applications in separate volumes provides the following advantages:

- The administrator can ensure that free space in the SYS volume is always available for NetWare's use.

- Security can be enhanced by dismounting volumes containing sensitive data, so that data can be stored off line when it is not being used.

- Performance improves when separate volumes hold other operating systems or large graphics and multimedia files. Placing these files in separate volumes lets the network administrator increase the block size or add optional file-name space support for other operating systems without impairing the performance of DOS files stored on other volumes.

- Fault tolerance is increased because the server can continue to provide services even when a volume is taken off line for repairs.

Network printing is one reason why additional free space in the SYS volume is needed. When printed output is sent to a network printer, it may first be stored on a NetWare server in directories called *print queues*. (Even with NDPS, the printer agent may use space on the server to hold a file before sending it to the printer.) Although NetWare 5.0 lets you place print queues in any volume, they are commonly placed in the SYS volume. For example, let's say a company has a NetWare server with a SYS volume that is almost filled with many large data files. If several users try to print large desktop publishing jobs on networked printers at the same time, they will flood the SYS volume with the printed output stored in the print queue. If the SYS volume runs out of space, the system cancels print jobs and sends error messages to the users. (If the SYS volume fills up, that can also corrupt the NDS database, because NetWare also uses the SYS volume for temporary storage.) The print jobs need to be resubmitted, or the network administrator must free up disk space. You can avoid such problems by keeping data files in separate data volumes and by allocating at least 500 MB for the NetWare 5.0 operating system files in the SYS volume.

If you are going to install online documentation on the SYS volume, you need to add another 60 MB, for a total of 560 MB.

If you do run out of space on a volume, you can increase the volume's size by adding another disk drive to the NetWare server and then directing NetWare to use empty space on the new drive to expand the existing volume. This process is called **spanning** a volume.

When a volume spans more than one disk drive, you may want to consider using a RAID (Redundant Array of Independent Disks) subsystem instead of simply two hard disks. With one volume spanning two disks, any problem with the hardware on either of the two disks will prevent the volume from mounting. (Mounting is the process NetWare uses to ready the hard disk partition to read and write data.)

When creating multiple volumes, you must use the following naming conventions:

- Each volume on a NetWare server must have a unique name.

- The volume name must be 2 to 15 characters long.

- Volume names cannot contain spaces or any of the following special characters: = < > ? " * + , : ; \ / | [ ]

Examples of valid volume names include DATA, ICS_GRAPHIC16, CTS-ENGINEERING, MAC_ATTAC, and UNIX@WORLD.

A colon must follow the volume name when specified as part of a path, and it is a common convention to write volume names when referred to in text with the colon—for example, SYS:, DATA:, CTS-ENGINEERING:. However, the colon is *not* part of the actual volume name.

A backslash or a forward slash must be used to separate the NetWare server name from the volume name. For example, the SYS volume on Server01 would be written as Server01\SYS: and the DATA volume on Server02 would be written as Server02\DATA:.

A **block** is the amount of data that is read or written to the volume at one time. The block size of a volume is assigned when the volume is created during installation. By default, NetWare creates the block size based on the volume size, as shown in Table 5-1.

Table 5-1   Default NetWare volume block sizes

Volume Size	Default Block Size
1–32 MB	4 KB
32–150 MB	8 KB
150–500 MB	16 KB
500–2,000 MB	32 KB
2,000+ MB	64 KB

A larger block size can speed up access time for large files, such as bit-mapped graphics images and CAD files. However, larger block sizes use more disk space, which makes them less efficient for storing many small files. NetWare 5.0 lets several files share one block. As Figure 5-2 shows, block suballocation divides any partially used disk block into 512-byte suballocation blocks, allowing unused space in that block to be allocated to another file, rather than being left unused.

 As long as block suballocation is enabled, there is generally no need to change the default block size.

In addition to block suballocation, NetWare provides two other tools to manage volume space. **File compression** reduces the size of a file by rewriting the file using a special coding technique. There are variations of this technique; the basic idea of file compression is to replace repeated characters or combinations of characters with a coded marker. For example, in the sentence "There the dog found the cat staring at the mouse" the three-character combination *the* is repeated four times. This combination can be replaced with a code such as X. Then the sentence can be stored as "Xre X dog found X cat staring at X mouse." When the file is used, it will be decompressed, replacing the codes with the original characters. If you want to use file compression on a NetWare volume, it must be enabled for the volume. File compression is enabled by default on NetWare volumes.

NetWare also supports **data migration**, which allows you to move files that have not been used for a long time to another type of storage medium, such as an optical disk. This frees up disk space on the NetWare volume. The filename, however, is still listed on the volume. If a user tries to open the file, it is then copied back from the optical disk to the volume before being opened. This technique enables little-used files to be stored off the volume but to still be available to the user. Data migration requires special hardware and software, and the default setting for a NetWare volume is data migration disabled.

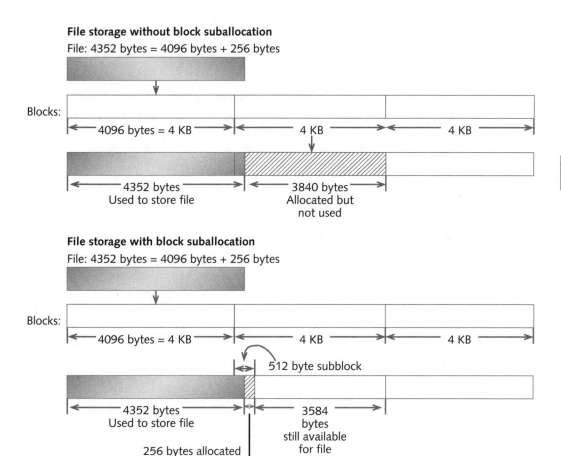

Figure 5-2   NetWare block suballocation

Directories and Subdirectories

The storage space in each NetWare volume can be organized into directories and subdirectories. A **directory** is a logical storage area on a volume. A **subdirectory** is a further division of a directory. In Windows 95/98, directories are called **folders**. Creating directories within a NetWare volume is like hanging folders in the drawer of a file cabinet. Directories and subdirectories let you keep files organized in a volume, just as folders let you organize files in a file cabinet's drawer. An important network administrator responsibility is to design a directory structure for each volume that will separate software and data according to functionality and use. NetWare's SYS volume contains several system-created directories that play important roles in the operation of the NetWare server. Novell also recommends an additional set of directories to help build a suitable directory structure to store software and data files. These directories are discussed in the following sections.

Required Directories When you install NetWare 5.0, six major directories are created, as shown in Figure 5-3. (NetWare also creates five other directories related to Java and the Internet, but these are beyond the scope of this discussion.) The NetWare operating system stores its required system files and utilities in the SYS volume by creating four main directories: **Login**, **Public**, **System**, and **Mail**. In addition, NetWare creates the **Deleted.Sav** and **Etc** directories. You need to understand how NetWare uses these required directories and where certain types of NetWare system files are stored. This section explains these directories and provides examples of their use by NetWare.

SYS

LOGIN   SYSTEM   PUBLIC   MAIL   ETC   DELETED.SAV

Figure 5-3   NetWare required directories

The SYS:LOGIN directory contains files and programs that can be accessed before logging in. You can think of this directory as NetWare's reception area. Just as you enter a reception area when you first go into a business office, when a user first connects to the network he or she is attached to the LOGIN directory of a NetWare server. Workstations gain access to the LOGIN directory only, and have limited access to files and programs stored in that directory. An important program in the LOGIN directory is LOGIN.EXE. Another important program that administrators often copy to the LOGIN directory is NLIST.EXE, which is by default in the PUBLIC directory.

When you visit an office building, you need to obtain permission from the receptionist before visiting someone's office. The NLIST.EXE program performs the receptionist's job of checking who is available to see you, by listing the names of all NetWare servers on the network. Next the receptionist needs to identify you to the person you want to see. LOGIN.EXE presents your user name and optional password to NDS and then, after you are identified as a valid user, gives you access to network resources.

The LOGIN and NLIST programs can be copied to a user's workstation and run from that workstation's local hard disk. This approach eliminates the need to change the active drive to a network drive in order to log in to the network. This option can be important when you are creating a DOS batch file and do not know what drive letter a workstation will be using for its network drive.

Many network administrators like to use the SYS:LOGIN directory to store common files and programs used by many workstations during the startup process. This technique lets you update a new release of these programs simply by copying the new software into the LOGIN directory rather than copying it to each workstation's hard disk drive.

The SYS:PUBLIC directory contains utility programs and files that are available to all network users after they have logged in. Many of these programs and files are necessary for users to be able to access and use network services. The NDIR.EXE, NLIST.EXE,

WHOAMI.EXE, NETUSER.EXE, and LOGOUT.EXE programs are all examples of NetWare utilities that may be run from the PUBLIC directory. For a network administrator, the PUBLIC directory is like a toolbox, containing many utilities you need to perform such network tasks as creating new users, managing files, assigning access rights, and working with printers.

The SYS:SYSTEM directory contains NetWare operating system files and utilities that are accessible only to users such as the Admin users who have been given supervisory privileges on the network. Novell uses the dollar symbol ($) in all filenames that contain system information. For example, the SYS$LOG.ERR file is the system error log.

Many NetWare system files are not accessible from the DOS DIR command; you need to use the NetWare NDIR command to display them when you work on the NetWare server. Only the network administrator should be given access rights to the SYSTEM directory, to prevent users from erasing or modifying system files and using commands that affect the functioning of the NetWare server.

Tip

Some network administrators move certain program files that they do not want the user to run, such as the Windows NWADMIN utility and the DOS NETADMIN utility, from the PUBLIC directory to the SYSTEM directory.

In NetWare 5.0 the SYS:MAIL directory is used by e-mail programs that use NetWare's Message Handling Service (MHS) to store data files. In earlier versions of NetWare, the MAIL directory of a server contained a subdirectory for each user, which is automatically created whenever a new user is added to the NetWare server. E-mail software used these subdirectories to pass electronic messages between users, but the NetWare operating system also needed them for storing user information such as personal login scripts. A NetWare 5.0 server stores personal user information such as login scripts in the NDS Directory database instead of in the SYS:MAIL directory. The SYS:MAIL provides compatibility with network clients that access the NetWare server using bindery emulation mode.

Because the operating system uses these directories, you should not allow users to access the MAIL directories to store their personal files, because this is likely to erase or change crucial NetWare system files. To back up the NetWare server and perform maintenance tasks, the network administrator needs to keep track of the MAIL directories.

As Figure 5-3 shows, in addition to the four major system directories you can also find ETC and DELETED.SAV directories on the SYS volume of a NetWare server. NetWare 5.0 automatically creates the SYS:ETC directory to store sample files to help the network administrator configure the server. The SYS:DOC directory is an optional directory for NetWare servers that NetWare creates when electronic versions of the NetWare manuals are installed.

To help users recover lost files, a network administrator should be aware of the purpose and use of the DELETED.SAV directory. The SYS:DELETED.SAV directory is automatically created on each NetWare volume and is the part of the NetWare file recovery

5

system that allows the recovery of a file even after the directory that contained the file has been deleted. When files are deleted from a NetWare volume, the blocks on the hard disk that contained the file's information are not immediately reused (as would happen on your local DOS drive). Instead, as NetWare requires more disk space, it reuses disk blocks from the files that have been deleted the longest, allowing you to recover files even after they have been deleted for some time. A file normally must be recovered in the directory from which it was deleted, but if that directory has been removed the file might still be found in the DELETED.SAV directory. In Chapter 7 you will have an opportunity to practice retrieving deleted files.

Suggested Directories   The six required directories just described are automatically created for you during installation and provide the NetWare operating system with the storage areas it needs to perform its functions. In addition, an organization will probably require storage areas in the NetWare server disk volumes. The network administrator is responsible for planning, creating, and maintaining the directory structure necessary to store the organization's data and software on the NetWare server. Novell suggests that four basic types of directories should be part of an organization's file system: DOS directories, application directories, user home directories, and shared directories. This section describes each type of directory and explains how it can be used to meet the storage needs of an organization.

DOS Directories   Before Windows 3.1x could be run, a version of DOS had to be running. With Windows 95, most of the DOS functions were replaced by Windows itself. However, Windows 95/98 still has some DOS-based commands and utilities, such as the DISKCOPY command. As a network administrator, you will probably encounter a mix of workstations that run different versions of DOS and Windows. Because each DOS version and Windows 95/98 run external commands written for that version only, you must provide a separate directory for each DOS version. One solution is for each workstation's local hard disk drive to contain a directory with the DOS commands used by that workstation. However, this requires each workstation to have a hard drive containing the DOS commands and increases the chance that a computer virus will accidentally erase or damage the DOS commands. To deal with this threat, network administrators commonly create subdirectories in the PUBLIC directory for each version of the DOS operating system being used on the network. Each subdirectory contains only the DOS external commands (those not contained in COMMAND.COM), such as DISKCOPY, XCOPY, and FORMAT, that the administrator wants available on the network. This technique saves the administrator from having to keep DOS directories on each workstation's hard disk and updating all workstation hard drives when a newer version of DOS is installed.

 The version of DOS built into Windows 95 and Windows 98 is MS-DOS 7.0.

In addition to a subdirectory for the DOS component of Windows 95/98, the DOS structure shown in Figure 5-4 provides for different machine types and DOS environments by establishing a directory level for each machine type and then dividing the machine types into subdirectories corresponding to DOS versions. This structure is necessary because some PC manufacturers, such as Compaq and IBM, have modified Microsoft DOS to provide special features for their own brands of computers. For example, IBM provides a specialized version of DOS, so the IBM_PC directory is further divided into two subdirectories—one for IBM's DOS version and one for the standard Microsoft DOS versions. Each of the IBM_PC subdirectories can be further subdivided into additional subdirectories for each DOS version. Using the version number for the directory name, as shown in Figure 5-4, lets NetWare locate the correct DOS directory automatically for the workstation to use when a user logs in.

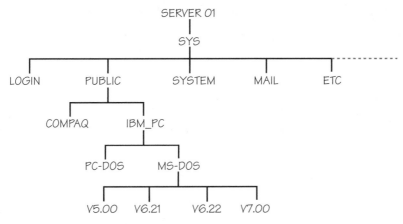

Figure 5-4   Recommended DOS directory structure

Application directories   In addition to creating the required NetWare directories, network administrators must create directories and subdirectories for the applications and data needed by network users. The first rule in organizing directories is to keep data and software separate whenever possible. This means you need to define a directory for each software application stored in the NetWare server. Software applications fall into two basic categories: general-purpose packages, such as Word or WordPerfect and Microsoft Excel or Lotus 1-2-3, and special-purpose or vertical applications such as payroll or order-entry software. Multiple users throughout an organization often need general-purpose software, so these applications are often stored in directories in the server's SYS volume. Special-purpose applications are often restricted to small groups of users or departments; such applications contain their own data directories and files and sometimes require large amounts of data storage. To restrict access or keep the SYS volume from filling up, some network administrators store special-purpose applications, such as payroll or inventory, in a separate data volume.

Home directories In addition to access to application directories, each user needs a private **home directory** in which to store files and documents. When planning disk storage needs, anticipate the space users need to store personal projects and files for their work. Generally, only the owner of a home directory has access rights to it; store files needed by multiple users in shared directory areas. The location of user home directories depends on the design of the directory structure. If the server has only one volume (SYS), they can be placed in a general-purpose directory named HOME or USERS. See Figure 5-5.

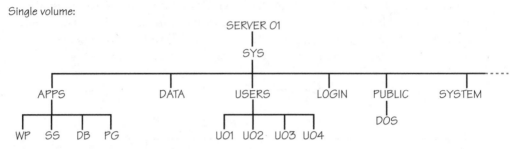

Figure 5-5 Novell suggested directories

Alternatively, you can place HOME or USERS (and all other data subdirectories) in the DATA directory, as Figure 5-6 shows. User home directories can also be separated by workgroup, as described later in this chapter.

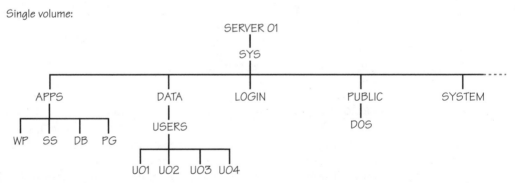

Figure 5-6 Using a DATA directory

If the server has more than one volume, use the additional volume(s) for data storage, and locate the home directories there. See Figure 5-7.

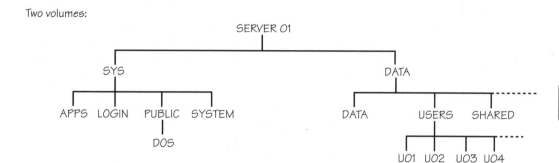

Two volumes:

Figure 5-7   Using a DATA volume

User home directories should be named with the user's login name. This lets the network administrator assign a drive letter to the user's home directory when the user logs in. In Chapter 13, you will learn how to use NetWare login scripts to automate the process of mapping drives to user home directories.

Shared directories   One benefit of using a network is being able to share files. As a network administrator, you will need to establish shared work directories that allow multiple users to work with common files and documents. Shared work directories enable one user to save a file and another user working on the same project to access it. Word processing documents and spreadsheet program worksheets stored in a shared directory are available to only one user at a time. Special software is needed to let multiple users access a file at the same time, to prevent one user's changes from overwriting someone else's changes. Figure 5-7 shows a general-purpose shared directory named SHARED, for use by all users. Later in the chapter you will learn how to create a departmental directory structure that includes shared directories for each workgroup.

Files

Files contain the actual blocks of data and software that can be loaded from the disk storage system into the computer's RAM. Every NetWare volume contains a **directory entry table (DET)** and a file allocation table (FAT) to keep track of each file's name and location on the disk volume. The DET also stores file attributes and **access rights**. Access rights control what operations a user can perform on a file or directory. **Attributes** are special flags that identify how the file is to be viewed or processed. Examples of common file attributes used in DOS and Windows are Read-Only, Hidden, and System. NetWare provides such additional attributes as Sharable and Delete-Inhibit. In Chapter 10 you will learn more about the file access rights and attributes available with NetWare.

NetWare by default supports DOS file-naming conventions with filenames of up to eight characters and an optional three-character extension. The NetWare DET, however, is not limited to DOS filenames, because NetWare servers must often store files from workstations running other operating systems such as Windows 95/98, Windows NT, Apple Macintosh, OS/2, and Unix. As a network administrator, you will need to know how to set up and manage file storage from workstations running a variety of operating systems. Because non-DOS systems support longer filenames with special attributes, additional logic must be added to the NetWare server, and the DET must be expanded for server volumes that will support files used by non-DOS systems. Because of the importance of the DET and FAT in accessing files from a NetWare volume, a second copy of both tables is automatically maintained to allow recovery if a disk error damages the primary tables.

Directory Paths

To access files, you need to specify the location of the directory or file within the NetWare file system. The **default drive** and **default directory** are the drive and directory you are currently using. A **directory path** is a list of file system components that identifies the location of the directory or file you want to access. A **complete directory path**, also called an **absolute directory path**, contains the NetWare server's name, volume name, directory, and all subdirectories leading to the target object. For example, the complete path to the U01 home directory, shown in Figure 5-5, is SERVER01/SYS:USERS\U01. A **partial directory path**, also called a **relative directory path**, lists only the locations leading from the default directory to the target object. Assume, for example, that your default directory is the SYS volume. In this case, the partial directory path is specified as \USERS\U01. As a network administrator, you will often need to use both complete and partial paths when working with the NetWare file system. This is true when using the Windows utilities as well as DOS. To drill down into various folders to locate a file, you need to know which folders to look into.

Complete Path

When specifying the complete directory path to an object, you start with the NetWare server's name followed by a slash and then the name of the volume followed by a colon. Then specify directories and subdirectories by using either a forward slash (/) or a backslash (\) to separate the directory and subdirectory names. Although a slash can be added between the volume and directory names, some programs misinterpret the volume name as a directory name. Therefore it is best *not* to include a slash after the colon in a volume's name.

To avoid confusion when you enter DOS paths (or enter paths into the Windows Run dialog), consistently use backslashes between directory and subdirectory names in NetWare paths because DOS does not accept forward slashes as part of directory paths on local disk drives.

DOS commands normally do not accept NetWare complete directory paths because they contain unfamiliar objects, such as the NetWare server name and volume name. For example, the following command output shows that the DIR command will display the directories in a NetWare path (here it is G:), but an attempt to use the DOS COPY command to copy files from drive A: to Eleanor Franklin's home directory, which is named EFRANKLN, fails.

```
G:\> DIR USERS


Volume in drive G is SYS
Directory of G:\USERS


EFRANKLN       <DIR>          12-15-98      9:10a

SSAMLSN        <DIR>          12-15-98      9:10a

EPLANK         <DIR>          12-15-98      9:10a

MPINZON        <DIR>          12-15-98      9:10a

GSAKHARV       <DIR>          12-15-98      9:10a

JMORGAN        <DIR>          12-15-98      9:10a


G:\> COPY A:\*.* SYS:USERS\EFRANKLIN
Too many parameters
```

The result of this COPY command is an error message that says, "Too many parameters." DOS cannot correctly interpret SYS as a valid part of the directory path. The same is true of Windows 95/98, when typing in a directory path such as in the Start menu's RUN dialog. Type G: in the preceding example and Windows knows exactly how to retrieve the information. Type CONSTELLATION\SYS, however, and an error message appears telling you that you have an incorrect path.

SYS File System NDS Objects

Two of the NDS objects you studied in Chapter 4 represent parts of the file system—the NetWare Server object and the Volume object. Each NetWare server in the network is represented by a NetWare Server object. For NetWare 5.0 servers, the NetWare Server object is automatically created and added to the Directory tree when NetWare 5.0 is installed on the server. The server must be named at the time NetWare 5.0 is installed, and this name is used as the name of the NetWare Server object. In Chapter 6 you will learn more about installing NetWare 5.0.

When a volume is created and named, NetWare also creates a Volume object and places it in the same context in the Directory tree as the NetWare Server object where the volume is physically located. The Volume object is named by combining the name of the NetWare server and the name of the volume. For example, when the SYS volume is created on Server01, a Volume object named Server01_SYS is placed in the same container holding the NetWare Server object Server01. In Chapter 6 you will learn about creating volumes.

Although NDS does not let you create objects representing directories and files, it does read the directory structure of a volume, which can be displayed in the Directory tree. As Figure 5-8 shows, Volume objects can be expanded to show the directories in the volume and the files in a directory. In Chapter 7 you will work with NetWare utilities that manage directories and files.

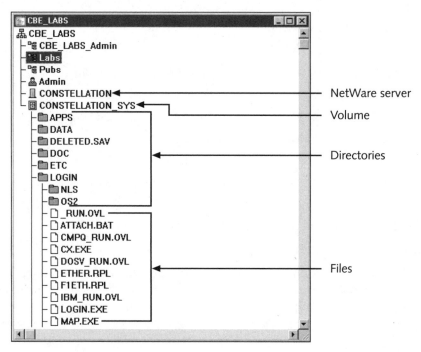

Figure 5-8   Directories and files in NDS Directory tree

DIRECTORY STRUCTURE

Once you understand the components of a file system, you can design a directory structure to meet the processing needs of an organization. Designing a directory structure is like creating a blueprint for a building. Just as the blueprint lets the builder determine the construction details and materials needed, the directory structure design lets the network administrator allocate storage space and implement the network file system. Designing the directory structure involves two steps:

1. Defining the directories and subdirectories needed

2. Placing those directories in the file system structure

Before you design an organization's directory structure, you need to analyze the processing needs of the users in the organization, to determine what directories will be needed. When creating the directory structure, be aware that there is no single best approach that all network administrators use. Instead, each network administrator develops his or her own unique style for defining and arranging directories. This section explains the concepts and techniques that will help you develop your own style for creating good directory structures.

Define Workgroups

5

The first step in designing a directory structure is to determine the storage required for the services the NetWare server will provide to the network users. To do this, you will work with the information systems personnel at Cunningham, Burns, and Evans Laboratories (CBE Labs), the same company you worked with in Chapters 1 and 4. Figure 4-23, in Chapter 4, shows the CBE Labs organizational chart.

To determine storage needs, you start by examining an organizational chart to determine the computer users and any workgroups. From the CBE Labs organizational chart, you can immediately see three main workgroups: administration, publications, and testing and evaluation. In addition, administration can be divided into marketing, finance, personnel, and information systems. Testing and evaluation can be divided into hardware, software, database (DBMS stands for database management system), and network.

Define NetWare Server Use

Although small networks may have only one NetWare server, a typical network has two or more. When more than one NetWare server is on the network, the use of each server must be defined. For example, Ted Simpson, the information systems manager at CBE Labs, has recommended using three NetWare servers instead of the single NetWare 3.2 server CBE Labs now uses. Management has approved buying two new servers that will run the NetWare 5.0 operating system. The old NetWare 3. 2 server will be kept. Ted needs to decide how to use the three servers.

The purpose of CBE Labs is to test computer components and then report the results, so the main server needs are for the testing and evaluation workgroup and for the publishing workgroup. Ted decides to first allocate one NetWare 5.0 server to testing and evaluation, and one NetWare 5.0 server to publishing. This leaves administrative tasks and company-wide requirements, such as e-mail, to be taken care of. Ted realizes that the testing and evaluation workgroup will need all the capacity of its NetWare server, but the publishing workgroup will use only part of the capacity of its server. By allocating one NetWare 5.0 server as a combined administration/publishing server, many administration needs can be filled. However, the finance department needs resources for the accounting system. This system is an older, DOS-based system that is already running on the NetWare 3. 2 server. Ted decides to leave that application where it is and to dedicate the NetWare 3. 2 server to finance.

Many network administrators create naming schemes for the NetWare servers in their networks. As you learned in Chapter 4, because CBE Labs president Joseph Cunningham served as an officer in the U.S. Navy, CBE Labs names servers after U.S. Navy aircraft carriers. The existing NetWare 3.2 server is named RANGER. The administration/publishing NetWare 5.0 server is named CONSTELLATION, and the testing and evaluation NetWare 5.0 server is named SARATOGA. The Server Planning Form in Figure 5-9 shows the three servers, their proposed functions, and the volumes they will contain.

NetWare Server Planning Form			
Created By:	Ted Simpson	Date:	9/15/99
Organization:	CBE Labs		
NetWare Servers:			
NetWare Server Name:	CONSTELLATION		
NetWare Operating System:	5.0		
Volumes:	SYS		
	DATA		
	CDROM		
Purpose:	CONSTELLATION is the main administration and publishing NetWare server.		
NetWare Server Name:	SARATOGA		
NetWare Operating System:	5.0		
Volumes:	SYS		
	DATA		
	CDROM		
Purpose:	SARATOGA is the main testing and evaluation labs NetWare server.		
NetWare Server Name:	RANGER		
NetWare Operating System:	3.2		
Volumes:	SYS		
Purpose:	RANGER is the secondary administration NetWare server and is used for accounting applications and data.		

Figure 5-9   CBE Labs Netware Server Planning Form

Both of the new servers, CONSTELLATION and SARATOGA, have two hard drives, which will become a SYS volume and a DATA volume. They also each have a CD-ROM drive, and NetWare 5.0 will treat a CD-ROM in this drive as a volume. Each CD-ROM will have a separate volume name, but for planning purposes these volumes will be referred to as CDROM. The existing NetWare server, RANGER, has only a SYS volume. Instead of a DATA volume, RANGER will use a DATA directory as part of the directory structure.

Define Directories

After you identify the network users and workgroups, you need to determine—through discussions with the users and department managers—what applications and data storage areas they will need. It is important to get users involved early in the directory design process, to make sure the result will anticipate and serve their needs.

Directories can be divided into four general categories: general-purpose applications, vertical applications, shared data, and home directories. A **general-purpose application** is a software program—such as a word processor, spreadsheet, or CAD product—that many different users access to create and maintain their own files and documents. A **vertical application** is a software program that performs a specialized process such as payroll, order entry, or manufacturing requirements planning. Vertical applications are normally restricted to a department or a limited number of users, and give multiple users access to shared database files within the application's directory structure.

Shared data areas lets users exchange files by saving the files where multiple users can access them. In designing directory structures, a network administrator can include a **local shared directory**, which restricts access to shared files, to the users of the workgroup concerned with them. The network administrator can also provide a **global shared directory** so that workgroups can share files.

You will follow this process for CBE Labs. Ted Simpson has discussed network usage with the CBE Labs staff and has gathered the following information:

- The finance department uses a DOS-based payroll application for weekly payroll processing. In addition, all users in finance use a spreadsheet package to work on budgets, and only the finance users share these budget spreadsheet files.

- Each user in testing and evaluation has his or her own computer and uses it to access test results stored in a specialized SQL (Structured Query Language) database. In addition, the testing and evaluation users periodically share word processing document files when working together on a report.

- Testing and evaluation users have a specialized hardware analysis program that they use to evaluate hardware.

- The publishing personnel use word processing and desktop publishing software to work on shared documents such as the company's main publication, the *C/B/E Networker*. In addition, the publishing personnel work with the testing and evaluation personnel to help format and print special test reports for customers.

- All staff members at CBE Labs need access to a word processing program to write their own correspondence and memos. To make work easier, everyone would like to share common word processing templates, forms, and customer lists.

- All staff members at CBE Labs need access to the company's e-mail program, a shared fax program, and Internet tools.

- CBE Labs has purchased a Windows 95-based software suite, Office97, which includes a word processor, an electronic spreadsheet, a presentation graphics program, and a database program. Enough licenses were purchased so that everyone at CBE Labs can use the suite.

Using information from his discussions, Ted has filled out the Directory Planning Form shown in Figure 5-10. Ted must now allocate volume space for the applications and data storage needs. The general-purpose software directories for CBE Labs include the software suite application that all employees need, the company's e-mail program, and the company's shared fax software. Vertical applications at CBE Labs include the payroll system that administration uses, the SQL database and the hardware analysis software that testing and evaluation uses, and the desktop publishing application that publishing uses. Ted decides to put application directories for the general-purpose software on the CONSTELLATION_SYS volume, along with the desktop publishing program. He also decides to put the testing and evaluation applications on the SARATOGA_SYS volume, and the accounting software on the RANGER_SYS volume. This arrangement puts each application on the NetWare server assigned to the workgroup using the software.

Ted plans to put data directories on the DATA volumes of CONSTELLATION and SARATOGA and in a DATA directory of RANGER. Figure 5-10 shows data needs. Shared directories include a SHARED directory for all users to contain common word processing forms, templates, and customer lists needed by all users; BUDGETS directories for general administration and finance; REPORTS directories for three administration workgroups, TESTDATA directories for each testing and evaluation workgroup to hold the results of the groups tests; and a REPORTS directory for testing and evaluation. Ted will also set up 11 workgroup-shared work directories to hold each workgroup's working papers. Although Ted could set up just one shared directory for the entire company, multiple directories will keep the files separate, making it easier for staff to locate and use only the files they need.

Directory Planning Form

Created By:	Ted Simpson	Date:	9/15/99
Organization:	CBE Labs		

Workgroups:

Workgroup Name:	Workgroup Members
Everyone	All CBE Labs users
Administration	13 Administration users
Publications	5 Publications users
Testing and evaluation	14 Testing and evaluation users
Marketing	3 Marketing users
Finance	3 Finance users
Personnel	1 Personnel user
Information systems	3 Information systems users
Hardware	3 Hardware users
Software	3 Software users
Database	3 Database users
Network	3 Network users

Directories:

Description	Type	Users	Estimated Size
WINOFFICE	general-purpose application	everyone	300 MB
e-Mail	general-purpose application	everyone	100 MB
Fax	general-purpose application	everyone	25 MB
Internet	general-purpose application	everyone	50 MB
Payroll	vertical application	finance	25 MB
SQL database	vertical application	testing & eval.	100 MB
Hardware analysis	vertical application	testing & eval.	50 MB
Desktop publishing	vertical application	publishing	50 MB
CBE shared	shared data	everyone	100 MB
Workgroup shared	shared data	11 workgroups	50 MB each
Test data	shared data	4 testing & eval. work-groups	100 MB
Reports	shared data	testing & eval.	100 MB
Payroll data	shared data	finance	250 MB
Desktop publishing documents	shared data	publishing	100 MB
Budgets	shared data	2 admin. workgroups	25 MB each
Reports	shared data	3 admin. workgroups	25 MB
Home directories for each user	private data	32 staff users	40 MB per user

Figure 5-10   CBE Labs Directory Planning Form

5

Design the Directory Structure

Once you have figured out which directories are needed, you are ready to design the layout and determine the location of the directories within the NetWare server's volumes. To design the directory structure for your NetWare server, you must first define the data and software directories your users need to perform their processing functions.

Then you organize these directories into a logical and easy-to-use structure that will provide a foundation for your network's file system. In this section, you learn how to analyze directory needs for an organization, as well as two major ways to organize a directory structure: department oriented and application oriented. In addition, this section gives you forms and techniques that will help you design and document your directory structures.

The Volume Design Form and Directory Design Form

As Figure 5-11 shows, the Volume Design Form is used to document each volume's directory structure and all directories branching from the root of the volume. The Volume Design Form can also show subdirectory structures. For example, the PRODUCT directory is treated this way in Figure 5-12. In addition to laying out the directory structure, the Volume Design Form contains fields for specifying NetWare version, total volume capacity, block size, and whether to enable block suballocation, file compression, and data migration on the volume. Notice that the planned block size is 64 KB. The larger block size is used with block suballocation to increase file storage efficiency on the volume.

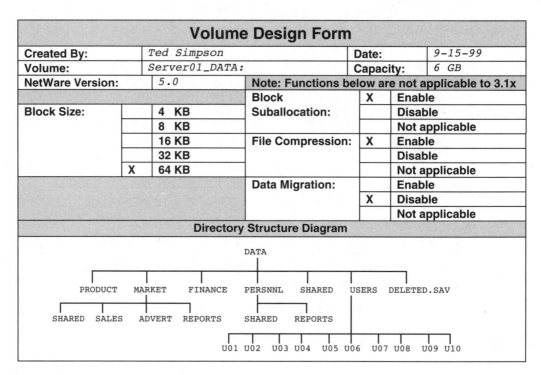

Figure 5-11 Sample Volume Design Form

When diagramming a directory structure, you will find it is often difficult to draw all directories and subdirectories for a volume on one sheet of paper. The Volume Design Form does not provide enough space for you to diagram more complex directories. Having separate forms for subdirectories lets you make alterations to a subdirectory without having to redraw an entire diagram. You should complete one Directory Design Form, shown in Figure 5-12, for each directory not fully documented on your volume design form.

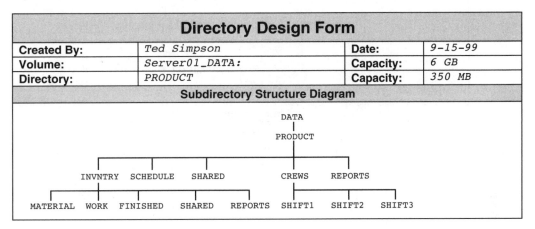

Figure 5-12 Sample Directory Design Form

Organizing the SYS Volume

The simplest method for organizing the SYS volume is to branch all directories from the root of the SYS volume, as Figure 5-13 shows. The lack of hierarchy in this directory design, however, makes it difficult to group directories by function or to manage and assign special trustee rights. In addition, storing all files in the SYS volume can cause the NetWare server to crash if not enough disk space is available for the operating system.

To avoid these pitfalls, many network administrators separate the SYS volume from data storage by using a DATA volume. This method not only frees up adequate space in the SYS volume for system functions, but also simplifies backup procedures and lets you perform maintenance activities on the DATA volume without taking the SYS volume off line.

Volume Design Form					
Created By:	Ted Simpson			**Date:**	9-15-99
Volume:	Server01_SYS:			**Capacity:**	4 GB
NetWare Version:	5.0		**Note: Functions below are not applicable to 3.1x**		
			Block Suballocation:	X	**Enable**
Block Size:		4 KB			**Disable**
		8 KB			**Not applicable**
		16 KB	**File Compression:**	X	**Enable**
		32 KB			**Disable**
	X	64 KB			**Not applicable**
			Data Migration:		**Enable**
				X	**Disable**
					Not applicable

Directory Structure Diagram

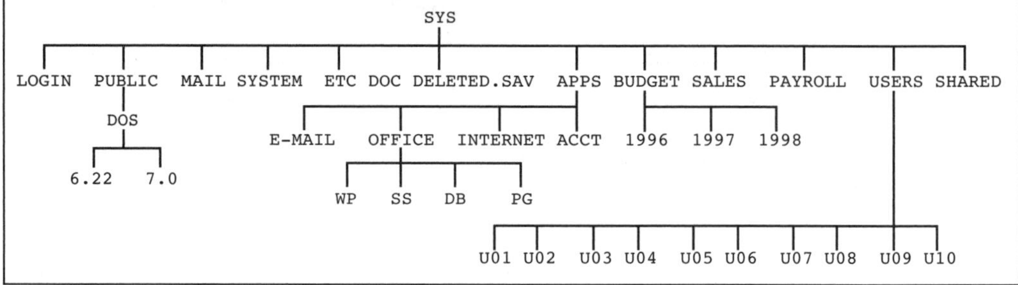

Figure 5-13 Simple SYS volume directory design

In a multiple-volume design, many network administrators place directories for the DOS operating system and general-purpose applications in the SYS volume. Figure 5-14 illustrates this multiple-volume approach applied to the CBE Labs SYS volume structure on the NetWare server CONSTELLATION. Notice that all the general-purpose application packages and special-purpose applications have been placed in separate subdirectories under the APPS directory. This will make it easy for the network administrator to assign access rights. The directories for CBE Labs' data will be located in a separate DATA volume. Because over time the data directories will grow in size, placing them in a separate volume will let the network administrator monitor and maintain adequate storage space in the DATA volume.

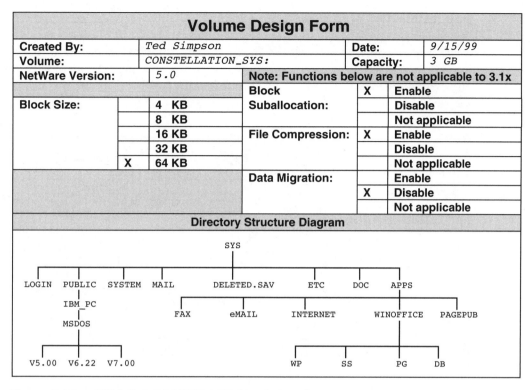

Figure 5-14   CBE Labs' CONSTELLATION_SYS: volume

Organizing the DATA Volume

Network administrators generally use two methods to organize directories in a DATA volume: by application or by department or workgroup. The method you select will depend on your personal preference and on the size and type of processing performed by the organization. Generally, smaller network file systems can be organized by using an application-oriented structure that branches all directories from the root of the volume. This keeps the design simple and easy to manage. In larger file systems involving multiple workgroups and many data directories, it is often easier to maintain security and locate data by using a departmental structure. This structure places data directories as subdirectories under workgroup directories. In some cases, a combination of both methods will work best for an organization.

Whatever design method you use for data directories, a good rule of thumb is not to exceed 6 subdirectory layers, and to have no more than 16 subdirectories in any one directory. This way, you can always see all directories on a computer monitor at the same time.

Application-Oriented Structure An **application-oriented structure** groups the directories by application rather than by department or workgroup. All user home directories, for example, can be placed in a common directory called USERS. The shared directories can then be grouped according to use, and applications not placed on the SYS volume can be placed in separate directories at the root of the DATA volume. Figure 5-15 shows the application-oriented method applied to the DATA volume.

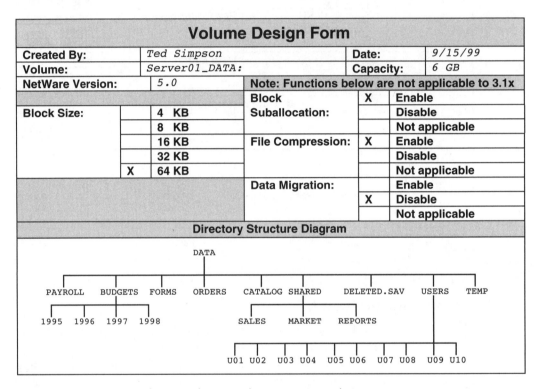

Figure 5-15   DATA volume with an application-oriented structure

The advantage of an application-oriented structure is that it is fairly shallow, which makes it easier to locate files without going through multiple layers of directories. In large directory structures, however, the shallow nature of the application-oriented structure can actually be a disadvantage, because it is difficult to know which departments use which directories. In an application-oriented structure, the network administrator will need to make more trustee assignments because rights will not automatically be granted for users to access the directories with the software applications they need.

Departmental Structure In a **departmental structure**, user home directories, shared work directories, and applications are located within the workgroups and departments that control them. Directories that contain files available to all users are located at the root of the volume. Figure 5-16 shows the organization of directories for a DATA volume using a departmental structure. A SHARED directory is located at the root of the DATA volume to contain files used by the entire organization. The SHARED work directories located in each workgroup's directory structure provide separate shared file access for each department. A major difference between the departmental- and application-oriented structures is the location of the user home directories. Notice in Figure 5-16 that the user home directories are located under each department directory rather than placed all together under a general USERS directory.

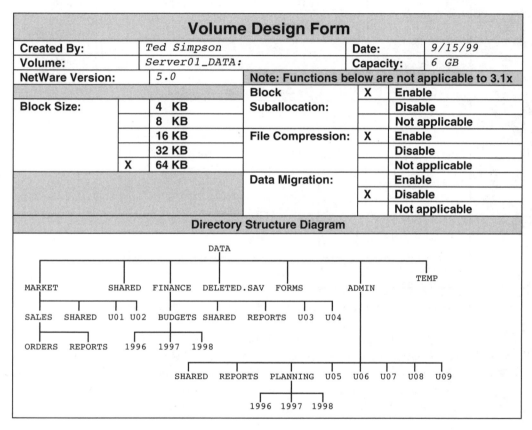

Figure 5-16 DATA volume with a departmental structure

Combined Structure It is also possible to combine the two approaches. A common way of doing this is to use the departmental structure for most of the volume organization but to consolidate all user home directories in a common USER directory. This has the advantage of maintaining a logical structure for creating directories associated with departmental functions, while making user directories easier to manage by locating them in one place. CBE Labs will use this approach for the CONSTELLATION_DATA: volume, as Figure 5-17 shows.

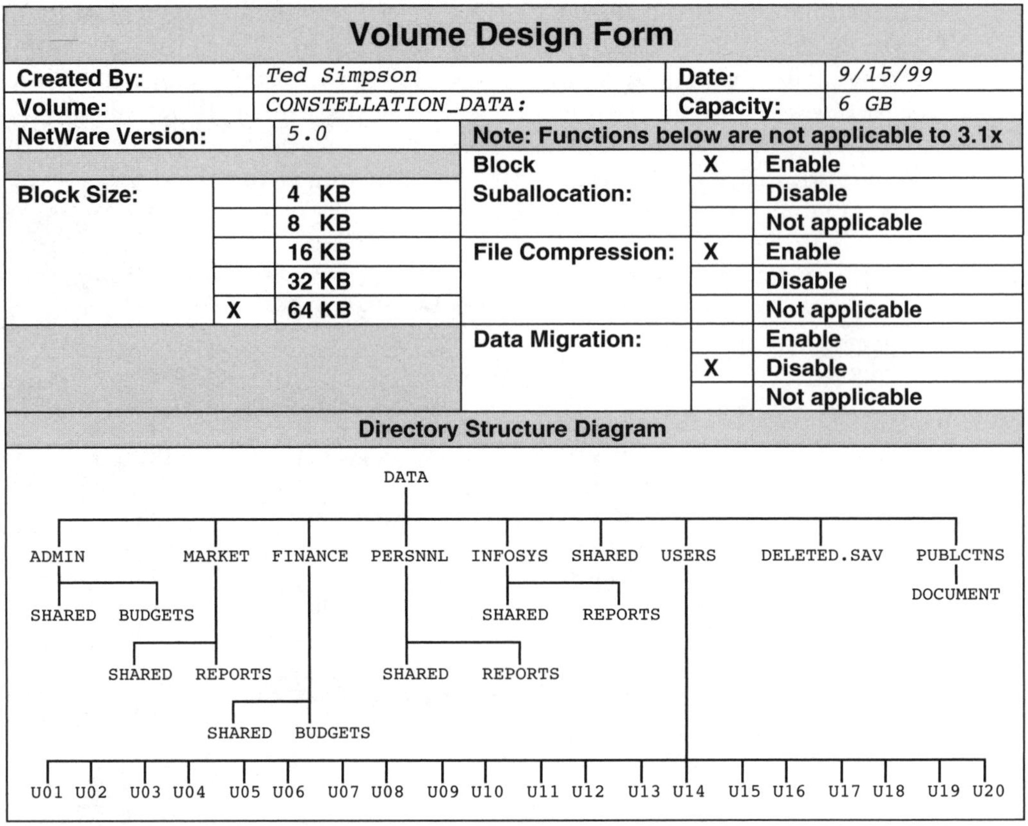

Volume Design Form

Created By:	Ted Simpson			Date:	9/15/99
Volume:	CONSTELLATION_DATA:			Capacity:	6 GB
NetWare Version:	5.0		Note: Functions below are not applicable to 3.1x		

			Block Suballocation:	X	Enable
Block Size:		4 KB			Disable
		8 KB			Not applicable
		16 KB	File Compression:	X	Enable
		32 KB			Disable
	X	64 KB			Not applicable
			Data Migration:		Enable
				X	Disable
					Not applicable

Directory Structure Diagram

Figure 5-17   CONSTELLATION_DATA: volume with a combined structure

The other CBE Labs volumes will be organized the same way, as shown in the directory structures of the SARATOGA_SYS: and SARATOGA_DATA: volumes in Figures 5-18 and 5-19. The RANGER_SYS: volume follows the same guidelines but also includes a DATA directory, because RANGER has no DATA volume. Figure 5-20 shows the RANGER_SYS: volume.

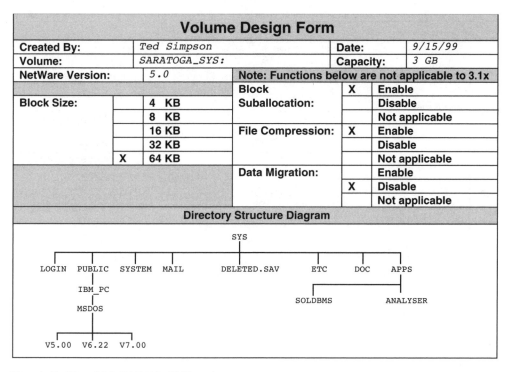

Figure 5-18   SARATOGA_SYS: volume

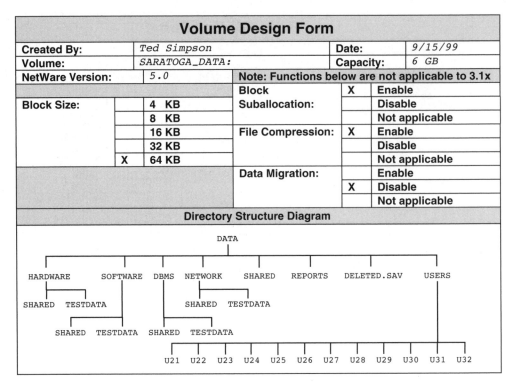

Figure 5-19   SARATOGA_DATA: volume

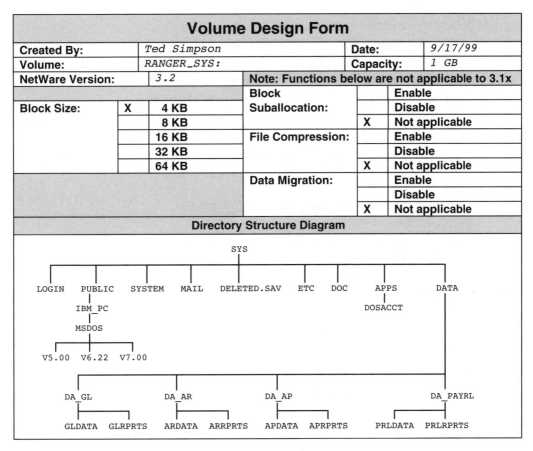

Figure 5-20 RANGER_SYS: volume

NetWare File and Directory Utilities

NetWare provides several ways to create and manipulate files and directories, as well as to view information on them. These include the Windows Explorer as well as the NetWare Services utility available through the Windows System Tray or when you right-click Network Neighborhood on the Windows desktop. NetWare also maintains support for **command line utilities**, programs you run by typing a command at the DOS prompt or from the Windows Start, Run window. One command line utility that remains useful is NDIR. This section describes the NetWare procedures using Windows and NDIR that provide information about the volumes and directory structures on a NetWare server.

Windows Explorer

You can view NetWare volumes and their contents by opening Windows Explorer, then selecting Network Neighborhood. You will then see your Directory tree object and the various servers available to you (depending on your rights). Double-click any server and the volumes within it appear on the right-hand listing.

For volume information, such as space used, purgeable space (space taken up by deleted files, which could be reused), or the number of directory entries: right-click the volume name and choose Properties. If you click the NetWare Volume Information tab, volume and directory information is presented as a pie chart, as in Figure 5-21.

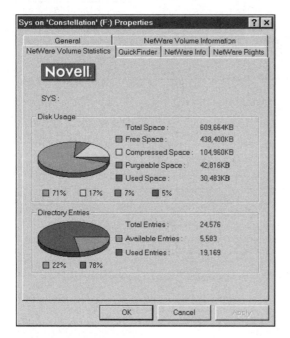

Figure 5-21   Checking volume information from Explorer

You can use Windows Explorer to reorder files by access date, size, or extension. This can simplify a copy or delete operation for multiple files or directories. As administrator, you can also modify user rights to directories by right-clicking the directory, choosing the Properties option, and selecting the NetWare Rights tab.

For file information, right-click any file stored in the NetWare volume and choose Properties. You can then view the file's attributes and your rights to it, as shown in Figure 5-22. As administrator, you can set rights for access to this file and change its attributes.

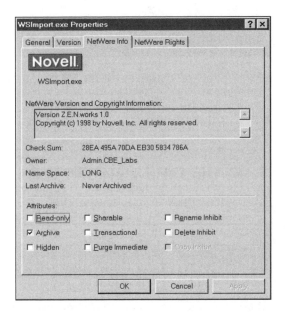

Figure 5-22   Checking file information from Explorer

The NDIR Command

NetWare's NDIR command in NetWare 5.0 is similar to, but much more powerful than, the DOS DIR command. The syntax of the NDIR command is:

```
NDIR [path] [/options] [/?] [/VER]
```

As shown in the syntax, the NDIR command has several parameters that you can use with it. These are listed in Table 5-2.

Table 5-2   NDIR command parameters

Parameter	Use This Parameter To:
path	See the directory path to the volume, directory, subdirectory, or file
/?	Access help about NDIR. If this parameter is used, all others are ignored
/VER	See the version number of the NDIR command. If this parameter is used, all others are ignored

The NDIR command has many options for sorting and display of files: by size, date of last access, or date; you can also display files created after or before a certain date. One of the most important NDIR options lets you display a list of files in directories and subdirectories by owner (that is, who created them), a capability that is currently not available with Windows Explorer. As administrator, you will need this capability to identify which users are using space on the network in which files. (NetWare Administrator can show you how much space is used, and Windows Explorer can show you who owns individual files, but you can't get both kinds of information simultaneously except through the command line utility NDIR.)

To display a list of files by owner, enter the following command at the DOS command line:

```
NDIR /SORT OW
```

NetWare will then list the files in the current directory by owner in alphabetical order. If you want to include all subdirectories as well, enter:

```
NDIR /SUB /SORT OW
```

If the directory listing is long (which is likely), you can redirect the output to a file with this command:

```
NDIR /SUB /SORT OW >dirlist.txt
```

where *dirlist.txt* can be any name you want to type so long as it is a valid filename for your server. (NetWare places the file in the directory from which you ran the command. You can then read the file using Notepad or another text editor.)

Once you have such a list, you can then examine it to determine who owns what files. You can then inform users of the files they have on the system, and get feedback on which ones can be deleted. Often people forget they have created and stored files in various locations, and other users are reluctant to delete them, so the files sit and take up space. A quick review using NDIR can find these files.

Table 5-3 lists some of the most useful options available with the NDIR command line utility.

The /sort option has a reverse function, /REV SORT *option*, in which option is one of the SORT *options* (AC, AR, CR, OW, SI. etc.). For example, NDIR /REV SORT SI would display a list of files sorted from largest to smallest (the reverse of the /SORT SI command).

Table 5-3   NDIR options

Option	Use This Option To
/VOL	See volume information
/SPA	See space information
/DO	See a list of directories only
/FO	See a list of files only
/FI	See a list of every copy of the specified files in the current directory and the directories listed in the current path
/SUB	Include all subdirectories below the specified directory
/DA	See date information
/DE	See file detail information
/R	See file attributes and user rights information
/COMP	See file compression information
/LONG	See long filenames in name spaces that support long filenames
/MAC	See Apple Macintosh files
/SORT	Sort the list of files in ascending order (A to Z, earliest to latest, smallest to largest)
/REV SORT *option*	Sort in descending order (Z to A, latest to earliest, largest to smallest)
/SORT AC	Sort by access date
/SORT AR	Sort by archive date
/SORT CR	Sort by creation or copy date
/SORT OW	Sort by owner
/SORT SI	Sort by size
/SORT UP	Sort by last update date
/SORT UN	Display without sorting (stop sorting)

The NetWare File Copy Utility

When you view your directories and files in the Windows Explorer, you can copy them in a variety of ways:

- Drag and drop the file or directory to a new location
- Right-click the file and select Copy, then Paste it to a new location
- Right-click the file, then select NetWare Copy

The first two perform a standard Windows copy operation. The NetWare Copy option is quite different, and should not be confused with Windows copy operations. NetWare

Copy preserves the rights specified for the file, whereas Windows ignores them and does not place them on the new copy of the file. Also, with NetWare Copy, all file attributes are preserved, whereas with standard Windows copy procedures NetWare file attributes are not carried over.

A file attribute is a flag, stored in the directory along with the file's name and location, that gives the file certain characteristics such as making it Read-Only, Hidden, or Sharable. By default, the NetWare Copy option copies all the file attributes supported by the target server or local hard disk. Using Windows copy procedures, in contrast, does not transfer NetWare file attributes.

Renaming Directories

A network administrator sometimes needs to change the name of an existing directory or subdirectory to make it more meaningful or to avoid conflicts with other directory or filenames. You can right-click the directory name in Windows Explorer, choose Rename, and type in the new name of the directory.

CHAPTER SUMMARY

❑ Designing and maintaining a directory structure is one of the most important jobs of a network administrator because it is the foundation of the file system on a server. The NetWare file system consists of four parts: NetWare server, volumes, directories, and files. When NetWare is installed on your servers, the seven required SYS volume and system directories are created automatically. The NetWare required directories include LOGIN, PUBLIC, SYSTEM, MAIL, DOC, ETC, and DELETED.SAV. Each serves a specific purpose. The LOGIN directory contains files and programs that are available to a workstation before the user logs in. The PUBLIC directory contains NetWare commands and utilities that are available to all users after logging in. The SYSTEM directory is the responsibility of the NetWare server administrator and contains operating system and administrator utilities. The MAIL directory is used by electronic messaging programs. The DOC directory is used by online electronic documentation. The ETC directory is used for sample and example files. The DELETED.SAV directory holds deleted files when the directory or subdirectory containing them is also deleted.

❑ In addition to the directories created by NetWare, the network administrator should create additional directories for Windows 95/98 and DOS, application software, shared data, and personal user home directories. There are two major methods of arranging these directories: by application and by department. Application-oriented structures are grouped around applications; departmental structures are grouped around workgroups. Application-oriented structures often work best in small and medium-size file systems; in large file systems with multiple workgroups and many directories and files, however, the departmental structure usually provides a better structure for directory organization.

❏ A path is used to specify the location of a file or directory in the NetWare file system. A complete path contains all components of the directory structure leading to the specified file or directory. When specifying a complete path, you use a slash to separate the NetWare server's name from the volume name and a colon to separate the volume and directory names. A partial path consists of the directories and subdirectories leading from your current default directory to the desired file or directory location.

❏ You can use the NDIR command line utility as well as Windows Explorer to provide information about files and directories in your Directory tree. The Novell Client for Windows adds some features to Windows to enhance working with the NetWare server. These include a NetWare Copy option that preserves all the NetWare attributes for files and directories. You can use Windows Explorer to access volume, directory, and file information on NetWare servers. The same tool can also rename and delete files and directories from NetWare volumes.

COMMAND SUMMARY

Command	Syntax	Definition
NDIR	NDIR *[path] [/options] [/?] [/VER]*	Displays network directory and file information including last date updated, size, and owner information. See Table 5-3 for details on these options.

KEY TERMS

absolute directory path

access rights

application-oriented structure

attributes

block

command line utilities

complete directory path

data migration

default directory

default drive

Deleted.sav directory

departmental structure

directory

directory entry table (DET)

directory path
Doc directory
Etc directory
file compression
folder
general-purpose application
global shared directory
home directory
local shared directory
Login directory
Mail directory
network file system
partial directory path
Public directory
relative directory path
spanning
subdirectory
vertical application
volume

REVIEW QUESTIONS

1. List three benefits of the NetWare file system.

2. List the file system components in sequence from major to minor.

3. A(n) _____ is a physical amount of storage on one or more hard disk drives or other storage media.

4. A volume can span up to _____ disk drives.

5. What fault tolerance capability should you consider before spanning a volume over multiple disk drives?

6. The maximum length of a volume name is _____ characters.

7. Identify each of the following as either a valid or invalid character in a volume name:

$ _____   + _____

_____   \ _____

, _____   . _____

(_____

8. _____ is the name of the required NetWare volume.

9. _____ is the directory containing NetWare utilities that all users can access before they log in.

10. The _____ directory contains files and utilities available only to the administrator.

11. When you compare a network file system to a file cabinet, which file system component corresponds to each of the following?

    cabinet: _____   **hanging folder:** _____

    drawer: _____   **manila file folder:** _____

12. The _____ directory contains the files used by all users after they log in.

13. The _____ directory is created in each volume to contain deleted files.

14. Briefly explain under what conditions files are placed in the DELETED.SAV directory.

15. List four types of Novell-suggested directories.

16. Given the directory structure shown in Figure 5-23, write a complete path to the JAN99.WK1 file.

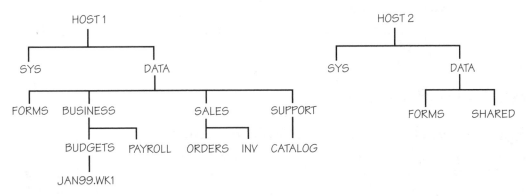

Figure 5-23

17. Use the directory structure shown in Figure 5-23 to write the steps to change your current directory from the FORMS directory of NetWare server HOST1 to the PAYROLL directory on HOST1.

18. In a(n) _____ directory structure, the user home directories are located in a common directory called USERS.

19. What is the first step in designing a directory structure?

20. Briefly describe at least one disadvantage of storing data files in the SYS volume.

21. Briefly explain two advantages of NetWare Copy over a Windows Copy.

For Questions 22 through 31, use the directory structure shown in Figure 5-23 and assume that your default directory is in the SYS volume of a NetWare server named HOST1.

22. Write the steps to display a list of all directories on the DATA volume, along with your effective rights.

23. Write the steps to find a file named BUDGET99.WK1 in the BUSINESS directory of the NetWare server HOST1.

24. What utility or utilities would you use to determine the amount of space used by deleted files in the DATA volume?

25. Write the steps to determine how much space in the DATA volume is occupied by the BUSINESS directory and all its subdirectories.

26. Write the steps to copy all files with the .DOC extension from the FORMS directory of the HOST2 NetWare server to the FORMS directory on the DATA volume of server HOST1.

27. Write the steps to list all files in the DATA volume that are larger than 1 MB.

28. Write the steps to rename the INV subdirectory of SALES to INVENTORY.

29. Write the steps to change your default directory to the FORMS directory of the HOST2 NetWare server.

30. Write the steps to list all the files in the ORDERS subdirectory on the DATA volume sorted by size.

31. Write the steps to list all the files in the CATALOG subdirectory that were updated after June 30, 1999.

HANDS-ON PROJECTS

Project 5-1: Checking Volume Information

In this project you use the Windows Explorer and/or NDIR to obtain volume information about a NetWare server on your network. As a network administrator, you need to know how to use the information this command provides to make such decisions as determining a location on the NetWare server in which there is room to install a new application.

1. Use Windows Explorer and/or NDIR to fill in the table that follows for each of the volumes on your NetWare server.

   Steps/utilities used: _____

	Bytes	Percent
Total volume space		
Space used by entries		
Deleted space not yet purgeable		
Space remaining on volume		

2. Use Windows Explorer and/or NDIR to determine the following information about the SYS volume.

   Steps/utilities used: _____

   Amount of space in use by compressed files: _____

   Amount of space saved by compressed files: _____

   Amount of space available in the volume: _____

3. Calculate the available amount of unused disk space without any deleted files being purged. Record the amount here:_____

4. Use the information from Step 3 to answer the following question: Will saving a 100 KB file on the SYS volume require reclaiming space from deleted files? Briefly explain your reasoning.

5. Using the information you recorded in Steps 1–3, write a memo to your instructor describing the result of your work. Include the information you recorded is Steps 1–3 in your memo.

Project 5-2: Checking Directory Space

Use Windows Explorer and/or NDIR to determine the amount of disk space available at the root of your NetWare server's SYS volume.

Steps/utilities used: _____

	Restrictions	In Use	Available
Volume			
User volume restrictions			
Directory restrictions at the root			

Turn in a copy of this form to your instructor.

Project 5-3: Checking Directory Information

Use Windows Explorer or NDIR to determine the amount of disk space used by each of the directories on the root of your NetWare server's SYS volume.

Steps used: _____

Enter the information you found in the following table.

Directory Name	Space Used

Turn in a copy of this form to your instructor.

Project 5-4: Checking Directory Structure

Use Windows Explorer to list the directory structure of the UAS\EXAMPLE directory. Use a copy of the Volume Design Form (see Figure 5-11 or Appendix B) to document all subdirectories in the UAS\EXAMPLE directory structure. Turn in a copy of this form to your instructor.

Steps used: _____

Project 5-5: Obtaining NetWare File and Directory Information

1. Use Windows Explorer or the NDIR command to determine which volume contains the UAS directory.

   Steps used: _____

   Volume containing UAS: _____

2. Use Windows Explorer or the NDIR command to display all files with the file-name extension .DOC that are located in the UAS\EXAMPLE directory structure.

   Steps used: _____

3. Use Windows Explorer or the NDIR command to display all files with the file-name extension .DOC that are located in the UAS\EXAMPLE directory structure, showing date information.

   Steps used: _____

4. Use Windows Explorer or the NDIR command to display all files with the file-name extension .DOC that are located in the UAS\EXAMPLE directory structure, showing attributes and rights information.

   Steps used: _____

5. Use Windows Explorer or the NDIR command to display all files with the file-name extension .DOC that are located in the UAS\EXAMPLE directory structure, showing detailed information for each file.

   Steps used: _____

6. Use Windows Explorer or the NDIR command to display all files with the file-name extension .DOC that are located in the UAS\EXAMPLE directory structure, displaying files only.

   Steps used: _____

7. Use Windows Explorer or NDIR to display all files with the filename extension .DOC that are located in the UAS\EXAMPLE directory structure, sorted by size.

   Steps used: _____

8. Use Windows Explorer or NDIR to display all files with the filename extension .DOC that are located in the UAS\EXAMPLE directory structure and that were last updated after January 1, 1999.

   Steps used: _____

9. Turn in your results to your instructor.

Project 5-6: Working with Explorer and NetWare Copy

In this exercise you will practice using the Windows Explorer and the NetWare Copy option to find files and then copy those files into the directories you have created. You will then use Explorer to verify that the files have been copied successfully into the specified directory locations.

1. Change to your ##ADMIN directory and create a subdirectory named LETTERS.

2. Suppose you need to copy all Microsoft Word document files from the SYS volume into the LETTERS subdirectory you just created. Because Microsoft Word uses a .DOC extension, you can use Windows Explorer Arrange option to find and display all the Word filenames. Record these steps and the path to the DOC files.

3. Use the NetWare Copy option to copy the .DOC files you recorded in Step 2 into the LETTERS directory you created. Record the steps you used.

4. Use Windows Explorer to rename the directory LETTERS to DOCS. Record the steps you used.

CASE PROJECTS

Case 5-1: Creating a Network File Structure for the Jefferson County Courthouse

The Jefferson County Courthouse network is proceeding according to plan. The network proposal is still for just the 12 users in the Social Services section. The 12 users include program administrator Janet Hinds, her assistant Tom Norihama, receptionist Lisa Walsh, department secretary Terry Smith, and 8 social workers. The group will use one NetWare 5.0 server.

From discussions with Janet, the following decisions have been made:

1. The NetWare server will have only one volume, a 6 GB SCSI drive.

2. The county is providing a license for a Windows-based suite of software that includes a word processor, an electronic spreadsheet, and a presentation graphics program. No personal database program is included in this package. This program is named Office99, and the three programs are abbreviated as WP, SS, and PG.

3. The county has purchased a database management system named DBSys and has contracted for an application to be developed in DBSys that can be used to track the social services workers' cases. DBSys requires a directory named DBSys, and the application requires a subdirectory named Tracker under that directory. In addition, a data directory named Trkrdata is required, and this directory must have three subdirectories named TForms, TTables, and TReports.

4. The staff needs a SHARED directory and a REPORTS directory that all members of the staff can access.

5. Each member of the staff requires a HOME directory that only he or she can access.

Create a proposed network file system for the Jefferson County Courthouse. Document your proposal with a NetWare Server Planning Form, a Directory Planning Form, Volume Design Forms, and Directory Design Forms as needed (see Appendix B). Turn in the proposal to your instructor in memo form, with copies of your work forms attached.

Case 5-2: Creating a Network File Structure for J. Q. Adams Corporation

The J. Q. Adams network development is proceeding according to plan. The network will use two NetWare 5.0 servers. One will be dedicated to administration and one to production. The J. Q. Adams Corporation organization chart is shown in Chapter 4, Figure 4-29.

From discussions with Donna Hulbert, the president of J. Q. Adams, the following decisions have been made:

1. Each NetWare server has two volumes: SYS and DATA. Each is a 4 GB SCSI drive.

2. The company has purchased a license for a Windows-based suite of software that includes a word processor, an electronic spreadsheet, and a presentation graphics program. There is no personal database program included in this package. This program is named Office99, and the three programs are abbreviated as WP, SS, and PG. This application will reside on the administration NetWare server.

3. The company has purchased an accounting system named AcctSys. This application and all its data will reside on the administration NetWare server. This application requires a program directory named AcctSys. It also requires a data directory named ASdata, and this directory must have subdirectories named AS_GL, AS_AP, AS_AR, and AS_PR.

4. The company has purchased an inventory tracking system that will reside on the production NetWare server. Named InvTrack, this application requires a program directory named InvTrack. In addition, it requires a data directory named ITdata, and this directory must have subdirectories named ITForms, ITTables, and ITRprts.

5. The staff needs a SHARED directory and a REPORTS directory that all members of the staff can access on the administration server.

6. Each member of the staff requires a HOME directory on the administration server that only they can access.

Create a proposed network file system for the J. Q. Adams Corporation. Document your proposal with a NetWare Server Planning Form, a Directory Planning Form, Volume Design Forms, and Directory Design Forms as needed (see Appendix B). Turn in the proposal to your instructor in memo form, with copies of your work forms attached.

5

6

INSTALLING NETWARE 5.0

In this chapter, you will learn:

♦ Describe the steps involved in installing NetWare on the server

♦ Identify and load common disk and LAN drivers

♦ Use the NetWare Install Wizard to create NetWare disk partitions and volumes

♦ Load and unload NetWare Loadable Modules (NLMs)

♦ Use NetWare console commands to check your server installation and configuration

♦ Install the software components that allow a Windows workstation to access the NetWare server

---

Now that you have designed your NDS Directory tree and network file system, you are ready to get down to the business of working with NetWare and setting up your network. A network administrator must know the software components that make the network operate and be able to configure the NetWare operating system. In this chapter you will learn about loading and running NetWare 5.0 on a server and the Novell Client software on the attached workstations.

NetWare installation can be divided into two major parts: server and workstation. The server installation includes loading the NetWare operating system on the hard drive of the server, setting up the NetWare partitions on each drive, creating volumes, loading the necessary drivers to access the network interface cards (NICs), and doing the initial work with the NDS Directory tree. Workstation installation involves loading the software and drivers on the workstations to enable them to access the NetWare server and use the network.

Although a Certified Novell Engineer (CNE) is expected to be able to install the NetWare NOS on a server, a Certified Novell Administrator (CNA) is only expected to be able to administer the installation after it is done. Therefore, in this chapter we will explain what NetWare installation accomplishes, so that you can understand the results of the installation and how it affects the network. However, we will not go through all the steps of the installation in detail.

On the other hand, a CNA is expected to be able to install client software on the workstations. The current Novell Client is available in versions for DOS, Windows 3.1x, and Windows 95/98. It makes full use of the 32-bit computing power of current microprocessors, as well as using memory more effectively. In this chapter you will learn how to install and configure Novell Client for Windows 95/98.

NETWARE NETWORK OPERATING SYSTEM INSTALLATION

There are eight main steps in installing NetWare 5.0 on a server:

1. Define and document the network layout and hardware configuration of your server.

2. Install NetWare server hardware and configure the hardware.

3. Partition and install DOS on the bootable hard drive.

4. Launch the NetWare Install Wizard and perform the steps under DOS.

5. Complete the NetWare installation under the NetWare NOS, including:
   - Load disk and CD-ROM drivers.
   - Load LAN drivers and protocols.
   - Create NetWare hard drive partitions and volumes.

6. Install Novell Directory Services.

7. Create and modify startup configuration files STARTUP.NCF and AUTOEXEC.NCF.

8. Choose optional installation options.

In the following sections, we will discuss these steps and their effects on the NetWare server.

Defining and Documenting the NetWare Server Environment

Before you start the NetWare server installation, you must properly document the network system and hardware configuration of your server. Chapters 4 and 5 covered the initial parts of the NetWare server installation plan, planning the NDS Directory tree, and preparing the network file system volume and directory design forms. Now you need to complete the plan by documenting the network layout and NetWare server hardware configuration.

Defining the Network Layout

Defining the network layout requires understanding and documenting the network system in which the NetWare server will be installed. A **network layout** consists of the following components:

- The NetWare server's name and internal network number
- The network topology and network cards used
- The IP address of each device on the network where the NetWare server is to be connected
- The frame type to be used on each network cable system

Most of this information you can obtain by walking around the existing network or by making decisions on installation. A good way to do this on existing networks is to make a simple pencil sketch of the network system, which will include the network layout information. Figure 6-1 illustrates a network plan consisting of a NetWare server attached to a single Ethernet 10BaseT hub.

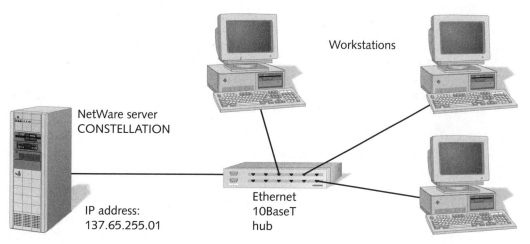

Figure 6-1   Network with a single NetWare server

A **NetWare server name** is a unique identification of the server, distinguishing it from other machines on the network. It is important for each NetWare server to have a name that is both meaningful and unique. When assigning a NetWare server name, consider including the location and function of the NetWare server as part of its name. For example, the primary NetWare server at F. D. Roosevelt Investments could be named FDR_Server01.

NetWare server names can be from 2 to 47 characters long and can include any alphanumeric character, hyphens, and underscores. You cannot use spaces in the server name. The following characters also are not allowed:

= < > [ ] " * + , ? | : ; / \

Valid NetWare server names include FDR_Server01, CONSTELLATION, and FDR_NW-50_Server. However, FDR Server01 (using a space instead of an underscore), FDR+Server01 (using the + symbol), and FDR[Server01] (using square brackets) are not valid names.

In addition, a NetWare server must be assigned a unique **internal network number**. The NetWare operating system uses this number for communication among its device drivers. Although you can assign your own internal network number, most installations use the random server number suggested by the NetWare installation program. Some network administrators use the server program's serial number as the internal network number. This keeps the serial number handy when you need to contact Novell for NetWare operating system software upgrades.

Both the NetWare server name and the internal network number are unique, so either is sufficient by itself to identify the NetWare server. However, they are used for different purposes: users refer to the NetWare server by name (while accessing resources in the tree, for example), whereas the network software uses the internal network number.

Chapter 3 defined a network address as a number assigned to each LAN system. The number is used to route packets between networks. With Novell IPX, a unique network address consisting of from one to eight hexadecimal digits must be assigned to each frame type used on each NIC. LAN addresses are necessary because several LANs may be connected to a common backbone to form an internetwork or may be joined via telephone lines to form a WAN. However, because TCP/IP has become standardized as the network protocol, NetWare now distinguishes resources using their unique IP addresses.

In addition to using IP addresses, a network must have one or more packet frame types assigned to it. As Chapter 3 explained, a frame type defines the formatting of the physical packet that is transmitted over the network. It does not matter if the network is IP-only, IPX-only, or a mixture of both. All typically use one or two packet frame types. To communicate on the network, all machines must use the same frame type. Several popular packet frame types are in use. NetWare 5.0 defaults to using Ethernet_II, which supports IP. The two most common Ethernet frame types used with NetWare in the past are IEEE 802.3 and IEEE 802.2. IEEE 802.2 is a more up-to-date frame type than 802.3 and is the default for NetWare 5.0 when using IPX. If you are installing a NetWare server on an existing network with machines that use IEEE 802.3, you can convert all workstations and servers to IEEE 802.2 or you can load both frame types on your new server.

Loading two frame types is a good temporary solution until you can get all machines converted to IEEE 802.2. This approach slows down performance, however, because each frame type must be treated as a separate logical network.

Adding a second NetWare server to an existing network creates a **multiple NetWare server network**, as Figure 6-2 shows. Although each NetWare server is given a unique name and IP address (or internal network number with IPX), they both use the same network address and frame type for the LAN cable system on which they communicate.

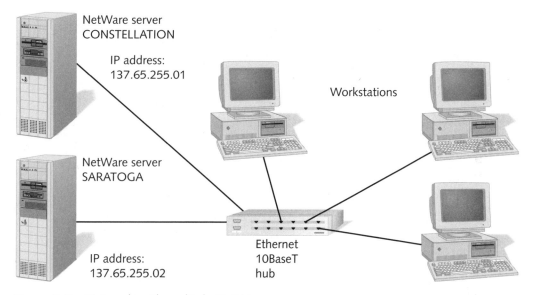

Figure 6-2   Network with multiple NetWare servers

Multiple networks can be connected to form an internetwork. As discussed in Chapter 3, an **internetwork** consists of networks connected by bridges and routers. Figure 6-3 illustrates an internetwork created by adding a different network topology to the system. Notice that each network cable system in the internetwork is assigned a different network address. The NetWare server SUPERIOR is referred to as an internal router because it transfers packets between networks in addition to performing its NetWare server activities.

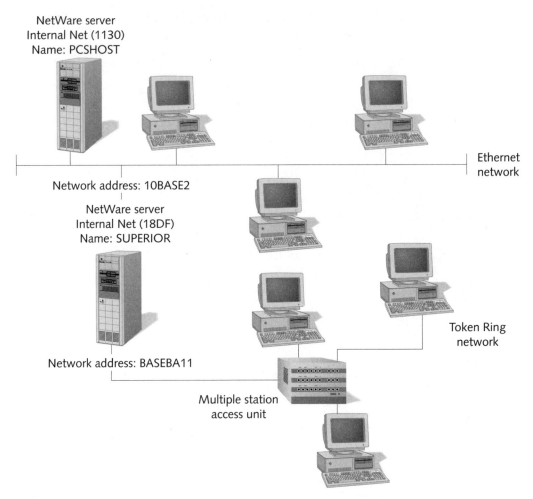

NetWare server
Internal Net (1130)
Name: PCSHOST

Network address: 10BASE2

NetWare server
Internal Net (18DF)
Name: SUPERIOR

Network address: BASEBA11

Ethernet
network

Token Ring
network

Multiple station
access unit

Figure 6-3   Sample internetwork with Token Ring and Ethernet

Completing the NetWare Server Worksheet

After you have identified the network system, you should record the NetWare server's name and internal network number, along with the network address and frame type for each network card to be placed in the NetWare server. During installation you also will need the following NetWare server hardware information:

- Name of the disk driver program for each disk controller card
- Each disk controller card's settings, including interrupt and I/O port
- Capacity and configuration of each hard drive attached to a disk controller
- Name of the network card driver program to be used with each network card

- Each network card's settings, including interrupt, I/O port, and memory address range

- IP information, including IP address, subnet address, and gateway

You can find this information in the documentation supplied with the NetWare server and network cards. If you cannot find it there, your hardware vendor can provide the necessary hardware settings. This information is best documented by completing a NetWare server worksheet like the one shown in Table 6-1. (A blank copy of this worksheet appears in Appendix B.)

6

NETWARE SERVER WORKSHEET							
Installed by:	Ted Simpson						
NetWare Server Name:	CONSTELLATION		**Internal Network Number:**		CBELAB01		
SYSTEM INFORMATION							
Computer Manufacturer:	HP		**Model:**		NetServer 5/133 LF		
CPU:	Pentium		**Clock Speed:**		133 MHz		
Memory Installed:	64 MB		**Bus:**		ISA/PCI		
DISK INFORMATION							
Disk Controller 1							
Type:	IDE		**Mfg:**		**Model:**		
Interrupt:	14 (E Hex)		**I/O Address:**	1F0	**DMA Channel:**	None	
Memory Address:							
Disk Driver Name:	IDEHD.CDM						
Drive Address	**Type**	**Mfg**	**Cyl/Hd /Sec**	**Speed/ Capacity**	**Partition Size** DOS	NetWare	**Mirrored with drive**
Disk Controller 2							
Type:	SCSI		**Mfg:**	Adaptec	**Model:**	2740	
Interrupt:	5		**I/O Address:**	340h	**DMA Channel:**	3	
Memory Address:							
Disk Driver Name:	AIC7770.CDM						
Drive Address	**Type**	**Mfg**	**Cyl/Hd /Sec**	**Speed/ Capacity**	**Partition Size** DOS	NetWare	**Mirrored with drive**
0	SCSI	HP		12 ms/2.03 GB	100 MB	1.9 GB	None
1	SCSI	HP		12 ms/2.03 GB		2.03 GB	None
NETWORK CARD INFORMATION							
Network Type	**Mfg**	**LAN Driver**	**I/O Port**	**Memory Address**	**IRQ/DMA**	**Frame Type**	**Network Address**
Ethernet	Intel	E100S.LAN	300	0D000	10/ None	802.2/ 802.3	CBELAB01
IP INFORMATION							
IP Address:	137.65.285.155		**Subnet Address:**	255.255.252.0	**Gateway:**	137.65.255.254	
NON-NETWORK DEVICE INFORMATION							
Device Name	**IRQ**	**I/O Port**	**DMA**	**Memory Address**			
COM1	4	3F8-3FF					

Table 6-1   NetWare Server Worksheet

The NetWare Server Worksheet has six main sections: identification, system information, disk information, network card information, IP information, and non–network device information. In the identification section, record the installer's name, the name of the NetWare server, and the internal network number.

In the system information section, enter the make and model of the computer, the microprocessor type, clock speed, memory capacity, and types of expansion slots. Although you won't need this information during NetWare installation, you do need to know that your NetWare server meets or exceeds the minimum requirements for the NetWare version you are installing (you learned the minimum requirements for a NetWare 5.0 server in Chapter 2). This information is also useful after initial installation if you install additional server options or upgrade the NetWare server software.

The disk information section of the NetWare Server Worksheet contains documentation for up to two disk controller cards in your NetWare server. You will need this information when you install the NetWare server. In addition, the capacity and partition size information for each disk drive is helpful in planning disk mirroring and duplexing. (Disk mirroring or duplexing requires that each mirrored NetWare partition be the same size.) The settings for the cylinder, head, and sector of IDE disk drives are stored in the CMOS. You may need this information to reconfigure the CMOS after a battery or system failure.

 Recording this information isn't just for your own knowledge. System failures frequently occur during vacations or weekends when the administrator is not accessible. Having hardware configuration information available on site can speed the recovery process and avoid user discomfort while the network is off line. Many common IDE/ATA drive specifications are now available on the Web at the drive vendor's Web site, as a further resource.

The NetWare server described in Table 6-1 contains both an IDE and a SCSI controller card. The IDE controller card manages the 3.5-inch floppy disk and a CD-ROM drive. The SCSI controller card manages a large-capacity drive for the SYS and DATA volumes, and a tape backup system.

You need the controller card information to load the correct disk driver software during installation and to provide NetWare with the necessary configuration parameters. In addition, knowing the hardware configuration information, such as interrupt, I/O port, and DMA channel, will help you avoid hardware conflicts when you install other hardware, such as LAN cards.

One of the first steps in installing NetWare on a server is loading the correct disk driver program to give the NetWare operating system access to the server's hard drives. The Install Wizard will auto-detect most common controllers and disk drives during the configuration process. You will need to verify that the Wizard has correctly identified your hardware, but you won't have to go hunting for drivers as in the past.

It is often the network administrator's job to install network cards in the NetWare server and workstation computers. The network card information portion of the NetWare server worksheet contains important information identifying the network cards to be installed in the server, along with their configurations. Your first concern is to obtain cards that are appropriate for the network system you are installing and to ensure that the network cards are certified by Novell to work with your version of NetWare.

 Do not trust a vendor's or reseller's promise that their "plug-and-play" PCI card will work with NetWare. Even when the card is listed as approved for NetWare, it may have only been tested with one brand of PCI systemboard. You may end up spending hours trying to get NetWare to recognize a "plug-and-play" card without success. Your best bet is to use known brands and to ask for configurations the reseller or hardware vendor has already tested.

Next you will need to identify the correct network card driver to load during NetWare installation. This will enable NetWare to send and receive packets. To help you load the correct driver, Novell has included network card drivers for many of the common network cards, shown in Table 6-2. If you have one of the network cards listed or if the documentation that came with your card tells you to use a certain driver, record the name of the LAN driver on the NetWare server worksheet.

Table 6-2   Common NetWare network interface card drivers

Cabling System	Network Interface Card	Driver Name
Ethernet	Intel Ethernet Pro 10	EPRO.LAM
	MicroDyne NE/2 MicroDyne NE/2T	NE2.LAN
	MicroDyne NE2-32	NE2_32.LAN
	MicroDyne NE1000 (Assy 950-054401) MicroDyne NE1000 (Assy 810-160-001)	NE1000.LAN
	MicroDyne NE1500T	NE1500T.LAN
	MicroDyne NE2000 MicroDyne NE2000T	NE2000.LAN
	MicroDyne NE2100 (Assy 810-000209)	NE2100.LAN
	MicroDyne NE3200	NE3200.LAN
	MicroDyne NE32HUB	NE32HUB.LAN
	SMC 8100	SMC8100.LAN
	SMC 8232	SMC8232.LAN
	SMC 8332	SMC8332.LAN
	3COM 3C503	3C503.LAN
	3COM 3C509	3C5X9.LAN
	3COM 3C770	3C770.LAN
Token Ring	MicroDyne NTR2000	NTR2000.LAN
	IBM Token Ring	TOKEN.LAN

To avoid hardware conflicts with other devices in the computer, each NIC installed in the NetWare server must be set to use a unique interrupt, I/O port, and memory address. Because you may need to enter these hardware settings when first installing the card driver, it is useful to document, on the NetWare server worksheet, the interrupt, I/O port, and memory address of each network card.

Because IP is NetWare's native protocol, you will need to record information about your computer's IP address for future reference. Each device using IP must have its own unique addressing information. If two devices have the same IP address, they will not be able to connect with the network..

 It's important to record your IP information. It is not easy to reconstruct the information if your network administrator is not available or months have passed since you configured your machine. Unlike drive specifications or drivers, this information cannot be obtained from a vendor's Web site or documentation, because each site has a unique IP address.

The determination and selection of IP addresses is beyond the scope of this book. Typically, these addresses are assigned by your MIS department or network administrator, to coordinate with the rest of your network's IP addresses as well as to facilitate connecting to the Internet. If your network is an isolated system that won't be connected to another IP network such as the Internet, you can use some defaults in assigning IP addresses: 128.0.0.1 for your IP address, 255.255.255.0 for the subnet mask, and you can leave the Gateway blank.

The non-network device information of the NetWare server worksheet lets you document other devices and controller cards that are currently in the system. This information helps you avoid any current or future hardware interrupt conflicts.

NetWare Server Installation

After you have identified the network system and hardware specifications and filled out the NetWare server worksheet, you are ready to roll up your sleeves and start the NetWare installation. The time spent planning and documenting the network and NetWare server environment will pay off by helping you avoid problems caused by loading wrong drivers or entering incorrect card configurations.

NetWare Server Preparation

Before installing the NetWare NOS, you must install all the necessary hardware. If your NetWare server is not shipped to you with all the hardware installed (such as disk drives, CD-ROMs, disk controller cards, and NICs), you will need to install and configure them. The manufacturer of the hardware will provide the necessary instructions and materials. (Typically, you will do this to add an additional hard drive or an NIC to the existing hardware.)

Before you launch the Install Wizard, you should know that NetWare 5.0's Server CD-ROM is bootable. Most CD-ROM drives require the operating system to load drivers in order to read data from a CD-ROM disc. However, the latest drives now include firmware that allows a CD-ROM drive to act as a boot drive, just as a floppy disk drive can. This specification, called El Torito, comes with some Compaq PCs as well as PCs from other vendors. If your hardware supports the El Torito specification on the CD-ROM drive, you can have the soon-to-be NetWare server system boot from the CD-ROM itself. This can eliminate having to create a DOS partition, because the Install Wizard will automatically create one for you. However, because the El Torito specification is quite new, your system may not contain a bootable CD-ROM drive. For this reason, we will cover the more common procedure of creating your own partition here.

6

The NetWare 5.0 Install Wizard will run only from DOS, not from Windows or the MS-DOS prompt in Windows. If you have Windows installed on the hard drive, you must remove it and create a new DOS partition before continuing. For this, you will need a DOS setup disk. Novell suggests a minimum DOS partition of 50 MB. However, it is recommended that you create a larger DOS partition to store a core dump for diagnostic purposes. Therefore, you should have at least a 100 to 150 MB DOS partition.

A core dump needs about 1 MB of disk space in the DOS partition for every 1 MB of RAM in the NetWare server. So the minimum is 64 MB of space, plus the 30 Novell recommends as a base, for a total of 100 MB for the DOS partition. More RAM will need more disk space.

It is best not to use the DOS that comes with Windows 95/98 or NT to create a boot disk or to format a DOS partition using FDISK and FORMAT. Some users have reported that NetWare will not install on a hard disk formatted and configured using Windows "DOS." Therefore, you must create your DOS partition using the DOS utilities on the NetWare 5.0 License disk or with an earlier version of DOS. DR-DOS, MS-DOS, and PC-DOS 3.x, 4.x, 5.x, 6.x, and 7.x are all compatible with NetWare 5.0. The floppy disk includes the appropriate COMMAND.COM, FDISK.EXE, FORMAT.EXE and EDIT.EXE files to create your partition. (You need EDIT to create CONFIG.SYS and AUTOEXEC.BAT files to load your CD-ROM drivers.)

Although DOS is initially used to boot the NetWare server, once NetWare is started NetWare functions as a completely separate operating system that directly controls the computer hardware.

The final step in preparing the NetWare server is making sure that the date and time have been set accurately in the CMOS. NetWare 5.0 will use this information when the NOS takes control of the server.

NetWare Installation Methods

You can install NetWare 5.0 from a CD-ROM in a CD-ROM drive in the server, or from a copy of NetWare 5.0 located on another server on the network (either from a CD-ROM in a CD-ROM drive or from files copied onto a server volume). If another NetWare server is available on the network, installing from files copied to a volume on that NetWare server is the fastest installation method. In this chapter, we assume that only one new NetWare server is available. Therefore, we will discuss using a CD-ROM in a CD-ROM drive for NetWare server installation. The CD-ROM drive should have been installed and configured as part of the hardware installation of the NetWare server.

 Don't forget that if you reformat the hard drive to create a new DOS partition and blank space for NetWare, you will also erase your CD-ROM drivers. Copy those to a floppy before reformatting.

Customizing the Installation

Novell provides two options for installing NetWare 5.0 on a new NetWare server: a simple installation and a custom installation. Simple installation means you accept the defaults that the Install Wizard provides for your network. Normally, these are perfectly acceptable on a small network. Customizing the installation gives the network administrator more control, by enabling him or her to specifically name or set configuration options that NetWare handles automatically during a simple installation. In this chapter, you will learn about the defaults as well as when you can customize a particular parameter.

The First NetWare 5.0 Server in the NDS Directory Tree

Now that the NetWare server is ready, you can install the NetWare 5.0 NOS. If this is the first copy of NetWare 5.0 installed in your network, this installation will create Novell Directory Services (NDS) for the network. This includes creating and naming the NDS Directory tree and the NDS administrator. When additional NetWare 5.0 servers are installed in the network, they are added into the existing NDS Directory tree and are administered by the previously created network administrator.

The Character-Based Portion of the Installation

You begin the NetWare installation by running the INSTALL.BAT program from the CD-ROM at the DOS prompt. This launches the character-based portion of the Install Wizard, which is responsible for the following functions:

- Initiating a NetWare server installation

- Letting the user select a New Server install or an upgrade of an existing NetWare NOS to NetWare 5.0

- Copying NetWare DOS files to the DOS partition of the bootup hard drive of the NetWare server

- Letting the user specify a language, mouse, and video type for the NetWare server

- Creating the **STARTUP.NCF** file to load appropriate hardware drivers

- Creating the **AUTOEXEC.NCF** file to load additional drivers

- Adding to the AUTOEXEC.BAT file the ability to automatically start the NetWare server

After you type Install and press [Enter], NetWare will display a screen showing the product logo and version number. The Install Wizard program will display the licensing agreement. If you accept this agreement, the Install Wizard will check to make sure the available hardware is capable of running NetWare, that is, if there is enough RAM and hard disk space, and if the processor is fast enough. If Install Wizard finds any deficiencies, it will alert you to them, but will not stop the installation. You will need to use the Tab key to highlight OK and then press [Enter] to acknowledge the deficiency. Install Wizard will move you on and ask you to specify what type of installation this is, upgrade or new server, as shown in Figure 6-4.

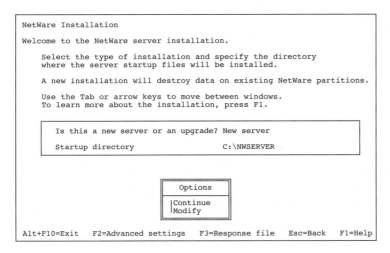

```
NetWare Installation

Welcome to the NetWare server installation.

    Select the type of installation and specify the directory
    where the server startup files will be installed.

    A new installation will destroy data on existing NetWare partitions.

    Use the Tab or arrow keys to move between windows.
    To learn more about the installation, press F1.


    Is this a new server or an upgrade? New server

    Startup directory                   C:\NWSERVER


                        Options
                       Continue
                       Modify

Alt+F10=Exit   F2=Advanced settings   F3=Response file   Esc=Back   F1=Help
```

Figure 6-4   New Server selection screen

Install Wizard also asks you if you want NetWare to place its startup files into the default directory of C:\NWSERVER. (You can choose to modify the default directory path, but this should rarely be necessary.) The default is for New Server, so you can choose Continue.

You must use the keyboard to access the Continue option, because in this part of the installation the mouse driver is not yet available.

You now specify the language that NetWare will use. The language configuration specifies the country, a code page to indicate the language to be displayed, and a keyboard mapping for keyboards other than standard U.S. English. Accept the defaults—Country Code 001 (United States), Code Page 437 (U.S. English), and standard U.S. keyboard—or modify these to match your country and language. See Figure 6-5.

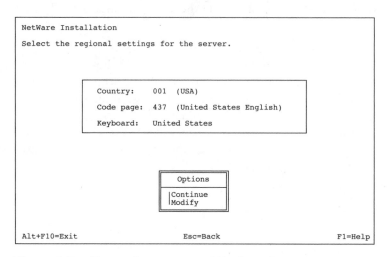

```
NetWare Installation

Select the regional settings for the server.



            Country:     001   (USA)

            Code page:   437   (United States English)

            Keyboard:    United States




                  Options
                 |Continue
                 |Modify


Alt+F10=Exit                 Esc=Back              F1=Help
```

Figure 6-5   Choose Language and Keyboard screen

When you start NetWare 5.0, it runs two special startup files: STARTUP.NCF and AUTOEXEC.NCF (the extension NCF stands for **NetWare Command File)**. These files are similar to the old DOS files CONFIG.SYS and AUTOEXEC.BAT. The installation program gives you a chance to add SET commands to STARTUP.NCF. **SET commands** are used to control NetWare performance parameters. STARTUP.NCF and AUTOEXEC.NCF are automatically created during installation, and the necessary commands are included in these files based on your actions during installation. You will have an opportunity to edit both files later in the installation, so there is no need to add special SET commands at this time.

NetWare also modifies the server's AUTOEXEC.BAT file so that the NetWare 5.0 NOS automatically starts when the server is rebooted. This is done by adding the line

SERVER.EXE

to the AUTOEXEC.BAT file. This is a convenience (it eliminates an extra step at booting) but also a security measure—there is less opportunity for someone to manipulate the server from the DOS prompt.

If you wish to access the DOS prompt instead of automatically launching NetWare 5.0, you can specify that the AUTOEXEC.BAT file not be modified to include SERVER.EXE as the last command. To do this, press F2 (Advanced settings) in the NetWare Installation screen shown in Figure 6-4, select the Load Server at Reboot option, and change it to NO (the default is YES).

NetWare now asks you to accept the mouse and video drivers for your system. Again, unless your worksheet specifies a different mouse or video (for example, VGA and not SVGA), accept these defaults as shown in Figure 6-6.

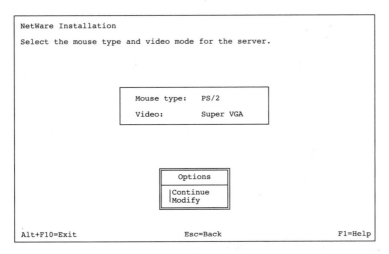

Figure 6-6   Choose mouse and video type screen

NetWare now performs an automatic hardware detection on your system. In Figure 6-7, the system includes an Adaptec 2940 SCSI host adapter (AHA2940). (The other two optional features you don't need to worry about in basic installations.) Your adapter should appear here. If it does not, or the adapter is different from the one you have listed on your worksheet, you can change this driver using the Modify option.

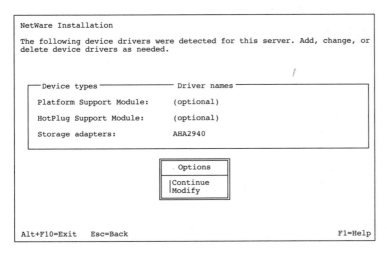

Figure 6-7   Specific adapter type screen

NetWare now looks for the specific devices attached to the host adapter as well as for any installed network cards. It will display the default choices onscreen, as shown in Figure 6-8.

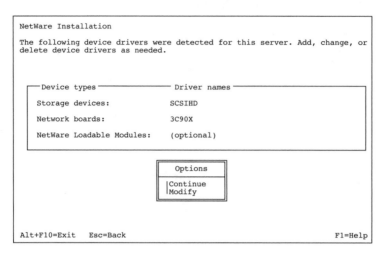

```
NetWare Installation

The following device drivers were detected for this server. Add, change, or
delete device drivers as needed.


  ┌─Device types ──────────── Driver names ─────────────┐
  │ Storage devices:            SCSIHD                   │
  │                                                      │
  │ Network boards:             3C90X                    │
  │                                                      │
  │ NetWare Loadable Modules:   (optional)               │
  │                                                      │
  └──────────────────────────────────────────────────────┘

                    ┌─── Options ───┐
                    │ |Continue      │
                    │ |Modify        │
                    └───────────────┘

 Alt+F10=Exit    Esc=Back                            F1=Help
```

Figure 6-8   Specify storage devices dialog box

Again, if these defaults match your system, you can continue. NetWare will then ask you about creating the SYS volume using the available free space on the hard drive. The default is to use all the remaining space on the drive, as shown in Figure 6-9. You can change this or accept it. (You can create additional volumes on other hard disks later in the installation.)

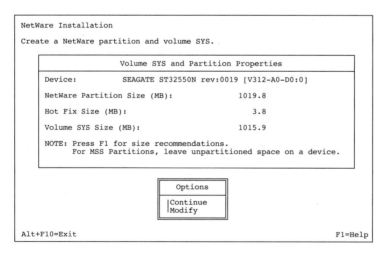

```
NetWare Installation

Create a NetWare partition and volume SYS.

        ┌──────── Volume SYS and Partition Properties ────────┐
        │ Device:          SEAGATE ST32550N rev:0019 [V312-A0-D0:0] │
        │                                                     │
        │ NetWare Partition Size (MB):        1019.8          │
        │                                                     │
        │ Hot Fix Size (MB):                     3.8          │
        │                                                     │
        │ Volume SYS Size (MB):               1015.9          │
        │                                                     │
        │ NOTE: Press F1 for size recommendations.            │
        │       For MSS Partitions, leave unpartitioned space on a device. │
        └─────────────────────────────────────────────────────┘

                    ┌─── Options ───┐
                    │ |Continue      │
                    │ |Modify        │
                    └───────────────┘

 Alt+F10=Exit                                        F1=Help
```

Figure 6-9   Specify volumes dialog box

NetWare asks that if you want to create an NSS (Novell Storage Services) volume, you leave some unpartitioned space on the hard disk. Typically, an NSS volume will be on its own drive, so don't worry if your SYS volume takes up the whole drive. (SYS cannot be an NSS volume.) NSS is new with NetWare 5.0 and is a method for creating volumes that are fast to mount even when in the hundreds or thousands of gigabytes. This is very useful for database volumes (which are often very large), since the database can't run until the whole volume mounts. With traditional volumes, NetWare takes a long time—hours, in some cases—to mount a multigigabyte volume.

If you press F3 on this screen, NetWare will display the default volume options page, as shown in Figure 6-10.

6

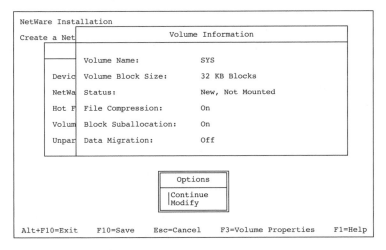

Figure 6-10 Volume Options page

This page lets you turn compression on or off (to save space, it defaults to "on"), and to specify the block size. Unless you have a reason to change the block size, accept the default NetWare chooses. After you accept the configuration for your SYS volume, NetWare will display a list of other storage devices and their drivers. This may include, for example, your CD-ROM driver (IDECD) and additional hard disk driver (SCSIHD), as shown in Figure 6-11.

```
NetWare Installation

The following device drivers were detected for this server. Add, change, or
delete device drivers as needed.


  ┌─Device types──────────────── Driver names ──────────────┐
  │                                                          │
  │  Storage devices:          IDECD,SCSIHD,SCSIMO           │
  │                                                          │
  └──────────────────────────────────────────────────────────┘



                      ┌─────────────────────┐
                      │      Options        │
                      │ ┌───────────────────│
                      │ │Continue           │
                      │ │Modify             │
                      └─┴───────────────────┘



Alt+F10=Exit    Esc=Back                              F1=Help
```

Figure 6-11   Other storage devices page

NetWare now automatically detects your network card and displays the appropriate driver. Again, if this information does not match your worksheet, you will need to change it.
However, NetWare 5.0 is quite good at detecting common network cards and includes a
wide range of drivers so you should not encounter many problems. Unfortunately, if there
will be difficulties, they will crop up here as NetWare attempts to communicate with the
board. If it cannot detect the card, NetWare will state that no card was found. This may
indicate a problem with the PCI card (try another brand—such as SMC or 3COM).

 If you find that no PCI network card will work in your particular system, don't
despair—you can still use an ISA-based card. This may reduce your network
performance somewhat, however.

Each LAN driver results in a LOAD *LANdriver* statement being created in the
AUTOEXEC.NCF file. The LOAD *LANdriver* command includes any module parameter values needed for the LAN driver to be loaded correctly. LAN drivers use the set
of module parameters listed in Table 6-3 to specify information about NICs. You can
modify the LOAD *LANdriver* commands after the installation process is finished by editing the AUTOEXEC.NCF file. Figure 6-12 shows an example of an AUTOEXEC.NCF
file with LOAD *LANdriver* commands.

Table 6-3 CDM Driver and LAN module parameters

Module Parameter	Use this parameter to
DMA = number	Set the DMA (direct memory access) channel
FRAME = frametype	Set the frame type used with the board
INT = number	Set the interrupt number (IRQ) used by the board
MEM = number	Set the memory address used by the board
NAME = name	Assign a name to this configuration of the board
PORT = number	Set the I/O (input/output) port used by the board
NODE = address	Set a node address for the board. Usually not needed since each board is encoded with a unique address
RETRIES = number	Set the number of retransmissions the board will make for frames that fail to reach their destination
SLOT = number	Specify the EISA, MCA, or PCI slot in which the board is installed on the system board

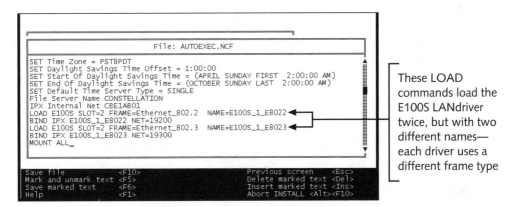

```
                        File: AUTOEXEC.NCF

SET Time Zone = PST8PDT
SET Daylight Savings Time Offset = 1:00:00
SET Start Of Daylight Savings Time = (APRIL SUNDAY FIRST  2:00:00 AM)
SET End Of Daylight Savings Time = (OCTOBER SUNDAY LAST  2:00:00 AM)
SET Default Time Server Type = SINGLE
File Server Name CONSTELLATION
IPX Internal Net CBE1AB01
LOAD E100S SLOT=2 FRAME=Ethernet_802.2  NAME=E100S_1_E8022
BIND IPX E100S_1_E8022 NET=19200
LOAD E100S SLOT=2 FRAME=Ethernet_802.3  NAME=E100S_1_E8023
BIND IPX E100S_1_E8023 NET=19300
MOUNT ALL_


Save file              <F10>       Previous screen    <Esc>
Mark and unmark text <F5>          Delete marked text <Del>
Save marked text       <F6>        Insert marked text <Ins>
Help                   <F1>        Abort INSTALL <Alt><F10>
```

These LOAD commands load the E100S LANdriver twice, but with two different names— each driver uses a different frame type

Figure 6-12 LOAD LANdriver commands in the AUTOEXEC.NCF file

The LOAD *DISKdriver* commands are located in STARTUP.NCF; the LOAD *LANdriver* commands are located in AUTOEXEC.NCF.

At this point, Install Wizard is ready to move out of the character-based screens and into GUI mode.

The NetWare 5.0 Portion of the Installation

A very significant point has now been reached in the installation of the NetWare 5.0 server. Up to this point, the installation has been running as a DOS process. But now the **SERVER.EXE** program is automatically run, and the NetWare 5.0 NOS takes over. The core of the NetWare operating system is the SERVER.EXE program. When installing NetWare, you use DOS to boot the server and then load the NetWare operating system by running SERVER.EXE. After the SERVER.EXE program loads into memory, it controls the computer, and DOS is no longer needed. After starting NetWare, you might want to remove DOS from memory to make more space (approximately 64 KB) available for NetWare file caching.

 If you want to retain the ability to return to DOS after downing the server, rather than rebooting the system, do not remove DOS.

Although the SERVER.EXE program provides the core NetWare services, such as file and printer sharing, it uses other modules to access hardware devices such as disk drives and network cards or to provide additional services such as communications to a mainframe. These modules are shown in Figure 6-13. For this reason, Novell refers to the SERVER.EXE program as a *software bus*. NetWare 5.0 is a very flexible system that lets the network administrator add and remove software drivers and services as required without needing to exit the server or reboot.

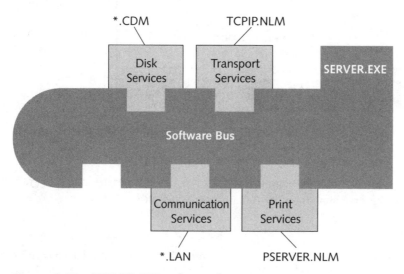

Figure 6-13   SERVER.EXE software bus

The final portion of the installation is controlled by the GUI-based Install Wizard (actually, by a Java application running on the Java Virtual Machine inside the NetWare OS). The wizard is responsible for the following functions:

- Naming the server
- Loading LAN protocols
- Creating NetWare hard drive partitions
- Creating NetWare volumes
- Installing the NetWare license
- Creating the NetWare server SYS: volume directory structure
- Copying the NetWare server files to the NetWare directories on the SYS: volume
- Copying optional NetWare NOS files to the NetWare server

The naming screen appears as the next item of the installation process, as shown in Figure 6-14.

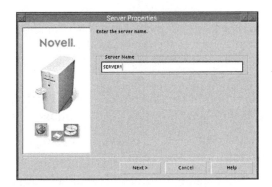

Figure 6-14   Entering the server name

You can now use your mouse if you need to highlight items and/or select them. If you use the keyboard, note that accepting the contents of a field and screen is a two-step process. For example, if you type the name of your server and press [Enter], you might expect to move to the next screen. However, with Install Wizard, this only moves the active component to the Next button at the bottom of the screen. To continue to the next screen, you'll need to press [Enter] again or click Next.

As we discussed earlier, you need to type a unique name for your server as described on your worksheet. Once you do, Install Wizard displays the Protocols selection screen shown in Figure 6-15.

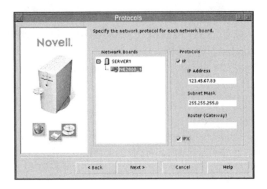

Figure 6-15   Defining the NDS tree

The network board is the one you configured during the earlier part of the installation. The protocol choices are IP and IPX. You can install either or both. For most networks, you will install IP only. In that case, your network administrator will have provided you with appropriate IP addresses. (If you choose to install IPX, it will default to use the 802.2 frame type and a random internal network number.)

The default frame type for NetWare 5.0 is Ethernet_II (which supports TCP/IP). If you choose to include IPX support, then NetWare also installs the Ethernet 802.2 frame type.

Each protocol you select here means it is bound to a LAN driver with a BIND protocol statement in the AUTOEXEC.NCF. The syntax of the BIND command is

```
BIND    protocol[TO]    LAN    driver    |    board    name    [driver
    parameters . . . ] [protocol parameters . . . ]
```

The BIND *protocol* command includes any parameter values needed. Several parameters can be used with BIND. See Table 6-4.

Table 6-4   BIND command parameters

Parameter	Use this parameter to:
protocol	Specify the network protocol—for example, IPX
LAN driver I board name	Specify the LAN driver name or the name assigned to the NIC in a LOAD LANdriver statement
driver parameter	Specify LAN module parameters used to identify an NIC. The simplest to use is the NAME = name parameter
protocol parameter	Specify parameters necessary for the protocol. For the IPX protocol, the NET=IPX external network number parameter is required

After the installation process is finished, you can modify the LOAD driver commands by editing the AUTOEXEC.NCF file. Figure 6-16 shows an example of an AUTOEXEC.NCF file with LOAD *LANdriver* commands. Each frame type driver that is bound results in a BIND *frametype* statement being created in the AUTOEXEC.NCF.

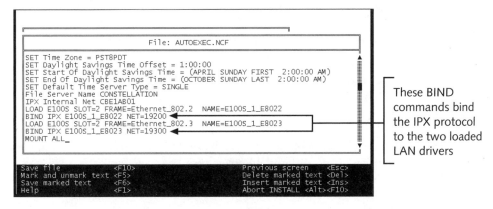

Figure 6-16   BIND commands in the AUTOEXEC.NCF file

Install Wizard now asks you to specify your time zone. Note that the list provided is based on Greenwich Mean Time and not alphabetically, so you may have to search a little to find your exact time zone. It is vital that you choose the right one so that NDS can remain correctly synchronized.

Next the wizard asks you to specify whether this new server will go into an existing NDS tree or into a new one. Choose New, and the wizard now asks you to describe this tree, as shown in Figure 6-17.

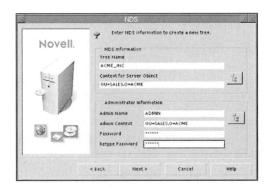

Figure 6-17   Describing the new NDS tree

This description includes a name for the tree as well as the name of the Admin User. Don't use a variation of the server name for the tree. Although such a variation may suggest a kind of symmetry, it will become a hurdle every time a user wants to determine whether he or she is looking at the server or the tree. (For example, if the CBELABS tree were named SARAT instead, and there was the server SARATOGA in the tree, then users could confuse SARAT the tree for SARATOGA the server, and vice versa.)

Once you type the name of the tree, the wizard will fill in most of the remaining fields with default information. Accept these unless you have a reason not to. (For example, in a multiserver internetwork, you may not want to have the new Admin the same Admin for the whole tree.) Type an appropriate password for the administrator, or the wizard won't let you continue. (There is no getting around passwords here.)

At this point, the wizard will summarize your NDS tree configuration. You should copy this information down on your worksheet before continuing.

Creating NetWare Partitions.   After NDS loads, Install Wizard will move to the section on volumes. You will confirm the NetWare SYS partition and configure any other volumes you want to create on available hard disk space, as Figure 6-18 shows.

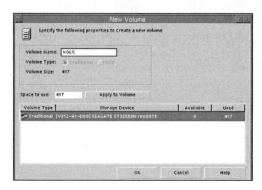

Figure 6-18   New Volume dialog box

The wizard will display all available space on all known drives as configured earlier. You can choose to create a single volume on a drive or multiple volumes on a single drive. (You can also have a volume span multiple drives, but this runs the risk of losing the volume if one drive goes bad.)

NetWare automatically assigns the **default volume name** SYS to the first volume you created. Subsequent volumes are given default volume names of VOL1, VOL2, VOL3, and so on. The name SYS cannot be changed—this is the volume where NetWare will copy the NOS files—but you can change the names of the subsequent volumes.

After you create the disk partitions and volumes, NetWare 5.0 gives you a chance to modify the volume parameters. These parameters include the volume name, the block size, the use of file compression, the use of block suballocation, and the use of data migration.

A NetWare volume that is **mounted** is available for use by users; a **dismounted** (or not mounted) volume is not available for use. The volume must be dismounted when changes are made to volume parameters.

All volume names except SYS can be modified at this point if you need to change a volume name. As discussed in Chapter 3, NetWare also uses a default block size based on volume size. You can change this, but you really don't need to as long as block suballocation is enabled. NetWare enables block suballocation by default, and there is no need to change this.

NetWare also enables file compression by default. File compression saves hard disk space, and normally you should leave it enabled. The NetWare file compression system uses a **data compression algorithm** to shrink the amount of disk space files need. Data compression algorithms typically substitute codes for repeating sets of characters. For example, the phrase "here, there, and everywhere" can be compressed, by using the substitution "x = ere" to "hx, thx, and everywhx," which saves the space of six characters. Because a header containing the coding information must to be added to the compressed file, this method is effective only on files that are larger than some minimum file size. NetWare 5.0 uses a minimum file size of 512 bytes and a default **minimum compression percentage gain** of 2% (the compressed file must be at least 2% smaller than the original). Also by default, NetWare 5.0 waits until a file has been unused for seven days before compressing it. Because file compression requires a lot of CPU work, file scans and compression are done between midnight and 6:00 A.M. by default. You can change the compression system defaults using SET commands.

The term NetWare **data migration** refers to the systematic moving of unused data to a storage device other than a volume. **Optical disks** are typically used for long-term storage because of their high capacities. Unlike file compression, which leaves the compressed file on the volume, data migration removes the file from the NetWare volume after copying it to the optical disk. Each NetWare volume has data migration disabled by default; leave it disabled unless you are working with data migration hardware.

Installing the Novell License.   After you accept your NetWare volume configuration, Install Wizard moves on to the licensing step. Your NetWare 5.0 license is on the LICENSE floppy disk in a file with the extension .NLF. NetWare now prompts you for the disk and then copies the license to the server. (Remember, you can only use this license once in a given tree. Try to reuse this license for another server, and through NDS NetWare will detect this attempt.)

 NetWare 5.0 lets you add users to your network by combining licenses on one server. For example, if you need a license for 35 users, you can combine a 25-user license and a 10-user license. This type of licensing offers considerable flexibility over an all-or-nothing approach where you would have to pay extra for a 50-user license to handle your 35 users.

Installing Optional NetWare Files. Install Wizard now displays a list of optional components you may want to install on your server, as shown in Figure 6-19.

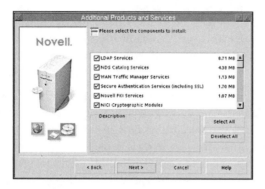

Figure 6-19 Selecting optional components

These options include enhanced security using PKI and cryptographic modules, support for the Lightweight Directory Access Protocol (LDAP), and others.

 Don't worry if you miss selecting a set of files at this point—you can add them later by running NWCONFIG.

At this point, the wizard will offer you the chance to do a "product customization" for the components you have selected to install. For most networks, it shouldn't be necessary to do customization. However, you may want to change an IPX internal network number, which frame type is used, or include a second language with the default one. You may want to turn compression off on a volume or change other configuration information such as the name of the NDPS broker. That's where the screen shown in Figure 6-20 comes in.

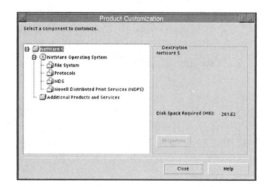

Figure 6-20 Product Customization screen

If the defaults are acceptable, you can continue with the installation. At this point, Install Wizard is ready to copy all the files required for the NetWare server. This will take 20 to 30 minutes, depending on your CD-ROM drive speed. When you return, you will see the screen shown in Figure 6-21. You can then reboot to start your new server.

Figure 6-21   Installation complete screen

Using NetWare Console Commands at the Server

Once you finish the installation and the NetWare server is running, you will also occasionally need to perform various maintenance activities on the server. These include reviewing or modifying the STARTUP and AUTOEXEC.NCF files, loading drivers and modules, sending messages to users from the console, enabling or disabling login from the server, making it possible to use long filenames, monitoring the network, and downing and starting the server.

Editing the STARTUP.NCF and AUTOEXEC.NCF Files

During installation, the STARTUP.NCF and AUTOEXEC.NCF files were created to record NetWare commands based on options chosen during installation. The STARTUP.NCF and AUTOEXEC.NCF files are run automatically each time the NetWare NOS is started and are used to configure the NetWare operating environment. STARTUP.NCF is located (as is SERVER.EXE) in the NWSERVER directory on the DOS boot partition, whereas AUTOEXEC.NCF is located on the SYS volume in the SYS-TEM directory. This means NetWare can read and execute the NetWare commands in STARTUP.NCF before the SYS volume is mounted, but the commands in AUTOEXEC.NCF can be read only after the SYS volume is mounted.

The STARTUP.NCF and AUTOEXEC.NCF files automate the server bootup process, and maintaining them is an important job of a network administrator. The following sections discuss the impact of the installation steps on these files and describe what commands are added to them during installation.

The STARTUP.NCF and AUTOEXEC.NCF files can be modified during installation, but, more importantly, they can be edited at any time after the installation is complete. You do this by loading the NWCONFIG NLM, by typing the command

NWCONFIG [Enter]

at the NetWare server console command line prompt. (The NetWare console is the monitor and keyboard attached to the NetWare server.)

 In the past, NetWare utilities required that you type LOAD before utilities such as NWCONFIG. The NetWare 5.0 operating system understands that you mean you want to load NWCONFIG even if you only type NWCONFIG. Don't worry: If you type in a wrong name for a utility, NetWare will simply say "Not Found" and return you to the command prompt.

Once you have NWCONFIG loaded, you can choose to edit these system files or to review their contents.

Loading Drivers and Modules

You will also need to load drivers or modules on the server. As mentioned earlier, you can use the LOAD command for this task, or in the case of NLMs, you can simply type the name of the module. When you use the LOAD command, you should understand its syntax:

LOAD [path]loadable_module_name [module_parameters]

When you can type the name of the NLM without using LOAD, you might wonder when you would use this LOAD command. You use it most often when the module is on a CD-ROM mounted on the server or on a floppy disk in the floppy drive. You also use it when other drivers are needed. The LOAD command and its parameters are more fully detailed in Table 6-5.

Table 6-5   LOAD command parameters

Parameter	Use this parameter to:
path	Specify the path to the loadable module you want to run
loadable_module_name	Specify the name of the loadable module you want to run
module_parameters	Specify parameters for the loadable module you want to run (these vary from module to module)

Loadable modules are of five types:

- Adapter drivers (.HAM)
- Disk drivers (.CDM)

- LAN drivers (.LAN)

- NLM programs (.NLM)

- Name space support modules (.NAM)

 If a driver that you need is not supplied by Novell on the NetWare 5.0 CD-ROM, you should have it on a floppy disk packaged with the controller card. During installation, put the disk in the A: drive, where the installation program locates the driver on the disk and loads it.

You may want to make a LOAD command a permanent part of your server each time it reboots. To do so, you will need to modify either the STARTUP.NCF file (for disk drivers) or the AUTOEXEC.NCF file (for LAN drivers.) For example, you would add a LOAD *DISKdriver* command to the NetWare STARTUP.NCF file for each driver. The LOAD driver command includes any module parameter values needed for the driver to be loaded correctly. Both disk drivers and LAN drivers use the shared set of module parameters listed in Table 6-5 to specify information about a disk controller card or NIC installed in the NetWare server.

NetWare 5.0 breaks up the older disk drivers into two parts using the **Novell Peripheral Architecture (NPA)**: the **Host Adapter Module (HAM)** and the **Custom Device Module (CDM)**.

Sending Messages

You can use the SEND *message text* console command to broadcast messages to users. This is particularly useful for posting warning messages just before you shut down a NetWare server or unload a network service such as PSERVER.

Enabling or Disabling Login

A pair of useful console commands are DISABLE LOGIN and ENABLE LOGIN. The DISABLE LOGIN command allows the NetWare server to be on the network, but not available to users, when you're performing maintenance tasks for which you don't want any user on the server. ENABLE LOGIN reestablishes the users' ability to use the server's resources. Chapter 14 covers these and other console commands in more detail.

Adding Name Spaces to Support Long Filenames

In addition to DOS filenames, NetWare 5.0 supports other client operating system file-naming conventions on a NetWare server through NetWare **name space** modules. NetWare 5.0 includes name space support for Macintosh and long filenames, and support for Unix files can be purchased from Novell. Name space NLMs use the extension .NAM. The Macintosh name space (MAC.NAM) is important if you have Macintoshes connected to your network. The long filename name space (LONG.NAM) is obviously important for Windows 95/98. For this reason, NetWare loads the LONG.NAM as a default for its volumes.

Adding a name space requires two steps:

1. Loading the appropriate name space .NAM module

2. Running the ADD NAME SPACE utility

The **ADD NAME SPACE utility** needs to be run only once on each volume for a given name space. The name space .NAM module must be loaded each time the NetWare server is booted, and the .NAM module supports all volumes with added name spaces on the NetWare server. The syntax of the ADD NAME SPACE command is

`ADD NAME SPACE name TO [volume_name]`

The ADD NAME SPACE command includes any parameter values needed. Several parameters can be used with ADD NAME SPACE; they are listed in Table 6-6.

Table 6-6   ADD NAME SPACE parameters

Parameter	Use this parameter to:
no parameter	Display the name spaces that are currently loaded on the NetWare server
name	Specify the name space module. The possible names are OS/2, MA (Macintosh), FTAM, and NFS
volume_name	Specify which volume the name space is being added to

To add Macintosh name space to the SYS volume, for example, you use the following commands at the console command prompt:

1. At the prompt, type LOAD MAC.NAM, and then press [Enter]. The MAC.NAM name space support module is loaded on the NetWare server.

2. At the prompt, type ADD NAME SPACE MA TO SYS, and then press [Enter]. The MAC name space is added to the SYS volume.

These two commands need to be run every time the NetWare server is booted, so they should be added to the AUTOEXEC.NCF file.

Using MONITOR

The **MONITOR utility** provides essential information about NetWare server performance and workstation connection information. It's a good idea to always have MONITOR running on the server.

To load the NetWare MONITOR utility, use the following commands:

1. At the prompt, type LOAD MONITOR and then press [Enter]. The MONITOR screen appears, as shown in Figure 6-22. This figure shows the contracted General Information window. (After a few seconds of inactivity, the full information screen appears.)

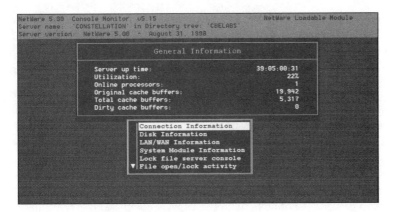

Figure 6-22 Monitor screen

2. Press [Tab] to expand the General Information window to see all the data in the window, as shown in Figure 6-23. You can press [Tab] a second time to toggle back to the compressed General Information window.

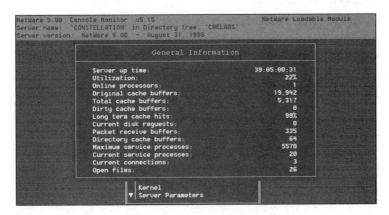

Figure 6-23 Expanded General Information screen in Monitor

 You can press the [Alt] + [Esc] key combination to move between the MONITOR screen and the console command prompt (or the screen of any other NLM that's loaded).

Downing the NetWare Server

Once your NetWare server is operational, you should test the startup files to be sure the NetWare server will start correctly the next time you use it. Although it is not something a network administrator needs to do often, you need to know how to properly stop and restart the NetWare server when you maintain hardware or upgrade software.

Downing the NetWare server is the process of stopping the server program by logging off all users, taking the server off line so it is no longer available to workstations, and dismounting all volumes to update the disk with any changes currently stored in the memory buffers. All these processes are accomplished by using NetWare's **DOWN command**.

Before using the DOWN command, you should issue the DISABLE LOGIN command to prevent users from logging into the NetWare server. Then use the SEND command to send a short message to any current users. Announce that the NetWare server will be shut down in several minutes and ask users to save their work and log out of the NetWare server.

If any users are logged into the NetWare server when you issue the DOWN command, the NetWare server displays a warning on the console, asking if you want to proceed. Continuing with the DOWN command can cause data in files being processed to be lost. To determine if the current users have any files open, you can use the NetWare MONITOR utility to view existing connections and view any open files. You can then either send a message asking the user to log out or cancel the user's session if no files are open.

Starting the NetWare Server

Starting the NetWare server involves booting the computer with DOS and then loading the SERVER.EXE program. The SERVER program starts by first loading the disk driver specified in the STARTUP.NCF file and then performing the commands in the AUTOEXEC.NCF file. These provide the server name, internal network number, and LAN drivers.

You can automate this server startup process by creating an AUTOEXEC.BAT file in the server's DOS partition that contains the following commands:

```
@ECHO OFF

CLS

CD\NWSERVER

PAUSE Use [Ctrl] [Break] keys to abort server startup

SERVER
```

The PAUSE command is optional. Issuing a PAUSE command in the server's AUTOEXEC.BAT file lets you stop the computer in the DOS mode before starting the SERVER program. This enables you to perform certain maintenance functions such as copying drivers and software upgrades to the NWSERVER directory before starting the NetWare server. However, the PAUSE command also requires that someone be present to respond to it. Some software that works with a UPS will down a server in the event of a power failure, followed by an automatic reboot when power is restored. The PAUSE command prevents a complete unattended automatic reboot.

The Directory Tree After Installation

After the first NetWare 5.0 server installation is complete, NDS is installed and the Directory tree has been created. At this point it consists of only the following:

- The [Root] has been created and named.

- The minimal set of Organization and Organizational Unit objects necessary to establish the NetWare server context have been created and named.

- The Admin User object has been created.

- The NetWare Server object for the NetWare server has been created.

- Volume objects for each volume on the NetWare server have been created.

- The [Public] trustee was created and given Browse rights at the [Root] object. This means that all users, as they are added, can browse the entire Directory tree. (The [Public] object and Browse rights are discussed in Chapter 10.)

- There are *no* groups created.

For example, Cunningham, Burns, and Evans Laboratories (CBE Labs) has installed its first NetWare 5.0 server. The server has an Intel 133 MHz Pentium CPU, 64 MB of RAM, one 3.5-inch floppy disk drive, two SCSI 20 GB drives, and an IDE CD-ROM drive. A 150 MB DOS partition has been created with MS-DOS 6.22.

CBE Labs decided to name its NetWare server CONSTELLATION and to use the IP address 137.65.285.155. CONSTELLATION has an Intel Smart Pro/100 LAN adapter. This requires the E100S.LAN driver, which is not available in the standard driver set provided by Novell. The E100S.LAN driver is on a disk that Intel provided with the card. CBE Labs uses two protocols: 802.2 and 802.3. Both types were bound to the E100S during installation.

The two SCSI disk drives are partitioned as two volumes: SYS and DATA. Each partition uses all the available space on its hard drive. Neither partition will be mirrored or duplexed.

CBE Labs named its Directory tree with the tree name CBELABS and created the Organization object CBE_Labs. The context for the NetWare server CONSTELLA-TION is .CBE_Labs. The network administration account will use the standard user name Admin, and the password will be APSTNDP (the first letters of the seven layers of the OSI model). The context for the Admin User object is also .CBE_Labs. CBE_Labs is in the Pacific Coast time zone, and daylight savings time is used. Because this is the first server on the network, it will be the time reference source for all other servers installed later. This is known as a **single reference time server (SRTS)**. Other types of time servers are discussed later in this chapter.

After the installation of NetWare 5.0, the CBE Labs Directory tree appears as shown in Figure 6-24. The [Public] trustee, although created, does not show up in the Directory tree because it is not a Directory tree object.

Figure 6-24   CBE Labs Directory tree with the NetWare
server CONSTELLATION

Network Time Synchronization: NetWare Time Servers

When only one NetWare server is on the network, you don't need to worry about different types of NetWare time servers. But with the addition of a second NetWare server on the network, time synchronization becomes important.

The goal is to use one common time throughout the network. There are four types of NetWare time servers: single reference, primary, reference, and secondary. As its name implies, a single reference time server (SRTS) is the only time reference on the network, and provides the time to all other servers and workstations on the network. The network administrator manually sets the time on an SRTS. A **primary time server (PTS)**, in contrast, synchronizes the official network time with other PTS NetWare servers and reference time servers through a "voting" process. After the "official" time is established, all servers adjust their internal clocks to it. The time is also provided to all secondary time servers and workstations. A **reference time server (RTS)** differs from a PTS by being able to synchronize with a time source (such as an atomic clock or radio clock) external to the network. Although reference time server NetWare servers vote with PTS machines to determine the "official" network time, they don't adjust their clock to it. This has the effect of pulling the "official" network time, which is an averaged time, toward the time of the RTS. Over time, the RTS time will become the "official" network time. Again, the time is also provided to all secondary time servers and workstations. **Secondary time servers (STS)** receive time information from secondary reference time server, primary time server, and reference time server NetWare servers and set their clocks accordingly. They then send the time to workstations.

Primary time servers and reference time servers must have at least one other primary time server or reference time server on the network with which to synchronize. Using primary time servers and reference time servers is most appropriate in WANs, especially when portions of the WANs are in different geographic locations.

A single reference time server (SRTS) is most appropriate for small LANs. If an SRTS is used, no primary time servers or reference time servers can exist on the network. When you add more servers to an NDS tree with an SRTS, each new server looks to the SRTS for timing information. If the SRTS fails, manual intervention is required to promote another server to being the SRTS. In a PTS/STS system, NDS automatically corrects this problem.

NOVELL CLIENT SOFTWARE INSTALLATION

After NetWare has been installed on the NetWare server, the next task is setting up the workstations that will be attached to the network. Assuming the wiring is already in place and tested, setting up a workstation to use the network involves installing and configuring the NIC and then installing the client software. As a network administrator, you will need to be familiar with these processes to upgrade workstation software and install new workstations on the network.

Installing the Network Card

To connect a workstation to the network, you must first obtain the network cards appropriate for the topology and system you are using. NetWare is compatible with most network cards on the market, but it is a good idea to obtain cards that have been certified by Novell. They have gone through an extensive testing process in the Novell labs. If you choose to use a non-PCI plug-and-play card, then before you install the card you need to determine the correct hardware settings—including interrupt number, I/O port, and memory address—to avoid conflicts with other devices in the workstation.

Network cards use either jumpers or software to store configuration settings. The software included on some network cards lets you store the card's configuration settings in the CMOS memory contained on the network card. Network cards designed for PCI bus machines have an automatic configuration process that calculates the hardware settings for you and stores them in CMOS memory on the systemboard. The network driver program retrieves these configuration settings when it runs on the workstation. Using the software setup process allows driver programs to be self-configuring and means you don't need to modify the driver program parameters for different computer configurations.

Software Components

For a workstation connected to the network to communicate with a NetWare server, it needs three software components:

- An NIC driver
- A protocol stack
- A network client

The **NIC driver** software performs the data link process that controls the network adapter card so it can send and receive packets over the network cable system. Information on the correct driver program for use with NetWare should be included in the manual that comes with the network card. In some cases, the workstation driver software is contained on a disk included with the network card. Sometimes you will be instructed to use one of the many workstation driver programs included with the Novell Client Software CD-ROM.

The second workstation component is the **protocol stack**, which includes the network and transport layers responsible for formatting the data within a network packet and routing that packet between networks. For example, NetWare 5.0 servers use TCP/IP.

The third workstation component is the **network client**, which carries out the session and presentation layer functions by providing access to the network from the local operating system.

Overview of ODI Drivers

To provide support for multiple protocols and to make it easier for network administrators to update card configurations and drivers, Novell developed the **Open Data Interface (ODI)** software and driver specifications. The ODI driver specifications are standards for network card companies to use in developing drivers that are compatible with Novell's ODI software. In addition, the ODI client software lets the workstation run multiple protocol stacks on the same network card. The ODI client software, for example, can communicate with a Unix host (using TCP/IP) while also communicating with a NetWare server (using the IPX protocol). The connections to both servers will use the same network cable system. The ODI standard also supports more than one NIC in a workstation, so that, for example, a workstation could be connected to both an Ethernet and a Token Ring network at the same time.

The ODI specification refers to an NIC driver as a **Multiple Link Interface Driver (MLID)**, reflecting ODI's ability to support multiple NICs in the workstation. In addition, ODI adds a fourth component to the three software components listed earlier: the link support layer. The **Link Support Layer (LSL)**, shown in Figure 6-25, is supplied by Novell to provide a connection within the data link layer between the protocol stack and the card driver so that more than one protocol stack can share the same network card. For example, as Figure 6-25 shows, the LSL lets you run both TCP/IP and IPX/SPX simultaneously over the same network card by passing both TCP/IP packets and IPX packets to the NIC driver. Figure 6-25 also shows the use of two NICs in the workstation.

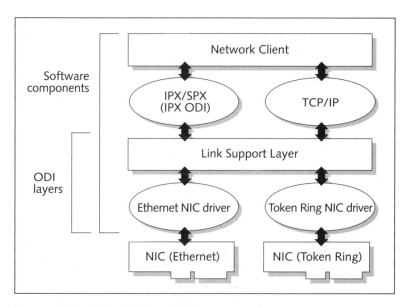

Figure 6-25   Workstation ODI components

The Network Client

The network client is the software that allows the workstation's operating system to communicate with the network. The Novell Client supports a variety of features that at this writing are not available in Windows NT: auto-reconnect, packet burst mode, and packet signatures. These advantages reduce network traffic, compared to an NT server.

Auto-reconnect means what its name suggests: If the workstation loses its connection to the server for whatever reason, the client software will try to reconnect automatically. You don't have to rerun the login program. In fact, since auto-reconnect occurs in the background, you don't have to reload your applications to continue working.

Packet burst mode provides faster communication to the NetWare server by allowing the workstation to receive a number of data packets at once before responding with an acknowledgment. Without packet burst mode, the workstation must acknowledge each data packet sent by the server before the next packet can be sent. Packet burst mode is especially effective on lightly used networks. When more workstations are accessing the network, large groups of packets can actually decrease performance for workstations that are waiting to use the network. For this reason, the packet burst mode is automatically adjusted by the Novell Client and NetWare server based on the network load.

Packet signatures ensure that packets are sent by authorized workstations. Before the packet signature system, another workstation could "forge" a packet and make the NetWare server think it came from a workstation that had higher privileges. Packet signatures prevent forged packets by requiring an encrypted code made up of the user's password and workstation connection number to verify that the workstation that originated the packet is authorized to do so.

NetWare 5.0 includes a client installation program called SETUP. This program can be found on the Novell Client Software CD-ROM. To start the workstation installation process, simply insert the disc into the CD-ROM drive. It should automatically launch the setup program. (If not, you can locate the program in the root directory on the disc.)

Novell's current network client software is included on the Client Software CD-ROM that comes with NetWare 5.0. It is also available for download free from Novell's Web site, *www.novell.com*. Novell Client software has two parts:

- The NetWare Input/Output System (NIOS)
- Client NetWare Loadable Modules (NLMs)

 The use of files named NetWare Loadable Modules with the Novell Client is unfortunate, because it is no longer possible to determine, by the file extension, files that can run only on a NetWare server. Until the Novell Client introduced NLMs for workstations, the extension .NLM always indicated a program file that would run only on a NetWare server. Don't worry, you won't be the first administrator to erase "extraneous" NLMs from a workstation only to discover they are required by the Novell Client.

If your network has workstations using Windows 3.1x, you must install the Microsoft Windows 32-bit extensions to use Novell Client for DOS/Windows. These extensions are available from Microsoft via the Internet. This chapter discusses the Novell Client for Windows 95/98.

The Novell Client for Windows 95/98 files are available in two forms. One form creates an installation directory for the Novell Client over a network. The other form is as a CD-ROM. This chapter covers the CD-ROM installation. The network installation is similar and faster because there is no need to access the CD-ROM during installation.

Novell Client for Windows 95/98 offers the **NetWare Provider for Windows 95/98**, which adds NetWare tools to the Windows 95/98 Network Neighborhood, Explorer, and System Tray programs. These features will be discussed as needed in later chapters.

Installing the Novell Client Software

With the Novell Client software, Novell provides an installation program that automates installation. For example, the CBE Labs network administrator needs to install Novell Client on a workstation.

The workstation already has the NIC and Windows 95/98 installed, and the Microsoft Client for Windows Networks was installed as part of the Windows 95/98 installation procedure. The NIC is attached to a network cable connection. With the Microsoft client installed, the workstation is capable of logging into a NetWare server in bindery emulation mode, but not of logging into an NDS Directory tree.

When it is installed, the Novell Client removes any existing NetWare network client. Although you could remove an existing client manually, the installation seems to proceed more smoothly when the Novell Client is allowed to handle the removal.

The Novell Client requires at least 6 MB of RAM. However, because Windows 95/98 requires a minimum of 16 MB of RAM, a workstation that can run Windows 95/98 can run the Novell Client. Novell Client also requires 6 MB of hard drive storage. The NIC must be installed and attached to a network cable connection. During the installation of Novell Client, you will need the Novell Client Software CD-ROM and the Windows 95/98 CD-ROM.

To install the Novell Client for Windows 95/98, use the following steps:

1. If the workstation is not running, start the workstation and let it boot Windows 95/98.

2. Insert the Novell Client Software CD-ROM into the CD-ROM drive. The Setup program automatically comes up, asking you to choose a language (English is the only one presented on products shipped in North America.)

3. Click English.

4. Choose Install Novell Client and then click Windows 95/98 Client as shown in Figures 6-26 and 6-27.

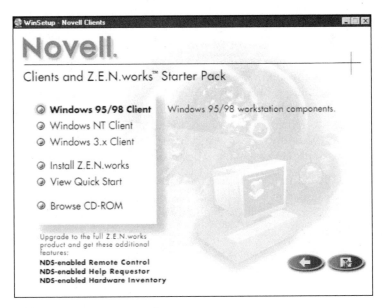

Figure 6-26   Platform options dialog box

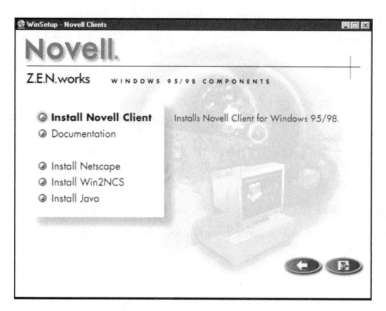

Figure 6-27   Client option dialog box

5. The Novell Client for Window 95/98 License Agreement dialog box opens. You can scroll through the license agreement to review it by using the vertical scroll bar on the dialog box.

6. Click the Yes button to accept the agreement and proceed.

7. The Setup program now asks you if you want to do a Typical or a Custom installation. Unless you have a good reason not to, leave the default as Typical and press Install. At this point, the Novell Client installation program removes any existing Novell client on the workstation. The Novell Client installation program does a thorough and effective job of removing the installed client, so you do not need to remove a previously installed Novell client before installing Novell Client for Windows 95/98. You can also view README files as described in the next section by clicking the View Readme button.

8. If the Novell Client installation program needs files from the Windows 95/98 CD-ROM, it will ask for them after it has copied files from the Novell Client CD-ROM. However, it does not always do so—but keep the CD-ROM handy just in case.

9. At this point, the installation process is automatic. Once the Novell Client for Windows 95/98 is installed, the program will display a message saying you should reboot for the changes to take effect. Click Yes to reboot the workstation.

10. After rebooting, the Novell Client for Window 95/98 loads and displays the Novell Login screen. If you have a valid username and password, you can enter them and log in to the network. Otherwise click Cancel.

The README.TXT File

The Novell Client files include a README.TXT text file, which contains the latest release notes available when the Novell Client files were approved for distribution. The Novell Client installation program lets you view the README file with Notepad. You can also print a copy for review. One important item in the Novell Client README.TXT file is that the primary documentation for Novell Client is the Novell Client Help file, which was copied to the workstation hard drive during installation. There is no separate printed documentation for the Novell Client.

 Always review the README file that comes with software packages for information that is not contained in the software manuals. README files contain the most recent configuration information and data about known problems with the software.

To view and print the Novell Client for Windows 95/98 README.TXT file, follow these steps:

1. In the Client Installation dialog box that asks for the type of installation (Typical, Custom, etc.), click the View README button. The README.TXT file is displayed in Notepad for viewing. (You may see a message saying the file is too large to open in Notepad. Then Windows will open WordPad instead. However, the current release notes don't require WordPad.)

2. Use the File, Print command to print a copy of the README.TXT file, and then close Notepad.

Customizing the Client

You can customize your particular installation of the Novell Client using various tools. First, you can open the Control Panel in Windows and double-click the Network icon to display the Configuration tab, which shows a list of your installed network components. These components include clients, adapters, protocols, and agents. An **adapter** is a hardware component used to connect the workstation to the network. For example, in Figure 6-28 the workstation's 3Com Etherlink III ISA NIC is an adapter. A **client** is the software that provides the network connectivity for the workstation, while a protocol (or protocol stack) is software that controls how the workstation communicates with the network and other workstations or NetWare servers on the network. In Figure 6-28, the client is Novell NetWare Client, and three protocols are being used: Novell's IPX 32-bit protocol for the Novell Client, the Microsoft IPX/SPX-compatible protocol, and the Microsoft TCP/IP protocol. Only the first of these is part of the Novell Client. Finally, an **agent** is client software that enables the workstation to use network services provided by server software on an applications server.

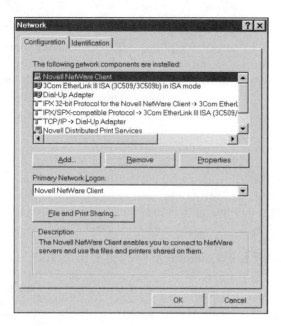

Figure 6-28   Network dialog box

The Novell Client and the IPX 32-bit protocol for the Novell Client are part of the Novell Client. You can access the settings for the Novell Client and protocol by clicking them in the list of installed components and then clicking the Properties button.

To display the Novell Client Properties dialog box, do the following:

1. Click Novell NetWare Client in the list of installed components in the Network dialog box.

2. Click the Properties button in the Network dialog box.

The Novell NetWare Client Properties dialog box is displayed, as shown in Figure 6-29.

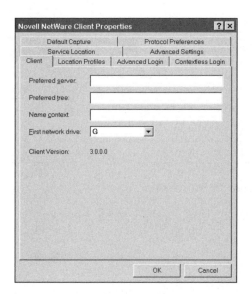

Figure 6-29   Novell NetWare Client Properties dialog box

Novell NetWare Client Properties Dialog Box Pages

The Novell Client Properties dialog box shown in Figure 6-29 has eight tabbed pages: Client, Location Profiles, Advanced Login, Contextless Login, Service Location, Advanced Settings, Default Capture, and Protocol Preferences.

Initially, when you open this dialog box, the Client page is displayed. This page contains the preferred connection settings for the workstation. The settings on the Advanced Login page control what appears in the display of the Novell NetWare Login dialog box, including how many tabbed pages to display to the user and the default settings for those pages. The Default Capture page includes property settings to control printer output for printed output from the workstation. The Location Profiles page lists any available profiles for this workstation. (An administrator can set up permanent drive mappings or print capture statements in a profile for this workstation, without regard for who logs in.) The Contextless Login page allows users to search for their valid user name within NDS. (Some users may have a difficult time remembering exactly what their context is within the tree and so cannot log in.) The Protocol Preferences page supports a choice between IP and IPX as the preferred protocol for this workstation. Which you choose will depend on the type of network you set up. The Advanced Settings page enables property settings for 67 parameters, which lets the network administrator fine-tune workstation connectivity to the network. Finally, the Service Location page covers items relating to using SLP applications on the workstation. This includes specifying which directory agents to use and the list of scope names that will be reported to those applications. These pages are summarized in Table 6-7.

Table 6-7   Novell NetWare Client Properties

Client Properties Page	Purpose
Client	Sets the workstation NDS connection preferences
Advanced Login	Controls the display of options on the initial Login screen
Default Capture	Sets the workstation defaults for printer output
Location Profiles	Displays available profiles for this workstation
Contextless Login	Allows users to search for their user names within the NDS tree
Protocol Preferences	Allows the administrator to set a preferred network protocol for this workstation (IP or IPX)
Advanced Settings	Sets property values of 67 Client parameters
Service Location	Sets the scope list and the list of directory agents for use by SLP applications

The Client Page.   As shown in Figure 6-29, the workstation connection settings include a server setting, a preferred tree setting, a user name context setting, and a first network drive setting. (It also displays what version of the Novell Client you are running.) The values you set are property values and are stored in the Windows 95/98 Registry. In fact, all settings you select for the Novell Client are stored in the Registry, which eliminates the need for a separate NetWare configuration file to store the property setting.

The Preferred server setting specifies which server the workstation will attach to for login purposes if the workstation is attaching to a bindery-based NetWare 3.1x server or a NetWare 5.0 server in bindery mode. When connecting in bindery mode, the Novell Client sends a request for the first available NetWare server as soon as it is loaded, then attaches to the first NetWare server that responds and makes that server the default NetWare server. By specifying a preferred server, the network administrator can control which NetWare server the workstation attaches to.

When logging into an NDS Directory tree instead of a NetWare server, the Preferred tree setting specifies which NDS Directory tree the workstation will use for login purposes. Thus, the Preferred tree setting serves the same function for NDS that the Preferred server setting does for bindery mode. (Of course, if your network has only one tree, then this tree will appear as the default for this setting.)

Note   In an NDS Directory tree, the User object will be assigned a default server based on Directory tree partitioning. The Preferred server setting can also be used to override the default server setting and thus enable the network administrator to control which NetWare 5.0 server is used to authenticate the user's login in an NDS environment.

A user must log into an NDS Directory tree in the proper context. This means that the context of the user's User object must be included in the login. The **Name context** setting specifies the default context for users logging into the network using the workstation. For example, the CBE Labs Admin User object is in the context .CBE_Labs, as shown in Figure 6-30. The network administrator can set the name context for the workstation to .CBE_Labs. This context will automatically be used for logins from the workstation, and the network administrator can log into the network as the Admin user by simply entering the login name of Admin. Without the name context setting, the user would also have to enter the correct context of his or her User object when logging in.

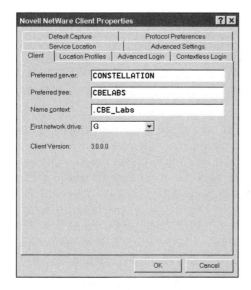

Figure 6-30   Completed Client page settings

After attaching to a NetWare server or an NDS Directory tree, the first available drive pointer is mapped to the SYS:LOGIN directory of the default NDS NetWare5.0 server for the Directory tree. The first network drive setting lets the network administration specify which drive letter will be mapped to the SYS:LOGIN directory. This mapping allows the user to access the NetWare LOGIN.EXE program for logging in.

The choice of the first network drive limits both the number of local drive letters available to the workstation and the number of drive letters available for network drive mappings. The F: drive has often been designated as the first network drive. However, as workstations use more local drives, the G: drive is often used as the first network drive.

Workstations are using more peripherals or hardware setups that require a local drive letter. Examples are CD-ROM drives, optical drives, and compressed hard disks that require a "host drive."

As part of the Novell Client for Windows 95/98 installation, the CBE Labs network administrator now enters the settings for the preferred and default login settings for users logging into the network from this workstation. The preferred tree is CBELABS, the name context is .CBE_Labs, and the first network drive will be G:. In addition, the network administrator will specify CONSTELLATION as the preferred server in case the user needs to log into the server in bindery mode.

To enter the Client page preferred and default settings, follow these steps:

1. The Preferred server text box should be active. If not, click it to activate it and then type CONSTELLATION to designate CONSTELLATION as the preferred NetWare server.

2. Click the Preferred tree text box to activate it. Type CBELABS to designate CBELABS as the preferred NDS Directory tree.

3. Click the Name context tree text box to activate it. Type .CBE_Labs to designate .CBE_Labs as the default context of the user's User object in the NDS Directory tree.

4. Check the First network drive text box to see if it is set to drive letter G:. If it isn't, then click the First network drive drop-down list arrow to display the drive letters in the drop-down list, then click G to set the G: drive as the first network drive. The completed Client page settings are shown in Figure 6-30.

The Advanced Login Page.   The Advanced Login page of the Novell Client Properties dialog box controls how the user interacts with the Novell Login dialog box during login. The default is for the Advanced button to appear. If the user clicks the Advance button, it displays the Novell Login dialog box as shown in Figure 6-31, where it has two tabbed pages: NDS and Script.

The Login part of the Novell Login dialog box always displays the Username and Password text boxes. The preferences set on the Client page of the Novell Client Properties dialog box are used to determine the user's default network connection. In Figure 6-31, user Admin is logging into the NDS Directory tree CBELABS. This connection is determined by the settings shown in Figure 6-30, where CBELABS is the name of the preferred NDS Directory tree.

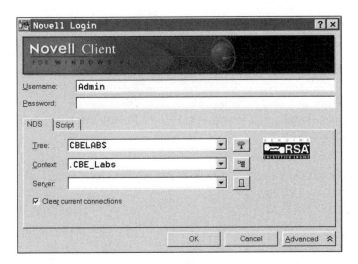

Figure 6-31   Novell Login dialog box

The display of the NDS and Script pages of the NetWare Login dialog box is controlled by the Advanced Login page of the Novell Client Properties dialog box. This page is shown in Figure 6-32.

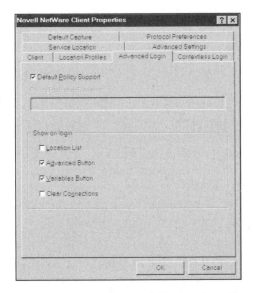

Figure 6-32   Advanced Login properties page

The Advanced Login page in Figure 6-32 shows the default settings for the page. There are three important results of these settings. First, the Location List and Clear Connections check boxes in the Show on Login area are unchecked. This indicates that these options will not appear on the Login dialog. The Advanced Button and Variables Button are both checked to be shown, so the user will have the option of clicking the Advanced button in the login screen to display both the NDS and the Script pages. (Once the user clicks the Script tab, the Variables button then appears in the Script page.)

A bug in the 3.0.0 version of the Client software allows the Clear Connections check box to appear in the Login dialog even if the administrator specifically removes this function from the Client.

With the defaults set in the NDS page, the user logs into the preferred tree, which is why the CBELABS tree is the connection shown in Figure 6-31, and any connections the user has to any Directory tree or NetWare server are disconnected during the new login. Also, the defaults on the Script page mean that one or both types of login scripts run (login and profile), that script results display automatically, and that the results window closes automatically as well.

You can use the settings on the Advanced Login page to control the following features:

- Which pages of the Novell Login dialog box are displayed to the user

- The default type of connection for the workstation

- How login scripts are handled on the workstation

- The default values of variables needed by the login script

- Whether new settings specified by a user during login should be saved

You will choose which pages of the Novell Login dialog box to display to a user depending on the user's needs. The NDS page is useful if the workstation is used to log into more than one network or NetWare server. If it is, then the user must be able to choose his or her login connection. However, if users of the workstation always log into the same network or NetWare server, there is no need to display this page. The need for the Script page is similar to that for the NDS page: If users of the workstation must change or vary the defaults specified in the Novell NetWare Client Properties dialog box, the page should be displayed. If the defaults will always be used, users do not need to see this page. Finally, the Variables button should be displayed only if users need to enter parameter values for their login script during login. If no variable values are needed (as is usually the case) or if the default parameter values are always used, there is no need to display the button.

The workstation that the CBE Labs network administrator is working with will be used by the Information Systems (IS) workgroup at CBE Labs. Because workgroup members need to be able to specify their network connection, control login script display, and enter login script variables during login, the network administrator needs to modify the settings on the Login page of the Novell Client Properties dialog box. Users of this workstation will normally log into the CBELABS Directory tree and clear previous connections, so there is no need to change these defaults. The user's User object property settings will determine which login script or profile script to use, so there is no need to specify a login script or profile script. Finally, login scripts and profiles scripts at CBE Labs normally don't need input values, so there is no need to set variable values.

To enter the Login settings, click the Advanced Login page tab of the Novell Client Properties dialog box to display the Advanced Login page, shown in Figure 6-33. The Advanced Button, Variables Button, and Clear Connections check boxes should be checked.

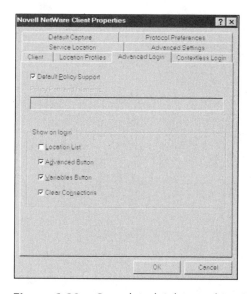

Figure 6-33   Completed Advanced Login page

The Default Capture Page.   The Default Capture page of the Novell Client Properties dialog box controls how print jobs are printed when using LPT ports. (If you use the Printers setup procedure in Windows, you won't need to worry about capturing any LPT ports.) This page is shown with default settings in Figure 6-34.

NetWare printing is discussed in detail in Chapter 12, so it isn't covered here. The important point to consider here is that most users won't require any changes in the Default Capture settings. Using the standard Windows Printer definition procedure is fine for both Novell Distributed Print Services (NDPS) and queue-based NetWare printing.

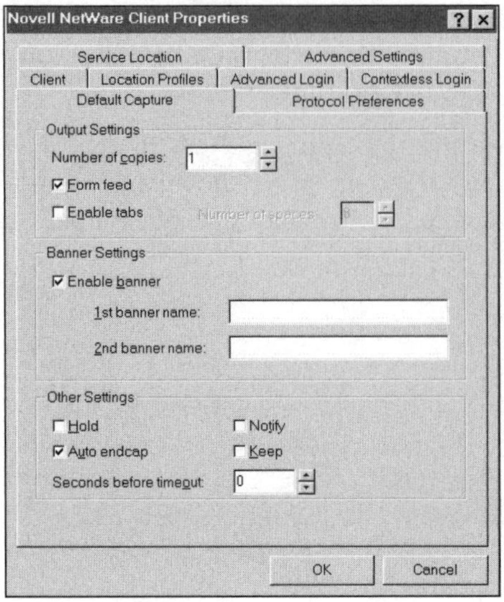

Figure 6-34   Default Capture settings page

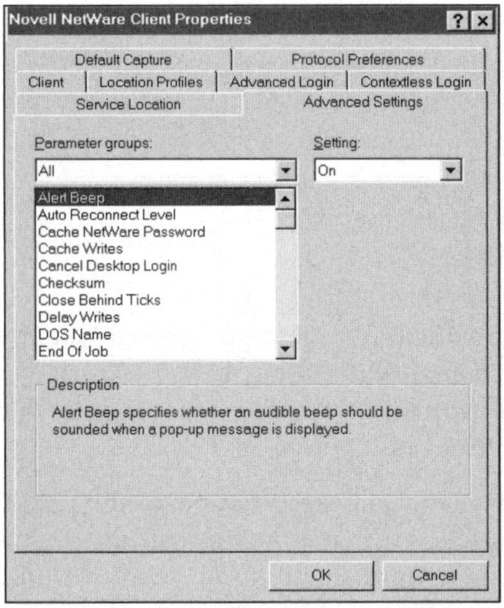

Figure 6-35   Advanced Settings page

The Advanced Settings Page. The Advanced Settings page of the Novell Client Properties dialog box lets you set property values for 67 Novell Client parameters, grouped into eleven parameter groups (or twelve parameter groups, if the All group is counted). The values you set, like the values you set in the other pages of the Novell NetWare Client Properties dialog box, are stored in the Windows 95/98 Registry. These property values include Preferred Tree, Preferred Server, Name Context, and First Network Drive values. Figure 6-35 shows this Advanced Settings page. The parameter groups used on the Advanced Settings page are detailed in Table 6-8.

Table 6-8   Novell Client parameter groups

Parameter Group	Used to Control:
All	All parameter settings
Connection	Parameter settings for the user's LAN connection
Environment, NETX Compatibility	Parameter settings related to the user's workstation and ensuring backward compatibility with settings for the NETX (older DOS) shell
File System	Parameter settings for access to files stored in volumes on NetWare servers
Packet Management	Parameter settings related to the packets that the work-station sends and receives on the network
Cache Performance	Parameter settings for the workstation's interaction with file caching on NetWare servers
Printing	Parameter settings for network printing
Troubleshooting	Settings for parameters that can help determine problem sources
Wide Area Network (WAN)	Parameter settings for user's WAN connections
Graphical Interface	Settings that control whether NetWare tools appear on the desktop, in the system tray, or in menus
SLP General	Settings on how the workstation uses the SLP protocol
SLP Times	Settings on timing related to the SLP protocol

 The Novell Client for DOS and Windows 3.1x uses the **NET.CFG** file, which is where the Novell Client property values are set for the Novell Client for DOS and Windows. Documentation on the NET.CFG file is in the Novell Client for DOS and Windows Help File.

An example of a parameter set on the Advanced Settings page is the NetWare Protocol parameter in the Connection parameter group, as shown in Figure 6-36.

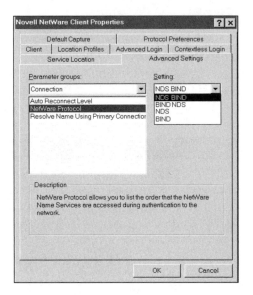

Figure 6-36 NetWare Protocol parameter settings

The NetWare Protocol parameter is used to control which type of network connection is used by the workstation. There are two options: NDS for Novell Directory Services and BIND for bindery. This first protocol listed is the first one that the Novell Client uses in connecting to the network. For example, in Figure 6-36 the NetWare protocol list is NDS BIND, which indicates that the workstation will first try to connect to an NDS Directory tree and then try to connect to a NetWare server in bindery mode if an NDS tree is not available. As the drop-down list in Figure 6-36 shows, there are four settings for the parameter. These settings are summarized in Table 6-9.

Table 6-9 NetWare Client Protocol parameter settings

Parameter Setting	Comments
NDS BIND	Client first attempts to connect to an NDS Directory tree; if that fails, attempts to connect to a NetWare server in bindery mode
BIND NDS	Client first attempts to connect to a NetWare server in bindery mode; if that fails, attempts to connect to an NDS Directory tree
NDS	Client attempts to connect to only an NDS Directory tree
BIND	Client attempts to connect to only a NetWare server in bindery mode

You have now customized and set the workstation's default Novell Client properties. You will need to reboot the workstation again for these defaults to take effect.

Updates to Novell Client Files

Novell updates NetWare files from time to time, sometimes to fix a known problem and sometimes to improve the functionality of the software. As a network administrator, you should regularly check for updates to NetWare files and implement these updates as they occur. Novell publishes a list of the current updates at the Novell Support Connection on its Web site at *http://support.novell.com*. Individual update files are also available through this site.

Novell Client Settings

After the Novell Client is installed, the network administrator may still need access to Novell Client parameter settings in order to modify them. As discussed during the Novell Client installation, the IP and IPX 32-bit protocol are part of the Novell Client. After you complete the installation, you can access not just the Novell Client settings but also the protocol settings through the Network icon in the Windows 95/98 Control Panel. Double-clicking the Network icon displays the Network dialog box, shown earlier in Figure 6-28.

 Windows needs the Microsoft IPX/SPX-compatible protocol shown in the Network dialog box in Figure 6-28 to work with the Novell Client components. This protocol is installed as part of the Novell Client installation, and if you remove it the other Novell Client components will also be removed.

For example, you can click the IPX 32-bit Protocol for Novell Client in the installed components list of the Network dialog box and then click the Properties button to display its Properties dialog box, as shown in Figure 6-37.

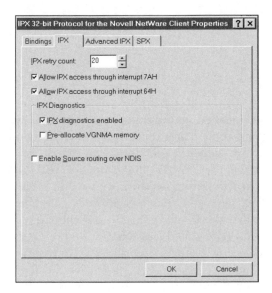

Figure 6-37   IPX protocol properties page

The IPX 32-bit Protocol for Novell Client Properties dialog box has four pages: Bindings, IPX, Advanced IPX, and SPX. Notice that by default the IPX page is initially displayed. The IPX page contains the basic settings for Internetwork Packet eXchange (IPX) parameters, and the defaults initially set normally work well with most NetWare 5.0 networks. As its name implies, the Advanced IPX page contains other parameter settings for the protocol. This page is important because it lets the network administrator select the frame types to use with the protocol. The default installation setting is to use all the frame types detected on the network. However, this may not be efficient if, for example, several frame types are used on the network but this workstation only needs to communicate with some of them. In this case, the network administrator can specify the frame types to be used, as shown in Figure 6-38.

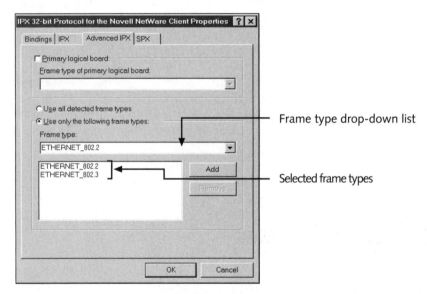

Figure 6-38   Advanced IPX page

The Advanced IPX page also allows the network administrator to specify whether the primary logical board is necessary. Each frame type that is used with an NIC is considered to be broadcast on a separate logical network, which is called a **subnetwork**. For example, in Figure 6-38 two frame types are in use: ETHERNET_802.2 and ETHERNET_802.3. Unless you are installing NetWare 5.0 in an existing network, you won't have any problems with different frame types. In most networks, you will use only one frame type. If you do use different types, remember that the frame types can use the same NIC. One physical NIC becomes two logical NICs (also called *logical boards*)—one for each frame type. One logical NIC is designated as the primary logical NIC or primary board. Novell Client 32 usually selects the primary board itself, normally the logical board using ETHERNET_802.2, which is the default frame type for NetWare 5.0 when an Ethernet NIC is used. If necessary, however, the network administrator can specify the primary board by checking the Primary logical board check box on the Advanced IPX page and then selecting the appropriate frame type.

The SPX page contains the settings for the Sequenced Packet eXchange (SPX) protocol, which is typically used with older NetWare utilities such as RCONSOLE. The Bindings page shows which client software uses this protocol.

The IPX 32-bit Protocol for the Novell NetWare Client Properties dialog box can be closed by clicking the OK button or the Cancel button. If settings have been changed, you must click the OK button to save the changes. Clicking the Cancel Button closes the dialog box without making any changes. Clicking the Close icon in the upper right-hand corner of the dialog box has the same effect as clicking Cancel.

Logging into the Network

When Windows 95/98 starts, the Novell Client is also started and the Novell Login dialog box, shown in Figure 6-39, is displayed.

Figure 6-39 Novell Login screen

 If the Novell Client screen does not appear, then you have a problem with a faulty network board, an incorrect Novell Client installation, or a bad cable or hub.

When the Novell Client dialog box appears, the name of the last user to log into the network using this workstation appears in the Username field. If the name is correct, you need to enter only the password, but if the name is incorrect, you must enter the correct user name. Once you specify the required Username and Password information, and then click the OK button, you log into the network.

The default settings for network connections, printer capture defaults, and scripts that were set during the Novell Client installation (or modified after the installation) in the Novell Client Properties dialog box are used during the login. If the Advanced Button appears in the login dialog box, then the user can override the defaults during login by specifying values on these pages.

To log into the network, you can use the following steps:

1. If the workstation is turned off, turn on the workstation.

2. If the workstation is turned on, click the Start button, select Programs, select Novell, and then click NetWare Login.

3. If necessary, click the Username text box to activate it and then type your user name.

4. If necessary, click the Password text box to activate it and then type your password.

5. If you need to change the default login settings, click the Advanced button to modify your NDS, Script, or Variable settings.

6. Click the OK button.

For example, now that the Novell Client installation on the new workstation is complete, the CBE Labs network administrator will use this workstation to log into the network as the user Admin. The workstation is currently turned off, so starting the computer and Windows 95/98 will also display the Novell NetWare Login dialog box.

To log into the network using the Novell Client, you can use the following steps:

1. Turn on the workstation. Windows 95/98 loads, and the Novell Login dialog box is displayed, as shown earlier in Figure 6-39.

2. Because the user name displayed in the Name text box, Admin, is correct, there is no need to change the user name.

3. The Password text box should be active. If not, click it to activate it.

4. Type the password, which will be displayed as a series of asterisks (********).

5. The workstation defaults are correct for the Admin user, so there is no need to change them. Click the OK button. During login, a script window will appear to display the login script. After the login script is complete, all windows will automatically close themselves. The user is logged into the network.

Logging into Additional NDS Directory Trees or NetWare Servers

The Novell Client permits a user to log into more than one NDS Directory tree. It also lets the user log into NetWare 3.1x servers that are not part of a tree or NetWare 5.0 servers that need to be attached in bindery mode. This can be done using the Novell Login dialog box, the Windows 95/98 Network Neighborhood program, the N in the System Tray, or the Windows 95/98 Explorer.

To use the Novell Login dialog box, the user must be able to specify the connection on the NDS page of the Novell Login dialog box. For example, Figure 6-40 shows the settings necessary for the CBE Labs network administrator to attach to the NetWare 3.2 server RANGER.

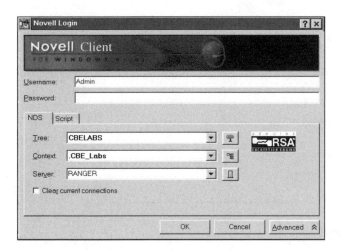

Figure 6-40   Logging into multiple directory trees or servers

The Directory tree or NetWare server must be specified. You can type them in, or you could choose them by clicking the browse buttons to the right of the fields and selecting the appropriate names from a list. In Figure 6-40, the NetWare 3.2 server name RANGER has been typed into the Server text box. The Clear current connections check box also must be deselected. This is important—otherwise the existing connection to the CBELABS Directory tree would be cleared and only a connection to RANGER would exist. With these settings, the user will attach to the NetWare 3.2 server RANGER without losing the current connection to the CBELABS network. With these settings made, you would now provide the user name and password. Clicking the OK button completes the login.

You can also attach to additional Directory trees and NetWare servers using Windows 95/98 Network Neighborhood or the N in the System Tray and Windows Explorer. The NetWare Provider for Windows 95/98 has added features to these utilities. Because Network Neighborhood is accessible through Explorer, you'll look at Explorer. Figure 6-41 shows Windows 95/98 Explorer with the Network Neighborhood section expanded to show the available Novell Directory Services trees and NetWare Servers available on the entire network. You attach to an additional Directory Tree or NetWare server by authenticating on that NDS tree or NetWare server.

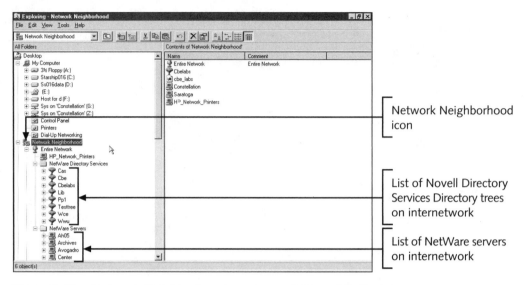

Figure 6-41   Network Neighborhood resources displayed in Explorer

Authenticating is the process of sending your user name and password to the NDS Directory tree or NetWare server and having them checked and validated. This may be done automatically or by having you provide your user name and password. Automatic authentication occurs when the Novell Client Cache NetWare Password parameter is set to "on." The Cache NetWare Password parameter is one of the Novell Client parameters controlled on the Advanced Settings page of the Novell Client Properties dialog box. The valid parameter values are "on" and "off," and the default value is "on." When password caching is enabled, Novell Client stores or "caches" your user name and password in the memory of your workstation (*not* on the hard drive). When you attempt to use a network resource that requires you to attach to another NDS Directory tree or NetWare server, the Novell Client automatically provides your user name and password and you are authenticated without any input from you. However, if password caching is disabled, you will be prompted to provide your user name and password.

For example, if CBE Labs network administrator Ted Simpson wants to attach to the NetWare 3.2 server RANGER, he would begin by locating RANGER in the list of NetWare servers in Explorer. He would then right-click the icon for RANGER, which would display the shortcut menu shown in Figure 6-42. He would then click Authenticate to attach to RANGER.

Figure 6-42   NetWare Server shortcut menu in Explorer

To attach to an additional NDS Directory tree or NetWare server, you can do the following:

1. Click the Start button, select Programs, select Novell, and then click NetWare Login.
2. Click the Advanced button to display the NDS page, and then enter the necessary information.
3. Enter the user name and password.
4. Click the OK button.

An alternative method is to use Explorer:

1. Launch Explorer; then expand the Network Neighborhood until the NDS Directory tree or NetWare server that you want to log in to is visible.
2. Right-click the NDS Directory tree or NetWare server icon to display the shortcut menu.
3. Click Authenticate. If NetWare password caching is enabled, your name and password will be automatically provided to the new resource. Otherwise, the Novell Login dialog box is displayed, and you must enter your login information and then click the OK button.

Viewing NetWare Resources

You can view a list of your NetWare connections using the extensions to Windows 95/98 Network Neighborhood and Explorer installed by the Novell Client. When you right-click the Network Neighborhood icon on the desktop or in Explorer, a shortcut menu appears, as shown in Figure 6-43.

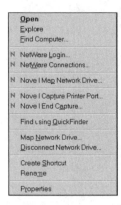

Figure 6-43   Network Neighborhood shortcut menu

If users want to view their current network connections, they can right-click Network Neighborhood, then select NetWare Connections. This displays the NetWare Connections dialog box shown in Figure 6-44. The user's current network connections are shown in this dialog box.

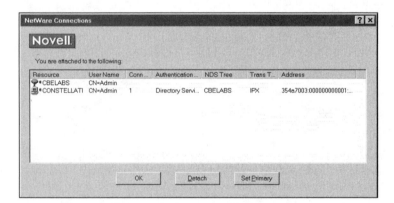

Figure 6-44   NetWare Connections dialog box

Logging Out of the Network

The most secure way to log out of the network is to use the Windows 95/98 Shut Down command. This command is selected by clicking the Start button on the Windows 95/98 taskbar and then clicking Shut Down. This displays the Shut Down Windows dialog box, which has several options. If you select the Shut down the computer? option, the Novell Client will log you out of any NDS Directory trees and NetWare servers you are attached to as Windows 95/98 runs its shutdown routine. If you select the Close all programs and log on as a different user? option, the Novell Client also closes all existing connections. In this case, however, the Novell Login dialog box is then displayed so that a new user can log in without rebooting the computer. In both cases, your user name and password are removed from memory if they were cached during your login.

To log out of the NDS Directory tree from the Start menu, you can do the following:

1. Click the Start button, and then click Shut Down.

2. In the Shut Down Windows dialog box, select the option you want.

3. Click the OK button.

If you want to log out of an NDS Directory tree (or NetWare server) without shutting down the computer, you can use Network Neighborhood or Explorer. It's easier to use the Network Neighborhood portion of the Explorer display. To log out of the NDS Directory tree, expand the Network Neighborhood tree until you can see the NDS Directory tree icon that you want to log out of. Right-click the icon to select it and display the shortcut menu shown in Figure 6-45. Click Logout to log out of the network. This is *not* a secure logout, because if NetWare password caching is enabled, your user name and password remain cached in memory. You will continue to see network resources in Explorer and Network Neighborhood, and if you try to use a network resource you will be automatically logged in again so that you can access the resource.

Figure 6-45   Logging out with the NDS directory tree shortcut menu

Verifying the Installation

After completing the server and workstation installation, you should reboot your workstation to load the new parameters. If you see a "NetWare server not found" message, the most common causes are a defective cable, a faulty Ethernet connector, an incorrect frame type, an interrupt being used by both the network card and some other device in either the server or the workstation, a faulty hub, or the IP protocol not being properly bound to the network card on the NetWare server.

Sometimes the reason for a problem can be so obvious that it escapes you. Take, for example, the case of a network administrator who spent some time looking for the cause of a "NetWare server not found" message only to discover that someone had broken into the NetWare server room and actually stolen the server. In this case the workstation was literally correct: The NetWare server could not be found!

Once you verify that the NetWare server and workstations are communicating correctly, you can continue setting up the network by establishing the NetWare server's directory structure, along with the user accounts and security, as described in the following chapters. Installation is an ongoing process that expands the network to incorporate additional workstations and enhances the NetWare server.

CHAPTER SUMMARY

◻ The NetWare installation process is divided into two major operations: installing the NetWare server software and installing the workstation software. Installing NetWare on a server can be divided into eight main steps. Step 1 is to plan the network layout and complete a NetWare server worksheet to document the network environment and NetWare server hardware configuration. Step 2 is installing and configuring the NetWare server hardware. Step 3 includes partitioning the boot drive and installing DOS. In Step 4 you complete the portion that runs under DOS. This includes loading the correct disk drivers, LAN drivers, and protocols, and creating drive partitions and volumes. In Step 5 you work with the main steps of the Install Wizard that runs under NetWare 5.0 itself. In Step 6 you install Novell Directory Services and create the NDS Directory tree. Step 7 is editing the STARTUP.NCF and AUTOEXEC.NCF startup files. Step 8 is choosing any installation options you want to use.

◻ For the NetWare server to connect to the network, disk drivers and NIC LAN drivers must be correctly loaded into the NetWare NOS. Similarly, network protocols must be bound to the NICs. The commands to bind network protocols to NIC are stored in the STARTUP.NCF and the AUTOEXEC.NCF files so that they will be run automatically when the NetWare server is booted. The MONITOR NLM provides a useful tool for monitoring the NetWare server's performance.

◻ To access the NetWare server, the workstation computer requires three software components. The first component is the network card driver, which provides the data link process of transmitting and receiving packets over the network cable system. The second software component is the protocol stack, which is responsible for formatting the packets through the network, transport, and session layers of the OSI model. In NetWare 5, TCP/IP is used as the default protocol. The third software component is the client software that provides an interface from Windows to the NetWare server. The Novell Client acts as a front end for Windows and directs all application and user requests for NetWare services to the network server. All three components are included with the installation process for the Novell Client. Novell Client software can also improve network performance and security by using packet burst mode and packet signatures.

❑ Novell Client software is available in versions for DOS/Windows 3.1x, Windows 95/98, and Windows NT. The client files are on the Novell Client/Z.E.N.works CD-ROM included with NetWare 5.0. They can also be downloaded free from Novell's Web site. Installation of Novell Client for Windows 95/98 is an auto-run function on the CD-ROM or you can choose to run SETUP from the Win95/98 directory on the CD-ROM. After installation, you can configure the Novell Client by setting parameters on pages of the Novell Client Properties dialog box. These settings can be modified through the Network icon in the Windows 95/98 Control Panel. The five Novell Client Properties pages are the Client page, which sets the connection preferences; the Advanced Login page, which controls the display of the Novell Login dialog box; the Default Capture page, which sets defaults for printed output; Location Profiles, which provides a selection of login profiles for this location; and the Advanced Settings page, which enables you to control the values of 67 parameters that affect the Novell Client. The parameter settings made in the Novell Client Properties dialog box are stored in the Windows 95/98 Registry; in the version of Novell Client for DOS/Windows 3.1x, these settings are stored in the NET.CFG file.

❑ Novell frequently issues updates and patch files to the NetWare NOS and Novell Client files. Periodically after installation, you will need to obtain and install any needed updates.

❑ The Novell Login dialog box provided with the Novell Client lets you log into NDS Directory trees and NetWare servers. You can log into more than one NDS Directory tree using the Novell Client. You can also log in through the extensions to Windows 95/98 added by the NetWare Provider for Windows 95/98. These same extensions enable you to view your current network connections through the Current NetWare Resources dialog box.

❑ After installing the workstation software, you should reboot the computer and attempt to log into the NetWare server. When first loaded, the Novell Client will attempt to attach to a Directory tree and a default NetWare server. If the workstation does not receive a response from a NetWare server within a few moments, it returns a "NetWare server not found" error message. The most common causes of the "NetWare server not found" error message are a bad cable, incorrect frame type, overlapping interrupt assignments, or the IP protocol not being properly bound to the network card on the NetWare server.

COMMAND SUMMARY

Command	Syntax	Definition
ADD NAME SPACE	*ADD NAME SPACE name [TO volume_name]*	Run once to create an additional name space on a volume. Needed to support the long filename space, which is used to support Windows 95/98 long filenames.
BIND	*BIND protocol [TO] LAN driver	board name [driver parameters . . .] [protocol parameters . . .]*	Allows NetWare to communicate with a LAN card by attaching a protocol stack to the card driver.
DISABLE LOGIN	*DISABLE LOGIN*	A NetWare console command that prevents users from logging in to the server. Users currently logged in are not affected. Use this command before you shut down the NetWare server, to prevent additional users from logging in after you have broadcast the warning message.
DISMOUNT	*DISMOUNT [ALL] [volume name]*	This console command takes the specified volume or all volumes off line, making them inaccessible to the network. It is usually used when you need to perform volume maintenance.
DOWN	*DOWN*	A NetWare console command that takes the server off line by stopping all network communication and dismounting all volumes. You receive a warning message if active connections to the server exist, and you can terminate the connections or cancel the command.
ENABLE LOGIN	*ENABLE LOGIN*	A NetWare console command that enables users to log into the NetWare server. After you use the DISABLE LOGIN command, use this command to restore logins

LOAD	*LOAD [path]* *Loadable_module_name* *[module parameters]*	Accesses and runs a NetWare Loadable Module (NLM) in the NetWare server's RAM. By default, modules are loaded from the SYS:SYSTEM directory. Modules remain in RAM until unloaded. Because NetWare is a multitasking operating system, many modules can be loaded at one time. Examples of module names include the INSTALL and MONITOR modules described in this chapter. (*Note*: If the NLM you wish to load is in the SYS:SYS-TEM directory, you only have to type the name of the module and press [Enter] for NetWare to load it.)
MONITOR	*LOAD MONITOR* or *MONITOR*	A NetWare Loadable Module that displays information regarding the performance of a NetWare server.
MOUNT	*MOUNT* *[volume name] [ALL]*	This console command enables you to mount a specific volume or all volumes. Mounting a volume loads the file allocation table and directory entry table into RAM. A volume must be mounted before it can be accessed by the network.
NWCONFIG	*LOAD NWCONFIG* or *NWCONFIG*	A NetWare Loadable Module that is used to set up and maintain NetWare disk drives and volumes, as well as perform system operations such as copying system and public files and creating or modifying the startup files.
SEND	*SEND "message"*	Send a message to all network users logged in to the network. You should issue this command to warn users that the NetWare server is going to be shut down.
UNLOAD	*UNLOAD module name*	Terminates execution of the specified module and removes it from memory.

6

KEY TERMS

adapter
Add Name Space utility
agent
authenticating
AUTOEXEC.NCF
client
Custom Device Module (CDM)
data compression algorithm
data migration
default volume name
dismounted volume
DOWN command
Host Adapter Module (HAM)
internal network number
internetwork
Link Support Layer (LSL)
minimum compression
    percentage gain
MONITOR utility
mounted volume
Multiple Link Interface Driver (MLID)
multiple NetWare server network
name context
name spaces
NET.CFG
NetWare Command File (NCF)
NetWare Provider for
    Windows 95/98
NetWare server name
network client
network layout
NIC driver
Novell Peripheral Architecture (NPA)
Open Data Interface (ODI)
optical disks

packet burst mode
packet signature patch
primary time server (PTS)
protocol stack
reference time server (RTS)
secondary time server (STS)
SERVER.EXE
SET commands
single reference time server (SRTS)
STARTUP.NCF
subnetwork

6

REVIEW QUESTIONS

1. List the eight major steps for installing NetWare on a NetWare server.

2. A(n) _____ is used internally by the NetWare operating system to communicate with its device drivers.

3. A NetWare server's name can be from _____ to _____ characters in length.

4. All devices that communicate with each other over a network cable system must use the same _____.

5. A network containing two NetWare servers is referred to as a(n) _____.

6. Multiple networks connected together by routers are called a(n) _____.

7. A NetWare server that connects two networks is referred to as a(n) _____.

8. Which of the following is an invalid IPX network address?
   _____ A _____ 10BASET _____ 1AB216A15 _____ 1EEE8025

9. List three types of NetWare Loadable Modules and their corresponding extensions.

10. When it creates a partition and volumes, NetWare by default uses the volume names of _____ and so on.

11. Describe the purpose of STARTUP.NCF and AUTOEXEC.NCF.

12. The _____ and _____ keys are used to switch the server console from one active module to another.

13. List the three workstation software components.

14. The Windows 95/98 _____ contains configuration settings used by the ODI drivers. These settings were previously contained in the _____.

15. List the five pages in the Novell Client Properties dialog box.

16. Describe how to install the Novell Client when using Windows 95/98 as the operating system.

17. Where are updated Novell files and patches available?

18. Why do you need to add the long filename space to a NetWare server supporting Windows 95/98?

19. List the four commands necessary to load the Macintosh name space support for the first time.

20. List the command(s) necessary to stop the NetWare NOS running on a NetWare server and return to the DOS prompt.

21. What command is used at the DOS prompt to start the NetWare NOS on a NetWare server?

HANDS-ON PROJECTS

Project 6-1: Performing a Complete NetWare 5.0 Installation

In this exercise you install NetWare 5.0 from a CD-ROM drive. At the end of this exercise, you will also have configured a NetWare server that you can access from a workstation attached to the network. To do this exercise, you will need the following components, which will be supplied by your instructor:

❏ Access to an Pentium 133 or later computer with at least 64 MB of RAM and a 1 GB hard disk

❏ An NIC and cable to connect to a network hub that has at least one other workstation attached to it

❏ A CD-ROM drive that can be attached to the NetWare server (or a CD-ROM drive that is shared on the network)

❏ A copy of a NetWare 5.0 Operating System CD-ROM

❏ A copy of the Novell Client for Windows 95/98 CD-ROM

❏ A non-Windows DOS boot disk containing the FDISK, FORMAT, and SYS commands

❏ A floppy disk containing your CD-ROM drivers

Once you have verified that your work area contains these components, use the following steps to install NetWare and initialize your NetWare server.

Step 1: Record NetWare Server Information

1. Sketch a diagram of the network system you are building, including all student NetWare servers and network topologies. Label the diagram with the following information:

   - Name of each NetWare server

   - IP address to be used for each server (indicate RANDOM if you are going to let the installation process select a number for you)

   - Network topology

   - Network card model and manufacturer

   - Ethernet frame type

2. Obtain a blank copy of the NetWare Server Worksheet shown in Table 6-1 (there is a copy in Appendix B).

3. Fill in the identification section by supplying a valid name for your server.

4. Fill in the system information section by identifying the disk controller card type, drive information, and correct NetWare disk driver to be used. Your instructor will tell you where to obtain this information. You might need the documentation sheet included with the computer and system manuals.

5. Fill in the network card information section by reading the settings off the network card or using the network card handout provided by your instructor.

6. Fill in the IP Information section with information provided by your instructor.

7. List any other equipment in the NetWare server in the non-network device information section, and check that no hardware interrupt conflicts exist.

Step 2: Install NetWare 5.0

In this step you use the CD-ROM drive to run the Install Wizard. Your instructor will provide instructions to supplement the description of the NetWare server installation given in this chapter. The following steps assume you have access to a CD-ROM drive as a drive letter on your computer:

1. Boot the computer with the DOS disk. This disk should contain the drivers that enable you to access a CD-ROM drive, either one attached to your computer or one shared on the network. Be sure the NetWare 5.0 CD-ROM is in the CD-ROM drive before you continue. If necessary, your instructor will give you directions for using the **FDisk**, **Format**, and **SYS** commands.

2. Change to the drive letter containing the NetWare 5.0 CD-ROM.

3. Type the command **INSTALL**. Follow the steps outlined in the chapter as supplemented by your instructor to complete the NetWare 5.0 installation. Your instructor will tell you about any special considerations you need to be aware of during installation. *Note on creating the server volumes:* Make the SYS volume size 500 MB, and create a DATA volume using all but 5 MB of the remaining disk space.

4. Record approximately how long this installation process took.

Step 3: Complete the Installation

Briefly identify each process you will need to perform to complete the NetWare server installation to the point where the server is available to the network and can be rebooted.

1. Use the hot-key sequence to return to the console prompt.
2. Record the contents of your STARTUP.NCF file.
3. Record the contents of your AUTOEXEC.NCF file.
4. Where is the STARTUP.NCF file stored?
5. Where is the AUTOEXEC.NCF file stored?

Project 6-2: Test the Installation

For this exercise you need access to a NetWare server console you have recently installed or to one provided by your instructor. Table 6-10 presents a set of console commands that were not discussed in the chapter. Try the commands on the console, and record the results. Write a short memo to your instructor in which for each of the console commands you:

1. Briefly describe its purpose and why you might use it after performing an installation.
2. Report and interpret the results of the console command.

Table 6-10   Selected NetWare console commands

Command	Purpose
SPEED	Use this command to display the speed of the NetWare server's processor. This speed is a relative number. For example, an Intel 33 MHz 80386 DX processor will have a SPEED result in a range around 320.
MEMORY	Use this command to display the amount of installed memory.
MODULES	Use this command to display a list of the modules that are currently running on the NetWare server. The output includes the name, description, and version number (for .DSK, .LAN and .NLM modules).
VOLUMES	Use this command to display a list of the mounted volumes on the NetWare server. The output uses the following flags: Cp–File compression is enabled Sa–Block suballocation is enabled Mg–Data migration is enabled

Table 6-10   Selected NetWare console commands (continued)

Command	Purpose
DISPLAY SERVERS	Use this command to display a list of all NetWare servers and services that are broadcasting Service Advertising Protocol (SAP) packets. Services will include NetWare servers, NDS, print servers, Storage Management Services (SMS) devices, and Structured Query Language (SQL) servers. The output includes the network address of the server and the number of hops to the server, where a hop is defined as the number of routers the packer must pass through to get to the destination.
DISPLAY IPX NETWORKS	Use this command to display a list of networks recognized by the NetWare server. The output includes the IPX external network number followed by the number of hops to the network and the time in tics (1/18th of a second) it takes for a packet to get to that address.

6

Project 6-3: Installing Novell Client for Windows 95/98 on a Workstation

In this exercise you install Novell Client for Windows 95/98 to enable your workstation to access the network NetWare server. To complete this exercise, you will need the following components, which will be supplied by your instructor:

❏ A workstation computer with a LAN card and CD-ROM drive

❏ A copy of the Novell Client for Windows 95/98 CD-ROM

❏ A copy of the documentation that came with the card

❏ The disk that was supplied with the network card (optional)

❏ The network card hardware settings (your instructor may give you a copy of the network card manual with the card settings indicated and may ask you to determine the hardware configuration given the jumper settings indicated in the diagram)

1. Use the documentation supplied by your instructor to fill in Table 6-11 with the configuration of your network card.

Table 6-11   NIC specifications

Network Interface Card Make and Model	Other Novell Cards Emulated	ODI Driver	Interrupt	I/O Port	Memory Address

2. Install Novell Client for Windows 95/98 on your workstation, following the steps outlined in this chapter.

3. Reboot your workstation with your newly installed Novell Client.

4. List two items you should check for if the workstation login cannot find the NetWare server on an Ethernet network.

Project 6-4: Checking for Updated Novell Client Files

In this exercise you check the Novell Support Connection Web site for the latest updates to your Novell Client. You download a copy of any update files and then update your Novell Client installation. To complete this exercise, you will need the following components, which will be supplied by your instructor:

❑ A workstation computer with a LAN card, a CD-ROM drive, a hard drive, and Windows 95/98 installed

❑ Novell Client for Windows 95/98 installed on the workstation

❑ Internet access at the workstation, and a Web browser with FTP capabilities

1. Use your Web browser to connect to the Novell Support Connection at *http://support.novell.com*.

2. Browse the Web site to see what information is available.

3. Download the most recent update file for Novell Client for Windows 95/98. Your instructor will provide additional information about where to store this file.

4. Your instructor will give you instructions on how to expand the contents of the file you downloaded and how to update the Novell Client for Windows 95/98 installation.

CREATING THE NDS DIRECTORY TREE STRUCTURE

After reading this chapter and completing the exercises you will be able to:

♦ Use NetWare commands and utilities to work with the NetWare Directory Services (NDS) Directory tree structure

♦ Create, move, rename, and delete container objects

♦ Create, move, and rename leaf objects

♦ Rename Directory trees

Once the server installation is complete, it's time to set up the NetWare Directory Services (NDS) Directory tree structure. You planned the NDS Directory tree in Chapter 4, and created the first portions of the Directory tree during the NetWare 5.0 installation in Chapter 6. Now you need to create the organizational structure of the tree and add network resources in their proper organizational context.

To do this job, you need to understand the NetWare commands and utilities used to create and maintain the NDS Directory tree. Chapter 4 introduced you to NDS trees and planning the directory service structure. This chapter gives you experience with the NetWare 5.0 commands and utilities to create, navigate, and display the actual Directory tree. Later, in Chapter 9, you will add users, groups, and organizational roles to the tree.

For example, the Cunningham, Burns, and Evans Laboratories (CBE Labs) network administrator has now installed the NetWare 5.0 servers. Now the rest of the NDS Directory tree organizational structure for CBE Labs needs to be created. We'll need to use NetWare commands and utilities that work with NDS during this process.

NETWARE COMMAND AND UTILITY GROUPS

There are six basic NetWare command and utility groups: command line utilities, menu utilities, graphical utilities, supervisor utilities, console commands, and NetWare Loadable Modules (NLMs). However, the emphasis in NetWare 5 is to perform most operations using Windows.

Command line utilities (CLUs) are NetWare commands executed from the DOS prompt. Once they were the main way to work with NetWare; now, Windows utilities have superseded them. For example, NDIR and NCOPY are CLUs.

Menu utilities are interactive programs that contain menus and help messages that help you perform more complex tasks. Like the command line utilities, menu utilities were based on DOS and so Windows-based utilities have superseded them in most cases.

Graphical utilities are Windows-based and interactive. These utilities take advantage of Windows menu, dialog box, and icon conventions to visually present choices, options, and tasks. The utilities also include help messages based on the Windows help system. These utilities are the most powerful in NetWare 5.0. An example of a NetWare graphical utility is NetWare Administrator, described later in this chapter.

Supervisor utilities are command line, menu, and graphical utilities that are by default stored in the SYS:SYSTEM directory. Supervisor utilities are used in system configuration and maintenance. Later chapters show you how to use supervisor utilities to do such network management tasks as checking system security and fixing system problems.

Console commands are NetWare commands executed from the NetWare server console prompt. Console commands are built into the NetWare operating system. Examples are commands such as LOAD, MOUNT, and BIND.

NetWare Loadable Modules (NLMs) are programs that run on the NetWare server. They are loaded and run at the console prompt. You can add functions such as network printing to the NetWare server by running NLMs. Three different kinds of NLMs used during NetWare's installation are:

- Disk drivers, such as IDE.HAM and SCSI.HAM
- LAN drivers, such as TOKEN.LAN and NE3200.LAN
- Other NLMs, such as NWCONFIG and MONITOR

In Chapter 14 you will work with the NetWare server console commands and NLMs to do additional tasks such as backing up the file system and configuring the server for improved performance.

NETWARE ADMINISTRATOR (NWADMIN)

You will use the Windows utility **NetWare Administrator** (frequently called NWAdmin) to manage the NDS Directory tree. NWAdmin provides the centralized administration that makes the network easy to manage and administer.

NWAdmin lets you browse the NDS Directory tree, to create NDS container and leaf objects, and to manage the object properties. You can rename objects, move objects, and delete objects within the Directory tree. You can also manage NDS partitions with NWAdmin.

To use NWAdmin to create and manage objects in the Directory tree, you must have the necessary trustee rights. The Admin user—the only user discussed in this chapter—has Supervisor rights (which grant all trustee rights) and can therefore create and manage any objects anywhere in the Directory tree. Chapter 10 discusses trustee rights and their assignment to users and groups in detail.

Displaying the Directory Tree

When you launch NWAdmin, it automatically displays the Directory tree in a single browser window, as Figure 7-1 shows.

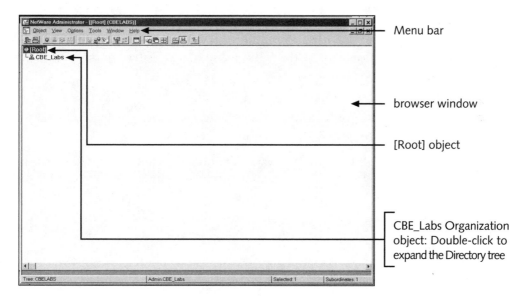

Figure 7-1   NetWare Administrator opening screen

Notice that in Figure 7-1 the initial screen shows only the [Root] and Organization objects, and does not expand the Directory tree further at this point.

To see the objects in a container object, use any of these methods:

- When the objects are *not* displayed, double-click the container object name or icon.

- Click the container object, click View on the menu bar, and then click Expand.

- Click the container object, then press the plus (+) key.

To hide the objects in a container object, use either of these methods:

- When the objects are displayed, double-click the container object or icon.

- Click the container object, click View on the menu bar, and then click Collapse.

- Click the container object, then press the minus or hyphen (-) key.

To change context, you can use either of these methods:

- Click View on the menu bar, click Set Context, and then type the new context.

- Click View on the menu bar, click Set Context, and then browse to the new context.

You can open additional browser windows so that you can simultaneously see different sections of the Directory tree (NWAdmin supports a maximum of 10 browser windows).

To open an additional browser window, click Tools on the menu bar, and then click NDS Browser. To close a browser window, click the Close button on the browser window. For example, the CBE Labs network administrator wants to open a second Directory tree browser window that starts at the CBE_Labs context. To create the CBE_Labs browser window, follow these steps:

1. If NWAdmin is not open, start it.

2. Click the CBE_Labs Organization object, and then click Tools on the menu bar. The Tools menu appears, as Figure 7-2 shows.

3. Click NDS Browser. NetWare Administrator displays a Set Context dialog box. The default is the name of your current Lab tree, as set by your instructor.

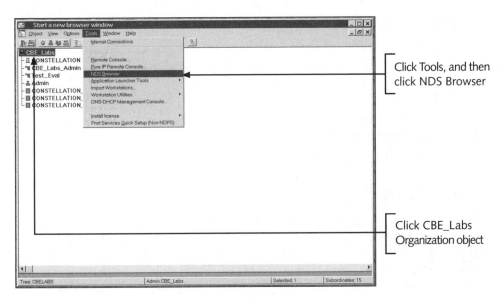

Figure 7-2 Opening a new browse window

4. Click the Browse button to the right of the Context field. Select the class CBE_Labs organizational unit to view the CBELABS tree. Click OK and a browse window similar to Figure 7-3 appears.

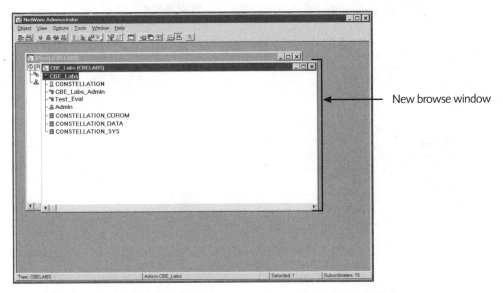

Figure 7-3 CBE_Labs browse window

The toolbar and status bar are configurable—you can choose whether or not to display them, and you can select the buttons on the toolbar and the status indicators on the status bar.

The browse window also lets you:

- Work with more than one NDS Directory tree
- Select and work with multiple User objects
- Expedite print services setup
- Use the Internet to contact Novell support services (for this you need an Internet connection on the workstation)

At the end of this chapter, we discuss working with multiple trees.

Limiting Views

As your NDS tree grows, it will fill with a variety of objects. Often you only want to see one type of object, or a couple, such as All Groups or All Groups and Users. You can do this using the Browser Sort and Include icon [🔢] on the button bar. If you click this button, NetWare Administrator shows a list of all the objects in the tree. You can also use the View menu, Sort and Include option, to access this list. By default, NetWare Administrator will include all object classes in the browser view, as Figure 7-4 shows.

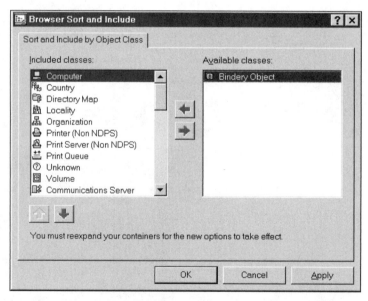

Figure 7-4   Display List dialog box

The Included Classes pane on the left in Figure 7-4 lists the objects you want to appear in your NetWare Administrator view. The objects listed in the right pane are excluded from view.

To hide one or more object classes, follow these steps:

1. Scroll through the list on the left, highlight the object class, then click the right arrow button in the center. This moves the object class from the display list on the left to the hide list on the right.

2. Once you have moved any objects you want to hide to the right pane, click OK.

3. Collapse and then re-expand the tree to refresh the view. Now when you display the containers, they will show only those object classes you have in the included list.

 You cannot use the Browser Sort and Include dialog box to display a long list of all users in the tree outside their containers. If you exclude the object classes Organization and/or Organizational Unit, then you will also exclude any and all object classes in those containers.

The Browser Sort and Include options persist only while you have the view open. Once you close the view, or exit NWAdmin, the default display of all object classes returns (unless you press the Save Preferences icon on the tool bar).

The Save Preferences icon [icon] is an on/off toggle that persists when you close NWAdmin. Leave it in the on position (depressed, or pushed in) and the current settings you have in NWAdmin remain when you open the utility again. Click it off to restore the default settings. You can also save the current setting from the Options menu, Save Settings on Exit option.

COMPLETING THE ORGANIZATIONAL STRUCTURE IN THE DIRECTORY TREE

NetWare actually creates the NDS Directory tree during the installation of the first NetWare 5.0 server in your Directory tree. NetWare needs to define the tree so it knows where to place (that is, in which context to place) the server object. When you install additional NetWare 5.0 servers into the Directory tree, you will again need to specify the context of each new NetWare server during its installation. This may require creating additional Organization or Organizational Unit objects in the Directory tree. You studied these aspects of Directory tree creation in Chapter 6, which covered NetWare 5.0 installation.

When the installation of all NetWare 5.0 servers is complete, the NDS Directory tree contains the following:

- The [Root] object
- One or more Country objects (optional)
- At least one Organization object
- One or more Organizational Unit objects (optional)

- A NetWare Server object for each NetWare 5.0 server installed

- A SYS Volume object for each NetWare 5.0 server installed

- A Volume object for each additional volume created during server installation (optional)

For example, suppose the CBE Labs administrator installed NetWare 5.0 on the server CONSTELLATION. This was the first server in the tree, so he created the CBELABS tree as well. Then he installed NetWare 5.0 on a second server, SARATOGA, and specified a new context for this server: Test_Eval.CBE_Labs. NetWare added this to the existing tree along with the new SARATOGA server object. After the CBE Labs network administrator installed NetWare 5.0 on the two CBE NetWare 5.0 servers, the CBE Labs Directory tree appeared, as shown in the CBE_Labs tree in Figure 7-5.

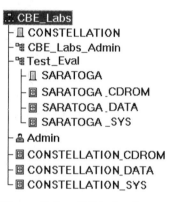

```
CBE_Labs
├─ CONSTELLATION
├─ CBE_Labs_Admin
├─ Test_Eval
│   ├─ SARATOGA
│   ├─ SARATOGA_CDROM
│   ├─ SARATOGA_DATA
│   └─ SARATOGA _SYS
├─ Admin
├─ CONSTELLATION_CDROM
├─ CONSTELLATION_DATA
└─ CONSTELLATION_SYS
```

Figure 7-5 CBE Labs directory tree after the installation process

CONSTELLATION was the first NetWare 5.0 server installed. During this installation, the administrator created the [Root] object and the name of the Directory tree, CBELABS. He did not create any Country objects. He created the Organization object CBE_Labs and located CONSTELLATION in the context .CBE_Labs. CONSTELLATION has two volumes: SYS and DATA. The administrator created and placed volume objects for each of these volumes in the same context as CONSTELLATION. During this installation process, he also created the User object Admin.

Because the administrator installed SARATOGA into the CBELABS Directory tree, he did not need to create a [Root] object or name the Directory tree. He did not create any Country or Organization objects during the installation, but did specify the new Organizational Unit object Test_Eval for the server, which NetWare created. He installed SARATOGA in the context Test_Eval.CBE_Labs. SARATOGA has three volumes: SYS, DATA, and CDROM. The administrator created and placed volume objects for each of these volumes in the same context as SARATOGA. Because the user Admin was already created, the administrator had no need to create an administrator account.

Now the CBE Labs network administrator needs to complete the organizational structure of the CBE Labs Directory tree by adding any necessary container objects to the Directory tree. The Directory tree must reflect the organization chart of CBE Labs, which Figure 7-6 shows.

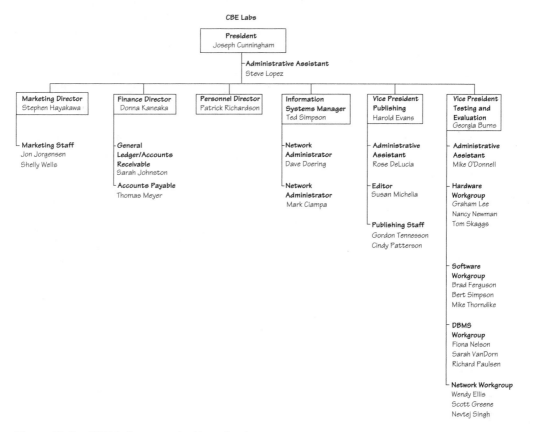

Figure 7-6   CBE Labs organization chart

Creating NDS Directory Tree Container Objects

Creating NDS Directory tree objects always uses the same basic procedure. To create an object, you can use any of these methods:

- Click the container object for the object, and then press [Insert].

- Click the container object for the object, click Object on the menu bar, and then click Create.

- Right-click the container object for the object, and click Create on the shortcut menu to bring up the New Object dialog box. Then, in the Class of New Object list, click the type of object you want and click OK. In the Create *ObjectType* dialog box, enter the necessary property values, and then click the Create button.

The type or class of objects listed in the New Object dialog box's Class of New Object list will vary—only types of objects that you can create will be displayed for you to choose from. When you choose an object type, the appropriate Create *ObjectType* dialog box for the object type will be displayed, where *ObjectType* is the name of the object you choose in the Class of New Object list. For example, if you are creating an Organization Unit object, the Create Organizational Object dialog box will be displayed.

To finish creating an object, you must supply the property values required in the Create *ObjectType* dialog box. This dialog box also gives you the options of (1) defining additional property values for the object you are creating, (2) immediately creating another object of the same type in the same container object, or (3) other choices, depending on which object is being created.

The [Root] Object

The [Root] object is the only exception to the steps just described for creating a new Directory tree object. You create the [Root] object *only* during installation of the first NetWare 5.0 server in the Directory tree. The [Root] object stores the name of the Directory tree. At this point, you cannot modify the [Root] object itself.

The Directory tree can be renamed by using the DSMERGE utility, discussed later in this chapter.

The Country Object

You can add Country objects to the Directory tree. As Chapter 4 discusses, Country objects are optional, and network administrators often prefer to use Organization objects with geographic names instead of Country objects. The names of Country objects are limited to a standard two-letter identifier, some of which Table 7-1 shows. The codes shown are CCITT X.500 standard country codes. Notice that the code for the United Kingdom (Great Britain) is GB, not UK. The Online Documentation shipped with NetWare 5.0 lists additional country codes.

You can create Country objects only immediately below the [Root] object. To add a Country object to a Directory tree, select Country in the Class of New Object list, and specify a country name.

Table 7-1   Examples of country codes

Country	Code	Country	Code
Australia	AU	Mexico	MX
Brazil	BR	New Zealand	NZ
Canada	CA	Philippines	PH
China	CN	Puerto Rico	PT
Denmark	DK	Russian Federation	RU
Egypt	EG	Saudi Arabia	SA
France	FR	Spain	ES
Germany	DE	Switzerland	CH
India	IN	United Kingdom	GB
Japan	JP	United States	US

For example, CBE Labs has just created a European branch with an office in England. The CBE Labs network administrator wants to create a United Kingdom Country object in the tree.

To create the United Kingdom Country object, follow these steps:

1. If NWAdmin is not open, start it.

2. Click the [Root] object, click Object on the menu bar, and then click Create.

3. The New Object dialog box is displayed, as Figure 7-7 shows. Notice that the list of object types displayed in the Class of New Object window varies depending on which types of new objects you can create within the container object. In this case, you can create only an Alias object, a Country object, or an Organization object.

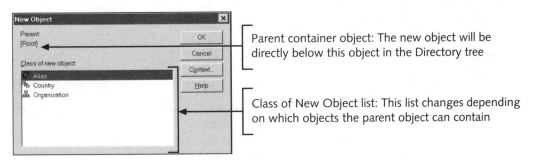

Figure 7-7   New Object dialog box for [ROOT] object

4. Click Country, and then click OK. The Create Country dialog box is displayed, as shown in Figure 7-8.

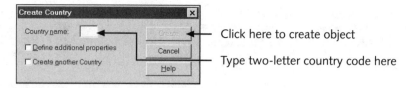

Figure 7-8   Create Country dialog box

5. In the Country Name text box, type the country code for the United Kingdom, which is GB.

6. Click Create. The GB Country object is added to the Directory tree, as shown in Figure 7-9.

Figure 7-9   GB Country object in directory tree

The Organization Object

You can add Organization objects directly below the [Root] or below a Country object in the Directory tree. To add an Organization object to a Directory tree, select Organization in the Class of New Object list, and specify a name for the organization.

For example, the CBE Labs network administrator wants to create the CBE_Labs_Europe Organization object below the GB Country object, to indicate the new European operation.

To create the CBE_Labs_Europe Organization object, follow these steps:

1. Click the GB Country object, click Object on the menu bar, and then click Create.

2. The New Object dialog box is displayed. The Class of New Object list of available objects includes the Alias and Organization objects, plus several others.

3. Click Organization, and then click OK. The Create Organization dialog box is displayed, as shown in Figure 7-10.

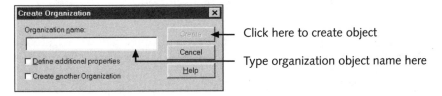

Figure 7-10   Create Organization dialog box

4. In the Organization Name text box, type CBE_Labs_Europe.

5. Click Create. Double-click the GB country object to display the CBE_Labs_Europe object, as Figure 7-11 shows.

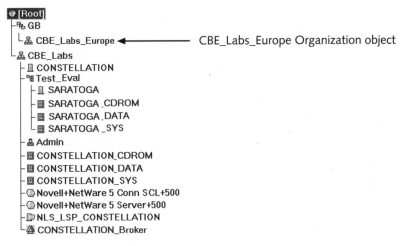

Figure 7-11   CBE_Labs_Europe object in directory tree

The Organizational Unit Object

You can add Organizational Unit objects directly below an Organization object or an Organizational Unit object in the Directory tree. To add an Organizational Unit object to a Directory tree, select Organizational Unit in the Class of New Object list, and specify a name for the organizational unit.

The CBE Labs organizational chart (see Figure 7-6) suggests that a number of possible Organizational Unit objects could be added to the CBE Labs Directory tree to complete the tree's organizational structure. If we assume that divisions headed by vice presidents will be in their own Organizational Units, and that divisions that report to the president are in the Administration Container (one possible design), we could design a tree with the following characteristics:

- You need to create the Organizational Unit objects CBE_Labs_Admin and Pubs below the CBE_Labs Organization object.

- You need to create the Organizational Unit objects Finance, InfoSystems, Marketing, and Personnel below the CBE_Labs_Admin Organizational Unit object.

- You need to create the Organizational Unit objects Hardware, Software, DBMS, and Network below the Test_Eval Organizational object.

The network administrator starts with the Organizational Unit object for CBE_Labs_Admin.

To create the CBE_Labs_Admin Organizational Unit object, follow these steps:

1. Click the CBE_Labs Organization object, click Object on the menu bar, and then click Create.

2. The New Object dialog box is displayed. Click Organizational Unit, and then click OK. The Create Organizational Unit dialog box is displayed, as Figure 7-12 shows.

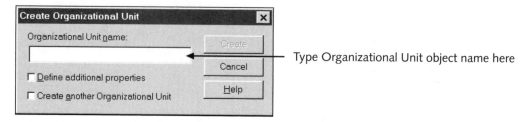

Figure 7-12   Create Organizational Unit dialog box

3. In the Organizational Unit Name text box, type CBE_Labs_Admin.

4. Click Create. The CBE_Labs_Admin Organizational Unit object appears in the Directory tree.

The network administrator took the following steps to create the other Organizational Unit objects needed to complete the Directory tree:

1. Repeat Steps 1 through 4 of the previous steps to add the Pubs Organizational Unit object to the tree.

2. Right-click the CBE_Labs_Admin organizational unit.

3. From the shortcut menu, select Create and then add four organizational units underneath CBE_Labs_Admin: Finance, InfoSystems, Marketing, and Personnel.

4. Now add organizational units beneath Test_Eval by right-clicking the Test_Eval organizational unit, choosing Create, and adding four organizational units underneath it: DBMS, Hardware, Network, and Software.

When you have added these objects, the organizational structure of the Directory tree is in place. You have created all necessary container objects, and you are ready to start adding leaf objects, such as User objects, in the containers (which you will do in Chapter 9). At this point, the CBE Labs Directory tree appears as Figure 7-13 shows.

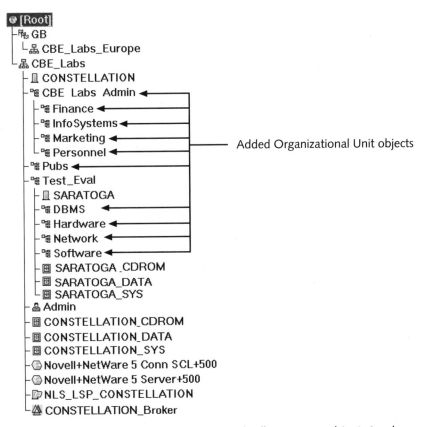

Figure 7-13   CBE Labs directory tree with all container objects in place

Viewing and Working with Container Object Properties

As you learned in Chapter 4, all Directory tree objects have properties, which are object characteristics that you can change. Each property stores one or more property values, which determine the characteristics of the objects. You can view properties by using an **object dialog box** for the object, each of which contains one or more **pages** of property values related to the object.

To view a container object's properties, you can use any of the following methods:

- Click the container object, and then press [Enter].
- Click the container object, click Object on the menu bar, and then click Details.
- Right-click the container object, and then click Details on the shortcut menu.

For example, the CBE Labs network administrator wants to enter some information about the CBE_Labs_Admin Organizational Unit object he just created.

To see the CBE_Labs_Admin Organizational Unit object properties, follow these steps:

1. Right-click the CBE_Labs_Admin Organizational Unit object, and then click Details. The Organizational Unit: CBE_Labs_Admin object dialog box is displayed, as Figure 7-14 shows.

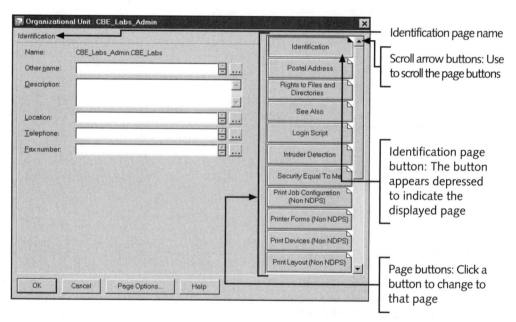

Figure 7-14   Organizational Unit: CBE_Labs_Admin object dialog box

The object properties are grouped into pages that are (1) identified by a screen name in the upper-left corner of the screen and (2) accessed by clicking the associated button in the scrollable button bar on the right side of the dialog box. For example, as Figure 7-14 shows, the Identification page is displayed and the Identification button is shown depressed, or pushed in (to indicate that it is selected) in the button bar. The Identification screen shows a group of Identification properties. You can change to another page by clicking the page's button. You can add, edit, or delete property values on a page by using the associated text box.

The CBE Labs network administrator needs to add the phone number and address for the marketing unit. The phone number is on the Identification page; the address information will go on the Postal Address page.

To add the CBE_Labs_Admin Organizational Unit's information, follow these steps:

1. Click the Telephone text box, and then type in the phone number 503-560-1548. *Do not press [Enter].*

2. Click the Postal Address button on the button bar. The Postal Address page appears, as Figure 7-15 shows.

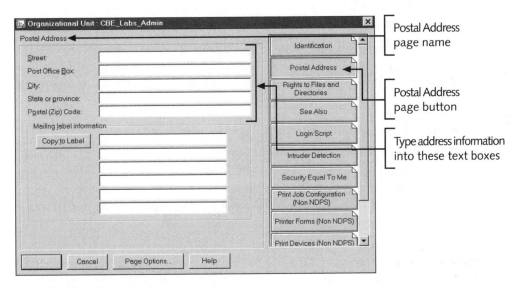

Figure 7-15   Postal Address page

3. Click the Street text box and then type 539 Lincoln Avenue.

4. Click the City text box and then type Portland.

5. Click the State or province text box and then type OR.

6. Click the Postal (ZIP) Code text box and then type 97205.

7. Click OK.

Working with Server-Related Leaf Objects

The first leaf objects added to the Directory tree are the Admin user object, NetWare Server objects for each NetWare 5.0 server installed into the Directory tree, and Volume objects for each volume created during installation. All these objects are created during the installation process. In Chapter 9, we'll work with User-related leaf objects. In this chapter we'll work with Server-related leaf objects.

As Chapter 4 discussed, there are three Server-related leaf objects: NetWare Server objects, Volume objects, and Directory Map objects. Before discussing Directory Map objects, we need to understand the idea of mapping a network drive. Network drive mapping is discussed in Chapter 8, so we'll postpone our discussion of the Directory Map object until that chapter. In this chapter we'll work with NetWare server and Volume objects.

If the only NetWare servers on the network are NetWare 5.0 servers, then all necessary NetWare Server objects and Volume objects have already been created and placed in their proper context. However, if any NetWare 3.x servers are on the network, the network administrator must create NetWare Server objects to represent each of them. In addition, the administrator must create a Volume object for each volume on the NetWare 3.x servers so that users can access the files on those volumes on the network.

The CBE Labs network contains one NetWare 3.2 server. Named RANGER, the server is used for running an accounting system in administration. RANGER has one volume: SYS. The CBE Labs network administrator needs to create the Directory tree objects for RANGER and the volume on RANGER.

The NetWare Server Object

NetWare Server objects representing NetWare 5.0 servers are added directly into their context during installation. If the tree was originally based on NetWare 4.x, then the tree already shows the NetWare 4.x servers. If the tree is new with NetWare 5.0, then with the addition of each new NetWare 4.x server to the tree, the tree automatically reflects the new object.

You must, however, manually add NetWare Server objects representing NetWare 3.x servers to the Directory tree. To add a NetWare Server object to a Directory tree, you select NetWare Server in the Class of New Object list. You must specify a name for the server.

For example, the CBE Labs network administrator needs to create the RANGER NetWare Server in the CBE_Labs_Admin Unit container.

The NetWare 3.x server must be running and on the network during the creation of the NetWare Server object that represents it. This is true for NetWare 5.0 as well. Therefore, your instructor will perform the following steps to show how to add a NetWare server to an existing tree. To represent RANGER in your CBE_Labs tree, use an Alias object for the equivalent CONSTELLATION server and volumes.

To create the RANGER NetWare Server object, follow these steps:

1. Click the CBE_Labs_Admin Organizational Unit object, click Object on the menu bar, and then click Create.

2. The New Object dialog box appears. Click NetWare Server and then click OK. The Create NetWare Server dialog box is displayed, as Figure 7-16 shows.

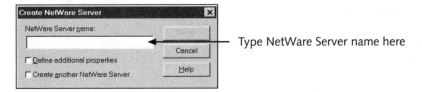

Figure 7-16   Create NetWare Server dialog box

3. Type RANGER in the Name text box (this needs to be an existing NetWare server on the network). Click the Create button.

4. If necessary, log in as Supervisor (if it is a NetWare 3.x server), using a valid password. The RANGER NetWare Server object has been added to the Directory tree.

The Volume Object

Like NetWare Server objects representing NetWare 5.0 servers, the installation program adds the Volume objects for NetWare 5.0 servers directly into their context. You must manually add Volume objects representing volumes on NetWare 3.x servers to the Directory tree. To add a Volume object to a Directory tree, select Volume in the Class of New Object list. Specify a name for the volume.

 You can create Volume (and Server) objects only when there is a physical volume (or server) on the network. This means that only your instructor will be able to perform the steps in this section. If necessary, represent the RANGER volumes in your CBE_Labs tree using an Alias object to the appropriate CONSTELLATION volumes.

For example, now that the CBE Labs network administrator has added the RANGER NetWare Server in the CBE_Labs_Admin Organizational Unit container, the administrator must now create the Volume object for the SYS volume on RANGER.

 The NetWare 3.x server must be running and on the network during the creation of the Volume objects that represent volumes on that server.

To create the SYS volume object, follow these steps:

1. Click the CBE_Labs_Admin Organizational Unit object, click Object on the menu bar, and then click Create.

2. The New Object dialog box is displayed. Click Volume, and then click OK. The Create Volume dialog box is displayed, as Figure 7-17 shows.

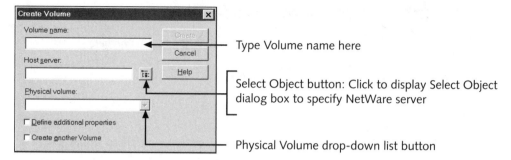

Type Volume name here

Select Object button: Click to display Select Object dialog box to specify NetWare server

Physical Volume drop-down list button

Figure 7-17 Create Volume dialog box

3. Type RANGER_SYS in the Name text box.

4. Click the Select Object button 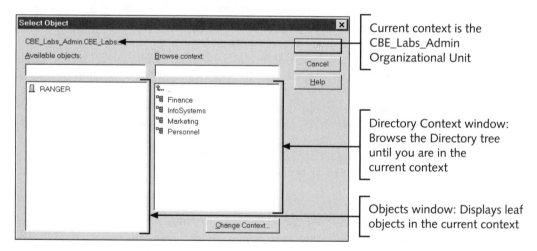 to the right of the Host Server text box. The Select Object dialog box is displayed, as Figure 7–18 shows.

Current context is the CBE_Labs_Admin Organizational Unit

Directory Context window: Browse the Directory tree until you are in the current context

Objects window: Displays leaf objects in the current context

Figure 7-18 Select Object dialog box

5. The Select Object dialog box is used to browse the Directory tree context to find an object. You browse the tree in the Directory Context window. In this case, the starting context is CBE_Labs_Admin.CBE_Labs. This is the correct context for the server RANGER that contains the SYS volume, so you do not need to browse the tree. You select an object in the Objects window. In the Objects window, click the NetWare Server object RANGER. The name of the selected object is displayed in the Select Object text box, as Figure 7–19 shows.

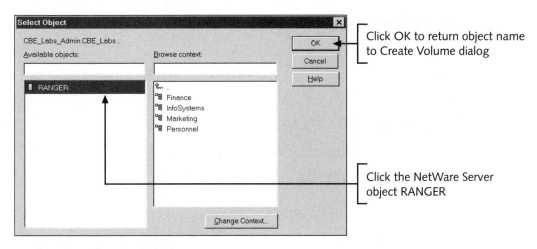

Figure 7-19   Selected object RANGER

6. Click OK. The host server name RANGER.CBE_Labs_Admin.CBE_Labs is displayed in the Host Server text box of the Create Volume dialog box, as Figure 7-20 shows.

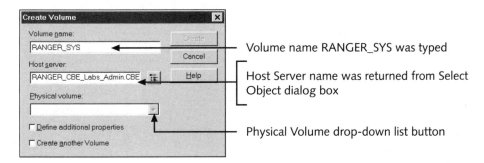

Figure 7-20   Host Server name RANGER

7. Click the drop-down list button to the right of the Physical volume text box. The drop-down list of volumes on RANGER is displayed, as Figure 7-21 shows.

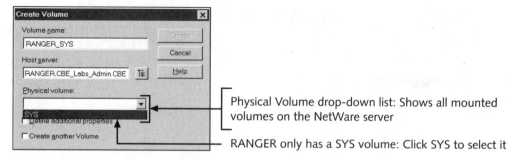

Physical Volume drop-down list: Shows all mounted volumes on the NetWare server

RANGER only has a SYS volume: Click SYS to select it

Figure 7-21   Selecting Physical volume on RANGER

8. Click SYS to select the SYS volume.

9. Click Create. The Volume object RANGER_SYS is created and added to the Directory tree. Figure 7–22 shows the CBE Labs Directory tree with the RANGER NetWare Server object and the RANGER_SYS volume.

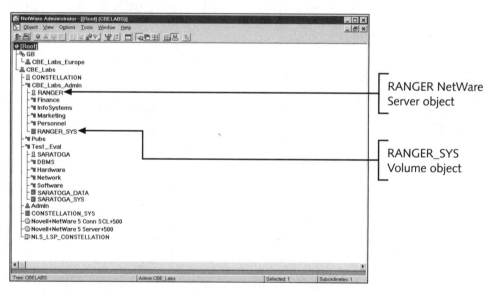

RANGER NetWare Server object

RANGER_SYS Volume object

Figure 7-22   Directory tree with NetWare server RANGER and RANGER_SYS volume

Viewing and Working with Leaf Object Properties

Viewing and working with leaf object properties is similar to viewing and working with container object properties.

To view a leaf object's properties, you can use any of the following methods:

■ Click the leaf object and then press [Enter].

- Click the leaf object, click Object on the menu bar, and then click Details.

- Right-click the leaf object and then click Details on the shortcut menu.

For example, the CBE Labs network administrator wants to see current volume statistics on the CONSTELLATION SYS volume. They can be seen by viewing the properties for the CONSTELLATION_SYS: volume.

To view the CONSTELLATION_SYS: volume object properties, follow these steps:

1. Right-click the CONSTELLATION_SYS Volume object and then click Details. The Volume: CONSTELLATION_SYS dialog box is displayed, as Figure 7-23 shows.

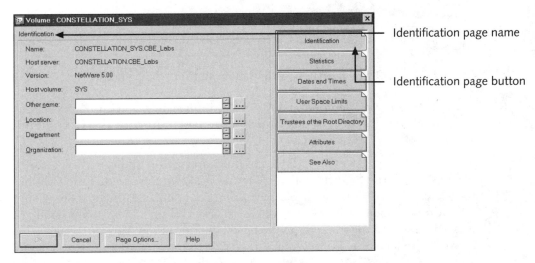

Figure 7-23   CONSTELLATION_SYS volume dialog box

Just as in the container object property dialog boxes, the object properties are grouped into pages. The first page displayed is the Identification page. This page shows the volume name, the name of the host server, the version of NetWare running on the host server, and the volume name on the server. You can enter other information such as the location of the volume, which department it is associated with, and which organization it belongs to.

To view the volume statistics, you would click the Statistics button to see the Statistics page.

To view the CONSTELLATION_SYS volume statistics, follow these steps:

1. Click the Statistics button. The Statistics page for the CONSTELLATION_SYS volume is displayed, as shown in Figure 7-24.

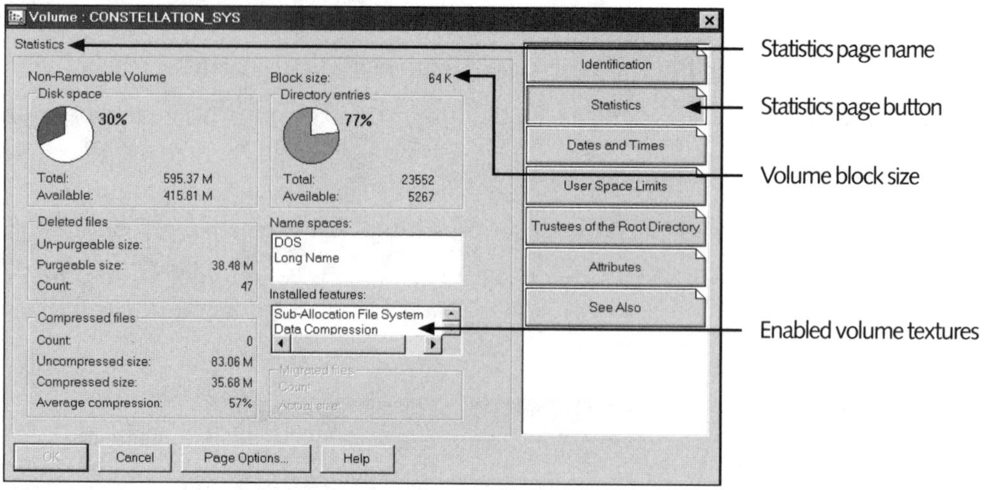

Figure 7-24 CONSTELLATION_SYS volume statistics dialog box

2. When you are done reviewing the information, click OK if you have changed, added, or deleted any information or click the Cancel button if nothing has been changed.

The Statistics page contains a lot of useful information about each volume. For example, looking at the Statistics page in Figure 7-24, we can see that the volume is using a 64 KB block size along with block suballocation and data compression. The page also tells you how many compressed files are on the volume, their compressed and uncompressed sizes, and the average percentage of compression. You can also see a visual and textual representation of how much disk space is free, and how many directory entries are still available. Figure 7-24 shows that both the DOS and LONG name spaces are available on this volume.

WORKING WITH THE ALIAS LEAF OBJECT

The Alias object is one of the Miscellaneous leaf objects. As Chapter 4 describes, the Alias object lets you place a leaf object in one container object that references another leaf object in a different container. This is usually done for convenience—it keeps the user from having to become familiar with complex complete names of objects in branches of the Directory tree. It is often done, for example, to let a user easily access printers, print queues, and print servers.

In the end-of-chapter exercises in this chapter, you may need to use the Alias object to simulate NetWare servers and their volumes. Some of the exercises are based on networks with more than one NetWare server. If your network computer lab has only one NetWare server, you can use Alias objects to complete the exercises. For example, if you need to create a second NetWare server named Server02 in a network environment with only one NetWare server named Server01, you would create an Alias object named Server02 that references Server01. This lets the Directory tree simulate two NetWare servers in the network.

MODIFYING AN NDS DIRECTORY TREE

As a network administrator, you will often need to modify an existing NDS Directory tree. Common modification tasks are renaming container and leaf objects, moving individual objects, moving sections of the Directory tree, deleting objects, renaming trees, and merging trees.

Renaming Objects

It is often necessary to rename an object. This is easy; you can rename all objects except the [Root]. To rename an object, click the object, click the Object menu, and then click Rename. Type in the new name and then click OK.

For example, the NetWare server SARATOGA should have been installed in the Test&Eval organizational unit; however, the limitations of the NetWare 5.0 installation process forced the CBE LABS network administrator to name the organizational unit Test_Eval. The administrator can now rename it Test&Eval.

To rename the Test_Eval Organizational Unit object:

1. Click the Test_Eval Organizational Unit object to select it.

2. Click Object on the menu bar and then click Rename. The Rename dialog box appears.

3. Type Test&Eval in the New Name text box, as shown in Figure 7-25.

4. Click OK.

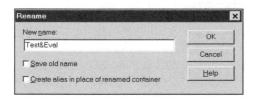

Figure 7-25   Renaming the Test_Eval Organizational Unit object

Moving Leaf Objects

You will often need to move a leaf object, such as a User object or a Printer object, from one container to another. Doing this, of course, changes the object's context, but NDS will automatically make the necessary changes in the property values.

To move an object, you can use any of these methods:

- Drag the object to its new context in the Directory tree.
- Click the object, then click Object on the menu bar, then click Move, then enter the new context and click OK.
- Click the object, click Object on the menu bar, click Move, and then browse to new context and click OK.

Deleting Objects

Managing and modifying the Directory tree will often require you to delete an object. Deleting most leaf objects, such as Users and Printers, presents no problem. Deleting a NetWare Server object, however, demands consideration of NDS partitions and replicas, which are discussed later in this chapter. Deleting a container object requires that you first delete or move all objects within that container object.

To delete an object, you can use any of these methods:

- Click the object and then press [Delete].
- Click the object, click Object on the menu bar, and then click Delete.
- Right-click the container object for the object, and then click Delete on the shortcut menu.

MANAGING DIRECTORY TREES

As a network administrator, you will occasionally need to work with the Directory tree as a whole, rather than with its component parts. This happens when you need to rename a Directory tree, or combine two Directory trees into one. For example, you may need to rename a Directory tree if the company name is changed. You may need to combine two Directory trees if there is more than one Directory tree on your internetwork, and management has decided to consolidate the trees for easier use.

DSMERGE.NLM

The utility used to manage Directory trees is **DSMERGE.NLM**. This NetWare Loadable Module is run by loading it at the console prompt with the console command:

```
LOAD DSMERGE [Enter]
```

When the module is loaded, it appears as shown in Figure 7-26.

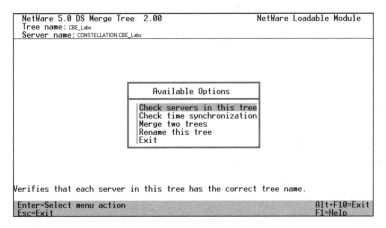

```
NetWare 5.0 DS Merge Tree  2.00              NetWare Loadable Module
Tree name: CBE_Labs
Server name: CONSTELLATION.CBE_Labs



                  ┌──────────────────────────────┐
                  │       Available Options       │
                  ├──────────────────────────────┤
                  │ Check servers in this tree    │
                  │ Check time synchronization    │
                  │ Merge two trees               │
                  │ Rename this tree              │
                  │ Exit                          │
                  └──────────────────────────────┘




Verifies that each server in this tree has the correct tree name.

 Enter=Select menu action                          Alt+F10=Exit
 Esc=Exit                                           F1=Help
```

Figure 7-26   DSMERGE NLM main menu

Renaming a Directory Tree

You can rename a Directory tree by using the Rename this tree menu item. You must load DSMERGE on the NetWare server where the Master replica of the [Root] partition is stored for this tree. When you choose the Rename this tree menu item, you are required to log into the tree from the server as the Admin user and use the complete name of the Admin account (i.e., .Admin.CBE_Labs, not just Admin). DSMERGE then asks you for the tree's new name. After you type it in, press [F10] to finish renaming the tree.

Managing Multiple Directory Trees

As a network administrator, you will also occasionally need to work with more than one Directory tree. NetWare's utilities include support for viewing and administering multiple trees.

Earlier, we discussed how when you first load NetWare Administrator, it displays a view of the NDS tree you had loaded the last time you used it. (If you are not now logged into that tree, it will display an error message.) If you now want to view a second tree, you can do so by closing the current view and opening a new one, or by opening a second view using the NDS Browser option. To do this:

1. Load NetWare Administrator if you haven't already done so. The utility displays your current NDS tree.

2. Choose Tools, NDS Browser. NetWare Administrator now asks you to specify which tree you want to view in the new window, as Figure 7-27 shows.

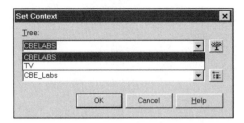

Figure 7-27 Select Tree and Context dialog box

 If you have only one NDS tree, you will not be able to complete Steps 3–6.

3. Choose another NDS tree from the list, or type its name into the TREE field. At this point, you'll notice we discussed this same procedure earlier for changing your context, only this time you are changing your NDS tree.

4. Choose OK to continue.

5. If you are not logged into the tree you specified, then the Novell Login dialog box appears. To continue, provide an appropriate name and password.

6. Assuming you were logged into this second tree, then NetWare Administrator now shows you a browser window similar to Figure 7-22, with [ROOT] at the top. You can now begin to administer this second tree using NWAdmin.

The Novell Login Utility

Novell Login also supports multiple trees. We discussed how the Login utility includes a TREE field where you can pick a new NDS tree to log into. (See Chapter 6 for details.) To log into that tree, you will still need the appropriate user name (such as ADMIN) and the correct password. (The same would be true of any of your users. To log into that tree and use its resources, they too would have to be defined in the second tree and have appropriate rights in that tree.)

NetWare Connections

The Novell System Tray tool gives you and your users a way to see which NDS trees you are connected to. Right-click the N icon in the System Tray, then choose NetWare Connections. NetWare displays a list of your connections, like Figure 7-28. You can see to which trees in the NDS Tree list you are connected. (For further details, see Chapter 6.)

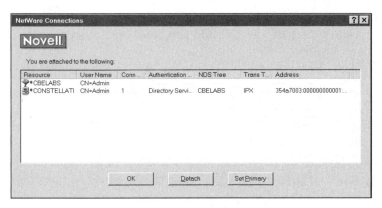

Figure 7-28 NetWare Connections dialog box

7

CHAPTER SUMMARY

◘ To set up and manage a network, NetWare network administrators must master the NetWare commands and utilities. This chapter described the different types of NetWare tools available to the network administrator: command line utilities, graphical utilities, supervisor utilities, menu utilities, console commands, and NetWare Loadable Modules (NLMs). Console commands and NLMs are used from the server's console; command line utilities, menu utilities, and graphical utilities run at the workstations.

◘ Graphical utilities use the Windows GUI. The term *supervisor utilities* refers to any utility stored in the SYS:SYSTEM directory that the network administrator uses for system administration. Console commands are NetWare commands that must be run from the NetWare server console prompt. NetWare Loadable Modules (NLMs) are programs and utilities that run on the NetWare server.

◘ The NetWare Administrator (NWAdmin) graphical utility is the preferred tool for working with the NDS Directory tree. It enables you to do everything you need to do with NDS, using an easy Windows interface.

◘ You can use NWAdmin to display portions or all of a Directory tree. You can also open additional browser windows to display different sections of the Directory tree in separate browser windows. A maximum of 10 browser windows can be open at one time.

◘ The Directory tree is initially created during the installation of NetWare 5.0 servers. After all NetWare 5.0 servers in a network have been installed, the Directory tree contains the [Root] object, one or more Country objects (optional), at least one Organization object, one or more Organizational Unit objects (optional), the Admin user object, a NetWare Server object for each NetWare 5.0 server installed, a SYS volume object for each NetWare 5.0 server installed, and a Volume object for each additional volume created during server installation (optional).

At this point, the network administrator needs to complete building the organizational structure of the Directory tree and add any NetWare 3.x servers and their associated volumes into the tree.

❐ To complete the organizational structure, you typically add container objects to the Directory tree. Container objects include the [Root], Country, Organization, and Organizational Unit objects. Using NWAdmin, you can create, rename, and delete container objects and manage their properties. You cannot, however, simply move a container object to another part of the tree.

❐ You can use NWAdmin to create, rename, and delete leaf objects in container objects, as well as to manage their properties. In this chapter, you added leaf objects for a NetWare 3.x server and its SYS volume.

❐ The server console utility DSMERGE.NLM is used to rename Directory trees. NetWare utilities, including NWAdmin, Novell Login, and the System Tray utility, also support multiple NDS trees both for administration as well as sharing resources.

COMMAND SUMMARY

Command	Syntax	Definition
DSMERGE	*Load DSMERGE*	NLM utility that lets you manage the NDS Directory tree. You can rename a Directory tree and merge two Directory trees into one. Menu options include: Check servers in this tree Check time synchronization Merge two trees Rename this tree

KEY TERMS

command line utility (CLU)
console commands
DSMERGE.NLM
graphical utilities
menu utilities
NetWare Administrator (NWAdmin)
NetWare Loadable Module (NLM)
object dialog box
pages
supervisor utilities

REVIEW QUESTIONS

1. Identify each of the following as being either a command line utility, graphical utility, console command, or NetWare Loadable Module (NLM):

   NDIR ————————————————————————————

   NWAdmin ————————————————————————

   DSMERGE ———————————————————————

2. Briefly explain the difference between a command line utility and a console command.

3. Briefly explain an advantage of a graphical utility over a command line utility.

4. Write the steps to display the Directory tree starting at the [Root] and showing all subordinate container and leaf objects.

For Questions 5 through 8, use the Directory tree for Washington Management Services shown in Figure 7-29 and assume that your initial context is [Root].

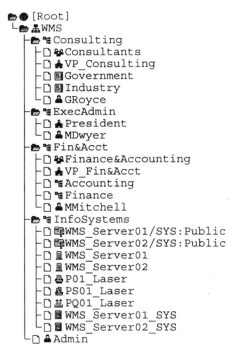

Figure 7-29   Washington Management Services directory tree

5. Write the steps to display only the context of the Consulting organizational unit container in NWAdmin.

6. Having changed context to the Consulting organizational unit container, write the steps to change context to the WMS organization container.

7. Write the steps to display the entire Directory tree without leaf objects in tree form regardless of the current context.

8. Write the steps to display the entire Directory tree with leaf objects in tree form regardless of the current context.

9. Explain how to display or hide the objects in a container object using NWAdmin.

10. Explain how to change context using NWAdmin.

11. Explain how to open an additional browser window or close an existing browser window using NWAdmin.

12. For each object listed, state whether at least one of that type of object must exist when you have completed the installation of all NetWare 5.0 servers in the network:

   [Root] object

   Country object

   Organization object

   Organizational Unit

   NetWare Server object for a NetWare 5.0 server

   NetWare Server object for a NetWare 3.x server

   Volume object for a NetWare 5.0 server

   Volume object for a NetWare 3.x server

   User object

   Group object

13. Explain how to create Directory tree objects using NWAdmin.

14. Match each of the following country codes with its corresponding country:

Country Code	Country
AU ———————	a. Saudi Arabia
CA ———————	b. United States
JP ———————	c. Canada
SA ———————	d. Australia
US ———————	e. United Kingdom
GB ———————	f. Japan

15. An object's properties are managed using the ——————— dialog box, which consists of one or more ——————— of property values.

16. Some dialog boxes used to create objects contain a Select Object button. Describe how to use the Select Object button to select an object.

17. Explain how to rename Directory tree objects using NWAdmin.

18. Explain how to move leaf objects using NWAdmin.

19. Explain how to delete leaf objects using NWAdmin.

20. When a new Directory tree is created during NetWare 5.0 installation, which partition is the [Root] object placed in?

21. A subtree is a container object that contains ―――――――――.

22. Describe the steps to move a container object to a new context in the Directory tree.

23. To rename a Directory tree, you must use the ―――――――――.

24. List the five steps that must be completed before merging two Directory trees.

HANDS-ON PROJECTS

Project 7-1: Using NWAdmin in Contexts

Your instructor has created an NDS Directory tree for your network environment, including a section based on the Franklin D. Roosevelt Investments (FDR) Directory tree discussed in Chapter 4 of this text. In this exercise, you use NWAdmin to display various contexts within the NDS Directory tree and to view Directory tree information within the FDR section of the Directory tree.

1. Log into your network using your normal login procedure.

2. Open NWAdmin.

3. Display a view of your current NDS tree.

4. Change your context to display the [Root] object.

   Steps used: ――――――――――――――――――――――――――

5. Change the view to display only the FDR_Admin organizational unit of FDR.

   Steps used: ――――――――――――――――――――――――――

6. Change the view of the tree to show the Directory tree from the [Root] down *without* leaf objects.

   Steps used: ――――――――――――――――――――――――――

7. Change the view of the tree to show the Directory tree from the [Root] down *with* leaf objects.

   Steps used: ――――――――――――――――――――――――――

8. Change the view of the tree to show the Directory tree from the FDR organization object down *without* leaf objects.

   Steps used: ――――――――――――――――――――――――――

9. Print your current view.

10. Change the view to show the Directory tree from the FDR organization object down *with* leaf objects.

    Steps used: ――――――――――――――――――――――――――

11. Print your current view.

12. Close NWAdmin and return to Windows 95/98.

Write a memo to your instructor listing the steps you used and describing the results of each new view. Attach a copy of your printouts from Steps 9 and 11.

Project 7-2: Viewing Directory Tree Information with DSMERGE

This project requires access to a NetWare 5.0 server console.

In this project you use the DSMERGE NLM utility to work with the NDS Directory tree.

1. At the NetWare server console prompt, type **LOAD DSMERGE** and then press **[Enter]** to start the DSMERGE NLM utility.

2. Choose **Check servers in this tree** in the DSMERGE main menu. List the name of each server shown:

3. Choose **Check time synchronization** in the DSMERGE main menu. Summarize the time synchronization in the network as described by DSMERGE.

4. To unload the DSMERGE utility, choose **Exit** in the DSMERGE main menu.

   Write a memo to your instructor describing your use of DSMERGE and the results you recorded.

CASE PROJECTS

Case 7-1: Creating the Jefferson County Courthouse Directory Tree Organizational Structure

In Chapter 4, you designed an NDS Directory tree for the Jefferson County Courthouse. The network administrator has installed the NetWare 5.0 Server and is ready to finish creating the Directory tree. Your job is to put your Directory tree plan into practice.

After discussing your design with the courthouse personnel, you agreed on the Directory tree design that Figure 7-30 shows.

```
🖿⬤ [Root]
 └🖿🛦JCCH
   ├☐ 🏢 JCCH_Server01
   ├☐ 🖳 SocServices
   ├☐ 🛦 Admin
   ├☐ 🖴 JCCH_Server01_DATA
   └☐ 🖴 JCCH_Server01_SYS
```

Figure 7-30   Jefferson County Courthouse directory tree

1. Start NWAdmin.

2. Locate the Jefferson County Courthouse organizational unit. This shows the courthouse tree after NetWare 5.0 server installation. The objects that would normally be created during a NetWare 5.0 installation—the NetWare server, its associated volumes, and the Admin user—are included in the organizational unit (except for [Root]).

3. Create the rest of the Jefferson County Courthouse Directory tree structure as shown in Figure 7-30.

4. Because you cannot add the server objects directly, describe the steps you would take to create those objects in the tree.

5. Print a copy of your completed Directory tree.

6. Write a memo to your instructor stating that you have completed this assignment. Attach a copy of your printed Directory tree. Turn in your memo to your instructor.

Case 7-2: Creating the J. Q. Adams Corporation Directory Tree Organizational Structure

In Chapter 4, you designed an NDS Directory tree for the J. Q. Adams Corporation. The network administrator has installed its two NetWare 5.0 Servers and is ready to finish creating the Directory tree. Your job is to put your Directory tree plan into practice.

After discussing your design with J. Q. Adams management personnel, you agreed on the Directory tree design shown in Figure 7-31. Notice that Figure 7-31 shows a third NetWare server: JQA_Server03 is a NetWare 3.2 server that will be used in Production to help with quality control. It has two volumes: SYS and DATA. Because this is a NetWare 3.2 server, the JQA_Server03 NetWare Server object and the associated Volume objects do not exist in the current Directory tree structure and will need to be added.

1. Start NWAdmin.

2. Locate your J. Q. Adams organizational unit subcontainer. This unit shows the J. Q. Adams network after installation of the NetWare 5.0 servers. The objects normally created during a NetWare 5.0 installation—the NetWare servers and their associated volumes—are not shown because a physical server must represent those on the network. The tree does show the Admin user.

3. Create the rest of the J. Q. Adams Directory tree structure as Figure 7-31 shows.

4. Print a copy of your completed Directory tree.

5. Write a memo to your instructor stating that you have finished this assignment. Attach a copy of your printed Directory tree. Turn in your memo and a copy of your printed Directory tree.

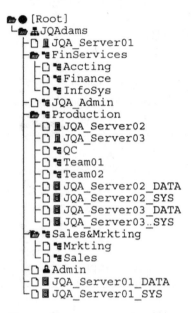

Figure 7-31 J. Q. Adams Corporation directory tree

8

CREATING THE NETWORK FILE SYSTEM

After reading this chapter and completing the exercises you will be able to:

♦ Create a network file system

♦ Describe the use of network and search drive pointers

♦ Establish a drive pointer usage plan for your network system

♦ Understand the concept of mapping drives

♦ Use the Windows 95/98 Explorer to create drive pointers and search drives to directories within a file system

♦ Use NetWare Administrator to create a Directory Map object

♦ Use NetWare utilities to work with files and directories in the NetWare file system

♦ Salvage and purge deleted files

Once the server installation is complete, it's time to set up the network file system. To do this important task, you need to understand the NetWare commands and utilities used to create and maintain the NetWare file system. Chapter 5 introduced you to some of these commands and utilities; this chapter will give you experience with some additional NetWare and Windows 95/98 commands and utilities used to manage the network file system.

The information in this chapter is divided into three major categories: directory management, drive pointers, and file management. In the directory management section you will apply certain Windows 95/98 commands, with which you are already familiar, to the NetWare file system to create the network directory structure, and will use NetWare Administrator to view and create directories. In the drive pointer section, you will use the Windows 95/98 Explorer to access network drives. When you install the Novell Client, it adds functions to Explorer, including network drive pointers. You will also use the DOS MAP command to manage drive pointers. The drive pointers section also suggests ways to plan the drive pointer usage in your network system. In the file management section you will learn about Windows 95/98 and NetWare utilities that help you manage files on your NetWare servers.

In the past, most NetWare management was done with proprietary DOS-based tools such as FILER, VOLINFO, NETUSER, and others. With NetWare 5, most tasks are performed in Windows with graphical tools. In essence, NetWare lets you use those tools for network file management as well.

 This book assumes that you are already comfortable with using Windows file and directory management tools. Windows file management is not covered in depth here.

DIRECTORY MANAGEMENT

In Chapter 5, you learned how to design the server's file system using volumes, directories, and subdirectories. In this section you will learn how to apply NetWare and Windows 95/98 commands when creating and maintaining directories and subdirectories for your server. These tasks are an important part of everyday network operations.

In this chapter, we'll continue to watch the network administrator for CBE Labs as he creates the new CBE Labs network. In Chapter 5, he planned the directory structure for each volume in the CBE Labs network. In this section, he will actually create the directory structures.

Recall that CBE Labs has two NetWare 5.0 servers, CONSTELLATION and SARATOGA, and one NetWare 3.2 server, RANGER. CONSTELLATION and SARATOGA each have a SYS and DATA volume, but RANGER has only a SYS volume. Because CD-ROMs provide their own directory structures, the network administrator doesn't need to worry about CD-ROM directory structures, only those for volumes on hard disks.

At CBE Labs, the administration and publishing workgroups use CONSTELLATION. Thus CONSTELLATION_SYS volume stores a major set of application software, including the company's e-mail, fax, and Internet software. In addition, CONSTELLATION_SYS stores a shared copy of the company's Windows 95-compatible desktop publishing software, PageMaker. CBE Labs also keeps a copy of the user workstations' software package Office97 on the volume so the software can be installed onto the users' PCs from the network instead of from disks.

The CONSTELLATION_DATA volume stores administration and publishing data. A SHARED directory is maintained at the root level so that users can easily transfer files to each other, and SHARED subdirectories are maintained for each administration section for file sharing among administration groups (the publishing workgroup has no access to these directories). Finally, private personal directories are maintained for each user in the administration and publishing workgroups under the USERS directory.

The lab workgroups use SARATOGA. Therefore the SARATOGA_SYS volume stores the application software the lab workgroups need and share, including an SQL database management system (DBMS) program and a program named Analyzer that evaluates hardware and software. The SARATOGA_DATA volume stores lab workgroup test and evaluation data and reports. As on CONSTELLATION_DATA, a SHARED directory is kept at the root level so that users can easily transfer files to each other, and SHARED subdirectories are kept for each lab workgroup for file sharing among groups. In addition, a REPORTS subdirectory holds the final lab reports; everyone at CBE Labs can access this directory. For example, the publishing group picks up copies of reports from this directory to publish in *The C/B/E NetWorker*. And as on CONSTELLATION_DATA, private personal directories are kept for each user in the lab workgroups under a USERS directory.

The Finance department uses RANGER, the NetWare 3.2 server, to run the legacy DOS-based accounting system. The RANGER_SYS volume contains the program files in the APPS\DOSACCT subdirectory, and the DATA directory holds the subdirectories for the data files for the program. There is no need for a SHARED directory or user directories on RANGER_SYS.

Chapter 5 showed the volume design forms for each volume in the CBE Labs network. For reference, Figures 8-1 and 8-2 show the volume design forms for the CONSTELLATION_SYS and CONSTELLATION_DATA volumes. (Blank copies of these forms are available in Appendix B.)

8

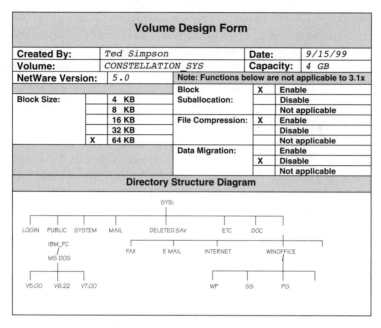

Figure 8-1   CONSTELLATION_SYS volume

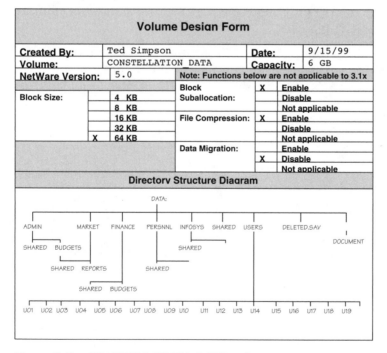

Figure 8-2   CONSTELLATION_DATA volume

Windows Directory Management Commands

In Windows 95 or 98, directories and subdirectories are also called **folders**. Folders are created by using the File, New, and Folder menu commands.

For example, the CBE Labs network administrator needs to create the PAGEPUB subdirectory to the APPS directory. To create the APPS directory and PAGEPUB subdirectory, follow these steps:

Only your instructor will be able to perform the following steps exactly as shown. You can follow along by using your own user directory as the Root of SYS.

1. Click Start, point to Programs, and click Windows Explorer to launch Explorer. If necessary, maximize the Explorer window to a full screen. The Windows 98 Explorer screen appears as Figure 8-3 shows.

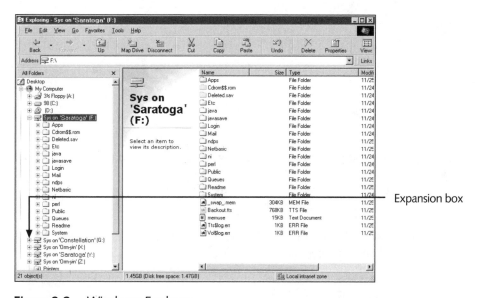

Expansion box

Figure 8-3   Windows Explorer

Some sites may use F: or another letter as the initial network drive. If necessary, substitute your network drive letter for G: in this exercise.

2. Click the expansion box (plus sign) in front of the Sys on Constellation (G:) drive to view the subdirectories of the CONSTELLATION_SYS volume, then click 'Sys on Constellation (G:)' to display the contents of the CONSTELLATION_SYS volume.

3. Click File, New, Folder to create a new folder (subdirectory) called Apps. The new folder appears in the Contents of the G:\ window. The title New Folder is highlighted in edit mode so that you can edit the folder name.

4. Type Apps as the new folder name, and then press [Enter]. The new folder is named.

5. Click the Apps folder, then click File, New, Folder. Type PAGEPUB as the new folder name and press [Enter].

6. Close Windows Explorer.

NetWare Administrator Directory Management

Directories and subdirectories can also be created by using the NetWare Administrator utility. Although directories are not NDS objects, directories can be created for Volume objects and other directories, and displayed in the NetWare Administrator tree view.

To view the directory structure for a Volume object in NetWare Administrator, follow these general steps:

1. Double-click the Volume object icon when the directories are not displayed.

2. Double-click each Directory icon to display the subdirectories (and files) in that directory.

3. Repeat Step 2 on each subdirectory until the entire directory tree is displayed.

To create a directory using NetWare Administrator, follow these general steps:

1. Click the Volume or directory that will contain the directory; then press [Insert].
   or
   Click the Volume or directory that will contain the directory, click Object on the menu bar, and then click Create.
   or
   Right-click the Volume or directory that will contain the directory; then click Create on the shortcut menu.

2. In the Create Directory dialog box, type the name of the directory; then click the Create button.

For example, the CBE Labs network administrator has created the first level of directories for the DATA volume (for your lab, your instructor will have created these) and now needs to create the subdirectories for the FINANCE directory. The first subdirectory he will create is the SHARED subdirectory.

To create the SHARED subdirectory from NetWare Administrator, follow these steps:

1. If necessary, double-click each container object to display all leaf objects.

2. Double-click the CONSTELLATION_DATA Volume object to display the first level of directory structure.

3. Click Object, then click Create. The Create Directory dialog box appears, as Figure 8-4 shows.

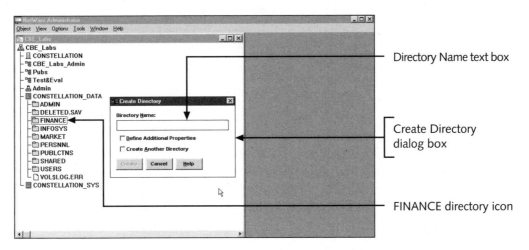

Directory Name text box

Create Directory dialog box

FINANCE directory icon

8

Figure 8-4   Create Directory dialog box

4. Type FINANCE in the Directory Name text box, and then click the Create button. The FINANCE directory is created.

5. Repeat Steps 3 and 4 to create a subdirectory of FINANCE called SHARED. After you finish creating it, double-click the FINANCE directory icon to display the new directory.

Creating the Directory Structure

Using the commands just discussed, the CBE Labs network administrator can now create the rest of the directories and subdirectories needed in the directory structures on each volume. Note that even though Figure 8-2 shows subdirectories for each user, he does not create them at this time. The user home directories are created when the User object is created for each user, which you will learn how to do in Chapter 9. Figure 8-5 shows the completed directory structure for the CONSTELLATION_SYS volume in the Windows 95 Explorer program. (Your instructor will complete this structure on the server. You can recreate a similar structure in your own home directory.)

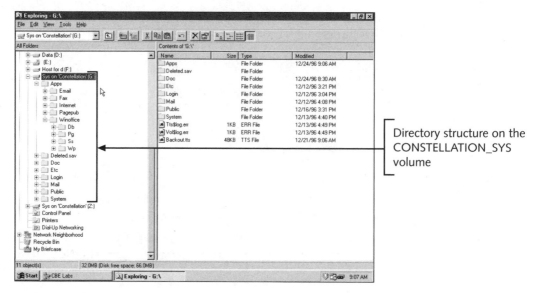

Figure 8-5   CONSTELLATION_SYS directory structure

Figure 8-6 shows the completed directory structure for the CONSTELLATION_DATA volume as displayed by NetWare Administrator.

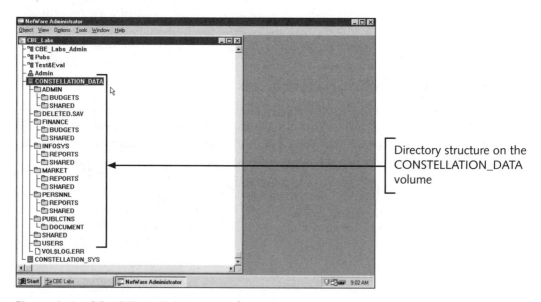

Figure 8-6   CONSTELLATION_DATA directory structure

Drive Pointers

In both NetWare and Windows environments, drive pointers play an important role in accessing files located on different devices and directories. A **drive pointer** is a letter of the alphabet that is used to reference storage areas in the file system. By default, Windows reserves the first five drive pointers (A–E) for storage devices on the local workstation. These letters are therefore often called **local drive pointers**. Letters A and B are reserved for floppy disk drives, C and D are normally used for hard disks, and E is often a CD-ROM, (although D and E are often reserved for CD-ROM drives or other external storage devices.)

The Windows Explorer with the NetWare Provider for Windows 95 extensions (included in the Novell Client), the NetWare N icon in the System Tray, and the Network Neighborhood icon are the major tools a network administrator uses to establish and maintain drive pointers. Used with the Novell Client, the Windows 95/98 Explorer also lets you create drive mappings.

To become a network administrator, you need to know how to use these tools to maintain network drive pointers. In addition, planning and implementing a proper set of network and search drive pointers are important steps in setting up a successful network environment. Later in this section you will read some tips and suggestions for organizing drive pointer usage for your file system.

> You may want to think of NetWare **drive mappings** as similar to Windows shortcuts. Just as a shortcut must point to a specific directory to find a given application, so too a NetWare drive pointer points to a directory for a NetWare application.

In the past, planning drive mappings was a crucial administrator task. Because there can only be a maximum of 26 drives (one for each letter), the administrator didn't have much room to play around. Worse, each time the administrator or a user installed a new application, it would often grab a mapping for itself. It isn't too hard to imagine a user with more than 16 applications plus another set of five or six data directories. Add all the local drive letters, and mappings became a scarce commodity.

Fortunately, with Windows drive mappings are in much less critical demand. Some sites require them, especially to support legacy programs. On other sites, you won't need any drive mappings at all. However, most sites require at least some search drive or regular drive mappings.

Network Drive Pointers

A **network drive pointer** can be one of three types: regular, root, or search. Regular and root drive pointers are usually assigned to directories containing data files; search drive pointers are assigned to network software directories.

Regular Drive Pointers

A **regular drive pointer** is assigned to a directory path and shows all directories and subdirectories leading to the storage area. A regular drive pointer should be assigned to each volume as well as to commonly used directories. This lets application software packages that cannot use NetWare complete paths access the data in any volume.

Root Drive Pointers

A **root drive pointer** looks to the user or application as if the default path were at the root of the drive or volume. Figure 8-7 shows an example of two drive pointers, using Windows Explorer. Notice how the search drive pointer displays the volume name, whereas the root drive pointer shows the exact name of the directory (and its path).

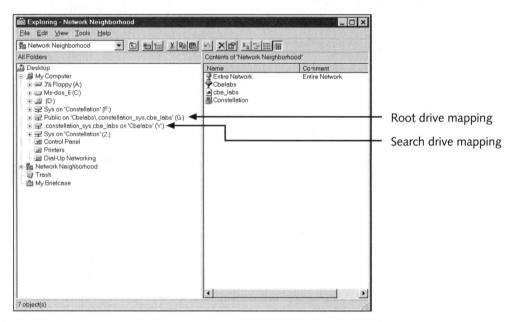

Root drive mapping

Search drive mapping

Figure 8-7 Root and search drive pointers in Windows Explorer

Search Drive Pointers

DOS programs use **search drive pointers** to locate files. Typically, the primary search drive will point to the NetWare 5 server's SYS:PUBLIC directory. For most applications, Windows shortcuts or menu options in the application provide the primary link to launch an application.

Windows 95/98 applications do not need search drives because the application icon parameters provide the path to the Windows application. Thus, as more workstations use Windows 95/98, there will be less need for NetWare search drives.

If your program requires a search drive, then you can select that option when mapping the drive. In the Map Drive dialog box shown in Figure 8-8, you can check the box for Map Search Drive.

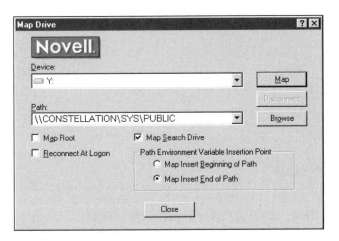

Figure 8-8   Marking a drive as a search mapping

NetWare only supports up to 16 search drives, as shown in Figure 8-9. This user limitation was one key reason operating systems moved away from the drive pointer model and to the Universal Naming Convention (UNC) used in Windows.

Network and Search Drive Pointers

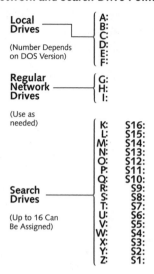

Figure 8-9   Drive pointer usage chart

Figure 8-8 shows the Novell Map Drive dialog box. In this dialog box, there is an option to reconnect the mapped drive at login, thus making the drive mapping permanent. Otherwise, the mapping only lasts until the user logs into NDS again.

Any changes a user makes to his or her drive mappings only apply to that user, not to other users on the network.

Planning Your Drive Mappings

Now that we have discussed the kinds of drive mappings NetWare uses, let's consider when and why you would use them. You need to plan a minimum set of standard drive pointers in your network blueprint. Then you implement these standard mappings, using a group or personal login script. Once users log in, they will find that their workstation automatically includes those mappings.

First determine what regular and root drive pointers you need to enable easy access to any shared and private files. Keep these drive pointers to a minimum, because most users cannot keep track of more than five different drive pointers. Typical drive pointers for each user should include the following:

- *A drive pointer to the root of each volume.* These drive pointers let users change to another volume quickly without drilling up and down through layers in Windows Explorer. When using a two-volume structure, many network administrators map one drive letter to the SYS volume and another drive letter to access the DATA volume.

- *A drive pointer to the shared work directories that are available to all users.* For example, if you create a shared directory named WORK on the root of the DATA volume, any user can access files in this directory by clicking on the mapping to the DATA volume. Similarly, if you create a shared word-processing forms directory named FORMS on the root of the DATA volume, then mapping a drive to the DATA volume will let any user access a common word-processing form.

- *A root drive pointer mapped to the user's home directory.* This drive letter, usually H for "home" or U for "user," is the starting point for users' personal data storage. Each user will take a different path. Making this drive letter a root drive prevents the user from accidentally changing the drive pointer to a different directory location. Users can create subdirectories within their home directories, for example, and then move around within those subdirectories, using Windows Explorer, without interfering with other users.

- *A root drive pointer mapped to the user's workgroup directory.* This drive pointer lets users access shared files within their workgroups. Users in the business department, for example, can have their L drive mapped to DATA:BUSINESS. The SALES department users can have their L drive mapped to the DATA:SALES directory. If you create a WORK directory for each department, every user in the system can get to his or her workgroup's shared work directory using the path L:\WORK.

- *Application drive pointers.* You may find that some legacy application packages require their own pointer. When you plan for these drive pointers, keep in mind that all users who run the application will want to have the same drive pointer letter. That is because the software often designates a specific drive letter for accessing its data and work files.

In addition to planning the regular drive pointers, the network administrator needs to plan search drive pointers to let users access utilities and software packages that are frequently used. When planning search drive usage, keep the total number of search drives to fewer than eight, to provide better performance and reduce the chance of conflicts with regular drive pointers.

As mentioned, users running Windows will not need search drives mapped to Windows applications, because the paths to these directories are already stored in the properties of the Windows folders or icons. As a minimum, most network administrators will want to create the following search drive mappings:

- Search drive to the SYS:PUBLIC directory

- Search drive to the network WINDOWS directory if Windows 95/98 is being run from the network

A properly planned set of drive pointers includes the search drives needed to run any legacy DOS-based software packages and utilities, along with a standard set of regular drive pointers that give users easy access to data storage directories containing files they need for work. The drive pointer planning form that Figure 8-10 shows includes the following drive pointers for each user:

- The H drive pointer to the user's home directory lets each user access his or her own private data easily.

- The J drive pointer mapped to each user's local department or workgroup lets users access their department's shared work files by using the path J:\WORK.

- The G drive pointer to the SYS volume gives each user access to software or utilities stored in the SYS volume.

- The I drive pointer mapped to the root of the DATA volume gives each user access to the global data structure for the organization. For example, a user can access the organization's global work directory with the path I:\WORK or access the organization's shared forms directory with the path I:\FORMS. If a department wants its own forms directory, that directory can be accessed with the path J:\FORMS.

- The K drive pointer is mapped to each user's shared workgroup data.

Drive Mapping Planning Form		
Organization:	**CBE Laboratories**	
Planned By:	**Ted Simpson**	
Date:	**9/15/99**	
GROUP:	**Everyone**	
Letter:	**Description of Use:**	**Path:**
S1:	NetWare Utilities	CONSTELLATION/SYS:PUBLIC
S2:		CONSTELLATION/SYS:
G:	Global SYS volume	CONSTELLATION/SYS:
I:	Global Data volume	CONSTELLATION/DATA:SHARED
GROUP:	**Marketing**	
Letter:	**Description of Use:**	**Path:**
H:	User data	CONSTELLATION/DATA:
		USERS/%Username
J:	Workgroup data	CONSTELLATION/DATA:MARKET
K:	Workgroup shared data	CONSTELLATION/DATA:
		MARKET/SHARED
GROUP:	**Finance**	
Letter:	**Description of Use:**	**Path:**
H:	User data	CONSTELLATION/DATA:
		USERS/%Username
J:	Workgroup data	CONSTELLATION/DATA:FINANCE
K:	Workgroup shared data	CONSTELLATION/DATA:
		FINANCE/SHARED
GROUP:		
Letter:	**Description of Use:**	**Path:**

Figure 8-10   Sample drive mapping planning form

Mapping Drive Pointers with Windows Explorer

You can create drive pointers in Windows 95/98 by using Windows Explorer. To create a drive pointer, in the folders list highlight the directory you want to map and then right-click on it to select the Novell Map Network Drive option.

Creating routine drive mappings in the user's login script saves the trouble of recreating them each session. To do this, you would use NetWare Administrator to include a MAP command in the user object's Login Script property.

For example, the CBE Labs network administrator could map the CONSTELLATION/SYS root directory to the K: drive by using Windows Explorer by following these steps:

1. To start Windows Explorer, click Start, Programs, Windows Explorer.

2. To display all the available network connections, click the Network Neighborhood expansion box. Click the expansion box in front of the icon for CONSTELLATION.

3. Right-click the folder icon for SYS to select it and display the shortcut menu.

4. Click N Novell Map Network Drive to display the Novell Map Drive dialog box that Figure 8-11 shows.

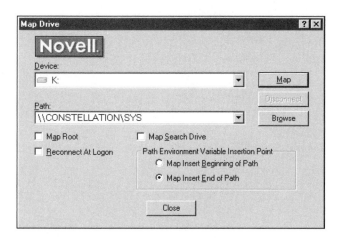

Figure 8-11   Map Network Drive dialog box with mapping

5. Click the Device drop-down list button, and then click K: to select the K: drive.

6. Click Map to create the drive mapping. The mapping appears in the list of drives under My Computer.

You can also map a drive by clicking the Tools Map Network Drive menu item. However, this action invokes a Windows program, not NetWare. So mapping a drive here would only apply to this workstation. Otherwise the process is similar to that of mapping with NetWare: Select the drive you want to map from the Drive: drop-down list. Select the mapping you want from the Path: drop-down list or type it into the Path: text box. When entering the mapping, you use **Universal Naming Convention (UNC)** paths. UNC paths include the server and volume name as part of the path by using double backward slashes in front of the NetWare server name, a single backward slash between the server and volume names, and a single backward slash between the volume name and the directory name (instead of a colon). The syntax looks like this:

`\\ServerName\Volume\Directory\Subdirectory`

Mapping Drives in Windows using NetWare

Now that you are familiar with the theory of drive mapping, you can learn how to create and manage those mappings within Windows. Keep in mind that many, if not most, of your applications will now be delivered or installed as icons on the Windows desktop. Thus, you won't need to map drives nearly as often as with previous versions of NetWare.

We've looked at drive mapping using native Windows tools. When you install NetWare Client32, you also install some significant enhancements to this basic function. In particular, you can now map root drives and search drives from the Windows desktop.

To map either of these drive types, right-click the Network Neighborhood icon on your Windows desktop. NetWare displays a menu as in Figure 8-12.

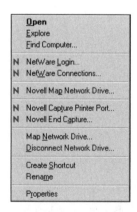

Figure 8-12   NetWare Client options menu

Note that this menu includes both a native Windows Map Network Drive option as well as options marked with the Novell N. If you choose the Novell version for mapping a drive, NetWare displays a dialog box similar to Figure 8-13.

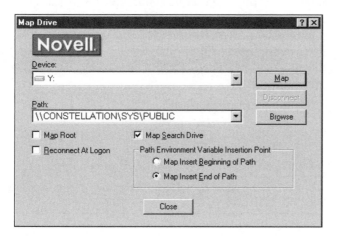

Figure 8-13   Mapping a search drive

Note that at the bottom of this dialog box are check boxes for Map Root or Map Search Drive. By default, NetWare performs a regular mapping unless you check either of these boxes. Type or browse to your drive path. Then choose OK. Your drive is now mapped. Again, if you want these mappings to become permanent, add them to the user's login script.

Removing Drive Mappings in Windows

Removing a drive mapping in Windows is simple. Right-click the icon of the mapped drive in Windows Explorer, and then choose Disconnect. NetWare automatically removes the mapping. You can perform the same function in the My Computer window.

The MAP Command

MAP is a versatile DOS command line utility that network administrators use to create, modify, and delete both regular and search drive pointers. Although you most often will be using the Windows desktop tools to handle pointers, you need to be familiar with the basic MAP command as used in login scripts to control a user's drive mappings at login. As you learned in Chapter 4, a login script is a file containing NetWare commands. The LOGIN.EXE program uses this file when a user successfully logs into a server. In this section you will learn the following required network administrator tasks by describing the purpose of each task, the syntax of the associated MAP command, and an example of its use.

The basic syntax of the MAP command is:

```
MAP [option] /VER [drive:=] [path] [?]
```

You can use several parameters with the MAP command, as listed in Table 8-1.

Table 8-1   MAP command parameters

Parameter	Use this parameter to:
drive:	Specify the drive letter.
path	Specify the path to the directory being mapped. Include: NetWare server name Volume name Directory path on volume
/?	Access help about MAP. If this parameter is used, all others are ignored.
/VER	See the version number of the MAP command. If this parameter is used, all others are ignored.

You can use several options with MAP, as listed in Table 8-2.

Table 8-2   MAP command options

Option	Use this option to:
INS	Insert an additional search drive mapping. You can also type the word INSERT.
DEL	Delete the drive mapping.
N	Use the next available drive letter for mapping. You can also use the word NEXT.
R	Create a root drive mapping. You can also use the word ROOT.
P	Map to a physical volume. This must be the first or second parameter listed.
C	Change the type of drive mapping from regular to search or search to regular.

Table 8-3 gives examples of using the MAP command to perform various tasks either at the DOS command line or in a user's login script:

Table 8-3 Examples using the MAP command

Task	Example
View current mappings	MAP [Enter]
Create regular drive mappings	MAP G:=CONSTELLATION_SYS: [Enter]
Create a root drive mapping	MAP ROOT J:=CONSTELLATION_SYS:APPS\OFFICE [Enter]
Change a drive mapping	MAP J:=J: [Enter] (This has the effect of changing the Root mapping shown in the example above into a regular drive mapping.)
Create a search drive mapping	MAP S16:=CONSTELLATION_SYS:PUBLIC [Enter]
Remove a drive mapping	MAP DEL J: [Enter] (This deletes the drive mapping on J.)

Creating Regular Drive Pointers

To use the MAP command to create a new drive letter, enter the command

```
MAP drive:=[path]
```

where *drive* can be any letter of the alphabet (A–Z). You can replace *path* with either a complete or partial NetWare path leading to the target directory. If you omit the path, the MAP command will assign the specified drive pointer to the current path. For example, if the CBE Labs network administrator wants to assign drive L to the DATA:MARKET directory on CONSTELLATION, he would use the following MAP command to specify a complete path:

```
MAP L:=CONSTELLATION/DATA:MARKET
```

You can also use an existing drive map as part of the path, as shown in the following command, which assigns the drive letter N to the DATA:MARKET\REPORTS directory by using the L drive pointer, which is mapped to the DATA:MARKET directory as a starting point:

```
K:\>MAP N:=L:REPORTS
```

Notice that there is no slash between the drive letter (L) and the path (REPORTS). Placing a slash in the command would cause the system to search the root of the DATA volume for the REPORTS directory. Because no REPORTS directory exists in the root of the DATA volume, an error message indicating an invalid path would be displayed.

If you use a local drive pointer (A–F), the MAP command asks if you want to override the local pointer with a network path. If you answer yes, the local drive pointer will access the network path rather than the local drive.

The command

    MAP N [*path*]

can be used to assign the specified path to the next available drive letter, proceeding from F (or whatever drive is assigned using the FIRST NETWORK DRIVE parameter) through Z. You can also use the word NEXT instead of just N. This command is useful when you want to map an unused drive letter to a directory path and you do not care what letter is used. Suppose, for example, you want to map a drive to the SHARED subdirectory of the MARKET directory. The MAP NEXT command, as shown in Figure 8-14, maps the next available drive letter, in this case H, to the USER subdirectory.

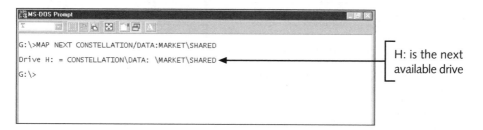

Figure 8-14   Creating regular drive mappings

Why Create Root Drive Pointers?

A root drive pointer looks to the user or application program as if the drive pointer were at the beginning of a drive or volume. Root drive pointers are useful for two reasons:

1. Some applications access files only from the root of a directory path. This can be a problem for a network administrator, because users are not usually given rights to the root of a volume and also because you might want to keep the application contained in a certain directory in the structure. NetWare solves this problem by letting the network administrator or users map a drive to a "fake" root containing the application.

2. Root drive pointers make it more difficult for a user or application to change the drive pointer to another location inadvertently. For example, if a user's home directory is mapped to a regular drive pointer and the user issues a CD\ command, the mapping of the drive pointer is changed to the root of the current volume. Root drive mappings, in contrast, appear to DOS as the beginning of a drive, causing CD\ to return to the directory to which the root drive is mapped to rather than going to the root of the volume.

Creating Search Drive Pointers

Search drives are pointers to directories where programs are stored on the network. A workstation will already have one or more search drives mapped to local directories. You can assign a maximum of 16 search drives, starting with S1 and ending with S16. You can add new search drives to the list by using the MAP command either to assign the next available search drive number or to insert the search drive between two existing search drives. The syntax of the MAP command that adds new search drives is as follows:

```
MAP INS S#: = [path]
```

When you add a search drive to the end of the list, you do not include the INS option and you replace # with the next available search drive number from 1 through 16. If you skip search drive numbers, the MAP command will automatically assign the next available number. When you add a new search drive, NetWare automatically assigns the next available drive letter, starting with Z for S1 and ending with K for S16. For example, suppose you have the following search drives mapped:

```
S1:=Z:. [CONSTELLATION\SYS:\PUBLIC]

S2:=Y:. [CONSTELLATION\SYS:\PUBLIC\IBM_PC\MSDOS\V7.00]

S3:=C:\DOS
```

The next available search drive is Search4 (S4). To map search drive S4: to the SYS:APPS\WINOFFCE directory, you can use the following map command:

```
MAP S4:=SYS:APPS\WINOFFCE
```

When adding new search drives, you cannot skip search drive numbers. For example, if you attempt to map the preceding search drive to S5 before S4 is mapped, NetWare automatically uses the next sequential search drive number, in this case S4, as Figure 8-15 shows.

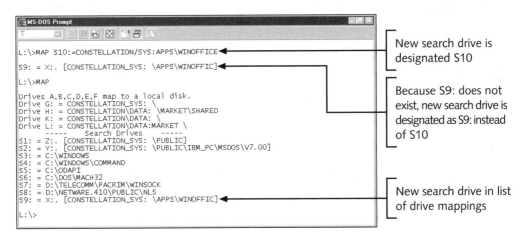

New search drive is designated S10

Because S9: does not exist, new search drive is designated as S9: instead of S10

New search drive in list of drive mappings

Figure 8-15 Adding a new search drive mapping

Because NetWare will not skip search drive numbers, you can use the command MAP S16:=[path] if you want to add a search drive to the end of the search list and cannot remember the number of the last search drive.

When inserting a search drive between two existing drives, include the INS option and replace # with the number of the search drive before which you want the new drive placed. When you set up search drives, assign the lower search drive numbers to the most commonly used paths. This makes the system more efficient by reducing the number of directories NetWare has to search through when it looks for a program file.

For example, assume you have the following search drives mapped:

S1:=Z:.[CONSTELLATION\SYS:PUBLIC]

S2:=Y:.[CONSTELLATION\SYS:PUBLIC\IBM_PC\MSDOS\V7.00]

S3:=X:.[CONSTELLATION\SYS:APPS\WINOFFCE]

Suppose you want to use the word-processing program located in the APPS\OFFICE97\WP directory and still maintain the other search drive mappings. To make the word-processing directory first in the search order, you could use the MAP INS command shown in Figure 8-16 to create a new Search1 mapping. This resequences the other search drives, as displayed by the MAP command.

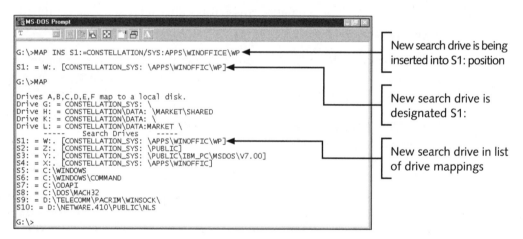

Figure 8-16   Inserting a search drive mapping

Notice that the drive letter W is assigned to the new search drive and that, although the other search drives are renumbered, they retain their drive letter assignments. The DOS MAP commands shown in Figure 8-16 illustrate the way the search commands affect the DOS path. NetWare keeps track of search drive numbers by their sequence in the DOS path. Because drive W is now the first drive in the path, it becomes S1.

Directory Map Objects

A **Directory Map object** is a server-related leaf object that the network administrator can use in a MAP command to simplify administration of the drive mappings. The Directory Map object contains the path that you would normally use in a drive mapping. By using the Directory Map object in a MAP command, you are providing the drive-mapping path as the path contained in the Directory Map object.

For example, the network administrator for CBE Labs wants to map a drive to the files shared among all CBE Labs personnel. These reports are stored in the CONSTELLATION/DATA:SHARED directory. To map a regular drive, the network administrator would use the following command:

```
MAP P:=CONSTELLATION/DATA:SHARED
```

To map a drive by using a Directory Map object, the network administrator first creates the Directory Map object and enters the volume and path data needed for the drive map. For example, he could create a Directory Map object named SharedFiles in the CBE_Labs_Admin Organizational Unit of CBE_Labs. He would then use the following MAP command:

```
MAP P:=.SharedFiles.CBE_Labs_Admin.CBE_Labs
```

If the network administrator later wants to move these files to another location, he can change the drive mapping by simply changing the Volume and Path property values stored in the Directory Map object. This is easier than finding every use of the regular mapping in all the login scripts that use the drive mapping. For this reason, you will usually want to create Directory Map objects for to use in drive mappings.

You can create Directory Map objects by using NetWare Administrator. After creating them, you can use them in any MAP command.

The CBE Labs network administrator wants to create a Directory Map object named SharedFiles in the CBE_Labs_Admin Organizational Unit container object. The Directory Map object will contain the path CONSTELLATION/DATA:SHARED.

To create the SharedFiles Directory Map object, follow these steps:

1. Launch NetWare Administrator.

2. Expand the Directory tree to show the CBE_Labs_Admin organizational unit and its contents.

3. Click the CBE_Labs_Admin Organizational Unit object, click Object on the menu bar, and then click Create.

4. The New Object dialog box is displayed. Click Directory Map and then click OK. The Create Directory Map dialog box is displayed, as Figure 8-17 shows.

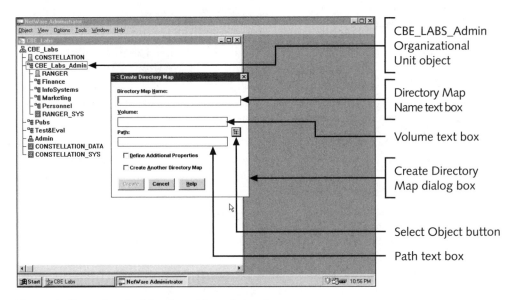

Figure 8-17   Create Directory Map dialog box

5. Type SharedFiles in the Directory Map Name text box.

6. Click the Volume text box to activate it, and then click the Select Object button 📇 to the right of the Volume text box. The Select Object dialog box is displayed.

7. Use the Select Object dialog box to browse the Directory tree to locate and select the CONSTELLATION_DATA Volume object. The name of the selected object appears in the Selected Object text box.

8. Click OK. The volume name CONSTELLATION_DATA. CBE_Labs appears in the Volume text box of the Create Directory Map dialog box.

9. Click the Path text box to activate it, and then click the Select Object button 📇 to the right of the Path text box. The Select Object dialog box is displayed.

10. Click the SHARED directory folder to select it. Click OK. NWAdmin fills in the Path text box of the Create Directory Map dialog box, as shown in Figure 8-18.

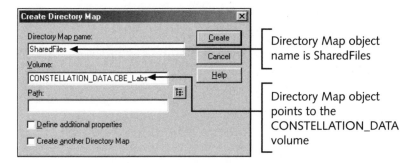

Figure 8-18 Create Directory Map dialog box

11. Click Create. The Directory Map object SharedFiles is created and added to the Directory tree, as shown in Figure 8-19.

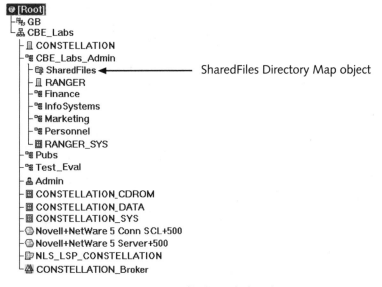

Figure 8-19 Directory tree with SharedFiles directory map

You cannot test your new mapping until you add the appropriate MAP command to your login script:

```
MAP P:=.SharedFiles.CBE_Labs_Admin.CBE_Labs
```

using NWAdmin. To do this, double-click your user object in your NDS tree. Click Login Script, and type in the MAP command shown above as the last line in the login script. Click OK to save this Login Script.

Then you will need to log back into NDS. You can now test the mapping using the following steps:

1. Open a DOS session by clicking Start, pointing to Programs, then clicking MS-DOS Prompt.

2. Type MAP [Enter] to view your drive mappings. The new mapping will be displayed.

FILE MANAGEMENT

After you have your network file system in place and have created drive mappings, you can now install applications and users can put their data on the network. The directories and subdirectories of the network file system are used for storing the application and data files. As a network administrator, you must manage these files and their directories. In this section, you will study some tools that will help you accomplish this.

Viewing NetWare Directory and File Attributes

To see information about directory and file attributes, run Windows Explorer. Select a network directory, and display its contents. Right-click on a file or directory, and you'll see a menu with the Properties option at the bottom. Click on this, and NetWare will display information about the current directory or file. The Properties option also provides a way to set various file or directory attributes. For example, Figure 8-20 shows the information about the CONSTELLATION/SYS:PUBLIC directory.

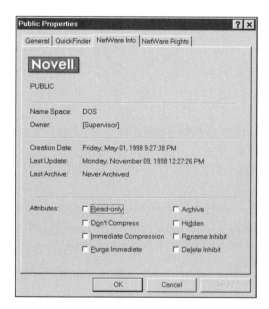

Figure 8-20   Directory Properties dialog box

Information about the file or directory—including the owner, attributes, and creation date and time—appears in the dialog box. Using the appropriate tab at the top, you can also display a list of trustees with rights to the directory, and the effective rights of the current user.

- The Owner field displays the name of the user who created the directory. Administrator authority is required to change the information in this field.

- The Creation Date field tells you the date and time the directory was created and can be changed only if you are logged in with Administrator authority.

- The Attributes section displays the attributes available for this directory or file. With a checkmark, it indicates which ones are active. As administrator, you can click the boxes to set or un-set any of these attributes. These include Read-only, Hidden, Compression variables, and Purge Immediate (used when you need the space.)

- The NetWare Rights tab displays the current effective rights field showing who has effective access rights in this file or directory. If you do not have administrator or equivalent rights, you cannot directly change the information in this field because it depends on the privileges assigned to your user name as well as any trustee assignments granted to you or a group you belong to. Chapter 10 will describe the information in this dialog box in more detail.

- The Inherited Rights and Filters option, also under the NetWare Rights tab, displays a list of access rights that the directory will allow to flow into it from its parent directories. Chapter 10 will describe the use of this field.

- The Trustees field, also on the NetWare Rights tab, lists all users and groups who have been assigned rights to this directory. Chapter 10 will explain assigning trustees to a directory in more detail.

For example, right-clicking a NetWare file and choosing Properties will display information about the file, as Figure 8-21 shows.

8

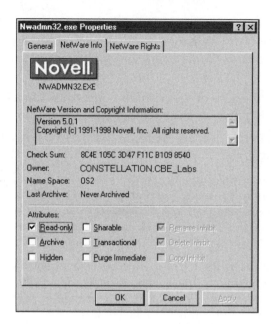

Figure 8-21 Displaying information about a NetWare file

The NetWare Info tab for a file offers many functions, similar to the directory options previously mentioned:

- The Attributes area lets you add or remove attribute flags by displaying a window of existing attributes for this file. You can then click to add or remove the appropriate attributes. Chapter 10 will describe the use of the NetWare file attributes.

- The Owner field identifies the user who originally created the file. Only an administrator user can change the contents of the Owner field. This is normally done if the name of the user who originally created the file is deleted from the system.

- The Name Space field shows whether the file uses DOS or Long File Name space (OS/2 uses a Long File Name space).

- On the NetWare Rights tab, the Inherited Rights and Filters and Trustees fields function the same way they do in the Directory Properties window.

- The Effective Rights field on the NetWare Rights tab is for information purposes only and cannot be changed, even by the administrator.

- On the General tab, the Size field shows the file size in bytes.

- The Created Date field (as well as the Modified and Accessed date fields in the case of files) is for informational purposes and cannot be changed.

> If you want to work with several files, use the mouse and the [CTRL] key to highlight each filename and then right-click and choose Properties. NetWare displays a similar set of tabbed properties dialogs as for a single file. This time, NetWare shows only the combination of rights/trustees for the selected files.

Windows-Based NetWare File Management

You can use the Windows 95/98 Explorer to copy, move, and delete both local and network files. You should already know how to use Windows Explorer to do these functions. Used with the NetWare Client 32 client, Windows Explorer can also be used to assign and control trustee rights, as Chapter 10 discusses.

In this section we'll discuss using the various Windows-based tools for file management.

Using NetWare Administrator to View Volume Information

NetWare Administrator lets you see information about a selected volume, as explained in Chapter 7. If you already have the Administrator running, it saves a step to use NWAdmin rather than Windows Explorer. The information provided is the same in both utilities. To view volume information in NWAdmin:

1. Right-click a volume object in your directory tree.

2. On the shortcut menu, select Details. NetWare displays an Object Properties dialog box for the volume.

3. Click the Statistics button on the right side of the dialog box. The Volume Information dialog box appears, as Figure 8-22 shows.

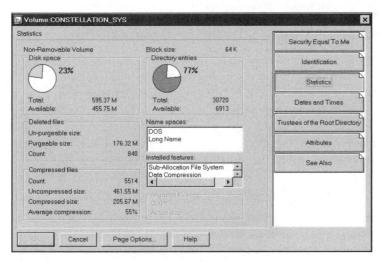

Figure 8-22   Volume Information dialog box

The Volume Information window shows the following items:

- Current use of space on the volume
- All loaded name spaces such as long filenames
- Details about compression
- Any installed features such as suballocation

The key information here is the available space on the volume. You will often need to track space carefully, to keep the volume from unexpectedly filling up.

Using Windows Explorer to View Volume Information

Explorer also allows you to see information about a selected volume. The general steps are:

1. Open Explorer.
2. Right-click the volume name you want.
3. Choose Properties on the menu.
4. Choose NetWare Volume Statistics. The Volume Statistics dialog box shown earlier in Figure 8-22 appears.

Again, you will see a variety of information about the current volume. One important aspect is the amount of space taken up by deleted files (called purgeable space). NetWare will recover this space automatically when it runs out of free space on the volume. Comparing the amount of purgeable space a volume has to its available space gives you an idea when this volume will be full.

Using Windows to Salvage and Purge Deleted Files

You can use Windows to salvage or purge files from network directories. (Naturally, you'll need appropriate rights in the directory you try to purge or salvage.) Salvaging a file is quite similar to the Windows UNDELETE function; you retrieve a file or files that have been deleted but you now want to restore. Salvaging has similar limitations to the UNDELETE command in that if you wait too long, you may not be able to salvage a file. A purge is like emptying the Recycle Bin—it irrevocably removes that file or files from the network volume. Once you run Purge on a directory or file, you cannot use Salvage to recover it.

To perform a Salvage or Purge operation, select the directory you want by opening either My Computer or Network Neighborhood, then double-clicking an appropriate network volume. Right-click the directory you want (the one that contained the file or files you want to recover), and NetWare presents a menu similar to Figure 8-23.

Figure 8-23   File Options menu

NetWare offers you a choice of Salvage or Purge. If you choose Salvage, the Salvage dialog box appears as Figure 8-24 shows. If there are no files you can salvage from this directory, then the Salvage Files window will be blank.

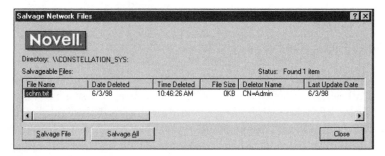

Figure 8-24   Salvage dialog box

 The importance of the Salvage feature is its ability to recover files that have been deleted even when the directory structure in which the file was stored no longer exists.

If you choose Purge, NetWare presents a screen almost identical to the one Figure 8-24 shows, listing all deleted files. You can choose one or more files to purge, or you can click Purge All. You can also choose Purge Subdirectories to purge deleted files from all subdirectories of the selected directory.

Caution! Once you purge a file, it is gone forever. So choose carefully when performing a Purge All or Purge Subdirectories operation.

Using NetWare Administrator to Salvage and Purge Deleted Files

To salvage deleted files using NetWare Administrator, in the NetWare Administrator browser window select the directory you want to work with. Then select the Salvage command on the Tools menu to display the Salvage Files dialog box, as Figure 8-25 shows.

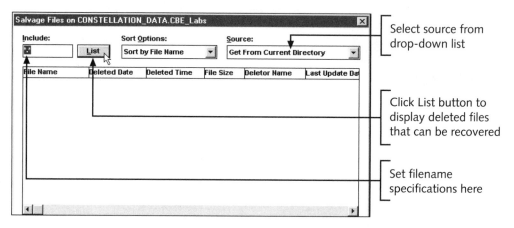

Figure 8-25   Salvage Files dialog box in NetWare Administrator

This dialog box has an Include: text box in which you can specify a search pattern, such as *.WK1, to view all deleted files with the .WK1 extension, or leave the default global pattern (*.*) to display all deleted files. When you have edited the search pattern, you click the List button to display all deleted files matching the pattern. You can use the Sort Options drop-down list to control how the displayed files are sorted, and the Source drop-down list to display files from the current directory or from the DELETED.SAV directory. Files to be salvaged are selected by clicking the first filename and then holding down [Ctrl] while clicking on other filenames to add them to the selection. (Holding down [Shift] and clicking on a second filename will select all files between and including the first filename selected and the second filename.) Once the files are selected, you click the Salvage button to salvage the files. A dialog box appears to show where the restored files will be placed. Figure 8-26 shows a file selected for recovery.

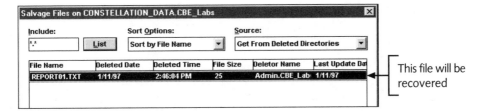

This file will be recovered

Figure 8-26   Selected files

Purging deleted files with NetWare Administrator works exactly like salvaging files, except after you have selected the files to be purged you click the Purge button instead of the Salvage button. A dialog box is then displayed to confirm the purge.

When you are low on disk space, purging deleted files can often improve the NetWare server's performance.

8

CHAPTER SUMMARY

❏ Directory management involves creating and removing directories and subdirectories on the various volumes in the network. This is known as creating and maintaining the directory structure for each volume. In Windows 95/98, directories are called *folders*. Tools used to create directories and subdirectories include the Windows 95/98 File, New, Folder command and the NetWare Administrator Create command.

❏ Drive pointers are letters assigned to local drives and network directories for working with the file system and accessing software stored in other directories. The drive pointers A–E are normally reserved for local drives. NetWare often uses drive pointers F–Z to point to directory locations. Regular and root drive pointers are assigned to directories that contain data files; search drive pointers are assigned to software directories.

❏ Users can add or delete drive mappings with the Windows NetWare utilities or by using Windows Explorer. The system tray N icon displays a menu with the option for Novell Map Network Drive. In Explorer or Network Neighborhood, right-clicking on the directory mapping you want will also display the Novell Map Network Drive option. When a user logs in, drive pointers are set through the login script.

❏ The MAP command is the utility network administrators use to create and maintain drive pointers in login scripts. As a network administrator, you should be able to use the MAP command to perform the following functions:

- View drive pointer assignments

- Create a regular drive pointer

- Create a root drive pointer

- Add a new search drive in the middle or at the end of the current search drive list
- Remove a regular drive mapping
- Remove a search drive mapping

❑ A Directory Map object is used in the NDS Directory tree to simplify the mapping of drive pointers in situations in which the mapped directory may change location in the file directory structure. By mapping a drive to the Directory Map object, the network administrator can change the drive pointer in just one place, the Directory Map object properties, when the directory location changes.

❑ A user or the network administrator can use the Windows 95/98 Explorer program and the Network Neighborhood icon to change a user's drive pointer mappings. Because drive pointers play a major role in the way users, applications, and menus, access the NetWare file system, it is important for a network administrator to establish standards for drive pointer usage, to prevent conflicts and software configuration problems. As a general rule you should use a drive pointer planning form similar to the one Figure 8-10 shows (a blank form can be found in Appendix B) to establish for each user a set of drive pointers that includes a regular drive pointer to the root of each volume, a root drive pointer to the user's home directory, and another root drive pointer to the shared work area for the user's workgroup. In addition to the required search drive to the SYS:PUBLIC directory, search drives need to be allocated for any legacy DOS-based software packages. A standard drive pointer usage plan makes accessing and maintaining the network file system much easier for both the users and the network administrator.

❑ File management involves copying, moving, and deleting files in the various directories. Several NetWare utilities are useful in file management. Purging files using Windows Explorer or NetWare Administrator permanently erases deleted files and frees up disk space. Otherwise NetWare maintains the deleted file on the volume until the disk is almost full and only then erases files to make room for new ones as necessary. When you are low on disk space, purging deleted files can often improve the NetWare server's performance.

❑ The primary tool used with the file system is the Windows Explorer. A network administrator needs to know what functions this utility performs and how to use it for the tasks this chapter describes. As a network administrator, you should know how to use Explorer to complete the following:

- Change the current directory using the browser
- Copy or move a directory structure
- Create directories
- Copy files
- Rename files and subdirectories
- Delete files and directory structures

- View volume information
- Salvage deleted files
- Purge deleted files

❐ You can use both Windows Network Neighborhood and NetWare Administrator to salvage and purge deleted files. The importance of the Salvage feature is its ability to recover deleted files even when the directory structure in which the file was stored no longer exists.

COMMAND SUMMARY

Command	Syntax	Definition
MAP	MAP d:=[path]	Creates regular drive mappings
	MAP N [path]	Creates a regular drive mapping using the next available drive letter
	MAP d:= [path]	Creates root drive mappings
	MAP S#:=[path]	Adds a search drive to the end of the search list
	MAP INS S#:=[path]	Inserts a search drive before an existing drive number
	MAP DEL d:	Removes either regular, root, or search drive pointers
	MAP C drive	Changes a search drive mapping to a regular drive mapping and vice versa

 This summary of the MAP command contains only basic parameters, not all possible options.

KEY TERMS

Directory Map objects
drive mapping
drive pointers
folders
local drive pointers
network drive pointers
regular drive pointers
root drive pointers

8

search drive pointers
Universal Naming Convention(UNC)

REVIEW QUESTIONS

1. Describe how to create a new directory in Windows 95/98.
2. Describe how to create a new directory using NetWare Administrator.
3. _____ drive pointers are used to reference data storage locations on the server.
4. _____ drive pointers are used to reference software storage directories on a server.
5. Write the steps to view all drive mappings.
6. Write the steps to create a new root drive pointer H that will point to the SERVER01/DATA:USERS\JOHN directory.
7. Write the steps to add a search drive pointer to the SERVER01/SYS:SOFTWARE\WP directory.
8. Write the steps to change the path of a search drive from the SYS:SOFTWARE\WP directory to the SYS:SOFTWARE\UTILITY directory without creating a regular drive pointer from the existing search drive.
9. Given the directory structure shown in Figure 8-27, write sample login script MAP commands to map drives to the marked areas.

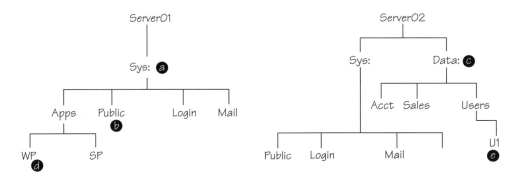

Figure 8-27   Sample directory structure

a. _____
b. _____
c. _____
d. _____
e. _____

10. What is (are) the advantage(s) of using a Directory Map object instead of a direct drive pointer mapping?

11. Describe how you would use a Directory Map object to create a drive pointer to directory (c) in Figure 8-27.

12. Describe how you would use a Directory Map object to create a drive pointer to directory (d) in Figure 8-27.

13. A user or network administrator can map drive pointers on a user's PC using the _____ or the _____.

14. Describe how a user can create a drive pointer mapping using Windows 95/98.

15. Deleted files can be recovered using the _____ function. This function is available in the _____ utility and the _____ utility.

16. To permanently remove deleted files from a volume, you would use the _____ function. This function is available in the _____ utility, and the _____ utility.

HANDS-ON PROJECTS

Project 8-1: Using Windows Explorer to Copy a Directory Structure

In this project you practice using the Windows Explorer utility to copy a sample directory structure from the SYS volume to a designated location in your home directory. The files and subdirectories in this structure will be used in subsequent Hands-on Projects and Case Projects.

1. Log into the network using your student user name.

2. Before copying all files and subdirectories from the CONSTELLATION_SYS:EXAMPLE directory to your home directory, you need to record the complete NetWare path to your directory. On the following line, record the complete path to your home directory, including server name, volume, and directory names:

   _____

3. Display the CONSTELLATION_SYS:EXAMPLE directory structure showing all directories and subdirectories in Windows Explorer.

4. Use the Network Neighborhood icon to change the default DOS prompt to point to your home directory.

   a. Right-click the **Network Neighborhood** icon.

   b. Choose **N Novell Map Network Drive**.

   c. Select your default network drive (F: or G:).

   d. Click **Disconnect**. NetWare will remove the current mapping.

   e. Click **Browse**. Locate your home directory in the tree, highlight it, then click **OK**.

f. Check the **Reconnect at Logon** box if you want to make this drive mapping permanent.

g. Click **MAP**.

NetWare now will remap the drive to your chosen directory.

5. Use the File, New command to create a directory for the sample structure at the beginning of your home directory, as Figure 8-28 shows.

Figure 8-28

6. Use Explorer to copy all files without attributes, along with all the subdirectories from the CONSTELLATION_SYS:EXAMPLE directory, into the area you created in Step 5. Record the steps you use:

_____

7. Use Windows to display the contents of your home directory and all subdirectories. Compare these directory listings with the one you produced in Step 3. Make sure all subdirectories are included.

8. Use Windows to display all files and attributes in the SAMPLE subdirectory. Record the commands you use:

_____

Project 8-2: Using Explorer to Copy Files

In this project you practice using Windows Explorer to copy files from one directory on the server to another directory location.

1. Start Explorer and change to your ##ADMIN directory.

2. Copy all files that end with a number from the EXAMPLE directory into a SAMPLE\BUDGETS subdirectory in your home directory. Record the Explorer steps you use to do this:

_____

Project 8-3: Using Explorer to Rename Files and Directories

In this project you practice using Windows Explorer to change the names of files and directories.

1. If you have not already done so, start Explorer and change to your ##NWTC directory.

2. In the SAMPLE\BUDGETS subdirectory, change the name of the worksheet file EARN01.WK1 by replacing the "01" in the filename with the current year (e.g., EARN1999). Change the name of the TAX02.WK1 file by replacing the "02" in the filename with last year (i.e. TAX1998).

3. Create a subdirectory under Budget called FORMS. Rename this subdirectory as CTIFORMS.

4. After completing the name changes, use Explorer to display a directory listing of the BUDGETS subdirectory.

5. Use Explorer to display the entire structure of your SAMPLE directory.

8

Project 8-4: Salvaging Files using NetWare Administrator

In this project you practice using the Salvage option of NetWare Administrator to recover deleted files. You first use Windows Explorer to delete the files from the SAMPLE\BUDGETS subdirectory, then salvage them with NetWare Administrator.

1. Start Windows Explorer.

2. Select the BUDGETS subdirectory. Record the complete path to this directory.

   _____

3. Select two files. Record the filenames:
   Files marked:

   _____

4. Delete the marked files.

5. Exit Windows Explorer.

6. Start NetWare Administrator.

7. Use the appropriate options to determine the amount of space available from deleted files in this volume. Record the name of the option, the steps you used, and the amount of space available:

   _____

8. Start the Salvage option in NetWare Administrator.

9. Change to the directory path you recorded in Step 2.

10. Set the Salvage option to sort files by deletion time.

11. Use the appropriate option to display all deleted files.

12. Mark and salvage the files you deleted in Step 4.

13. Exit NetWare Administrator.

Project 8-5: Using the MAP Command

In this project you use the login script MAP command to create both regular and search drive mappings, then test the search drive. After each of the map descriptions in Step 1, record the MAP command you plan to use to create that drive mapping. Do not execute these MAP commands until Step 3.

1. Write MAP commands for the following sample directory areas:

   a. A regular drive pointer to the SAMPLE subdirectory of your student directory:

   _____

   b. A root drive pointer to JCunningham's home directory, located in the USERS directory:

   _____

   c. A search drive pointer after the last existing search drive that points to the WIN32 subdirectory of the CONSTELLATION_SYS\PUBLIC directory:

   _____

2. Use MAP commands to create the drive mappings you defined in Step 1.

3. What letter is used by the first search drive mapping? _____

4. Use Windows Explorer to test your search drive mapping.

5. Delete your search drive mapping. Record the steps you use:

   _____

6. Use Network Neighborhood functions to display the revised search drive list.

Project 8-6: Creating a Directory Map object with NetWare Administrator

In this project you create a Directory Map object using NetWare Administrator.

1. Start NetWare Administrator.

2. Select the Test&Eval Organizational Unit in the CBE_Labs tree.

3. Create a Directory Map object named Network Budgets that maps a drive pointer to your BUDGETS subdirectory.

4. Exit NetWare Administrator.

5. Write a MAP command to use the Network Budget Directory Map object in a search drive mapping. (If you did Project 8-5, use the same drive letter you used there). Record your command:

_____

6. Use MAP commands to create the drive mapping you defined.

CASE PROJECTS

Case 8-1: Setting Up a Drive Pointer Environment for the J. Q. Adams Corporation

The J. Q. Adams Corporation would like you to set up a drive pointer environment for the administrative users of its network. To be able to access his or her home directory directly without accidentally changing to another location, each user needs a drive pointer. In addition, all users in each department need to be able to easily access the shared work directory for their department as well as access the organization's work directory and word-processing forms. The users in the sales department need a special drive pointer to run the order entry system. All users in the company need to be able to run either the word-processing or spreadsheet application software stored in a directory called SOFTWARE on the server's SYS volume, as well as to use NetWare and DOS commands.

1. Complete a copy of the drive pointer planning form shown in Figure 8-10. (You can copy a blank form from Appendix B.) Assume a standard NetWare SYS volume was created for the server, with a USERS directory at the root of SYS.

2. Describe the MAP commands you would use to implement the drive pointers you planned in Step 1.

_____

8

9

MANAGING USERS, GROUPS, AND LOGIN SECURITY

> **After reading this chapter and completing the exercises you will be able to:**
>
> ♦ List the three types of NetWare security, and describe how login security can be used to restrict access to the server
>
> ♦ Create new users, groups, organizational roles, and profiles, and assign access restrictions using the NetWare Administrator and UIMPORT utilities
>
> ♦ Describe how the NetWare accounting system can be used to charge for network services and to keep track of total system usage and growth
>
> ♦ Use the DSREPAIR utility to check for and fix possible problems in the NDS database

Giving users convenient access to the server and at the same time protecting sensitive or private information and services are the primary functions of a network security system. NetWare 5.0 provides capabilities and tools for the network administrator to establish a sophisticated security system that will meet these needs in a LAN environment. As a network administrator, you will be expected to know how to use these capabilities and tools to perform the following security system functions:

- Create users and groups

- Determine what administrative functions can be delegated to user accounts and how to assign these privileges

- Protect user accounts from unauthorized use

- Use NetWare accounting to track system usage and charge users for network services

- Assign appropriate trustee rights to control access to NDS and the Directory tree

- Assign appropriate trustee rights and file attributes to control access to the file system

- Secure the server console from unauthorized access

To provide these functions, NetWare security can be described as having three levels: login security, trustee rights security (NDS and file system), and console security. These are illustrated in Figure 9-1.

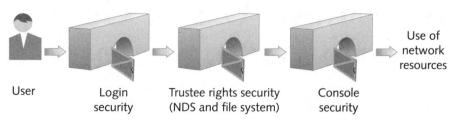

User   Login   Trustee rights security   Console   Use of
        security   (NDS and file system)   security   network
                                                                     resources

Figure 9-1   NetWare system security

You have already worked with login security, which controls initial access to the server, in Chapter 1, when you had to enter a valid user name to log into a server and when you used the SETPASS utility to make your account more secure with an optional password. In this chapter, you will learn more about login security and how to use NetWare utilities such as NetWare Administrator and UIMPORT to create users and groups, assign privileges, and establish access restrictions. In Chapter 10 you will learn how trustee rights (NDS and file system) security can give users the access rights they need to perform their work without affecting other users and can limit access to Directory tree objects, directories, and files that contain sensitive or secure information. Chapter 14 contains techniques and commands to make the server console secure from unauthorized access.

LOGIN SECURITY

Login security is sometimes called "initial access security" because it controls a user's access to a server. The login security system of NetWare 5.0 consists of five components that together let users access the server and do their work:

- User names
- Passwords and password restrictions
- Time restrictions
- Station restrictions
- Account restrictions

User Names

When NetWare 5.0 is first installed and started, one user name and account, Admin, is automatically created, and the Admin User object is added to the Directory tree. The Admin user has access to all network services, the entire NDS Directory tree, and the entire file system.

Initially the network administrator logs in as Admin and then creates the NDS Directory tree, the directory structure, other users, groups, and access restrictions. In this section you will learn to assign user names and access privileges and properly construct the user environment.

After creating the NDS Directory tree and network file system, the network administrator next needs to create a User object in the Directory tree for each user. After creating the User object, the administrator can assign access to network resources by granting access privileges to the User object.

User names can be up to 64 characters in length. NetWare 5.0 defaults to having long filename support, so there is no problem with longer user names. However, you may want to limit the length of user names to make them easier for users to type at login time.

One of the first considerations in creating user names is developing a consistent way to construct a user name from each user's actual name. Two common methods are used to construct user names. One is to use the first letter of the user's first name followed by the first seven letters of his or her last name, for a total of eight letters. For example, the user name for Mary Read is MREAD. The advantage of this method is that the user name is very similar to the user's actual name. The disadvantages are that most last names must be truncated and frequently two or more users have the same first initial and last name. For example, the user name for Michael Read would also be MREAD.

The second common method for creating user names is to use the first three letters of the user's first name, followed by the first three letters of the user's last name. In this method, Mary Read's user name becomes MARREA. This way, user names are uniformly of a consistent length and there is a smaller chance of duplicates. A disadvantage is that the user names are less recognizable. Whichever system you choose, be as consistent as possible.

NetWare 5.0 also lets a network administrator assign special manager and operator privileges to user accounts so they can perform such basic network administrative functions as creating and maintaining user accounts and working with printers. Delegating responsibility lets the network administrator concentrate on more important network functions.

Even if you do not want to delegate basic jobs to other users, you can use this capability to create user names that you yourself use to perform certain functions without having to log in as Admin. Logging in as Admin every time you need to do a network task that does not require administrator privileges increases the risk of accidentally damaging files or introducing viruses into the network. (Because the Admin user name has all access rights to the entire network file system, if your workstation is infected by a computer virus the virus software can copy itself into other network files and possibly erase network data.)

One property of the User object is security equivalence. Assigning a security equivalent to the Admin user privilege level gives a user the same privilege level and authority as the Admin user. Of course, this status should be limited to a few users. Most network administrators, however, establish at least one administrator-equivalent user to act as backup, sometimes called a "back door," in case the Admin account is inadvertently disabled or deleted. Later in this chapter you will learn how to use NetWare Administrator (NWAdmin) to tell you which users on your server have been granted administrator equivalency.

By granting appropriate privileges, you can create **workgroup managers**, who can create and manage new users and groups without having access to the entire server, and **user account managers**, who can modify but not create user accounts. The main purpose of creating users with these types of privileges is to let the network administrator delegate control of workgroups or departments to other capable users. In a large network, this reduces the amount of time the network administrator must spend performing these basic tasks.

You can also designate users as **printer operators**, which lets a user control jobs on a printer. Being a printer operator allows the user to perform such printer functions as changing forms, stopping the printer to clear paper jams, restarting the printer at a specific page number, and canceling a print job.

When a user logs in, the NetWare operating system checks his or her user account to see which level of privileges is assigned to that account.

Passwords

Although user names and assigned privileges provide initial access to the server and delegate network management duties, they do little to prevent unauthorized access to restricted information or server functions. Networks need additional security to restrict who can use the server, to protect the information and the integrity of the server environment. After user names, the next barrier in a security system is passwords on user accounts. You create the password for the Admin account during installation.

In NetWare 5.0, passwords can be up to 39 characters long; if you let users change their own passwords, you can increase password security by requiring some or all of the password restrictions described in the following paragraphs.

NetWare provides additional security against guessed user names and passwords. Rather than displaying a message that an attempted login user name is invalid or does not exist, NetWare will simply deny the login attempt. This feature makes it more difficult for people to guess user names, because they can never be sure if they have entered a correct user name and wrong password or if they have just entered an incorrect user name.

Set Minimum Password Length

To prevent the use of passwords that are short and easy to guess, most network administrators follow Novell's recommendation of a five-character minimum for password length. In this chapter, you will learn how to change the minimum length of passwords assigned to existing or newly created users.

Force Periodic Password Changes

After a while, a user's password can become known to coworkers and no longer provides protection against unauthorized access to that user's account. Having users periodically change passwords reduces this problem. NetWare lets you force selected user accounts to change passwords by limiting the time period a password remains valid. NetWare's default of 40 days between password changes may be too frequent for most users. If the time period between password changes is too short, users often record their current password near their work areas where it can easily be found and used (under the keyboard and in a desk drawer are common hiding places). As network administrator, you can increase the time between password changes, to improve server security. In addition, encourage good password and login habits by periodically reminding users not to record password information near workstations and to log out whenever they leave workstations unattended.

Require Unique Passwords

Another way to increase password security is to require users to enter a different password each time they change their password. When you require unique passwords, the server keeps track of the last 10 passwords that have been used by a user and rejects a new password that repeats one of the previous 10. NetWare's unique passwords option prevents users from alternating among a few favorite passwords, and therefore makes it more difficult for an intruder to log in using a known password. Network administrators often combine this option with forced periodic password changes, to provide increased safety on security-sensitive user accounts such as the Admin account or an account assigned to a payroll clerk.

Limit Login Grace Periods

When a password has been set to expire, the user has six **grace logins** to begin using the expired password. This default six-login grace period prevents users from being accidentally locked out from the network after their passwords expire, and it also keeps users from using an expired password indefinitely. Each time a user logs in after password expiration, NetWare displays a reminder that the current password has expired and states the remaining number of grace logins. Six grace logins are adequate for most server installations, but the network administrator or user account manager can change this number on an individual basis or change the default value assigned to all new user names when they are created.

Time Restrictions

Time restrictions enable the network administrator or user account manager to increase a user's account security by limiting the times during which the account can be used. This prevents someone who knows a user's password from logging in and accessing the network after business hours. Time restrictions can be set in half-hour increments. For example, a network administrator can restrict a payroll clerk to use the server only between 8 a.m. and 4:30 p.m. on weekdays. Time restrictions are important on high-security accounts, such as a payroll clerk's, because they keep intruders from accessing sensitive payroll information during nonbusiness hours.

Station Restrictions

Station restrictions can limit the number of times a user account can be concurrently logged into the server and can specify from which workstations a user can log into the network. The NetWare default is that a user can log in from any workstation and be logged into the network at several workstations simultaneously. The Admin user or other users with appropriate administrator privileges can change these defaults.

Setting a user name to be valid for logging in simultaneously from several workstations lets a network administrator create a general-purpose user name for multiple users. In most situations, however, limiting user accounts to one workstation at a time is important for the following reasons:

- Logging in from multiple workstations can cause software errors with some programs because certain control files are not sharable and therefore cannot be accessed simultaneously from more than one location by the same user.

- Restricting the user name to one workstation at a time helps users who move between multiple workstations remember not to leave a workstation unattended—and thus open to access by unauthorized users.

- Limiting a user account to access from a single workstation prevents an intruder who knows a user's name and password from logging in at an unattended workstation and gaining unauthorized access to the server.

Restricting a user account to a specific network and workstation node address increases security for highly sensitive information. A payroll clerk, for example, can be required to log in only on the workstation located in his or her office and only during normal office hours. For an intruder to access the payroll data, he or she would need to know the payroll clerk's user name and password to enter the payroll clerk's office during normal business hours, and to log into the server from the clerk's workstation. These limitations prevent all but a very bold intruder or a very well-trusted employee from making such an attempt, and his or her actions would likely be noticed by other employees.

Of course, if your Admin password is generally known to network users, all security efforts are in vain—anyone with the Admin password can log in from any workstation and have access to the entire network. So you might want to enhance Admin account security by requiring any administrator-equivalent user names to access the network from only two workstations that you can constantly monitor. Having your Admin account operate from two different workstations, or having an administrator-equivalent user name that operates on a separate workstation address, lets you access the server with administrator privileges if one workstation is out of order.

Account Restrictions

Account restrictions are conditions defined by the administrator to restrict user accounts. When an account is locked, no one can log in to the server with that user name until the account is reactivated. A network administrator needs to know how account restrictions can be used and how to reactivate a user account after any of the following limitations has locked it:

- The user account expired.

- The number of grace logins is exceeded.

- The account's balance is depleted.

- The predetermined number of incorrect password attempts has been made.

Account Expiration Date

NetWare's account expiration date is used to set a date after which the user account becomes disabled. This is a good way to establish temporary user accounts that you do not want accessed after a certain date. Student user accounts, for example, can be set to expire at the end of a semester or school year. After the expiration date, if a user attempts to log in with an expired user name, NetWare requires a password and then displays a message that the account has been disabled. Figure 9-2 shows a login attempt with an expired user name. Note that before issuing the error message NetWare requires you to enter the password.

NetWare's practice of requiring a user to enter a password before issuing any error messages makes it harder for an intruder to guess user names and passwords.

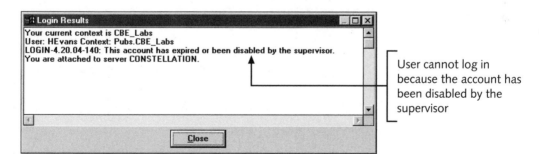

Figure 9-2   Expired user name

Number of Grace Logins Exceeded

Users who are forced to change their password after a specified number of days are granted a fixed number of logins with the old password after it has expired. Figure 9-3 shows the Change Password dialog box.

Enter a new password

Figure 9-3 Change Password dialog box

If a user fails to enter a new password within the granted number of grace logins, the account will be disabled until the Admin or user account manager either assigns a new password or extends the number of grace logins. Figure 9-4 shows a login attempt after a user's grace logins are used up.

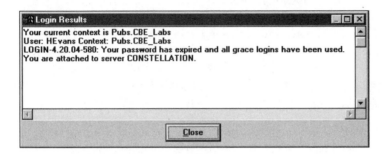

Figure 9-4 Grace logins expired

Depleted Account Balance

If the accounting feature is enabled on a server, records are kept of usage for such services as disk blocks read or written. Users can be "charged" for these services, and the charges are then deducted from the amount in the user's balance field. You can assign the following conditions:

- A balance to an individual user account that determines for how much time the user can access the network

- A credit limit that allows the user to draw on an account balance up to the limit

- Unlimited credit to the user

- A default credit limit and account balance that is granted to each new user created

When the amount in a user's account balance falls below his or her credit limit, the user's account is disabled until a user with administrator privileges increases the balance or provides more credit.

Intruder Detection

Unlike account restrictions that can be set individually for each user, NetWare's intruder detection is a feature that the network administrator turns on or off for all users in a container object. Thus intruder detection is configured individually for each Organization object or Organizational Unit object in a Directory tree.

Intruder detection locks an account when a user fails to enter the correct password within the number of attempts the administrator has specified. The purpose of intruder detection is to prevent someone who knows a user name from trying to log into that user's network account by repeatedly entering likely password combinations. The intruder detection feature lets you place a maximum on the number of times a user can try to enter his or her current password within a specified time period, and then set a length of time that the account will be locked when the specified number of attempts has been exceeded. Only a user with administrator privileges for the container object can release a locked account before the specified time interval. Figure 9-5 shows an example of intruder detection locking up a user account after three login attempts.

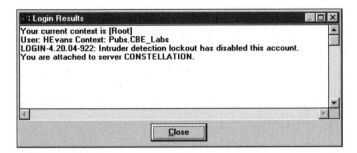

Figure 9-5   Intruder detection lockout

MANAGING USERS AND GROUPS

Now that you understand how login security works with user accounts to protect the NetWare environment, you are ready to create and manage users and groups. You will also learn about managing the network using user profiles and organizational roles.

User-Related Leaf Objects

As you learned in Chapter 4, user-related leaf objects have properties that enable you to manage the users on your network. User-related leaf objects include the User object, the Group object, the Organizational Role object, and the Profile object. These objects are summarized in Table 9-1.

Table 9-1   User-related leaf objects

Object Icon	Object	Purpose
🧍	User	Represents a network user
👥	Group	Represents a group of users
🏛	Organizational Role	Represents a position in an organization
📋	Profile	Provides information about groups of users that are not organized as a group

User-related objects, like other Directory tree objects, are created and managed using the NWAdmin utility you worked with in earlier chapters.

Users

Users, also called end users, are the people in the organization who use network resources such as computers and printers. The User object is used to represent and manage each network user and is represented in the Directory tree by the user icon shown in Table 9-1. Two properties, Login Name and Last Name, are mandatory and must be specified when you create each user. Login security is applied to each user through property settings assigned to each User object.

The User object Admin and an associated user account are created during NetWare 5.0 installation. The network administrator uses this user account to create other users. The User object for each user is created in the organizational unit of the Directory tree that represents the user's location in the organization.

To finish creating an object, you must supply the property values required in the Create *ObjectType* dialog box. In this dialog box, you are also given the options of (1) defining additional property values for the object you are creating, (2) immediately creating another object of the same type in the same container object, or (3) defining user defaults for the object.

For example, the CBE Labs network administrator needs to create user accounts for the network users at CBE Labs. The CBE Labs organizational chart, shown in Figure 1-8, shows the users who need accounts. Figure 9-6 shows the current Directory tree for CBE Labs.

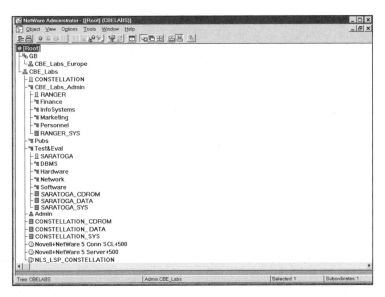

Figure 9-6   Current CBE Labs Directory tree

CBE Labs uses the user's first initial and full last name for login names. Although this creates user names longer than eight characters, CBE Labs management believes it's easier for users to remember.

It is tempting to use the same user name for NetWare as for e-mail. This makes it simple for people to remember. However, it also makes it much simpler for hackers to undermine network security. Because e-mail addresses reveal the user name, then the hacker has half of the puzzle solved for breaking in. Weigh the need for security against ease of use before making such a standard.

You will create the User objects for president Joseph Cunningham and administrative assistant Steve Lopez in the context CBE_Labs_Admin.CBE_Labs. User objects for all employees in the marketing, finance, personnel, and information systems departments will be created in their respective Organizational Unit containers. User objects for vice president Harold Evans and all employees in publishing will be created in the Pubs Organizational Unit container. The User objects for vice president Georgia Burns and administrative assistant Mike O'Donnell will be created in the context Test&Eval.CBE_Labs, with all employees in Labs having their User object created in their respective workgroup.

Creating More Than One Object

When creating more than one of the same type of object, you can use the Create Another *Object Type* option in the Create *Object Type* dialog box to repeat the object creation process without having to start over in the browser window. In this case, the CBE Labs network administrator needs to create multiple users in each container object. By using the Create Another User option, he can create all the users in a container object without leaving the Create User dialog box.

Creating Home Directories

At CBE Labs, each user has his or her own **home directory**, a directory reserved for the user's personal files. Each user has home directory privileges in only his or her home directory. It is easiest to create home directories at the same time the user's User object is created. This is done by using the Create Home Directory option in the Create User dialog box.

The directory name of the user's home directory will be the same as the login name. (Keep in mind that older NetWare servers typically use only the first eight characters of a user's login name as the home directory name.)

Creating User Objects

The CBE Labs network administrator is ready to create accounts for the CBE Labs users. He starts by creating the User objects for Joseph Cunningham and Steve Lopez.

To create the User objects for Cunningham and Lopez, follow these steps:

1. Launch NetWare Administrator and log in using your Admin username and password.

2. Expand the Directory tree in the browser window so that you can see all the objects in the tree.

3. Click the CBE_Labs_Admin Organizational Unit object, click Object on the menu bar, and then click Create.

4. The New Object dialog box is displayed. Click User, then click OK. The Create User dialog box appears, as Figure 9-7 shows.

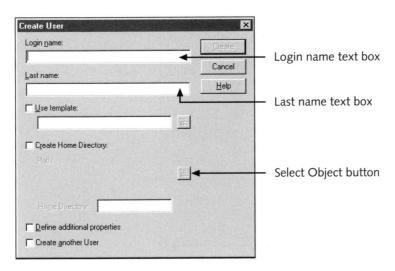

Figure 9-7   Create User dialog box

5. Because we want to create more than one user in this context, click the Create another User check box.

6. Because each user will have a home directory, click the Create Home Directory check box.

7. Click the Login Name text box to activate it, then type JCunningham. The login name is required to create the User object.

8. Click the Last Name text box to activate it, then type Cunningham. The last name is required to create the User object.

9. Joseph Cunningham's login name, JCunningham, appears in the Home Directory text box. This will be the directory name of his home directory. To specify the path for the home directory, click the Select Object button 🔢. The Select Object dialog box is displayed.

10. Use the Select Object dialog box to browse the Directory tree context to find an object. In this case, the starting context is CBE_Labs_Admin. The new context will be the Users directory on CONSTELLATION_DATA.CBE_Labs. Browse through the Directory tree until the Select Object dialog box appears, as Figure 9-8 shows, with the context of CONSTELLATION_DATA.CBE_Labs, and the Users directory as the selected object.

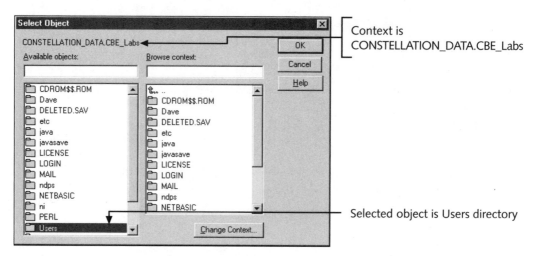

Context is
CONSTELLATION_DATA.CBE_Labs

Selected object is Users directory

Figure 9-8 Specifying path to user's home directory

11. Click OK. The path to Joseph Cunningham's home directory appears in the Create User dialog box, as Figure 9-9 shows.

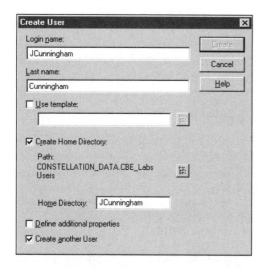

Figure 9-9 Completed Create User dialog box

12. Click the Create button. The JCunningham User object is created and added to the Directory tree, and the home directory is created on the CONSTELLATION_DATA volume.

13. Because you selected the Create Another User option, the Create User dialog box reappears. Repeat Steps 7–9 using the login name SLopez and the last name of Lopez.

14. After you create the User object for Steve Lopez, the Create User dialog box appears again. Because there are no more users to be created in this context, click the Cancel button.

15. Close and redisplay the CBE_Labs_Admin branch of the Directory tree. The User objects now appear as Figure 9-10 shows.

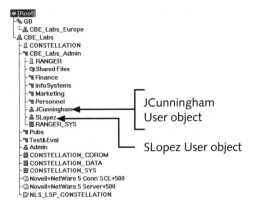

Figure 9-10 CBE Labs Directory tree with User objects

Managing User Object Property Values

Once a User object is created, you can set property values for the object to manage a user's access to network resources. You worked with object properties in Chapter 7, where you added postal office data for the CBE_Labs_Admin Organizational Unit. In this chapter you will work with the property values that specify a user's identity and control login security. In Chapter 10 you will work with user trustee right assignments to network resources through the Directory tree and the file directory structure.

You can set property values for each User object as you create it if you check the Define Additional Properties check box when you create the User object. Alternatively, as in this example, the network administrator can create the User objects and then set property values later.

To view a User object's properties, you can use any of these methods:

- Click the User object, and then press [Enter].
- Click the User object, click Object on the menu bar, and then click Details.
- Right-click the User object, and then click Details on the shortcut menu.

For example, the CBE Labs network administrator wants to enter some data for Joseph Cunningham to the property settings of the JCunningham User object.

To view the JCunningham User object properties, follow these steps:

1. Right-click the JCunningham User object, and then click Details. The User: JCunningham object dialog box appears, as Figure 9-11 shows.

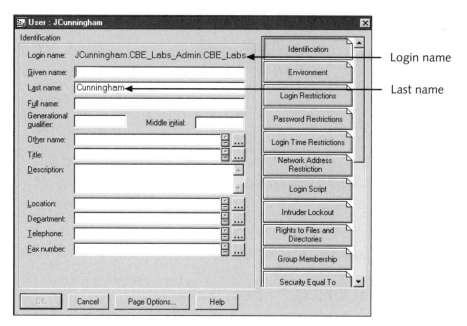

Figure 9-11   User: JCunningham object dialog box

The object properties are grouped into pages identified by a screen name in the upper-left corner of the screen and are accessed by clicking the associated button in the scrollable button bar on the right side of the dialog box. For example, as Figure 9-11 shows, the Identification page appears and the button bar shows the Identification button as depressed or pushed in (to indicate that it is selected). The Identification screen shows a group of Identification properties. You can change to another page by clicking the page's button. By using the associated text box, you can add, edit, or delete property values on a page.

User Identification Page Properties

Figure 9-11 shows the properties on the Identification page. You set the Login name and Last name properties when you create the User object. You can modify the Last name property on this page, but to change the Login name you must rename the User object. Additional information on this page includes more name data, organizational role data, and telephone numbers. NetWare uses the Full name property to display the user's full name during login.

The CBE Labs network administrator needs to add additional identifying information about Joseph Cunningham.

To add Joseph Cunningham's identification information, follow these steps:

1. Click the Given name text box, and then type the name Joseph. Do not press [Enter].

2. Click the Full name text box, then type the name Joseph Cunningham. *Do not press [Enter].*

3. Click the Title text box, then type the title President. *Do not press [Enter].*

4. Click the Department text box, then type the department name Administration. *Do not press [Enter].*

5. Click the Telephone text box, then type the phone number 503-560-1540. *Do not press [Enter].*

6. Click the Fax number text box, then type the phone number 503-560-1541. *Do not press [Enter] or click OK.* The Identification page now appears as in Figure 9-12.

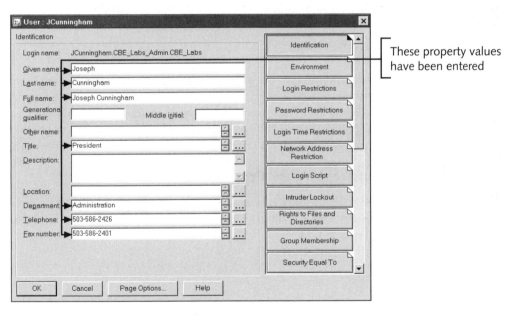

Figure 9-12 Completed Identification page

User Environment Page Properties

The second page in the User object properties is the Environment page. The Environment page properties include language, home directory, and default server data. If the user is logged in to the network, the user's network address is displayed. Figure 9-13 shows the Environment page.

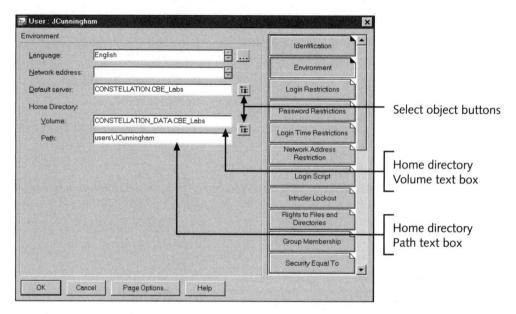

Figure 9-13 Environment page

If your network supports multiple languages, the Language property lets you specify which language the user sees displayed in NetWare dialog boxes, menus, and commands. The Home Directory Volume and Path properties let you create a home directory for the user or modify the location of a previously created home directory. The Default Server property is used to specify which NetWare server receives messages for the user from other users.

User Postal Address Page Properties

The Postal Address page properties include street address, post office box, city, state, and ZIP code information along with an area to create a mailing label. The Postal Address page is shown in Figure 9-14.

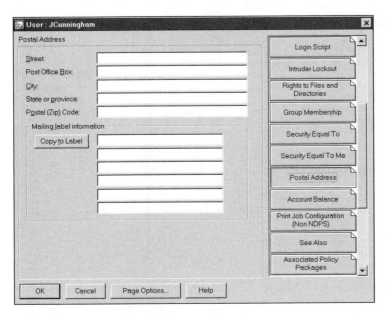

Figure 9-14   Postal Address page

The CBE Labs network administrator needs to add the postal address for Joseph Cunningham.

To add Joseph Cunningham's postal address, follow these steps:

1. Use the down scroll arrow to scroll through the page buttons until the Postal Address button appears.

2. Click the Postal Address button on the button bar. The Postal Address page is displayed.

3. Click the Street text box, then type 539 Lincoln Avenue. *Do not press [Enter].*

4. Click the City text box, then type Portland. *Do not press [Enter].*

5. Click the State or Province text box, then type OR. *Do not press [Enter].*

6. Click the Postal (ZIP) Code text box, then type 97205. *Do not press [Enter] or click OK.* The Postal Address page now appears as shown in Figure 9-15.

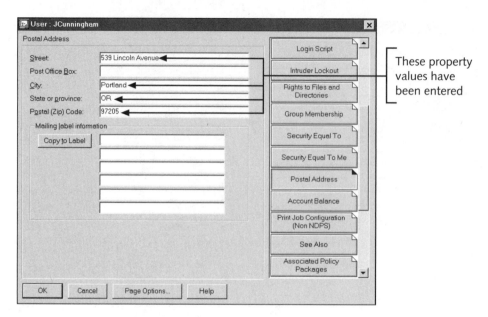

These property values have been entered

Figure 9-15 Completed Postal Address page

User Password Restrictions Properties

The first component of login security is creating a user name. You did this when you created the User object. The next component is creating a password and setting password restrictions. This is done on the Password Restrictions page, as shown in Figure 9-16.

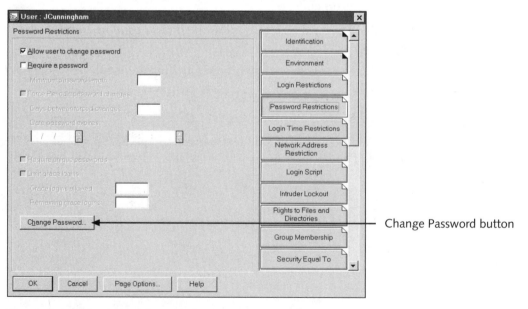

Change Password button

Figure 9-16 Password Restrictions page

The Password Restrictions page lets the network administration implement the steps of password security discussed earlier in this chapter. Use this page to require a password, set a minimum password length, force periodic password changes, require unique passwords, and limit the number of grace logins. This page also contains a Change Password button that is used to set a new password for a user.

A common practice is to create an initial password but set the password expiration date so that the password has already expired. This forces the user to change the password on one of their first logins. This procedure lets users set their own passwords and keeps other users from logging in on an account without a password.

The CBE Labs network administrator needs to set password restrictions for Joseph Cunningham. In addition, he will set a password of TP14CBE (Test Password One for CBE Labs) on the account to prevent anyone else from using the account.

To add Joseph Cunningham's password restrictions, follow these steps:

1. If necessary, use the scroll arrows to scroll through the page buttons until the Password Restrictions button appears.

2. Click the Password Restrictions button on the button bar. The Password Restrictions page is displayed.

3. Click the Require a Password text box. *Do not press [Enter].*

4. Click the Minimum Password Length text box. Change the default minimum password length of 5 to the new length of 6. *Do not press [Enter].*

5. Click the Force Periodic Password Changes check box. The NetWare default days (40) between forced changes appears in the Days Between Forced Changes text box, and the current date and the time the User object was accessed appear in the Expiration Date and Time spin boxes. In the Days Between Forced Changes text box, type 120. Use the Expiration Date spin box arrows to set the date to yesterday's date. Use the Expiration Time spin box arrows to set the time to 11:59:59 PM. *Do not press [Enter].*

6. Click the Require Unique Passwords check box. *Do not press [Enter].*

7. Click the Limit Grace Logins check box. The number of NetWare default grace logins (6) appears in the Grace Logins Allowed text box and the Remaining Grace Logins text box. Set the Grace Logins Allowed and the Remaining Grace Logins to 3. *Do not press [Enter].*

8. Click the Change Password button. The Change Password dialog box is displayed, as Figure 9-17 shows.

9

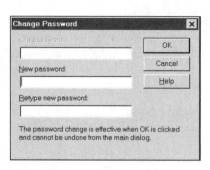

Figure 9-17   Change Password dialog box

9. Type CBELABS in the New Password text box. Click the Retype New Password text box; then type CBELABS. Click OK.

10. The Password Restrictions page now appears as shown in Figure 9-18. *Do not press [Enter] or click OK.*

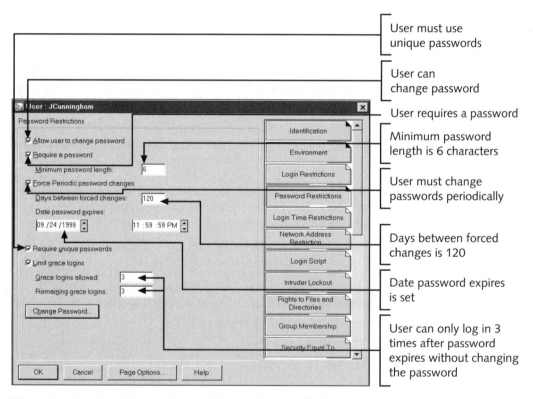

Figure 9-18   Completed Password Restrictions page

User Login Time Restrictions Properties

Time restrictions on user accounts are controlled on the Login Time Restrictions page, shown in Figure 9-19. The Login Time Restrictions page lets the network administration specify which times a user can and cannot log in to the network.

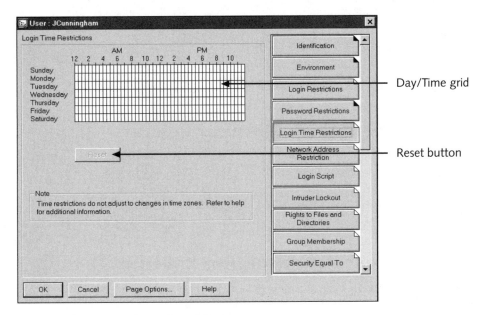

Figure 9-19   Login Time Restrictions page

CBE Labs policy is that all users are restricted from logging in between midnight and 6:30 a.m. The CBE Labs network administrator needs to set these times for Joseph Cunningham.

To add Joseph Cunningham's login time restrictions, follow these steps:

1. If necessary, use the scroll arrows to scroll through the page buttons until the Login Time Restrictions button appears.

2. Click the Login Time Restrictions button on the button bar. The Login Time Restrictions page is displayed.

3. Click and drag the time block from Sunday at 12 midnight (in the upper-left corner of the grid) to Saturday at 6:30 AM. *Do not press [Enter].*

4. The Login Time Restrictions page now appears, as Figure 9-20 shows. *Do not press [Enter] or click OK.*

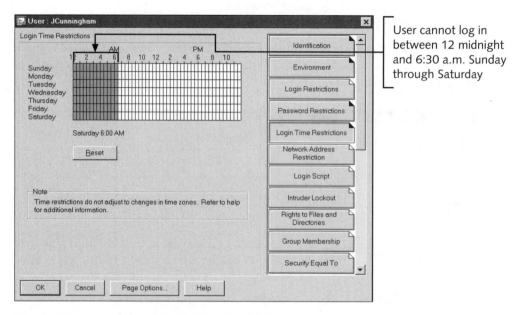

Figure 9-20   Completed Login Time Restrictions page

User Network Address Restrictions Properties

Network workstation restrictions are controlled on the Network Address Restriction page, as Figure 9-21 shows.

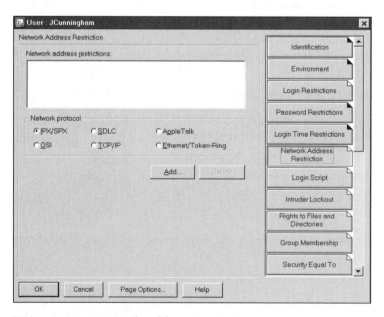

Figure 9-21   Network Address Restriction page

The Network Address Restriction page lets the network administration specify which workstations a user must use in order to log into the network, as well as the network protocol being used.

CBE Labs policy is that all users have unrestricted workstation address access. This lets them check their e-mail from any workstation. The CBE Labs network administrator does not need to set a workstation address restriction for Joseph Cunningham.

User Login Restrictions Properties

The account restrictions are controlled on the Login Restrictions page, as Figure 9-22 shows.

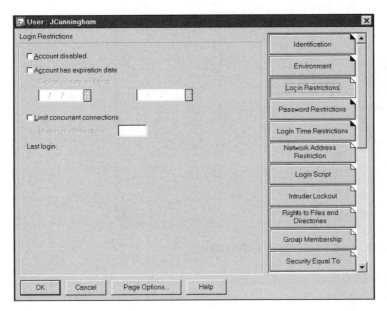

Figure 9-22 Login Restrictions page

The Login Restrictions page lets the network administrator disable an account or set a date and time at which the account will expire and become disabled. The Network administrator can also limit the number of concurrent user connections to the network, to prevent having too many users from being on the system at one time, or to limit the number of users because of licensing requirements.

The CBE Labs network administrator needs to limit the number of concurrent connections for Joseph Cunningham to one.

To add Joseph Cunningham's account restrictions, follow these steps:

1. If necessary, use the scroll arrows to scroll through the page buttons until the Login Restrictions button appears.

2. Click the Login Restrictions button on the button bar. The Login Restrictions page is displayed.

3. Click the Limit Concurrent Connections check box. The NetWare default maximum connections (1) appears in the Maximum Connections text box. Don't change this number. *Do not press [Enter].*

4. The Login Restrictions page now appears, as Figure 9-23 shows. *Do not press [Enter] or click OK.*

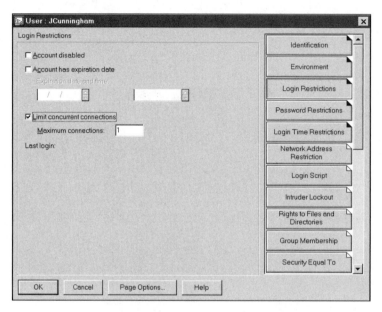

Figure 9-23 Completed Login Restrictions page

The network administrator has completed entering all the property settings necessary for Joseph Cunningham. Clicking the OK button at the bottom of the User: JCunningham object dialog box now will implement all the settings.

5. Click OK.

Now the CBE Labs network administrator enters the same types of property values for Steve Lopez. The steps are the same as those used for Joseph Cunningham and are not repeated here.

NWAdmin lets you change multiple objects at the same time. For example, if all User objects include the same fax phone number, you can change this number for all User objects simultaneously. To do so, select all User objects in the Directory tree, open a User dialog box (which will let you change only shared properties, not unique ones), and then change the fax phone number. This is a much more efficient way to make changes to multiple objects than changing each one separately.

Using Template Objects

Creating User objects one at a time can be a time-consuming task if there is a large number of users to be created. Often you will find yourself recreating the same property settings over and over again. This happens, for example, with users in the same workgroup or in the same container object in a Directory tree. To simplify User object creation, NetWare 5.0 lets you create a set of default, or common, settings for all User objects in a container object by creating a **Template object** for the container. You can have as many templates in a container as you need, but each has to have a unique name. The settings in the user template apply to any User object created in that container *after* the user template object is created.

The Template object for a container object is created like any other new object in the tree. To create a user Template object, click the container object, click Object on the menu bar, and then click Template.

For example, the CBE Labs network administrator needs to create user accounts for the CBE Labs personnel in the finance department. The User objects created are contained in the Finance Organizational Unit object. Because all these accounts will share many property settings, the network administrator will create a USER_TEMPLATE User object first to define the common property settings. The individual User objects will be created based on this template, so the administrator will not have to reenter the property values for each User object. Of course, property values unique to each User object, such as Given name, Full name, and Title, must still be entered individually for each user.

The CBE Labs network administrator is ready to create the USER_TEMPLATE User object for the Finance Organizational Unit users.

To create the USER_TEMPLATE User object for the Finance Organizational Unit and enter the initial property settings, follow these steps:

1. If necessary, launch NetWare Administrator and expand the Directory tree in the browser window so that you can see all the objects in the tree.

2. Right-click the Finance Organizational Unit object and choose Create, then click Template, and then click OK. The Template object dialog box appears.

3. Type in the name USER_TEMPLATE for the User object to be added to the Finance organizational Unit object. Check the Define Additional Properties box, then click Create.

4. Click the Department text box, then type the department name Finance. *Do not press [Enter].*

5. Click the Telephone text box, then type the phone number 503-560-1544. *Do not press [Enter].*

6. Click the Fax number text box, then type the phone number 503-560-1541. *Do not press [Enter] or click OK.*

7. If necessary, use the down scroll arrow to scroll through the page buttons until the Postal Address button appears. Click the Postal Address button on the button bar. The Postal Address page is displayed.

8. Click the Street text box, then type 539 Lincoln Avenue. *Do not press [Enter]*.

9. Click the City text box, then type Portland. *Do not press [Enter]*.

10. Click the State or Province text box, then type OR. Do not press [Enter].

11. Click the Postal (ZIP) Code text box, then type 97205. Do not press [Enter] or click OK.

The CBE Labs network administrator now needs to set the Home directory location for the new users.

To create the Home directory path settings for the USER_TEMPLATE User object, follow these steps:

1. If necessary, use the scroll arrows to scroll through the page buttons until the Environment button appears. Click the Environment button on the button bar. The Environment page is displayed.

2. To specify the path for the home directory, click the Select Object button to the right and below the Home Directory check box. The Select Object dialog box is displayed.

3. Use the Select Object dialog box to browse the Directory tree context to find an object. In this case, the starting context is Finance.CBE_Labs_Admin. The new context will be the USERS directory on CONSTELLATION_DATA.CBE_Labs. Browse through the Directory tree until the USERS directory appears, as Figure 9-24 shows.

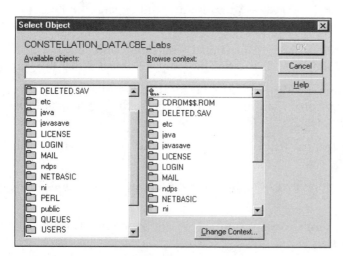

Figure 9-24   Specifying path to Finance user's home directory

4. Select the USERS directory, then click OK. The path to Finance user's home directory appears on the Environment page, as Figure 9-25 shows.

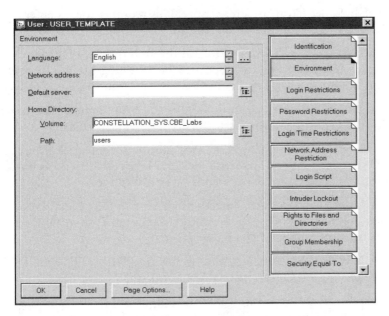

Figure 9-25   Command Environment page

The CBE Labs network administrator is now ready to set the default or common login security property values for user accounts in the Finance Organizational Unit. These steps parallel the steps he took in setting up Joseph Cunningham's account earlier in this chapter, and you can refer to those steps if you have questions about the following steps.

To create login security initial property settings for the USER_TEMPLATE User object, follow these steps:

1. If necessary, use the scroll arrows to scroll through the page buttons until the Password Restrictions button appears. Click the Password Restrictions button on the button bar. The Password Restrictions page is displayed.

2. Click the Require a Password check box. *Do not press [Enter].*

3. Click the Minimum Password Length text box. Set the minimum length to 6. *Do not press [Enter].*

4. Click the Force Periodic Password Changes check box. Set the Days Between Forced Changes to 120. Use the Expiration Date spin box arrows to set the date to yesterday's date. Use the Expiration Time spin box arrows to set the time to 11:59:59 PM. *Do not press [Enter].*

5. Click the Require Unique Passwords check box. *Do not press [Enter].*

6. Click the Limit Grace Logins check box. Set the Grace Logins Allowed to 3. *Do not press [Enter]*.

7. Check the box, Set Password after Create. This requires you to enter a password for each user you create using this template.

8. If necessary, use the scroll arrows to scroll through the page buttons until the Login Time Restrictions button appears. Click the Login Time Restrictions button on the button bar. The Login Time Restrictions page is displayed.

9. Click and drag the time block from Sunday at 12 midnight (in the upper-left corner of the grid) to Saturday at 6:30 AM. *Do not press [Enter]*.

10. If necessary, use the scroll arrows to scroll through the page buttons until the Login Restrictions button appears. Click the Login Restrictions button on the button bar. The Login Restrictions page is displayed.

11. Click the Limit Concurrent Connections check box. The NetWare default maximum connections of 1 appears in the Maximum Connections text box. Don't change this number. *Do not press [Enter]*.

12. Now you have created all default settings for the USER_TEMPLATE User object in the Finance Organizational Unit container. Click OK.

13. Expand the Finance Organizational Unit to update the display of the leaf objects in the container. The USER_TEMPLATE User object is now displayed, as Figure 9-26 shows.

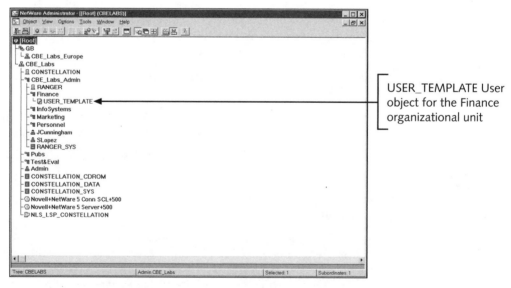

Figure 9-26   USER_TEMPLATE User object

Creating User Objects Using the USER_TEMPLATE User Object

Once a USER_TEMPLATE User object is created, you can use it to create user accounts for users in the container object. For example, the CBE Labs network administrator needs to create accounts for Donna Kaneaka (Finance Director), Sarah Johnston (General Ledger/Accounts Payable), and Thomas Meyer (Accounts Payable). Because all the common information is already in the USER_TEMPLATE User object, adding them requires only creating the unique information for each account.

To create the User objects for Kaneaka, Johnston, and Meyer, follow these steps:

1. If necessary, launch NetWare Administrator and expand the Directory tree in the browser window so that you can see all the objects in the tree.

2. Click the Finance Organizational Unit object to select it, click Object on the menu bar, and then click Create.

3. The New Object dialog box is displayed. Click User, and then click OK. The Create User dialog box appears. Check both the Use Template check box and the Create Home Directory check box.

4. Click the Select Object button next to the Template field. You can now browse through the tree to locate USER_TEMPLATE. Highlight it and click OK.

5. Because we want to create more than one user in this context, click the Create another User check box.

6. Click the Login Name text box to activate it; then type DKaneaka.

7. Click the Last Name text box to activate it; then type Kaneaka. Donna Kaneaka's login name of DKaneaka appears in the Home Directory text box, and the Volume and Path are correctly specified.

8. Set a user password for DKaneaka of at least six characters.

9. Click the Create button. The DKaneaka User object is created and added to the Directory tree, and the home directory is created on the CONSTELLATION_DATA volume.

10. Because you selected the Create Another User option, the Create User dialog box reappears. Repeat Steps 5–8 twice, the first time using the login name SJohnston and the last name of Johnston, and the second time using the login name TMeyer and the last name of Meyer.

11. After you create the User object for Thomas Meyer, the Create User dialog box reappears. Because there are no more users to be created in this context, click the Cancel button.

12. Close and redisplay the Finance branch of the Directory tree. The User objects now appear as Figure 9-27 shows.

9

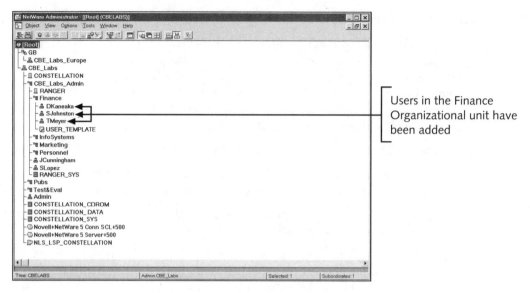

Figure 9-27 CBE Labs Directory tree with Finance User objects

Of course, the unique property settings for each user still need to be added. The CBE network administrator now attends to these details.

To add Donna Kaneaka's unique information, follow these steps:

1. Right-click the DKaneaka User object, then click Details. The User: DKaneaka object dialog box is displayed, as Figure 9-28 shows. Note that the default Department, Telephone, and Fax number are already entered and displayed.

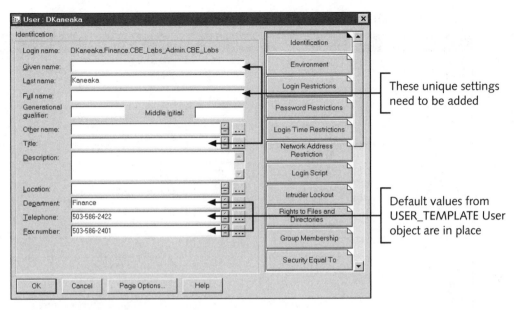

Figure 9-28   User: DKaneaka object dialog box

2. Click the Given name text box, then type the name Donna. *Do not press [Enter].*

3. Click the Full name text box, then type the name Donna Kaneaka. *Do not press [Enter].*

4. Click the Title text box, then type the title Finance Director. *Do not press [Enter].*

5. You have now entered all unique property values for Donna Kaneaka. All other property values that needed to be set were set to the default values from the USER_TEMPLATE User object. Click OK.

6. Repeat Steps 1–5 for Sarah Johnston and Thomas Meyer.

At this time the CBE Labs network administrator creates USER_TEMPLATE User objects for the other Organizational Unit objects in the CBE Labs Directory tree. Using these, the user accounts are created. Table 9-2 shows a complete list of USER_TEMPLATE User objects and the User objects for CBE Labs, including the ones just created.

Students should use Table 9-2 and Figure 7-6 (in Chapter 7) to complete the CBE-LABS tree. The following sections assume that these objects have been created. In addition, students should specify a random phone number for each user created.

Table 9-2   USER_TEMPLATES and Users for CBE Labs

Organizational Unit	User Objects Created	Title
CBE_Labs_Admin	JCunningham	President
CBE_Labs_Admin	SLopez	Administrative Assistant
Finance	USER_TEMPLATE	
Finance	DKaneaka	Finance Director
Finance	SJohnston	
Finance	TMeyer	
Marketing	USER_TEMPLATE	
Marketing	SHayakawa	Marketing Director
Marketing	JJorgensen	
Marketing	SWells	
Personnel	USER_TEMPLATE	
Personnel	PRichardson	Personnel Director
InfoSystems	USER_TEMPLATE	
InfoSystems	TSimpson	Information Systems Manager
InfoSystems	DDoering	Network Administrator
InfoSystems	MCiampa	Network Administrator
Pubs	USER_TEMPLATE	
Pubs	HEvans	Vice President for Publishing
Pubs	RDeLucia	Administrative Assistant

Table 9-2 USER_TEMPLATES and Users for CBE Labs (continued)

Organizational Unit	User Objects Created	Title
Pubs	SMichelia	Editor
Pubs	GTennesson	
Pubs	CPatterson	
Test&Eval	USER_TEMPLATE	
Test&Eval	GBurns	Vice President for Testing and Evaluation
Test&Eval	MODonnell	Administrative Assistant
Hardware	GLee	
Hardware	NNewman	
Hardware	TSkaggs	
Software	BFerguson	
Software	BSimpson	
Software	MThorndike	
DBMS	FNelson	
DBMS	SVanDorn	
DBMS	RPaulsen	
Network	WEllis	
Network	SGreene	
Network	NSingh	

9

Enabling Intruder Detection

In NetWare 5.0, intruder detection is enabled or disabled for each container object and applies only to User objects in that container. You start or stop intruder detection by using the Intruder Detection page in the Organization object or Organizational Unit object dialog box, as Figure 9-29 shows.

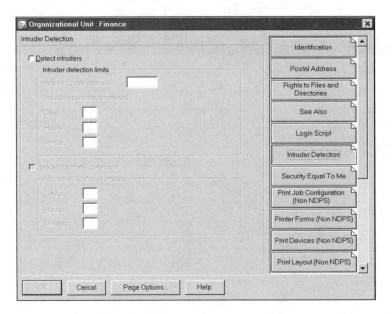

Figure 9-29   Intruder Detection page

When intruder detection is enabled, the network administrator can limit the number of times a user can try to log in within a certain period before being labeled as an intruder, and can set how long the account will be locked if the intruder detection limit is exceeded.

For example, the CBE Labs network administrator wants to enable intruder detection for the user accounts for the CBE Labs personnel in the finance department.

To enable intruder detection for the Finance Organizational Unit, follow these steps:

1. Right-click the Finance Organizational Unit object, then click Details. The Organizational Unit: Finance object dialog box appears.

2. If necessary, use the scroll arrows to scroll through the page buttons until the Intruder Detection button appears. Click the Intruder Detection button on the button bar. The Intruder Detection page is displayed.

3. Click the Detect intruders check box. *Do not press [Enter].*

4. Use the Incorrect Login Attempts text box to set the number of allowed login attempts to 5. Do not change the Intruder Attempt Reset Interval. *Do not press [Enter].*

5. Click the Lock Account After Detection check box. Do not change the Intruder Lockout Reset Interval. *Do not press [Enter].* The completed Intruder Detection page appears, as Figure 9–30 shows.

6. Click OK.

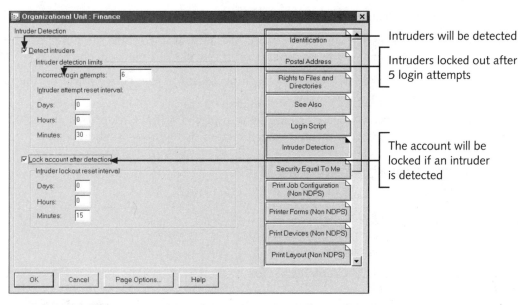

Figure 9-30   Completed Intruder Detection page

Groups

The Group object represents and is used to manage groups of related users and is indicated by the icon 👥. You must specify the Group Name when you create a group.

Groups are useful when you want to assign the use of some network resource to several users. For example, at CBE Labs, all users who work in the laboratories need access to the SARATOGA_SYS:APPS, SARATOGA_DATA:SHARED, and SARATOGA_DATA:REPORTS directories. These users also share access to a laser printer. Rather than assigning the access rights for these resources to individuals, the network administrator can create a group named Lab_Staff and assign the access rights to the group. All members of this group automatically get access to the resources.

You can create groups as needed in appropriate container objects. You can assign users to a group regardless of the Group object's context and the User object's context. Group membership can also be a property value in a USER_TEMPLATE-type User object. Access to network resources can be granted to all users by assigning the [Public] trustee to a resource; Chapter 10 discusses this procedure. In this chapter, we'll work with using groups to control network resource allocation.

For example, the CBE Labs network administrator is ready to create the Lab_Staff group and add users to it.

To create the Lab_Staff group within the Test&Eval container, follow these steps:

1. If necessary, launch NetWare Administrator. Expand the Directory tree in the browser window so that you can see all the objects in the tree.

2. Click the Test&Eval Organizational Unit object, click Object on the menu bar, and then click Create.

3. The New Object dialog box is displayed. Click Group, then click OK. The Create Group dialog box is displayed, as Figure 9-31 shows.

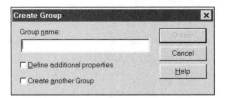

Figure 9-31   Create Group dialog box

4. Click the Group Name text box to activate it, then type Lab_Staff.

5. Click the Create button. The Lab_Staff group is created.

6. The Lab_Staff Group object now appears in the Directory tree, as Figure 9-32 shows.

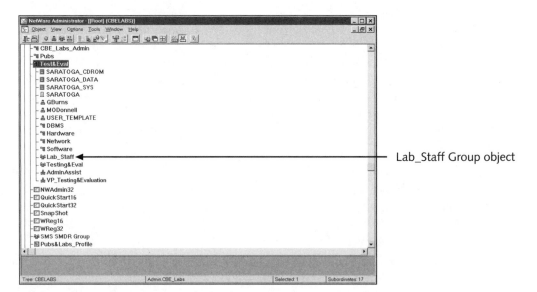

Figure 9-32   CBE Labs Directory tree with Group object

You can add users to a group in two ways:

- In the User: *UserName* object dialog box, you can add the user into a group on the Group Memberships page.

- In the Group: *GroupName* object dialog box, you can add members to the group on the User Members page.

For example, the CBE Labs network administrator needs to add Georgia Burns, Vice President for Testing and Evaluation, and Mike O'Donnell into the Lab_Staff group. To illustrate the two ways of adding users to groups, we'll add Georgia from the User: *UserName* dialog box and Mike from the Group: *GroupName* dialog box.

To add Georgia Burns and Mike O'Donnell into the Lab_Staff group, follow these steps:

1. Double-click the GBurns User object. The User: GBurns object dialog box is displayed.

2. If necessary, use the scroll arrows to scroll through the page buttons until the Group Membership button appears. Click the Group Membership button on the button bar. The Group Membership page is displayed, as Figure 9-33 shows.

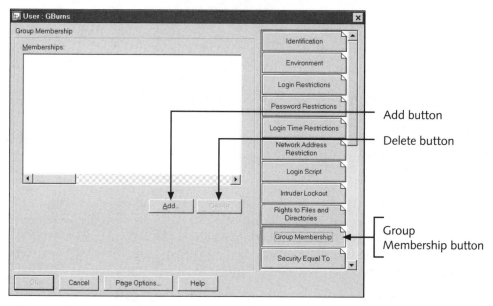

Figure 9-33   Group Membership page

3. Click the Add button. The Select Object dialog box is displayed.

4. Click the Lab_Staff Group object in the Objects list to select it, then click OK. The group name Lab_Staff.Test&Eval.CBE_Labs appears in the Groups Memberships list.

5. Click OK.

6. Double-click the Lab_Staff Group object. The Group: Lab_Staff object dialog box is displayed.

7. Click the Members button on the button bar. The Members page is displayed, as Figure 9-34 shows. Notice that GBurns is listed as a member of the group.

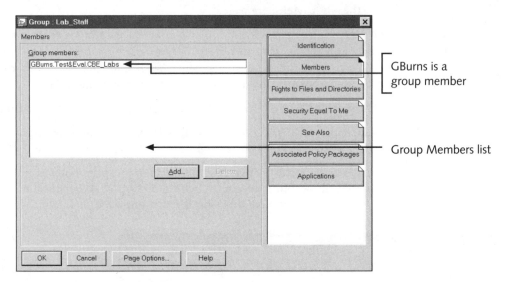

Figure 9-34 Members page

8. Click the Add button. The Select Object dialog box is displayed.

9. Click the MODonnell User object in the Objects list to select it, then click OK. The name MODonnell.Test&Eval.CBE_Labs appears in the Group Members list.

10. Click OK.

At this point, the CBE Labs network administrator adds all other members of Testing&Eval to the group. The easiest way to do this is to add members from the Members page in the Lab_Staff group object dialog box because you can add all the members from here without having to open the User object dialog box for each member. The following sections in this chapter assume that you have added all group members. If you haven't done so, do so now.

In addition, the CBE Labs network administrator now creates the other groups needed in the CBE Labs Directory tree and adds the group members to each group. Table 9-3 shows the Group objects and the members of each group.

 The following sections assume that you have added all objects and memberships shown in Table 9-3. If you haven't done so, do so now.

Table 9-3 Groups and Group Membership for CBE Labs

Group	Context	Members
Executives	CBE_Labs_Admin.CBE_Labs	JCunningham, HEvans, GBurns
Admin_Assists	CBE_Labs_Admin.CBE_Labs	SLopez, RDeLucia, MODonnell
Admin_Staff	CBE_Labs_Admin.CBE_Labs	JCunningham, SLopez, SHayakawa, JJorgensen, SWells, DKaneaka, SJohnston, TMeyer, PRichardson, TSimpson, DDoering, MCiampa
Pub_Staff	Pubs.CBE_Labs	HEvans, RDeLucia, SMichelia, GTennesson, CPatterson
Lab_Staff	Test&Eval.CBE_Labs	GBurns, MODonnell, GLee, NNewman, TSkaggs, BFerguson, BSimpson, MThorndike, FNelson, SVanDorn, RPaulsen, WEllis, SGreene, NSingh
Hardware_Staff	Hardware.Test&Eval.CBE_Labs	GLee, NNewman, TSkaggs
Software_Staff	Software.Test&Eval.CBE_Labs	BFerguson, BSimpson, MThorndike
DBMS_Staff	DBMS.Test&Eval.CBE_Labs	FNelson, SVanDorn, RPaulsen, GBurns
Network_Staff	Network.Test&Eval.CBE_Labs	WEllis, SGreene, NSingh

Organizational Roles

The Organizational Role object is used to represent a position in an organization structure such as president, chief information officer (CIO), or production manager and is represented by the icon 🏛 . The Organizational Role object is useful for recording and managing rights and resources assigned to an organizational role in the organization—whoever is assigned to that position automatically gets those rights and resources. You must specify the Organizational Role name when you create the Organizational Role object.

The power of the Organizational Role is found in the fact that although the individuals who fill organizational roles change, the responsibilities and rights associated with the role usually don't. By assigning access to network resources to an organizational role rather than to a user, it is easy to make sure that only the user or users in an organizational role have appropriate rights for that position.

For example, at CBE Labs Georgia Burns is Vice President for Testing and Evaluation. In this position, she should have access to all files in the SARATOGA_DATA: HARDWARE, SARATOGA_DATA:SOFTWARE, SARATOGA_DATA:DBMS, SARATOGA_DATA:NETWORK, SARATOGA_DATA:SHARED, and SARATOGA_DATA:REPORTS directories and all their subdirectories. Rather than assigning the access rights for these directories to her individually, the network administrator can create an Organizational Role named VP_Test&Eval and assign the access rights to the Organizational Role. By assigning GBurns to this role, she is automatically given access to the directories.

Organizational Role objects can be created as needed in appropriate container objects. You can assign users to an organizational role regardless of the Organizational Role object's context and the User object's context.

The CBE Labs network administrator is ready to create the VP_Testing&Evaluation Organizational Role and assign Georgia Burns to that role.

To create the VP_Testing&Evaluation Organizational Role, follow these steps:

1. If necessary, launch NetWare Administrator. Expand the Directory tree in the browser window so that you can see all the objects in the tree.

2. Click the Test&Eval Organizational Unit object, click Object on the menu bar, and then click Create.

3. The New Object dialog box is displayed. Click Organizational Role, then click OK. The Create Organizational Role dialog box appears.

4. Type VP_Testing&Evaluation.

5. Click the Create button. The VP_Testing&Evaluation organizational role is created. Close and redisplay the Test&Eval branch of the Directory tree. The Organizational Role object appears as shown in Figure 9-35.

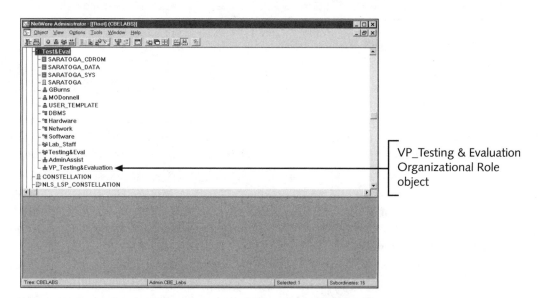

Figure 9-35   CBE Labs Directory Tree with Organizational Role object

The CBE Labs network administrator now assigns Georgia Burns to the organizational role of VP_Testing&Evaluation. Once assigned, Georgia has all the rights associated with that organizational role.

To assign Georgia Burns to the organizational role of VP_Testing&Evaluation, follow these steps:

1. Double-click the VP_Testing&Evaluation Organizational Role object. The Organizational Role: VP_Testing_&_Evaluation object dialog box is displayed, as Figure 9-36 shows.

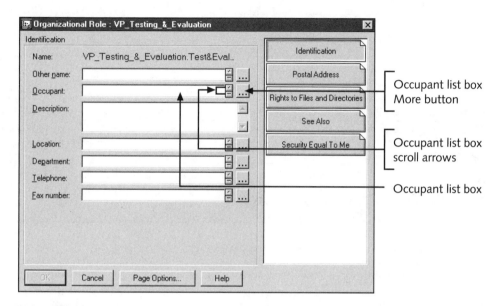

Figure 9-36   Organizational Role: VP_Testing_&_Evaluation object dialog box

2. To display the Occupant dialog box, click the More button ... to the right of the Occupant text box.

3. Click the Add button. The Select Object dialog box is displayed.

4. Use the Select Object dialog box to browse the Directory tree context to find an object. In this case, the starting context is Test&Eval.CBE_Labs. This is correct. Click the User object for GBurns in the Object list window; then click OK. Georgia Burns is added as the occupant of the VP_Testing_&_Evaluation position.

5. Click OK in the Occupant window.

6. Click OK in the Select Object dialog box.

At this point, the CBE Labs network administrator adds all organizational roles to the NDS Directory tree. Table 9-4 shows all organizational roles that will be used in the CBE Labs Directory tree, including Georgia Burns's role as VP_Testing_&_Evaluation.

The following sections in this chapter assume that you have created the organizational roles and assigned occupants as shown in Table 9-4. If you have not done so, do so now.

Table 9-4 Organizational roles for CBE Labs

Organizational Role	Context	Occupant
President	CBE_Labs_Admin.CBE_Labs	JCunningham
AdminAssist	CBE_Labs_Admin.CBE_Labs	SLopez
VP_Publishing	Pubs.CBE_Labs	HEvans
Editor	Pubs.CBE_Labs	SMichelia
AdminAssist	Pubs.CBE_Labs	RDeLucia
VP_Testing_&_Evaluation	Test&Eval.CBE_Labs	GBurns
AdminAssist	Test&Eval.CBE_Labs	MODonnell
Marketing_Director	Marketing.CBE_Labs_Admin.CBE_Labs	SHayakawa
Finance_Director	Finance.CBE_Labs_Admin.CBE_Labs	DKaneaka
Personnel_Director	Personnel.CBE_Labs_Admin.CBE_Labs	PRichardson
Information_Systems_Manager	InfoSystems.CBE_Labs_Admin.CBE_Labs	TSimpson
Network_Administrator	InfoSystems.CBE_Labs_Admin.CBE_Labs	DDoering, MCiampa

Profiles

Use the Profile object to run login scripts and assign resources to groups of users. You can write login scripts for Organization objects, Organizational Unit objects, and User objects but not for Group objects. The Profile object gives the network administrator a tool for creating login scripts for groups. The icon for the Profile object is 📑. The Profile Name must be specified when you create a profile. The Profile object also lets the network administrator assign directory and file trustee rights to the profile, so that all users who share the profile will also share those access rights.

The Profile object is most useful when a container object login script cannot be easily applied to a set of users who need to share common network resources. This often happens when the set of users is a subset of those in the container or the set of users consists of users from two or more containers.

For example, to use Lab data for publications, some CBE Labs personnel in both the Pubs Organizational Unit and the Test&Eval Organizational Unit will need access to the SARATOGA_DATA:SHARED and SARATOGA_DATA:REPORTS directories. These people include SMichelia and GTennesson in Pubs and GLee, BFerguson, FNelson, and WEllis in Test&Eval. These users need a Profile object so that a specialized login script can be created for them and specialized directory and file access can be set up if necessary.

The CBE Labs network administrator decides to create a Pubs&Labs_Profile Profile object.

This new Profile object will need file and directory rights as well as various trustee assignments. These will be covered in a later chapter.

To create the Pubs&Labs_Profile Profile object, follow these steps:

1. If necessary, launch NetWare Administrator. Expand the Directory tree in the browser window so that you can see all the objects in the tree.

2. Click the CBE_Labs Organization object, click Object on the menu bar, and then click Create.

3. The New Object dialog box is displayed. Click Profile, then click OK. The Create Profile dialog box appears.

4. Type Pubs&Labs_Profile.

5. Click the Create button. The Pubs&Labs_Profile profile is created. Close and redisplay the CBE_Labs branch of the Directory tree. The Profile object now appears as Figure 9-37 shows.

9

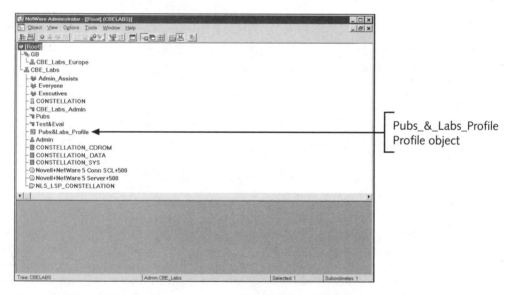

Figure 9-37 CBE Labs Directory tree with Profile object

The CBE Labs network administrator now assigns Susan Michelia to the Pubs&Labs_Profile profile. Once assigned, Susan will use the profile's login scripts and have all the rights associated with the profile.

To assign Susan Michelia to the Pubs&Labs_Profile profile, follow these steps:

1. Double-click the SMichelia User object (you may need to expand your tree to display this object). The User: SMichelia object dialog box is displayed.

2. If necessary, use the scroll arrows to scroll through the page buttons until the Login Script button appears. Click the Login Script button on the button bar. The Login Script page is displayed, as Figure 9-38 shows.

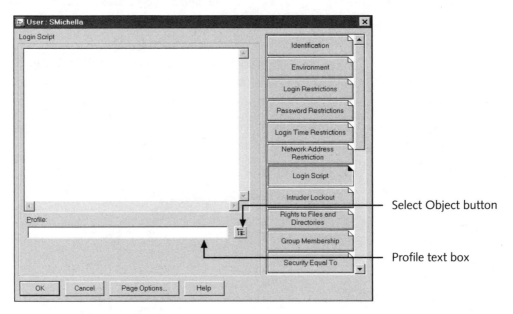

Figure 9-38 Login Script page

3. Click the Select Object button to the right of the Profile text box. The Select Object dialog box is displayed.

4. Use the Select Object dialog box to browse the Directory tree context to find an object. In this case, the starting context is Pubs. The context for the Pubs&Labs_Profile object, however, is .CBE_Labs. Browse until the context is .CBE_Labs and the Pubs&Labs_Profile object is displayed. Click the Pubs&Labs_Profile object in the Objects window, then click OK. The Pubs&Labs_Profile profile is displayed in the Profile text box, as Figure 9-39 shows.

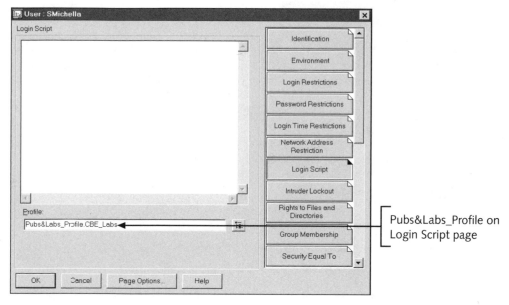

Figure 9-39   Completed Login Script page

5. Click OK.

6. A warning dialog box is displayed, as Figure 9-40 shows, stating that the user does not have needed rights to the Profile. These rights will be assigned in Chapter 10. Click the Yes button to acknowledge that you know the user does not have the necessary rights and to save the profile.

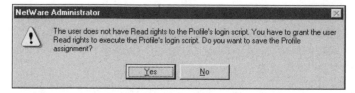

Figure 9-40   Rights warning dialog box

At this point, the CBE Labs network Administrator adds the Pubs&Labs_Profile profile to the Login Script page property settings of all other users who need to share it. The following sections in this chapter assume that you have configured these login scripts. If you haven't done so, do so now.

NETWARE ACCOUNTING

NetWare's accounting features let the network administrator track resources used on a network and charge users for their use. You can monitor user login and logout activity, charge customers for resource usage on the server, or monitor server usage to facilitate planning for server expansion.

Charging for Server Usage

NetWare's accounting functions can be used to record server usage by the following categories:

- Disk activity
- Connect time
- Disk storage space consumed
- Service requests

Records of server usage track growth and provide a way to charge users for services.

A teacher in a local school system used NetWare accounting to help motivate students to achieve better grades by rewarding good scores with additional credit on the server. Having credit on the server let students run games and simulations from the server during their break time.

Types of Charges

The disk activity charge includes the number of disk blocks read, the number of disk blocks written, or both. The amount charged can vary depending on time of day.

The disk storage figure lets you charge for each block of disk space occupied by a file owned by a user. This charge is assigned once per day. The network administrator can select the time of day and charge rate to be used.

After you have determined the charge rate, you can give your users a balance based on the amount paid for the month, remove the unlimited credit privilege, and optionally assign a credit limit. When a user's credit limit is exceeded, the server displays a message indicating that the user's account balance has been exceeded and then grants the user several minutes to complete his or her work and log out. At this point, the user's account is disabled and the user cannot log in again until the balance field is updated or additional credit is assigned.

Despite the emphasis on contemporary graphical utilities, the character-based ATOTAL program remains the primary means of accessing accounting data in NetWare 5.0. Figure 9-41 shows a sample of ATOTAL output. To run the ATOTAL program, the user must have established accounting on the server as described in the section, "Implementing Accounting on the Server," later in this chapter. Once this is done, the user opens an MS-DOS window, selects the drive letter mapped to the server's SYS volume, and enters ATOTAL.

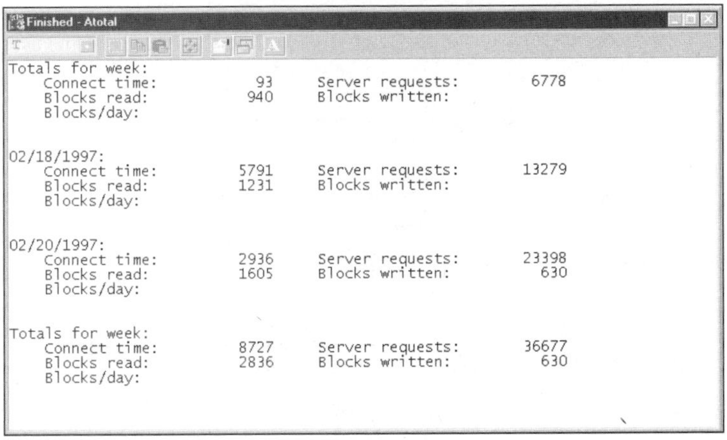

```
Finished - Atotal                                                          _ □ ×
T          □   
Totals for week:
     Connect time:         93     Server requests:       6778
     Blocks read:         940     Blocks written:
     Blocks/day:

02/18/1997:
     Connect time:        5791    Server requests:      13279
     Blocks read:         1231    Blocks written:
     Blocks/day:

02/20/1997:
     Connect time:        2936    Server requests:      23398
     Blocks read:         1605    Blocks written:         630
     Blocks/day:

Totals for week:
     Connect time:        8727    Server requests:      36677
     Blocks read:         2836    Blocks written:         630
     Blocks/day:
```

Figure 9-41   The ATOTAL DOS utility is used to display usage totals

Planning for Expansion

One aspect of NetWare accounting that can be helpful for all network administrators is the ability to monitor server usage and employ that information in planning for future server expansion. As usage on your server grows, you will eventually need to consider adding more disk storage, a faster disk system, more memory, or even a faster server computer. If you do not anticipate and justify these needs, you will probably have a hard time obtaining the budget for network improvements when you need them. With NetWare's accounting functions, you can gather usage information and then use a spreadsheet program to graph the server usage information to illustrate disk access, storage capacity, and server requests for each week. By extrapolation, the graph you can then draw will project your server expansion needs for budgeting purposes.

Implementing Accounting on a Server

Because accounting tracks usage of resources on each NetWare server, it must be implemented on each NetWare server individually. This is done in the NetWare Server object dialog box. As Figure 9-42 shows, the NetWare Server object dialog box has an Accounting button at the bottom of the page. When you click this button, you are prompted to confirm the installation of accounting on the server; and on your confirmation, accounting is installed.

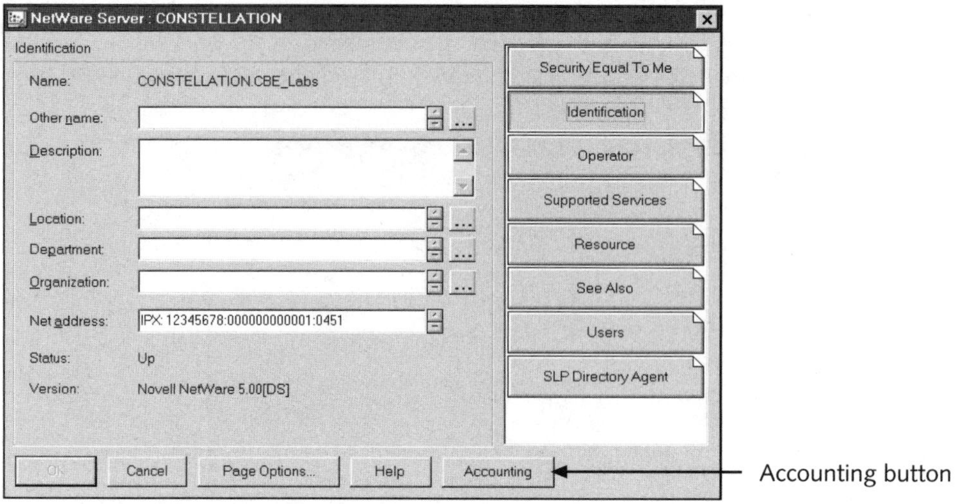

Figure 9-42   Installing accounting on NetWare server

Once accounting is installed, five pages are added to the NetWare Server object dialog box and the corresponding page buttons are added to the page button list:

- Blocks Read
- Blocks Written
- Connect Time
- Disk Storage
- Service Requests

Charging for Blocks Read

The Blocks Read page lets you enter the charge ratio you want to use for each block read for various specified time periods. Selecting this page displays the Blocks Read page that Figure 9-43 shows.

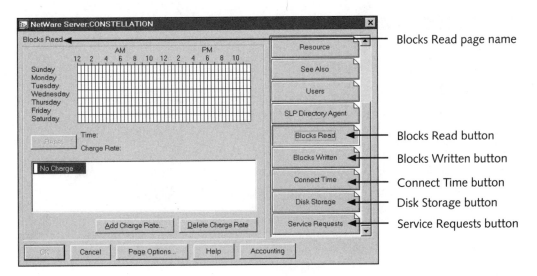

Figure 9-43   Blocks Read page

Notice that a grid shows days and times at the top of the page on the screen, and the box at the bottom of the page shows the existing charge rates. The initial assignment is no charge for all time periods. To set a charge rate, first create the rate and then apply it to the time periods.

For example, the CBE Labs network administrator needs to set a charge ratio of 38 cents for each block read during CBE Labs normal business hours of Monday through Friday, 8 a.m. to 5:30 p.m. He starts with the NetWare server CONSTELLATION.

To add the blocks read charge to CONSTELLATION, follow these steps:

1. Right-click the CONSTELLATION NetWare Server object, then click Details. The NetWare Server: CONSTELLATION object dialog box is displayed.

2. Click the Accounting button to install accounting. When the Accounting dialog box is displayed to confirm the installation, click the Yes button. Five new pages and page buttons are added to the NetWare Server dialog box.

3. If necessary, use the scroll arrows to scroll through the page buttons until the Blocks Read button appears.

4. Click the Blocks Read button in the button bar. The Blocks Read page is displayed.

5. Click the Add Charge Rate button. The Add Charge Rate dialog box is displayed, as shown in Figure 9-44.

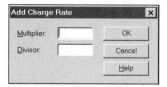

Figure 9-44 Add Charge Rate dialog box

6. Type the number 8 in the Multiplier text box.

7. Click the Divisor text box to activate it, then type in the number 1.

8. Click OK. The new rate is added to the list of rates.

9. Click (and keep the left mouse button down) the Monday at 8 cell in the day and time grid, then drag the highlight to cover from Monday at 8 AM through Friday at 5:30 PM. The day and time grid now appears as Figure 9-45 shows.

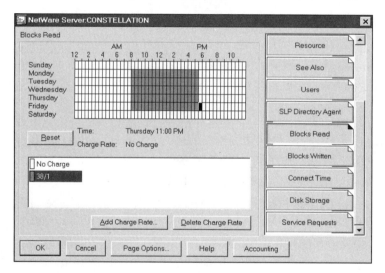

Figure 9-45 Completed Blocks Read page

10. Click OK.

Charging for Blocks Written

The Blocks Written page lets you enter the charge ratio you want to apply to each block written during the time period specified. The method of specifying charges is the same as for blocks read.

Charging for Connect Time

The Connect Time page lets you enter the charge ratio you want to apply to each minute a user is connected to the server during the time period specified. The method of specifying charges is the same as for blocks read.

Charging for Disk Storage

The Disk Storage Charge Rates option lets you enter the charge ratio you want to apply to each block of disk space used per day. The method of specifying charges is the same as for blocks read.

Charging for Service Requests

The Service Requests page lets you enter the charge ratio you want to apply to each server request a user made during the time period specified. The method of specifying charges is the same as for blocks read.

Removing Accounting from a NetWare Server

To remove accounting from a server, use the same Accounting button you used to install it. When accounting is installed, however, clicking the Accounting button will remove the accounting feature (you are prompted to confirm the removal of accounting, just as you were prompted to confirm the installation of accounting).

Managing User Account Balances

When accounting is enabled on a NetWare server, user account balances are managed using the Account Balance page in the User object dialog box, as Figure 9-46 shows.

9

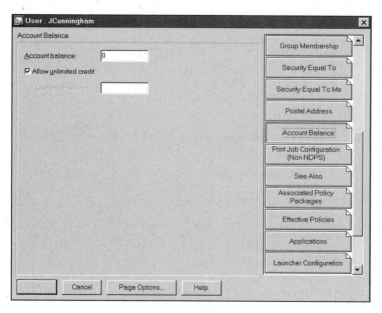

Figure 9-46 Account Balance page

If a user has no restrictions on his or her usage of server resources controlled by NetWare accounting, the Allow Unlimited Credit check box is checked. This is the default for newly created User objects, but, of course, you can control this with the settings in a USER_PROFILE User object used to create new accounts. You can also control this for new user accounts created using the UIMPORT utility, as discussed later in this chapter.

If a user does not have unlimited use of the resources, you uncheck the Allow Unlimited Credit check box and then set an initial account balance and a low balance limit. The initial account balance will be decreased as the user uses chargeable resources until the low balance limit is reached. At that point, the user cannot use additional chargeable resources until his or her account balance is increased.

NETWARE UTILITIES AND COMMANDS

This section covers the ATOTAL and UIMPORT command line utilities, and the DSREPAIR NetWare Loadable Module; these are used in managing users and groups.

The ATOTAL Command Line Utility

As mentioned in the section "Types of Charges," the ATOTAL utility provides usage summary information for chargeable network resources. The syntax of the ATOTAL command is

```
ATOTAL [/C] [/?] [/VER]
```

As the syntax shows, the ATOTAL command has several parameters, listed in Table 9-5. Figure 9-41 showed sample output from the ATOTAL utility.

Table 9-5   ATOTAL command parameters

Parameter	Use This Parameter to
/C	Scroll continuously through output instead of pausing after each page of output data.
/?	Access help about ATOTAL. If this parameter is used, all others are ignored.
/VER	See the version number of the ATOTAL command. If this parameter is used, all others are ignored.

The UIMPORT Command Line Utility

The **UIMPORT (user import) utility** is a batch-oriented, command line utility, which means that it uses a command file, called the **import control file**, that contains statements. These statements are used to create specified user accounts from data contained in a **data file**. Both UIMPORT import control and data files are ASCII text files. The import control file consists of a list of statements containing keywords and parameters that the UIMPORT program uses to determine how to create the specified user accounts. UIMPORT is a good way to create and delete users quickly when you are setting up a group consisting of many user accounts.

The syntax of the UIMPORT command is

```
UIMPORT [control filename] [data filename] [/VER] [/?]
     [ALL] [ATTR] [/C]
```

As the syntax shows, you can use several parameters with the UIMPORT command. Table 9-6 lists these parameters.

Table 9-6   UIMPORT command parameters

Parameter	Use This Parameter to
Control *filename*	Specify the name of the file containing information about loading the data in the data file.
Data *filename*	Specify the name of the file containing the data that will become the User object property values.
/VER	Display the version number of the UIMPORT command. If this parameter is included with any other parameter, the others are ignored.
/?	Displays help for UIMPORT. If this parameter is included with any other parameter, the others are ignored. (Except for the /VER parameter. If both /? And /VER are included, then the first one is the operative parameter and the other is ignored.)
ALL	Use with the /? parameter to display both sets of help screens—General and Attribute.
ATTR	Use with the /? parameter to display valid commands, keywords, default values, and property names for use in the control file. (For example, type UIMPORT /? ATTR to display this list.)
/C	Scroll continuously through output instead of pausing after each page of data.

The UIMPORT Data Files

The data file supplies User object property values separated by commas and enclosed in quotation marks.

The UIMPORT Import Control File

The UIMPORT import control file has two sections. The **import control section** contains control parameters that tell UIMPORT which options to use. The **fields section** tells UIMPORT which User object properties have values in the data file.

Table 9-7 shows the import control section control parameters.

Table 9-7   UIMPORT control parameters

Parameter Values	Possible Value	Default	Comments
CREATE HOME DIRECTORY	Y, N	N	Y = Create a home directory N = Don't create a home directory
DELETE MAILBOX DIRS	Y, N	N	Used when moving a user's mailbox to a new messaging server, or when changing the user's mailbox ID. Y = Delete the mailbox directories N = Don't delete the directories

Table 9-7 UIMPORT control parameters (continued)

Parameter Values	Possible Value	Default	Comments
DELETE PROPERTY	Any ASCII character string		Used to delete property values from a User object. Including this character string in a data field will cause the current property value to be deleted. *Cannot* be used to delete: • Volume restrictions • Password • Home directory
HOME DIRECTORY PATH	Any path		Used to specify the path to the home directory. The path must be enclosed in quotes. *Must* be used together with HOME DIRECTORY VOLUME.
HOME DIRECTORY VOLUME	Any volume name		Used to specify the volume for the home directory. The volume must be enclosed in quotes. *Must* be used together with HOME DIRECTORY PATH.
IMPORT MODE	C, U, B, R	B	Used to control UIMPORTS actions. C = Create new objects only U = Update existing objects only B = Both C and U R = Remove objects
MAXIMUM DIRECTORY RETRIES	Any number	5	Used to specify how many attempts UIMPORT makes to get the object ID of a newly created user when creating home and mailbox directories. This is necessary when the User object is created on one server and the directory is located on another because the replica on the second server must contain the User object data. Because updating the replica takes some time, a number of retries may be necessary to allow the replica to be updated.
NAME CONTEXT	Any context	Current context	Used to specify the NDS context where the User objects will be located.
QUOTE	Any character	" (quotes)	Used to specify the character used to enclose data file values with spaces.

9

Table 9-7 UIMPORT control parameters (continued)

Parameter Values	Possible Value	Default	Comments
REPLACE VALUE	Y, N	N	Used to specify whether a data value should replace or be added to data values in a multivalued property setting. Y = Replace current value N = Insert as an additional value
SEPARATOR	Any character	, (comma)	Used to specify the character used to delineate data fields in the data file.
USER TEMPLATE	Y, N	N	Used to specify whether or not to use the USER_TEMPLATE values when new User objects are created.

For example, the CBE Labs network administrator could have created the user accounts and User object for the employees in the Pubs Organizational Unit using UIMPORT. If he had done so, he could have used the following import control section:

```
IMPORT CONTROL
  CREATE HOME DIRECTORY = Y
  HOME DIRECTORY PATH = "USERS"
  HOME DIRECTORY VOLUME = "CONSTELLATION_DATA.CBE_Labs"
  NAME CONTEXT = ".PUBS.CBE_Labs"
  USER TEMPLATE = Y
```

Table 9-8 shows the definitions for many of the basic fields used in the fields section. There is a field for most of the properties in the User object—the exceptions are login time restrictions and network station restrictions. The fields are arranged according to the page in the User object dialog box that they appear on: Identification page, Environment page, and so on. Single-value properties, such as *Last name*, can have only one setting value in the field. Multivalued properties, such as *Group membership*, can have more than one value in the field. Because the default value of the REPLACE VALUE control parameter is *N*, values will be *added* to multivalued fields unless you specify the REPLACE VALUE control parameter as Y in the import control section.

Table 9-8 Basic UIMPORT field definitions

User Object Dialog Box Page	Field (Property)	Single-Valued or Multivalued	Comments
IDENTIFICATION	NAME	Single-valued	User's Login Name. An entry for this field is required.
IDENTIFICATION	LAST NAME	Single-valued	User's last name. An entry for this field is required.
IDENTIFICATION	GIVEN NAME	Single-valued	User's first or given name.
IDENTIFICATION	FULL NAME	Single-valued	User's full name.
IDENTIFICATION	GENERATIONAL QUALIFIER	Single-valued	User's generational qualifier such as Jr., III, etc.
IDENTIFICATION	INITIALS	Single-valued	The initial letter of the user's middle name.
IDENTIFICATION	OTHER NAMES	Multivalued	Other names that are used to identify the user.
IDENTIFICATION	TITLE	Multivalued	Titles that are associated with the user.
IDENTIFICATION	DESCRIPTION	Single-valued	A description of any type about the user.
IDENTIFICATION	EMAIL ADDRESS	Multivalued	User's email address.
IDENTIFICATION	LOCATION	Multivalued	User's work locations.
IDENTIFICATION	DEPARTMENT	Multivalued	Departments the user works for.
IDENTIFICATION	TELEPHONE	Multivalued	User's phone numbers.
IDENTIFICATION	FAX NUMBER	Multivalued	User's fax telephone numbers.
ENVIRONMENT	LANGUAGE	Multivalued	Language directories used for utilities messages for the user.
ENVIRONMENT	DEFAULT SERVER	Single-valued	Server for user's NetWare network messages.
ENVIRONMENT	HOME DIRECTORY	Single-valued	User's home directory location specified as *VolumeName:Path*. If used, this field value replaces any entry in the import control section.
LOGIN RESTRICTIONS	ACCOUNT DISABLED	Single-valued	If user's account is to be disabled, use Y in the field. The default is N.
LOGIN RESTRICTIONS	ACCOUNT HAS EXPIRATION DATE	Single-valued	Date user's account will expire. Use MM/DD/YY format.
LOGIN RESTRICTIONS	MAXIMUM CONNECTIONS	Single-valued	Number of simultaneous logins for user. Enter 0 for unlimited.

9

Table 9-8 Basic UIMPORT field definitions (continued)

User Object Dialog Box Page	Field (Property)	Single-Valued or Multivalued	Comments
PASSWORD RESTRICTIONS	ALLOW USER TO CHANGE PASSWORD	Single-valued	If user can't change his or her password, use N in the field. The default is Y.
PASSWORD RESTRICTIONS	REQUIRE A PASSWORD	Single-valued	Y = a password *is* required N = a password is *not* required
PASSWORD RESTRICTIONS	MINIMUM PASSWORD LENGTH	Single-valued	The minimum number of characters in the user's password.
PASSWORD RESTRICTIONS	DAYS BETWEEN FORCED CHANGES	Single-valued	The maximum number of days the user can keep the same password.
PASSWORD RESTRICTIONS	DATE PASSWORD EXPIRES	Single-valued	Date password will expire. Use MM/DD/YY format.
PASSWORD RESTRICTIONS	REQUIRE UNIQUE PASSWORDS	Single-valued	Y = unique passwords *are* required N = unique passwords are *not* required
PASSWORD RESTRICTIONS	GRACE LOGINS ALLOWED	Single-valued	Number of grace logins after password expires. 0 = no limit
PASSWORD RESTRICTIONS	REMAINING GRACE LOGINS	Single-valued	Used only with the MODIFY option, a number can be entered if the remaining grace logins is different than the normal number of grace logins allowed. Normally this number is set equal to the number of grace logins allowed.
PASSWORD RESTRICTIONS	PASSWORD	Single-valued	The user's initial password.
MAILBOX	MAILBOX LOCATION	Single-valued	The NDS Messaging Server object name with user's mailbox, using the complete name if the object is in a different context from where the user's User object will be created.
MAILBOX	MAILBOX ID	Single-valued	The directory name of the user's NetWare MHS directory. Generally, the same as the user's login name, shortened to 8 characters (without spaces or special characters) if necessary.

Table 9-8   Basic UIMPORT field definitions (continued)

User Object Dialog Box Page	Field (Property)	Single-Valued or Multivalued	Comments
FOREIGN E-MAIL ADDRESS	FOREIGN E-MAIL ADDRESS	Single-valued	The user's e-mail address on a non-MHS mail system. Format is Type:Value, where Type is the messaging protocol, and Value is the user's e-mail address on the foreign system.
FOREIGN E-MAIL ADDRESS	FOREIGN E-MAIL ALIAS	Single-valued	The user's e-mail address in a non-MHS mail format. Format is Type:Value, where Type is the messaging protocol, and Value is the user's e-mail address on the foreign system.
LOGIN SCRIPT	LOGIN SCRIPT	Single-valued	Use the path (in DOS form) and filename of an ASCII text file containing the login script.
LOGIN SCRIPT	PROFILE	Single-valued	NDS Profile object name, using the complete name if the Profile object is in a different context than where the user's User object will be created.
GROUP MEMBERSHIPS	GROUP MEMBERSHIP	Multivalued	NDS Group object name of each group the user belongs to, using the complete name if the Group object is in a different context than where the user's User object will be created.
SECURITY EQUIVALENCES	SECURITY EQUAL TO	Multivalued	NDS object name of each object to which the user is equal in security access, using the complete name if the object is in a different context than where the user's User object will be created.
POSTAL ADDRESS	STREET ADDRESS	Single-valued	The user's street address.
POSTAL ADDRESS	POST OFFICE BOX	Single-valued	The user's post office box designation.
POSTAL ADDRESS	CITY	Single-valued	The user's city.
POSTAL ADDRESS	STATE OR PROVINCE	Single-valued	The user's state or province.
POSTAL ADDRESS	POSTAL (ZIP) CODE	Single-valued	The user's ZIP code (5-digit or 4- + 5-digit format) or Canadian postal code.
POSTAL ADDRESS	MAILING LABEL INFORMATION	Multivalued	Use this field once for each line of information in the mailing label. Maximum of 6 lines.

9

Table 9-8   Basic UIMPORT field definitions (continued)

User Object Dialog Box Page	Field (Property)	Single-Valued or Multivalued	Comments
ACCOUNT BALANCE	ACCOUNT BALANCE	Single-valued	The user's beginning account balance.
ACCOUNT BALANCE	ALLOW UNLIMITED CREDIT	Single-valued	If user has unlimited account credit, use Y in the field. The default is N.
ACCOUNT BALANCE	LOW BALANCE LIMIT	Single-valued	The minimum balance the user must have to use chargeable network resources.
SEE ALSO	SEE ALSO	Multivalued	NDS object name of any other object associated with the user, using the complete name if the object is in a different context than where the user's User object will be created.
	SKIP		A special field name that causes UIMPORT to ignore a data field in the data file.

For example, because the users in the Pubs Organizational Unit have a USER_TEMPLATE object that controls most property values, the CBE Labs network administrator needed to use only the following field definition section when he created the user accounts and User objects for the employees in the Pubs Organizational Unit using UIMPORT:

```
FIELDS
   NAME
   LAST NAME
   GIVEN NAME
```

The complete import control file would have been

```
IMPORT CONTROL
   CREATE HOME DIRECTORY = Y
   HOME DIRECTORY PATH = "USERS"
   HOME DIRECTORY VOLUME = "CONSTELLATION_DATA.CBE_Labs"
   NAME CONTEXT = ".PUBS.CBE_Labs"
   USER TEMPLATE = Y

FIELDS
   NAME
   LAST NAME
   GIVEN NAME
```

The data file would have been an ASCII text file containing the following lines:
"DKaneaka","Kaneaka","Donna"
"SJohnston","Johnston","Sarah"
"TMeyer","Thomas","Meyer"

The UIMPORT utility, although DOS-based, remains the primary means of importing extensive lists of network users in NetWare 5.0.

The DSREPAIR NLM Utility

DSREPAIR is a NetWare Loadable Module (NLM) that is used to check and, if necessary, repair the NDS database partition stored on a NetWare server. As with all NLMs, the DSREPAIR utility is loaded at the server console prompt with the load command. The syntax is:

```
LOAD [path] DSREPAIR [-U]
```

Table 9-9 shows the DSREPAIR utility options.

Table 9-9   DSREPAIR options

Option	Use This Option to
path	Specify the path to DSREPAIR.NLM if needed.
-U	Run an unattended repair and then unload DSREPAIR automatically.

DSREPAIR works only with Directory Services database information on the NetWare server it is run on. When DSREPAIR is loaded, a menu of Available Options appears, as Figure 9-47 shows.

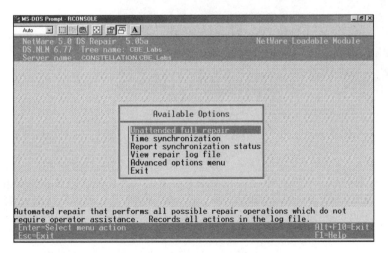

Figure 9-47   DSREPAIR Available Options menu

The main menu options are these:

- *Unattended full repair.* DSREPAIR will do every operation it can that does not require input from the network administrator. This option checks the Directory Services database for problems and repairs any problems that it can.

- *Time synchronization.* All NetWare servers listed in the NDS database partition and replicas on the server are checked, and the NDS version and time synchronization status for each NetWare server are reported. When a replica of the [Root] partition is located on the NetWare server, every NetWare server in the Directory tree will be included in the report.

- *Report synchronization.* All replicas in the Directory tree's replica table are checked, and their synchronization status is reported.

- *View/Edit repair log file.* A log of DSREPAIR actions is kept in a file. The default file for the log is named DSREPAIR.LOG and is stored in the SYS:SYSTEM directory.

- *Advanced options menu.* The repair operations that are run automatically under the menu choice Unattended Full Repair can be run individually using this option. Log file configuration information can also be entered here. See Figure 9-48.

- *Exit*

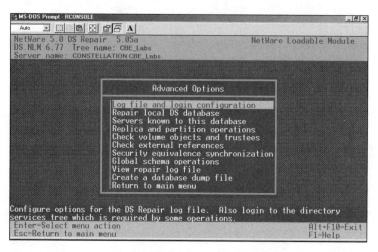

Figure 9-48   DSREPAIR Advanced Options menu

The –U option enables the network administrator to run an unattended full repair without making menu choices. When the command LOAD DSREPAIR –U is entered at the console prompt, DSREPAIR is loaded, the unattended full repair is run, and DSREPAIR is unloaded without any further instructions from the network administrator.

CHAPTER SUMMARY

❏ The NetWare security system lets a network administrator limit access to data and services on the server in three different ways: login security, file system security, and console security. The login security system this chapter describes consists of user names, passwords, time restrictions, station restrictions, and account restrictions. User names can be a maximum of 47 characters and often consist of the user's first initial followed by the last name, or of the first three letters of the first and last names, combined to make user names of six letters. User names can be given privileges to let users perform special administrative functions such as creating users or working with printers. Administrator equivalent users have the same rights as the Admin account, and by granting rights you can create users that can manage workgroups and user accounts. A printer operator privilege gives users control of the printing system.

❏ NetWare provides additional security by letting the network administrator establish password requirements and access restrictions. Password requirements that can be placed on each user account include requiring passwords of a specified minimum length, forcing users to change passwords within a specified number of days, and requiring users to select a different or unique password rather than alternating among a few favorite passwords. Time restrictions let a network administrator increase the security on an account by specifying what times the user can be logged into the server. Station restrictions provide further security by restricting a user account to one or more workstation addresses. Account restrictions, along with intruder detection, provide additional methods to disable a user's account when certain limits such as account expiration date or a maximum number of login attempts are reached.

❏ The network administrator uses NetWare Administrator to create and secure user and group accounts. User-related leaf objects include the User object, the Group object, the Organizational Role object, and the Profile object.

❏ The User object represents a user of the network and contains property settings controlling login security for the user. These settings include home directory creation, password restrictions, login time restrictions, network address restrictions, and login restrictions. The network administrator can create a user Template object for each container object. This user template object stores default property settings for all User objects created in that container. Intruder detection shuts a user out of the network after a specified number of failed login attempts. Intruder detection must be enabled for each individual container object.

❏ The Group object represents a group of network users and contains property settings that assign appropriate network resources to members of the group. Assigning resources to the group instead of to each user lets the network administrator more easily control who has certain system rights and privileges.

❏ The Organizational Role object represents a position in an organization chart and contains property settings that give network privileges to any user assigned to the

9

role. Because the privileges are associated with the position instead of the user, it is easy to reallocate them to a new user who takes over that role in the organization.

Like the Group object, the Profile object allows the administrator to assign network resources to groups of users. The Profile object, however, can be associated with a login script, whereas the Group object can't.

❑ NetWare accounting lets the network administrator establish charge rates for such services as blocks read, blocks written, connection time, disk space used, and server requests made. Using this feature, NetWare will deduct charges from the user account balances until the user account balance exceeds the credit limit, at which time the user account is disabled until the administrator assigns a new balance or increases the credit limit. The administrator uses the ATOTAL command line utility to prepare reports on use of chargeable network resources.

❑ The UIMPORT command line utility lets the network administrator easily create large numbers of users from a text file, called the data file, that contains the data needed for User object property value settings. UIMPORT uses an import control file to specify parameters for the user account creation. This file consists of two sections: the import control section, which tells UIMPORT which control parameters to use, and the field section, which specifies which properties have setting values in the data file.

❑ The DSREPAIR console utility is an NDS repair utility stored in the SYS:SYSTEM directory. The administrator uses it to fix problems with the NDS database, including replicas and replica synchronization.

COMMAND SUMMARY

Command	Syntax	Definition
ATOTAL	*ATOTAL [/C] [/?] [/VER]*	Command line utility used to summarize accounting charges for the chargeable resources on the NetWare servers.
DSREPAIR	*Load [path] DSREPAIR [-U]*	NLM utility that lets you repair the NDS database. You can also check time synchronization and replica synchronization. The -U option unloads the NLM after an unattended full repair. Menu options include: ■ Unattended full repair ■ Time synchronization ■ Replica synchronization ■ View/Edit repair log file ■ Advanced options menu ■ Exit

UIMPORT	*UIMPORT [control file] [data file] [/C] [ALL] [/?] [ATTR] [/VER]*	Command line utility that enables you to create user accounts from data in an ASCII text data file. Import options and data field specifications are contained in the control file, which has two sections: import control and fields. Import control parameters and field definitions are too extensive to list here—see Tables 9-7 and 9-8.

9

KEY TERMS

ATOTAL utility
data file
fields section
grace login
home directory
import control file
import control section
intruder detection
NetWare Accounting
printer operators
Template object
UIMPORT utility
user account managers
workgroup managers

REVIEW QUESTIONS

1. Identify each of the following as being either a command line utility, graphical utility, console command, or NetWare Loadable Module (NLM):

   ATOTAL _____

   UIMPORT_____

   DSREPAIR _____

2. List the three levels of NetWare security.

3. NetWare keeps track of user names, passwords, and other access restrictions in the _____.

4. List the five login security components that together give you network access.

5. List the users and groups that exist after NetWare is first installed on a network server.

6. A user name can be up to _____ characters in length.

7. Briefly explain the guidelines for user names in NetWare 5.0.

8. List three restrictions you can assign to password security.

9. Give an example of how time restrictions can be used to help secure a payroll clerk's workstation.

10. Briefly describe two ways in which station restrictions can be used to provide better security.

11. List the four ways an account can be disabled.

12. List the four types of charges that can be tracked with NetWare's accounting functions. (*Hint*: One type consists of two charges.)

13. The _____ charge rate is most useful if you are charging customers for access to your database file.

14. The _____ charge rate is most useful if you are charging customers for the amount of the server's processing time they use.

15. The _____ charge rate can be used to prevent users from staying logged into the server.

16. Which two utilities can be used to create users?

17. Which utility can be used to create groups?

18. The _____ page of the User object dialog box is used to create or change a user's password.

19. The _____ page of the User object dialog box is used to set time restrictions on a user's account.

20. The _____ page of the User object dialog box is used to set the number of concurrent connections a user can have.

21. The _____ User object is used to specify default User object property settings within a container object.

22. Intruder detection is enabled using the _____.

23. List three ways to add users to groups.

24. Discuss why the Organizational Role object is useful.

25. Discuss why the Profile object is useful.

26. The NetWare _____ utility summarizes accounting charges.

27. The NetWare _____ utility can repair a damaged NDS database.

HANDS-ON PROJECTS

Project 9-1: Using NetWare Administrator to Create Users, Groups, Organizational Roles, and Profiles

In this project you use NetWare Administrator to create three users and two groups and then assign the users to groups. All user and group names you create must be preceded by your student number to separate them from users and groups created by other students.

1. Log in using your assigned student user name (it must have workgroup manager privileges).

2. Launch NetWare Administrator.

3. In your assigned home directory, create a subdirectory named USERS. In the Software container of the Test&Eval.CBE_Labs organizational unit, create a new organizational unit called PRACTICE. In the new PRACTICE container, create three users called ##USER1, ##USER2, and ##USER3. (Replace the number symbols with your assigned student number.) Assign each of these users a home directory in your USERS subdirectory.

4. Give ##USER1 your full name.

5. For all accounts, assign login restrictions so that a password is required to use each account. Use a common password of ##PASSWORD for all three accounts. Be sure to replace the number symbols with your assigned student number.

6. For all three accounts, set the accounts to expire on tomorrow's date.

7. In your ##PRACTICE container, create two groups called ##GROUP1 and ##GROUP2. Be sure to replace the number symbols with your assigned student number.

8. Use the ##USER1 object dialog box to add ##USER1 to ##GROUP1. Use the ##USER2 and ##USER3 object dialog boxes to add these users to ##GROUP1.

9. Using the ##GROUP2 object dialog box, add all three users to ##GROUP2.

10. In your ##ADMIN organizational unit, create an organizational role named ##ORGROLE1. Be sure to replace the number symbols with your assigned student number.

11. Assign ##USER1 to occupy ##ORGROLE1.

12. In your ##ADMIN organizational unit, create a profile named ##PROFILE1. Be sure to replace the number symbols with your assigned student number.

13. Assign ##USER2 and ##USER3 to ##PROFILE1.

14. Exit NetWare Administrator.

15. At the DOS prompt, change your default directory path to the ##ADMIN\USERS directory.

9

16. Use NetWare Administrator to obtain a list of trustee assignments for each of the user home directories; then rerun the command redirecting the output to a printer.

17. Log out.

18. Log in as ##USER1.

19. Launch NetWare Administrator and attempt to change User 2's first name. Record the result here: _____ .

20. Exit NetWare Administrator.

21. Log out.

22. Log in using your assigned ##ADMIN user name.

23. Use NetWare Administrator to delete all the objects created in this exercise and the home directories created for ##USER1, ##USER2, and ##USER3.

24. Exit NetWare Administrator and log out.

Project 9-2: Setting Time and Station Restrictions

In this project you determine your current workstation's network and node address and then use NWAdmin to create and restrict a user to logging in from only this station during a specified time period.

1. Log in using your ##ADMIN user name.

2. Launch NetWare Administrator.

3. Use the Environment page of the ##ADMIN User object dialog box to determine the network and node address of the workstation on which you are working. Record your workstation address information here:

   Network address: _____ Node address: _____

4. In your ##PRACTICE container, create user name ##BILL with a home directory in the ##ADMIN\USERS directory.

5. Do not require a password for ##BILL's account, but set login restrictions so that ##BILL can log in from two workstations at the same time.

6. Use the Network Address Restriction page to restrict ##BILL to the network and node address recorded in Step 3.

7. Log out.

8. Log in as user ##BILL from your current workstation.

9. Go to another workstation and attempt to log in as ##BILL. In the following space, record any messages you see.

10. Return to your workstation and log out as ##BILL. Log in using your ##ADMIN user name.

11. For the ##BILL User object, use the Login Time Restrictions page to prevent Bill from logging in during the current hour.

12. Exit NetWare Administrator.

13. Try logging in from your current workstation as ##BILL. Record the message you receive: _____

14. Log in with your ##ADMIN user name, delete the ##BILL user account, and remove the ##BILL home directory.

Project 9-3: Enabling Intruder Detection

In this project you use NetWare Administrator to enable intruder detection for your ##ADMIN organizational unit. Because administrator privileges are necessary to enable intruder detection, you will need to log into the server with a user name that has administrator equivalency to do this exercise. Your ##ADMIN account should already have the appropriate privileges. If not, your instructor will direct you regarding which user name to use.

1. Log in using the administrator-equivalent user name.

2. Launch NetWare Administrator.

3. In your ##PRACTICE container, create a user named ##JOHN without a home directory. Set a password of PASSWORD on the ##JOHN account.

4. Open the ##ADMIN organizational unit object dialog box, and use the Intruder Detection page to enable intruder detection. Record the settings in the following blanks (do not make any changes to these fields):

Incorrect Login Attempts: _____

Intruder Attempt Reset Interval:
_____ Days _____ Hours _____ Minutes

Intruder Lockout Reset Interval:
_____ Days _____ Hours _____ Minutes

5. Set Incorrect Login Attempts to **3**; then close the dialog box.

6. Log out.

7. Attempt to log in as ##JOHN using an incorrect password. Repeat this until you get a message that you are locked out of the system. Record the message here:

_____

8. Log in as ##ADMIN, and delete the ##JOHN account.

CASE PROJECTS

Case 9-1: Using NetWare Accounting to Track Network Usage

Assume that you are working as a lab assistant for your college network administrator and that the administrator would like you to keep track of server usage in order to develop a budget for future server needs. The previous network administrator had installed accounting and established a charge rate for blocks read. Your network administrator explains that a charge ratio is needed before NetWare will track server usage, but because the previous administrator did not want to have the users charged, he set up a charge at a time when no one should be using the server. Your network administrator wants you to document the charge ratio set up by the previous administrator for future reference. The network administrator also wants you to run the ATOTAL program each day and then use this information to create three separate graphs: one for blocks read, one for storage used, and one for the number of server requests made.

To perform this activity, you will need to decide on an arbitrary accounting charge rate and the times you want to charge for network services, along with the charge ratio used. Record the information in Table 9-10.

Table 9-10 Using NetWare Accounting Tables

Charge Ratio	Day	Times

To complete the assignment, you will need to run the ATOTAL program each day for the next three days and create graphs similar to the ones in Figure 9-49 showing NetWare server usage.

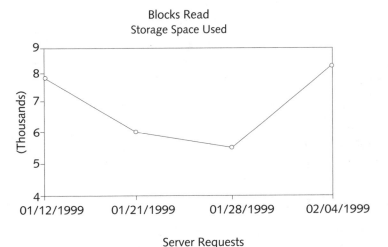

Blocks Read
Storage Space Used

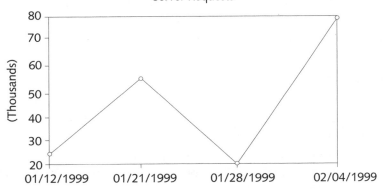

Server Requests

Figure 9-49   NetWare Server usage graphs

Case 9-2: Creating Users with UIMPORT

In this case study you create a template called USER_TEMPLATE to create users for the J. Q. Adams Company. Assume that you are the network administrator for the J. Q. Adams Company and that you need to create users in the sales department. As a network administrator, you know that templates can simplify the task of creating users by enabling the administrator to define and use templates that contain account information common to all users in a department. (In NetWare, only a administrator-equivalent user can create templates.) However, although you can create templates in your portion of the tree, you cannot run the UIMPORT utility in your test network. For this exercise, you will practice creating appropriate files for the UIMPORT utility only. In all cases, substitute your assigned student number for the number symbols (##).

In order to perform this case project, you will use the J.Q. Adams directory tree you worked on in the exercises in Chapter 8, as shown in Figure 9-50.

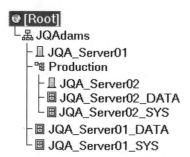

Figure 9-50   J.Q. Adams installation

Part 1: Creating User Templates

A user template object contains such information as home directory location, groups the users belong to, account balance information, and password requirements. You have decided to use a template to create the users for Team01 in the production department.

1. Launch NetWare Administrator.

2. Locate the JQAdams organizational unit.

3. Locate the Team01 Organizational Unit object in the Production container of that tree.

4. Create a Template object named USER_TEMPLATE in the Production container. Use the following settings:

   a. Set an initial account balance of 0. On the Account Balance page, mark the Allow Unlimited Credit text box. This provides unlimited credit to users.

   Require all users to have a password of at least five characters and force periodic password changes so that after 120 days the users have to invent a new password that is different from the previous 10 passwords the user has chosen. When a password expires, each user should be given three grace login times before his or her account is disabled.

5. Create a new user in the Team01 Organizational Unit using the USER_TEMPLATE. Use "Ben Avery" as the user's Full Name and "BAvery"as the login name. After you create the user object, check to see how the default property settings have been created.

6. Exit NWAdmin.

Part 2: Creating New Users with UIMPORT Files

Now that the Team01 template is created, you are ready to create the Team 01 users. Create the following users for the Team 01 by creating the appropriate UIMPORT files:

FULL NAME	USERNAME
Ned Lynch	NLynch
Ann Bonny	ABonny
George Moon	GMoon

1. Run Notepad from your Windows desktop.

2. Type the following:

   IMPORT CONTROL

         CREATE HOME DIRECTORY = N

         NAME CONTEXT = ".JQAdams"

         USER TEMPLATE = Y

   FIELDS

         NAME

         LAST NAME

         GIVEN NAME

3. Close and save the document in text format by choosing **File**, **Save As**, then naming the file. Save it on your local C: drive. (Remember, the name isn't important because you will simply specify it when you run your UIMPORT command as explained earlier in the chapter.)

4. Start a new document in Notepad for the UIMPORT data file. Enter the name, last name, and given name for each user you want to create. Remember, only one user per line, and use quote marks around each entry and commas after the name and last name entries.

5. Save this document on your local C: drive with an appropriate name (again, it doesn't matter what name you choose, since you would normally just specify it when you run UIMPORT).

Write a memo to your instructor showing the contents of the UMIPORT files you used in this exercise. Turn in this memo to your instructor accompanied by a copy of your data files on disk.

10

MANAGING TRUSTEE ASSIGNMENTS AND FILE ATTRIBUTES

After reading this chapter and completing the exercises you will be able to:

♦ Identify the components of NetWare trustee rights (NDS and file system) security

♦ Describe how effective rights are obtained from a combination of trustee assignments, group rights, and inherited rights

♦ Describe how the Inherited Rights Filter (IRF) modifies effective rights in a directory or file

♦ Use NetWare utilities to grant trustee rights and determine user effective rights

♦ Work with NetWare file and directory attributes

A fter user accounts have been created and secured, the next level of NetWare security involves giving users access to NDS and to the NetWare file system. This is the trustee assignments and file attributes security level. Initially, new users have rights only to work in their home directories and to run programs from the SYS:PUBLIC directory. An important responsibility of a network administrator is to provide users with the rights to access the network NDS objects, directories, and files they need and still protect sensitive network information.

Trustee assignment controls who has rights to access network resources after the user has logged on to the network. Access rights are like a set of keys provided to a new employee. Just as keys give access to rooms, access rights give users access to the directories that contain files they need to use.

You can also protect directories and files in NetWare security. In addition to controlling access to them through trustee assignments, the network administrator can also assign directory and file attributes to a directory, file, or group of files. These attributes, described later in this chapter, can be attached as another means of limiting user access.

In this chapter, you will learn how to use access rights and attributes to give users the effective access to network resources that they need to perform their work.

 Most software applications allow file sharing for workgroup computing. Thus the network administrator needs to balance file system security and integrity with providing shared access to directories that contain files used simultaneously by more than one workstation.

TRUSTEE ASSIGNMENTS

In this section you will learn about trustees, rights, and assignments, and how to use them in planning Directory tree and file system security. You'll also become familiar with NetWare and Windows tools for managing trustee assignments.

Trustees, Rights, and Assignments

A **trustee** is a user who has been given access to NDS objects, directories, or files. The user is called a trustee because the user is responsible for the security of the objects, directories, or files to which he or she has access.

The term **rights** describes the type of access the user has been given. For example, the file system **File Scan right** lets users see directory and file listings, and the **Read right** lets users see (but not change) the contents of a file. NetWare 5.0 has object rights, property rights, directory rights, and file rights. Table 10-1 summarizes these rights, which will be discussed in more detail later in this chapter.

Table 10-1 Types of NetWare 5.0 Trustee rights

Type of Rights	Trustee Access
Object rights	Trustee can work with an NDS Directory tree object as a whole but can't work with the properties of that object.
Property rights	Trustee can work with the properties of an NDS Directory tree object but must first be granted necessary Object rights to the object.
Directory rights	Trustee can work with a file system directory—and generally the files in that directory, although this can be blocked by assigned File rights and the file's Inherited Rights Filter (discussed later in this chapter).
File rights	Trustee can work with a file.

The terms **grant** and **assign** are used interchangeably to describe giving rights to a trustee. Thus, you make the user JCunningham a *trustee* of the CBE Labs Directory tree by *granting* or *assigning* him specific NDS Object rights. The term **trustee assignment** refers to the rights given to the user. The *trustee assignments* given to JCunningham determine what access he has to the NDS Directory tree objects and the network file system directories and files.

A **trustee list** is the set of trustee assignments for an NDS object, directory, or file; it is used to determine who can access the object, directory, or file. The trustee list of an NDS object is stored in a property of the object, the **access control list (ACL)**.

As a network administrator, you will use trustee assignments to control which users have access to the network resources. In controlling access to those network resources through how you grant rights to trustees, you maintain network security by giving access *only* to users who need it. Trustee assignments are the network administrator's main tool for controlling network resources and maintaining system security after a user has logged into the network.

 The notation for Novell rights is typically to use only the first letter of the right enclosed in brackets, as shown in Table 10-2. This notation is used in this chapter as well. When we say that All rights are granted, we use the notation [All], rather than specifying each right individually.

Object Rights

Object rights give the user access to NDS objects. They do not, however, give access to the properties of the objects. Table 10-2 summarizes the NetWare 5.0 object rights.

Table 10-2   NetWare 5.0 Object rights

Right	Effect on Object
Supervisor [S]	Grants the user all rights to the object, and also grants the user all Property rights to the object.
Browse [B]	Lets the user see the object in the Directory tree and have the object's name show up in search results.
Create [C]	Applies only to container objects. Lets the user create new objects in the container but not create Property rights for the objects.
Delete [D]	Lets the user delete the object from the Directory tree. If the object is a container object, it must be empty before it can be deleted.
Rename [R]	Lets the user rename the object.
Inheritable [I]	Lets all rights be inheritable within the container (the NetWare 5.0 default). Applies only to container objects. If this right is deselected, then rights are not inherited by child containers.

The **Browse right** enables users to see objects in the Directory tree. By not granting this right, the network administrator can control which parts of the Directory tree users can see. For example, consider the CBE Laboratories Directory tree that Figure 10-1 shows.

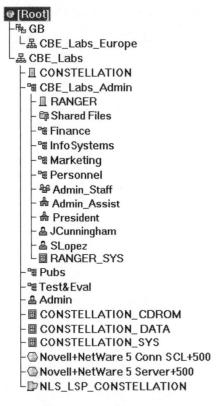

Figure 10-1   CBE Labs Directory tree

Users in the Test&Eval and Pubs organizational units may not need to see some other sections of the Directory tree, such as the Finance, Marketing, and Personnel organizational units. By controlling the Browse right for users in Test&Eval and Pubs, the network administrator can make the three organizational units invisible to those users.

The **Create right**, which applies only to container objects, lets users create objects in a container object. However, it does not allow the user to set property values in the objects. The **Delete right** lets users delete a Directory tree object. However, before you can delete a container object you must delete all objects in it—you cannot delete a container object with objects in it. The **Rename right** lets users change the name of an object, which changes the object's complete name.

The **Inheritable right** changes the way rights flow down the NDS tree. By default in NetWare 5.0, all rights flow down (are inheritable) from a parent container to its child containers or leaf objects. The Inheritable right applies only to container objects. If the Inheritable right is removed, the container's child containers will not inherit the rights granted to the parent container.

Using the Inheritable right, an administrator can effectively create a dead-end container for special purposes. Typically, however, the Inheritable right is left at the default, active setting.

The **Supervisor right** gives the user all the other Object rights. In addition, it gives the user Supervisor rights to all properties of the object. Thus a user with Supervisor rights to an object can also change any property settings for that object.

Property Rights

Property rights let the user access the property settings of NDS objects. Before you can grant Property rights to a user, the user must, of course, have Object rights to the object. Table 10-3 summarizes the NetWare 5.0 Property rights.

Table 10-3 NetWare 5.0 Property rights

Right	Effect on Property
Supervisor [S]	Grants the user all rights to the property.
Compare [C]	Lets the user compare a value to the value of the property, not to the value itself. Included in Read.
Read [R]	Lets the user see the value of the property. Includes Compare.
Write [W]	Lets the user change, add, or delete the value of the property. Includes Add or Delete Self.
Add or Delete Self [A]	Lets the user add or delete him- or herself to or from the user list in objects that have user lists. The user can't change other property values. Included in Write.

The **Compare right** lets users test the values of the property against a reference value—for example, whether a printer in the NDS tree is a color printer or not. When the user with Compare rights tests a property value (such as color), a True (equals test value) or a False (doesn't equal test value) response can be returned, although the value stored in the property setting is never displayed. The **Read right** lets the user actually see the value of the property setting. The Compare right is included in the Read right, so that when you grant the Read right you also grant the user the ability to make comparisons.

Although the Read right lets the user see the value of the property setting, it doesn't allow the user to change the value. To change values, the user must have the **Write right**. With the Write right, the user can add, modify, or delete a value. A special case of the Write right is the Add or Delete Self right. The **Add or Delete Self right** enables a user to add him- or herself to the ACL property (if the object has one). An example of an object with an ACL property is a Group object; having the Add or Delete Self right to a Group object means that the user can add (or remove) him- or herself to (or from) the group. The Write right includes the Add or Delete Self right.

As with Object rights, the Supervisor Property right gives the user all rights to the property. It is important to note that Property rights can be assigned for each object property individually, so that different users can have different access to an object's property values. In addition, granting the Supervisor Object rights to an object normally grants the Supervisor Property rights to all the object's properties (this can, however, be changed by using the Inherited Rights Filter, discussed later in this chapter).

Directory and File Rights

Directory rights control access to the directories and subdirectories in the network file system, whereas **File rights** control user access to the files in these directories and subdirectories. The same eight rights are used for both Directory rights and File rights. Note that the rights can be assigned to individual files as well as to directories. A user normally has the same access to files in a directory as to the directory itself. This can be modified using File rights on specific files or by using an Inherited Rights Filter on the file (discussed later in this chapter). Table 10-4 summarizes the NetWare 5.0 Directory and File rights.

Being able to assign access rights to a specific file means the network administrator can let users update a certain file or database within the directory while blocking rights to other files that exist in that storage area.

The Read right and File Scan right are often used together to enable users to access files or run programs in a specified directory. All users are given Read and File Scan rights to the SYS:PUBLIC directory. Having the Create right to a directory lets a user create subdirectories as well as new files in the specified directory. The Create right lets a user copy files into the directory as long as no other file in the directory has the same name. Granting the Create right to an existing file might seem meaningless, but it does let the user salvage the file if it is deleted.

Be aware that assigning the **Erase right** to a directory lets a user not only erase files but also remove the entire directory and its subdirectories. There is an important difference between the Write right and the Modify right. The Write right lets the user change or add data to an existing file; the **Modify right** lets a user change a file's name or attributes only—it has nothing to do with changing the contents of the file. The **Access Control right** lets a user determine which users can access the directory or file by granting access rights to other users. Because allowing users to grant rights to other users can make it difficult for the network administrator to keep track of file system security, normally you should not give the Access Control right to other users.

Table 10-4   NetWare 5.0 Directory rights and File rights

Right	Effect on Directory	Effect on File
Supervisor [S]	Grants all rights to the specified directory and all subdirectories.	Grants all rights to the specified file.
Read [R]	Lets the user read files or run programs in the directory.	Lets the user read or run the specified file or program without having Read rights at the directory level.
Write [W]	Lets the user change or add data to files in the specified directory.	Lets the user change or add data to the specified file without having Write rights at the directory level.
Create [C]	Lets the user create files and subdirectories.	Lets the user salvage the specified file if it is deleted.
Erase [E]	Lets the user delete files and remove subdirectories.	Lets the user delete the specified file without having Erase rights at the directory level.
Modify [M]	Lets the user change file and subdirectory names and use Explorer to change the attribute settings on files or subdirectories.	Lets the user change the name or attribute settings of the specified file without having Modify rights at the directory level.
File Scan [F]	Lets the user obtain a directory of file and subdirectory names.	Lets the user view the specified filename on a directory listing without having File Scan rights at the directory level.
Access Control [A]	Lets the user grant access rights to other users for the specified directory.	Lets the user grant access rights to the specified file without having Access Control rights at the directory level.

Having the Supervisor right is not quite the same as having all rights, because it applies to all subdirectories and cannot be changed at a lower directory. The Supervisor right also differs from the other rights in that only the Admin user or another user who has Supervisor rights to the directory can assign it.

Users who have the Access Control right in a directory but not the Supervisor right can accidentally restrict themselves from working in the directory by assigning themselves fewer rights to the directory or a subdirectory than they need. To avoid this, grant the Access Control right to a user only when it is absolutely necessary for the user to assign rights to other users.

By looking at specific situations, you will understand better what access rights are necessary to perform functions in the network file system. Table 10-5 lists typical operations that users need to perform on files and directories and the access rights required to perform these operations.

Table 10-5   Rights required for common functions

Task	Typical Command or Program	Rights Required
Read a file	WordPad	Read
Obtain a directory listing	Windows Explorer	File Scan
Change the contents of data in a file	WordPad	Write
Write to a closed file using a text editor that creates a backup file	EDIT (DOS)	Write, Create, Erase, Modify (Modify not required if creating a new file)
Execute a program file	WordPad	Read
Create and write to a new file	WordPad	Create
Copy a file from a directory	Windows Explorer	Read, File Scan
Copy a file into a directory	Windows Explorer	Create
Copy multiple files to a directory with existing files	Windows Explorer	Create, File Scan
Create a subdirectory	Windows Explorer	Create
Delete a file	Windows Explorer	Erase
Salvage deleted files	Windows Explorer or NetWare Administrator	Read and File Scan on the file and Create in the directory or on filename
Change attributes	NetWare Administrator	Modify
Rename a file or subdirectory	Windows Explorer	Rename
Change the Inherited Rights Filter	NetWare Administrator	Access Control
Make or change a trustee assignment	NetWare Administrator	Access Control

Directory trustee assignments are kept track of in the **directory entry table (DET)** of each volume. A DET for a file or directory can hold up to six trustee assignments. If you assign more than six trustees to a directory, an additional entry in the DET is made for that directory name. It is a good idea, however, to keep trustee assignments to six or fewer for each directory. You can usually do this by assigning a group as a trustee and then making users who need access to that directory members of the group. File trustee assignments are also tracked in the DET. If you assign more than six trustees to a file, you need an additional entry in the DET for that filename.

Assigned Rights, Inherited Rights, and Effective Rights

Assigned rights are rights granted directly to a user or another NDS object. It is always a user who can actually use and exercise trustee rights. However, a user can gain access to trustee rights in six ways:

- A trustee assignment is made to the *user.*

- The user is a member of a *group,* and the group has trustee assignments.

- The user occupies an *organizational role,* and the organizational role has trustee assignments.

- The user's User object is located in a *container object* that has trustee assignments.

- The user has been given *security equivalence* to another user who has trustee assignments.

- Subordinate container objects and directories inherit the user's trustee assignments granted in a parent container object or directory. This inheritance applies, however, only if no rights are specifically assigned for that object or directory. A subsequent assignment of rights is discussed in more detail below.

The rights that a user actually has to an object, an object's properties, a directory, or a file are called **effective rights**. Effective rights are the functions a user can perform on an object or property, or in a specific directory or file. In many cases, a user's effective rights are the same as his or her trustee assignments. However, a user's effective rights are a combination of the rights gained through the six methods just listed, modified by the network administrator's ability to restrict rights that a user otherwise would have. Later in this chapter, we'll discuss how to restrict effective rights.

Now we will look at ways of gaining effective rights. Although techniques for managing all trustee assignments are similar, it's easier to understand trustee assignment management by discussing Object and Property rights separately from Directory and File rights. We'll start with Object and Property rights management, and then discuss managing Directory and File rights.

Managing Object Rights and Property Rights

When you are assigning Object rights and Property rights, you make the assignment using either the object (A) to which access is being granted, or the object (B) that is getting access to Object A. For example, if you want a user to have rights in a container object, the trustee assignment can be granted to the user either in the container object's object dialog box or in the user's object dialog box.

Rights Assigned to the User

The simplest and most straightforward way for a user to gain effective rights is to be granted a trustee assignment. You will look at a simple example and then see how trustee assignments are actually made, using the CBE Laboratories example.

EXAMPLE 10-1: Assigning user Trustee rights at F. D. Roosevelt Investments Inc.

F. D. Roosevelt Investments Inc., or FDR as it is commonly referred to, is a small investment brokerage house that manages a variety of mutual funds. Investors can invest in the mutual funds through any of several investment options offered by the company.

FDR has three business units: Administration, Sales, and Investments. Figure 10-2 shows the FDR organizational chart, and Figure 10-3 shows the NDS Directory tree for FDR.

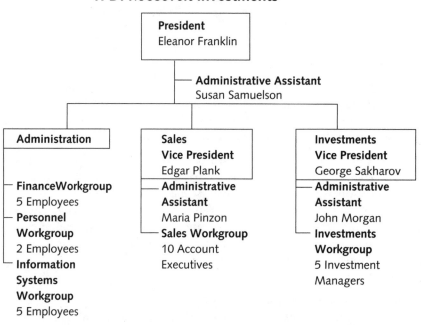

F. D. Roosevelt Investments

Figure 10-2 F. D. Roosevelt Investments Inc. organizational chart

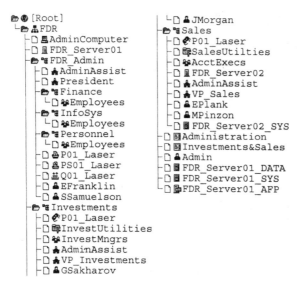

```
🗁🌐[Root]                        └🗋 👤JMorgan
 └🗁👤FDR                        🗁🏢Sales
   🗋🖥AdminComputer             🗋🖨P01_Laser
   🗋🖳FDR_Server01              🗋📇SalesUtilties
  🗁🏢FDR_Admin                  🗋👥AcctExecs
    🗋👤AdminAssist              🗋🖳FDR_Server02
    🗋👤President                🗋👤AdminAssist
   🗁🏢Finance                   🗋👤VP_Sales
     └🗋👥Employees              🗋👤EPlank
   🗁🏢InfoSys                   🗋👤MPinzon
     └🗋👥Employees              🗋🖳FDR_Server02_SYS
   🗁🏢Personnel                🗋📘Administration
     └🗋👥Employees             🗋📘Investments&Sales
    🗋🖨P01_Laser               🗋👤Admin
    🗋🖨PS01_Laser              🗋🖳FDR_Server01_DATA
    🗋🖨Q01_Laser               🗋🖳FDR_Server01_SYS
    🗋👤EFranklin               🗋🖳FDR_Server01_APP
    🗋👤SSamuelson
  🗁🏢Investments
    🗋🖨P01_Laser
    🗋📇InvestUtilities
    🗋👥InvestMngrs
    🗋👤AdminAssist
    🗋👤VP_Investments
    🗋👤GSakharov
```

Figure 10-3   FDR Directory tree

Paul Drake, the lead account executive at FDR, needs the ability to manage NDS objects in the Sales organizational unit. He will be granted the Supervisor object right to the Sales Organizational Unit object. The Supervisor object right gives the trustee the Supervisor right to all properties of that object, as Figure 10-4 shows.

	Trustee Assignments		Objects: 🖳 Sales
P Drake:	User	Object Rights	[S]
	Effective Rights		[SBCDR]
	User	Property Rights: All Properties	[ ]
	Effective Rights		[SCRWA]

Figure 10-4   Paul's Object and Property rights

Now consider another example: implementing object and property rights at CBE Laboratories. Georgia Burns, the CBE Labs vice president for testing and evaluation, is very knowledgeable about network administration. To expedite administration of the Test&Eval branch of the CBE Labs Directory tree, it has been agreed that she will be given the rights to administer the Test&Eval branch. Thus she must be given the Supervisor right to the Test&Eval Organizational Unit object. Figure 10-5 shows the Test&Eval branch of the CBE Labs Directory tree.

10

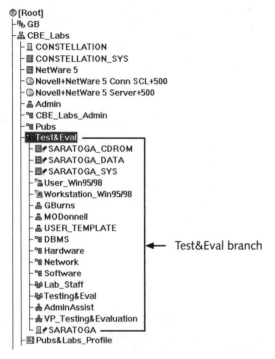

Figure 10-5   Test&Eval branch of CBE Labs Directory tree

Assigning Trustee Rights to an Object from the Object Itself

When you assign trustee rights from an object, you select the object and then open a dialog box that displays the trustees of the object.

To grant property and object trustee rights to an object from the object itself, follow these general steps:

1. Click the object name or icon to select it. Then click Object on the menu bar, and click Trustees of this Object to display the Trustees of *Objectname* dialog box.

   or

   Right-click the object name or icon to select it and display the shortcut menu. Then click Trustees of this Object to display the Trustees of *Objectname* dialog box.

2. Use the settings controls in the Trustees of *Objectname* dialog box to manage trustees and trustee rights assignments.

You will use this method to give Georgia Burns her trustee assignment to the Test&Eval Organizational Unit object.

To grant Georgia Burns Trustee rights to the Test&Eval Organizational Unit object from the Test&Eval Organizational Unit object, follow these steps:

1. If NetWare Administrator is not open, launch it. If necessary, log in with the appropriate Administrator privileges.

2. Click the Test&Eval Organizational Unit object to select it, then click Object on the menu bar. The Object menu appears, as Figure 10-6 shows.

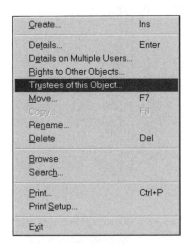

Figure 10-6   Trustees of this Object command on Object menu

3. Click Trustees of this Object on the Object menu. The Trustees of Test&Eval dialog box is displayed, as Figure 10-7 shows.

   The object is a trustee of itself. Checked check boxes indicate that the right is granted; empty check boxes indicate that it is not. Grayed-out check boxes indicate that the right is not applicable to the selected object—this usually occurs when no objects have been selected.

4. Click the Add Trustees button to display the Select Object dialog box.

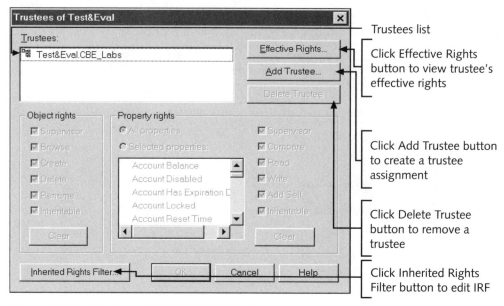

Trustees list

Click Effective Rights button to view trustee's effective rights

Click Add Trustee button to create a trustee assignment

Click Delete Trustee button to remove a trustee

Click Inherited Rights Filter button to edit IRF

Figure 10-7   Trustees of Test&Eval dialog box

5. Select the GBurns User object (you may need to browse the tree to locate it), then click OK. GBurns is made a trustee of the Test&Eval Organizational Unit object, as Figure 10-8 shows. *Do not close the Trustees of Test&Eval dialog box at this time.*

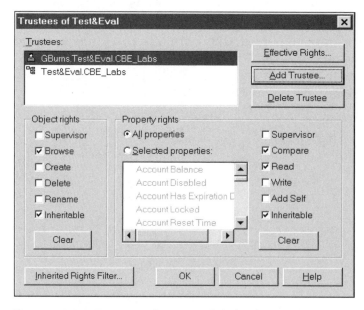

Figure 10-8   Trustees of Test&Eval dialog box

Now that Georgia Burns is a trustee of the Test&Eval Organizational Unit, her specific rights can be assigned. Note that in Figure 10-8 the default rights granted are the Browse Object right and the Compare and Read Property rights to all properties. These rights would enable her to see the object in the Directory tree and to see all the values of the property settings for the object. Remember that the Compare right is included in the Read right, so nothing is gained by assigning the Compare right in addition to the Read right.

Also notice in Figure 10-8 that you can assign Property rights for each property individually by using the Selected Properties radio button. This gives the network administrator total control of exactly what each trustee can do with the properties of the object.

Georgia Burns needs the Supervisor Object right. This includes the Supervisor Property right to all properties, but it's a good idea to explicitly grant the Supervisor Property right to all properties in the dialog box as well—this serves as a visual reminder of the rights granted to the trustee.

To grant Georgia Burns Object rights and Property rights to the Test&Eval Organizational Unit object, follow these steps:

1. Click the GBurns.Test&Eval.CBE_Labs trustee to select it in the Trustees list, if it isn't selected already.

2. In the Object Rights box, click to select the Supervisor check box, and click to deselect the Browse check box (although it isn't necessary to deselect the Browse right, doing so presents a clearer picture of the trustee's rights).

3. In the Property Rights box, click the All Properties radio button to select it, if it isn't selected already.

4. In the Property Rights box, click to select the Supervisor check box, and click to deselect the Compare check box and Read check box (although it isn't necessary to unselect the Compare and Read rights, doing so presents a clearer picture of the trustee's rights). The Trustees of Test&Eval dialog box now appears as Figure 10-9 shows.

5. Click OK to close the Trustees of Test&Eval dialog box.

The Trustees of *ObjectName* dialog box gives the network administrator a quick way to check a trustee's effective rights to an object. To check the effective rights, select the trustee in the Trustees list, and then click the Effective Rights button.

10

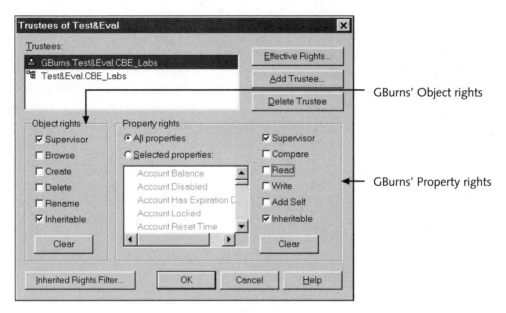

Figure 10-9   GBurns' Object and Property rights to Test&Eval

To view Georgia Burns's effective Object rights and Property rights to the Test&Eval Organizational Unit object, follow these steps:

1. Select the Trustees of this Object menu option again.

2. Click the GBurns.Test&Eval.CBE_Labs trustee to select it in the Trustees list, if it isn't selected already.

3. Click the Effective Rights button to display the Effective Rights dialog box, as Figure 10-10 shows.

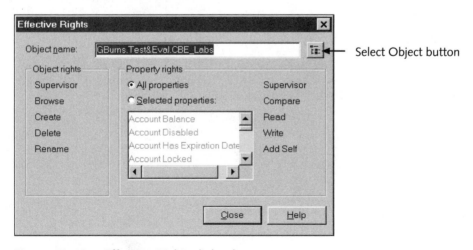

Figure 10-10   Effective Rights dialog box

Notice that Georgia Burns has all Object and Property rights to the Test&Eval Organizational Unit object. Rights not assigned would be grayed out.

Also notice the Select Object button. You can use this button to check the effective rights of other objects in the Directory tree to the current object.

4. Click the Close button to close the Effective Rights dialog box. The Trustees of Test&Eval dialog box appears.

5. Click Cancel to close the Trustees of Test&Eval dialog box.

Assigning Trustee Rights to an Object from a Trustee Object

Alternatively, you can assign trustee rights from the object that is being granted the trustee assignment. To do so, select the Trustee object and then open a dialog box that displays the trustee assignments of the Trustee object.

To grant property and object Trustee rights to an object from a Trustee object itself, follow these general steps:

1. Click the object name or icon to select it. Then click Object on the menu bar, and click Rights to Other Objects to display the Search Context dialog box.
   or
   Right-click the object name or icon to select it and display the shortcut menu. Then click Rights to Other Objects to display the Search Context dialog box.

2. Use the Search Context dialog box to set the search context for the search for the trustee's rights to other objects in the Directory tree and to search for the trustee rights.

3. Use the settings controls in the Rights to Other Objects dialog box to manage trustees and trustee rights assignments.

When the trustee assignment is made from the User object (or other Trustee object), NetWare first searches the Directory tree to find and list the objects for which the user has rights assigned. The context for this search—the whole tree or a branch of it—is specified as part of the search. Searching the Directory tree takes time, so it is faster to limit the area of the tree that needs to be evaluated. Normally, you should limit the search context to only the part of the Directory tree that includes the objects for which you are granting trustee rights to the user.

Let's see how this method could be used to give Georgia Burns her trustee assignment to the Test&Eval Organizational Unit object. We will start with removing her prior trustee assignment.

To grant Georgia Burns Trustee rights to the Test&Eval Organizational Unit object from the GBurns User object, follow these steps:

1. If NetWare Administrator is not open, launch it.

2. We will need to remove the trustee assignment we made earlier to GBurns. Highlight the Test&Eval object, then choose Object, Trustees of this Object.

3. In the Trustees of Test&Eval dialog box, highlight GBurns in the Trustees list.

4. Click Delete Trustee.

5. Choose Yes to accept this. This removes our previous trustee assignment.

6. Click OK to close the Trustees of Test&Eval dialog box.

7. Expand the tree to locate and click the GBurns User object to select it, then click Object on the menu bar. The Object menu appears, as shown in Figure 10-11.

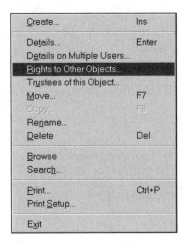

Figure 10-11   Rights to Other Objects command on Object menu

8. Click Rights to Other Objects on the Object menu. The Search Context dialog box is displayed, as Figure 10-12 shows.

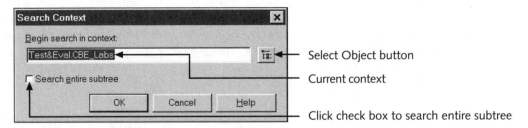

Figure 10-12   Search Context dialog box

9. Click the Select Object button to display the Select Object dialog box. In the Select Object dialog box, select the CBE_Labs Organization object, then click OK.

10. The Search Context dialog box is displayed, with CBE_Labs in the Context to Begin Search text box. Click the Search Entire Subtree check box to select it, then click OK. The program searches for object trustee assignments for Georgia Burns, and then the Rights to Other Objects dialog box is displayed for User: GBurns, as Figure 10-13 shows. Note that there are no Assigned Objects because we are illustrating the initial assignment of trustee rights to the Test&Eval Organizational Unit object to Georgia Burns.

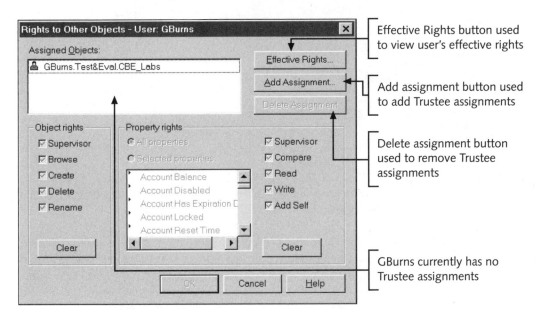

Figure 10-13   Rights to Other Objects—User: GBurns dialog box

11. Click the Add assignment button to display the Select Object dialog box.

12. Browse the tree to locate and click the Test&Eval Organizational Unit object, then click OK. GBurns is assigned trustee rights to the Test&Eval Organizational Unit object, as Figure 10-14 shows. Save the assignment by clicking OK.

Georgia Burns's specific Object and Property rights could also be assigned from the Rights to Other Objects dialog box. The Rights to Other Objects dialog box uses exactly the same methods of granting specific Object rights and Property rights to trustees that are used in the Trustees of *ObjectName* dialog box. Note that in Figure 10-14 the Rights to Other Objects dialog box shows that the same default Object rights of Browse object and the same default Property rights of Compare and Read property to all properties are granted. The specific steps for granting Georgia Burns Object and Property rights would be exactly the same as those already shown, so we will not repeat them.

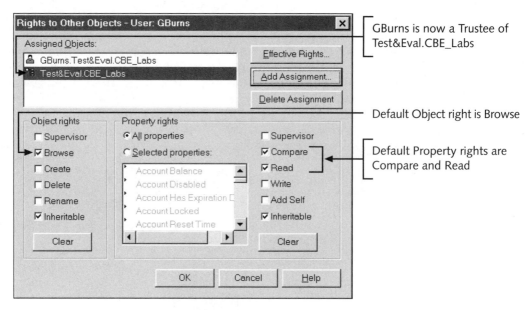

Figure 10-14   GBurns assigned as trustee of Test&Eval.CBE_Labs Organizational Unit object

The Trustees of *ObjectName* dialog box works in the same way as the Rights to Other Objects dialog box. One difference is that you use the Trustees dialog box to check a trustee's effective rights to an object. To check the effective rights, select the object in the Assigned Objects list, and then click the Effective Rights button.

Rights Assigned to a Group

Groups consist of users who have common network requirements. Grouping users can simplify trustee assignments. When a group is made a trustee of an object, all members of that group are also considered trustees of the object and thus have the same rights as the group. A user's effective rights in a directory then combine his or her own trustee assignment with any rights he or she has as a group member.

A special case of a group is **[Public]**. When [Public] is made a trustee of an object, *every* object in the NDS Directory tree—users, groups, organizational units, and so on—inherits the same [Public] rights to the object. In addition, [Public] rights are available to users who have loaded the NetWare client software but haven't logged into the network yet. When you install NetWare 5.0, the [Public] becomes a trustee of the [Root] object and gets the Browse Object right [B]. Thus, by default, anyone with access to your network can see your whole Directory tree *before* logging into the network!

If you don't want all users, logged in or not, to see your Directory tree, you must delete [Public] as a trustee to the [Root] of the Directory tree.

Novell recommends making a container object an object's trustee rather than giving the [Public] object the trustee rights to an object. This narrows the granting of rights to only the users, groups, and other objects in that container. Granting rights only to a specific container also means that users have to be logged in before receiving rights, which would not be the case with granting rights to [Public].

Now you will look at two examples of using groups to assign trustee rights.

EXAMPLE 10-2: Assigning group Trustee rights at F. D. Roosevelt Investments Inc.

FDR has removed the [Public] trustee assignment from the [Root] of the Directory tree and has granted the AcctExecs group the Browse Object right [B] and Compare and Read Property rights [CR] for the Sales Organizational Unit. This lets the group see all objects in their branch of the Directory tree and read the object property values.

In addition, the AcctExecs Group is being given the right to let group members add themselves to access control lists (ACLs) for objects in the Sales Organizational Unit object. This will be especially useful for printing problems, because all members of the group will then have more control of the printing process using the workgroup's laser printer.

What effective rights does Maria Pinzon, the administrative assistant for sales, have to the Sales Organizational Unit object? As Figure 10-15 shows, because Maria doesn't have any trustee assignments as a user, her effective rights are determined by her group membership.

10

	Trustee Assignments		Object:	🖳 Sales
MPinzon:	User	Object Rights	[	]
	Group AcctExecs	Object Rights	[B	]
	Effective Rights		[B	]
	User	Property Rights:		
		All Properties	[	]
	Group AcctExecs	Property Rights:		
		All Properties	[CR A	]
	Effective Rights	All Properties	[CR A	]

Figure 10-15   Maria's Object and Property rights to Sales object

What effective rights does Paul Drake have to the Sales Organizational Unit object? As shown in Figure 10-16, Paul's Supervisor Object right [S] and Supervisor Property right [S] still give Paul rights to the object and its properties.

Trustee Assignments		Object:	🖳 Sales	
PDrake:	User	Object Rights	[S]	
	Group AcctExecs	Object Rights	[B]	
			[SBCDR]	
	User	Property Rights:		
		All Properties	[S]	
	Group AcctExecs	Property Rights:		
		All Properties	[CR A]	
	Effective Rights	All Properties	[SCRWA]	

Figure 10-16   Paul's Object rights to Sales object

For another example, let's return to CBE Labs. The Testing & Evaluation Staff workgroup of CBE Labs has asked permission to link some of the servers it tests into the CBE Labs network. After much consideration, permission has been granted. To facilitate management of the servers and their associated volumes in the CBE Labs Directory tree, the NetWare servers and their associated volumes will be placed in the Network Organizational Unit object.

The members of the Lab_Staff group will have Supervisor rights to the Network object. This will let them create and manage objects as necessary in this section of the Directory tree.

The process for assigning rights to groups is the same as for assigning rights to individual users. Just as with individual users, Object rights and Property rights are granted using either the object to which access is being granted or the object that is receiving the trustee assignment. The same steps detailed earlier for granting Georgia Burns trustee rights to the Test&Eval Organizational Unit object are used to grant the Lab_Staff group a trustee assignment to the Network Organizational Unit. We'll use the method of granting the trustee assignment from the object that the rights will access, and we'll also use the shortcut menu to open the Trustees of *ObjectName* dialog box.

To grant the Lab_Staff group trustee rights to the Network Organizational Unit object from the Network Organizational Unit object, follow these steps:

1. If NetWare Administrator is not open, launch it.

2. Browse the tree to locate and right-click to select the Network Organizational Unit object. The object shortcut menu appears, as Figure 10-17 shows.

   Notice that the object shortcut menu includes both the Rights to Other Objects command and the Trustees of this Object command. You can use the object shortcut menu to display either the Rights to Other Objects dialog box or the Trustees of *ObjectName* dialog box.

3. Click the Trustees of this Object command on the object shortcut menu. The Trustees of Network dialog box is displayed.

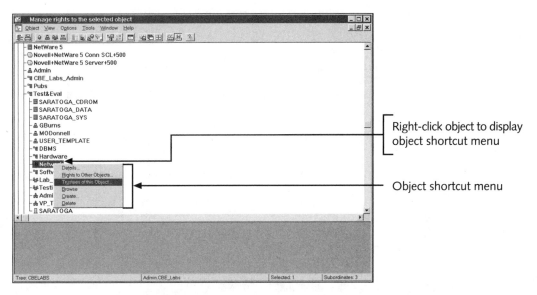

Right-click object to display object shortcut menu

Object shortcut menu

Figure 10-17   Object shortcut menu

4. Click the Add Trustee button to display the Select Object dialog box.

5. Select the Lab_Staff Group object, then click OK. The Lab_Staff group is made a trustee of the Network Organizational Unit object, as Figure10–18 shows. Do not close the Trustees of Network dialog box at this time.

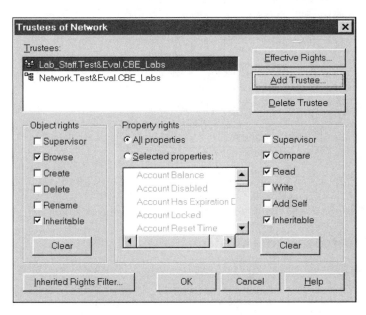

Figure 10-18   Trustees of Network dialog box

10

The steps for granting the Lab_Staff group specific Object rights and Property rights are the same as for granting specific rights to Georgia Burns.

To grant the Lab_Staff group Object rights and Property rights to the Test&Eval Organizational Unit object, follow these steps:

1. Make sure the Lab_Staff.Test&Eval.CBE_Labs trustee is selected in the Trustees list. If it isn't, click it to select it.

2. In the Object Rights box, click the Supervisor check box to select it, then click the Browse check box to unselect it.

3. In the Property Rights box, make sure that the All Properties radio button is selected. If it isn't, click it to select it.

4. In the Property Rights box, click the Supervisor check box to select it, then click the Compare check box and Read check box to unselect them. The Trustees of Network dialog box now appears as Figure 10-19 shows.

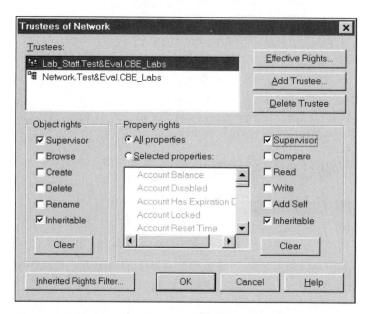

Figure 10-19   Network group's Object and Property rights to Network

5. Click OK to close the Trustees of Network dialog box.

Rights Assigned to an Organizational Role

You can also create assigned rights by granting trustee assignments to an Organizational Role object. These rights will be available to any user who occupies this organizational role. The advantage of this method is that when a new person takes over a job, you don't have to take away trustee assignments from one user and create them for another—you simply change the occupant of the position. Because the trustee assignments belong to the position, they are available only to the person(s) occupying the position.

The user's effective rights are the combination of his or her (1) user trustee assignments, (2) group memberships, and (3) organizational roles occupied.

You will start by looking at the FDR example, and then you will look at CBE Labs.

EXAMPLE 10-3: Assigning organizational role Trustee rights at F. D. Roosevelt Investments, Inc.

Edgar Plank is the FDR vice president for sales and as such is the occupant of the VP_Sales organizational role in the FDR Directory tree. He is also a member of the AcctExecs group, which has the Browse Object right [B] and Compare and Read Property rights [CR] for the Sales Organizational Unit. Edgar has no trustee assignments granted directly to him.

The VP_Sales Organizational Role object is granted the Create, Delete, and Rename Object rights [CDR] and the Supervisor Property right to all properties [SCRWA].

What effective rights does Edgar Plank have to the Sales Organizational Unit object? As Figure 10-20 shows, because Edgar doesn't have any trustee assignments as a user, his effective rights are determined by his group membership and the organizational role he occupies.

	Trustee Assignments		Object:	▢▤ Sales
EPlank:	User	Object Rights	[ ]	
	Group AcctExecs	Object Rights	[B]	
	OrgRole VP_Sales	Object Rights	[CDR]	
	Effective Rights		[BCDR]	
	User	Property Rights: All Properties	[ ]	
	Group AcctExecs	Property Rights: All Properties	[CR A]	
	OrgRole: VP_Sales	Property Rights: All Properties	[S]	
	Effective Rights	All Properties	[SCRWA]	

Figure 10-20   Edgar's Object rights to FDR object

Paul Drake does not occupy any organizational role defined in the Directory tree.

What effective rights does Paul Drake have to the Sales Organizational Unit object? As Figure 10-21 shows, Paul's Supervisor Object right [S] and Supervisor Property right [S] still give Paul rights to the object and its properties.

Trustee Assignments			Object:	🖳 Sales
PDrake:	User	Object Rights	[S]	
	Group AcctExecs	Object Rights	[B]	
	OrgRole None	Object Rights	[ ]	
	Effective Rights		[SBCDR]	
	User	Property Rights:		
		All Properties	[S]	
	GroupAcctExecs	Property Rights:		
		All Properties	[CR A]	
	OrgRole: None	Property Rights:		
		All Properties	[ ]	
	Effective Rights	All Properties	[SCRWA]	

Figure 10-21   Paul's Object rights

For another example, you will consider the trustee assignments made at CBE Labs. Georgia Burns, the vice president for testing and evaluation, should be granted Supervisor Object and Property rights to the Test&Eval branch of the CBE Labs Directory tree because of her acknowledged skill as a network administrator. At CBE Labs, however, network administration skills are a requirement for this position. This means that whoever occupies the position of vice president for testing and evaluation can administer the Test&Eval branch of the Directory tree. Therefore, it makes sense to make the supervisor Object and Property rights trustee assignment for that branch to the VP_Testing&_Evaluation Organizational Role object. Then, whoever occupies that organizational role will automatically have the needed rights. Furthermore, the network administrator won't have to delete the trustee assignment for one User object and assign it to another.

The CBE Labs network administrator has not removed the [Public] trustee assignment to the [Root] object. Taking this into account, Figure 10-22 shows Georgia's effective rights to the Test&Eval organizational Unit object after the trustee assignment has been shifted.

The CBE Labs network administrator needs to delete the trustee assignment for the GBurns User object to the Test&Eval Organizational Unit object and then add the VP_Testing&_Evaluation Organizational Role object as a trustee. Because the GBurns User object occupies the VP_Testing&_Evaluation organizational role, Georgia Burns will still have the same access to network resources as before.

GBurns:	User	Object Rights	[	]
	[Public] trustee	Object Rights	[B	]
	Group: LabStaff	Object Rights	[	]
	OrgRole: VP_Testing_&_Evaluation	Object Rights	[S	]
	Effective Rights		[SBCDR	]
	User	Property Rights: All Properties	[	]
	[Public] Trustee	Property Rights: All Properties	[	]
	Group: LabStaff	Property Rights All Properties	[	]
	OrgRole: VP_Testing_&_Evaluation	Property Rights: All Properties	[S	]
	Effective Rights	All Properties:	[SCRWA	]

Figure 10-22   Georgia's Object rights

Make trustee assignments for organizational roles in exactly the same way as you would for users and groups, using either the Trustees of *ObjectName* dialog box or the Rights to Other Objects dialog box. You can also delete trustee assignments using either the Delete Trustee button in the Trustees of *ObjectName* dialog box or the Delete Assignment button in the Rights to Other Objects dialog box.

To delete Property and Object trustee rights to an object from the object itself, follow these general steps:

1. Click the object name or icon to select it. Then click Object on the menu bar and click Trustees of this Object to display the Trustees of *Objectname* dialog box.
   or
   Right-click the object name or icon to select it and display the shortcut menu. Then click Trustees of this Object to display the Trustees of *Objectname* dialog box.

2. Click the trustee in the Trustees list to select it, then click the Delete Trustee button.

To delete Property and Object trustee rights to an object from a Trustee object itself, follow these steps:

1. Click the object name or icon to select it. Then click Object on the menu bar and click Rights to Other Objects to display the Search Context dialog box.
   or
   Right-click the object name or icon to select it and display the shortcut menu. Then click Rights to Other Objects to display the Search Context dialog box.

2. Use the Search Context dialog box to set the search context for the search for the trustee's rights to other objects in the Directory tree and to search for these trustee rights.

3. Click the object in the Assigned Objects list to select it, then click the Delete Assignment button.

To delete the trustee assignment to Georgia Burns and grant the VP_Testing_&_Evaluation organizational role trustee rights to the Test&Eval Organizational Unit object from the Test&Eval Organizational Unit object, follow these steps:

1. If NetWare Administrator is not open, launch it.

2. Click the Test&Eval Organizational Unit object to select it, click Object on the menu bar, and then click the Trustees of this Object command on the Object menu. The Trustees of Test&Eval dialog box is displayed.

3. Click the trustee GBurns.Test&Eval.CBE_Labs in the Trustees list, as Figure 10-23 shows.

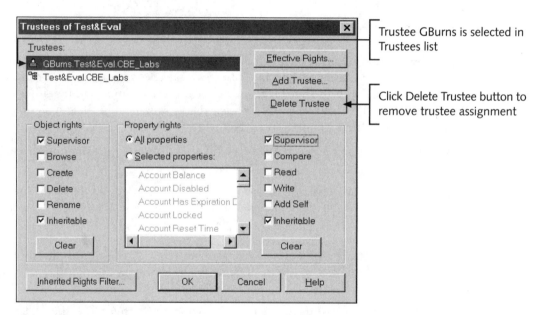

Figure 10-23   GBurns selected in Trustees of Test&Eval dialog box

4. To delete the trustee GBurns.Test&Eval.CBE_Labs from the Trustees list, click the Delete Trustee button. Click Yes to confirm the deletion.

5. To display the Select Object dialog box, click the Add Trustee button.

6. Browse the tree to locate and select the VP_Test&Eval Organizational Role object, then click OK. The VP_Testing&_Evaluation Organizational Role object is made a trustee of the Test&Eval Organizational Unit object.

7. In the Object Rights area, click the Supervisor check box to select it, then click the Browse check box to unselect it.

8. In the Property Rights area, make sure that the All Properties radio button is selected. If it isn't, click it to select it.

9. In the Property Rights area, click the Supervisor check box to select it, then click the Compare check box and Read check box to unselect them. The Trustees of Test&Eval dialog box now appears, as Figure 10-24 shows.

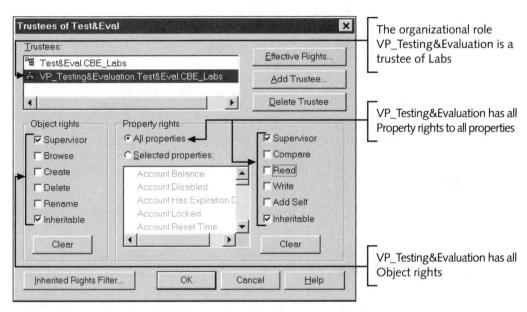

Figure 10-24   VP_Testing_&_Evaluation Organizational Role object's Object and Property rights to Test&Eval

10. Click OK to close the Trustees of Test&Eval dialog box.

Security Equivalence and Rights Assigned to a Container Object

You can grant trustee rights to container objects—the [Root] object, Country objects, Organization objects, and Organizational Unit objects. These rights will be directly available to any user, group, or organizational role that is in the container object, because each object in a container object has **security equivalence** to the container object. When Object A is security equivalent to Object B, Object A is granted all the rights that Object B has been granted. Therefore, because the User object GBurns is located in the Test&Eval Organizational Unit container, GBurns is security equivalent to Test&Eval.CBE_Labs and automatically has all rights granted to Test&Eval.CBE_Labs.

Actually, it is a little more complex than this. An object in a container is security equivalent to all the container objects in the object's complete name. So GBurns is also security equivalent to CBE_Labs, as Figure 10-25 shows.

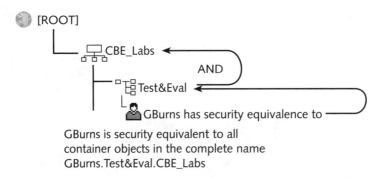

GBurns is security equivalent to all
container objects in the complete name
GBurns.Test&Eval.CBE_Labs

Figure 10-25   Security equivalence and container objects

Assigning rights to container objects is a powerful way to control trustee assignments. Every object in the container object, or in child container objects in the Directory tree, has the access rights of the trustee assignments granted to the container. Thus all users, groups, and organizational roles, for example, in a container have the same access to network resources created by the trustee assignments to the container.

As usual, we'll start by looking at the FDR example; then we'll look at CBE Labs.

EXAMPLE 10-4: Assigning container object Trustee rights at F. D. Roosevelt Investments Inc.

Although the network administrator for FDR has removed the [Public] trustee from the [Root] of the Directory tree, he still wants to let the users browse the tree. To do this, he has assigned the Browse Object right [B] to the FDR Organization object. He has also assigned the Compare and Read Property rights [CR] to all properties to the FDR Organization object, so that users can see the setting values for the objects in the Directory tree.

Edgar Plank, the FDR vice president for sales, occupies the VP_Sales organizational role in the FDR Directory tree and is a member of the AcctExecs group. Edgar has no trustee assignments granted directly to him.

What effective rights does Edgar Plank have to the FDR Organization object? Edgar doesn't have any trustee assignments as a user, and the rights he has because of his group membership and organizational role occupancy are only for the Sales Organizational Unit. As Figure 10-26 shows, his effective rights are determined by the rights granted to the FDR Organization object and by his security equivalence to this object because it is part of his complete name—EPlank.Sales.FDR.

Trustee Assignments		Object:	FDR	
EPlank:	User	Object Rights	[	]
	Group AcctExecs	Object Rights	[	]
	OrgRole VP_Sales	Object Rights	[	]
	Container: FDR		[B	]
	Effective Rights		[B	]
	User	Property Rights:		
		All Properties	[	]
	Group AcctExecs	Property Rights:		
		All Properties	[	]
	OrgRole: VP_Sales	Property Rights:		
		All Properties	[	]
	Container: FDR	Property Rights:		
		All Properties	[CR	]
	Effective Rights	All Properties:	[CR	]

Figure 10-26   Edgar's Object rights

You can see another example of effective rights with the Test&Eval Organizational Unit. To let all the CBE Labs employees in Test&Eval see the objects in the Test&Eval Organizational Unit, you need to make the trustee assignment only to the Test&Eval Organizational Unit object itself. However, it turns out that NetWare automatically makes a container object a trustee of itself, but leaves Object and Property rights undefined. Undefined rights are indicated by grayed boxes next to the Object and Property rights lists, as Figure 10-27 shows.

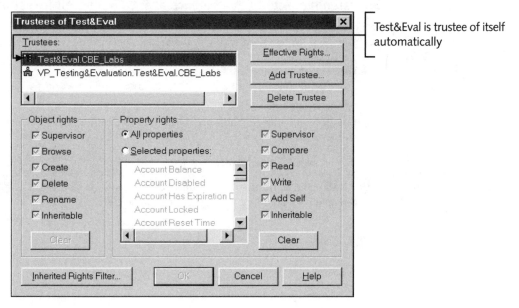

Test&Eval is trustee of itself automatically

Figure 10-27   Test&Eval Organizational Unit object as a trustee of itself

Thus any rights the network administrator wants to grant to objects in the container, typically the Browse Object right [B] and the Compare and Read Property rights [CR], must be assigned by the network administrator. To change the trustee rights for a container object, we would use the process for assigning rights already discussed.

Rights Assigned Directly by Security Equivalence

Any object in a container object is automatically security equivalent to the container object because of its context in that container. However, you can also create security equivalence by directly assigning it on an object's Security Equal to page in the object's Object dialog box. Granting access rights using the Security Equal to page is similar to granting access rights by making a user a member of a group. It is also important to note that security equivalence of Object A to Object B grants Object A only the rights *specifically granted* to Object B, not to any rights that Object B has because of security equivalence. That is, if Object B is security equivalent to Object C, Object A does not have the rights that Object B obtains by being security equivalent to Object C.

A common use of security equivalence is to grant select users Supervisor privileges on the network by making them security equivalent to the Admin user.

 Although an object is security equivalent to all container objects in the object's complete name, the container objects are not listed in the Security Equal To list on the Security Equal To page.

EXAMPLE 10-5: Assigning security equivalence at F. D. Roosevelt Investments Inc.

Eleanor Franklin is the president of FDR. She has asked the network administrator for FDR to grant her Supervisor privileges on the network so that she can check whatever she needs to whenever she needs to. To do this, the network administrator has made her security equivalent to the Admin object. Regardless of whatever other rights Eleanor has assigned to her, her security equivalence to Admin grants her full supervisory rights throughout the network.

Edgar Plank, the FDR Vice President for Sales, has also been made security equivalent to the Admin user. Although he occupies the VP_Sales organizational role in the FDR Directory tree and is a member of the AcctExecs group, Edgar has no trustee assignments granted directly to him.

What effective rights does Edgar Plank have to the Investments Organizational Unit object? Edgar doesn't have any trustee assignments as a user, and the rights he has because of his group membership and organizational role occupancy are only for the Sales Organizational Unit. As Figure 10-28 shows, however, his security equivalence to Admin grants him full access to the Investments object.

Trustee Assignments		Object: 🖳 Investments	
EPlank:	User	Object Rights	[ ]
	GroupAcctExecs	Object Rights	[ ]
	OrgRole VP_Sales	Object Rights	[ ]
	Container: FDR	Object Rights	[ ]
	Security Equivalence: Admin	Object Rights	[SBCDR]
	Effective Rights		[SBCDR]
	User	Property Rights: All Properties	[ ]
	Group AcctExecs	Property Rights All Properties	[ ]
	OrgRole: VP_Sales	Property Rights: All Properties	[ ]
	Container: FDR	Property Rights: All Properties	[ ]
	Security Equivalence: Admin	Property Rights: All Properties	[SCRWA]
	Effective Rights	All Properties:	[SCRWA]

Figure 10-28   Edgar's Object rights to Investments object

Now you will look at an example at CBE Labs. Ted Simpson is the information systems manager for CBE Labs, and as such he needs to have the security equivalence of the Admin user.

To make Ted Simpson security equivalent of the Admin user, follow these steps:

1. If NetWare Administrator is not open, launch it.

2. Double-click the TSimpson User object in InfoSystems.CBE_Labs_Admin. CBE_Labs to display the User: TSimpson object dialog box.

3. If necessary, use the scroll arrows to scroll through the page buttons until the Security Equal To button appears.

4. Click the Security Equal To button on the button bar. The Security Equal To page is displayed, as Figure 10-29 shows.

   Notice that although Ted Simpson has security equivalence to the container objects InfoSystems, CBE_Labs_Admin, and CBE_Labs, none of these is listed in the Security Equal To list. The security equivalence to container objects is not displayed in this list.

   Group memberships, however, also give a member a security equivalence to the group, and that security equivalence does appear in the Security Equal To list.

10

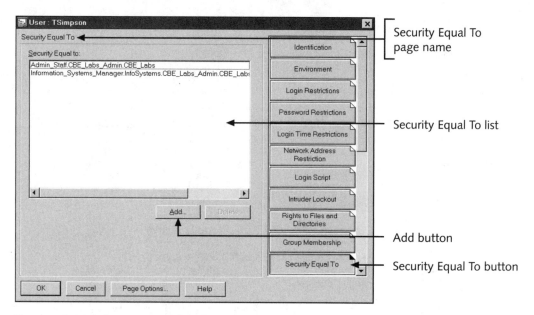

Figure 10-29 Security Equal To page

5. Click the Add button to display the Select Object dialog box. Browse the tree to locate and select your Admin user object, similar to Figure 10-30.

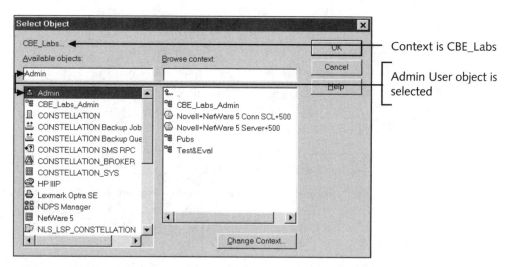

Figure 10-30 Selecting Admin object

6. Click OK. The Admin.CBE_Labs object is added to the Security Equal To list, as Figure 10-31 shows.

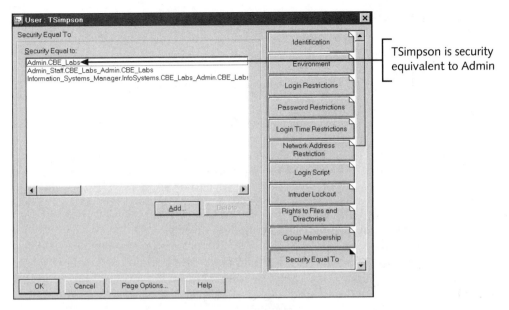

TSimpson is security equivalent to Admin

Figure 10-31   Completed Security Equal To page

7. Click OK to close the User: TSimpson Object dialog box.

Users should not be able to add themselves to their own Security Equal To list. Otherwise they could assign themselves security equivalence of the Admin user or another network administrator.

Inherited Rights

So far we've discussed trustee assignments made directly to the user, or to a group or organizational role associated with the user. We've also discussed trustee assignments made to the [Public] trustee and object security equivalence to container objects and leaf objects as a way to gain access to network resources.

Generally, the user's effective rights are the sum of all these rights. However, calculating a user's effective rights is actually a little more complex than this, because of inherited rights.

Inherited rights in a Directory tree are rights available in one container that were actually granted to a container higher in the Directory tree. These rights will be available to any object in the lower container object. Figure 10-32 shows these relationships.

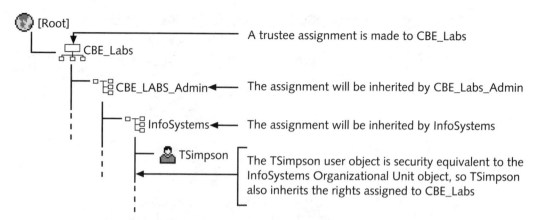

Figure 10-32   Inherited rights and container objects

Inherited rights are available in the Directory tree because an object is security equivalent to each container in its complete name. However, inherited rights differ from security equivalence because inheritance works only if no direct trustee assignments are made to an object.

EXAMPLE 10-6: Inherited rights at F. D. Roosevelt Investments Inc.

Maria Pinzon, the administrative assistant for sales, is a member of the AcctExecs group but has no trustee assignments granted directly to her. AcctExecs has the Browse Object right [B] and the Compare, Read, and Add Self Property rights [CRA] for all properties to the Sales Organizational Unit. No rights are granted to the [Public] trustee.

The FDR network manager has just granted the Browse Object right [B] and the Compare and Read Property rights [CR] for all properties to the FDR Organization object.

What effective rights does Maria have to the Sales Organizational Unit object? Because Maria has specific trustee assignments for the AcctExecs group, the rights granted to the FDR Organization object have no effect on her rights in the Sales Organizational Unit, as Figure 10-33 shows.

Trustee Assignments		Object:	⬚⬛ Sales	
MPinzon:	User	Object Rights	[	]
	Group AcctExecs	Object Rights	[B	]
	[Public] trustee	Object Rights	[	]
	Container: Sales	Object Rights	[	]
	Container: FDR	Object Rights	NO EFFECT	
	Effective Rights		[B	]
	User	Property Rights:		
		All Properties	[	]
	Group AcctExecs	Property Rights:		
		All Properties	[CR	A]
	[Public] Trustee	Property Rights:		
		All Properties	[	]
	Container: Sales	Property Rights:		
		All Properties	[	]
	Container: FDR	Property Rights:		
		All Properties	NO EFFECT	
	Effective Rights	All Properties:	[CR	A]

Figure 10-33   Maria's effective rights in Sales

What effective rights does Maria have to the Investments Organizational Unit object? Maria's group membership has no specific rights granted here. Therefore, her rights are those inherited from the trustee assignments granted to the FDR Organization object, as Figure 10-34 shows.

10

Trustee Assignments		Object:	⬚⬛ Investments	
MPinzon:	User	Object Rights	[	]
	Group AcctExecs	Object Rights	[	]
	[Public] trustee	Object Rights	[	]
	Container: Sales	Object Rights	[	]
	Container: FDR	Object Rights	[B	]
	Effective Rights		[B	]
	User	Property Rights:		
		All Properties	[	]
	Group AcctExecs	Property Rights:		
		All Properties	[	]
	[Public] Trustee	Property Rights:		
		All Properties	[	]
	Container: Sales	Property Rights:		
		All Properties	[	]
	Container: FDR	Property Rights:		
		All Properties	[CR	]
	Effective Rights	All Properties:	[CR	]

Figure 10-34   Maria's effective rights in Investments

In the FDR example just given, Maria inherited the Property rights from the FDR container object. However, Property rights are inherited only if they are granted to all properties of the object. For example, if the FDR Organization object had been granted only the Compare and Read Property rights [CR] to object names instead of to all properties, containers lower in the Directory tree would not inherit these rights.

Thus, if no trustee assignment is made for a user or group in a container, the user or group will inherit the rights from the parent container(s). A user's effective rights in a container can be modified by making a new trustee assignment to either the user or to a group to which the user belongs. The rights specified in the new trustee assignment will override the inherited rights for that group or user name in the specified container, as in Maria's rights to the Sales Organizational Unit.

The Inherited Rights Filter

As discussed, when you make a specific trustee assignment in a container, this assignment overrides any rights inherited from a parent container. You can also block rights from being inherited even if no specific trustee assignment is made. When you do not want trustee assignments to be inherited by a lower container, NetWare lets you prevent rights from being inherited by providing each container object and directory with what is called an **Inherited Rights Filter (IRF)**. The IRF blocks selected rights from passing into the lower container object structure. When you first create a container, the IRF allows all rights to be inherited. Thereafter, removing rights from the IRF prevents the container or directory from inheriting rights no longer specified in the IRF.

The IRF filters rights inherited from a higher container object, but does not affect a trustee assignment made in the current container object.

An IRF is created for every object (and, as you will learn later, for every directory and file) and is used to determine which rights a trustee inherits. You can picture the IRF as a series of gates—one for each right. Figure 10-35 shows these relationships.

Initially, as Figure 10-35 shows, the IRF allows all rights to be inherited—all the gates are open. This also can be seen in the Inherited Rights Filter dialog box used in NetWare Administrator, which Figure 10-36 shows.

Object Rights IRF:

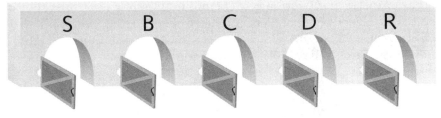

Property Rights IRF:

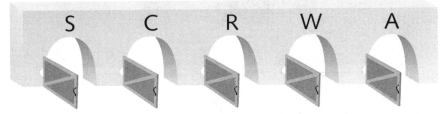

Figure 10-35   Inherited Rights Filter for Object rights and Property rights

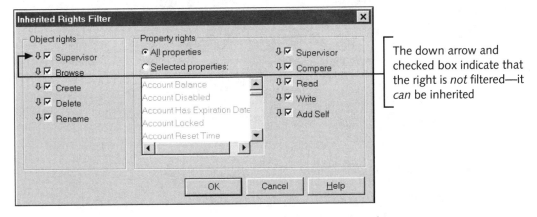

Figure 10-36   Inherited Rights Filter dialog box in NetWare Administrator

In the Inherited Rights Filter dialog box in Figure 10-36, all the check boxes are checked and a downward pointing arrow appears next to each check box. A checked check box with a downward pointing arrow indicates that the right is not being filtered. That is, the gate is open and the right can be inherited.

To filter a right—to prevent it from being inherited—deselect the appropriate check box in the Inherited Rights Filter dialog box for the object. This "closes the gate" and stops inherited rights from getting through.

For example, the Lab_Staff group at CBE Labs now has supervisory rights to the Network Organizational Unit object. The group does not want other users to be able to modify this object or its properties. Therefore, the group will use the IRF for the Network object to block the Create, Delete, and Rename Object rights [CDR] and the Supervisor, Write, and Add Self Property rights [SWA] from being inherited. Then the "gates" to Network will appear as Figure 10-37 shows.

NetLab Object Rights IRF:

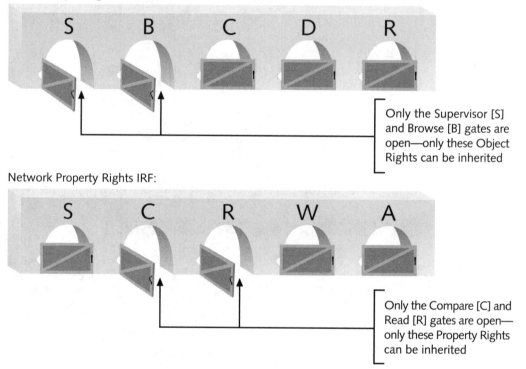

Only the Supervisor [S] and Browse [B] gates are open—only these Object Rights can be inherited

Network Property Rights IRF:

Only the Compare [C] and Read [R] gates are open— only these Property Rights can be inherited

Figure 10-37   Inherited Rights Filter for Object rights and Property rights for Network

You can access the IRF for an object through the Trustees of *ObjectName* dialog box.

To modify the Inherited Rights Filter for Object and Property trustee rights of an object, follow these general steps:

1. Click the object name or icon to select it. Then click Object on the menu bar, and click Trustees of this Object to display the Trustees of *Objectname* dialog box.
   or
   Right-click the object name or icon to select it and display the shortcut menu. Then click Trustees of this Object to display the Trustees of *Objectname* dialog box.

2. Click the Inherited Rights Filter button.

3. Use the settings controls in the Inherited Rights Filter dialog box to manage inherited Object and Property rights.

To set the Inherited Rights Filter for the Network Organizational Unit object, follow these steps:

1. If NetWare Administrator is not open, launch it.

2. Browse the tree to locate and click the Network Organizational Unit object to select it; then click Object on the menu bar.

3. Click Trustees of this Object on the Object menu. The Trustees of Network dialog box is displayed, as Figure 10-38 shows.

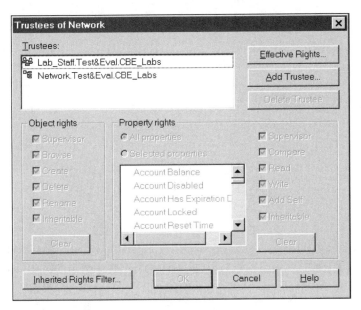

10

Figure 10-38 Trustees of Network dialog box

4. Click the Inherited Rights Filter button to display the Inherited Rights Filter dialog box.

5. In the Inherited Rights Filter dialog box, click the Create, Delete, and Rename Object rights check boxes to deselect them. Then click the Supervisor, Write, and Add Self Property rights check boxes to deselect them. The Inherited Rights Filter dialog box now appears as Figure 10-39 shows.

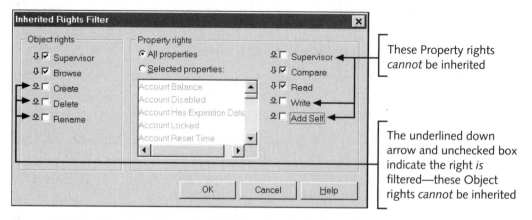

These Property rights *cannot* be inherited

The underlined down arrow and unchecked box indicate the right *is* filtered—these Object rights *cannot* be inherited

Figure 10-39   Completed Inherited Rights Filter dialog box for NetLab

Notice in Figure 10-39 that each downward pointing arrow has been replaced with an arrow with a line under it for all rights that are being filtered out. This symbol and the unchecked check box indicate a filtered out or blocked ability to inherit a trustee right.

6. Click OK to return to the Trustees of Network dialog box.

7. Click OK.

The Inherited Rights Filter only reduces rights and never adds to them.

When you are calculating a trustee's effective rights for an object, you must subtract any Inherited Rights filtered out by the object's IRF. Remember, however, that the IRF blocks only inherited rights, not what rights can be directly granted to an object. Moreover, remember that if trustee rights are directly granted to an object, this grant itself stops all inherited rights so that the IRF has no effect in this case. The IRF blocks only inherited rights when such rights can, in fact, be inherited.

Now you will consider an example at FDR Investments.

EXAMPLE 10-7: Inherited rights at F. D. Roosevelt Investments Inc.

Maria Pinzon, the administrative assistant for sales, is a member of the AcctExecs group but has no trustee assignments granted directly to her. AcctExecs has the Browse Object right [B] and the Compare, Read, and Add Self Property rights [CRA] for all properties to the Sales Organizational Unit only, not to other branches of the Directory tree. There are no rights granted to the [Public] trustee.

The FDR network manager has granted the Browse Object right [B] and the Compare and Read Property rights [CR] for all properties to the FDR Organization object. However, because the Investments group has decided that it doesn't want users reading property values for objects in the Investments organizational unit, the network manager has also implemented an IRF for the Investment Organizational Unit object that blocks all Property rights except Supervisor [CRWA].

What effective rights does Maria have to the Investments Organizational Unit object? Maria's group membership has no specific rights granted here. Therefore, her rights are those she inherits from trustee assignments granted to the FDR Organization object, minus those blocked by the IRF, as Figure 10-40 shows.

	Trustee Assignments	Object:				Investments
MPinzon:	User	Object Rights	[		]	
	Group AcctExecs	Object Rights	[		]	
	[Public] trustee	Object Rights	[		]	
	Container: Investments	Object Rights	[		]	
	Container: FDR	Object Rights	[	B	]	
LESS	IRF: Investments	Object Rights	[		]	
	Effective Rights		[	B	]	
	User	Property Rights: All Properties	[		]	
	Group AcctExecs	Property Rights: All Properties	[		]	
	[Public] Trustee	Property Rights: All Properties	[		]	
	Container: Investments	Property Rights: All Properties	[		]	
	Container: FDR	Property Rights: All Properties	[	CR	]	
LESS	IRF: Investments	Property Rights: All Properties	[	CRWA	]	
	Effective Rights	All Properties:	[		]	

Figure 10-40   Maria's effective rights in Investments

In the FDR example just given, Maria inherited the Compare and Read Property rights [CR] to Investments from the FDR container object. However, the IRF blocks these Property rights, so Maria has no Property rights to Investments.

Handle the Supervisor right carefully in IRFs. Although the Supervisor right cannot be removed from an IRF for a directory or file (as you'll learn later), it can be removed from an IRF for an object. This lets you split administrative duties throughout the Directory tree. For example, the CBE Labs organization in Great Britain could be managed by a different person from whoever manages the CBE Labs organization in the United States. Blocking the Supervisor right appropriately using IRFs would make sure each of the two network administrators would have control of only his or her portion of the CBE Labs Directory tree.

There is a potential problem here, however. If no trustee was assigned Supervisor rights to an object and then the object's IRF blocked inherited Supervisor rights, then the object would be cut off from anyone's control. To help prevent this problem, Novell has designed the NetWare 5.0 utilities so that you cannot block the Supervisor Object right unless some object has been granted specific Supervisor rights to the object.

Unfortunately, the Supervisor right can be assigned to any object, including the object that will have the IRF set. For example, you could assign the Supervisor Object right to the Test&Eval Organizational Unit object in the CBE Labs Directory tree and then block the Supervisor right in the Test&Eval Organizational Unit object's IRF. Because the Supervisor object right had been assigned, this would be permitted. But doing so would cut off the Test&Eval branch of the tree because a user cannot access the granted Supervisor right— you can't log in as an Organizational Unit, only as a User. Thus be very careful to assign an object's Supervisor Object right to a user before using the object IRF.

In general, IRFs should be used only when absolutely necessary. A network administrator can usually control access to network resources by directly assigning trustee rights without using IRFs.

Managing Directory Rights and File Rights

Directory rights and File rights control access to the network file system resources. The same concepts and techniques that you learned for trustee assignments of Object rights and files can be applied to Directory rights and File rights.

Trustee assignments for directories and files can be made to the same objects that can have trustee assignments for objects and properties. When you are assigning Directory and File rights, the assignment is made using either the user's User object or the directory or file object dialog box. You can also use the NetWare Client 32 extensions to Windows Explorer to manage Directory and File rights.

Granting trustee rights to a directory automatically grants the same rights to all files in that directory. To change the trustee rights for a file within that directory, you must change the rights assigned for that specific file.

 Although granting the Supervisor Directory or File right [S] automatically grants all Directory and File rights, many network administrators also specifically grant all the other rights as well when granting the Supervisor right [S].

Rights Assigned to the User

Just as with Object and Property rights, the simplest and most straightforward way for a user to gain effective rights is to be granted a trustee assignment as a user. A simple example follows; then you'll see how trustee assignments are actually made using the CBE Laboratories example.

EXAMPLE 10-8: Assigning user directory and file Trustee rights at F. D. Roosevelt Investments Inc.

Figure 10-41 shows the Volume Directory Structure Design Form for the FDR_SERVER01_DATA volume.

Volume Design Form

Created By:	*Network Administrator*		Date:	*9/15/1999*
Volume:	*FDR_SERVER01_DATA*		Capacity:	*2 GB*
NetWare Version:	*5.0*		Note: Functions below are not applicable to 3.1x	

		Block Suballocation:	X	Enable
Block Size:	4 Kbytes			Disable
	8 Kbytes			Not applicable
	16 Kbytes	File Compression:	X	Enable
	32 Kbytes			Disable
X	64 Kbytes			Not applicable
		Data Migration:		Enable
			X	Disable
				Not applicable

Directory Structure Diagram

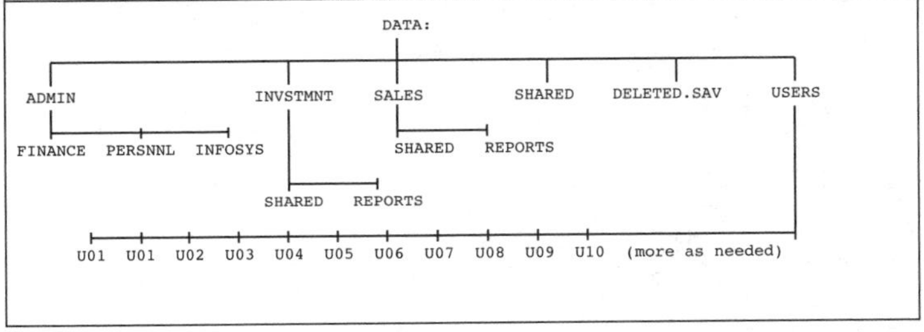

```
                          DATA:
       _____|_____
      |          |          |         |          |        |
    ADMIN     INVSTMNT     SALES     SHARED  DELETED.SAV  USERS
    ___|___                  |___
   |   |   |                SHARED  REPORTS
FINANCE PERSNNL INFOSYS      |___
                           SHARED  REPORTS

    +---+---+---+---+---+---+---+---+---+---+
   U01 U01 U02 U03 U04 U05 U06 U07 U08 U09 U10  (more as needed)
```

Figure 10-41   FDR_SERVER01_DATA: volume

Paul Drake, the lead account executive at FDR, needs to be able to manage the SALES directory and its subdirectories on the FDR_SERVER01_DATA volume. He will be granted all rights—including the Supervisor right—to the SALES directory. When the Supervisor right is granted in the directory, it gives Paul the Supervisor right to all files in that directory, as Figure 10-42 shows.

	Trustee Assignments	Object: ⬚ SALES	
PDrake:	User	Directory Rights	[S]
	Effective Rights		[SRWCEMFA]
	User	File Rights:	[S]
		may be modified for each file as needed	
	Effective Rights		[SRWCEMFA]

Figure 10-42   Paul's effective rights in SALES

Now you'll consider another example: implementation of Directory and File rights at CBE Laboratories. Georgia Burns will also be given all rights (Supervisor [S] and all others) so that she can administer the SARATOGA_SYS and SARATOGA_DATA volumes.

Figure 10-43 shows a recommended directory structure of SARATOGA_SYS. Figure 10-44 shows a recommended directory structure of SARATOGA_DATA.

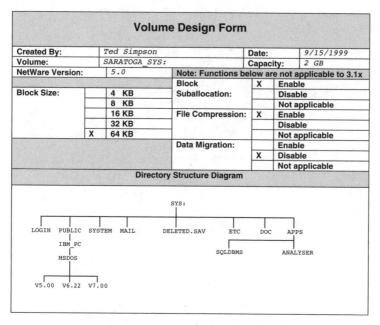

Figure 10-43 Volume Directory Structure Design Form for SARATOGA_SYS: volume

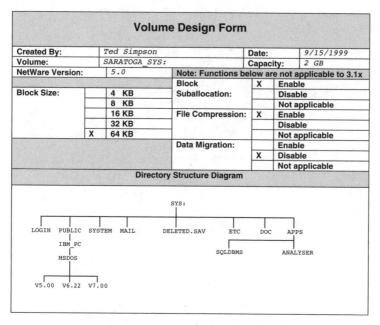

Figure 10-44 Volume Directory Structure Design Form for SARATOGA_DATA volume

Assigning Trustee Rights to a Directory or File from a Trustee Object

You begin by making the trustee assignment to Georgia Burns. As with Object rights, you're assigning trustee rights from the object being granted the trustee assignment. This varies from the previous procedure, however, because you do this from the object's object dialog box.

To grant directory and file trustee rights to an object from a Trustee object itself, you follow these general steps:

1. Click the object, then press [Enter].
   or
   Click the object, click Object on the menu bar, and then click Details.
   or
   Right-click the object, then click Details on the shortcut menu.

2. Switch to the Rights to Files and Directories page.

3. Click the Find button to open the Search Context dialog box and search the Directory tree for existing trustee assignments in the desired context.

4. Click the Add button and use the Select Object dialog box to select the directory or file for which the trustee rights are being granted.

5. Click the appropriate check boxes in the Rights section to select or deselect the rights to be granted.

6. Click OK.

When the trustee assignment is made from the User object (or other Trustee object), NetWare can first search the Directory tree to find and list the directories and files for which the user has rights assigned. The context for this search—all of the tree or a branch of it—is specified as part of the search. Searching the Directory tree takes time, so it is faster to limit the area of the tree that needs to be evaluated. Normally, you should limit the search context to only the part of the Directory tree that includes the objects for which you are granting trustee rights to the user. This step is not required for adding a new trustee assignment, but it is helpful to see what assignments have already been made so that you aren't inadvertently duplicating a previous assignment.

Now you will see how this method could be used to give Georgia Burns her trustee assignment to the root of the SARATOGA_DATA volume, SARATOGA_DATA:\.

To grant Georgia Burns trustee rights to the SARATOGA_DATA:\ directory, follow these steps:

1. If NetWare Administrator is not open, launch it.

2. Right-click the GBurns User object, then click Details. The User: GBurns object dialog box is displayed.

3. If necessary, use the down scroll arrow to scroll through the page buttons until the Rights to Files and Directories button appears.

4. Click the Rights to Files and Directories button on the button bar. The Rights to Files and Directories page is displayed, as Figure 10-45 shows.

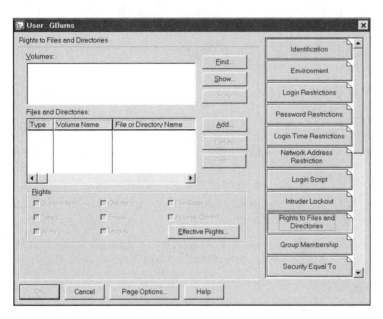

Figure 10-45 Rights to Files and Directories page

5. Click the Find button. The Search Context dialog box appears. If necessary, click the Select Object button to locate the Test&Eval context. In the Select Object dialog box, select the Test&Eval Organizational Unit, then click OK.

6. The Search Context dialog box is displayed with Test&Eval.CBE_Labs in the Context to Begin Search text box. Click the Search Entire Subtree check box to select it, then click OK. A search is done for directory and file trustee assignments for Georgia Burns, and these are then displayed in the Volumes list and Files and Directories list. As Figure 10-46 shows, the only existing trustee assignment for GBurns is to her home directory on the SARATOGA_DATA volume. Notice that if you are using an alias for SARATOGA_DATA, the NetWare Administrator screen shows the actual server and volume name: CONSTELLATION_DATA.

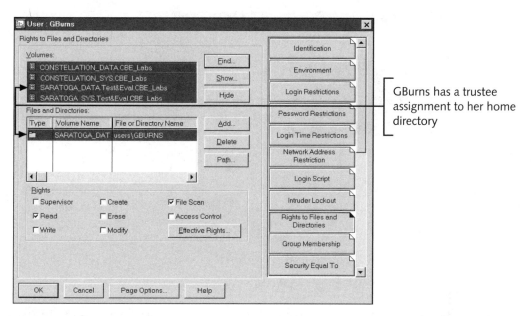

GBurns has a trustee assignment to her home directory

Figure 10-46   User: GBurns dialog box showing current directory and File Trustee rights

The NDS configuration in your test network may vary from the one shown in the figures. For example, if there is no actual second server in your test network, you will have only an Alias to represent RANGER or SARATOGA. In those cases, the actual assignment will be to the CONSTELLATION_DATA volume, even though NetWare Administrator and other Novell utilities may show the alias's name.

7. Click the Add button to display the Select Object dialog box.

8. Select the SARATOGA_DATA Volume object, then click OK. GBurns is assigned default trustee rights of Read [R] and File Scan [F] to the root of the SARATOGA_DATA:\ directory.

If you are using an alias for SARATOGA_DATA, NetWare Administrator now does not show this assignment. This is only temporary. When you save this configuration and then reopen this page, the assignment will show the "true" server and volume name, not the SARATOGA_DATA alias.

9. Click all the unchecked check boxes in the Rights section to assign GBurns all Trustee rights to this directory. The User: GBurns object dialog box appears as Figure 10-47 shows.

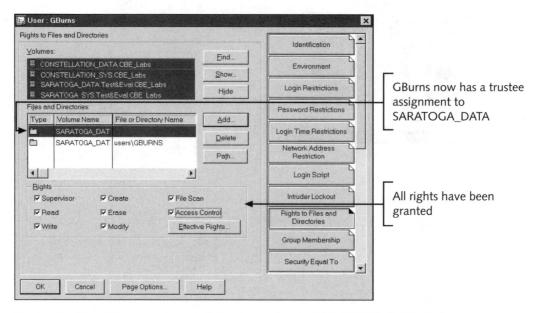

Figure 10-47   GBurns assigned all Trustee rights to SARATOGA_DATA:\ directory

    10. Click OK.

Assigning Trustee Rights to a Directory or File from Windows Explorer

The Novell Client software includes extensions to the Windows Explorer program that let you manage most directory and file rights from Explorer, with one important exception (see Note).

You cannot assign the Supervisor right [S] to a directory or file through Explorer. This must be assigned in NWAdmin.

To grant directory and file trustee rights to an object from Windows Explorer, you follow these general steps:

    1. Launch Explorer.

    2. If necessary, create a drive mapping to the volume that contains the directory or file. (You can also go through Network Neighborhood to locate the volume.)

    3. Expand the branch of the Explorer tree that contains the drive mapping until the directory or file is displayed.

4. Click the directory or file to select it, click File, and then click Properties to display the *ObjectName* Properties dialog box.

5. Click the NetWare Rights tab to display the NetWare rights page.

6. Expand the displayed NDS Directory tree until the object for which the trustee assignment is to be made is displayed.

7. Click the Add button.

8. In the Trustees list, click the object name to select it.

9. Click the check boxes to assign the appropriate rights.

10. Click OK.

The Novell Client extensions to Explorer enable the NDS directory tree to be fully displayed with all the proper icons. Being able to Browse the Directory tree easily in Explorer makes this method quickly accessible when you're using Explorer to check directory structure and contents. The inability to assign the Supervisor right [S], however, somewhat limits the usefulness of this method—you can use it effectively only when you're not concerned about granting the Supervisor right [S].

You will look at one example: you'll again show how Georgia Burns would have her rights to the SARATOGA_DATA:\ directory assigned. This is exactly the same assignment you've already made—we're simply illustrating a third way to do it.

10

To grant Georgia Burns trustee rights to the SARATOGA_DATA:\ directory, follow these steps:

1. Launch Explorer.

2. Expand Network Neighborhood branch to show the CBELabs tree, then expand CBELabs to locate the SARATOGA_DATA volume (or, if you are using an alias, to locate CONSTELLATION_DATA). Click the SARATOGA_DATA (or CONSTELLATION_DATA) icon to select it, click File, and then click Properties, as Figure 10-48 shows.

   The SARATOGA_DATA on Test&Eval Properties dialog box is displayed, as Figure 10-49 shows.

Figure 10-48   File, Properties command

Figure 10-49   SARATOGA_DATA on Test&Eval Properties dialog box

Notice that the NetWare Volume Information page is initially displayed, show-ing volume statistics such as Total Space and Available Space on the volume.

3. Click the NetWare Rights tab. The NetWare Rights page is displayed as Figure 10-50 shows.

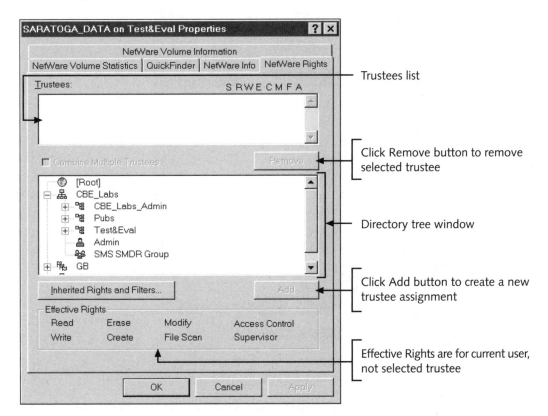

Figure 10-50   NetWare Rights page

This page includes a Trustees list, a window displaying the Directory tree, and a list of the effective rights of the current user. Note that the effective rights are for the current user, not for a trustee. In this case, the current user is DAuer, the CBE Labs network administrator; because he has security equiva-lent to the Admin user, he has all rights including Supervisor.

4. In the Directory tree window, expand the Directory tree until the GBurns User object is visible, then click the GBurns User object to select it, as Figure 10-51 shows.

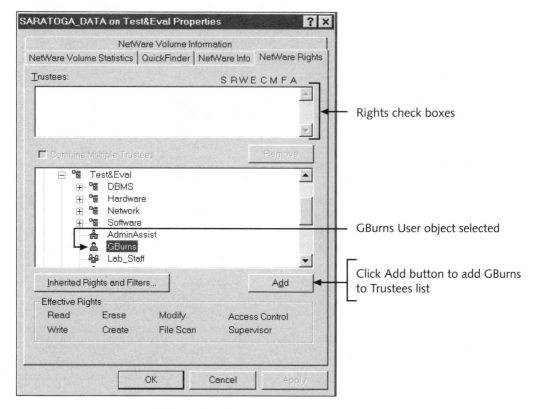

Figure 10-51 Selecting GBurns User object

5. Click the Add button. GBurns.Test&Eval.CBE_Labs is added to the Trustees list, with default rights of Read [R] and File Scan [F].

6. Click GBurns.Test&Eval.CBE_LABS in the Trustees list to select GBurns. Click the check boxes for all the unselected rights to grant them to GBurns. Note that the check box for the Supervisor right [S] is grayed out, which means that the Supervisor right [S] cannot be granted using this method. The dialog box now appears as Figure 10–52 shows.

7. Click OK.

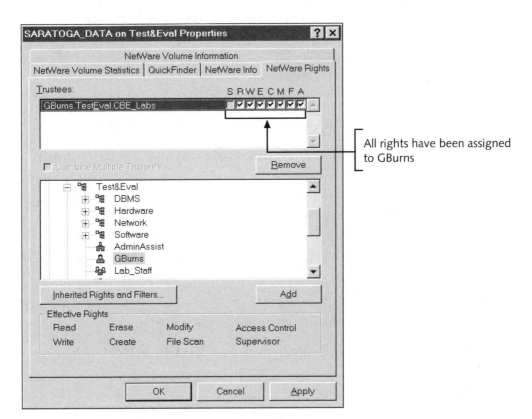

Figure 10-52   Granting Trustee rights to GBurns

Rights Assigned to Groups, Profiles, and Organizational Roles

Directory and file rights can also be assigned to groups and organizational roles, just as Object and Property rights were assigned. In addition, you can grant trustee rights to Profile objects. You have already learned that the Profile object is similar to the Group object, with the particular advantage of being able to have its own login script. The ability to also assign Directory and File rights to a Profile object gives the network administrator a convenient method of assigning Directory and File rights to those who use the Profile objects login script.

The same methods discussed earlier of assigning Directory and File rights to users are used for granting rights to groups and organizational roles. When you decide whether to assign rights to an organizational role, a group, or individual users, the same advantages still apply: It is easier to administer rights to organizational roles and groups. By granting rights to organizational roles and groups, users automatically get appropriate rights if they need them, and removing a user from a group or organizational role effectively removes the user's rights.

For example, Georgia Burns has decided to give the Lab_Staff group Read and File Scan rights [RF] to the SARATOGA_DATA volume. The Lab staff keeps its data in this volume, and these rights will let everyone see what files exist and open and read them. However, [RF] rights will not let users change, delete, or rename the files, so Georgia must grant these additional rights to the appropriate users. One case is the Lab_Staff group, which also needs such rights to the NETWORK directory (and its subdirectories). Georgia will therefore grant the Lab_Staff group Write, Create, Erase, and Modify rights [WCEM] to the NETWORK directory. Because trustee assignments made in one directory are inherited by (flow down to) subdirectories, the Network group will inherit the same rights in the NETWORK\SHARED, NETWORK\TESTDATA, and NETWORK\REPORTS subdirectories.

Rights Assigned to Container Objects and Security Equivalence

You can assign Directory and File rights to container objects just as you assigned Object and Property rights. Again, for granting rights to container objects use the same methods used for assigning Directory and File rights to individual users.

Security equivalencies also work the same. If Object A is security equivalent to Object B, Object A is granted all the Directory and File rights that Object B has been granted. For example, because the CBE Labs information systems manager Ted Simpson is security equivalent to the Admin user, Ted Simpson effectively has the same Directory and File rights as the Admin user. This gives Ted all rights including the Supervisor right [S] to all directories and files on all volumes of all CBE Labs servers.

Inherited Rights and the Inherited Rights Filter

Inherited rights work almost the same for Directory and File rights as they do for Object and Property rights, with one important exception: The IRF cannot block the Supervisor right [S] for Directory and File rights. You can visualize the IRFs for Directory and File rights as Figure 10-53 shows.

Directory rights IRF:

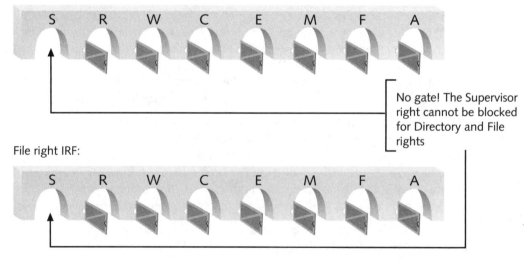

File right IRF:

Figure 10-53 Inherited Rights Filter for Directory rights and File rights

The IRF for a directory or file is accessed through the *ObjectName* object dialog box.

To use NetWare Administrator to modify the Inherited Rights Filter for Directory or File trustee rights of a directory or file, follow these general steps:

1. Click the directory or filename or icon to select it. Then click Object on the menu bar, and click Details to display the *ObjectName* object dialog box.
   or
   Double-click the directory or filename or icon to select it and display the *ObjectName* object dialog box.
   or
   Right-click the object name or icon to select it and display the shortcut menu, then click Details to display the *ObjectName* object dialog box.
   or
   Click to select the directory or file and then press [Enter].

2. Click the Trustees of this Directory or Trustees of this File button.

3. On the Trustees of this Directory or Trustees of this File page, use check boxes in the Inheritance filter area to set the IRF. A checked box enables the right to be inherited; an unchecked box blocks inheritance.

4. Click OK.

Notice that the method of setting the IRF for directories and files is the same as the method of setting the IRF for objects and properties. The IRF default is all check boxes checked, which lets all rights be inherited, and you must uncheck a check box to block the inheritance of the right. The only difference is the Directory and File Supervisor right [S], which cannot be blocked.

For example, the Lab_Staff group at CBE Labs wants only those users who have specifically been granted rights to the SARATOGA_DATA:NETWORK directory to be able to use that directory. You will create the necessary IRF to do this.

To set the Inherited Rights Filter for the SARATOGA_DATA:NETWORK directory, follow these steps:

1. If NetWare Administrator is not open, launch it.

2. Expand the Directory tree until the directories on the SARATOGA_DATA volume are visible. Click the NETWORK Directory object to select it, then click Object on the menu bar, then click Details.

3. Click the Trustees of this Directory button. The Trustees of this Directory page is displayed, as Figure 10-54 shows.

10

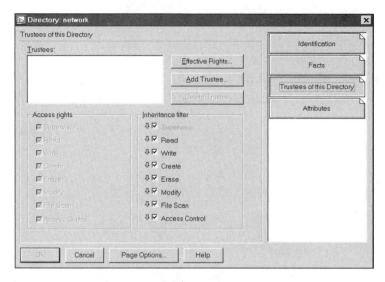

Figure 10-54   Trustees of this Directory page

4. Looking at the Inheritance Filter area, notice that all the check boxes are checked. The Supervisor right [S] check box is checked and grayed out, indicating that you cannot change the setting for this right.

5. Click each of the other check boxes to block those rights from being inherited, as Figure 10-55 shows.

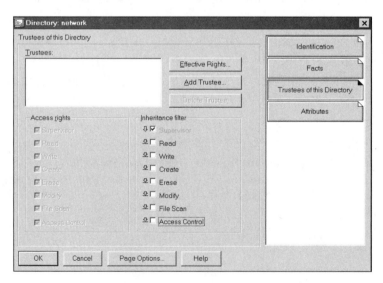

Figure 10-55   Completed Trustees of this Directory page

Notice that in Figure 10-55 each downward pointing arrow has been replaced with an arrow with a line under it for all rights that are being filtered out. This symbol and the unchecked check box indicate a filtered out or blocked ability to inherit a trustee right.

6. Click OK.

Just as with Object and Property rights, a user's effective rights are a combination of his or her assigned rights and inherited rights. Again, it is always a *user* who actually uses trustee rights. You can calculate a user's effective Directory or File rights to a particular directory or file as follows:

1. Combine the assigned rights from trustee assignments made to:

   - The *user*
   - The user as a member of a *group*
   - The user as a member of a *profile*
   - The user as an occupant of an *organizational role*
   - The user as an occupant of a *container object*
   - The user as security equivalent to other objects

   If the user has assigned rights granted to the directory or file, the assigned rights take precedence over inherited rights, inherited rights do not apply, and the IRF has no effect. This combination of rights is the user's effective rights.

2. If the user has no assigned rights granted, the user's trustee assignments granted in a parent container object or directory are inherited. The inherited rights must be checked against the IRF for the directory or file. The inherited rights not blocked by the IRF are the user's effective rights.

EXAMPLE 10-9: Inherited Directory Rights at F. D. Roosevelt Investments Inc.

Maria Pinzon, the administrative assistant for sales, is a member of the AcctExecs group, but has no trustee assignments granted directly to her. AcctExecs has the Read, Write, Create, Erase, Modify, and File Scan Directory rights [RWCEMF] to the FDR_SERVER01/DATA:SALES directory. There is an EVERYONE group at FDR, and Maria, along with everyone else, is a group member. The EVERYONE group has Read and File Scan rights [RF] to the FDR_SERVER01/DATA:\ (the [Root] directory on the DATA volume). No directory or File rights are granted to the [Public] trustee. No other trustee assignments affect Maria directly, but IRFs may limit her inherited rights.

What effective rights does Maria have to the FDR_SERVER01/DATA:SALES directory? Because Maria has specific trustee assignments to SALES from the AcctExecs group, the rights granted to the EVERYONE group to the [Root] directory have no effect on her rights in the SALES directory, as Figure 10-56 shows.

Trustee Assignments		Object:	📁SALES	
MPinzon:				
User	Directory	[		]
Group AcctExecs	Directory	[	RWCEMF	]
[Public] trustee	Directory	[		]
Group: EVERYONE	[Root] of DATA	[	R F	]
IRF:	Directory	[		]
Effective Rights			[	RWCEMF	]

File rights for all files in the directory are the same, because there are no assignments of file rights that would override the directory rights assigned.

Figure 10-56   Maria's effective rights in SALES

What effective rights does Maria have to the FDR_SERVER01/DATA:ADMIN directory? Because Maria has no specific trustee assignments to ADMIN from the AcctExecs group, the rights granted to the EVERYONE group to the [Root] directory will be inherited subject to an IRF. There is no IRF for ADMIN. Figure 10-57 shows Maria's rights in the ADMIN directory.

Trustee Assignments		Object:	📁ADMIN	
MPinzon:				
User	Directory	[		]
Group AcctExecs	Directory	[		]
[Public] trustee	Directory	[		]
Group: EVERYONE	[Root] of DATA	[	R F	]
IRF:	ADMIN	[		]
Effective Rights			[	R F	]

File rights for all files in the directory are the same, because there are no assignments of file rights that would override the directory rights assigned.

Figure 10-57   Maria's effective rights in ADMIN

What effective rights does Maria have to the FDR_SERVER01/DATA:INVSTMNT directory? Because Maria has no specific trustee assignments to INVSTMNT from the AcctExecs group, the rights granted to the EVERYONE group to the [Root] directory will again be inherited subject to an IRF. INVSTMNT does have an IRF, which blocks the Read, Write, Create, Erase, Modify, File Scan, and Access Control Directory rights [RWCEMFA]. Figure 10-58 shows Maria's rights in the INVSTMNT directory.

Trustee Assignments		Object:	📁INVSTMNT	
MPinzon:				
User	Directory	[		]
Group AcctExecs	Directory	[		]
[Public] trustee	Directory	[		]
Group: EVERYONE	[Root] of DATA	[R	F	]
IRF:	Directory	[RWCEMFA	]	
Effective Rights			[		]

File rights for all files in the directory are the same, because there are no assignments of file rights that would override the directory rights assigned.

Figure 10-58   Maria's effective rights in INVSTMNT

In this case, the IRF completely blocks any rights Maria would have had in the INVSTMNT directory. She cannot see or use this directory, any of its subdirectories, or any of the files in any of those directories.

Planning Directory Tree and File System Security

Computing effective rights can be a complex task when multiple container, profile group, and user trustee assignments are involved. Good strategies in planning Directory tree and file system security include using as few trustee assignments as possible and keeping the use of IRFs to a minimum. If you need to use an IRF, that may indicate you should rethink your assignment of rights, the organization of your Directory tree, or the directories in your file system. Imagine, for example, that you are a network administrator for a company and that your predecessor created a directory structure in which word processing document files were stored in subdirectories of the SOFTWARE\WP directory, as Figure 10-59 shows.

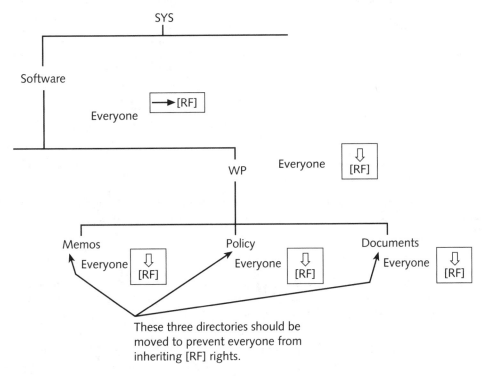

These three directories should be moved to prevent everyone from inheriting [RF] rights.

Figure 10-59   Directory structure

Your predecessor also created a Group object named EVERYONE (all users are added to the group) and made the EVERYONE group a trustee of SOFTWARE with [RF] rights. This means that all users inherit [RF] rights to the document subdirectories. This creates a security problem because all users have the ability to read any document. To eliminate this problem, you set the IRFs of the document subdirectories to block the inherited rights and then grant appropriate users the necessary trustee assignments to these subdirectories. Although this solution will work, it does not address the real problem: Data directories and software directories should be in separate locations. The best solution in this example is to move the document subdirectories to another location in the file system.

To help keep the trustee assignment security as simple and effective as possible, a network administrator should follow two simple strategies when planning trustee assignment security:

1. Plan rights from the top down.

2. Plan trustee assignments in this order: groups, profiles, organizational roles, and container objects.

Remember that rights are inherited from parent container objects into subordinate container objects and from parent directories into subordinate subdirectories and files.

Planning the NDS Directory tree and the network directory structure from the top down takes advantage of this principle. The following guidelines can help you implement a top–down strategy:

- At the top of your directory structure, place directories that are least frequently accessed. Place the most frequently accessed directories at the bottom.

- Start planning rights at the department or highest-level directory, and work down to the subdirectories and files within it.

- Grant only the rights needed by the user or group at any given level of the Directory tree or the file system.

- Use the inheritance principle. Use IRFs to protect objects and directories against trustees inheriting unwanted rights, but keep IRFs to an absolute minimum.

- Create and use an EVERYONE group.

When planning trustee assignments, start by assigning rights to the groups and profiles that have the most users. It is often helpful to create an EVERYONE group and assign common trustee rights for all users to this group. Next assign rights to other groups and profiles. It helps to think of profiles as simply another type of group—a group created specifically to enable assignment of resources on login via the login script. Thus profiles often group together exactly those users who can benefit from common directory and file trustee assignments. Organizational roles can also be thought of as a type of group, albeit often a group that has only one member. Use organizational roles for the allocation of specialized resources needed by the occupants of that role. Container objects provide the basis for yet another type of group: people who share a common location in the organizational schema. Their common resource needs can provide the basis for trustee assignments.

Finally, make individual user trustee assignments. This keeps user trustee assignments to a minimum. You will usually find some group or organizational role to which it is more appropriate to assign trustee rights. Some network administrators go to the extreme of never making trustee assignments to users; they make the trustee assignment to a group name instead, and then make the user who needs the access rights a member of that group.

When assigning trustee rights to groups and users, follow the same pattern as when you planned the rights assignments:

1. Assign rights to groups, starting with the group EVERYONE.

2. Assign rights to profiles.

3. Assign rights to organizational roles.

4. Assign rights to container objects.

5. Assign rights to individual users.

DIRECTORY AND FILE ATTRIBUTES

Attributes are flags or codes that can be associated with files and directories. They indicate to the NetWare operating system what type of processing can be performed on the associated file and directory.

Attributes apply only to file system components (directories and files). They do not apply to NDS objects.

To provide additional protection against accidental change or deletion, the network administrator often places attributes on directories and files. Attributes are also used to specify special processing such as making a file shareable or purging all files that are deleted from a specific directory. Attributes override user effective rights in a directory or file. If a file is flagged with the Read Only attribute, the only operations you can perform on the file—no matter what your effective rights are—are Read and File Scan. Assume, for example, a user has the Supervisor Trustee right [S] to the SALES directory and therefore would inherit all access rights to the files and subdirectories in the SALES structure. If a file named ZIPCODE.DAT is stored in the SALES directory and is flagged with the Read Only attribute, this user has only read access to the ZIPCODE.DAT file. Because this user has a Supervisor [S] trustee assignment to the SALES directory, however, he or she can use the Modify right to remove the Read Only attribute and then change or even delete the ZIPCODE.DAT file.

Attributes

Table 10-6 lists all attributes NetWare 5.0 uses, along with their corresponding abbreviations and whether they can be applied to directories, files, or both.

Table 10-6   NetWare 5.0 directory and file attributes

Attribute	Applies To	Abbreviation
Archive Needed	File	A
Can't Compress	File	Cc
Compressed	File	Co
Copy Inhibit	File	Ci
Delete Inhibit	File, Directory	Di
Don't Compress	File, Directory	Dc
Don't Migrate	File, Directory	Dm
Don't Suballocate	File	Ds
Execute Only	File	X
Hidden	File, Directory	H
Immediate Compress	File, Directory	Ic
Index	File	I
Migrated	File	M
Normal	File, Directory	N
Purge	File, Directory	P
Read Only	File	Ro
Read Write	File	Rw
Rename Inhibit	File, Directory	R
Shareable	File	Sh
System	File, Directory	Sy
Transactional	File	T

Of these 20 attributes, 4 are from DOS: Archive Needed [A], Hidden [H], Read Only [Ro in NetWare, just R in DOS], and System [Sy in NetWare, just S in DOS]. NetWare supports the 4 DOS attributes and adds 16 additional attributes.

NetWare 5.0 also enable the Read Audit and Write Audit attributes, but NetWare does not use them. Although these attributes can be assigned to files, Novell has not yet defined their use. As a result, network administrators do not use these attributes.

Archive Needed

The **Archive Needed [A]** attribute is assigned automatically to files when the contents of a file are modified and is one of the four DOS attributes NetWare supports. Copy or backup utilities can remove this attribute after the file is copied to another storage location. This attribute is important in controlling what files are copied to a backup disk. It is possible to back up only the files that have been changed since the last backup.

Can't Compress

The **Can't Compress [Cc]** attribute is a status flag that shows the file can't be compressed using NetWare's file compression because the compression wouldn't save a significant amount of disk space. Although displayed on attribute lists, the Cc attribute can't be set by a user—NetWare automatically sets it.

Compressed

Like Can't Compress, the **Compressed [Co]** attribute is also a status flag that is displayed in attribute lists but can't be set by the user. The Co attribute shows that the file is compressed using NetWare's file compression.

Copy Inhibit

10

The **Copy Inhibit [Ci]** attribute is used to protect specified files from being copied by Macintosh users. Setting this attribute prevents Macintosh computers running the Apple Filing Protocol v2.0 and above from copying the file.

Delete Inhibit

The **Delete Inhibit [Di]** attribute prevents a file or directory from being deleted. If assigned to a file, the file's contents can be changed or the file renamed, but the file cannot be deleted unless a user who has been granted the Modify right [M] first removes the Delete Inhibit attribute. The Delete Inhibit attribute is often useful to protect an important data file from accidentally being deleted yet still enables its contents to be changed. Consider setting the Delete Inhibit attribute on many of your organization's permanent files, such as customer, payroll, inventory, and accounting files. Setting the Delete Inhibit attribute on a directory prevents the directory's name from being removed but will not prevent the contents of the directory or its files and subdirectories from being deleted. You might want to protect the fixed parts of your organization's directory structure from being modified by flagging all main directories with the Delete Inhibit attribute.

Don't Compress

The **Don't Compress [Dc]** attribute is used to keep files or directories from being compressed by NetWare's file compression system. The Dc attribute can be set by the user.

Don't Migrate

Migration is used to move files that haven't been used for a long period of time to secondary storage mediums such as DAT tape or optical disks. NetWare 5.0 has two attributes that work with migration systems. The first is **Don't Migrate [Dm]**, which is set by the user to keep a file from being migrated regardless of how long it has been on a volume without being used. For example, you don't want NetWare system files migrated even if you haven't used them. The Dm attribute can be set for directories as well as files. When the attribute is set for a directory, none of the files in that directory will be migrated. For example, by setting the *ServerName*/SYS:SYSTEM directory Dm attribute, you don't have to set the Dm attribute for every file in SYSTEM.

Don't Suballocate

NetWare's block suballocation scheme is used to save disk space, and normally you should use block suballocation. If certain files shouldn't be stored using block suballocation, you use the **Don't Suballocate [Ds]** attribute to prevent the use of block suballocation when storing those files.

Execute Only

Whereas the Copy Inhibit attribute keeps Macintosh files from being copied, the **Execute Only [X]** attribute is used to protect software files from being illegally copied. The Execute Only attribute can be set only on .EXE and .COM files by an administrator-equivalent user. Once set, Execute Only cannot be removed, even by the administrator. As a result, do not assign Execute Only to files unless backup copies of the files exist. Certain program files will not run when they are flagged Execute Only, because these programs need to copy information from their program files into the workstation's memory—the Execute Only attribute prevents this. Because the Execute Only attribute cannot be removed, to get rid of it you need to delete the file and reinstall it from another disk.

Hidden

The **Hidden [H]** attribute is a DOS attribute used to hide files and directories from DOS utilities and certain software applications. However, the NDIR and NCOPY commands will display hidden files and directories—and show the H attribute, when it is enabled. One simple way to help protect software from illegal copying is to use the Hidden attribute to make the software directories and files hidden from normal DOS utilities. If you move the NCOPY and NDIR commands from the SYS:PUBLIC directory to the SYS:SYSTEM directory or some other location, standard users will not have access to them.

Another way to protect the NCOPY and NDIR commands from unauthorized use is to place an IRF on the files in question to prevent users from inheriting the [RF] rights to these files and then make a specific trustee assignment to a special group. Only members of the special group can then use the NCOPY and NDIR commands.

The Hidden attribute can be especially useful when you have Windows workstations. With Windows it is very easy for users to explore the directory structure using the Explorer. By hiding directories and files, you can make the file structure much less accessible.

Immediate Compress

The **Immediate Compress [Ic]** attribute is set for files and directories that you want to be compressed as soon as possible. Before compressing the file, NetWare 5.0 will normally wait until the file has not been used for a specific period of time.

Index

The **Index [I]** attribute is automatically set by NetWare when a file reaches a certain size relative to the block size on the volume. (As a minimum, this would be any file that exceeds 64 FAT entries.) Since indexing is handled by NetWare, users cannot modify the Index attribute.

Migrated

The second of the two NetWare 5.0 attributes that work with migration systems, the **Migrated [M]** attribute is a status flag set by NetWare after a file has been migrated. A file that appears in a listing with the M attribute has actually been moved to another storage medium and is no longer physically on the volume. When you try to work with such a file, it must first be retrieved from the other storage medium and recopied to the volume. If the other storage medium is easily accessible, such as a DAT tape already in the DAT tape drive, the retrieval can be fairly quick. However, if the file is stored on a medium that is not easily accessible, such as a DAT tape stored in a different building, you will have to retrieve the storage medium yourself first and place it in the appropriate drive before it can be recopied to the volume.

Normal

If none of the attributes are set, the file or directory is considered to be **Normal [N]**.

Purge

As described in Chapter 8, NetWare enables deleted files to be retrieved with the Salvage command in NetWare Administrator until either the server reuses the deleted file's space, or the directory is purged using the Purge command in NetWare Administrator. Space from files that have been purged is no longer available to the operating system, so the

10

file can't be recovered with the Salvage command. You can assign the **Purge [P]** attribute to either a file or a directory if you want the NetWare server to immediately reuse the space from deleted files. When you assign it to a file, the Purge attribute purges the file as soon as it is deleted, making that space immediately available to the system for reuse. When you assign Purge to a directory, any file deleted from the directory is automatically purged and its space reused. The Purge attribute is often assigned to directories that contain temporary files, in order to reuse the temporary file space as soon as the file is deleted. The Purge attribute can also be assigned, for security reasons, to files that contain sensitive data, preventing an intruder from salvaging and then accessing information from these files after they have been deleted.

Read Only

The **Read Only [Ro]** attribute applies only to files. It protects the contents of a file from being modified. The Read Only attribute performs a function similar to opening the write protect tab on a disk. Files containing data that is not normally changed—such as a ZIP code file or a program file—are usually flagged Read Only. When you first set the Read Only attribute, the Rename Inhibit and Delete Inhibit attributes are also set by default. If for some reason you want to let the file be renamed or deleted but do not want its contents changed, you can remove the Rename Inhibit and Delete Inhibit attributes.

Read Write

The **Read Write [Rw]** attribute applies only to files. It is the opposite of Read Only, and indicates that the contents of the file can be added to or changed. When files are created, the Read Write attribute is automatically set, letting the contents of the file be added to or changed. When file attributes are listed, either Rw or Ro will be listed.

Rename Inhibit

You can assign the **Rename Inhibit [R]** attribute to either files or directories. When assigned to a file, it protects the filename from being changed. During installation, many software packages create data and configuration files that may need to be updated and changed, but those filenames must remain constant for the software package to operate properly. After installing a software package that requests certain file or directory names, it is a good idea to use the Rename Inhibit attribute on these files and directories to keep someone from changing the file or directory name and causing an error or crash in the application. Using the Rename Inhibit attribute on a directory keeps that directory's name from being changed, while still enabling files and subdirectories contained within that directory to be renamed.

Shareable

When files are created, they are available to only one user at a time. Suppose, for example, you create a spreadsheet file called BUDGET98.WK1 on the server and a coworker opens this file with a spreadsheet program. If you try to access the BUDGET98.WK1 file, you will receive an error message that the file is in use or not accessible. With spreadsheet files and word processing documents, if more than one user can access the file at one time any changes one user makes can be overwritten by another user. Program files and certain database files, however, should be made available to multiple users at the same time. For example, you would want as many users as have licenses to be able to run the word processing software you just installed, or perhaps have access to a common database of customers. To let a file be opened by more than one user at a time, the **Shareable [Sh]** attribute for that file must be enabled. Normally you need to flag all program files Shareable after performing an installation.

In addition to Shareable, most program files are also flagged as Read Only [Ro], to prevent users from deleting or making changes to the software. To prevent multiple users from making changes to the file at the same time, most document and data files are not flagged as shareable.

System

The **System [Sy]** attribute is a DOS attribute that also is often assigned to files and directories that are part of the NetWare operating system. (Print queues in the older Print Services were actually subdirectories in the SYS:SYSTEM directory and were flagged with the System attribute.) Like the Hidden attribute, the System attribute hides files from the DOS utilities and application software packages but also marks the file or directory as being for operating system use only. NetWare utilities display directories and files with the System and Hidden attributes set if the user has the File Scan right.

Transactional

The **Transactional [T]** attribute can be assigned only to files and is used to indicate that the file will be protected by the **Transaction Tracking System (TTS)**. The TTS ensures that when changes or transactions are applied to a file, either all transactions are completed or the file is left in its original state. The TTS is particularly important for database files—when a workstation is updating a record and crashes before the update is complete, the integrity of the file is protected. Assume, for example, that a NetWare server is used to maintain an on-line order entry system containing customer and inventory files. When an order is entered, at least two transactions are necessary: one to update the customer's account balance and the other to record the inventory item to be shipped. Suppose that while you are entering the order, the workstation you are using crashes after it updates the customer balance and therefore fails to record the item on the shipping list. In this case, TTS cancels the transaction and restores the customer's balance to its original amount, enabling you to reenter the complete order. Because TTS is a feature used by application software, using the Transactional attribute does not implement TTS protection—you also need to have the proper system design and application software.

10

Setting Attributes for a Directory or File from the Directory or File Object Itself

You've already read about how to use NetWare Administrator to grant trustee assignment and rights to directories and files. You can also use NetWare Administrator to set directory and file attributes. You do this by selecting the directory or file object in the NDS Directory tree and then opening the *ObjectName* object dialog box. The *ObjectName* object dialog box for a directory or file contains an Attributes page, with a set of check boxes to set attributes. For files, NetWare also displays another set of check boxes (which cannot be changed by the user) that show whether a file can or can't be compressed (Cc attribute), is or isn't compressed (Co attribute), and is or isn't migrated (M attribute).

To set directory and file attributes from the directory or file object itself, follow these general steps:

1. Click the Directory or File object, then press [Enter].
   or
   Click the Directory or File object, click Object on the menu bar, and then click Details.
   or
   Right-click the Directory or File object, then click Details on the shortcut menu.

2. Switch to the Attributes page.

3. Click the appropriate check boxes in the Directory Attributes or File Attributes section for the attributes to be set.

4. Click OK.

For example, the network administrator at CBE Labs has decided to protect the files in the CONSTELLATION/SYS:PUBLIC directory from accidental erasure and renaming by using Delete Inhibit (Di) and Rename Inhibit (R). Setting these attributes means that users cannot delete or rename the files in the PUBLIC directory. CBE Labs does not migrate files. If migration were used, the Don't Migrate (Dm) attribute would also have to be set for this directory—otherwise rarely used but still needed NetWare system files would be removed from the volume.

To set directory attributes for the CONSTELLATION_SYS:PUBLIC directory from the CONSTELLATION_SYS:PUBLIC directory object, follow these steps:

1. If NetWare Administrator is not open, launch it. Expand the tree until the directories of the CONSTELLATION_SYS volume are visible.

2. Right-click the CONSTELLATION_SYS:PUBLIC directory and select Details to display the Directory: PUBLIC object dialog box.

3. Click the Attributes button on the button bar. The Attributes page is displayed, as Figure 10-60 shows.

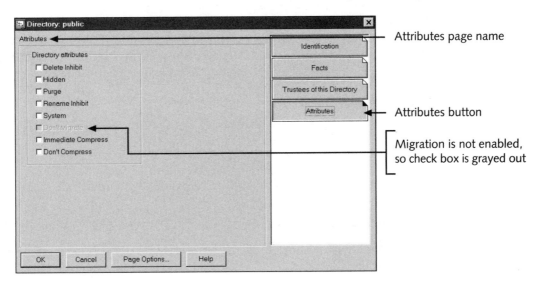

Figure 10-60   PUBLIC Attributes page

4. Click the Delete Inhibit and Rename Inhibit check boxes in the Attributes section to set the Delete Inhibit and Rename Inhibit attributes. The Directory: PUBLIC object dialog box appears as Figure 10-61 shows.

10

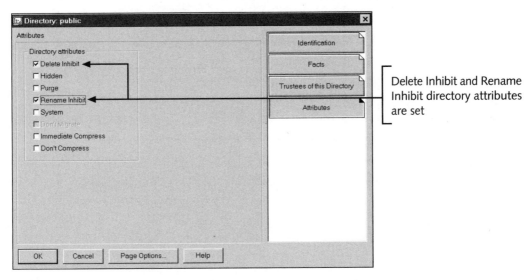

Figure 10-61   Completed CONSTELLATION_SYS:PUBLIC directory

5. Click OK. Do not close *NetWare Administrator*.

The NDIR.EXE file in the CONSTELLATION/SYS:PUBLIC directory is a frequently used file. However, the file is subject to compression if not used for seven days. Although NetWare's compression and decompression utilities are fast enough so that the user wouldn't notice much delay in opening the file, the CBE network administrator has decided to set the Don't Compress attribute on the file. This will keep the file uncompressed and ready to use.

To set file attributes for the NDIR.EXE file in the CONSTELLATION_SYS:PUBLIC directory from the NDIR.EXE file object, follow these steps:

1. Expand the Directory tree until the files in the CONSTELLATION_SYS:PUBLIC directory are visible.

2. Double-click the NDIR.EXE File object to select it and display the CONSTELLATION/SYS:\PUBLIC\NDIR.EXE object dialog box.

3. Click the Attributes button on the button bar. The Attributes page is displayed, as Figure 10-62 shows.

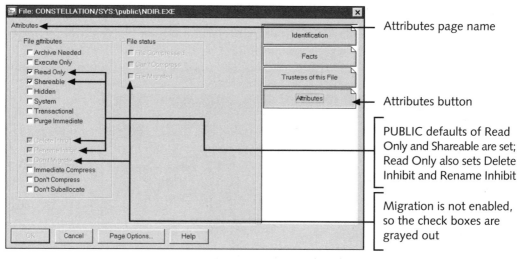

Figure 10-62   CONSTELLATION/SYS:\PUBLIC\NDIR.EXE Attributes page

Note that by default the files in the PUBLIC directory are set as Read Only [Ro], which automatically also sets them as Delete Inhibit [Di] and Rename Inhibit [R]. By default, the files are also set as Shareable [Sh].

4. Click the check box in the Attributes section to set the Don't Compress attribute. The Directory: CONSTELLATION_SYS:\PUBLIC\NDIR.EXE object dialog box appears as Figure 10-63 shows.

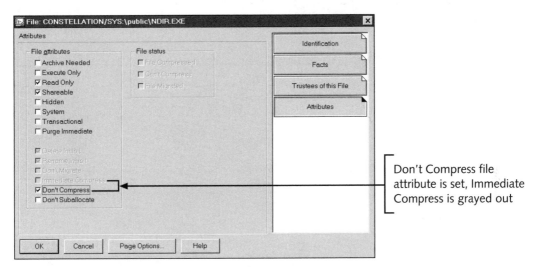

Figure 10-63   Completed CONSTELLATION/SYS:\PUBLIC\NDIR.EXE Attributes page

5. Click OK.

Setting Attributes for a Directory or File from Windows Explorer

Just as the Novell Client extensions to the Windows Explorer program enable you to manage most Directory and File rights from Explorer, you can also manage most directory and file attributes. This is an effective way of setting many attributes without launching NetWare Administrator. Table 10-7 shows which directory and file attributes can be set in Explorer.

Table 10-7   NetWare 5.0 directory and file attributes in Explorer

Attribute	Applies To	Set Directory (Folder) Attribute in Explorer	Set File Attribute in Explorer
Archive Needed [A]	File	YES for files in it	YES
Copy Inhibit [Ci]	File		YES
Delete Inhibit [Di]	File, Directory	YES	YES
Don't Compress [Dc]	File, Directory	YES	
Don't Migrate [Dm]	File, Directory		
Don't Suballocate [Ds]	File		
Execute Only [X]	File		
Hidden [H]	File, Directory	YES	YES
Immediate Compress [Ic]	File, Directory	YES	
Index [I]	File		
Normal [N]	File, Directory		
Purge [P]	File, Directory	YES	YES
Read Only [Ro]	File	YES for files in it	YES
Read Write [Rw]	File	YES = No Ro	YES = No Ro
Rename Inhibit [R]	File, Directory	YES	YES
Shareable [Sh]	File		YES
System [Sy]	File, Directory		
Transactional [T]	File		YES

To set directory and file attributes to a directory or file from Explorer, follow these general steps:

1. Launch Explorer.

2. Expand the Network Neighborhood branch of the Explorer tree until the directory or file is displayed.

3. Click the directory or file to select it.

4. Click File, then click Properties to display the *ObjectName* Properties dialog box.
   or
   Click the Properties button on the toolbar.

5. Click the NetWare Info tab to display the current attribute settings.

6. Click the check boxes to set the appropriate attributes.

7. Click OK.

The CBE Labs Network Administrator needs to set the same directory attributes for the SARATOGA/SYS:PUBLIC directory that he set for the CONSTELLATION/SYS: PUBLIC directory. He also needs to set the attributes for the NDIR.EXE file in the SARATOGA/SYS:PUBLIC directory. You will use Explorer to set these attributes.

Remember, if your test network uses aliases for SARATOGA and RANGER, these will not appear in Windows Explorer. Only physical volumes and servers will appear in Explorer.

To set directory attributes for the SARATOGA/SYS:PUBLIC directory from Explorer, follow these steps:

1. Launch Explorer.

2. Expand the Network Neighborhood icon to show the SARATOGA server icon. Expand this to show the SARATOGA_SYS volume icon. Click the SARATOGA_SYS icon to select it; then click the Properties button.

3. Click the NetWare Info tab to display the current attribute settings, as shown in Figure 10-64. This page shows the name space, owner, and date information about the directory (folder).

10

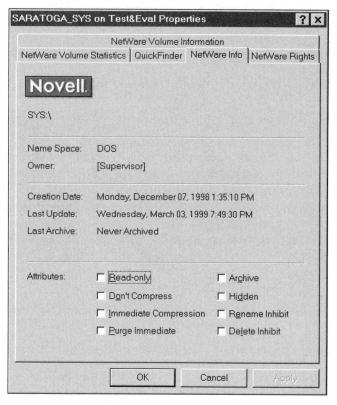

Figure 10-64   NetWare Info page

4. Click the Delete Inhibit and Rename Inhibit check boxes in the Attributes section to set the Delete Inhibit and Rename Inhibit attributes. The NetWare Folder page appears, as Figure 10-65 shows.

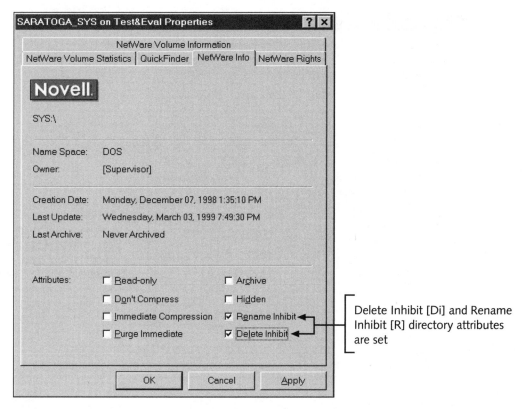

Delete Inhibit [Di] and Rename Inhibit [R] directory attributes are set

Figure 10-65   Completed NetWare Info page

> 5. Click OK. Don't close Explorer at this time.

Now let's set the file attributes for NDIR.EXE.

To set file attributes for the NDIR.EXE file in the SARATOGA/SYS:PUBLIC directory from Explorer, follow these steps:

1. If you haven't already done so, expand the Network Neighborhood to show the SARATOGA server icon. Expand this to show the SARATOGA_SYS volume icon in the PUBLIC directory. Click the NDIR.EXE file icon in the right-hand window, click File, and then click Properties.

2. Click the NetWare Info tab. The NetWare Info page is displayed, as Figure 10-66 shows.

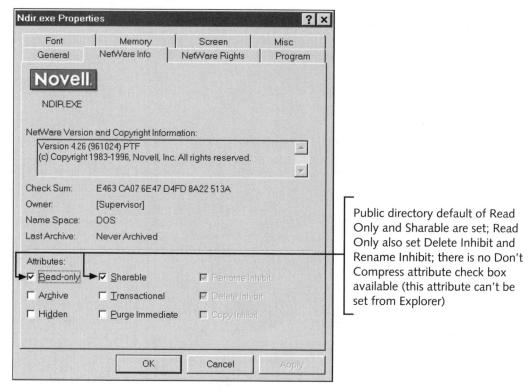

Figure 10-66 NetWare Info tab

This page shows the name space, owner, and date information about the file. Notice that the default Read Only and Shareable settings show up, with the associated Rename Inhibit and Delete Inhibit check boxes checked and grayed-out. Also notice that there is no check box for the Don't Compress attribute. The NetWare Info page does not contain as comprehensive a set of settings as the File object Attributes page in NetWare Administrator.

3. Click OK.

The FLAG Command

The NetWare command line utility for managing attributes is the FLAG command. The syntax of the FLAG command is

```
FLAG path [[ + | - ] attribute] [/option] [/?] [/VER]
```

Several parameters can be used with FLAG, as listed in Table 10-8.

Table 10-8 FLAG command parameters

Parameter	Use This Parameter to:
path	Specify the directory path to the directory or file you want to work with. This parameter is mandatory.
+	-	Add attributes (+) or delete attributes (-). You can add and delete attributes in the same command.
attribute	Specify one or more directory or file attributes.
/?	Access help about FLAG. If this parameter is used, all others are ignored.
/VER	See the version number of the FLAG command. If this parameter is used, all others are ignored.

Also, several options can be used with FLAG, as listed in Table 10-9.

Table 10-9 FLAG command options

Option	Use This Option to:
/C	Let the output scroll continuously.
/D	View details for a directory or file.
/DO	View or change directories only.
/FO	View or change files only.
/NAME=name	Change the directory or file owner.
/M=mode	Modify the search mode used by executable files.
/S	Search the specified directory and all subdirectories below it.

The set of *attribute* symbols that can be used with the FLAG command is shown in Table 10-10.

10

Table 10-10   NetWare 5.0 directory and file attributes used with FLAG command

Attribute		Used with Directories	Used with Files
ALL		YES - Includes Di, H, Ic, P, Ri and Sy for directories	YES - Includes A, Ci: (Macintosh files), Di, Dc
[A]	Archive Needed		YES
[Ci]	Copy Inhibit		YES - Macintosh files only
[Di]	Delete Inhibit	YES	YES
[Dc]	Don't Compress	YES	YES
[Dm]	Don't Migrate	YES	YES
[Ds]	Don't Suballocate		YES
[H]	Hidden	YES	YES

Certain attribute symbols that you learned about earlier show up as file status flags in the output of the FLAG command. These symbols are shown in Table 10-11. You cannot set these attributes, but you should be able to recognize them in the output.

Table 10-11   NetWare 5.0 file attributes used as status flags

Attribute	
[Cc]	Can't Compress
[Co]	Compressed
[M]	Migrated

The /M=Mode option is a rarely used option that sets a search mode for executable files. It will not be covered in this chapter.

If you use the FLAG command by itself with no parameter, a list of all files in the current directory and their attribute status is displayed.

You use the FLAG command to view or change the attributes of files in the specified directory. You can replace the path with either a complete or partial path leading to the desired file or files. If you specify no path, you access files in the current directory. The filename in the path can be replaced with the name of the file you want to access, or you can use global (*) and wildcard (?) characters to access several files. If no filename is specified, the FLAG command will affect all files in the specified path. To see a list of the attributes on all files in the current directory, simply type FLAG and press [Enter]. Replace the flag list field with the letters, separated by spaces, of the attributes you want to set.

CHAPTER SUMMARY

❐ Just as a physical building, such as a warehouse, needs to be secured with locks and keys, the NetWare NDS and file systems must also be secured. Trustee assignments provide access rights that, like keys, give users entry to the Directory tree and server storage areas they need to access. Four types of rights can be assigned: Object rights, Property rights, Directory rights, and File rights. Object rights are rights to the objects in the NDS Directory tree, and Property rights are rights to the properties of those objects. Directory rights are rights to the directories and subdirectories in the NetWare file system, and File rights are rights to the files in those directories.

❐ Object rights provide access to objects in the NDS Directory tree. There are five Object rights: Supervisor, Browse, Create, Delete, and Rename. The Supervisor right grants all the other Object rights to the trustee and also grants all Property rights for the object. The Browse right enables the user to see the object in the Directory tree. The Create right applies only to container objects and lets the user create new objects in that container. It does not, however, let the user create Property rights for those objects. The Delete right lets the user delete the object from the Directory tree, and the Rename right lets the user rename the object.

❐ Property rights give access to the property settings of an object in the Directory tree. There are five Property rights: Supervisor, Compare, Read, Write, and Add or Delete Self. The rights may be granted for all properties of an object, or for selected properties. One user may have varying rights to different properties of an object. The Supervisor right grants the user all rights to the property. The Compare right lets the user compare a value to the property setting but not actually see the property setting. The Read right lets the user see the property setting and includes the Compare right. The Write right lets the user change the values of the property setting and includes the Add or Delete Self right, which lets the users add or delete themselves from a user list if the object has a user list property.

❐ Directory and File rights provide access to the file system directories and files, respectively. There are eight access rights for directories and files: Supervisor, Read, Write, Create, Erase, Modify, File Scan, and Access control. The Supervisor right can be assigned only by an administrator-equivalent user and provides a user with all rights to the directory and all subdirectories, including the right to assign the Supervisor right to other users. In addition, because the Supervisor right cannot be revoked or blocked at any lower level, assigning the Supervisor right is a good way to make a user act as administrator of a portion of the directory structure. The File Scan right lets users see the directory or file in the file system, whereas the Read right lets users actually read or use a file. The Write right lets users change the contents of a file, the Create right lets users create new files or salvage deleted ones, and the Modify right lets users change attributes or rename

10

a file or subdirectory. The Access Control right lets a user assign other rights, except Supervisor, to other users. Trustee assignments grant rights to users. Trustee assignments can be made to User objects, Group objects, Profile objects, Organizational Role objects, and Container objects. Effective rights for a user are a combination of rights given to a user's name combined with the rights given to any other object with which the user is associated. Granted trustee rights are then inherited by (1) all container objects in the Directory tree subordinate to the container to which the trustee assignment was made or (2) the subdirectories and files within the directory for which the trustee assignment was made. As a result, a user's effective rights often consist of inherited rights that have flowed down to a container object, directory or file from a trustee assignment made in a higher-level container object, or directory.

❏ An Inherited Rights Filter (IRF) exists for each object, directory, and file to control what rights the object, directory, or file inherits from higher-level objects and directories. When an object, directory, or file is first created, the IRF enables all rights to be inherited. Later you can remove rights from the IRF to block those rights from being inherited.

❏ Several utilities are used to set and view trustee assignments and the IRFs. The main graphics utility is the NetWare Administrator. The Client 32 extensions to Windows Explorer can also be used to manage trustee assignments.

❏ Attributes play an important role in file system security because they let you protect directories and files from such operations as deletion, renaming, and copying. Attributes can also be used to control file sharing, suballocation, compressing, purging, and migrating. Directory attributes include Delete Inhibit, Don't Compress, Don't Migrate, Hidden, Immediate Compress, Normal, Purge, Rename Inhibit, and System. File attributes include Archive Needed, Copy Inhibit, Delete Inhibit, Don't Compress, Don't Migrate, Don't Suballocate, Execute Only, Hidden, Immediate Compress, Purge, Read Only, Read Write, Rename Inhibit, Sharable, System, and Transactional. File status flags, which are displayed but which you cannot set, are Can't Compress, Compress, and Migrated.

❏ The same graphical utility—NetWare Administrator—used to set and view trustee assignments is used to set and view attributes. The Novell Client extensions to the Windows Explorer again enable Explorer to be used to manage some attributes. The FLAG command line utility provides a comprehensive tool for managing directory and file attributes from the DOS prompt.

COMMAND SUMMARY

Command	Syntax	Definition
FLAG		When used without any options, the FLAG command will display the attribute settings of all files in the current directory. To set attributes on one or more files, replace the path with the path and name of a file or use global file identifiers such as * and replace attributes with one or more of the following attribute flags separated by spaces (those attributes marked [Dir] work with directories as well as files):

ALL	Set all attributes [Dir]
A	Archive needed
Ci	Copy Inhibit
Di	Delete Inhibit [Dir]
Dc	Don't Compress [Dir]
Dm	Don't Migrate [Dir]
Ds	Don't Suballocate
H	Hidden [Dir]
Ic	Immediate Compress [Dir]
N	Normal [Dir]
P	Purge [Dir]
R	Rename Inhibit [Dir]
Ro	Read Only
Rw	Read Write
Sh	Shareable
Sy	System [Dir]
T	Transactional
X	Execute Only

Options that can be used include:

/C	Continuous output
/D	View details
/DO	Directories only
/FO	Files only
/M = mode	
/NAME = name (change the owner)	

Change the owner

/S	Include subdirectories

10

KEY TERMS

Access Control right [A]
access control list (ACL)
Add or Delete Self right [A]
Archive Needed [A]
assign
assigned rights
attributes
Browse right [B]
Can't Compress [Cc]
Compare right [C]
Compressed [Co]
Copy Inhibit [Ci]
Create right [C]
Delete right [D]
Delete Inhibit [Di]
directory entry table (DET)
Directory rights
Don't Compress [Dc]
Don't Migrate [Dm]
Don't Suballocate [Ds]
effective rights
Erase right [E]
Execute Only [X]
File rights
File Scan right [F]
grant
Hidden [H]
Immediate Compress [Ic]
inherited rights
Inherited Rights Filter (IRF)
Migrated [M]
Modify right [M]
Normal [N]
Object rights
Property rights
[Public]
Purge [P]

Read Only [Ro]
Read right [R]
Read Write [Rw]
Rename Inhibit [Ri]
Rename right [R]
rights
security equivalence
Shareable [Sh]
Supervisor right [S]
System [Sy]
Transaction Tracking System (TTS)
Transactional [T]
trustee
trustee assignment
trustee list
Write right [W]

10

REVIEW QUESTIONS

1. Identify each of the following as being either a command line utility, graphical utility, console command, or NetWare Loadable Module (NLM):

   FLAG_____

   Explorer _____

   NetWare Administrator _____

2. _____ define a user's access to NDS and the NetWare file system.

3. List the four types of rights.

4. What is the purpose of Object rights?

5. The _____ right enables a user to see an object in the NDS Directory tree.

6. The _____ right enables a user to create NDS objects in a container object.

7. What is the purpose of Property rights?

8. The _____ right enables a user to compare a value to a property setting but not to see the value itself.

9. The _____ right enables users to add themselves to a user list if the object has one.

10. What is the purpose of Directory rights?

11. The _____ Directory right enables a user to see file and subdirectory names.

12. The _____ Directory right enables a user to rename the directory.

13. The _____ Directory right enables a user to assign rights to other users.

14. What is the purpose of File rights?

15. The _____ File right enables a user to salvage a file if it is deleted.

16. The _____ File right enables users to read a file if they do not have the necessary Directory rights.

17. The _____ File right enables a user to change data within an existing file.

18. The _____ Directory right cannot be revoked or blocked within the directory structure in which it is defined.

19. _____ consists of a subset of the access rights and controls what functions a user can perform in a directory or file.

Figure 10-67 shows the NDS Directory tree for FDR Investments. Use this Directory tree as the basis for answering Questions 20-25. [Public] has no rights in the tree.

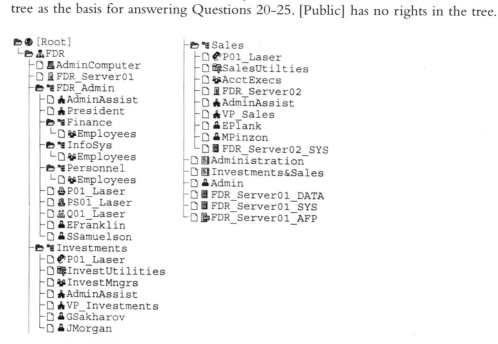

Figure 10-67 FDR Directory tree

20. You work in administration and have been given the [BCD] rights to the FDR Organization object and the [SBCDR] rights to the FDR_Admin organizational unit. What are your effective rights in the Finance.FDR_Admin.FDR organizational unit? Why do you have these rights?

21. You work in administration and have been given the [BCD] rights to the FDR Organization object and the [SBCDR] rights to the FDR_Admin organizational unit. What are your effective rights in the Sales.FDR organizational unit? Why do you have these rights?

22. You work in sales and are a member of AcctExecs. You have been given the [B] right to the FDR Organization object and the [BCDR] rights to the Sales.FDR organizational unit. In addition, AcctExecs has the [S] right to Sales.FDR. What are your effective rights in the Sales.FDR organizational object? Why do you have these rights?

23. You are the new VP for investments and are a member of InvestManagers. You have been given the [B] right to the FDR Organization object and the [B] right to the Investments.FDR organizational unit. In addition, InvestManagers has the [CD] rights to Investments.FDR. As VP for investments you have the [R] right for Investments.FDR. What are your effective rights in the Investments.FDR organizational object? Why do you have these rights?

24. Given that you are a member of the AcctExecs group that has been granted the [RWF] rights to a directory called BUSINESS and have a trustee assignment of [RCF] to the BUSINESS directory, what are your effective rights in the BUSINESS directory?

25. Assume you have been given a trustee assignment of [RCF] to the BUSINESS directory and a trustee assignment of Erase and Write to the BUSINESS\SPDATA\BUDGETS subdirectory. What are your effective rights in the BUSINESS\SPDATA subdirectory?

For Questions 26–28, use the following rights assignment information: You have a trustee assignment of [WCE] to the BUSINESS directory and a trustee assignment of [EW] to the BUSINESS\SPDATA\BUDGETS subdirectory. In addition, you belong to a group that was granted the [RF] rights to the BUSINESS directory.

26. What are your effective rights in the BUSINESS\SPDATA\BUDGETS subdirectory?

27. Assume all rights except [R] and [F] are removed from the IRF of the BUSINESS\SPDATA subdirectory. What are your rights in the BUSINESS\SPDATA subdirectory?

28. What are your rights in the BUSINESS\SPDATA\BUDGETS subdirectory?

Questions 29–37 all deal with Taft Distribution, Inc. and its personnel. Rights granted in one question are assumed to still be granted in following questions, and rights deleted in one question are assumed to still be deleted in following questions.

29. Write the commands to give the user JMann the [WCEMA] rights to the SERVER01/DATA:BUSINESS\BUDGETS directory and the ADMIN group the [RWF] rights to the SERVER01/DATA:BUSINESS directory.

30. Explain the steps in Explorer or NWAdmin to remove the Modify and Access Control rights from the trustee assignment made for the user JMann in the DATA:BUSINESS\BUDGETS directory.

31. Explain the steps in Explorer or NWAdmin to display all the trustee assignments in the DATA:BUSINESS directory.

32. Explain the steps in Explorer or NWAdmin to determine your effective rights in the BUSINESS\SPDATA directory.

33. Explain the steps in Explorer or NWAdmin that would prevent users and groups from inheriting rights in the BUSINESS\USER subdirectory.

34. Explain the steps in Explorer or NWAdmin to assign the user JMann the [E] and [M] rights in the BUSINESS\SPDATA subdirectory.

35. Explain the steps in Explorer or NWAdmin to delete the trustee assignment made to the user JMann in the BUSINESS\SPDATA\BUDGETS subdirectory.

36. Assume the user JMann was given a trustee assignment of [RWCEMF] to the BUSINESS\SPDATA directory and initially had a trustee assignment of [RWCF] in the BUSINESS\SPDATA\BUDGETS subdirectory. What are JMann's effective rights in the BUSINESS\SPDATA\BUDGETS subdirectory after his trustee assignment to BUDGETS was deleted in Question 35?

37. State whether the user JMann gained or lost rights in the BUDGETS directory and explain why.

38. When you set the Read Only attribute, what other attributes are also set by default?

39. Which of the following attributes are used with directories?

    Archive needed _____

    Copy inhibit _____

    Delete inhibit _____

    Don't compress _____

    Don't migrate _____

    Don't suballocate _____

    Execute only _____

    Hidden _____

    Immediate compress _____

    Purge _____

    Read only _____

    Read write _____

    Rename inhibit _____

    Shareable _____

    System _____

    Transactional _____

40. Write a FLAG command setting the attributes to enable software files in a SYS:SOFTWARE\WP directory to be used by more than one user at a time and also to prevent the files from being deleted or changed.

41. Explain the steps in Explorer or NWAdmin in setting the directory attribute that will prevent deleted files in the SYS:SOFTWARE\TEMP directory from being salvaged.

42. Explain the advantages of setting the Purge attribute on a directory.

HANDS-ON PROJECTS

These projects assume that each student has been given a home directory for classwork in the CONSTELLATION_SYS\USERS\##ADMIN format.

Project 10-1: Working with Access Rights

The objective of this project is to provide you with practice assigning access rights to a directory and then attempting to perform several disk operations in that directory to see how the access rights affect use of the file system. In the following steps, make sure to substitute your assigned student number for the number (or pound, or space) symbols (##).

1. Log in using your assigned student user name and change to your ##ADMIN directory.

2. Create directories called CHAP10 and SP within your ##ADMIN directory.

3. Use Explorer to copy all files with the .TXT extension from your local Windows directory to the CHAP10 and SP subdirectories.

4. Use NWAdmin to create a user named ##USER10 anywhere in your CBELabs tree.

5. Use NWAdmin to assign ##USER10 the Access Control right to CHAP10 and Read and File Scan rights to ##ADMIN\SP.

6. Log out.

7. Log in as ##USER10 and change to the ##ADMIN\CHAP10 directory.

8. Log out and log in as administrator. Use Explorer to view the files. Record your results.

9. Use NWAdmin to grant ##USER10 only File Scan rights to CHAP10.

10. Log in as ##USER10 and repeat Step 8. Record your observations.

11. Try to read the contents of a file by using the TYPE *filename* command. Record the results.

12. Log in as administrator and use NWAdmin to give ##GROUP10 the Read right to the CHAP10 directory.

13. Log in as ##USER10 and repeat Step 11. Record your observations.

14. Try creating a subdirectory called PRACTICE. Record your observations.

10

15. Log in as administrator and use NWAdmin to give ##USER10 only the Create and Access Control rights to the CHAP10 directory.

16. Log in as ##USER10 and repeat Step 14. Record the results.

17. What two ways could you use to make the directories visible?

18. Try using Explorer to copy the SP.BAT file from SYS:SOFTWARE.NTC\SP to the CHAP10 directory. Record your results.

19. Try using Explorer to copy all files from the SYS:SOFTWARE.NTC\DB subdirectory in the CHAP10 directory. Record your results.

20. Log in as administrator and add the File Scan right to ##GROUP10 so that ##USER10 has effective rights of [RCFA] in the CHAP10 directory. Log in as ##USER10 and then repeat Step 19. Record your observations.

21. Log in using your assigned ##ADMIN user name and delete any users and groups you created in this exercise.

Project 10-2: Using the Inherited Rights Filter

In this project you create a directory structure and two users and then use NetWare utilities to grant trustee assignments and set up an IRF in order to observe how effective rights are inherited.

Part 1: Create Directory Structure and Users

1. Log in using your assigned student user name, and change to your ##ADMIN directory.

2. If you have not already done so, create a directory in your ##ADMIN work area named CHAP10.

3. Create two directories in the CHAP10 directory named ORDERS and USERS.

4. Create two users called ##CLERK1 and ##CLERK2 anywhere in your CBELabs tree. Create home directories for these users in the CHAP10\USERS directory.

5. Create a group named ##CLERKS. Make both ##CLERK1 and ##CLERK2 members of this group,

6. Give the group ##CLERKS Read and File Scan rights to the CHAP10 directory.

7. Make ##CLERK1 a manager of the CHAP10 directory structure by granting the user name the Supervisor right.

8. Make ##CLERK2 a trustee of the CHAP10 directory with the [WCEM] rights.

9. Log out.

Part 2: Check Effective Rights

1. Log in as ##CLERK2.
2. Use Explorer or NWADMIN to record your effective rights in the directories listed in the following table.

Directory Path	Effective Rights
CHAP10	
CHAP10\ORDERS	
CHAP10\USERS	

3. Log out.

Part 3: Modify Trustee Assignments

In this part of the project you observe how making a new trustee assignment to the group of which a user is a member will change the effective rights inherited by the user to a subdirectory.

1. Log in using your assigned student user name, and change to your ##ADMIN directory.
2. Use Explorer or NWADMIN to assign the ##CLERKS group no rights to the CHAP10\ORDERS subdirectory.
3. Log out.
4. Log in as ##CLERK2
5. Record your effective rights in the CHAP10 directory.
6. Record your effective rights in the CHAP10\ORDERS subdirectory.
7. Why didn't your effective rights in the CHAP10 directory flow down to the CHAP10\ORDERS directory?
8. Log out.

Part 4: Using IRFs to Change Effective Rights

1. Log in using your assigned ##ADMIN user name.
2. Use NWADMIN to remove all rights except File Scan and Supervisor from the IRF of the CHAP10\USERS directory.
3. Use NWADMIN to enable the CHAP10\ORDERS directory to inherit only Read and File Scan rights.
4. Log out.
5. Log in as ##CLERK2.

10

6. Use Explorer or NWADMIN to record your effective rights in the subdirectories shown in the following table.

Directory Path	Effective Rights
CHAP10	
CHAP10\ORDERS	
CHAP10\USERS	

7. Log out.

8. Log in as ##CLERK1.

9. Use Explorer or NWADMIN to record your effective rights in the subdirectories shown in the following table.

Directory Path	Effective Rights
CHAP10	
CHAP10\ORDERS	
CHAP10\USERS	

Project 10-3: Using Explorer to Work with Directory Attributes

The objective of this project is to provide you with experience using Windows Explorer to set directory attributes.

1. Log in using your assigned ##ADMIN user name.

2. Start Explorer.

3. Change to your ##ADMIN directory.

4. Create a new directory named MENUS.

5. Add the Don't Compress attribute to the MENUS subdirectory.

6. Use a FLAG command to display the directory attributes. You should see the Don't Compress attribute.

7. Use Explorer to remove the MENUS directory.

8. Log out.

CASE PROJECTS

Case 10-1: J. Q. Adams Company Security

Assume that you are the network administrator for J. Q. Adams. Lois, John, and Ann are employees of J. Q. Adams who all work in the business department. Figure 10-68 shows the business department's directory structure.

Users must have all rights to their home directories, including Supervisor and Access Control, to complete these projects. Your instructor or network administrator may need to set this for you.

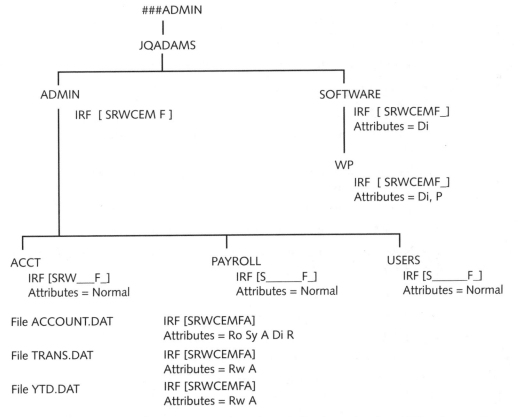

Figure 10-68   J. Q. Adams business department directory structure IRF assignments

10

Step 1: Creating a Structure

To perform this project and answer the questions, you first need to create the directory structure for J. Q. ADAMS in your ##ADMIN student work area by performing the following steps:

1. Log in using your assigned student user name.

2. Using NetWare Administrator, create the directory structure shown in Figure 10-68.

3. Set the IRFs for each of the directories as indicated in Figure 10-68.

4. Set the Delete Inhibit attribute on each of the directories in the JQADAMS structure.

5. Obtain a hard copy of your JQ ADAMS directory structure, including the IRFs for each directory.

6. Use NWAdmin to display the attributes for each of your JQADAMS directories and subdirectories.

7. Use the Print Screen key to print the screen showing your directory attributes.

Step 2: Working with Files

In this project you need to create the general ledger files for the ACCT directory and use FLAG commands to set attributes necessary to meet the requirements specified in the problem.

1. Use Notepad to create the ACCOUNT.DAT file in the ACCT directory with the following contents:

   This is the Accounts Database.

   General ledger accounts and their descriptions are stored here.

2. Use Notepad to create the TRANS and YTD files shown in Table 10-12.

   TRANS.DAT:

   This is the Accounts Transaction file.

   Debit and Credit entries are stored here.

   YDT.DAT

   This is the year-to-date summary file.

   End of year totals are stored here.

Table 10-12   File and directory attribute requirements

Directory/File	Attribute Requirements
ACCOUNT.DAT	Protect the file from being changed and enable shared access.
TRANS.DAT	Protect the file from being erased or renamed, but allow changes to the contents.
YTD.DAT	Protect the file from being erased or renamed, but allow changes to the contents.
SOFTWARE:	Hide this directory.
SOFTWARE\WP:	Immediately purge any deleted files.

3. Use the appropriate utility to set the file and directory attributes as described in Table 10-12. Record each command or utility you used.

ACCOUNT.DAT file: _____

TRANS.DAT file: _____

YTD.DAT file: _____

SOFTWARE: _____

SOFTWARE\WP: _____

4. Use the NDIR command to obtain a hardcopy of all files in the ACCT directory.

5. Use NWAdmin to display the directory attributes. Use the Print Screen key to print the screen.

Step 3: Creating Users and Groups

In this project you will create the users and groups needed for the J. Q. Adams business department. Be sure to replace the number symbols (##) in each user name with your assigned student number.

1. Create the group ##ADMIN in an appropriate part of the JQADAMS tree. Assign the group [RF] rights to the JQADAMS directory. (This will be the default setting.)

2. Create the user accounts shown in Table 10-13 having home directories in the JQADAMS\USERS subdirectory. Make all users members of the ADMIN group.

Table 10-13   J. Q. Adams User Accounts

User	User and Home Directory Name
John Combs	##JCombs
Lois Kent	##LKent
Ann Bonny	##ABonny

Step 4: Assigning Trustee Rights

In this project you use NetWare Administrator to grant trustee assignments for the JQADAMS directory structure to the business department users you created.

1. Launch NetWare Administrator.

2. Because John is the administrator of the business department, grant him the Supervisor right in the JQADAMS\ADMIN\USERS subdirectory.

3. Make Ann a trustee of the payroll directory by giving her all rights to the PAYROLL subdirectory.

4. Make Lois a trustee with [RWFCE] rights to the ACCT directory.

5. If you haven't already done so, grant the ##ADMIN group [RF] rights to the JQADAMS directory.

6. Obtain a hard copy of the trustee assignments for each of the JQADAMS directories.

Step 5: Determining Effective Rights

In this project you use the appropriate NetWare commands to answer questions regarding the user's effective rights to the directory structure. Following each question are lines for you to record what command you used to determine the rights and who you were logged in as when you used the command. In addition, explain why the user or group has these rights and how the rights were obtained.

1. What are John's rights in PAYROLL? :

   Command used: ————————————

   Logged in as: ————————————

   In the following space, explain how John got these rights:

   _____

   _____

2. In the following space, explain what you would do if you no longer wanted John to have all rights to the PAYROLL subdirectory but still have Supervisor rights in the other subdirectories of the JQADAMS structure:

   _____

   _____

3. What are Ann's rights in the ACCT directory? ————————————

   Command used: ————————————

   Logged in as: ————————————

   In the following space, explain how Ann got these rights:

   _____

   _____

4. What are Ann's rights in the PAYROLL directory? ————————

   Command used: ————————

   Logged in as: ————————

   In the following space, explain how Ann got these rights:

   _____

   _____

5. What are Lois's rights in the ACCT directory? ————————

   Command used: ————————

   Logged in as: ————————

   In the following space, explain how Lois got these rights:

   _____

   _____

6. Are Lois's rights in the ACCT subdirectory sufficient for her to keep the files updated? ————————

   If not, explain why:

   _____

   _____

   If not, provide her with the necessary rights. Record here how you did it:

   _____

7. Log in as John and determine what his effective rights are to the ACCOUNT.DAT file: ————————

   Command used: ————————

   Logged in as: ————————

8. Try to use Notepad to change the contents of the ACCOUNT.DAT file. Record your results in the following space:

   _____

9. Explain briefly what John must do if he needs to add information accounts to the ACCOUNT.DAT file:

   _____

   _____

10. Use the appropriate utility to implement the solution you defined in Step 9. Record the option you used here: ————————

11. Ann needs to be able to post payroll transactions to the TRANS file. Briefly explain what steps you should follow to enable Ann to post to the TRANS file but not give her access to the other files in the ACCT directory.

10

11

INSTALLING APPLICATIONS

After reading this chapter and completing the exercises you will be able to:

♦ List and define the three levels of NetWare compatibility

♦ Describe the three types of network-compatible programs

♦ Create the file structure necessary for installing network applications

♦ Use NetWare commands to install software and grant users the rights they need to run software

♦ Install and test applications

♦ Use the Application Launcher and snAppShot to distribute and manage applications

Your responsibilities as a network administrator will include installing, configuring, and testing application software. Because access to applications will be your users' primary concern on the network, proper management of those applications is critical. Typical tasks of setting up rights, paths, and configuration can be handled more easily in NetWare 5.0, thanks to the Application Launcher tool and NetWare Administrator.

Because software packages have such a wide variety of specialized installation programs and procedures, it is not possible to provide a detailed set of rules and techniques that will work for installing all applications. Refer to the installation instructions that come with each application to work out the details of installing that product on the server. There are, however, several general steps that should be followed for most software installations. This chapter describes the following eight steps of software installation:

1. Determine NetWare compatibility.

2. Determine single-user or multiuser capability.

3. Determine and create the appropriate directory structure.

4. Perform the application installation procedure.

5. Set appropriate directory and file attributes.

6. Provide user access rights.

7. Modify configuration files.

8. Test the software.

We cannot overemphasize the importance of controlling software licensing on the network. Before adding any software on the server, make sure you do not violate the terms of the software license agreement. Read the software license agreement to determine if it is legal to run the software from a server and be sure you have the correct number of licenses to cover the number of users who will be accessing the application at one time. As the administrator, you will be held responsible if the organization you work for is found in violation of the software license, so you need to make certain that the software you install on the server does not violate copyrights.

NetWare 5.0 introduces a desktop management architecture and tool set called **Z.E.N.works** (for **Zero Effort Networking**). Z.E.N.works includes the Application Launcher (previously called NetWare Application Launcher or NAL) and extends its capabilities. The Application Launcher leverages NDS to make it easier to set up applications on a workstation. Using NWAdmin, you can set up an Application object such that the next time users log in, NetWare will create a new shortcut on their desktops for an application so they can run it. Z.E.N.works goes much further. It provides a way of totally configuring a user's workstation during the NetWare login process. Z.E.N.works is a major advance in network management that reestablishes Novell as a leader in network operating systems.

Although we will discuss Z.E.N.works only briefly here, it is an extremely powerful tool. It can be used to create a virtual desktop for each user, including all setup and configuration details for applications, and distribute it to any desktop from which the user logs in. Users will no longer have to consider just one computer "their" system. Using Z.E.N.works, any workstation could become "their" system. (You will learn more about using Z.E.N.works to manage a network in Chapter 14.)

DETERMINING NETWARE COMPATIBILITY

When you install an application on a NetWare server, it is important to first determine the application's level of NetWare compatibility. Most applications are designed and written for use on networks and can be installed by following the network installation instructions included with the software package. Because NetWare is very compatible with DOS, most older applications and legacy software will also run flawlessly from the server even though they were originally written for a standalone computer. Certain programs, however, cannot be installed on a NetWare drive, and others will not run properly after installation. In this section, you will learn about the three basic levels of NetWare compatibility and how they affect the installation procedure: NetWare-incompatible, NetWare-compatible, and NetWare-aware.

NetWare-Incompatible

Certain applications are designed to work only from a local workstation's hard drive. This is often true of older applications—especially those that have copy protection systems built into the software or installation program. Some of these copy protection systems require a special disk containing the software license number to be in the disk drive of the machine running the program. Sometimes these applications run when installed on a server; the workstation running the software, however, needs to have the original disk. Other software installation procedures involve writing information, such as the software license, directly to the hard drive of the computer in which the software is installed. Because these installation programs write directly to the local computer's hard drive, they cannot be used to install the software onto the server. As a result, these software packages either fail to be installed into the NetWare file system or do not run properly if copied into a NetWare directory.

Today almost all commercially available software packages are designed to run from either a network server or a workstation's local hard drive. (Exceptions include CD-ROM-based titles.) Some software companies, however, have designed their programs to run from a server only when you purchase the network version of the application. When you try to copy the workstation version of one of these programs to the server and then run the program from an attached workstation, an error message informs you that the application cannot be run from a network drive. This problem is easily solved by purchasing a network upgrade for the software package, which allows the number of workstations specified in your license to access the software from the server at the same time.

NetWare-Compatible

Thousands of software applications are certified by Novell as being NetWare-compatible. **NetWare-compatible** means that the software can be installed in the NetWare file system and will then run properly from any workstation just as if it were running from that workstation's local disk drive. Although many programs are not specifically designed for NetWare, the Novell Client makes the NetWare file system appear as a local drive. Most applications, therefore, are not aware of the fact that they are being run from a server rather

11

than the local hard disk. To deal with these programs, the administrator usually uses NetWare drive mappings to establish regular or search drives in order to install and run these programs from the server. To determine if a software package you are considering is NetWare-compatible, refer to one of the following sources:

- Novell's Internet site (*www.novell.com*)

- A regional Novell sales office

- The supplier of the application

NetWare-Aware

Many software applications today are designed to take advantage of the features found in network operating systems. They therefore often include special NetWare installation options such as setting up network printing or creating separate work and configuration files for each user. These software packages are referred to as being **NetWare-aware**.

 When Windows is installed on networked workstations, Microsoft Windows applications can automatically take advantage of many network functions. A user running the Microsoft Word application on a networked workstation, for example, can choose to send output directly to a NetWare printer or access a document file, either using a drive pointer that has been previously mapped to the NetWare file system or through exploring Network Neighborhood.

When you are buying an application that is NetWare-aware, check with the supplier about software license requirements. Some NetWare-aware software products have built-in limitations on the number of users that can access the application at one time, based on your license agreement. To increase the number of users who can run the software applications with these built-in limitations, you need to obtain additional license disks that you then install on the server. For software packages that do not have built-in software license counters, the purchaser is expected to obtain licenses to accommodate the number of users who need to run the software concurrently. It is the administrator's responsibility to do this.

 Network metering software is available to let an administrator limit the number of users who can run a specified program at the same time. Installing this type of license-counting software can greatly assist you in enforcing software license agreements on your network.

Licenses come in many varieties. The most common in enterprise use are site, corporate, concurrent, and per-seat licenses. Site licenses permit any number of users at a given location to use the software. A corporate license is similar, but it covers an entire organization. Concurrent licensing is a way for companies to save money by buying only the number of licenses they need at any one time. For example, if a company has 20 people in its accounting department, but only 10 people work each shift, the company could purchase a 10-user concurrent license. A per-seat license provides for every user; if you have 20 possible users, you would buy 20 seat licenses.

Microsoft does not offer concurrent licensing. You must buy a license for each possible user of Microsoft software when used in an enterprise environment. You will need to discuss with a Microsoft representative if you qualify for a site or corporate license to help reduce the cost. (Fortunately, Microsoft is one of only a few companies to do this. Most support concurrent licensing.)

Many applications, because they have no internal mechanism to limit access, work for an unlimited number of users on the network. Installing and using such software without buying enough licenses for the number of active users is a direct violation of the software's licensing agreement. Vendors and the Software Publishers Association are conducting impromptu audits of educational and commercial sites to verify valid licensing. Fines for violations usually are in the tens of thousands of dollars. It is simply not worth that risk to copy programs to the network for everyone's use without licenses. Even if a user commits the error, it is your job as administrator to check on newly installed programs and verify license compliance.

DETERMINING SINGLE-USER OR MULTIUSER CAPABILITY

After you determine that a software package is compatible with your NetWare server, the next step toward installation is to determine the capability of the application in terms of the number of users it supports. There are three types of programs that run on a network: single-user, multiple-user, and multiuser. This section describes the three capabilities and explains how they relate to installing and using the application on your network.

Single-User

Many NetWare-compatible software packages are designed to operate from the workstation's local disk drive and are therefore limited to being run by only one user at a time. These are called **single-user applications**. This limitation can be imposed by a software license or by the way the application is designed. Many software programs use temporary files to store the system information the program needs to operate. Because single-user software applications are designed to be used by only one user at a time, when two users try to access the application simultaneously, the information written to the temporary file for the second user can overwrite control information needed by the first user. This causes the software application to issue error messages or to crash.

Figure 11-1 illustrates the attempt by two users at CBE Labs, Jon Jorgenson and Shelly Wells, to run a single-user spreadsheet program. Jon starts the program first and opens a file named BUDGET.XLS on a network disk drive. Information about the file, including the file's name, is then written to the temporary file in the spreadsheet software directory. Shelly then starts the spreadsheet program and opens a file called SALES.XLS on a workstation's local hard drive. The spreadsheet program next writes control information from the SALES files to the same temporary file used to store the control information for the BUDGET file. The result is that the control information for Jon is erased, causing his spreadsheet program to crash or produce an error message when the file information is needed.

11

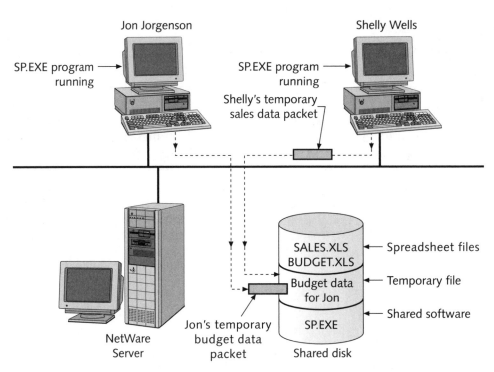

Figure 11-1   Single-user application

Even if a software application supports only one user at a time, there are still advantages to placing it on a server rather than on a local workstation. One advantage is that it can be used by more than one user, as long as it is not done simultaneously. Another advantage is that it prevents users from modifying the configuration files or illegally copying the software to another machine. When a software program is installed on a NetWare server, you can use access rights and file attributes to prevent files from being changed or copied.

A disadvantage of running certain applications from a server can be the additional load placed on the network. For example, running Aldus PageMaker over a network can significantly slow down other network operations because of the large amount of application software and other data loaded during normal program operation. The best way to determine where to place applications to maximize their performance is to load the application on both a server and a workstation and compare its speed during normal operation.

The first step in deciding to place a single-user software package on the server is to consult the license agreement to be sure it is legal for you to run the program from a server. Even though a single-user application can be run by only one user at a time, some software companies consider simply placing their applications on a server a violation of the copyright agreement and may require you to get a network license in order to use the program legally even for one user.

Multiple-User

A **multiple-user application** is either NetWare-aware—and therefore designed to support multiple users—or is designed with enough flexibility so that the application can be set up to keep each user's work files separated. Figure 11-2 illustrates a multiple-user application. Both Thomas Myer and Sarah Johnston of CBE Labs are running a multiple-user word processing application and are working with document files on their local hard drives. Because the word processing software is designed for multiple users, Thomas's control information for the LETTER1 document file is kept in a temporary file that is separate from the control information for Sarah's MEMO2 document file. Keeping each user's temporary and configuration data in separate files is one way multiple-user software applications support simultaneous use of a program.

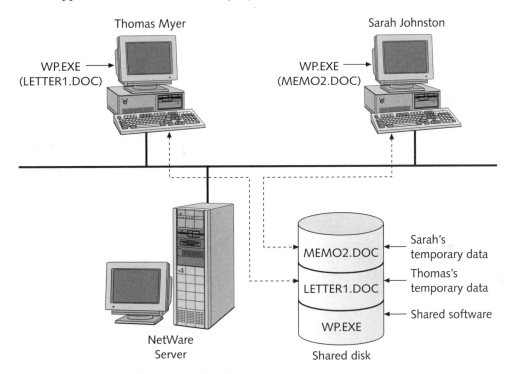

Figure 11-2   Multiple-user application

Some applications that are designed for use by a single user on a local workstation can be adapted to support multiple users on a network. This is done by setting up a search drive to the software directory, flagging the program files as sharable, and then providing separate work directories for each user's configuration files. This complicated procedure can be difficult if you are not very familiar with the program or don't have the advice of someone who has reconfigured an application in this way.

Most network system software (such as NetWare), and general-purpose software applications (such as word processors, desktop publishing, spreadsheets, and database management software) are accessed simultaneously by many users. Thus the administrator needs to maintain only one copy of an application on the server rather than keep track of multiple copies installed on separate workstations. NetWare-aware programs are designed to support multiple users simultaneously and, if you get the correct number of licenses for the number of users, can be installed by following the instructions for your network system. Multiple-user applications enable users to manage data and document files located anywhere in the network file system. A user in the finance department, for example, can access a spreadsheet program to create a graph showing projected sales for the quarter, whereas a user in the accounting department can run the same spreadsheet software to do a cash flow report.

Although a multiple-user application lets more than one user run the program at the same time to work on separate files, it does not allow two or more users to access the same file simultaneously. Two users can, for example, use the same word processing program, but they cannot access the same document file and make changes to it simultaneously. The first user must finish his or her changes and close the file before the next user can access the document to view or change it.

Some programs, such as Microsoft Word, allow two or more users to open a single document. However, the program notifies the second and additional users that they are opening a document that already has been opened by another user. The second and following users will not be able to save the file by its original name but can save it with a new name, in the same directory or in a different directory as the original file.

Multiuser

A **multiuser application** is a special type of multiple-user software that enables more than one user to access the same file simultaneously. Multiuser applications are often required in a database system when more than one user needs to access data. This situation occurs, for example, in an order entry system—like the one shown in Figure 11-3—when two or more records in the Orders database need to be updated by clerks processing orders at the same time. In this illustration, Sarah Johnston and Thomas Myer from CBE Labs receive calls at the same time from different customers placing orders. Customer 4 orders 10 subscriptions; Customer 2 orders 3. Because the Orders program is designed to enable more than one user to access the Orders database, Sarah can be writing Customer 4's order to disk at the same time Thomas is updating Customer 2's order information, which is stored in a separate database record.

Application systems with multiuser programs—such as order entry systems or airline reservation systems—often use programs that include special features to prevent one user's changes from overwriting changes made by another user. **Record locking** is one of the features included with most multiuser applications to protect the database records from corruption in the event that two users access the same record simultaneously. Record locking lets a multiuser program prevent users on the network from editing a specific record in a file while it is being updated. While a sales clerk is working with Customer 4, for example, no other user on the network can edit Customer 4's order information.

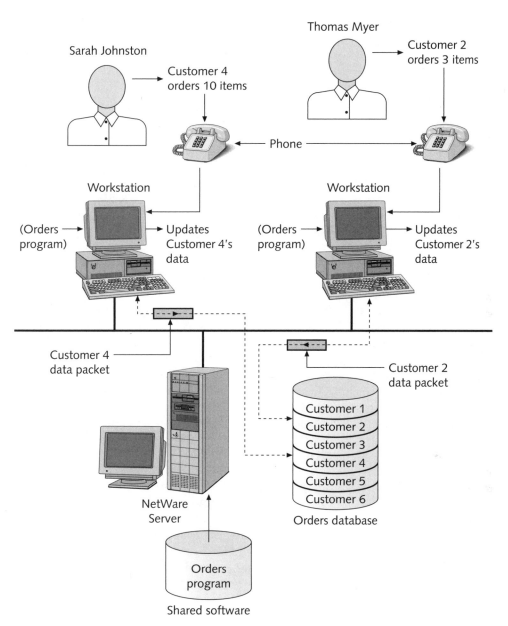

Figure 11-3   Multiuser application

In addition to record locking, NetWare includes a feature called the **transaction tracking system (TTS)**. The TTS, working with record locking, enables software packages to recover data if a workstation crashes in the middle of processing a transaction. Assume, for example, that Sarah's computer crashes after Customer 4's order has been written to disk but before the customer's accounts receivable data is updated. Transaction tracking lets Sarah return the customer order information to its preorder status and then re-enter Customer 4's order. Without transaction tracking, Customer 4's order could accidentally be placed twice and the account balance updated only once. To let the application implement the record locking and transaction tracking features of NetWare, application software must be written to use special multiuser instructions.

 Integrated network applications such as Microsoft Office use a process in Microsoft Windows called dynamic linking. This process allows a master document file to consist of multiple object documents. Each object document can then be accessed by a different user, and the master document can be updated automatically with any changes made to the object documents.

DETERMINING THE APPROPRIATE DIRECTORY STRUCTURE

After you determine the NetWare compatibility level of the application with which you are working, the next step is to decide where the application belongs in the organization's directory structure. Where you place an application's directory in the file system is determined to a large extent by your directory structure design and by what type of application you are installing. This section offers suggestions for placing an application's directory, based on whether the application is single-user, multiple-user, or multiuser.

 Although the examples here show the SYS volume as the location for applications, this is by no means the only location possible for these files. For security reasons, some administrators limit access to the SYS volume and then create an APPS volume specifically to contain application directories.

Single-User Applications

Because single-user applications are used by only one user at a time, access to them is usually restricted to just a few users in an organization. Therefore a single-user application is best stored in a location of the directory structure that is closest to the users who will be running the application. A single-user payroll application for CBE Labs, for example, is normally used by one or two users in the finance department. The logical destination for the directory containing the payroll software and data is therefore within the finance department's shared directory structure, as Figure 11-4 shows.

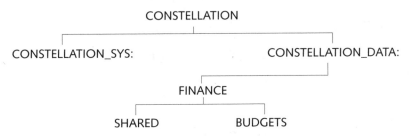

Figure 11-4 Single-user application directory structure

Multiple-User Applications

General-purpose multiple-user applications such as word processors, spreadsheets, graphics, or database software applications that many users in an organization access to maintain their own separate files are often placed in a common directory in a network volume such as the SYS volume, as Figure 11-5 shows. This directory structure lets the administrator use the inherited rights principle (described in Chapter 10) to easily provide Read and File Scan rights to the general-purpose applications for all users to the APPS directory.

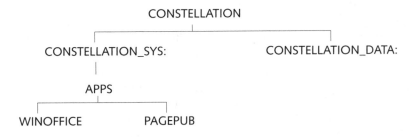

Figure 11-5 Multiple-user application directory structure

 Because of their large size and complex interaction with local workstation hardware, Windows 95 and Windows 98 typically are not installed and run from the network.

Multiuser Applications

As noted earlier, multiuser applications must be specially written to take advantage of such network features as record locking and transaction tracking. As a result, multiuser applications are usually designed for specific database-oriented applications that handle such tasks as order entry, reservations, or inventory control. Because of the specialized nature of multiuser applications, you can often base their location on the users of each application. For example, CBE Labs may locate programs that the entire marketing group needs in the SHARED directory, as shown in Figure 11-6. Employee review, however, which is accessed only by personnel department users, can be located within the PERSNNL directory structure, as Figure 11-6 shows.

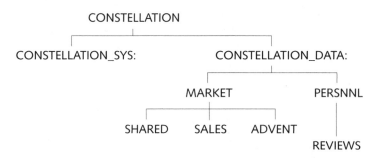

Figure 11-6   Multiuser application directory structure

Temporary and Configuration Files

Many NetWare-aware software programs need to store configuration information and temporary files for each user. Before you install an application, therefore, it is important to study the installation instructions to determine what options you have for placing temporary and user configuration files. Temporary files are usually created when a user starts the application and are deleted when the application program is terminated. Configuration files, in contrast, are permanent files that are normally used to store software settings such as printer type and default data storage path for each user. With separate configuration files, each user can customize the application to accommodate his or her normal usage. Most NetWare-aware software installation programs let the administrator specify where the user's temporary and configuration files will be stored. Before installing software applications, you need to decide where these files will be stored. One option is to store these files on the workstation's local hard disk drive. Using the local hard disk has the advantages of keeping user files separate and reducing demands on the network. A disadvantage, however, is that to use the customized settings, the user must run the software from his or her assigned workstation.

Because temporary files involve much more disk activity than configuration files do, a good compromise, when possible, is to store configuration files on the network and to keep the temporary files on the local hard disk. When you store configuration files on the server, you can place them in each user's home directory, or place all user configuration files for the software package in a common configuration directory.

PERFORMING THE APPLICATION INSTALLATION

Installing applications generally involves running a SETUP or INSTALL program that asks you for several items of information, including the location of the software disk, the drive or directory path into which you want to install, the location of work and configuration files, printer types, and specialized software configuration parameters. Although software configuration parameters depend on the application being installed, as administrator you need to provide the installation program with a path to the appropriate directory locations and select the proper printers and ports that will work on the network. This section describes some installation considerations you need to be aware of when selecting directories and printers.

Planning Drive Pointer Usage

Before running the installation program for a software product, you must determine if the program requires any NetWare drive mappings to run. Most Windows applications now support the **Universal Naming Convention (UNC)** for mapping drives and therefore do not require any drive mappings. With UNC, you simply specify the name of the server, the name of the volume, then the directory path to access a file. For example:

```
\\CONSTELLATION\SYS:APPS\WP
```

specifies the server CONSTELLATION, the volume SYS, and the directory path APPS\WP to find a file.

With older software, for Windows to find and start the program, you had to specify a drive letter, then the directory path:

```
G:\APPS\WP
```

For example, various versions of Intuit's Quicken and QuickBooks still require specific drive mappings to find their data files automatically.

The drawback to drive mapping is that all possible users of an application must map a drive on their workstation to that directory, which often requires using the same drive letter. This mapping therefore must be included in the users' login scripts. With Novell's Application Launcher, it is much easier to do this drive mapping dynamically, as you'll learn later in this chapter.

 To determine if your program requires drive mappings, open the application and find a dialog box with a browse feature (such as File, Open). If the program provides a browse dialog box to search through Network Neighborhood, it supports UNC. If it provides only a listing of drive letters, then it does not support UNC and you will have to map a drive letter for this application.

The following explanation is for those programs that do require drive mappings. Application installation programs need to know the path to the directory that will contain the application program files as well as the location of the user configuration and temporary files. Because each user who runs this application will need access to the application and configuration files, you should plan to use a drive pointer that will be mapped to the same volume for all users. This is important because if the drive letter you select is mapped to a different volume for some users, the directory path will not be found on the specified drive letter when these users try to run the application, and the application will terminate.

Suppose, for example, that you plan to place configuration files in the SYS:SOFTWARE\ WP\SETUP directory, and during installation you specify the path to the configuration files as G:\SOFTWARE\WP\SETUP, because drive G is currently mapped to the SYS volume. Assume that after you install the application, a user who has drive G mapped to the DATA volume attempts to run the application. Because the DATA volume does not contain the \SOFTWARE\WP\SETUP directory, the application program will terminate, because it cannot locate the user configuration files. For users to be able to run the application package, therefore, the paths specified for software configuration and temporary files absolutely must use a drive letter that will be mapped to the same path for all users. You can do this by setting up standard drive mappings in the container login script file, as described in Chapter 13.

When installing software that is not NetWare-aware, you might need to use the MAP ROOT command (see Chapter 8) for the drive letter you plan to use to contain the application directory. Mapping a root drive is necessary with installation programs that are not NetWare-aware because some installation programs have been known to create their own directory structure at the root of the drive letter you specify. Mapping a root drive will cause these installation programs to create the application directory within the directory structure to which you have mapped the root drive, rather than at the root of the NetWare volume.

If you wanted, for example, to install a payroll application that is not NetWare-aware in the FINANCE directory shown in Figure 11-4, you would first select a drive letter, such as P, to be used for the payroll application and then map a root drive P pointer to the FINANCE directory, using the following command:

```
MAP ROOT P:=DATA:FINANCE
```

Now when the installation program attempts to create a payroll directory in path P:\, it will actually be making the directory in the FINANCE directory structure.

Specifying the Directory Path

Your first step, before running an installation program, is to be sure the drive mappings you plan to use for the application and configuration files have been established. Immediately after starting, most software installation programs will ask you to specify the path to the directory in which the application program files are to be installed. Later during the installation process, you may also have options to enter paths for both temporary and configuration files. When entering the paths, be sure to specify the drive pointers you defined when planning your directory structure.

Figure 11-7 shows a screen that appears during installation of the Corel WordPerfect application, which includes the paths for installing the application on a network drive. Notice that the F network drive letter is being used for installing the software. Suppose the COREL\SUITE8 directory of the volume is mapped to drive F, and the default directory for user document files is located on drive H. In order to use the application, each user will need to have his or her drive F letter mapped to the volume that contains the COREL\SUITE8 directory, along with a drive H pointer mapped to the default document directory.

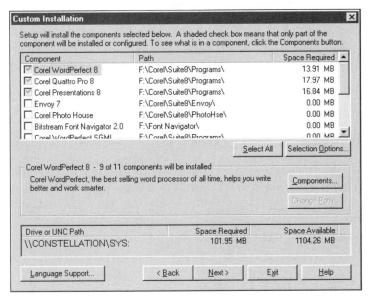

Figure 11-7   Choosing WordPerfect in Custom Installation screen

Specifying Printer Types and Ports

Most applications enable you to select one or more printer types, along with the port used for hard copy output. Multiple-user applications that include word processors and spreadsheets let the installer select many printer types for the user to choose. In these cases, you select the printer types that will be available on the user's workstations or can be shared on the network. If the application is NetWare-aware or complies with Windows requirements, you will be able to select a printer name for your print setup. (NetWare printing is covered in Chapter 12.) All contemporary Windows software supports printing to your defined Windows printers—which can include NetWare printers as well.

Installation programs for single-user applications may limit you to only one printer type during installation. To enable multiple users to run a software package that is installed for only one type of printer, you may want to place the selected printer on the network. Doing so will let all users access the same printer type. The best solution is to select the best printer type you can afford for this application and then place that printer on the network, as Chapter 12 describes. The printed output from the program can then be redirected to the network printer, so that the output will be directed to the correct printer type no matter which user is operating the program.

SETTING APPROPRIATE DIRECTORY AND FILE ATTRIBUTES

After you run the software installation program, you need to make sure the application directory and files are secure. If the software is designed for multiple users, you need to provide for shared use. If the installation program is NetWare-aware, it may set the necessary file and directory attributes for you. You may, however, want to add attributes to increase file security or provide extra functions such as transaction tracking. This section discusses which attributes are appropriate for what applications. Table 11-1 summarizes the attribute settings for each application type.

Table 11-1   Attribute settings

Application Type	Data Files	Application Program Files
Single-user Example: Payroll	Read Write nonsharable	Read Only nonsharable (some software programs may allow multiple users to access them even if flagged nonsharable)
Multiple-user Example: word processor	Read Write nonsharable	Read Only Sharable
Multiuser Example: database system	Read Write Transactional Sharable (requires the program to provide record locking and transaction tracking)	Read Only Sharable

You can use the function of the Sharable attribute on a document file to let multiple users access that file at the same time, as Chapter 10 describes. This attribute is usually set on record-locking database files.

Single-User Applications

Because only one user at a time can use a single-user application, both data files and executable program files require no special attributes—except possibly the Read Only attribute, to protect them from accidental erasure or modification by a user or a software virus. The Read Only attribute is important for applications in which users need Erase, Modify, or Write access rights to work with data or temporary files stored in the application's directory. Setting the Read Only attribute, however, sometimes causes application errors for certain software products that store configuration information in the program files. Make sure you test the application after setting any Read Only attributes, to be sure users can perform their necessary functions. An alternative to using the Read Only attribute is to use the Delete Inhibit and Rename Inhibit attributes to protect application files from being renamed or erased and still allow changes to be made. Setting these attributes on a file allows users to change the contents of the file but keeps them from renaming or deleting the file.

Even though program files in a single-user application are not flagged Sharable, in some applications two or more users can run the application at the same time, causing program problems or corrupt data files. Test a newly installed application by running it from two different workstations, to find out if more than one user can access the programs simultaneously. If more than one user can run the programs at the same time, you need to develop a procedure to prevent multiple access, or else install the application in a separate directory for each user. If multiple users need access to the same data files, replace the single-user application with a NetWare-aware application designed for multiple users.

Multiple-User Applications

The major difference in attribute settings between a multiple-user application and a single-user application is that the files that run the multiple-user application should be flagged Sharable to let more than one user access the software simultaneously. Because most multiple-user applications are NetWare-aware, they are designed for shared access, and the installation process may not require you to use Explorer to set the Sharable attribute. Check the installation instructions, however, to see if you need to set any additional attributes after installation. As for single-user applications, data files for multiple-user applications must be left nonsharable and Read Write to prevent multiple users from overwriting each other's changes. Leaving the data files nonsharable allows only one user at a time to access and modify information in a specific file.

 As mentioned earlier, some applications such as Microsoft Word, when used on a network, let two or more users open a document file at the same time even when the file is not flagged Sharable. However, only the first user to open the document can save changes to the document under its original name. Changes made by the second user can be saved to a different filename. If the second user tries to save the file using its original name, an "Access denied" error message is displayed.

Multiuser Applications

As already stated, a multiuser application is a special form of a multiple-user application that lets more than one user update the same data file simultaneously. The major difference in attribute settings between multiple-user and multiuser applications is that the data files to be shared should have the Sharable attribute set for multiuser applications, to enable multiple users to access and update the database records simultaneously. In addition, to enable TTS on a shared database system, the database files (such as .DAT or .DBF files) need to be flagged with the Transactional attribute in addition to being made Sharable. Executable files also require special attention, as Figure 11-8 shows.

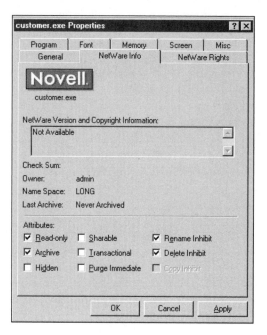

Figure 11-8   Setting multiuser file attributes

Notice that the CUSTOMER.EXE file is flagged Delete Inhibit (DI) and Rename Inhibit (RI). These additional attributes prevent files from being accidentally deleted or renamed by users who have been given Erase or Modify access rights. Flagging the CUSTOMER.EXE program file (or any .EXE or .COM file) Read Only will keep a user or a software virus from copying, changing, or deleting it.

All Applications

In addition to the attributes already described, you might want to use NetWare's Hidden attribute to make it more difficult for users to copy program files illegally onto a local disk. To prevent an executable file from being copied, you can right-click the filename in the NDS tree in NetWare Administrator. Choose Details, then click the Attributes tab to open the dialog box shown in Figure 11-9. You can then check the Execute Only attribute for the file. This prevents the program file from being copied but still lets it be run.

The disadvantage of the Execute Only attribute is that once set on a file it cannot be removed, even by the administrator. Therefore, make sure to have original installation disks or a working backup of the application file. Software applications that open their executable program files in the read mode to access messages and other information will not run correctly when the Execute Only attribute is set. Because the Execute Only attribute allows the program files to be opened only in run mode, these programs crash when they attempt to read from their program files. After you set the Execute Only attribute, make sure to test the application.

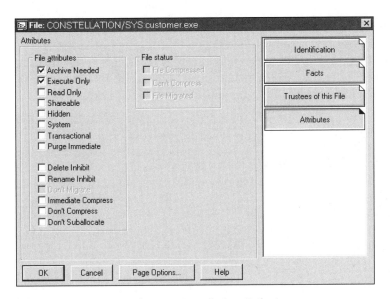

Figure 11-9   Using the Execute Only attribute

Another directory attribute to consider in this context is Purge. Flagging directories that contain temporary files with the Purge attribute will cause the NetWare operating system to immediately reclaim the space used by a temporary file when the temporary file is deleted. Because you would probably never want to salvage a temporary file, flagging temporary file directories with the Purge attribute can help improve system performance and provide more time before NetWare will need to reuse space occupied by other deleted data files—ones that might be more likely to need salvaging.

PROVIDING USER ACCESS RIGHTS

To use a newly installed application, users need access rights to the software directory along with appropriate drive mappings. As an administrator, you need to determine the minimum set of access rights that will let users work with the application software yet keep them from changing or deleting programs or files that must remain unaltered. To separate application software from the data, the administrator must also define regular and search drives that will let users run application software from the directory containing data files. This section discusses several considerations and techniques that will help you plan and provide user access.

Access Rights

At a minimum, all users will need Read and File Scan rights to the directory containing an application. Whenever possible, assign trustee rights to groups rather than to individual users—this makes it easier to add or change access rights later. In addition, you may need to assign additional rights for either of the following two conditions:

- If you are storing temporary files in the application software directory, you will need to provide users with at least the Create and Erase rights to this directory. In addition, if the software application needs to rename temporary files, you must assign the Modify right. This creates a security problem, however, because users with the Modify right can change the attributes on program files. You can prevent this change either by placing temporary files in a different directory (if possible) or by using the Inherited Rights Filter (IRF) on each of the program files, enabling them to inherit only Read and File Scan rights.

- If you store the user configuration files in the software directory and you want users to be able to customize their configuration settings, you will need to provide users with at least the Write right. If you place user configuration files in a separate directory, then assign the users Read, File Scan, Write, Create, Erase, and Modify rights to the directory that contains the configuration files.

Drive Mappings

In order for users to run application software that does not support UNC (the Universal Naming Convention), and to access data files, you need to establish both search and regular drive pointers. (These drive mappings will need to be included in the login script files, as described in Chapter 13, or launched using the Application Launcher). Regular drive pointers should provide users easy access to the directory location containing their data, with a maximum of three directory layers. The regular drive pointers consist of a drive pointer to the root of the volume, a drive pointer to the user's workgroup, and a drive pointer to the user's home directory. These drive pointers should be sufficient to access most application data files. If a data directory is accessed by users in multiple departments, however, a special drive mapping to that directory should be established for all users who need to use the data.

Search drive mappings should be established for all general-purpose software directories. When planning search drive mappings, try to keep the total number of search drives for any user to eight or fewer. You can do this by using the Application Launcher to insert a search drive mapping for the application being run and then deleting that search drive mapping when the program terminates.

Modifying Configuration Files

A final step of installing an application may involve modifying the CONFIG.SYS files on all workstations that will be running an application. As an administrator, you need to know the statements that might be added to the CONFIG.SYS file of each workstation on the network. Installation programs often modify the CONFIG.SYS of the workstation in which you install the software, but the other workstations that will run this application from the network will also need to have their CONFIG.SYS files modified in order to use the application.

 Although many administrators believe that Windows 95/98 no longer uses either the CONFIG.SYS or AUTOEXEC.BAT files, that is not true. You will seldom find software for Windows 95 or 98 that will require changes to those files, but it is still possible. For example, Internet News Reader adds a statement to the AUTOEXEC.BAT file, as does Corel's WordPerfect 7.

Table 11-2 shows three common CONFIG.SYS statements with examples. The FILES statement increases the number of file handles available to DOS. A file handle contains information on each file that is currently open. Most network software will require at least 25 file handles. The BUFFERS statement increases the number of disk blocks that DOS will keep in memory. When NetWare drives are accessed, this number can be kept quite low, because most information comes from the network and each block takes up to 532 KB of RAM on the workstation. Between 12 and 15 blocks will be enough for most network workstations. The SHELL statement increases the environment space available to hold the DOS paths and search drives. In addition, certain software variables and directory locations are stored here. Because of this, it is often necessary to increase the space to at least 1024 bytes for most network workstations. If you receive the message "Out of Environment Space," you should increase the environment space by an additional 256 bytes.

Table 11-2 Common CONFIG.SYS statements

Statement	Example
FILES=n	FILES=25
BUFFERS=n	BUFFERS=15
SHELL=[path]COMMAND.COM/P/E:n	SHELL=COMMAND.COM/P/E:1024 The /E:1024 parameter defines 1024 bytes of environment space.

11

TESTING THE SOFTWARE

After the installation process has been completed, the administrator needs to complete the following steps to test the software:

1. Test the application while logged in with Supervisor rights.

2. Test the application while logged in with a user name of a user who will use the application.

3. Test the application from each user's workstation to ensure that workstations are properly configured.

4. Check users' effective rights in relevant directories and program files.

First, test the application while logged in with Supervisor rights. Right-click Network Neighborhood on the desktop to establish the drive mappings you defined for the application software. Use Explorer to go to the data directory, and double-click the appropriate icon to start the application. Test as many functions of the application as possible, including data entry, file access, and printing.

When you are confident the application is installed correctly and the correct drive mappings have been defined, log out and then log back in with a user name that will run the application. Repeat the tests you ran as administrator, to make sure users have been granted the rights necessary to work with the application. After you have confirmed that the software will run from your workstation when you log in as a user, go to each user's workstation and test the application to be sure the workstation configurations support the application properly. Finally, check the user's effective rights in each of the directories and program files to make sure users cannot erase or change crucial files.

THE APPLICATION LAUNCHER

A feature of NetWare 5.0 and the Novell Client software is the **Application Launcher** (formerly the Novell Application Launcher or NAL), which is part of the Z.E.N.works software included with NetWare 5.0. The Application Launcher helps administrators configure and manage applications. Once configured, users can launch the application from an Application Launcher window on their desktops or from the Windows Explorer, Start menu, System Tray, or even from an icon on the desktop. This relieves the users from needing to know on which server, volume, and directory an application is installed, and it also relieves the administrator from much of the detail of managing applications on the network.

Support for the Application Launcher is included with both the Novell Client for Windows 95/98 and the Novell Client for DOS and Windows 3.x. However, the Z.E.N.works installation is separate from the NetWare 5.0 installation (but is included on the Novell Client CD-ROM). This installation task is performed by a CNE (Certified NetWare Engineer), rather than a CNA (Certified NetWare Administrator), and therefore is not covered here.

Why use the Application Launcher to start applications, rather than creating the desktop shortcut icons familiar to most Windows users? There are many reasons. First, using Windows to create the icons requires visiting each workstation to manually create them. This is a major investment in time and effort. Second, any changes you need to make to these applications may require revisiting every desktop in order to reconfigure the icons. (Even worse, you might try asking users to do the reconfiguration on their own.) Finally, determining who uses a particular workstation so you can configure the appropriate icons would be a challenge. Instead, the Application Launcher lets you set up all this from your central console using NDS and user/group/container relationships.

Z.E.N.works is included with NetWare 5.0, but only as a starter pack. Additional functionality must be purchased for it to operate fully. The full version of Z.E.N.works offers:

- Remote control through NDS to resolve software problems.

- Help Requester so users can interact with a network help desk system via e-mail.

- Hardware inventory with the gathered workstation information placed into NDS.

To use the Application Launcher, you need to define an Application object. First, you launch NetWare Administrator, and select the Organization or Organizational Unit container in which to locate the Application object. Next, right-click the object and select Create to display the available NDS objects as shown in Figure 11-10. Select the Application object and click OK to display the Create Application Object window.

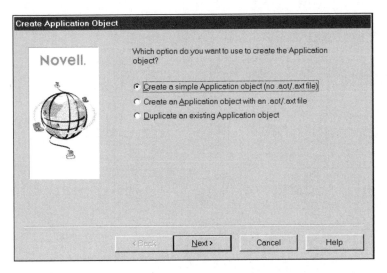

Figure 11-10 Creating an Application object

Older versions of NetWare Administrator offered Application object types for DOS and for the various Windows versions. NetWare 5.0's NetWare Administrator now incorporates this information as part of a single Application object type.

Choose Create a simple Application object, then click Next. The NetWare Administrator asks you to name the Application object you are creating. For example, if you are going to distribute a word processor (such as Microsoft Word), you could type Word Processor or Word97 as the name.

You can now specify the network path to the program itself. If you need to, you can browse through your network directories to locate the program. Finally, check the box marked Define additional properties so you can associate this Application object with a container object. Now click Finish.

NetWare Administrator now creates the new Application object in the tree. It then opens the object's dialog box. Click the Associations tab, and then the Add button to display the list of available objects. Choose an appropriate container object to associate with this application. This should be a container within which are the users who need this application. Click OK when you are finished.

After you select the type of application you want to create, as mentioned before, you enter the name of the application as you want it to appear on the NDS tree, enter the location of the file to be executed, check the Define additional properties box, and click Create. NetWare Administrator creates the new Application object and displays the Application Identification dialog box, as Figure 11-11 shows.

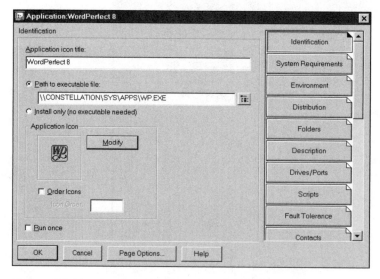

Figure 11-11   Application Identification dialog box

You can now configure your application by selecting the buttons (pages) in the right-hand column of the Application Identification dialog box. The key pages are:

- *Identification*—This page lets you change the application's icon, the title of the icon, and the path to the executable files.

- *System Requirements*—On this page you can specify any operating system, RAM, or processor requirements for the application. If the application requires a given amount of free space on a network or local drive—for example, for a swap file a typical part of Windows and Windows applications)—you can also specify that here. Any user clicking this application's Application icon in the Application Launcher window must be doing so from a workstation that meets these requirements, or NetWare will not let the user open the application. For example, if your version of WordPerfect requires Windows 98 and not Windows 95, you can specify this through the System Requirements page, as Figure 11-12 shows.

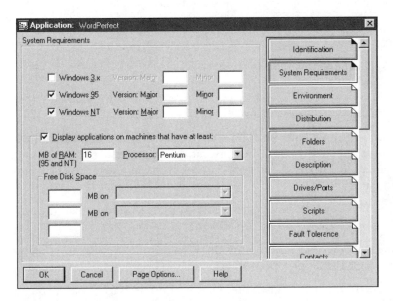

Figure 11-12   Application System Requirements page

- *Environment*—On this page you can enter any command-line parameters that the application needs.

- *Description*—Here you can write a description of the application for users who may be unfamiliar with it. Users can then refer to this page for any information they might need.

- *Drives/Ports*—This page enables you to specify the required search, root, or standard drive mappings for the application, rather than doing this through a login script. You can also define special printer requirements for use with the older queue-based printing service in NetWare, as described in Chapter 12. Figure 11-13 shows the Drives/Ports page.

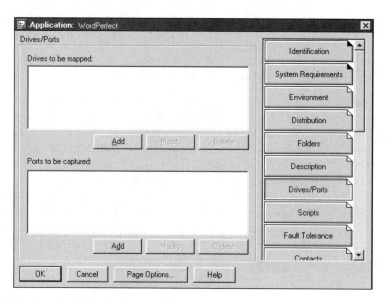

Figure 11-13 Application Drives/Ports page

- *Scripts*—You can specify login script commands that are executed either before or after the application executes.

- *Fault Tolerance*—This page lets you specify one or more additional locations for program files needed to run the application. In essence, this lets users continue to run an application if the server on which the application was originally installed fails.

- *Contacts*—This page lets you specify whom users should contact if they encounter problems with the application.

- *Associations*—Here you can identify the User, Group, Profile, or container objects that can access the Application object.

- *File Rights*—If you scroll down and choose the File Rights page, you can specify any rights to directories or files the user needs to access this program and its data files, as Figure 11-14 shows. (For example, you can specify rights to a QuickBooks directory containing your current financial records.)

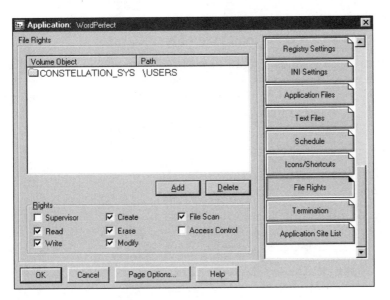

Figure 11-14   Application File Rights page

All these pages are available for further configuring the application even after you finish creating your new object.

The final step in configuring an Application object is to click OK. Your new object will appear in the NDS tree.

Automating the Application Launcher

Now that you have the Application object in the NDS tree, you'll want to give each user who wants the program a way to view and access this object. Here is where the Application Launcher comes in. You need to change the appropriate container login script to run the Application Launcher and display the application's icon, as follows:

1. If it isn't already running, open NetWare Administrator.

2. Right-click the container object in the NDS tree within which are listed the users you want to give access to the application.

3. Select the Details option, then choose the Login Script tab. NetWare Administrator displays the container's current login script. (It may be blank if you haven't defined it before.)

4. Type this line at the very end of the login script (substitute your own server's name for CONSTELLATION):

```
@\\CONSTELLATION\SYS\PUBLIC\NAL.EXE
```

You can also add the line:

`@\\CONSTELLATION\SYS\PUBLIC\NALEXPLD.EXE`

if you want to give the user rights to run the Application Explorer. This provides multiple ways to access distributed applications (from a folder on the desktop or from Windows Explorer). Notice how the Application Launcher's old name (NAL) still shows up in the abbreviated name of the executable file. Of course, you'll need to substitute your server's name in the path.

5. To display the container object's Applications dialog box, click the Applications tab.

6. Click Add to locate and add the application you just created to this container object.

7. Mark one or more of the desktop locations where you want users to run the application from. These locations include the System Tray, the Start menu, and as a desktop icon. Click OK to accept these changes.

The next time the appropriate users log into the network, the Application Launcher will run and the new application will be available to them.

Using Templates

You can also create Application objects that require a much more elaborate configuration than just running an .EXE file. For example, before they will start, some programs require additional DLLs to be present in the local Windows directory.

To handle this situation, Novell has developed the **snAppShot** program. This program runs while you install an application on a test workstation. The snAppShot software then saves this configuration as an **Application Object Template (AOT)** file. The template thus identifies the location of any files, plus any changes to the workstation Registry, needed to duplicate the installation on another workstation.

 The snAppShot program also can create a user-editable version of the AOT file. This is called the *Application Object Text Template* or *AXT*. Although this gives you the advantage of making any changes you want to the configuration, the AXT file is slower to process than the AOT file.

Run the snAppShot program on a workstation with no other applications installed (to get a clear picture of what gets installed). This test system should have Windows 95/98 already installed as well as Novell Client.

1. Run the SNAPSHOT.EXE program from the SYS\PUBLIC\SNAPSHOT directory using either the Start button, Run option, or Windows Explorer.

2. Choose Standard to create a new application profile.

3. The program will now ask you to name the application you are installing. It will ask for two different names: one as it will appear in NetWare Administrator's NDS tree, the other as it will appear on users' desktops. You can use the same name (the default) or two different ones. (You might use two different ones: for example, a generic "Spreadsheet" or "WordProcessor" name for the user side, versus "Excel2000" and "Word8.0" on the NDS side.) Click Next after you have entered the names for the application.

Some programs use the plus (+) sign in their names, such as Visual C++. Others use a dot or period (.) such as in version numbers. NDS does not recognize these characters and will not create an Application object if they are used in the NDS name. Because NDS will read the name from the .AOT or .AXT file you create with snAppShot, you cannot type a name using these characters in snAppShot, either.

4. You can now specify the destination path for snAppShot's intermediate application files. The default is to the local drive of the Admin's workstation. You will find it preferable to keep these on a network drive, so type \\CONSTELLATION\ SYS\SYSTEM\SNAPSHOT*appname* where *appname* is the name you have chosen for your application in Step 2. (You can click the Browse button, but it supports only mapped drives. Using the UNC notation as shown above is a more universal way to access the location.) Click Next, then Yes to confirm the application's directory to continue.

5. The program now asks you where you want to place the application's .AOT file. Notice that NetWare creates the default path you specified in Step 4. Keep the default location in all cases unless you have a specific reason not to. Click Next to continue.

6. The program asks you which drive to scan to create its initial "snapshot." Typically, this is Drive C:, which is the default. If you want to use a different drive, or are going to install the program components on multiple drives, click Add. NetWare will display a list of your current mapped drives from which to choose. You can add as many drives as you need for scanning. Click Next to continue.

7. The program displays a summary of the options you chose for this application in Steps 2 through 6. Choose Next to continue. NetWare now performs the scan of your local drive, Windows Registry, and .INI files so it knows what your configuration was like before the installation of the new application.

You can choose Save Preferences in this dialog box to save the generic set of specifications for snAppShot. This includes the drives and locations on the drives to scan and the destination directory for application files. Once you have saved these generic preferences, you can choose Express in Step 2 above to generate another snAppShot application file. You'll then only have to specify the application-specific information to continue, rather than the generic items.

11

8. Click the Run Application Install button. NetWare displays a browse window for you to select the new application's SETUP.EXE, INSTALL.EXE, or other setup program.

9. Click Open to continue. You can now run the application's Install program. As you are performing the setup steps, write down the destination path for the program files. (For Windows programs, this is most often C:\Program Files.) Once you complete the installation, click Next in the snAppShot dialog box to continue. The snAppShot program now runs another scan of your local drive, Registry, and .INI files so it can determine the changes made by the application's installation process. It saves these in the .AOT file. At the same time, it saves the application's files in a compressed format with the extension .FIL. This can take up to an hour, depending on the size of the program and the complexity of the application program installation.

 Many Windows applications require a system reboot to reinitialize the Registry settings so the program can run. The snAppShot program accommodates this as well.

10. If the installation program requires you to restart the workstation, then do so. (If not, move on to Step 11.) Rerun the snAppShot program. It will say that it found an unfinished discovery process and ask you if you want to continue it. Click Yes to continue.

11. At this point, snAppShot will give you a chance to print a listing of the application's template configuration. This is a good idea for documenting your network configuration. Click Print, then choose your network printer to print a copy of the application's template configuration.

12. Click OK, then click Finish. NetWare closes the snAppShot program.

Creating a Template-Based Application

Now that you have created an application template (.AOT) file, you are ready to create an application from this template in NetWare Administrator. First, run NetWare Administrator, then locate and right-click the container where you want to place the Application object. Select Create, then Application, then click OK. In the dialog box that opens, click Create an Application object with an .aot/.axt file. Click Next.

You can now select the path and .aot file you want to use for your new application. Once you specify the path to the .AOT file, click Next. (You also can use the Browse button to explore your network to locate the file.) Click Next again to accept the default configuration, then click Finish. NetWare Administrator will now use information from the template to complete the new Application object.

At this point, you again use NetWare Administrator to associate this object with a container so appropriate users can run the application. This time, however, when users log in NetWare will do an automatic setup for the workstation to run the program. Performing this task will cause some delay, so an onscreen message tells users that the system is performing a scheduled task before displaying their desktop.

With the setup complete, users will find the new application's icon on their desktops, ready to start.

Creating a Fault-Tolerant Application

All too often, a much-needed application fails because the physical server on which it is installed is down for one reason or another. In the past, this meant the user simply had to wait until the server again became available in order to access the program.

With Application Launcher, you can define an additional location for the application, so users can run it even when the original server is down. The neat trick is that this is done behind the scenes in NDS, rather than by having multiple icons on the desktop. The same icon used to launch the program on the original server also will run the backup version.

For example, suppose the Word97 application is on the server CONSTELLATION. The server requires routine maintenance, so you want to have a way for users to continue to run the application without having to manually find the application on another server. You have installed a second copy of the Word97 software on the server SARATOGA. You can add this fault tolerance information to your Application object by following these steps:

1. Open NetWare Administrator (if it isn't already running.)

2. Right-click your Application object from the appropriate container.

3. Choose Details, then click the Fault Tolerance tab to display the object's Fault Tolerance dialog box.

4. Click the Enable Fault Tolerance button. (This button will only be enabled if you have two or more NetWare servers in your tree.)

5. Click the Add button to specify the path to the second installation of the program.

6. Type the appropriate path to the second application.

7. Click OK, then click OK again to accept these changes.

Now, if the server CONSTELLATION was downed, for example, users clicking the WordPerfect icon in the Application Launcher window would automatically start the version of the software on the available SARATOGA server instead.

11

This fault tolerance feature also can balance load demand on servers. For example, if there is an application that most of your users want first thing in the morning, such as e-mail or scheduling, you can define a second version on another server. Then, if the first server is slow in responding to the request for the application, NetWare automatically shifts to the second server to get the application.

If you right-click an Application Launcher icon, a shortcut menu with two commands will appear: Open and Properties. The Open command will start the application; the Properties command will display the description information about the application.

CHAPTER SUMMARY

❐ Installing application software can generally be divided into eight steps. The first step is determining the application's level of NetWare compatibility. Some software is not compatible with networks and will run properly only if installed on the local hard drive of a workstation. Because NetWare is designed to work closely with DOS, any legacy DOS applications will run from a NetWare server without any special features or modifications. Today many software companies design their products to be aware of network features and take advantage of running from a server.

❐ After you determine that an application will run on a NetWare server, the second installation step is to determine whether the application has single-user, multiple-user, or multiuser capability. A single-user application lets only one user at a time operate the software and access the data. A multiple-user application, such as a word processor or spreadsheet program, supports multiple users running the software but allows only one user to access a specific file at a time. A multiuser application—usually a database system that tracks such information as order entry or inventory—will support multiple users accessing the same file simultaneously.

❐ The third step in the installation process involves determining the application software directory. Shared multiple-user applications, such as word processors and spreadsheets, are usually stored in a general-purpose software directory located in the SYS volume. In a departmentalized directory structure, single-user applications and special-purpose multiuser applications are often stored in a subdirectory of a department's workgroup directory structure.

❐ After you decide on the location of the application's directory, the fourth step is to run the installation program and copy the application files into the selected directory path. This process usually involves entering such information as the source and target drives, the path in which to store temporary and configuration files, the type of printer and port, and special settings needed by the particular application.

❐ Once an application's files have been copied, the fifth step is to set file and directory attributes, to secure the files and allow shared access to multiple-user applications. You can protect files from illegal copying by flagging them with the Hidden or Execute Only attribute. The directory structure can also be protected by flagging directories Delete Inhibit and Rename Inhibit. To improve performance, you can use the Purge attribute to flag directories that contain temporary files. This recovers the file space immediately after file deletion rather than making temporary files available for salvaging.

❏ After the file and directory attributes have been set, the sixth step involves granting trustee assignments to enable users to run the applications. To let all users run the general-purpose application software, you can create an organizational unit with all users in that unit. Then assign the unit Read and File Scan rights to the SYS:SOFTWARE directory. In single-user and special-purpose multiuser application directories, it is sometimes also necessary to give users Write, Create, Erase, and Modify rights, to let them work with configuration and data files stored in the same directory as the application. Whenever possible, keep configuration and data files in a separate directory. This avoids the necessity of assigning extra rights to the software directories.

❏ Once you grant trustee rights, the seventh step is to verify any changes to the workstation's AUTOEXEC.BAT and CONFIG.SYS files. Although most Windows 95/98 programs no longer modify these files, some still do. Both files are stored at the root of the C: drive and can be viewed using Notepad. In many cases, programs that modify these files store backup versions of the files before modification, often with the extension .BAK, .OLD, or .000. You can compare the backup files to the modified files to see what changes have been made by the installation program.

❏ After the software installation is complete, the last step is to test the installation. First run the programs while logged in with Supervisor rights. After you are confident the software has been installed correctly, log in as a user of the application and test each task the users will be expected to perform. The final test of the application is to run the software from each workstation, to make sure the configuration files are correct. After all testing has been completed, you will be ready to proceed to automating the user environment with login scripts, as Chapter 13 describes.

❏ A key feature of the Novell Client software is support for Application Launcher. Application Launcher lets administrators distribute appropriate application icons to user desktops rather than requiring a visit to each workstation to configure them. This also relieves the users from needing to know which server, volume, and directory an application is installed on, and it also relieves the administrator from much of the detail of managing applications on the network.

❏ Administrators use NetWare Administrator to configure appropriate Application objects for automatic distribution to their users via commands defined in the appropriate container login scripts.

❏ Application Launcher includes a program called snAppShot, which captures the state of a workstation after the installation of a program. Using this information, Application Launcher can later perform the same tasks repeatedly on users' workstations, saving the administrator the trouble of performing multiple configurations.

11

Application Launcher also provides increased fault tolerance for application access by allowing a second or additional software locations to be defined for the same program icon on the desktop. Z.E.N.works and its workstation management functions are covered further in Chapter 14.

Key Terms

Application Launcher
Application Object Template (AOT)
Application Object Text Template (AXT)
multiple-user application
multiuser application
NetWare-aware
NetWare-compatible
NetWare-incompatible
record locking
single-user application
snAppShot
transaction tracking system (TTS)
Universal Naming Convention (UNC)
Z.E.N.works

Review Questions

1. What is the first step an administrator needs to complete before installing an application?

2. After you have copied the application files into the NetWare directory with the installation program, what is the next step to perform?

3. If you see the message "Out of Environment Space" when running a DOS or Windows 3.x application, you need to place the ———————— statement in the ———————— file.

4. List and define the three levels of NetWare compatibility.

5. A(n) ———————— application type enables multiple users to run the software, but only one user at a time can access a specific data file.

6. A(n) —————————— application type enables multiple users to access the same file simultaneously.

7. Which of the following would be acceptable locations in which to install a spreadsheet application that will be used by several users in a company? For each unacceptable location, briefly explain why that directory path would *not* make a good location.

   a. SYS:SYSTEM\SS

   b. SYS:PUBLIC

   c. SYS:APPS\SS

   d. DATA:BUSINESS\SS

   e. SYS:SS

8. What are two important directory locations that the administrator usually needs to provide during an installation procedure?

9. The —————————— attribute should generally be set on all program files.

10. The —————————— attribute should also be set on multiple-user program files.

11. The —————————— attribute can be set on .EXE and .COM files to prevent them from being copied.

12. What directory attribute might you consider setting on the software directories to secure them from curious users browsing the network?

13. At a minimum, users will need the —————————— and —————————— access rights to run application software.

14. Briefly explain why it is important that the drive letter you specify in the directory path for the application's work files be one that is mapped to the same location for all users.

15. Briefly explain why it is important first to test an application while logged in with Supervisor rights and then to test it again while logged in as a user.

16. Assume you install a database application that is designed to be used on a stand-alone PC on the server. Give one reason why you should not make the database file sharable.

17. When would you not want to make program files sharable?

18. Where do you use an Application Object Template?

19. What program do you use to create an AOT file?

20. Briefly explain why it is important to have application fault tolerance.

11

HANDS-ON PROJECTS

Project 11-1: Testing a Single-User DOS Application

In this project you experiment with creating and sharing a DOS-based application program intended for use by a single user. The objective of this exercise is to demonstrate that a single-user application can often be accessed by more than one user at the same time although the files are not flagged Sharable. To complete this exercise, you will need to coordinate your activity with one or more students or have access to two different workstations from which you can log in and test the application. Your instructor will tell you how to divide the class into teams.

1. Identify the other student(s) with whom you are to work, and exchange user names.

2. In his or her ##ADMIN work area, one team member should create a SOFTWARE directory that contains subdirectories for word processing (WP) and spreadsheet (SS) applications.

3. Copy the following programs from your local computer to the WP directory:

   `EDIT.HLP`

   `EDIT.COM`

   If your computer is running Windows 95/98, the files are found in the WINDOWS\COMMAND subdirectory.

4. Grant [RFWCEM] rights for this directory to all team members. (See Chapter 5 for details on granting rights.)

5. Each team member should log in and map a drive to the shared WP software directory.

6. From one team member's workstation, run the Notepad program and create a document file that contains a list of five movies you have seen during the last year.

7. Save the document with the name MOVIES.TXT.

8. Use Explorer to record the attributes set on each of the three files in the following list. On the following lines, record the steps you use:

Filename	Attribute(s)
EDIT.HLP	_____
EDIT.COM	_____
MOVIES.TXT	_____

9. Each team member should now change to the WP drive and use the Notepad program to access the MOVIES document. Do you think Notepad will enable multiple users to open the same document without the Sharable attribute? Does Notepad enable all team members to access the MOVIES document file?

10. An important reason for making document files nonsharable is to protect changes made by one user from being overwritten by another user. In this step, each team member should use Notepad to call up the MOVIES document and then place his or her name at the top of the document.

11. One user should save his or her document. Then another user should save his or her changes. Does Notepad enable each user to save his or her changes? What is the name of the user who saved his or her document first? What is the name of the user who saved his or her document last?

12. Access the MOVIES document. Which user's changes were saved?

13. If both users were able to save their documents, record the name of the user whose changes now appear in the document.

14. Based on this test, how should the Notepad program be used on the network? Write down the recommendations you would make.

Project 11-2: Creating an Application Object

In this project you will define a WordPerfect 8 Application object in the CBE_Labs_Admin container. (Your instructor will have installed the Z.E.N.works starter pack on your lab server so you can run this exercise.) Take the following steps:

1. Start NetWare Administrator and browse to the **CBE_Labs_Admin** container, in which you want to locate the Application object.

2. Right-click your **CBE_Labs_Admin** container object, and click **Create** on the shortcut menu to display the available objects.

3. Double-click **Application** (or click **Application**, then click **OK**) to display the Select Application Type window.

4. If it isn't already highlighted, click **Create Simple Application Object**, and then click **Next** to display the Object Name dialog box.

5. Type the name of the application as you want it to appear on the NDS tree in the Name text box; in this case, **WordPerfect 8.**

6. In the Path to executable file text box, type the location of the file to be executed. Hypothetically, this would be \\CONSTELLATION\SYS\APPS\WP\WP.EXE. Because we don't have this application installed, select the **\\CONSTELLATION\SYS\PUBLIC\ZENVER.EXE** program instead.

7. Click the **Define additional properties** check box to display the Application Identification window.

8. Click **Finish**. NWAdmin creates this new application object and displays the Application Identification dialog box shown earlier in Figure 11-11.

9. You can now configure your application by selecting the pages outlined earlier from this window. For example, you may want all users of WordPerfect 8.0 to store data files in a particular location. You might also want to designate a specific printer port for the application. More importantly, you may know that the application requires

11

systems with 32 MB of RAM or more. For this exercise, you will set a minimum RAM requirement.

10. To set a system requirement of 32 MB of RAM, click the **System Requirements** tab to display that page.

11. Click the check box marked **Display Applications on machines that have at least**...

12. In the field labeled MB of RAM, type **32** for 32 MB. Now Application Launcher will test any workstation prior to running WordPerfect 8.0 to make sure that the system has that much RAM. If it doesn't, then Application Launcher will not run the program.

13. Click the **Associations** tab to display the Associations dialog box.

14. Click **Add** and browse to select the **CBE_Labs_Admin** container object. Click **OK**. Now all users under this container will be able to run the application.

15. Click **OK** to accept these changes to your WordPerfect 8 application object.

16. Click the **CBE_Labs_Admin** object again to display its Details dialog box.

17. Select the **Login Script** tab. Type the following commands for running Application Launcher for users in this container:

    ```
    @\\CONSTELLATION\SYS\PUBLIC\NAL.EXE
    ```

    ```
    @\\CONSTELLATION\SYS\PUBLIC\NALEXPLD.EXE
    ```

18. Save your changes by clicking **OK**.

19. If you want, you can offer the WordPerfect program from the user's Start menu, Desktop, or System Tray by selecting the **Applications** tab.

20. Save your changes by clicking **OK**, then exit NetWare Administrator.

21. Test your new Application object by logging in as a user in CBE_Labs_Admin such as PRESIDENT.

22. Record the onscreen activity that occurs during your login.

23. Locate the WordPerfect 8 icon and click it. What are the results?

CASE PROJECTS

Case 11-1: Creating an Application Object for the Jefferson County Courthouse

In this project you use Application Launcher to define an application object for the Jefferson County Courthouse Directory tree.

1. If necessary, start the PC workstation. Start Windows 95/98, and run NWAdmin.

2. Click the **Jefferson County Courthouse** container to display that part of the NDS tree.

3. Select the container object in which to locate the Application object. What container object will that be? _____

4. Right-click the container object, then select **Create** on the menu to display a list of available object types.

5. Click **Application**, then click **OK**. Select **Create a Simple Application**.

6. Type **Microsoft Excel** in the Application Icon Title line. Select a path to the file if your system has Excel installed on it. If not, select an appropriate executable file from the NetWare PUBLIC directory.

7. Configure the application by using the pages from the Properties window. All users will have access to this application.

Turn in a copy of your data disk to your instructor.

Case 11-2: OfficePro

The OfficePro company specializes in providing word processing services for other businesses. Currently it employs five word processing staff members, each of whom has his or her own personal computer. Recently OfficePro installed a NetWare network to enable its employees to share laser printers and to have access to common documents. In addition, OfficePro obtained a NetWare-aware version of its word processing software, which will enable all users to share the same software package and provide them with special network capabilities. Rita Dunn, manager of OfficePro, has recently asked you to install the new word processing program on OfficePro's server and has provided you with the installation notes for the software package (shown in Figure 11-15). Rita Dunn also gave you a copy of OfficePro's current server directory structure (shown in Figure 11-16). Your job is to add the necessary directories to support the word processing application software, install the package, and provide the necessary rights for the users.

11

The LetterPerfect word processing software can either be installed on a local hard disk or a Novell NetWare file server. When using the network installation option, you will need to provide the install program with the type of network to install onto in addition to the location of software, temporary, and configuration files. Follow the instructions below when installing the LetterPerfect software on your network system.

Software Files:

The installation program will ask for the drive and directory to contain the LetterPerfect software package program and work files. Users will need to have a search drive mapped to this directory in order to run the package from any drive or directory in the network file system. All users will need a minimum of Read and File scan rights to this directory unless you plan to keep configuration files in this directory, in which case refer to the following configuration file instructions.

Configuration Files:

Each user must be supplied with a three-letter user name that allows the software to separate user configuration files by naming the file LPxxx.CFG where "xxx" is the three-letter user name. By default each user configuration file will be stored in the directory from which the LetterPerfect software is started. However, if a user enters a different three-letter user name or starts the LetterPerfect software from a different directory, a new LPxxx.CFG file will be created with default configuration information. If you wish to place configuration files in a separate directory, you will need to supply the installation program with the drive and path to the directory that is to contain the user configuration files. In this case, the user LPxxx.CFG configuration files will be stored in that directory rather than the default directory. All users will need to have a minimum of Read, Write, File Scan, and Create rights to this directory. Be sure the drive letter you use when entering the location for user configuration files is available when the user runs the LetterPerfect software.

Temporary Files:

Temporary files are used to contain control information such as current filename and location information while the user is running the LetterPerfect software. By default temporary files will be stored in the directory from which the user starts the LetterPerfect software and will be erased when the application is terminated. If you wish you can choose to have temporary files stored in an alternate directory on either the file server or local computer hard disk. Because temporary filenames include the user's three-letter user name, multiple-user temporary files can be placed in the same directory. Users will need a minimum of Read, File Scan, Write, Create, and Erase rights in the directory used to store temporary files. Be sure the drive letter you use when entering the location for user temporary files is available when the user runs the LetterPerfect software.

Figure 11-15   Word processing installation notes

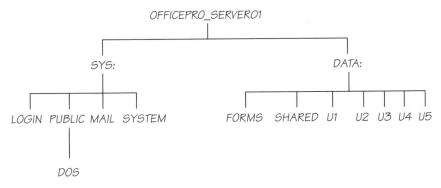

Figure 11-16 OfficePro directory structure

1. Use a copy of the Volume Design Form (see Appendix B) to design a directory structure that will support the network word processing application.

2. Record any necessary drive mappings including the drive and the path.

3. Document the trustee rights for each directory you defined in Step 1.

4. Record any NetWare Administrator or Explorer commands you need to use to establish special file or directory attribute settings.

11

12

NETWARE PRINTING

In this chapter, you will learn:

- Describe the two primary printing architectures supported by NetWare 5.0—Novell Distributed Print Services (NDPS), and the older QMS (Queue Management Services)

- Identify and describe the NetWare printing components of these two architectures and their relationships to each other

- Use NetWare Administrator to create, configure, and work with the NDPS Manager, gateways, and printer agents

- Configure Windows workstations to direct printer output to the new NetWare printer

- Manage print jobs using NetWare Administrator or the Novell Printer Manager

---

Printer sharing is an important benefit of a network. Among its advantages are cost savings, increased work space, flexible printer selection, and printer fault tolerance. To become a network administrator, you need to know the NetWare printing system and the NetWare printing utilities that let you set up, customize, and maintain the printing environment on your network. NetWare 5.0 supports two printing architectures: Novell Distributed Print Services (NDPS) and the older print queue/print server approach called Queue Management Services (QMS). The default printing process for NetWare 5.0 is NDPS, but QMS or a combination of approaches may also be used.

In this chapter you'll learn about these two architectures and the NetWare printing concepts and skills you will need to implement a sophisticated network printing environment for your organization.

NDPS: A NEW APPROACH TO PRINT SERVICES

Most users are familiar with managing printing from a standalone PC. If the correct printer driver is installed, the printer is connected to the proper port, and the printer is on, then a typical Windows 95/98 application can print to it. The printer driver will translate the application's data into the appropriate printer code so the printer can print it.

Print services on the network become more complex. Physically, a server-attached printer appears much like the standalone system. However, the printer is quite differently configured to run with the server. Also, multiple workstations send print jobs to this one printer, rather than just one user on one workstation.

In the past, Novell used **Queue Management Services (QMS)** to provide print services. In QMS, the various print jobs that users sent were stored in a holding area called the **print queue**. The administrator defined a **print server** that would look in this holding area and see if **print jobs** were waiting. If jobs were lined up, the print server also knew what printer handled the jobs in that queue. (You could have a laser printer queue, a dot matrix queue, a color printer queue, etc.) The print server then sent the print job to the appropriate printer when the printer was ready, as Figure 12-1 shows.

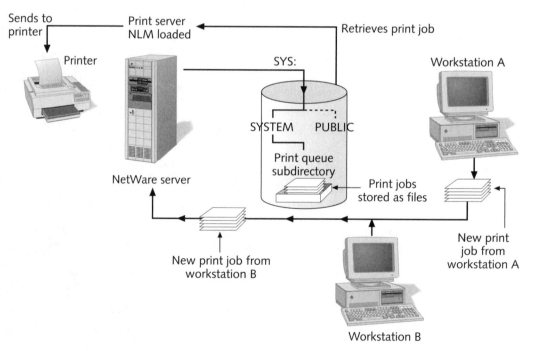

Figure 12-1   QMS printing

Although QMS was reliable, setting it up was often complex. This initial setup of the several objects—print queues, printer objects, and print servers—and configuring them to work together often made administrators reluctant to add more printers or tailor the service to more closely meet user needs.

With Windows 95, the concept of the Printer object was introduced. Users became accustomed to defining Printer objects. Unfortunately, with QMS there are three objects to be defined—Printer, Print Server, and Print Queue—and users and administrators often had to keep track of all three. With this system, troubleshooting could be difficult and time consuming, because administrators often had to physically visit several workstations, print devices, and servers.

Novell Distributed Print Services (NDPS) uses a different approach to setting up, managing, and troubleshooting network printing, using one NDPS Printer agent object rather than three different objects, and one utility, NetWare Administrator, rather than many different utilities. NDPS provides more services and is simpler to use than queues, thus reducing the time spent by administrators managing printing, and removing many network printing problems for users.

From the user's perspective, the NDPS Printer object is the only object they have to deal with when printing over the network, as Figure 12-2 shows. This is closer to the Windows 95/98 approach to defining printers.

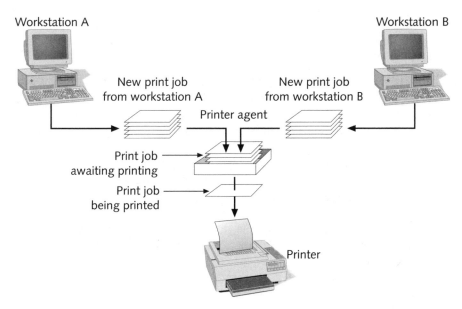

Figure 12-2   NDPS printing

We will explain later on about the actual components in the architecture of NDPS. For now, we can say that NDPS has some key advantages over the old QMS. These advantages include:

- *Automatic detection of NDPS-aware printers.* NDPS printers can be plugged into the network cable or hub and automatically announce their presence. This makes them immediately available for printing. (See the section later in this chapter called "Creating a Public Access Printer Agent.")

- *Automatic download of drivers to clients.* NDPS will distribute appropriate printer drivers to the workstation automatically when a user logs in. This eliminates the common complaint that a user can access a printer but doesn't have the correct driver for it.

- *Bidirectional communications with printers.* **Bidirectional communication** lets clients, printers, and administrators exchange information about printers and print jobs. With bidirectional communication, you can manage NDPS printers from NetWare Administrator, rather than through a proprietary management tool (such as software supplied by a printer vendor that works only with that vendor's printers) or from the printer's own keypad. Users can view the status of print jobs in real time as well as determine error conditions or see when the printer is just out of paper. In the past, this information could only be found out by going physically to the printer or by using a proprietary tool supplied by the printer vendor. Bidirectional communication also enables more options—such as via e-mail, pop-up dialogs, or recording in an event log—for notifying users and administrators about the status of printing tasks. Third-party software also provides support for fax notices and pager notification.

NDPS is installed by default with NetWare 5.0 as the preferred printing process; however, NetWare 5.0 offers the option to install the QMS process as well. NDPS also offers backward compatibility with the NetWare 4.x and 3.x queue-based system on mixed networks. That is, NDPS itself continues to support existing queues and printers attached to workstations. The NetWare Administrator also includes a setup wizard for traditional queue-based printing. You can also choose to run *both* NDPS and print queue services. The drawbacks of using both methods would be added management complexity and server resources devoted to duplicate services.

 Although NDPS is the default, the NetWare 5.0 Install Wizard gives you the option of choosing not to install NDPS. This option is available in the Product Customization screen displayed near the end of the installation procedure, as discussed in Chapter 6. However, we suggest you install NDPS unless you have a specific reason not to.

You should choose to run NDPS in most NetWare trees. As you'll see, NDPS offers advantages even with printers that do not directly support NDPS. The primary circumstance for *not* choosing NDPS and installing QMS would be having no printer drivers shipped with

NetWare 5.0 (i.e., for older printers that do not provide bidirectional communication, or with printers that require unusual drivers.)

Before getting into the specifics of setting up NDPS, you should have an overall knowledge of the components of NetWare printing and the types of printer attachments.

TYPES OF NETWORK PRINTERS AND METHODS OF ATTACHMENT

Before you can implement a network printing environment, you need to understand the basics of network printers. In this section, you will learn about the basic types of printers and methods of attachment in network printing.

Although there is a huge number of different printer models and configurations, most printers commonly found on networks come in three types: dot matrix, laser, and ink-jet (although dot matrix printers are slowly disappearing). Each requires a different print job format. As a network administrator, you will need to know the types and models of printers used on your network so that you can correctly configure network printing. A word processing program, for example, might support both laser and ink-jet printers. If a user tells the program to use the ink-jet printer, but sends the job to the laser printer, the print job will either not print, or will print garbage characters.

Up to five printers can be attached directly to the server and are called **local printers**. A **direct printer** is attached directly to the network cable using its own network interface card and software.

> NetWare also supports a third kind of printer—the remote printer. As with earlier versions, NetWare 5.0 includes a Windows 95/98 program called NPRINTER. When run on a workstation, NPRINTER makes a locally attached printer act as a network printer. This provides some flexibility in locating printers around the network. However, using NPRINTER is generally discouraged because of the demands it makes on the workstation. (In effect, the workstation may be useless until a print job is done.) Setting up and running NPRINTER is not part of the CNA requirements.

You must consider the printer attachment method when you configure the network printing environment. Many network administrators use a combination of printer attachments based on the type of printer and its expected usage. In this section, you will learn about each of the printer attachment options and how they affect network printing.

Local printers are attached directly to one of the printer ports of the NetWare server. Output is sent directly from the server to the local printers through the local printer ports. Local printers can be attached to the parallel (LPT) or serial (COM) ports of the server. The advantages of a local printer include printing performance that is faster than that of network printers and a reduction in network traffic.

12

You can attach a printer directly to the network cable by obtaining a special network card for the printer. Many printer manufacturers offer optional network cards that can be installed in their printers to enable the printer to be attached directly to the network cable, as Figure 12–3 shows.

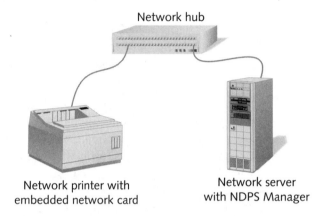

Network hub

Network printer with embedded network card

Network server with NDPS Manager

Figure 12-3   Direct network-attached printer

With the direct attachment option, the printer can print jobs sent directly from a workstation. This offloads the printing tasks from the server and thus may actually improve network performance. (Novell claims, however, that the newer generation of server hardware with Pentium-class processors can handle both printing and file service tasks with no degradation of performance.)

The disadvantage of direct printer attachment is the modest extra cost of the network attachment option needed for each printer. Most administrators, however, prefer the direct network-attached printer as it provides the flexibility to locate the printer close to users (as opposed to next to the server, which may be in a secure room or at least more isolated from users). It also means that troubleshooting and repair can be done without interfering with the server.

DEFINING THE PRINTING ENVIRONMENT

The first task a network administrator needs to perform when establishing a network printing environment, whether NDPS or queue-based, is to define the printing needs supported by the network. Defining the printing environment involves the following steps:

1. Define the printing requirements of each user's applications.

2. Determine the best printer locations and which types of attachments to use.

3. Determine the best location for Printer objects in the tree.

In this section, you will learn about each of these steps and how to apply them to defining a network printer environment for your organization by filling out a Print Services Definition Form.

Defining Printer Requirements

The first step in defining a printing environment is to identify the number and types of network printers that will be needed. You start by analyzing the requirements of each user's application software and printing needs. You can record the model and type along with the users and applications for each network printer that will be attached to NDPS.

 Try to keep the printing system as simple as possible by standardizing the make and model of printer to be used for dot matrix, laser, and ink-jet printer types.

For example, consider a print services definition for the marketing and finance departments of CBE Labs. The finance department uses a spreadsheet program to manage budget data, along with a payroll and general ledger accounting system. The finance department needs a high-speed laser printer to print accounting reports and payroll checks. Each member of the marketing department uses a personal computer to enter orders and produce price quotations. Price quotations need to be printed on company stationery. What is needed is a laser printer with stationery in tray 1 and standard paper in tray 2. Invoices are printed on one printer that has invoice forms always loaded, and sales reports are printed on a second printer that has standard printer paper. The marketing department has new presentation software that helps users produce attractive handouts for sales presentations. For these they need access to a color printer.

From the preceding information, a Print Services Definition Form like the one in Figure 12-4 can be filled in (a blank version of this form is included in Appendix B). The form defines one NDPS Manager, named NDPS_Manager, which controls six printers and printer agents. As you can see on the form, the finance department needs two printers on the network, a fast laser printer for accounting and spreadsheet applications and a high-resolution laser printer for word processing documents and graphs. Three printers have been defined to meet the printing needs of the marketing department: one laser printer for printing price quotations and two for invoices and sales reports. With two printers, users won't need to change back and forth between invoice forms and standard paper for reports. In addition, users in both the marketing and finance departments need to send presentation output and graphs to a color ink-jet printer.

12

PRINT SERVICES DEFINITION FORM

Prepared by: <u>David Doering</u>   Date: <u>9/15/99</u>

NDS Tree: <u>CBE_Labs</u>   Organization: <u>CBE_Labs</u>

Organizational Unit: _____   Server host: <u>CONSTELLATION</u>

                                                              (for NDPS Manager)

Manager Name: <u>NDPS_MANAGER</u>

Printer Name	Printer Type	Make/Model	Attachment Type	Location	Users/Applications	Public or Controlled Access?	Printer Agent
FIN_Laser_0	Laser	HP LaserJet 4			*finance* documents		
FIN_Laser_1	Fast laser	Lexmark Optra SE			*finance* accounting		
Color_Ink_2	Color ink-jet	Lexmark 3200 Jetprinter			*all* presentations		
MRK_Laser_3	Laser	HP LaserJet 4			*marketing* documents		
MRK_Laser_4	Laser	HP LaserJet 5			*marketing* invoices		
MRK_Laser_5	Laser	Okidata OkiPage 20DX			*marketing* reports		

Figure 12-4   Beginning to fill out Print Services Definition form

Defining NDPS Manager and NDS Tree Information

Your first task is to decide on which server in your tree you want to place (host) your NDPS Manager. Typically this is decided for you, because the NetWare install program automatically chooses the first NetWare 5.0 server installed in your tree. You may include a second server when you need to have a locally attached printer on the server. In the space at the top of the form, record the name of your NDPS Manager and its information.

Next identify the container objects within which you are going to place your NDPS Printer objects. This will help you when you are assigned access rights to printers and distributing drivers to users in those containers.

Defining Printer Location and Attachment

Once printer requirements are defined, the next consideration is the location of each printer—including how it will be attached to the network. Use the following guidelines when planning locations and attachment methods for printers:

- Determine whether the printer is to be locally attached to the server, or directly attached to the network.

- Place the printer close to the user who is responsible for it.

- Identify the printer agent for each printer.

- Use a direct attachment option if possible for each network printer.

Notice in Figure 12-5 that in addition to the attachment type, the Public or Controlled Access option is also identified. This, plus the printer agent information, will be needed when you define your printers in NetWare Administrator. Notice that the color ink-jet printer (the Lexmark 3200) is locally attached to the LPT1 port of the server. Depending on the location of the server, this can provide access to the printer to both marketing and finance department users. Also, it is less common for ink-jet printers to have a direct network-attachment option.

12

PRINT SERVICES DEFINITION FORM

Prepared by: David Doering   Date: 9/15/99

NDS Tree: CBE_Labs   Organization: CBE_Labs

Organizational Unit: _____   Server host: CONSTELLATION

                                            (for NDPS Manager)

Manager Name: NDPS_MANAGER_____

Printer Name	Printer Type	Make/Model	Attachment Type	Location	Users/Applications	Public or Controlled Access?	Printer Agent
FIN_Laser_0	Laser	HP LaserJet 4	Direct	*finance dept.*	*finance* documents	Controlled	PAFINL0
FIN_Laser_1	Fast laser	Lexmark Optra SE	Direct	*finance dept.* *payroll*	*finance* accounting	Controlled	PAFINL1
Color_Ink_2	Color ink-jet	Lexmark 3200 Jetprinter	Local LPT1	*info systems*	*all* presentations	Controlled	PACOLOR2
MRK_Laser_3	Laser	HP LaserJet 4	Direct	*marketing dept.* office area	*marketing* documents	Controlled	PAMRKL3
MRK_Laser_4	Laser	HP LaserJet 5	Direct	*marketing dept.* office area	*marketing* invoices	Controlled	PAMRKL4
MRK_Laser_5	Laser	Okidata OkiPage 20DX	Direct	*marketing dept.* office area	*marketing* reports	Controlled	PAMRKL5

Figure 12-5   Completed Print Services Definition form

Naming Printers

NetWare 5.0 allows printer names of up to 47 characters that can contain any number of ASCII characters, including spaces and special characters. One way to create meaningful printer names is to define one- to three-character codes for each of the printer information fields. Each printer name could consist of the combined codes for the three listed items, separated by dashes (-) or underscores (_). The printer name FIN_Laser_0, for example, identifies the HP LaserJet 4 printer that is located in the finance department.

Windows 95/98 may have trouble handling special characters, which means that you should only use letters and numbers in names, not dashes, under-scores, and so on. Therefore, the printer name in the preceding example becomes FINLASERJET4.

You may also want to create names using an identifier for:

- Location

- Printer model

- Attachment type/printer number

The printer location can be a three- to four-character field that identifies the name of the department or place where the printer is located. FIN, for example, can be used to iden-tify a printer located in the finance department; a room number, such as 209A, can be used to identify a printer located in a specific room or office. If a printer is moved, its name can be changed to identify its new location. Avoid using a user's name or workstation model to identify a printer. These labels often change and can leave the printer with a name that no longer identifies its location.

A three- to five-character code representing the make or use of the printer can be included in its name to help you remember what type of printer output can be sent to this printer. For example, INV can represent the printer to which invoices are sent; HP4SI can repre-sent an HP LaserJet 4Si printer that is available for general use.

You can include an attachment code—L for local or D for direct—and a printer number, if desired. The printer number value ranges from 0 to 255 and corresponds to the printer number assigned during configuration of the print server. The code L1, for example, iden-tifies printer 1 as locally attached to the printer server; D2 identifies printer 2 as directly attached to the network.

 After you define printer names, it is a good idea to label each physical printer with its assigned name. This will make it easier for both you (the network administrator) and users to identify them.

Now that you have defined your overall printing environment, it's time to set up that environment in the following sections.

Labeling Public or Controlled Access

You should also identify which of your printers are controlled access and which are pub-lic access printers. (We'll explain these concepts later in this chapter.) Knowing if a printer is public or controlled access can make troubleshooting easier. It can also serve as a task list for creating printer objects as you set up your NDPS printing environment.

12

Identifying the Printer Agent

Whether your printers have an NDPS Printer object or not depends on whether you have public or controlled access to that printer. But all NDPS printers will have a printer agent associated with them. Record the names of the printer agents as you create them; this information can come in handy for troubleshooting later on.

NDPS COMPONENTS

Novell Distributed Print Services (NDPS) has four components:

- Printer agents
- NDPS broker
- NDPS Manager
- NDPS gateways

A fifth component, appropriate client software, is included with the Novell Client package. (NDPS requires the Novell Client 2.2 or higher. NetWare 5.0 ships with Novell Client 3.0.)

A NetWare 5.0 directory tree needs only one broker and one NDPS Manager. It can have as many printer agents as there are printers on the network. It may have one or more gateways, depending on the brand of printers and on whether they are NDPS-compliant or not. Each of these elements will be discussed in the following sections, and are illustrated in Figure 12-6.

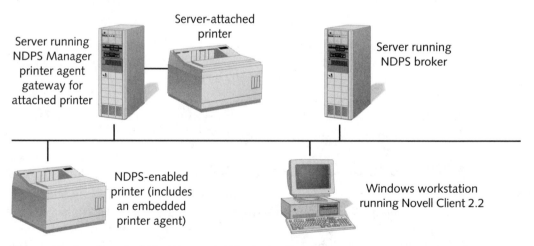

Figure 12-6   A typical NetWare 5.0 NDPS installation

Printer Agents

Printer agents are the core component in NDPS. Printer agents link a client workstation to the printer itself. They put print jobs into a queue and then send those jobs on to the printer itself. Each printer has its own printer agent. When a user sends a print job to the printer, the printer agent handles the job going to the printer. The printer agent also communicates with the NDPS broker to send the user a message saying the job is done. (The printer agent can also communicate with a gateway if the printer is not NDPS-aware.) The NDPS Manager monitors the printer agents.

A printer agent can be either a NetWare Loadable Module (NLM) loaded on the NetWare server or an embedded part of the printer itself. (At this writing, there are no vendors offering printers with embedded printer agents. It is likely, however, that more vendors will offer this option in the near future.)

If the network printer is a model with the embedded printer agent (your dealer will tell you), then in a simple network you need only plug that printer into the network to begin using it. (As mentioned earlier, everyone on the network will have access to this printer.) It is convenient, but it lacks any security control over who can print on this printer. More importantly, it lacks the interactivity possible with NDPS printers. This interactivity includes customizable notification as well as drivers downloadable through NetWare Administrator using NDPS.

A printer agent will typically be run as an NLM, because only the newest model printers will have embedded agents. Other than having to create the printer agent on the server, working with a server-based agent is identical to working with a printer-based agent. NetWare requires an NDPS Manager in the tree before you can create agents and Printer objects, so let's look at it next.

NDPS Manager

The **NDPS Manager** is an NLM run on a host server in the NetWare 5.0 tree. It provides a way to create and manage printer agents. One NDPS Manager in the tree can support any number of printer agents, so you will typically create only one such manager per tree. NetWare will automatically load the manager on the first NetWare 5.0 server you install in your tree and will load it after you create the first printer agent for your tree.

 If you plan to attach a printer directly to a NetWare 5.0 server, then you will need to install the NDPS Manager on that server. Otherwise the NDPS Manager could not send jobs to that printer. If necessary, you may need to create a second NDPS Manager in a tree to support a server-attached printer.

NDPS Broker

NetWare also automatically creates and loads an **NDPS broker** as part of the NDPS configuration. Strictly speaking, the broker can work with more than just printing services. In the future, Novell hopes that other services will take advantage of the broker's features. These include:

- *Resource Management Services (RMS)*—provides clients with automatic downloading of printer drivers and fonts.

- *Event Notification Services (ENS)*—provides various delivery methods for messages on print job status or printer problems or maintenance requirements.

- *Service Registry Services (SRS)*—provides support for NDPS-enabled (public access) printers (public access printers are covered in more detail later in this chapter).

 NetWare creates the NDPS broker on the first NetWare 5.0 server installed in the tree. NetWare won't install a second broker on any other server until the first broker is more than three network segments away from the second.

As you configure NDPS, NetWare automatically connects the agents and gateways (covered in the next section) to the broker. No user intervention is required.

NDPS Gateways

An **NDPS gateway** allows NDPS to communicate to non-NDPS-aware printers. Gateways are not a requirement for NDPS, but are a solution for non-NDPS-aware printers; that is, for printers that lack an embedded printer agent. When all printers include embedded printer agents, gateways will no longer be necessary. Because many printers today are not NDPS-aware, we will cover the use of gateways in NetWare 5.0.

Gateways also provide support for queue-based, Unix, Macintosh, and mainframe-attached printers. Once configured and loaded, the gateway is a low-maintenance item. NetWare 5.0 comes with three gateways (NLMs). You may have to run more than one, depending on the brand of printers you use. They include:

- HP gateway—for Hewlett-Packard printers

- Xerox gateway—for Xerox brand printers

- Novell gateway—for most other brands of printers that are not NDPS-enabled

Novell anticipates that additional vendors will create gateways for their printers, for example, a Lexmark gateway for its Optra line of network printers.

NDPS-Ready Clients

Because the NDPS architecture is fairly new, older Novell client software may not recognize its services. When run on these older client workstations, utilities such as NetWare Administrator simply won't display NDPS options or features (if they run at all).

This, of course, means that when you are ready to configure your network's print services, you will need to run the NetWare Administrator on a workstation with an appropriate NDPS-ready client.

To avoid problems, then, you should upgrade your administrator workstation (and preferably most user workstations) to use a Novell Client newer than version 2.2 and preferably the version 3.0 included with NetWare 5.0. (It is on the CD-ROM labeled Novell Client Software.)

CONFIGURING NDPS

Now that we have outlined the NDPS architecture, its requirements, and looked at how to define your network print services, we'll discuss the tasks associated with configuring and managing NDPS. These include:

- Creating the NDPS Manager
- Choosing a printer type
- Creating printer agents
- Selecting a gateway
- Creating an NDPS Printer object
- Configuring workstations
- Managing print jobs

Before you begin, physically install the printer on the network by attaching the 10BaseT cable from the printer to the network hub. (We'll assume a network-attached printer for this discussion.) Perform a power-on self-test to verify the printer is working normally.

For most classroom situations, there is only one network printer. Because NDPS also supports only one NDPS Manager and one printer agent for this printer, you will most likely follow along as the instructor demonstrates this installation procedure.

Creating the NDPS Manager

To create an NDPS Manager, you will run the NetWare Administrator from the SYS:\PUBLIC\WIN32 directory on a Windows 95/98 workstation with the latest Novell Client installed.

If you try to run an older version of the NetWare Administrator, or run the WIN32 version on an older client, NDPS options and objects won't appear in the menus or will fail to run properly.

12

Continue with the installation and configuration as follows:

1. Log in to the network using your Administrator account, then start NetWare Administrator.

2. Choose the container in which you want to place your NDPS Manager object. A convenient one is the same container as your server object. (Don't confuse this placement of the Manager object in the tree with the installing and running of the Manager software on a NetWare server.)

3. Right-click the container you want, click Create, then choose the NDPS Manager object type.

If NDPS Manager does not appear in the list of available objects, then you are running either the older version of NetWare Administrator or an older client.

4. Click OK. NetWare Administrator displays the Create NDPS Manager Object dialog box shown in Figure 12-7.

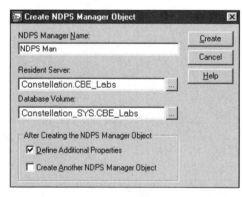

Figure 12-7 Create NDPS Manager dialog box

5. Type a name for your NDPS Manager. This could be as simple as NDPS_MAN.

6. Choose the resident (host) server on which you want to run your NDPS Manager. Use the Browse button to the right of the Resident Server field to help locate the server in your tree. You cannot place two NDPS Managers on the same server.

7. Once you specify the server, decide on which volume of that server you want to place the NDPS database. Any volume will do; the SYS volume is fine unless you want to limit the amount of data placed there. Again, the dialog box provides you with a Browse button to the right of the Database Volume field to search the tree for the volume.

8. Check the box marked Define Additional Properties if you want to automatically go to the NDPS Manager's Details dialog box after creating the object itself. This will let you start the process of creating a public access printer agent.

9. If you are satisfied with your NDPS Manager definition, click the Create button to continue. NDS will now create the NDPS Manager object in the tree. If you checked the Define Additional Properties box, then you will be at Step 2 of the Creating a Public Access Printer Agent procedure, described in the next section.

To automatically load the NDPS Manager each time the server is booted, you can use the NWCONFIG command from the server console as follows:

1. Go to the server, and at the system console screen type NWCONFIG, and press Enter.

2. Select the option NCF File Options, then the option to Edit the AUTOEXEC.NCF file.

3. At the end of the file, add the command: NDPSM *manager_name_and_context* where *manager_name_and_context* is the name of your NDPS Manager and its context. This will automatically load the NDPS Manager each time you reboot the server after NDPS installation.

4. Press [F10] to save the file, then exit NWCONFIG by pressing [Esc] twice, then [Enter].

For example, if you placed an NDPS Manager called NDPS_MAN in the container CBE_Labs, the command would be *NDPSM NDPS_MAN.CBE_LABS.*

12

Creating Printer Agents

At this point, you are ready to create printer agents for each printer. First, you will want to choose which type of printer you want to install. NetWare and NDPS support two types of access to printers on the network: public access and controlled access. A **public access printer** is available to anyone attached to the network. (We mentioned earlier that only NDPS-enabled printers attached directly to the network can be public access printers. By default, all other printers will be controlled access printers.) There are two reasons to make an NDPS printer public access:

- No configuration is necessary. You don't have to define the printer in the NetWare Administrator as a Printer object; you can just plug the printer into the network cable and power it on.

- Every user has immediate access to the printer without specifying this right in the NetWare Administrator.

Using public access printers is advisable in the following circumstances:

- When you have a high-trust/low-risk network, such as in a workgroup or small office

- When you don't need the improved print job notification capability of NDPS
- When you don't need to distribute printer drivers to many desktops
- When you have an NDPS-enabled printer

A **controlled access printer**, as you might expect, is accessible only to certain users and/or groups as defined by the administrator. A controlled access printer therefore has key advantages over a public access printer:

- Tighter security on who uses the printer
- Easier management of print jobs and the printer
- Option to automatically distribute printer drivers to users

A controlled access printer does, however, require creating and configuring an NDS object. Because most printers are not NDPS-enabled, and because in most networks use of printers needs to be managed, in most situations you will create and administer controlled access printers.

First, we'll describe creating a public access printer, then move on to creating an NDPS controlled access printer.

Creating a Public Access Printer Agent

The general steps to create a public access Printer Agent object are as follows:

1. From NetWare Administrator, double-click the NDPS Manager you just created. The NDS configuration screen for that manager appears.

2. On the Identification page, click the Printer Agent List button, then click New. (If the New button is grayed, your NDPS Manager did not load at the server. To fix this, go to the server console and enter LOAD NDPSMAN to load it manually.) The Create Printer Agent dialog box shown in Figure 12-8 opens. Notice that NetWare has already filled in the NDPS Manager name field for you. (This would not be true for a controlled access printer agent.)

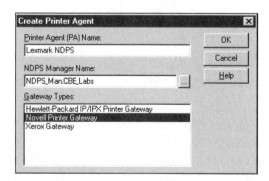

Figure 12-8   Create Printer Agent dialog box

3. Type a name for your printer agent. (NetWare would provide the name for a controlled access printer agent.) You can name the agent anything you want, but it is helpful to indicate what printer it supports or its location. For example, you might choose *HP5MPA* for an HP LaserJet 5M printer agent or *ADMINHP* for an HP LaserJet in the administration area.

4. Select the appropriate gateway as described in the next section.

Selecting a Gateway

As mentioned earlier, NetWare 5.0 includes gateways from HP, Xerox, and a generic one from Novell. The general steps to select a gateway are as follows:

These steps require a running NDPS Manager on CONSTELLATION. Otherwise, you will see an error message that the Manager is not loaded.

1. From the Create Printer Agent dialog box shown in Figure 12-8, click the type of gateway you need from the Gateway Types list and then click OK. (You will select the gateway based on what brand of printer you have. Use the Novell gateway for all other printer brands.) NetWare then displays one of three dialog boxes depending on which gateway you chose. Both the HP and the Novell gateway dialog boxes include a list of printers at the top of the dialog box. The Xerox dialog box is actually a wizard typical of many Windows programs. The wizard provides its own onscreen instructions, so here we'll focus on the HP and Novell dialog boxes.

2. Select the printer (such as "HP LaserJet 5" or "Apple LaserWriter") from the Printer Types list. If you have the Novell gateway, skip to Step 6.

3. Next, in the HP gateway dialog box, choose which type of connection the printer uses to attach to the network. This will be either IPX or IP. (It won't be both.) Remember, we are setting up an HP network-attached printer and not a server-attached printer.

If your printer is server-attached, you will use the Novell gateway instead. Do this only when the printer does not support a network attachment. A server-attached printer will demand resources on that server, while today's network-attached printers are just as fast, without using server resources.

4. Finally, in the HP gateway dialog box, you can select the printer from the list of those the NetWare Administrator is already aware of. You can also specify the printer's IP address (as shown in the HP printer's menu panel) directly. (If your printer is not listed, try selecting an earlier version of the same model. However, some printers are not listed because NDPS does not currently support them.

Check the Novell Web site, *www.novell.com*, to identify supported as well as problem printers.)

5. Choose OK. Skip to Step 12 to continue.

6. In the Novell dialog box, highlight the Novell Port Handler type, then click OK. Another dialog box appears in which you can specify the connection type and port type for the agent, as shown in Figure 12-9.

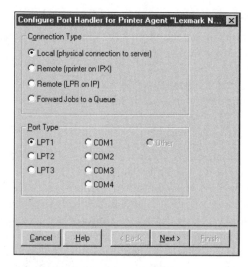

Figure 12-9   Specifying connection and port type

7. Select the connection type based on whether the printer is server-attached (local) or network-attached (RPRINTER or LPR). The fourth option, sending jobs to a queue, is for QMS-compatibility and won't be covered here.

8. When the printer is server-attached, choose the Local option. (This will also require specifying a port in the lower part of the dialog box.) When your network-attached printer runs in RPRINTER or RP mode, choose the Remote (rprinter or IPX) option. (Check the printer's documentation for support for this mode.) When your network-attached printer supports the Unix-style LPR mode (usually with TCP/IP), choose the Remote (LPR or IP) option.

9. If you chose the Local option, then you will need to specify the port type. This can be an LPT or COM port, depending on where you physically connected the printer.

10. If you chose one of the Remote options, then choose Other in the Port Type area.

11. Click Next to continue. NetWare will now ask you to specify details about the COM port, if you selected one in the Port Type area.

12. To finish creating your gateway, NetWare asks you to select which set of printer drivers you want to include. (This is optional, so you can skip this if you want.) Typically, you will include the Windows 95/98 software. You can also include the Windows NT versions as well as the Windows 3.x drivers if needed. This information is important to the automatic download and configuration functions available through NDPS. Otherwise, users would have to manually configure their workstations for these new printers.

13. Once you select your printer drivers, you can then click Continue. NetWare presents you with a Details screen for that printer. If the information is correct, click OK, then click OK again to create the gateway (or to recognize the gateway functions in the HP or XEROX NDPS-compatible printer for this printer agent). You also will then complete the creation of your printer agent.

Like the NDPS Manager software, the gateway and printer agent software also loads automatically once you complete the configurations. Unlike the NDPS Manager, you don't have to reconfigure the server's NCF files to have these components load each time the server starts. The NDPS Manager does this for you.

Creating a Controlled Access Printer Agent

Creating a controlled access printer agent is in essence adding an NDPS Printer object into the tree. At that point, NDPS will recognize the Printer object and provide all the security and management controls the administrator chooses for this printer. Setting up two of the components of the NDPS Printer object—the printer agent and the gateway—are identical to the procedures for the public access printer agent described earlier. The general steps are as follows:

 These steps assume you have an NDPS-compatible printer connected to the network. A locally attached (server-attached), non-NDPS-compatible printer using the Novell Gateway will demonstrate some, but not all of the functions in these steps. In particular, automated workstation configuration may not work for such printers because NDPS may not have the appropriate drivers.

1. Run NetWare Administrator.

2. Right-click the container that includes the users you want to have access to this printer.

3. Choose Create and then choose NDPS Printer from the list. Click OK. NetWare shows you the Create NDPS Printer dialog box shown in Figure 12-10.

12

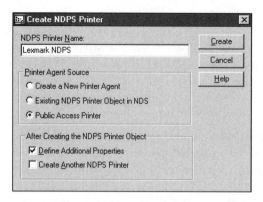

Figure 12-10   Create NDPS Printer dialog box

4. Give the new printer a descriptive name. As outlined earlier, NetWare 5.0 allows printer names up to a maximum of 47 characters. They can contain any number of ASCII characters, including spaces and special characters.

 Windows 95/98 and some utilities have trouble handling special characters such as dashes and underscores in printer names. For this reason, you may want to use letters and numbers in names, not dashes, underscores, or other special characters, even though NetWare itself handles them just fine.

5. Choose either to create a new printer agent or use an existing printer agent. (Typically, you'll choose to create a new one.)

6. Check the box marked Define Additional Properties if you want the NetWare Administrator to display your new object's Details dialog box after it finishes creating the object. (You could then begin to specify appropriate controls for this printer, such as defining the printer's Access Control list to include certain users, groups, or container objects.)

7. Click Create to continue. NetWare now displays the dialog box shown earlier in Figure 12-8. You can then follow through on the remaining steps discussed under Public Access Printer Agents to complete the controlled access printer.

After you follow through on the creation of printer agents, you are ready to configure your users' workstations for those printers. This is covered in the next section.

Configuring Workstations for Printers using NDPS

You can manually or automatically configure workstations to use NDPS printers. The manual operation uses the Novell Printer Manager (NWPMW32.EXE for Windows 95/98) on each desktop. The automated process uses the NDPS Broker to perform the configuration during the user's next login.

Manually Configuring Workstations for Printers

To manually configure a workstation for an NDPS printer:

1. Run the NWPMW32.EXE program from the CONSTELLATION\SYS\PUBLIC\WIN32 directory. If this is a new workstation, the main part of the dialog box will be blank. Once you configure a printer for this workstation, it will appear in this dialog box, as Figure 12-11 shows.

Figure 12-11   Novell Printer Manager dialog box

2. Choose the Printer menu, then choose New. The utility displays the Novell Printers dialog box. Click Add. The utility now displays a list of all the Printer objects in the Directory tree to which the logged-in user has rights. You may need to click the Browse button and explore your NDS tree to locate the appropriate Printer objects.

3. Highlight the printer you want, then click Install. The Printer Manager will now install the appropriate driver software on your workstation. Click OK, then Close to exit the Printer Manager.

 The Novell Printers dialog box has a button labeled Filter. This button opens a dialog box that lets you filter out printers that may not be the type you want. This is a valuable tool in large networks where many printers may be online. If you only wanted to see printers that support color output, you could use the filtering function to locate them.

4. If you want, you can now highlight the printer in the list and click on Set as Default Printer to make this printer object the workstation's default. You can now exit this dialog box and return to the Novell Printer Manager.

You will now see the Printer object in the Novell Printers dialog box. By clicking the printer, you or the workstation's user can manage print jobs as described later in this chapter.

Automatic Workstation Configuration

One advantage of NetWare 5.0 is its ability to easily and automatically configure workstations for printing. To automatically configure workstations:

1. Open NetWare Administrator and right-click the container containing the user objects whose workstations you want to configure. Select Details.

2. Click the NDPS Remote Printer Management tab on the right side of the dialog box. Click the Add button in the field labeled Printers To Install To Workstations. The NetWare Administrator will display a list of the available printers. You may need to use the Browse button to locate the appropriate Printer object.

3. Highlight the printer you want, then click OK.

You also have the option here of making this the default printer for each workstation, by clicking the Set As Default button.

4. Click the Update Driver button. NetWare displays a message that the next time users in that container log in, their workstations will be updated with this printer driver. Click OK to accept this, then OK again to close the dialog box.

NDPS will now ensure that the next time the user logs in, the appropriate drivers and printer configuration will be made on the workstation.

Managing Print Jobs

The administrator can manage print jobs using either the Novell Printer Manager or the NetWare Administrator. Users can run the Printer Manager, then double-click the appropriate Printer object to view the status of their print jobs, delete them, or put them on hold. If users have access to the NetWare Administrator, they can also do similar tasks, with the limitation that users can only monitor and modify their own print jobs, whereas administrators or Print Managers can handle all jobs.

To manage jobs using the NetWare Administrator:

1. Double-click the appropriate Printer object in the tree.

2. Choose Jobs, then choose Jobs List.

3. Highlight the print job for which you want details.

4. Click Information.

The NetWare Administrator now displays a dialog box showing you the status of the job, including job owner, submission date, and size of the job. You can delete this job by clicking the Jobs menu and selecting Cancel Printing.

If you need to reorder print jobs, such as when a senior manager wants a report generated immediately, you can highlight the rush job, then move the job to the top of the queue. To reorder print jobs:

1. Open NetWare Administrator, then double-click the appropriate Printer object in the tree.

2. Click the Printer Control tab on the right side of the dialog box.

3. On the Printer Control page, click the Jobs button, then click the Job Options button.

4. Select Reorder, then highlight the name of the rush job and specify its new position in the queue.

If you want to move the rush job to another printer (assuming the new printer uses the same driver as the first one), you can choose Copy or Move from the Job options, rather than Reorder as in Step 3 of the preceding list.

Assigning Managers and Operators

12

For many sites, having an assistant or two who can handle print jobs can save valuable time. This frees the administrator to deal with more important tasks. Assigning access control in the NetWare Administrator requires only a few steps. There are two types of printer assistants that you can define:

- Manager—a Print Manager can add or delete users for a particular printer object. A Print Manager can also define notification methods and recipients, and create, modify, or delete the printer configuration.

- Operator—a Print Operator can pause, restart, or delete print jobs as well as reorder them.

To assign either type, run NetWare Administrator, then double-click the Printer object you want. Click the Access Control tab on the right side. The dialog box has two windows for listing Managers and Operators, as Figure 12-12 shows. (By default, the Administrator has rights to all functions.) Choose the list you want, and press Add. (Click the Browse button to locate the users if necessary.) Select the user you want to make a manager or operator, and then choose OK.

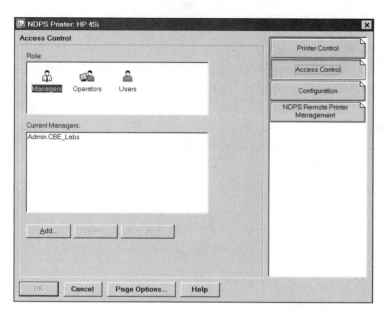

Figure 12-12   Setting up Print Managers and Operators

The next time that user logs in, he or she can function as a manager or operator.

CHAPTER SUMMARY

❏ An important task of the network administrator is establishing and maintaining a network printing environment that will provide users with access to a variety of printers. As a network administrator, you will be expected to know the printing concepts and utilities described in this chapter and be able to implement and maintain a NetWare printing environment consisting of either Novell Distributed Print Services (NDPS) or Queue Management Services (QMS). NDPS includes printer agents, which are software entities that control specific printers, at its core. It also has an NDPS Manager to handle all printer agents in the tree. Printer agents can either be embedded in an NDPS-aware printer or run from the server. When the printer agent is run from the server, it uses a gateway to communicate with its printer. The current version of NDPS includes three gateways to interact with HP, Xerox, or generic printer agents. NDPS also uses a broker to provide notification services as well as automatic distribution of printer drivers to workstations.

❏ In queue-based printing, print jobs go from the workstation to a holding area called a print queue. A print server then takes jobs from the queue and sends them to the appropriate printer. The first task in establishing the printer environment is defining the printing requirements for each user's applications, determining the types and number of printers necessary to meet these requirements, and determining the location of the printers on the network and whether they will be locally attached to the print server or attached to the network. The next step in defining the printer environment is developing a naming system for printers and print service objects that will make it easy for you to identify the printer location, type of printer, and method of attachment. After you have defined the printing environment, you must install the printing system. The NetWare Administrator performs most of the work involved with setting up and maintaining the NetWare printing system.

❑ With NDPS, after a broker, a manager, appropriate gateways, and printer agents are defined and loaded, workstations can be automatically configured for the network printer at login time. Once operational, a Windows workstation can be quickly configured for network printing using the Add Printer wizard.

❑ Print job management is handled through either the NetWare Administrator or through the Novell Printer Manager. Using either tool, users can view real-time status of their print jobs and can pause, resume, or delete their print jobs. Using the NetWare Administrator, users can be assigned to serve as print managers or operators. Managers can set up basic print services, whereas operators handle print jobs only for a defined set of users.

KEY TERMS

bidirectional communication
controlled access printer
direct printer
local printer
Novell Distributed Print Services (NDPS)
NDPS broker
NDPS gateway
NDPS Manager
print job
print queue
print server
printer agent
public access printer
Queue Management Services (QMS)

12

REVIEW QUESTIONS

1. The _____ is the primary network printing component that handles transferring a print job to a printer.

2. When is an NDPS gateway required?

3. Describe any limitations on using a server-attached printer with NDPS.

4. What utility do you use to install and configure NDPS printing?

5. How many NDPS Managers are required in each NDS tree?

6. When will NetWare create an additional NDPS broker in an NDS tree?

7. List two common ways of attaching a printer to the network.

8. List the three items of information that should be included in a printer's name.

9. List in sequence the minimum steps required to set up a networked printing environment.

10. The _____ utility contains a Quick Setup feature that can be used to quickly perform the steps necessary to set up a QMS network printing environment.

11. What type of printer requires no configuration in order for users to send print jobs to it?

12. Describe when a public access printer would be useful on a network.

13. After you define an NDPS Manager, what must you do for the manager software to load?

14. To print using Windows 95/98, the _____ permits you to create a printer.

15. Describe how to change the order in which print jobs are printed.

16. Write the procedure to delete a print job before it finishes printing.

17. Write the procedure to update user workstations in the CBE_LABS_ADMIN container with a driver for the HP 1170 Color Ink Jet printer.

HANDS-ON PROJECTS

For Projects 12-1 and 12-2, you need to log in with a user name that has ADMIN equivalency in order to establish the printing environment. If you do not have this equivalency on your server, or if your lab does not have an appropriate printer configuration, you will need to use aliases to indicate where you would place the appropriate objects in your test tree or simply record the appropriate steps you would take, then turn in this report to your instructor.

Project 12-1: Creating Print Services

Your assignment is to add a printer into the CBE_Labs tree.

1. Fill out an appropriate Print Services Definition Form (see Appendix B) using the following parameters:

   ■ Install the printer into the PUBS container.

   ■ Indicate the appropriate NDPS Manager you will use.

   ■ Use an HP 4Si printer with a direct attach connection.

2. Configure the appropriate gateway for use with this printer. Indicate any special requirements to work with this printer.

3. Define the printer as a controlled access printer. Indicate the steps required to provide users within the PUBS container with access to this printer, as well as to update them with appropriate drivers automatically.

4. Test your configuration by logging in as an appropriate user and sending a print job from Notepad stating, "This is a test of the HP 4SI Printer by ###," where the pound signs are your ID number.

5. Turn in this information to your instructor.

Project 12-2: Creating Print Services

In this project, you will add a printer that requires the use of the Novell Gateway.

Again, your assignment is to add a printer into the CBE_Labs tree.

1. Fill out an appropriate Print Services Definition Form (see Appendix B) using the following parameters:

   ■ Install the printer in the Test&Eval container.

   ■ Indicate the appropriate NDPS Manager you will use.

   ■ Use a Lexmark Optra SE with a direct network attachment.

2. Configure the Novell Gateway for use with this printer. Indicate any special requirements to work with this printer.

3. Define the printer as a controlled access printer. Indicate the steps required to provide users within the Test&Eval container with access to this printer as well as to automatically update them with appropriate drivers.

4. Test your configuration by logging in as an appropriate user and sending a print job from Notepad stating, "This is a test of the Lexmark Optra Printer by ###," replacing the pound signs with your ID number.

5. Turn in this information to your instructor.

12

Project 12-3: Managing Print Jobs from NetWare Administrator

In this project you learn how to manage print jobs using NetWare Administrator and the Novell Printer Manager on a Windows 95/98 workstation. This exercise assumes that Windows 95/98 has the latest Novell Client installed and that there is a network printer available for print jobs. (Your instructor will set this up and tell you the printer name if it is available.)

1. Log in using your assigned student user name.

2. Double-click **My Computer**, then double-click the **Printers** folder. Record the defined printers, then right-click each printer icon and select **Properties/Details**. Record the details about each printer.

3. Close the Printers folder.

4. Use Notepad to create a short document—maybe describing your plans for this coming weekend.

5. Use the Print option of Notepad to send output to the network printer.

6. Double-click the network printer in NetWare Administrator. Verify and record the job information and the status of your print job.

7. Indicate in another memo how you would change the priority of this print job. Print this memo as well.

CASE PROJECTS

Case 12-1: Creating a Printing Environment for the Jefferson County Courthouse

In this project you create a printing environment for the Jefferson County Courthouse Directory tree created in Case 7-1. Refer back to that project if necessary.

Part 1: Create and Configure Print Services

1. If necessary, start the PC workstation and start Windows 95/98.

2. Click the **Start** button.

3. Run the NetWare Administrator from the Programs/Novell menu or from your desktop icon shortcut.

4. Expand the Jefferson County Courthouse organizational unit to display the tree's container objects.

5. Select the container object **SOCSERVICES** as the location for the Printer object.

6. Click **Object** on the menu bar, and click **Create** to see a display of the available objects.

7. Click **NDPS Printer**, then click **OK**.

8. Type **SSHP5** as the name of the printer.

Part 2: Create and Configure the Printer Agent

1. If necessary, click **Create a New Printer Agent** to select it.

2. Check the **Define Additional Properties** box.

3. Click **Create**.

4. Click the **browse** icon near the NDPS Manager Name field.

5. Select the class's existing NDPS Manager as defined by your instructor.

6. Select the appropriate gateway for this printer. Then click **OK**.

7. Make appropriate adjustments to the gateway configuration, including selecting appropriate drivers for your classroom printer(s) as defined by your instructor.

8. Click **OK** to continue.

9. Select the Printer Agent object from your tree.

10. Right-click it and choose **Details**.

11. Click **Access Control**.

12. Click **Users**. Verify who has access to this printer.

13. Turn in a report of your configuration and a printout of the NDS tree to your instructor.

Case 12-2: Creating a Printing Environment for the J.Q. Adams Company

In this project you create a printing environment for the J. Q. Adams Company Directory tree created in Case 7-2. Refer back to that project if necessary.

Part 1: Create and Confirm the Printer

1. If necessary, start the PC workstation, and start Windows 95/98.

2. Run the NetWare Administrator.

3. Locate the J. Q. Adams Company organizational unit in your NDS tree.

4. Select the container object **SALES&MRKTING** as the location for the printer object.

5. Right-click the container object and select **Create**.

6. Select **NDPS Printer** and click **OK**.

7. Type **SMHP5** as the name of the printer.

Part 2: Create and Configure the Printer Agent

1. Click **Create a New Printer Agent**.

2. Check the **Define Additional Properties** box.

3. Click **Create**.

4. Type **PA###** as the name of the printer agent, replacing the ### with your student number. (You may need to use an alias for this in your tree.)

5. Click the **browse** icon near the NDPS Manager Name field, then locate and select the NDPS Manager.

6. Click the appropriate gateway for your printer. Configure it as needed.

7. When you are done, click **Finish**.

12

Part 3: Create and Configure the Printer Object

1. To locate the printer object, select the container object **SALES&MRKTING**.
2. To see a display of the available objects, click **Object** on the menu bar, and click **Create**.
3. Click **NDPS Printer**.
4. Type **SSMHP5R0** as the name of the printer.
5. Type the name of the printer agent as you defined it in Part 2, Step 4 of this project.
6. Check the **Define Additional Properties** box.
7. Click **Create**.
8. Click the **browse** icon next to the NDPS Manager Name field.
9. Choose the appropriate NDPS Manager object.
10. Select the appropriate gateway for the printer, as well as appropriate printer drivers, then click **OK**.
11. Click **Access Control**, then click **Users**. Note who the users are for this printer.

Part 4: Automate the Driver Delivery

1. To configure the printer driver delivery, select the container object **SALES&MRKTING**. Right-click this object, then select **Details** on the menu.
2. Click the **NDPS Remote Printer Management** button.
3. Click the **Add** button under Printers To Install To Workstations field.
4. Select the printer you created in Part 3 as the printer.
5. Click **OK**, then click the printer in the window, then click **Update Driver**, then click **OK**, and then click **OK** again to exit the dialog box.
6. Log in as a user in the J. Q. Adams organization, then view your printer configuration.
7. Report the results to your instructor.

CHAPTER

13

LOGIN SCRIPTS

After reading this chapter and completing the exercises you will be able to:

♦ Identify the four categories of login script files and how they are used

♦ Identify the purpose and correct syntax of login script commands

♦ Write container login scripts to meet the needs of a typical network organization

♦ Write user and profile login scripts to meet the personal processing needs of users

Once the network directory structure has been established and secured, the user accounts created, and the applications installed, the next challenge for the network administrator is to make this complex system easy to access and use. Administrators can configure Windows 95/98 workstations with user profiles, which allow several users to share the same hardware, but have different workstation configurations. Novell's Z.E.N.works provides an additional means to configure workstations remotely. A third way is to use login scripts, which run at the time the user logs into the network. Login scripts make it possible for users to log into a server and access network services by establishing drive mappings, providing informational messages, and executing special programs.

Establishing the user environment is an important aspect of a network administrator's job. In this chapter, you will learn about login scripts and how to establish the necessary login scripts for your network system.

The Windows User Profiles option will not be covered here. However, you should know that Novell's login process does not override local configurations set in the Windows User Profiles option. If users assume they can log into any workstation without checking on the presence/absence of a user profile on that workstation, they may be surprised when they cannot access their home directories.

Novell discourages the use of personal login scripts (a login script defined for each user). The preferred method is to simplify login by using container or group login scripts. Otherwise, any significant changes to your network configuration may require you to also change every user's login script. (You'll learn more about this later in the chapter.)

NetWare Login Scripts

As you learned in previous chapters, any drive mappings you establish while you are logged into a server are effective only until you log out. The next time you log in, you must again map each drive pointer you want to use. Requiring users to do this takes time away from productive work. NetWare saves you from this hassle with **login scripts**, which contain a set of commands NetWare must perform each time you log into the server. A NetWare login script is a file that contains a set of valid NetWare login command statements, as Figure 13-1 shows.

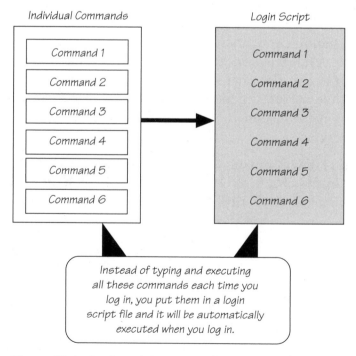

Figure 13-1   Login script compared to commands

Each login script command statement must contain a valid login script or NetWare command. The command statements in a login script file form a program that the Novell Client software processes after a user has logged in. Figure 13-2 shows a container login script that contains statements to map drive pointers for all users and displays a message that greets users when they log in.

```
MAP DISPLAY OFF
DISPLAY "Welcome to the CBE Labs Network"
MAP ROOT H:=CONSTELLATION/DATA:USERS\%LOGIN_NAME
MAP ROOT I:=CONSTELLATION/SYS:\PUBLIC
MAP J:= CONSTELLATION/SYS:APPS\EMAIL
DRIVE H:
```

Figure 13-2   Sample login script

A limited number of commands can be used in login script programs. Before you can design and write login script programs, you need to understand the individual command statements. The following sections present valid login script command statements and how they are used.

Some login script command statements, such as MAP, have corresponding NetWare command line utilities. Although the syntax and purpose of these commands are very similar to those of the command line utilities, the login script commands include special options or variables that are not available with the corresponding command line utility.

Login Script Variables

Many login script commands allow you to use variables as part of the command line. A **login script variable** contains a value that will vary with each user's login. One common use of a login script variable, for example, is to map a drive letter to each user's home directory. If each user's home directory has the same name as his or her user name, the following login script command, included in the User object container login script, will map the drive letter H to the home directory of each user when he or she logs in:

```
MAP ROOT H:=CONSTELLATION/DATA:USERS\%LOGIN_NAME
```

Notice that the variable %LOGIN_NAME is preceded by a percent sign (%). This identifies LOGIN_NAME as a variable rather than the name of a directory. The Novell Client will substitute the name of the user who is currently logging in for the %LOGIN_NAME variable in the MAP command statement. It will then map the H drive letter to the user's specified home directory. For example, let's say someone logs in with the user name GBurns. The login program will substitute the name GBurns for the variable %LOGIN_NAME, creating the statement

```
MAP ROOT H:=CONSTELLATION/DATA:USERS\GBURNS
```

13

Login script variables can be divided into several types, based on their use. **Date variables** contain information about the current month, day, and year in a variety of formats, as shown in Table 13-1. Date variables are useful for displaying current date information. The login script can also check for a specific day in order to perform special setup instructions. By including a DAY_OF_WEEK variable, you can write a login script command that sends a message reminding users of a weekly 2:30 P.M. meeting when they log in each Tuesday. The value of a date variable is stored as an ASCII string of a fixed length. The DAY variable represents the day number of the current month and may contain only the values 01 to 31. The NDAY_OF_WEEK variable represents the day number of the week, with Sunday being day number 1 and Saturday being day number 7.

When using the DAY variable in an IF statement, it is important to include the leading 0 in front of day numbers 01 through 09 and then enclose the day numbers in quotation marks (e.g., IF DAY>"09"THEN...).

Table 13-1   Date variables

Variable	Description
DAY	Day number of the current month (possible values 01–31)
DAY_OF_WEEK	Name of the current day of the week
MONTH	Number of the current month (possible values 01–12)
MONTH_NAME	Name of the current month
NDAY_OF_WEEK	Current weekday number (possible values 01–07)
SHORT_YEAR	Last two digits of the current year (1997 would be 97)
YEAR	Full four-digit year

The **network variables** shown in Table 13-2 can be used to display or check the network address and name of the current server of the user who is logging in. The **time variables** shown in Table 13-3 offer a variety of methods to view or check the login time. The GREETING_TIME variable is most often used to display welcome messages. The difference between the HOUR24 variable and the HOUR variable is that the HOUR variable requires inclusion of the AM_PM variable to specify if the time is before or after noon. The HOUR24 variable is based on a 24-hour system, in which 12 represents noon and 13 represents 1 P.M. If you want to specify a time in the login script, the HOUR24 variable is often easier to use. If you want all users who log in before 3 P.M. to be notified of a special meeting, for example, you could write login script commands that use the HOUR24 variable to compare the current login hour to 15. If HOUR24 is less than 15, the login script commands could then display a notice of the meeting.

Table 13-2   Network variables

Variable	Description
NETWORK_ADDRESS	Network address of the cabling system to which the user's workstation is attached (expressed as an eight-digit hexadecimal number)
FILE_SERVER	Name of the current file server

Table 13-3   Time variables

Variable	Description
AM_PM	Day or night (AM or PM)
GREETING_TIME	Time of day (possible values: Morning, Afternoon, or Evening) Most commonly used in welcome message
HOUR	Current hour of day or night (possible values 01–12)
HOUR24	Current hour in 24-hour mode (possible values 01 for 1 A.M. through 24 for midnight)
MINUTE	Current minute (possible values 00–59)
SECOND	Current second (possible values 00–59)

The **user variables** (see Table 13-4) let you view or check the user's login name, full name, last name, or the hexadecimal ID given to the user. As described earlier, the LOGIN_NAME variable is commonly used to map a drive letter to a user's home directory, provided the name of the user's home directory is the same as the user's login name. The FULL_NAME variable can be used to personalize greeting messages by including the user's name as part of the message.

Table 13-4   User variables

Variable	Description
FULL_NAME	User's full name
LOGIN_NAME	User's unique login name
USER_ID	Hexadecimal number assigned by NetWare for the user login name
LAST_NAME	User's last name

The **workstation variables** MACHINE, OS, and OS_VERSION, shown in Table 13-5, were most commonly used in the container login script when a search drive was mapped to the correct DOS version used on the workstation. (With the arrival of Windows 95/98 and low-cost hard disk space, most network administrators no longer store OS files on the network.) The STATION variable contains the connection number assigned to the user's workstation. Some software packages can use it to separate user temporary files when the station number is included as part of the temporary filename. The P_STATION variable contains the actual node address of the workstation that is logging in and can be used in login script files to cause certain processing to be performed on specific workstations. For example, suppose the workstation address 0800DC03D7D27 is used to run CAD software. You could include in the login script commands that use the P_STATION variable to check for station address 0800DC03D7D27, establish the necessary drive mappings, and then start the CAD software.

Table 13-5 Workstation variables

Variable	Description
OS	Workstation's operating system (default value MSDOS)
OS_VERSION	Workstation's operating system version (example: v6.20)
MACHINE	Long machine name that can be assigned in the NET.CFG file (example: IBMPC)
P_STATION	12-digit hexadecimal node address of the network card in the workstation
SMACHINE	Long machine name that can be assigned in the NET.CFG file (example: IBM)
STATION	Connection number of the current station
NETWARE_REQUESTER	Version of the VLM requester
NETWORK_ADDRESS	12-digit hexadecimal network number of the cabling system
SHELL_TYPE	Workstation's shell version number

Login Script Commands

Like any programming language, NetWare login scripts include commands that make the computer do certain processing tasks. Also like any programming language, login script commands are written according to rules that must be followed in order for the commands to be processed. These rules are commonly referred to as the **syntax** of the programming language. This section shows you the valid syntax of each NetWare login script command and gives examples of how to use it to perform common login functions. Before you turn to the individual login script commands, you should be aware of the following general rules that apply to all login script commands:

- Only valid login script command statements and comments can be placed in a login script file. (Otherwise, NetWare will issue an error message saying it could not process that line in the login script.)

- Login script command lines can contain a maximum of 150 characters.

- Long commands can be allowed to "wrap" to the next line if there isn't enough room on one line.

- The Novell Client software reads the login script commands one line at a time, and only one command is allowed on any command line.

- Commands can be entered in either uppercase or lowercase letters. Variables that are enclosed in quotation marks, however, must be preceded by a percent sign (%) and typed in uppercase letters.

- Comments (remarks) are entered by preceding the text either with the REM command or with one of two symbols, an asterisk (*) or a semicolon (;).

The MAP Command

The MAP command is the most important login script command. You can use it to establish automatically the regular and search drive mappings a user may need to work with applications on the NetWare server. The syntax and use of the MAP login script command are very similar to the MAP command line utility described earlier. In the login script version, however, you can use identifier variables and relative drive letters as part of the MAP command syntax, as follows:

```
MAP [option] [drive:=path;drive:=path] [variable]
```

You can replace *option* in the MAP command with one of the parameters shown in Table 13-6.

Table 13-6 MAP command options

Optional Parameter	Description
ROOT	Makes a drive appear as the root of a volume to DOS and the application programs
INS	Used with search drives to insert a new search drive at the sequence number you specify and then renumber any existing search drives
DISPLAY ON/OFF	Turns on or off the results of the map statements on the screen
ERRORS ON/OFF	Turns on or off any MAP error messages that may be displayed on the screen
C	Changes a search drive mapping to a regular drive mapping
P	Maps a drive to the physical volume of a server instead of to the volume object's name
N	Maps the next available drive
DEL	Removes the specified drive mapping

13

You can replace *drive* with any valid network, local, or search drive. In addition to specifying a drive letter, you can use a relative drive specification, such as *1, to indicate the first network drive, *2 the second network drive, and so on. If the workstation's first network drive letter is G, *1 will be replaced with G and *2 will be replaced with H. However, if a workstation's first network drive is L, *1 will be replaced with L and *2 will be replaced with M. Replace *path* with a full directory path beginning with a DOS drive letter or NetWare volume name.

With the login script version of the MAP command, you can place additional drive mappings on the same line by separating them with semicolons. If you want to map the G drive to the SYS volume and the K drive to the DATA volume, for example, you can issue the following MAP command statement:

```
MAP G:=SYS:; K:=DATA:
```

In NetWare 5.0, you can choose between specifying the physical volume name and the NDS object name for the volume. For example:

```
MAP G:=SARATOGA\SYS:
```

will map the drive to the physical volume name. The command:

```
MAP G:=SARATOGA_SYS:
```

will map the drive to the NDS volume object. Both commands work the same.

 When you want to remove a drive mapping, you can use the command MAP DEL (for Map Delete). For example, MAP DEL G: will remove whatever mapping existed for drive letter G.

If you aren't sure what drive letter to use, NetWare supports the variable N in the MAP command. For example, the command:

```
MAP N SARATOGA\SYS:
```

will map the next available drive letter on the workstation to the SYS volume. This avoids accidentally removing an existing drive mapping that might exist on the workstation.

Finally, you can also use the MAP command with a Directory Map object in NDS. A Directory Map object simply contains the exact path to a NetWare volume, directory, and/or subdirectories as the administrator defines it. The MAP command can then reference this Directory Map object instead of a path to create the drive mapping.

 Using a Directory Map object in a MAP command is helpful because it lets you, as administrator, change the location of data, applications, or other network utilities without having to redo the MAP commands in one or more login scripts. Instead, you simply change the reference in the Directory Map object itself, and all the scripts will now locate the changed path.

For example, suppose you wanted to have a general e-mail storage area on the network. You know that over time this will fill up and you may want to migrate it to another volume. You would run NetWare Administrator, and create a Directory Map object called MAILFILE, with the path SARATOGA_SYS:MAILFILE as its initial location at the root of the SYS volume. Then you could include the command:

```
MAP N MAILFILE
```

in a container login script that will map the next available drive letter on the workstation to the Directory Map object MAILFILE. If, in the future, you want to move the MAILFILE directory to VOL1, then you only have to change the path in the Directory Map object to SARATOGA_VOL1:MAILFILE and the container login script MAP command will still be valid.

Notice that you do not put a colon at the end of the Directory Map object's name as you would after the path for a regular MAP command.

As mentioned earlier, you can include login script variables in the MAP statement. Commonly used variables include %LOGIN_NAME, %OS, %OS_VERSION, and %MACHINE. The %OS, %OS_VERSION, and %MACHINE variables are often used for DOS- and Windows 3.11-based clients to map a search drive to a specific DOS directory based on the version of DOS being used on the workstation logging in. For example, Figure 13-3 displays the CBE directory structure, which stores three different versions of DOS. You can use the following MAP command statement in a login script file to map the second search drive to the appropriate DOS version for the workstation currently logging in:

```
MAP S2:=CONSTELLATION/SYS:PUBLIC\%MACHINE\%OS\%OS_VERSION
```

13

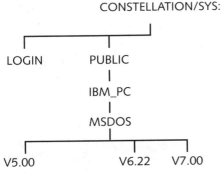

Figure 13-3   CONSTELLATION directory structure

Other special MAP command statements include MAP DISPLAY OFF or MAP DISPLAY ON and MAP ERRORS OFF or MAP ERRORS ON. By default, MAP DISPLAY is set to ON, displaying the results of each MAP command in the login script. The MAP DISPLAY OFF command prevents the map commands from being displayed on the user workstation while they are executed. This MAP command is often included at the beginning of a login script command to reduce the amount of information displayed on the user workstations. You can use the MAP ERRORS OFF command to prevent the display on a user's workstation of error messages generated by MAP commands that specify invalid paths. This command is useful if you include drive mapping commands in a login script that you know will not be valid for all users. Rather than have a user be confused by error messages that do not affect him or her, include the MAP ERRORS OFF command before the MAP commands that contain the invalid drive paths.

The CONTEXT Command

Accessing network resources is much easier when you set the current context of your client to the container that holds the objects you need to use. One way to do this is to use the Advanced button in the Novell Login utility to specify the context you want. Rather than go through this effort, you can set your preferred context within your user login script. The CONTEXT login script command lets you change the workstation's current context to the preferred default container when you log in. For example, the following command used in a login script would set the context to the CBE_Labs container:

```
CONTEXT .O=CBE_Labs
```

The WRITE Command

The WRITE command is used to place simple messages enclosed in quotation marks (" ") on the screen of the workstation. In addition to text, messages can contain identifier variables and special control strings, as shown in the following WRITE command syntax:

```
WRITE "text [control string] [%variable]"
```

In addition to replacing the *text* parameter with any message you want displayed when the user logs in, you can add the control characters shown in Table 13-7 anywhere in the text string. Notice that all options must be preceded by a backslash (\). Any options preceded with a forward slash (/) will be ignored and treated as normal text that appears on the screen.

Table 13-7 Control characters for WRITE

Character	Default Value
\r	Inserts a return and line feed
\n	Inserts a blank line
\"	Inserts an embedded quotation mark within the text
\7	Inserts a beep sound on the speaker

Login script variables can also be placed in the text by capitalizing all characters of the variable name and preceding them with a percent sign (%). As with the MAP command, the login script processor will substitute the value of the variable into the text string before displaying the string on the workstation. Login script variables often used with the WRITE statement include %GREETING_TIME and %FULL_NAME. The %GREETING_TIME variable contains the current time expressed as either Morning, Afternoon, or Evening. For example, the CBE network administrator may include a welcome message at the beginning of their login scripts similar to the following:

```
WRITE "Good %GREETING_TIME %FULL_NAME Welcome to the CBE
    Labs network"
```

You can make sure that all users see and acknowledge important messages by including the following PAUSE statement in your login script:

```
WRITE "Server will be coming down today, March 1, at 5 P.M.
    for a maintenance call."
PAUSE
```

When the PAUSE command is executed, NetWare stops the login script processing and displays the message "Strike any key when ready…" on the screen.

The DISPLAY and FDISPLAY Commands

The DISPLAY and FDISPLAY commands show the contents of an ASCII text file on the screen during the execution of the login script. The proper syntax of either command is:

```
[F]DISPLAY [directory path] filename
```

If the filename specified is in the current directory, or if a search drive has been established to the directory containing the filename, the directory path is not needed. To show the WELCOME.MSG file stored on the CONSTELLATION_DATA: volume in the PUBLCNTS\DOCUMENT directory at CBE Labs, for example, you can place the following FDISPLAY command in your container login script:

```
MAP INS S1:=CONSTELLATION/DATA:
FDISPLAY S1:\PUBLCNTS\DOCUMENT\WELCOME.MSG
PAUSE
```

It is important to follow the DISPLAY command with a PAUSE statement. This gives the user time to read the message file. The difference between DISPLAY and FDISPLAY is that the FDISPLAY command filters and formats the contents of the specified filename so that only the ASCII text itself is displayed. FDISPLAY will not display tabs. The DISPLAY command, in contrast, displays the exact characters contained in the file, including "garbage" characters such as printer or word processing edit codes. It is usually more appropriate to use FDISPLAY for displaying files that have been created with word processing packages. If you use a word processing package, however, make sure to save the file in ASCII text format or it's possible that even if FDISPLAY is used, it will not be readable.

13

Suppose the CBE network administrator wants to display a schedule of events for each day of the week. At the beginning of the week he receives the schedule for the following days. He can use the FDISPLAY command to display the appropriate day's message by creating files named after weekdays. For example, MONDAY.MSG contains Monday's schedule, and so on. He can then use the following DAY_OF_WEEK login script variable to display the appropriate day's schedule:

```
FDISPLAY S1:\PUBLCTNS\DOCUMENT\%DAY_OF_WEEK.MSG
```

IF/THEN/ELSE

The IF login statement is used to customize a login script to perform special processing when a condition—such as a specific day, time, or station—exists. It may also be used in a container or group login script to perform some function for a specific user. The syntax of a simple IF statement is as follows:

```
IF condition THEN command
```

The *condition* parameter is replaced with a conditional statement that has a value of either true or false. Conditional statements usually consist of an identifier variable and a value enclosed in quotation marks. Table 13-8 shows examples of several commonly used conditional statements.

Table 13-8   Sample conditional statements

Condition	Description
MEMBER OF "group"	This statement is true if the user is a member of the specified group.
DAY_OF_WEEK = "Monday"	This statement is true if the name of the day is Monday. Either uppercase or lowercase letters may be used.
DAY = "05"	This statement is true on the fifth day of the month. Valid day values range from 01 to 31. It is necessary to include the leading zero for day numbers less than 10.
MONTH = "June"	This statement is true for the month of June. Either uppercase or lowercase letters may be used.
NDAY_OF_WEEK = "1"	This statement is true on Sunday, which is a 1. Valid numbers range from 1 to 7.

You can replace the *command* parameter with any valid login script command statement. The following is an example of a simple IF statement with a single condition:

```
IF DAY_OF_WEEK = "FRIDAY" THEN WRITE "Hurrah, it's Friday!"
```

More complex IF statements can consist of multiple commands followed by the END statement. The syntax of a multiple-command IF statement is as follows:

```
IF condition THEN
  command 1
  command 2
  command n
END
```

In a multiple-command IF statement, all commands between the IF statement and the END statement are performed when the condition is true. For example, in a container login script, if you want to map certain drive pointers for the marketing department users of CBE Labs, you can use an IF statement similar to this one:

```
IF MEMBER OF "MARKETING" THEN
  MAP ROOT H:CONSTELLATION/DATA:USERS\%LOGIN_NAME
  MAP ROOT L:CONSTELLATION/DATA:MARKET
  MAP INS S1:CONSTELLATION/SYS:APPS\SP
```

Sometimes it is desirable to combine multiple conditions using AND or OR. When using OR to connect two conditions, the login command statements will be performed if either condition is true. If you want all members of either the marketing or finance groups to be informed of a weekly meeting, for example, you can use the following condition:

```
IF MEMBER OF "MARKETING" OR MEMBER OF "FINANCE"
```

Use the word AND when you want both statements to be true before the commands are processed. For example, say you want to remind all finance users of a meeting on Monday morning. Before displaying the reminder, you want to make sure the user is a member of the finance department, the day is Monday, and the login time is before 10 a.m. You can use AND to connect these three conditions, as shown here:

```
IF MEMBER OF "FINANCE" AND DAY_OF_WEEK = "MONDAY" AND HOUR24
  < "10" THEN
  WRITE "Remember the meeting at 10 A.M."
  PAUSE
END
```

The optional word ELSE is an important feature of the IF statement because it lets you perform either one set of commands or another based on the condition. An example of an IF/THEN/ELSE command is shown in the following login script segment. All members of the finance department will have their drive pointers mapped to the FINANCE directory of the CONSTELLATION/DATA volume. All other users will have their drive pointers mapped to the SHARED Directory of the CONSTELLATION/DATA volume.

```
IF MEMBER OF "FINANCE" THEN
  MAP ROOT K:=CONSTELLATION/DATA:FINANCE
ELSE
  MAP ROOT K:=CONSTELLATION/DATA:SHARED
END
```

13

Some IF commands can become quite complex, consisting of IF commands within IF commands. Placing one IF command within another IF command is called **nesting**. NetWare lets you nest as many as 10 levels of IF statements. When nesting IF statements, make sure each IF statement has a corresponding END statement, as the following script segment shows. Indenting IF statements as shown makes this job easier as well as more accurate.

```
IF MEMBER OF "FINANCE" THEN
  MAP ROOT K:=CONSTELLATION/DATA:FINANCE
  IF LOGIN_NAME="DKaneaka" THEN
       MAP I:=CONSTELLATION/DATA:ADMIN
  END
ELSE
  MAP ROOT K:=CONSTELLATION/DATA:SHARED
END
```

The first nested IF statement checks to see whether the user is a member of the finance department. If the user is a member of that group, the login script then checks to see if the login name is DKaneaka. If it is, an I: drive is mapped. However, if the user was not a member of the finance department, then a K: drive is mapped to CONSTELLATION/DATA:SHARED. Although indenting is not necessary for the IF statement to work, lining up the IF and associated ELSE and END statements and then indenting the commands to perform is standard programming practice, and makes complex IF statements much easier to read and maintain.

The DRIVE Command

The DRIVE command is used to set the default drive for DOS and Windows 3.11 clients to use after the user logs in. The syntax for the DRIVE command is as follows:

```
DRIVE drive:
```

Replace the *drive:* parameter with either a local or a network drive letter. Be sure the drive letter has been mapped to a directory path in which the user has the necessary access rights. Most network administrators use the drive near the end of the login script to place the user in either his or her home directory drive. The DRIVE statement has no effect on Windows 95/98 or NT clients.

The EXIT Command

The EXIT command stops execution of the login script and returns control to the client computer. Therefore, no additional login script commands are processed after the EXIT command is executed. When working with DOS and Windows 3.11 clients, you can also use the EXIT command to pass a command to DOS. For example, you could use the EXIT command to automatically start Windows on exiting the login script, as follows:

```
EXIT "WIN"
```

Replace "WIN" with any statement, up to a maximum of 14 characters enclosed in quotation marks, that you want passed to the DOS command prompt. Typically, this is the name of a program you want to run.

You cannot include a program name after the EXIT command as outlined here if the login script will be run on Windows 95/98 workstations. To gain a similar ability, use the @ command as in *@program_name*.exe, then on the next line enter the EXIT command.

The INCLUDE Command

The INCLUDE command lets you process login script commands that are stored in another file and then return to the login script statement following the INCLUDE command. It is similar to the CALL statement in DOS. The filename specified in the INCLUDE command must contain valid login script commands stored in standard ASCII text format. The proper syntax of the INCLUDE command is as follows:

```
INCLUDE [path] filename [NDS object]
```

If the *filename* parameter containing the login script commands is not located in the SYS:LOGIN or SYS:PUBLIC directory, you will need to replace the path with the complete directory path leading to the specified filename.

The INCLUDE command can be used to make your primary login script file shorter and easier to understand by including other login script files as modules or subroutines that are called from the primary script. For example, let's suppose CBE Labs wants to establish a special login script process for all finance department users. Rather than placing many commands in the container login script or having to maintain a complex login script for each finance user, you can create a file named FINANCE.LOG, containing all finance login script commands, in the CONSTELLATION/DATA:FINANCE directory. After you create the FINANCE.LOG file, you can use an INCLUDE command in the container login script, as shown here, to call the FINANCE.LOG file whenever a user logs in:

```
IF MEMBER = "FINANCE" THEN
   INCLUDE FINANCE.LOG
END
```

The FIRE PHASERS Command

The purpose of the FIRE PHASERS command is to fire a phaser blast—make a noise with the PC speaker to alert the operator to a message or condition encountered in the login process. (You can also abbreviate the command simply as FIRE.) You can control the length of the phaser blast by including a number of times to "fire" the sound, as shown here:

```
FIRE [PHASERS] n [TIMES]
```

You can replace *n* with a number from 1 to 9 representing how many times the phaser sound will be made. The words PHASERS and TIMES are optional and can be omitted from the FIRE login script command. The FIRE PHASERS command is often used with the IF statement to notify the user of a certain condition.

13

The REM Command

Comment (remark) lines can be placed in the login script. The Novell Client will skip any line that begins with REM, REMARK, an asterisk (*), or a semicolon (;). Using comments in your login script can make the script much easier for you or another administrator to read and understand. It is a good idea to precede each section of your login script with a comment identifying the function of that section, as in the following example:

```
REM Login Script
REM Written by Dave Doering
;
* Preliminary Commands
MAP DISPLAY OFF
;
```

The CLS Command

The CLS command is used simply to CLear the Screen. Normally it is a good idea to precede messages by clearing the screen and firing a phaser blast. This gets the user's attention and makes the message easier to read. You may want to follow the message with another CLS to remove the message from the screen. If you do, be sure to follow the message with a PAUSE command (and before the second CLS command) or the user will not get time to read it.

The BREAK ON/OFF Commands

The BREAK ON command lets the user stop execution of the login script by pressing the Ctrl-Break key combination during the running of the script. BREAK OFF is the default setting in NetWare, so if you want users to stop the script you must insert the command BREAK ON in the script. (The command only applies to that particular script, not to any scripts yet to be run.)

One example of using the BREAK ON command is to provide users with a "window" in the login script during which they can press Ctrl-Break to exit that login script.

The NO_DEFAULT Command

The NO_DEFAULT command prevents the Novell Client software from executing the default login script. You can put it in either the container or profile login script. The syntax is:

```
NO_DEFAULT
```

TYPES OF LOGIN SCRIPTS

To understand how NetWare stores and processes login scripts, you first need to be aware of the types of login scripts and their purposes. The NetWare login script system consists of four types of login script files: container, profile, user, and default. The four types of login script files let the network administrator provide a standard environment for all users and still provide flexibility so the network administrator can meet individual user needs. The **container login** script file lets the network administrator establish a standard configuration for each user in that container. The commands it contains are executed for all users of that container when they first log in. **Profile login scripts** execute for all members of a group, not just those in one container. You can set up a group and then assign any users to it. Individual user requirements can then be met with **user login script** files. Each user has his or her own personal login script file, which contains additional statements that are executed for that user after the container and profile login script commands are executed. The **default login script** is a set of commands that establishes a default working environment for each user who does not have a container, profile, or user login script.

To become a CNA, you need to know how these login script files work. This will enable you to configure a reliable and efficient login script system for your network. Figure 13-4 contains a flowchart that shows the relationships among the login script files.

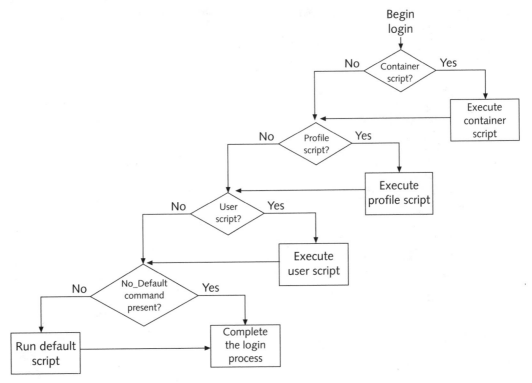

Figure 13-4   Login script flowchart

Notice that once you create the login script for a container, its commands are performed for all users in that container when they log in. Once all commands in the container login script have been executed, NetWare will determine whether the user is assigned to a Profile object. If the user object has a profile script defined, NetWare will execute the login script commands included in that profile script. Finally, NetWare will execute commands in either the user login script or the default login script.

To prevent default login script commands from being executed, you must either create a personal login script for each user that contains the EXIT command or include the NO_DEFAULT command in the container or profile login script.

If you keep the default workstation policy of showing the Advanced button in the Novell Login screen, users can bypass all these scripts or run one of their own creations from a local drive. You set this policy in the Novell Client32 Properties dialog on the Advanced Login page.

Container Login Scripts

Each container object has a Login Script property that may be used to enter login script commands that will be executed for each User object in that container. That is, the login script of a particular parent container will be executed whenever any User object in that container connects to the network. For example, in Figure 13-5 a container login script for the object CBE_Labs_Admin would apply whenever the User objects JCunningham or SLopez logged into the network.

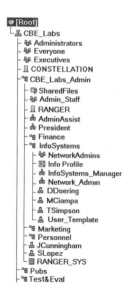

Figure 13-5   CBE Labs NDS tree

Note that a container login script applies only when that container is a direct parent of a User object. Again in Figure 13-5, a container login script in CBE_Labs would not apply to the User objects JCunningham or SLopez; only the container login script found in the direct parent of these users (in CBE_Labs_Admin) would be executed when they log in.

Although container login scripts are properties of container objects, the script itself is stored in NDS.

The container login script should include all the necessary commands to set up a standard working environment for all the users in that container. It may include drive mappings for users' home directories and search drives to applications and the PUBLIC directory, setting DOS environment variables, messages to all users in the container, commands to start specific applications or menus, and any other commands that would apply to all users of the container.

Profile Login Scripts

Profile login scripts apply to a "group" of selected users. That is, a profile login script will let you create a set of login commands that only selected users will execute. Thus a profile login script lies between a container script (which applies to all users in a container) and a user login script (which applies to only one user). It may establish mappings to specific applications or data that this group requires as well as set up a unique printer for their use.

The users who make up a "group" need not be part of a specific container or be located in a particular part of the NDS tree. Instead, a Profile object is created, and a login script for that Profile object is then entered. Then, the individual User object is made a trustee of the Profile object with at least the Read right to the login script of the Profile object. Thus any user to be added to this "group" would simply be given Read rights to the Profile object's Login Script. Anytime the user logs in, the Profile login script would then be executed.

Profile login scripts are intended for multiple users who are not all part of the same container object. In Figure 13-6, suppose that users DDoering, TSimpson, and MCiampa need the same login script as SLopez. Since we want these four users to have the same login script, but don't want to make that script part of the CBE_Labs_Admin container script, we can create a Profile object and these four users can be given Read rights to that object and have the profile login script assigned to them. Then anytime they log in, the profile login script would be executed. (Only one profile login script is executed per user.)

```
● [Root]
└─ 品 CBE_Labs
    ├─ 器 Administrators
    ├─ 器 Everyone
    ├─ 器 Executives
    ├─ ▯ CONSTELLATION
    ├─ ▫ CBE_Labs_Admin
    │   ├─ ⬚ SharedFiles
    │   ├─ 器 Admin_Staff
    │   ├─ ▯ RANGER
    │   ├─ 🖧 AdminAssist
    │   ├─ 🖧 President
    │   ├─ ▫ Finance
    │   ├─ ▫ InfoSystems
    │   │   ├─ 器 NetworkAdmins
    │   │   ├─ ▤ Info Profile  ◄──────  Profile object with shared login script
    │   │   ├─ 🖧 InfoSystems_Manager
    │   │   ├─ 🖧 Network_Admin
    │   │   ├─ 👤 DDoering ◄─┐
    │   │   ├─ 👤 MCiampa ◄─┤
    │   │   ├─ 👤 TSimpson ◄─┤
    │   │   └─ 👤 User_Template │  ──  Users running shared login script
    │   ├─ ▫ Marketing         │
    │   ├─ ▫ Personnel         │
    │   ├─ 👤 JCunningham       │
    │   ├─ 👤 SLopez ◄─────────┘
    │   └─ ▤ RANGER_SYS
    ├─ ▫ Pubs
    └─ ▫ Test&Eval
```

Figure 13-6   Profile login script users

User Login Scripts

User login scripts are for commands that apply to individual users. These scripts are located in the Login Script property of each User object. They contain such commands as special drive mappings or unique environment variables for a specific program that only that user would run.

 User login scripts are strongly discouraged and are often used only as a last resort. They can become very difficult to maintain. Many network managers have spent untold hours trying to track down a network problem only to later discover that a user changed his or her login script, which created the problem. In addition, if a change affects all users, it is very tedious to individually change each user's login script.

Many network administrators prefer to place most commands in container or profile login scripts, to reduce the need for user login scripts whenever possible.

 To prevent users from modifying their own login scripts, remove the Write right from the user's login script using NetWare Administrator.

Default Login Scripts

The final type of login script is the default login script. These login script commands are built into the Novell Client software and are executed only if there is no container, profile, or user login script. The purpose of the default login script is to provide the user with the basic drive mappings.

Because the default login script is contained in the Novell Client, it cannot be modified.

The statements that make up the default login script for the Novell client include the following:

MAP *1:=SYS: (maps the first network drive to the SYS volume)

MAP INS S1:=SYS:PUBLIC   (maps the first search drive to PUBLIC directory)

Once the network administrator has established a container login script that contains the basic drive mapping for the network, it is important to disable the default login script. Failure to do so will cause drive mappings made in the container login script either to be overwritten or duplicated. There are three ways to stop the default login script from being executed:

1. Put the NO_DEFAULT statement in the container or profile login script.

2. Create a user login script that contains only the command EXIT.

3. Put the EXIT statement in the container login script. This will cause the Novell Client software to terminate and prevent the execution of a profile, user, or default script. However, this method has the drawback of preventing any profile login scripts from executing.

If you want to prevent NetWare from running the default login script for a user, you need to give that user a personal login script. This can be as simple as a single EXIT command on one line in the script. Otherwise, NetWare will run the default login script.

13

IMPLEMENTING LOGIN SCRIPTS

Once you understand the syntax and function of the login script commands, and the way login scripts are stored and executed, your next task is to apply login scripts to setting up a network environment for each user's workstation when they log in. Implementing a login script system for your network requires four basic steps:

1. Identify the login script requirements for each container and user.

2. Write the script commands.

3. Enter the script commands.

4. Test the login script.

Identifying Login Script Requirements

To design a login script system, you start by identifying a standard set of regular and search drive mappings that all users will need to run software and access data in the network file system. Next, identify any special setup needs for each workgroup in the organization. Finally, identify any special setups that are unique for individual users.

If most of the user workstation setup needs are the same for groups of users (and they generally are), you can meet them through the container and profile commands. If your network has many special or individualized setup requirements, you might try to decide if you want to create a container or profile login script that contains only the essential commands, such as mapping a search drive to SYS:PUBLIC. Then you implement user login scripts to handle the workstation setup for each individual user.

Just as network administrators differ in the ways they design a directory structure, they also implement login script systems differently, depending on their preferences and experience. The important thing is to develop a workable strategy that meets both the needs of your organization and your personal preferences.

Writing Login Scripts

After you identify your login script needs and strategy, the next step is to write the necessary login script commands. You may find it helpful to use a login script worksheet, as Figure 13-7 shows. (A blank form of this worksheet can be found in Appendix B.) The worksheet is divided into sections by REM statements that define the start of each section. The first part contains sections that all users execute. The Preliminary Commands section can contain any initializing commands. The command MAP DISPLAY OFF, for example, will prevent MAP commands from displaying results on the workstation and will clear the screen. The Preliminary Commands section can also be used to clear the screen and display a greeting for the user. The #C:COMMAND /C CLS command used in the example will clear the screen by running the CLS command from the DOS COMMAND.COM program located in the root of the local workstation's C drive. The #C: preceding the statement sends the login program to the root of the C drive to run the COMMAND.COM program. Thus the #C:COMMAND.COM /C CLS command will not work if the workstation does not boot off its local hard disk. If your network contains workstations that do not have hard drives, you will need to place the #COMMAND /C CLS command in the DOS Setup section of the script after you map a search drive to the correct DOS directory, described as follows.

The Common Application Search Drive Mappings section contains the search drive mappings to DOS-based application packages that are to be accessed by all users. In the example login script in Figure 13-7, all CBE Lab users will be able to run the microcomputer applications.

Login Script Worksheet

Designed by:	Date:

Container context:

```
REM Preliminary Commands
MAP DISPLAY OFF
#C:\COMMAND /C CLS
WRITE "Good %GREETING_TIME, %FULL_NAME"
```

```
REM Common Application Search Drive Mappings
MAP INS S3:=CONSTELLATION/SYS:APPS\WINOFFICE
MAP INS S4:=CONSTELLATION/SYS:APPS\PAGEPUB
```

```
REM Common Regular Drive Mappings
MAP H:=CONSTELLATION/DATA:USERS\%LOGIN_NAME
MAP K:=CONSTELLATION/:DATA:SHARED
```

```
REM Mapping for Workgroups
IF MEMBER OF "MARKETING" THEN
        MAP ROOT L:=CONSTELLATION/DATA:MARKET
        #CAPTURE Q=MAREPS570R1Q1 TI=10 NB NT NFF F=3
END

IF MEMBER OF "FINANCE"  THEN
        MAP ROOT L:=CONSTELLATION/DATA:FINANCE
        IF DAY_OF_WEEK = "TUESDAY" AND HOUR24 < "09" THEN
                WRITE "Remember training at 8:30 A.M."
                PAUSE
        END

END
```

```
REM End of Login Script Commands
DRIVE H:
MAP DISPLAY ON
EXIT
```

13

Figure 13-7   Sample login script worksheet

The Common Regular Drive Mappings section contains drive pointers that will be available for all users. On many networks, for example, a drive pointer would be mapped to each NetWare volume. The Mapping for Workgroups section contains commands based on the workgroup of which the user is a member. In the example, the user who is a member of the marketing workgroup will have his or her home drive mapped to the MARKET directory. A user who is a member of the finance workgroup will receive a drive pointer to the FINANCE directory.

The End of Login Script Commands section can contain any commands that all users will perform before they exit the login script. In the example, the DRIVE H: command will place all users in their home directory before turning the MAP display on and exiting from the container login script. Because the EXIT command was not included in the sample container login script, NetWare will next execute either the user or the default login script commands.

Entering Login Scripts

After you write and check the login script, the next step is to enter and test it. As a network administrator you will need to know how to use NetWare Administrator to create and maintain the three types of login scripts—container, profile, and user—over which you create the user's work environment (you will not work with default login scripts).

Entering Container Login Scripts

To enter a container login script, follow these steps after logging in with administrator privileges:

1. Launch NetWare Administrator.

2. Select the container for which you want to create the login script. In this example, you'll create a container login script for the CBE_Labs_Admin container.

3. Use the right mouse button to click CBE_Labs_Admin and select Details to display the Identification window, as shown in Figure 13-8.

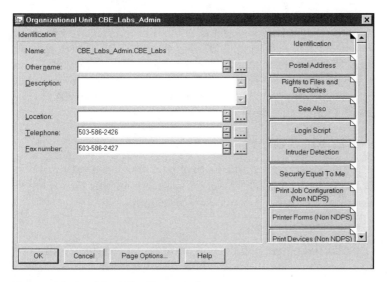

Figure 13-8   Identification window

4. Click Login Script to go to the Login Script window, as shown in Figure 13-9.

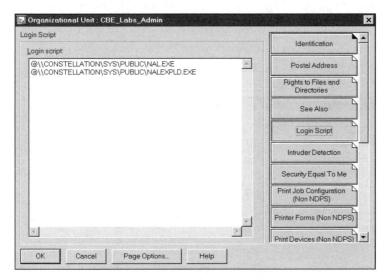

Figure 13-9   Login Script window

5. Type your login script. (A sample login script is shown in Figure 13-2.)

6. Click OK when finished to save the script and return to the browser window.

Users with appropriate rights to modify the container login script also can edit it using Network Neighborhood. Right-click the appropriate container object shown in Network Neighborhood, and select the Edit NDS Container Login Script option. NetWare will then display an edit screen showing you the existing (if any) container login script for that container. You can then add or remove commands from the script. When you are finished, click OK to save the script and return to the desktop.

Entering Profile Login Scripts

Entering a profile login script first requires that you create a Profile object and then assign the users Read rights to the Login Script property. In this example you will create a profile that contains the users SLopez and SJohnson.

1. Start NetWare Administrator.

2. Select the container under which you want to create the Profile object. In this example you'll create it under CBE_Labs_Admin.

3. Select Create on the Object menu, and the New Object list appears.

4. Select Profile from the New Object list. Click OK.

5. Enter the name of the profile you want to create. You'll use Group_1.

6. Check the Define additional properties box, then click Create.

7. If necessary, browse and select the Group_1 Profile object, then select Details on the Object menu to see the Profile window, as shown in Figure 13-10.

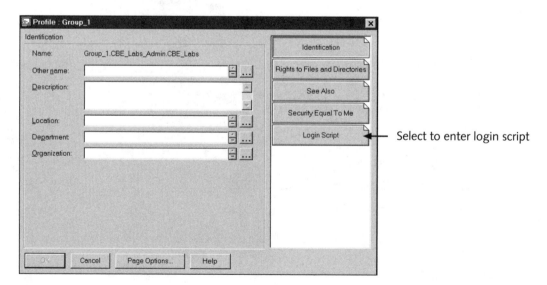

Figure 13-10   Profile window

8. Click the Login Script button to see the Profile login script window.

9. Type your profile login script, and click OK to save the script and return to the browser window.

Once you have created the Profile object and entered the login script, you assign the user to the profile script as follows:

1. Locate and select the User object you want to assign to this profile login script. In this example, you'll select SLopez.

2. Select Details on the Object menu.

3. Click Login Script and the Login Script window appears, as shown in Figure 13-11.

4. Enter the name of the Profile object in the Profile field. Type Group_1.CBE_Labs_Admin.CBE_Labs or browse the NDS tree and select Group_1 using the button to the right of the field.

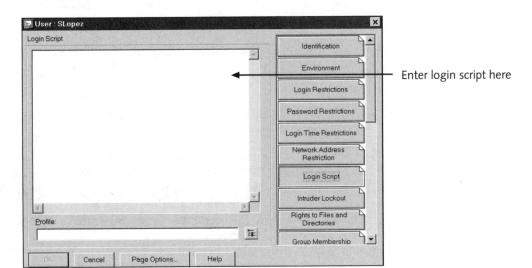

Figure 13-11   User Login Script window

5. Click OK, then confirm the change by clicking Yes.

The last step is to grant the user (SLopez) Read rights to the Profile object (Group_1).

1. Select the Profile object Group_1.

2. Select Trustees of this Object on the Object menu.

3. Click Add Trustee and indicate the user you want to add (SLopez), then click OK.

4. Click Selected Properties and then select Login Script. Place a check mark next to the Read property. Click OK.

Entering User Login Scripts

Entering a user login script requires only that you select that User object and type in the script.

1. Start NetWare Administrator.

2. Select the user for whom you want to create the login script. In this example, you'll create a user login script for JCunningham.

3. Use the right mouse button to click JCunningham, and select Details to display the Identification window.

4. Click the Login Script button to go to the Login Script window.

5. Type your login script.

6. Click OK to save the script and return to the browser window.

You also can modify your own login script using the System Tray N icon utility or by right-clicking your NDS tree icon shown in Network Neighborhood, as follows:

1. Double-click the System Tray "N" icon or open Network Neighborhood, and right-click the NDS tree icon.

2. Choose the User Administration option, then Edit Login Script, as shown in Figure 13-12. Note that the System Tray version adds the phrase "*for name-of-tree*" along with the words User Administration. (If you are logged in as ##Admin, you may see the Edit NDS Container Login Script option instead. You will need to use NetWare Administrator to modify other login scripts.)

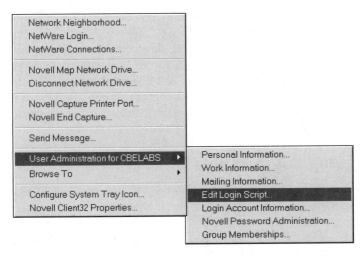

Figure 13-12 Edit Login Script and User Administration options

3. NetWare now displays an Edit Login Script window, as shown in Figure 13-13, where you can add or remove commands from your login script.

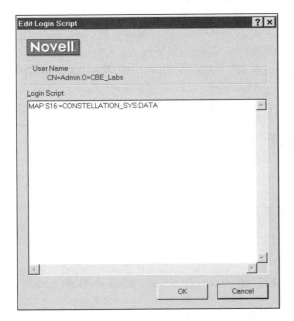

Figure 13-13 Edit Login Script dialog box

4. Click OK to save your changes and return to the desktop.

As an administrator you can remove the Edit Login Script option from the menu if you don't want users to be able to view or modify their own login scripts. Choose Start, Settings, Control Panel, open the Network icon, and double-click Novell NetWare Client to display the Properties page. Click Advanced Settings, then scroll to the Show Edit Login Script Item. Click to highlight this item, use the down arrow on the Settings pane to highlight OFF, then click OK to save the setting. Restart the workstation for the change to take effect.

Testing and Debugging Login Scripts

After the login scripts have been entered, you should test the login script system for at least one user in each workgroup by logging in with that user's name and checking to be sure all commands are executed properly. If your container login script does not use either the No Default or the EXIT command, it is important to prevent the default login script commands from being executed before you test the login script files. This is done, as described earlier, by placing the EXIT statement in each user's login script.

To test login scripts, you need to log in with a user name from each workgroup you have defined. After logging in, determine whether all commands are being executed properly by first looking for any error messages on the screen. Next use the Novell System Tray utility (the N icon) to verify your drive mappings. Select the Novell Map Network Drive option, then choose the dropdown menu box for selecting the drive letter. This displays the current list of mapped drives. You also can double-click the My Computer icon on the desktop to display mapped drives. Finally, you can use the DOS MAP command to display this list.

Verify that there is a drive mapping to SYS:PUBLIC in the My Computer dialog box. If there is a drive mapped to just SYS, then try opening it to view the different directories in it. Then try opening the PUBLIC directory. If the directory doesn't appear, or you cannot open it, then the user doesn't have enough rights to SYS:PUBLIC. Check to see whether the user login script or AUTOEXEC.BAT file has overwritten the mapping to the SYS:PUBLIC directory. If the search mapping for the PUBLIC directory has been overwritten, the drive letter, usually Z, will appear with the regular drive mappings. Search drives can be overwritten by the user login script containing MAP S#:=[path] commands or by a DOS PATH statement in an AUTOEXEC.BAT file following the LOGIN command.

If you cannot change to the PUBLIC directory, then the user does not have Read and File Scan rights to SYS:PUBLIC. The most common reason for a user not having access rights to SYS:PUBLIC is that the default server the user is attached to does not exist in his or her container. You can correct this problem by using NetWare Administrator to make the user's parent container a trustee of SYS:PUBLIC.

If the Windows 95/98 My Computer dialog box contains duplicated drive mappings to the SYS:PUBLIC directory, the most likely problem is that the default login script is causing a second drive mapping to be made. You can correct this problem by adding NO_DEFAULT to the user's container login script.

When all login scripts have been debugged, document drive mappings and other special setup commands that are performed for each workgroup or user.

 Because users need to know certain drive mappings to effectively access data and applications through the network file system, it is important that you give users the documentation or training they will need to use the workstation environment provided by the login script. The time spent in documenting and training users in how to use the system will pay off later in fewer problems and support calls.

Running Login Scripts with the Novell Client for Windows 95/98

Running a different login script with the Novell Client requires only a few steps. The user has the choice of running no scripts at all, or running a different one.

1. Start the Novell Client by right-clicking the N icon in the System Tray, then choosing NetWare Login.

2. Click the Advanced button. The Novell Client displays a set of tabs.

3. Click the Script tab. You now can choose not to run any scripts at all by unmarking the box marked Run Scripts. You also can specify a path to a different user or profile login script or both. The files must contain valid login script commands and must be in text format. These can be on your local drive.

4. To run the scripts, click OK.

13

Chapter Summary

❏ Establishing a workstation environment that makes the network easy to use is an important responsibility of the network administrator. NetWare provides a powerful way to automate workstation activities through login scripts. NetWare login script files contain commands that provide drive mappings and other workstation setup functions that are executed during the login process. You can use the login script commands to map drive letters, set the DOS environment of a workstation, display messages and files, execute other programs, and execute certain commands based on whether a given condition is true or false. Using login script variables with commands enables you to create general-purpose login scripts that work for multiple users. Login script variables can be divided into several types, including date variables such as DAY_OF_WEEK and MONTH_NAME, time variables such as HOUR24, user variables such as LOGIN_NAME, and workstation variables such as OS and OS_VERSION. An example of a login script command with a variable mapping a drive pointer to the home directory of each user is MAP ROOT H:=DATA:USERS\%LOGIN_NAME.

The percent sign in front of a variable name tells NetWare to substitute the value of the variable into the login script command when it is executed.

❑ The Novell Client software can execute four types of NetWare login script files: the container login script, the profile login script, the user login script, and the default login script. The container login script is executed for each user of that container when the user first logs in. After the container login script is executed, the login script processor will look for a profile login script. A profile login script enables users scattered across the tree to be considered as one group. If no profile login script exists, the Novell Client looks for a user login script. If no user login script file exists, the login script processor will execute the default login script commands stored in the Novell Client. Most login script commands should be stored, whenever possible, in the container login script. By including the EXIT command in the container login script, you can prevent NetWare from executing user or default login script statements. If you do not place an EXIT command at the end of the container login script, then either the user or default login script will run. If your user does not have a login script, and you do not want the default login script to run for that user, then insert the NO_DEFAULT command in the container login script. Creating a login script for each user disables the default login script and provides additional security.

❑ NetWare Administrator is used to create and maintain the three types of login scripts—container, profile, and user—through which you create the user's work environment. (You will not be able to modify the system's default login script.)

COMMAND SUMMARY

Command	Syntax	Definition
#	#[path] filename [parameter]	Executes the specified DOS program and returns control to the login script program. The Novell Client remains in memory while the requested program is being run.
BREAK ON BREAK OFF	BREAK ON/OFF	BREAK ON allows users to halt the execution of the login script by pressing Ctrl+Break. BREAK OFF, the default, prevents users from doing this.
CLS	CLS	Clears the login screen of its current contents.
CONTEXT	CONTEXT context_reference	Specifies a context to change to as the default for this workstation after login. Otherwise the Novell Client sets the context to that of the User object.

DISPLAY	*DISPLAY [path] filename*	Types the contents of the specified filename to the screen. If the filename specified is not in the current directory or search drive, include the full NetWare path to the specified filename. The DISPLAY command shows all characters in the file, including tabs and other printer control characters. (See FDISPLAY.)
DRIVE	*DRIVE drive:*	Changes the default drive in login script execution. This must be used, for example, to enable a subsequent command to run correctly.
EXIT	*EXIT "command line"*	Ends the login script processing and exits.
FDISPLAY	*FDISPLAY [path] filename*	Like the DISPLAY command, except that the FDISPLAY command filters any tab or printer control characters, making files that contain these control characters more readable.
FIRE PHASERS	*FIRE [PHASERS] n [TIMES]*	Produces a phaser sound on the PC speaker the number (n) of times specified, up to nine.
IF...THEN... ELSE	*IF condition(s) [AND/OR [condition] THEN commands [ELSE COMMAND] [END]*	The IF statement enables you to specify commands to be executed only when the specified condition is true. If the condition is false, commands following the ELSE statement will be executed. Each IF statement must conclude with an END statement and can contain up to 10 additional nested IF statements.
INCLUDE	*INCLUDE [path] filename or INCLUDE NDS_object_name*	Causes the login processor to obtain commands from the file specified. If the file is not in the current directory or search drive, you need to specify the complete NetWare path leading to the desired file. If you specify an object name instead, NetWare will also run the included object's login script commands. The object must have a defined login script for this to work.
MAP	*MAP [option] [drive:=path] [variable]*	Creates both regular and search drive mappings from the login script. The path statement can contain identifier variables preceded by percent signs, e.g., %MACHINE, %OS, %OS_VERSION, %LOGIN_NAME. Special MAP commands include MAP DISPLAY OFF/ON, and MAP ERRORS OFF/ON.

13

NO_DEFAULT	*NO_DEFAULT*	Prevents the Novell Client from running the generic default login script if the user has no user login script. This command can be used in container or profile login scripts.
PAUSE	*PAUSE*	Suspends login script processing until the user presses Enter on the keyboard.
REM	*REM[ARK] [text]*	Enables comments to be placed in login script files.
WRITE	*WRITE "text[control string][%variable]"*	Displays the message string enclosed in quotation marks on the console. Special control codes, such as /r for a new line, along with identifier variables preceded by percent signs, can be included within the quotation marks.

KEY TERMS

container login script
date variables
default login script
login script
login script variable
nesting
network variables
profile login script
syntax
time variables
user login script
user variables
workstation variables

REVIEW QUESTIONS

1. Briefly describe the importance of login scripts to a DOS-based workstation.
2. The CONTEXT command would most likely be found in a _____ login script file.
3. The _____ command is used to write the contents of an ASCII text file to the display screen.
4. The _____ command lets you execute login script statements contained in a specified ASCII text file.

5. The _____ command is used to display a brief message on the screen.

6. The _____ login script is executed before the profile login script.

7. The default login script is executed if _____.

8. Suppose you notice that a user has two drive mappings to the SYS:PUBLIC directory. Explain the most likely reason for this problem.

9. List two ways you can prevent the default login script commands from being executed.

10. The _____ utility is used to create and maintain the login scripts.

11. Suppose the first network drive on your workstation is L. What drive letter would the login script command MAP *3:=DATA: use to access the DATA volume?

12. Write a login script command that will display a welcome message containing today's date, including the name of the day, the month, the day, and the year.

13. Write a condition that can be used to determine if a user is logging in on the third day of the week.

14. Write a MAP command that uses identifier variables to map H as a root drive pointer to the user's home directory located in the DATA:USERS directory path.

15. Write a search mapping to the SYS:PUBLIC directory and appropriate DOS version, assuming the directory structure shown in Figure 13-14.

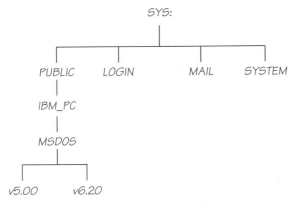

Figure 13-14 Directory structure for Question 15

16. The _____ login script command can be used to change to the user's home directory on drive H.

17. Will executing the EXIT command from the container login script prevent the default login script commands from being executed when a user has no user login script file?

18. Assume the home directories for the sales department are stored in the DATA:SALES\USERS directory. Write an IF statement for the container login script that will map H as a root drive to the correct home directory path for each sales department user.

19. Identify and correct any errors in each of the following login script commands:

TURN MAP DISPLAY OFF

MAP S2=SYS\PUBLIC\%MACHINE\%OS\%OSVERSION

WRITE "Good %Greeting_Time," %Login_name

HANDS-ON PROJECTS

Project 13-1: Documenting the Container Login Script on Your Server

In this project you demonstrate your knowledge of login script commands by examining the login scripts on your server and explaining the purpose of each of its commands.

1. Log into the server using your assigned student user name.

2. View a container, profile, and user login scripts with NetWare Administrator and record the scripts. If the login script is empty, describe typical commands that would go into such a script.

3. Next to each login script command, briefly describe the command's function in the login script.

Project 13-2: Practicing with Login Script Commands

In this project you practice writing and testing several login script commands by creating a practice user and then providing that user with a user login script.

1. Log in using your assigned student user name.

2. Run Windows Explorer.

3. Use Explorer to view and document the directory structure of your assigned server.

4. Create a new user named ##USER, where ## represents your assigned student number.

5. Change to your ##ADMIN directory, and create a subdirectory called WORK. Grant the new user Read, File Scan, Write, Create, and Delete rights to your ##ADMIN\WORK directory.

6. Enter all the required drive mappings in the user's login script that will let this user execute NetWare utilities and DOS external commands.

7. Log out and test the login script you have created, by logging in as ##USER.

8. Log in using your assigned student user name. Run NetWare Administrator and open your own user object. Select your ##Admin Login Script page.

9. Write the necessary command to display the daily message file based on the day of the week. For example, on Monday the login script should display a message called MONDAY.MSG, on Tuesday display TUESDAY.MSG, and so on. Record the command here: _____

10. Assume the user's birthday is today and include an IF statement that will display a short "Happy Birthday" message along with phaser fire (sound blasts) on today's date. Record the IF command here: _____

11. Write a command to map a root drive to your \##ADMIN\WORK directory. Record the command here: _____

12. At the end of the user login script, write an EXIT command to run the SESSION program. Assume this is on a Windows 95/98 workstation. Record the EXIT command here: _____

13. Test the login script you have created by logging in as ##ADMIN again.

14. Use the My Computer dialog or other appropriate options to check the drive mappings.

15. Print a hard copy of the login script to be checked by your instructor.

CASE PROJECT

Case 13-1: Designing a Container Login Script for J. Q. Adams

In this project you will write a container login script for the J. Q. Adams Corporation. Create a container login script to perform the following functions:

1. Create a drive mapping to each volume on the JQA_Server01 NetWare server.

2. Include a search drive mapping to the WP and SS subdirectories of WinOffice for all users.

3. For production department users, provide a drive mapped to the InvTrack Itdata subdirectory and root drive mapping to InvTrack subdirectory.

4. Before noon on Mondays, display a message for all production department users reminding them of the weekly meeting in conference room 210A.

5. Turn in a copy of your data disk to your instructor.

6. For extra credit, what step or steps would you have to take to actually execute this login script using the existing CONSTELLATION server and volumes?

13

14

MANAGING THE NETWORK

After reading this chapter and completing the exercises you will be able to:

♦ Describe essential NetWare console commands and NetWare Loadable Modules (NLMs) used to manage the network from the server

♦ Fix volume problems using the VREPAIR NLM

♦ Fix NDS problems using the DSREPAIR NLM

♦ Use the ConsoleOne Java utility to create a User object in your tree

♦ Perform remote console management to access the server console from a workstation attached to the network

♦ Use Novell Licensing Services (NLS) to install an additional license certificate on the server

♦ Use NetWare's Storage Management System (SMS) to back up network data

♦ Use Z.E.N.works and the Application Launcher to configure and distribute an application to user desktops

♦ Use Z.E.N.works to create and administer Workstation and Policy Package objects

In the previous chapters of this book, you learned how to install and configure a NetWare network. However, once a network is up and running, the work has just begun. Managing the network is a daily task, and although many of these activities take place at the workstation, at times you must access the server console to perform various commands and load modules, such as during installation of NetWare or server-based applications. It becomes even more important for the network administrator to know how to use the server console to perform a variety of tasks. In this chapter you will learn additional commands and options that are important for monitoring, backing up, and securing the server. You will also learn how to access the server console from another workstation attached either directly to the network or via a modem. Finally, you will study the tasks involved in managing the network.

STARTING THE SERVER

A NetWare server's primary hard disk contains at least two disk partitions; one for DOS and one for NetWare. Initially the server starts from the DOS partition (the C drive) by running a program called SERVER.EXE, which is stored in the C:\NWSERVER directory.

The SERVER.EXE program provides the core NetWare services such as file sharing, as well as a software bus for NLMs. Most network services such as Novell Distributed Print Services (NDPS) and Novell Directory Services (NDS), along with device drivers, are provided by loading NLMs.

As the SERVER program loads, it reads commands from the STARTUP.NCF file—which is also stored in the NWSERVER directory. This file contains the names of the disk drivers and other configuration commands. After the SERVER program loads its disk drivers, it mounts the SYS volume. It then reads the commands in the AUTOEXEC.NCF file (which is stored in the SYSTEM directory of the SYS volume). The AUTOEXEC.NCF file contains commands that identify the server's name, internal address, and any NLMs, such as the network card drivers, that must be loaded for server operation.

Once the SERVER program executes all the commands in the AUTOEXEC.NCF file, and all NLMs have initialized, the server is up and running. You can press the [Ctrl] + [Esc] key combination to view a window showing all active NLM screens that you can view.

You can type the number of the screen you want to view. For example, to change to the System Console screen, enter "1" and press [Enter] to display the console prompt. An alternate way to switch between console screens is to press the [Alt] + [Esc] combination to display screens until you come to the screen you want.

Be careful when pressing the [Alt] + [Esc] combination if you have the Java-based ConsoleOne tool loaded on the server. When the screen is inactive for a period of time, ConsoleOne temporarily stores its images on the hard disk. If you toggle through the server screens pressing [Alt] + [Esc], you will halt at the ConsoleOne screen and will have to wait from 20 to 30 seconds or more (depending on how fast your hard drive is) while ConsoleOne retrieves itself from the hard disk. If you use ConsoleOne, it is preferable to press the [Ctrl] + [Esc] combination, then select your screen.

CONSOLE OPERATIONS

Server operations fall into two major categories: console commands and NetWare Loadable Modules. **Console commands** are similar to DOS commands on a workstation in that they are built into the core server operating system program (SERVER.EXE). NetWare Loadable Modules (NLMs), as you learned in earlier chapters, are similar to applications run on a workstation. In this section you will learn about the console commands and several of the most common NLMs.

Console Commands

Many different console commands are available to you in NetWare 5.0. To make the system easier to understand, the commands are classified here by function: installation, configuration, maintenance, and security.

Installation Commands

Table 14-1 shows the installation commands. These are most frequently used when you first install NetWare on the server, expand the system, or install a separate application, such as the e-mail and messaging software from Novell called GroupWise.

Table 14-1 Installation commands

Command Syntax	Description
ADD NAME SPACE *name volume_name*	Adds space to a volume's directory entry table in order to support other operating system file naming conventions. Replace *name* with MAC or OS/2. Replace *volume_name* with the volume to which the specified name space is to be added.
BIND *protocol* TO *driver\board_name* [*driver_parameters*]	Attaches a *protocol* to a LAN card. Replace *protocol* with protocol name (e.g., IPX or IP). Replace *driver\board_name* with either the name of the card driver program or an optional name assigned to the network board. Optionally replace *driver_parameters* with the hardware settings that identify the network interface card (e.g., I/O port and interrupt).
LOAD [*path*]*module_name* [*parameters*]	Loads an NLM in the file server's RAM. Optionally replace *path* with the DOS or NetWare path leading to the directory containing the module to be loaded. Replace *module_name* with the name of the NLM you want to load. Optional *parameters* can be entered, depending on the module being loaded.
SEARCH [ADD *path*] SEARCH [DEL *number*]	Adds or removes a directory path from the search path used by the LOAD command when NLMs are being loaded. When no parameters are specified, the current server search paths are displayed. To add a search path, replace *path* with the DOS or NetWare path leading to the directory from which you want to load NLMs. To delete an existing search path, replace *number* with the number of the search path to be deleted.

14

Before Windows 95 was introduced, filenames were limited to eight characters and a three-character extension (this is called 8.3 notation). This limitation on the original DOS operating system was also used in the NetWare file system. The 8.3 notation required cryptic abbreviations rather than fuller names. For example, WNFLS699.DOC in the 8.3 DOS notation can now be written as Working_Notes_for_Lum_Seminar_June_1999.DOC instead.

The ADD NAME SPACE command is used to let you use non-DOS filenames, such as those used with Windows 95/98, Macintosh, or Unix, in a NetWare volume. The ADD NAME SPACE command modifies the directory entry table (DET) in the specified volume to allow storage of non-DOS filenames. This command needs to be executed only once for each volume in which the non-DOS files are stored. Replace the *name* parameter with the name of the name space module you loaded. Common names are LONG and MAC. Replace the *volume_name* parameter with the name of the volume to which you want to add the specified name space.

To use long filenames for a Windows 95/98 client, NetWare by default automatically loads the LONG name space module. This module permits filenames up to 256 characters in length.

The LOAD command reads an NLM into memory and executes it. By default, the LOAD command searches for the requested module in the SYS:SYSTEM directory unless you specify a different path. Valid paths can include NetWare volume names as well as local drive letters. When a module is loaded into memory, it remains there until the console operator ends the program or uses the UNLOAD command to remove the software from memory. You can place optional parameters after the LOAD command depending on the requirements of the module being loaded.

NetWare 5.0 does not require you to use LOAD before the name of the NLM if you are running any NLM stored in the SYS:SYSTEM directory (most NLMs are stored there). However, if you are loading a third-party NLM from a CD-ROM or a floppy disk, you will still need to use the LOAD command.

A simple example is to load the MONITOR utility, which provides important status screens on the functioning of the server. To do this, type:

```
LOAD MONITOR [Enter]
```

and NetWare loads the Monitor NLM and displays its main dialog box. (As noted earlier, because the MONITOR NLM is stored in the SYS:SYSTEM directory, you actually need only type MONITOR and press [Enter] to load this NLM.)

Another example is loading a LAN driver. During an ordinary installation, the Install Wizard creates all the LOAD commands in the AUTOEXEC.NCF file so the administrator need not add them. However, the LAN driver frequently needs to be changed (for upgrading the LAN card), so the process of manual configuration is important to know.

When you load a LAN driver, for example, you can include the *I/O port* and *option name* parameters in the LOAD command. For example, to access an E100S Ethernet LAN driver for a card that is in system board slot 2 and assign it the name E100S_1_8022, the network administrator would use the following LOAD command:

```
LOAD E100S SLOT=2 NAME=E100S_1_8022
```

You can later use the name E100S_1_8022 to reference this card driver, as described under the BIND command. Several popular NLMs and their associated parameters are described in more detail in the section on NLMs.

The BIND command attaches a protocol stack to a network card, which lets workstations using that protocol communicate with the server. The syntax is BIND *protocol* TO*driver | board_name* [*driver_parameters*]. Replace the *protocol* parameter with the name of the protocol stack you want to attach to the card. Replace *driver | board_name* with either the name of the card driver loaded previously with the LOAD command or the name you assigned to the card driver when you loaded it. If you have loaded the driver program more than once on different cards or with different frame types, you can replace *driver_parameters* with a combination of any of the parameters shown in Table 14-2 that uniquely identify the driver program to which you want to bind the specified protocol.

Table 14-2   BIND driver parameters

Parameter Syntax	Description
ADDR=*number*	Identifies the network (IP) address used by the driver.
DMA=*number*	Identifies the DMA channel the LAN driver is using. Use the same DMA channel that you used when you loaded the driver for the board.
FRAME=*name*	Identifies the frame type used when the driver program was loaded.
INT=*number*	Identifies the interrupt the driver is using for the network board. Bind the protocol with the same interrupt that you used when you loaded the LAN driver.
NET=*network_address*	Assigns a network address consisting of one to eight hexidecimal digits to the LAN card.
MEM=*number*	Identifies the memory address used when the driver was loaded.
PORT=*number*	Identifies the I/O port number the driver is using for the network board.
SLOT=*number*	On a PCI computer, the slot identifies the network board used when the LAN driver was loaded.

14

Use the *driver_parameters* item to specify options unique to the protocol being loaded. When using the IP protocol, you are required to specify a network address for use with the cable system to which the card is attached. For example, when the network administrator for CBE Labs needed to use the BIND command to attach the IP protocol stack with a network address of 137.65.211.155 to an E100S driver assigned to an Ethernet card in the system board slot 2, he used the following statement:

```
BIND IP TO E100S SLOT=2 ADDR=137.65.211.155
```

If you assigned a name to the E100S network driver assigned to the Ethernet card when you loaded it with the LOAD command, the BIND command could use the name assigned to the driver to specify uniquely the correct card. (See the LOAD command for an example of naming a network card driver.) To bind IP to a card driver named E100S_1_E8022, you would enter the following command:

```
BIND IP TO E100S_1_E8022 ADDR=137.65.211.155
```

The SEARCH ADD statement tells NetWare where to look for files. Unless you use a specific path, the NetWare server operating system normally checks for modules and files in the SYS:SYSTEM directory. However, just as the MAP INS S1:=path statement lets you add another directory to the search path of a workstation, you can use the SEARCH ADD statement to specify an additional directory path that contains files or programs for the server to use. Using the SEARCH ADD statement to add directory paths for the server does not affect the search drive mappings of the workstations.

As Figure 14-1 shows, you can enter the SEARCH command by itself to display a list of all active search paths and their corresponding numbers. The SEARCH DEL *number* command shown in Figure 14-1 deletes an existing search drive by specifying the number of the search drive to delete. When you restart a server, all current search paths are removed, so you need to include SEARCH ADD statements for all necessary directories in the AUTOEXEC.NCF startup file.

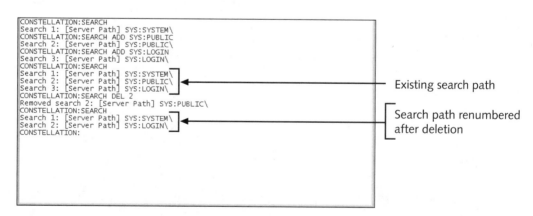

Figure 14-1   Sample SEARCH commands

Configuration Commands

You use the configuration console commands shown in Table 14-3 to view the configuration of the server and associated network cards. The information obtained by using these commands helps the network administrator identify the configuration of LAN cards and protocols, view other servers and networks, change the server date and time, and expand the network.

Table 14-3   Configuration commands

Command Syntax	Description
CONFIG	Displays configuration information about each network card, including hardware settings, network address, protocol, and frame type.
DISPLAY [IPX] NETWORKS	Shows all networks to which the file server has access, including the number of routers (hops) and the time in ticks ($\frac{1}{18}$ sec.) it takes to reach each network.
DISPLAY [IPX] SERVERS	Shows all servers in the file server's router table, including the number of routers (hops) to get to each server.
LIST DEVICES	Indicates all devices currently registered with the NetWare operating system.
MEMORY	Displays the total amount of memory available to the file server computer.
NAME	Displays the name of the file server.
PROTOCOL	Displays all protocols that are currently in use.
SET	Lets you view or change current file server environment settings.
SET TIME [*month/day/year*] [*hour:minute:second*]	Lets you change the file server's current system date and time.

14

The CONFIG command displays information about the server and network card configuration, as Figure 14-2 shows. Notice that in addition to displaying the server's name and internal network address, the CONFIG command displays the following information about each network adapter in the server:

- Name of the LAN driver
- Current hardware settings, including interrupt, I/O port, memory address, and direct memory access (DMA) channel
- Node (station) address assigned to the network adapter
- Frame type assigned to the network adapter
- Board name assigned when the LAN driver was loaded
- Protocol stack that was bound to the network adapter
- Network address of the cabling scheme for the network adapter

```
IPX internal network number: CBE1AB01
      Node address: 000000000001
      Frame type: VIRTUAL_LAN
      LAN protocol: IPX network CBE1AB01
Server Up Time:  2 Hours 43 Minutes 32 Seconds

Intel EtherExpress(tm) PRO LAN Adapter
      Version 1.48     September 16, 1994
      Hardware setting: I/O ports 300h to 30Fh, Interrupt Bh
      Node address: 00AA005F0E36
      Frame type: ETHERNET_802.2
      Board name: EPRO_E8022
      LAN protocol: IPX network 00019200

Intel EtherExpress(tm) PRO LAN Adapter
      Version 1.48     September 16, 1994
      Hardware setting: I/O ports 300h to 30Fh, Interrupt Bh
      Node address: 00AA005F0E36
      Frame type: ETHERNET_802.3
      Board name: EPRO_E8023
      LAN protocol: IPX network 00019300

Tree Name: CBELABS
Bindery Context(s):
<Press ESC to terminate or any other key to continue>
```

Figure 14-2 Sample output from CONFIG command

Use the CONFIG command before installing memory boards or network adapters in the server so that you have a current list of all hardware settings on the existing boards. This will help you select unique interrupt and I/O address settings for the new cards. You can also use the CONFIG command to determine the network address of a cable system before you add another server to the network. If you accidentally bring up another server using a different network address for the same cable system, router configuration errors between the servers will interfere with network communications.

The DISPLAY NETWORKS or the DISPLAY IPX NETWORKS command lists all network addresses and internal network numbers on the IPX network system, as Figure 14-3 shows. In addition to showing the address of each network, the DISPLAY NETWORKS command shows the amount of time required to access the network, measured by the number of hops and ticks required to reach each network from the current server. Each **hop** is a router that must be crossed to reach the given network. Each **tick** is a time interval of ⅟₁₈ of a second.

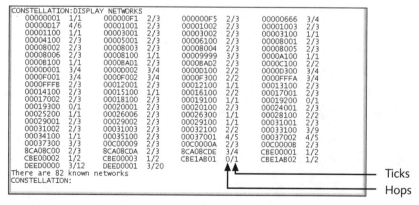

Figure 14-3 Sample DISPLAY NETWORKS command

The DISPLAY SERVERS or DISPLAY IPX SERVERS command is useful for determining whether the server is properly attached to an IPX multiserver network. When a server is first attached to a network, it sends a broadcast to all machines on the network, advertising its presence. From these broadcasts, the servers and workstations on the network build router tables that include the names of all servers and routers on the network. The DISPLAY SERVERS command lists all servers that have been inserted into the router table.

 Unlike IPX/SPX, TCP/IP does not broadcast available services across the network. Although this has the advantage of lowering network traffic, it also means there's no easy way to view what is out on the network, as you can with IPX. Currently you need to use the Java-based ConsoleOne utility at the server to view a list of IP-only servers and networks. You can also run NetWare Administrator to view services available in NDS. NetWare 5.0 also offers an optional service called the Service Location Protocol which has various console commands for displaying information.

For example, suppose when the network administrator for CBE Labs tried to add the server RANGER to the network, he encountered some difficulties. First, RANGER did not appear in other servers' (CONSTELLATION and SARATOGA) router tables and RANGER did not "see" the other servers on the network. The administrator discovered that this problem arose because the IPX protocol was not bound to the network card.

Another frequent cause for failing to "see" a server is that a network card is using a different frame type from that of other servers. If this is the cause, then the administrator needs to load another frame type onto the card (or change the original frame type).

A third cause of problems in server communications is a conflict in memory addresses for the card and some other device within the server. For example, if a network card has the same memory address as the mouse, the server will not be able to process any network packets. You can use the CONFIG command to check for such conflicts.

The DISPLAY IPX SERVERS and DISPLAY IPX NETWORKS commands are still useful for troubleshooting in mixed IP/IPX networks. A server configured to use only IPX on an all-IP network could essentially vanish from the other servers' routing tables. The same can be true of a single IP server on an all-IPX network.

The LIST DEVICES command lists information about all storage device drivers attached to the server, including disk drives, tape drives, and CD-ROMs. Information includes device number, description, and the NetWare assigned device ID, as Figure 14-4 shows, and can be useful when you are checking to see if all devices are loaded.

14

```
SARATOGA:list devices
  2. [VO25-A1-D2:1] SANYO CRD-820P rev:1.04.
  3. [VO25-A1-D2:0] QUANTUM FIREBALL_TM3840A.
  1. [VO25-A0-D1:0] ST32122A.

SARATOGA:
```

Figure 14-4   Sample LIST DEVICES command

The MEMORY command lets you determine the total amount of memory available to the server. This is a quick way to verify the amount of memory available without opening the server.

 The NAME command simply displays the name of the server on the console. You can use it to confirm the name of the server console on which you are working.

As Figure 14-5 shows, the PROTOCOL command displays all protocols registered with the server, along with the network frame types associated with the protocol. Initially, only the IP and IPX protocols are registered with the NetWare operating system.

```
CONSTELLATION:PROTOCOL
The following protocols are registered:
  Protocol: IPX  Frame type: VIRTUAL_LAN    Protocol ID: 0
  Protocol: IPX  Frame type: ETHERNET_802.2  Protocol ID: E0
  Protocol: IPX  Frame type: ETHERNET_802.3  Protocol ID: 0
CONSTELLATION:
```

Figure 14-5   Sample PROTOCOL command

 The PROTOCOL command also has a variation called PROTOCOL REGISTER, which you can use to register additional protocols and frame types. The syntax for adding the new types is PROTOCOL REGISTER *protocol frame id#*, where *protocol* is the name of the protocol, *frame* is the name of the frame type to be bound, and *id#* is a special protocol identification number (PID), that identifies data coming from a network board through a designated communications protocol such as IPX. You use PROTOCOL REGISTER only when you are using a new cable medium, such as changing from 10Base2 to 10BaseT network cables.

Use the SET command to view or change settings for the configuration categories that Figure 14-6 shows.

```
SARATOGA:set
Settable configuration parameter categories
    1. Communications
    2. Memory
    3. File caching
    4. Directory caching
    5. File system
    6. Locks
    7. Transaction tracking
    8. Disk
    9. Time
    10. NCP
    11. Miscellaneous
    12. Error Handling
    13. Directory Services
    14. Multi-processor
    15. Service Location Protocol
    16. Licensing Services
Which category do you want to view:
```

Figure 14-6   SET configuration options

Use the SET TIME command to change the current server time or date. The following commands show three variations of using SET TIME to change the NetWare server's current date and time to 3 p.m., October 30, 1999 (the third variation uses two SET TIME commands):

```
SET TIME 10/30/99 3:00p.m.

SET TIME October 30, 1999 3:00p.m.

SET TIME October 30, 1999
SET TIME 3:00p.m.
```

Maintenance Commands

The maintenance commands shown in Table 14-4 are the console commands that the network administrator commonly uses to control access to the server and volumes, to broadcast messages, look for network problems, and shut down the server for upgrades or maintenance.

14

Table 14-4   Maintenance commands

Command Syntax	Description
CLEAR STATION *number*	Terminates the specified workstation connection number in the command.
CLS/OFF	Clears the file server console screen.
DISABLE/ENABLE LOGIN	Prevents or enables new user logins.
DOWN	Closes all files and volumes, disconnects all users, and takes the file server off line.
MODULES	Lists all currently loaded modules starting with the last module loaded.
MOUNT *volume_name* [ALL] DISMOUNT *volume_name* [ALL]	Places a volume on or off line. Replace *volume_name* with the name of the volume you want mounted or use ALL to mount all NetWare volumes.
SCAN FOR NEW DEVICES	Registers new devices that have been switched on since the server was booted.
SEND *"message"* [TO] *username|connection_number*	Sends a message to a specified user. Replace *message* with a message (enclosed in quotes) you want sent. Replace *username|connection_number* with either the name of the currently logged in user or the connection number assigned to the user. The *connection_number* can be obtained from the Connection option of the MONITOR NLM.
TRACK ON/TRACK OFF	Displays service advertising packets that are sent or received.
UNBIND *protocol* [FROM] *driver|board_name*	Removes a protocol from a LAN card. Replace *protocol* with the name of the protocol stack (e.g., IPX) you want to remove from the card. Replace *driver|board_name* with either the name of the driver program that has been loaded for the network card or the name assigned to the network card by the LOAD command.
UNLOAD *module_name*	Removes a NetWare Loadable Module from memory and returns the memory space to the operating system. Replace *module_name* with the name of the currently loaded module, as in the MODULES command.

Use the CLEAR STATION command to terminate a workstation's connection to the server. A connection to a server is made when the workstation runs the Novell Client. The connection continues to be active, whether or not a user is logged in to the server, until the workstation is restarted or turned off. If a user is logged in when the connection is cleared, data can be lost due to incomplete updating of files that are open at the time the station's connection to the server breaks off.

Each NetWare operating system is designed to support a maximum number of connections depending on the license purchased. If your server reaches the maximum number of connections and you need more connections, then you can use the CLEAR STATION command to terminate unused connections, making room for other workstations to log in to the server.

 A better way to handle this situation (too few connections available) is to run the MONITOR utility. Use this tool to examine current connections on the network. Select any unused connections, and press [Del] to clear them.

You can use the CLS and OFF commands to clear the server console screen, letting you see new console messages more easily. A common practice is to use the CLS or OFF command before loading new modules or recording error messages.

Another use for the CLEAR STATION command is to force workstations to log out of the server before you down the server or perform a backup. For example, the administrator for CBE Labs comes into work on a holiday and, after completing his work, decides to back up the system. Before terminating a connection, he uses MONITOR to see if any data files are open and he also uses the SEND command to send a message to the user of that station to close the open files and log out.

The DISABLE LOGIN command stops new users from logging in to the server. Before downing the server, the administrator issues the DISABLE LOGIN message, to keep any additional CBE Labs users from logging in. He then uses the SEND command to send a message to all connected users, telling them the server will be down after the specified time period, so they should close all files and log out. If he does not issue the DISABLE LOGIN command, new CBE Labs users may log in to the server after the message is broadcast, unaware that the server is about to be downed.

 The ENABLE LOGIN command is the counterpart to DISABLE LOGIN. ENABLE LOGIN is most useful when the administrator's account has been disabled by intruder detection. (For example, if you forgot the password and tried too many times to guess at it before looking it up.) To reenable the account, type ENABLE LOGIN at the server console.

14

The DOWN command deactivates the NetWare server operating system and removes all workstation connections. Before issuing the DOWN command, disable new logins and broadcast a message to all users. You can then use the MONITOR command to be sure all connections are logged out before you enter the DOWN command. Figure 14-7 shows the command sequence.

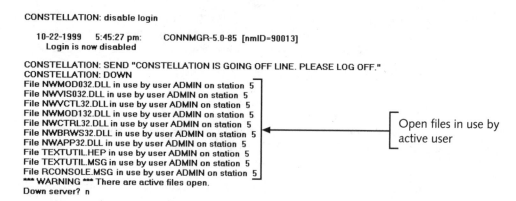

Figure 14-7 Command sequence for downing a server

If active sessions exist, the NetWare operating system will issue a warning message asking you if you want to terminate active sessions. If you see this message, you should cancel the DOWN command and use the MONITOR utility to determine which connections have open files. Then send messages to those users to log off. If no one is at the workstation and data files have been left open, you will need to go to the station yourself to close the open files and log off for the user. Remind users that they should not leave their workstations unattended while data files are open.

As mentioned, NLMs are external programs that are loaded into the memory of the server computer to add functionality to the NetWare core operating system. The MODULES command lists all the currently loaded modules with their names, version numbers, and release dates. The modules are listed in sequence, starting with the last module loaded and ending with the first module loaded. In addition to showing what modules have been loaded, the MODULES command also lets you quickly check the version number and date of a module. You need this information to determine NetWare compatibility or to look for network problems known to be caused by defective versions of certain modules.

The MODULES command also supports the use of the * wildcard. For example, if you wanted to view only those modules beginning with the letters NW, you would type MODULES NW*. This saves you from having to scan through dozens of NLMs that may be loaded on a typical NetWare 5.0 server.

The Novell Support home page (*www.support.novell.com*) is a good place to check for information regarding problems with NLMs. This site also provides information on obtaining corrected versions of the defective modules. America Online and CompuServe both have informal areas discussing NetWare and problem resolution. The Novell site also has forums for such discussions.

Mounting a volume is the process of loading information from the volume's directory entry table (DET) into the server's RAM. This makes the volume available for access by users and the server's operating system. The MOUNT command is needed to mount a volume that did not mount correctly when the server was started or has been taken off line with the DISMOUNT command. Normally the MOUNT ALL command is inserted into the server's AUTOEXEC.NCF startup file during installation; it attempts to mount all volumes when the server is brought up. In some cases, such as after a server crash, some volumes may not mount, because of errors in their file allocation tables (FATs) or DETs. When this happens, you need to correct the problem and then use the MOUNT command to bring the repaired volume on line.

The SCAN FOR NEW DEVICES command causes the NetWare operating system to check for any new devices that have been brought on line since the server was started. The most common use for this command is if you have external tape and CD-ROM devices attached to the SCSI interface. If you do not turn on a tape drive or CD-ROM device when the server is started, it will not be available for use unless you issue the SCAN FOR NEW DEVICES command. The SCAN FOR NEW DEVICES command lets the NetWare operating system register new devices without your having to restart it.

You use the SEND command on the server console to transmit a message to a work-station (or to all workstations) currently logged into the network. The most common use of the SEND command is to ask users to log off before downing the server. You can send messages either to a user's login name or to a connection number, by enclosing the message in quotation marks and following it with the connection number or user name. If you do not give an address or name, NetWare understands this to mean that you want the message sent to *all* users logged into the network.

The SEND message appears on the user's workstation unless the user issued the SEND /A=N DOS command to prevent all messages from being displayed. The SEND /A=C command allows messages from the server to be displayed and ignores messages from other workstations. You should discourage users from using the SEND /A=N command, because it can result in data loss if you bring the server down without their knowledge.

14

Use the TRACK ON command to view SAPs (Service Advertising Protocols) and router information packets either received by or sent from your server, as Figure 14-8 shows. All IPX servers, including older print servers, periodically send out SAPs to inform other machines of their presence. In addition to SAPs, IPX servers periodically (approximately once each minute) send out special packets called router information packets (RIPs). The RIP contains a list of all network addresses and the number of ticks and hops required to reach each network from the sending server.

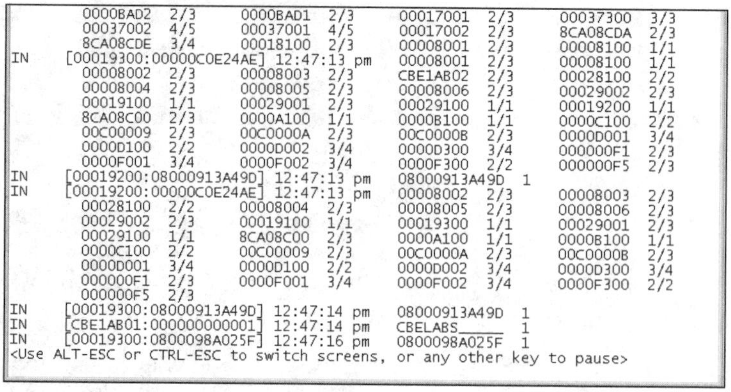

```
        0000BAD2  2/3    0000BAD1  2/3    00017001  2/3    00037300  3/3
        00037002  4/5    00037001  4/5    00017002  2/3    8CA08CDA  2/3
        8CA08CDE  3/4    00018100  2/3    00008001  2/3    00008100  1/1
IN      [00019300:00000C0E24AE] 12:47:13 pm    00008001  2/3    00008100  1/1
        00008002  2/3    00008003  2/3    CBE1AB02  2/3    00028100  2/2
        00008004  2/3    00008005  2/3    00008006  2/3    00029002  2/3
        00019100  1/1    00029001  2/3    00029100  1/1    00019200  1/1
        8CA08C00  2/3    0000A100  1/1    0000B100  1/1    0000C100  2/2
        00C00009  2/3    00C0000A  2/3    00C0000B  2/3    0000D001  3/4
        0000D100  2/2    0000D002  3/4    0000D300  3/4    000000F1  2/3
        0000F001  3/4    0000F002  3/4    0000F300  2/2    000000F5  2/3
IN      [00019200:08000913A49D] 12:47:13 pm    08000913A49D  1
IN      [00019200:00000C0E24AE] 12:47:13 pm    00008002  2/3    00008003  2/3
        00028100  2/2    00008004  2/3    00008005  2/3    00008006  2/3
        00029002  2/3    00019100  1/1    00019300  1/1    00029001  2/3
        00029100  1/1    8CA08C00  2/3    0000A100  1/1    0000B100  1/1
        0000C100  2/2    00C00009  2/3    00C0000A  2/3    00C0000B  2/3
        0000D001  3/4    0000D100  2/2    0000D002  3/4    0000D300  3/4
        000000F1  2/3    0000F001  3/4    0000F002  3/4    0000F300  2/2
        000000F5  2/3
IN      [00019300:08000913A49D] 12:47:14 pm    08000913A49D  1
IN      [CBE1AB01:000000000001] 12:47:14 pm    CBELABS_____  1
IN      [00019300:0800098A025F] 12:47:16 pm    0800098A025F  1
<Use ALT-ESC or CTRL-ESC to switch screens, or any other key to pause>
```

Figure 14-8 Sample output from TRACK ON command

Other servers on the network use this router information to maintain their local router tables. Use the TRACK ON command to display any SAPs and RIPs with the name and network address of the sender. This information can help you determine what is happening on the network and whether the server in question is functioning properly. For example, if a server is sending but not receiving any packets, that means the server is using the wrong frame type, other servers on the network are not functioning, or there is a problem with the network cable system.

After you issue the TRACK ON command, the console screen displays all SAPs that are being sent or received. You can press the [Alt]+ [Esc] key combination to change back to the console prompt or to any other module. To end the TRACK ON command, press [Alt]+ [Esc] or [Ctrl]+ [Esc] to return to the console prompt. Then enter the TRACK OFF command.

TRACK ON only displays information generated by IPX devices, not from IP networks. If you have an all-IP network, TRACK ON will display nothing. Use the UNBIND command to unload a protocol stack from a LAN driver. This will cause the server to stop communicating with other machines using that protocol. The most common use of the UNBIND command is to take a defective server off the network. Assume, for example, that the network administrator had bound the IPX protocol to a LAN driver, yet used the wrong network address. Almost immediately, the servers on the network will begin to signal that the router is calling the network a different name. To stop this problem, the administrator uses the UNBIND command to remove the protocol from the network card and then reissues the BIND command using the correct network address, as Figure 14-9 shows.

```
        NCP Service Address.

IP LAN protocol bound to SMC Ethernet Adapter Server Driver v7.02 (980307)

 2-10-1999   6:25:07 am:     NCP-5.0-66  [nmID=30017]
     The Network Address [UDP  123.45.123.01:0524] has been registered as an
     NCP Service Address.

CONSTELLATION:unbind IP from SMC_802

 2-10-1999   6:25:33 am:     TCPIP-4.20-110
     Unbound local IP address 123.45.123.1 from board 1.

IP LAN protocol unbound from SMC Ethernet Adapter Server Driver v7.02 (980307)

 2-10-1999   6:25:33 am:     NCP-5.0-66  [nmID=30017]
     The Network Address [UDP  123.45.123.01:0524] has been deregistered as an
     NCP Service Address.

 2-10-1999   6:25:33 am:     NCP-5.0-66  [nmID=30017]
     The Network Address [TCP  123.45.123.01:0524] has been deregistered as an
     NCP Service Address.

CONSTELLATION:
```

Figure 14-9   Sample output from UNBIND command

The UNLOAD command terminates an NLM and removes it from the server's memory. If your server has a marginal amount of memory, it may be necessary to remove modules to make space for file caching. Another common use for the UNLOAD command is to disconnect the server from a network card so you can test or fix a problem without downing the server and affecting users on different networks.

Assume, for example, that the CBE Labs server has both token ring and Ethernet cards in it, and the network administrator for CBE Labs needs to down the token ring network for maintenance. If he disconnects the server computer from the token ring cable, a string of error messages from the LAN driver, indicating that the card is not connected, will tie up his server console. To prevent this, he instead uses the UNLOAD TOKEN command to remove the TOKEN LAN driver before disconnecting the cable from the server. Although the users on the Ethernet network will not be affected, he is sure to notify all users on the token ring network that they need to log off before he unloads the TOKEN LAN driver and disconnects the server, or else valuable data might be lost. After doing the necessary work on the token ring network, he reestablishes communications with the token ring users by using the LOAD command to load the TOKEN LAN driver module and then using the BIND command to bind IPX to the token driver. The users on the token ring network can then log back in and resume using the server.

Securing the Console

Securing the NetWare server console is necessary to keep unauthorized users from entering console commands or loading NLMs. Depending on your organization, the need for NetWare server console security can range from keeping the server in a separate room to providing maximum security from intruders who are attempting to gain access to your network. Locking the server room is one of the first measures of NetWare server security that can be put in place. The SECURE CONSOLE command lets you provide extra protection against unauthorized use of the server console.

The SECURE CONSOLE command prevents several types of breaches in security:

- Removes DOS
- Prevents NLMs from being loaded from any directory other than the SYS:SYSTEM directory
- Prevents keyboard entry into the operating system debugger
- Prevents the use of the SET TIME command to change date and time from the console (a console operator or supervisor can still change the date and time by using the FCONSOLE utility from a workstation)
- Prevents a module from being loaded from a DOS partition, floppy drive, or NetWare volume

Keep in mind that SECURE CONSOLE also prevents an administrator from running certain commands that might be needed for legitimate reasons. For example, SECURE CONSOLE prevents the administrator from running the NetWare debugger to restart a crashed server. It also can prevent an administrator from running a LOAD command using the CD-ROM as a source for new software. Thus, you may not want to run SECURE CONSOLE as a default on your server.

Removing DOS provides both extra memory and extra security for the NetWare server. The network administrator at CBE Labs may remove DOS from the NetWare server CONSTELLATION for several reasons. First, removing DOS from the NetWare server's RAM frees up additional memory. Second, removing DOS prevents access to any DOS devices on the NetWare server. For example, this would prevent someone from loading an NLM from one of the server's DOS drives.

An intruder could access or alter information in the NetWare server CONSTELLA-TION at CBE Labs by loading a special NLM from the console that directly accesses data files. Because the SECURE CONSOLE command allows NLMs to be loaded only from the SYS:SYSTEM directory, an intruder will not be able to load the offending module from a DOS drive or some other directory on the server in which he or she has rights. The only way an intruder can load a module after the SECURE CONSOLE command has been issued is to have necessary rights to copy the module into the SYS:SYSTEM directory. Of course, for this part of the SECURE CONSOLE command to effectively prevent unwanted loading of NLMs, you must make sure no one has rights to SYS:SYSTEM and that your accounts are secure.

Some security and accounting features depend on date and time for their enforcement. Suppose, for example, Thomas Meyer in finance at CBE Labs has his user name secured both by a password and by a restriction on when and from what workstation he can log in. An intruder learns Thomas's password and gains access to the workstation on a weekend. Because the intruder has the equivalent of a master key, he or she gains access to the NetWare server console and uses the SET TIME command to change the date and time to a normal weekday. The intruder can then access or change the payroll data files. The SECURE CONSOLE command would prevent this by disabling the SET TIME command.

> The only way to "unsecure" a "secured" console (that is, to undo the SECURE CONSOLE command) is to restart the server.

NetWare Loadable Modules

A major strength of NetWare is its use of NetWare Loadable Modules (NLMs) to add functionality to the operating system. As discussed previously, the SERVER.EXE program provides the core NetWare services and acts like a software bus, letting you add NLMs to support hardware devices and software functions such as print servers and electronic messaging. Because NLMs play such an important role in tailoring the NetWare network, it is important for a CNA to become familiar with the standard NLMs included with the NetWare operating system.

As Table 14-5 shows, NLMs can be classified into five general categories based on their function. Each category has its own extension. In this section you will learn what you need to know about each of these NLMs in order to manage your server environments effectively.

Table 14-5   NLM categories

Category	Extension	Description
Host adapter drivers	.HAM	Communicates with controller boards.
Peripheral drivers	.CDM	Controls access to specific devices such as hard disks, CD-ROM drives, or tape subsystems.
LAN drivers	.LAN	Controls network cards.
Name space modules	.NAM	Contains logic to support filenaming conventions, such as Macintosh, Unix, or Windows long filenames.
General-purpose modules	.NLM	Adds additional services and functions to the network operating system.

14

Host Adapter Drivers

When you first start the NetWare operating system by running the SERVER.EXE program, it does not have a way of directly controlling the disk drives on the server until a Host Adapter Module is loaded. This module, which has a .HAM filename extension, lets the system talk to the IDE or SCSI controller card installed in the server. You won't see a specific request in the install process for this driver. Instead, NetWare automatically detects what cards are in the system and then asks you to confirm this finding. The operating system then loads the correct HAM driver for the adapter card.

Peripheral Drivers

Once NetWare recognizes the adapter card, it still needs to understand how to control the individual types of hard disks, CD-ROM drives, or other peripherals attached to that card. This service is provided by Custom Device Modules, which use the extension .CDM. The Install Wizard automatically loads the correct CDM after you identify the peripherals you have on your server.

 Although it might seem simpler if all adapters included only one type of hardware, some adapters, such as SCSI, can include both CD-ROM drives and hard disks on the same adapter. A single, efficient driver would be challenged to work with both types and still be effective.

Accessing the DOS partition of the hard disk and floppy disk drives does not require the disk driver. The DOS partition is available through the local DOS operating system unless it is removed with the SECURE CONSOLE command. However, the DOS partition and local drives typically are inaccessible from the server console without a third-party tool.

The command to load the appropriate CDM for your server's peripherals is later placed in the STARTUP.NCF file. Then, when the SERVER.EXE program starts, it will load the correct disk drive to access the NetWare volumes.

LAN Drivers

Before a server can access the network cable, you must load a LAN driver for the network controller card and bind a protocol to that LAN driver. Standard network drivers all have the extension .LAN and you can find them in the SYS:SYSTEM directory after you have installed the NetWare operating system files. If your network card does not use a standard driver, you should find the correct driver software on a disk that comes with the network card.

Name Space Modules

As mentioned, name space modules add logic to the NetWare operating system that let it support non-DOS filenames. By default, NetWare supports standard DOS eight-letter filenames and three-letter extensions plus the long filename specifications that Windows 95/98 uses. NetWare includes special NLMs, called *name space modules*, which can interpret Unix and Apple Macintosh filenames on a NetWare server. Table 14-6 shows two name space modules that are included with NetWare and that you can find in the SYS:SYSTEM directory with the .NAM extension. When you use name space support, you need to load the appropriate .NAM modules after the disk driver in the STARTUP.NCF file. Later in this chapter you will learn how to add and remove name space support from a volume.

Table 14-6   NetWare name space modules

Name Space Module	Description
MAC.NAM	Supports the Apple Macintosh filenaming conventions.
NFS.NAM	Supports the Unix system filenaming conventions.

General-Purpose Modules

In addition to special modules for controlling disk and network cards, a number of general-purpose NLMs are included in NetWare's SYS:SYSTEM directory. They have the file-name extension .NLM and provide a wide range of capabilities, as Table 14-7 describes. The rest of this section describes the modules a CNA uses to manage network servers.

Table 14-7   General-purpose NLMs

Module	Description
CDROM.NLM	Provides support for CD-ROM commands.
NWCONFIG.NLM	Used to work with NetWare partitions, volumes, and system files.
MONITOR.NLM	Used to monitor file server performance, hardware status, and memory usage.
VREPAIR.NLM	Checks the specified volume for errors and enables the operator to write corrections to the disk.
DSREPAIR.NLM	Corrects problem in NDS tree.
REMOTE.NLM	Provides the ability to view and operate the NetWare server console from a remote workstation. Requires a password.

CDROM   The CDROM module lets a server use a CD-ROM device attached to a device driver as a read-only volume. To attach a CD-ROM device to your server, you will need both the CD-ROM device plus the necessary drivers for use with your NetWare server. Most CD-ROM devices attached to NetWare servers today use a SCSI controller card along with associated SCSI disk driver software. You may need to load additional support modules. For example, NetWare loads the CD9660.NSS module, which handles the file format of most PC-formatted CD-ROMs. (The module CDHFS.NSS supports the Macintosh NFS-formatted CD-ROMs.)

Sharing CD-ROMs that contain desktop publishing clip art, sound files, and video for multimedia applications is an important function of the NetWare server in most organizations.

The network administrator wants to make a CD-ROM available to users on the NetWare server SARATOGA at CBE Labs. He will use the LOAD CDROM command to mount a CD-ROM as a NetWare read-only volume. Each user can map a drive letter to the CD-ROM volume and access files as for any NetWare volume.

> The CD-ROM module uses the new Novell Storage Service (NSS) to mount the volume. NSS uses only a tiny amount of memory so the impact of mounting CD-ROMs is quite different from the memory needed to mount a regular hard disk volume (under 1 MB for any size CD-ROM).

Typically, more than one CD-ROM title may be useful for network users. In this case, a seven-bay CD-ROM tower (with seven CD-ROM drives) can be attached to the NetWare server. For an even greater numbers of titles, CD-ROM (and now DVD-ROM) jukeboxes are available that support from 100 to 500 discs per jukebox depending on the configuration.

Whereas the NetWare CDROM NLM is adequate for mounting a single CD-ROM drive, handling a tower or jukebox is best done using a third-party package. These provide both single-drive-letter access to the entire tower or jukebox as well as better title management for these discs.

NWConfig   NWConfig works in a similar fashion to the Install Wizard you used in creating your server. (In fact, NWConfig used to be called Install in previous versions of NetWare.) You use the NWConfig module to perform such tasks as creating NetWare partitions and volumes on existing hard drives, copying all system and public files in the SYS volume, and creating or editing the STARTUP.NCF and AUTOEXEC.NCF files.

Suppose the NetWare server CONSTELLATION at CBE Labs is filling up and the network administrator needs to add disk space with a new volume. He must first add a new hard drive to the server. He can then run NWConfig to create the new volume and add it to the server.

MONITOR   The MONITOR utility module is one of the most powerful NLMs supplied with the NetWare operating system. In fact, you may want to keep it loaded at all times, to stay on top of changing server conditions. For example, you can use it to view information on server performance, current connections, disk access, or network traffic, as well as to modify server parameters.

> If you choose to have MONITOR loaded full time, when you leave the server unattended (such as overnight), switch from MONITOR to the server console screen. If the server has problems during the night, any possible error messages could then be left visible on the screen. Otherwise, only the frozen MONITOR screen would be visible.

After you load the MONITOR utility, it displays the General Information screen. If you leave MONITOR running with no keyboard activity for 10 seconds, the General Information screen expands, as Figure 14-10 shows (press [Tab] to toggle between normal and expanded screens). This expanded screen displays information regarding the server's available memory and performance. The Utilization field shows the percentage of time the processor is busy. In most cases, utilization should be less than 70%. The Server up time field measures the length of time the server has been running since it was last started. The Online processors field displays the number of processors this server has. The Original cache buffers field contains the number of buffers (in blocks of 4 KB) that were available when the server was first started. The Total cache buffers field contains the number of buffers currently available for file caching.

```
NetWare 5.00  Console Monitor  v5.19          NetWare Loadable Module
Server name:  'CONSTELLATION' in Directory tree: 'CBELABS'
Server version:  NetWare 5.00  -  August 31, 1998
┌─────────────────────────────────────────────────────┐
│                  General Information                  │
│                                                       │
│         Utilization:                         22%      │
│         Server up time:               39:05:00:31     │
│         Online processors:                     1      │
│         Original cache buffers:           19,942      │
│         Total cache buffers:               5,317      │
│         Dirty cache buffers:                   0      │
│         Long term cache hits:                99%      │
│         Current disk requests:                 0      │
│         Packet receive buffers:              335      │
│         Directory cache buffers:              64      │
│         Maximum service processes:          5570      │
│         Current service processes:            20      │
│         Current connections:                   3      │
│         Open files:                           26      │
│                                                       │
│            ┌─────────────────────┐                    │
│            │   Kernel            │                    │
│          ▼ │   Server Parameters │                    │
│            └─────────────────────┘                    │
└─────────────────────────────────────────────────────┘
```

Figure 14-10   Monitor General Information screen

If the number of total cache buffers is less than one-third of the original cache buffers, the server is running low on memory and you should either unload modules or add more RAM as soon as possible.

The Dirty cache buffers field shows the number of buffers that have had modifications but are waiting to be written to disk. A large number of dirty cache buffers indicates that the disk system is bogging down and that you may need a faster disk or an additional disk controller card. The Current disk requests field shows how many requests for disk access are currently waiting to be processed. Like the dirty cache buffers, you can use this number to determine whether disk performance is slowing down the network.

The following statistics are hidden until the expanded General Information screen appears:

The Long term cache hits field displays a statistical average for the cache hit rate since the server has been up. This lets you see patterns over time, and the Short Term cache hits statistic lets you determine any spiking that may occur during peak loads.

The Current disk requests number indicates how well your I/O channel is working. If this number increases over time, your channel may be a bottleneck. The value in the Packet receive buffers field indicates the number of buffers established to process packets that have been received by the server and are waiting to be serviced. The Directory cache

14

buffers value indicates the number of buffers reserved for disk directory blocks. Increasing the initial number of directory cache buffers available when the server first starts can sometimes improve the performance of the server when it is first started. The Maximum service processes value indicates the number of task handlers allocated for station requests, and the Current Service Processes value represents the number of task handlers currently activated. Current connections is the number of connections currently in use. Before you down the server, you can use the Open files field to determine whether any files are currently open.

> The server Utilization, Total cache buffers, and Dirty cache buffers statistics together can give you a quick picture of your server's health. The utilization should stay under 70% (it can go higher for a minute or two), the Total cache buffers figure should be at least 50% of the Original cache buffers figure, and the Dirty cache buffers figure should be less than 30% of the Total cache buffers figure.

In addition to the General Information window, the MONITOR utility has several options that you can use to view information about the performance and operation of your server. Some of the most important of these options are the Connections option, the Storage Devices option, and the LAN/WAN Drivers option.

Selecting the Connections option displays a window that shows all active connections and the user names currently logged in. If no user is logged in to a given connection number, the message "NOT-LOGGED-IN" will appear next to the connection number. To view information about any connection, select the connection number and press [Enter]. A window showing connection information for the user logged in to that connection will be displayed. Also displayed are the names of any currently open files, as Figure 14-11 shows. Notice that the window shows the network address, the number of requests, kilobytes read and written, and currently open files for the selected user name.

```
NetWare 5.00  Console Monitor v5.19                    NetWare Loadable Module
 Server name:  'CONSTELLATION' in Directory tree:  'CBELABS'
 Server version: NetWare 5.00 - August 31, 1998

                        Connection Information For ADMIN

            Status:                                    Normal    ▲
            Network address:                    137.65.208.107:0 █
            Connection time:                           1:08:59
            Requests:                                      346
            Kilobytes read:                              1,088
            Kilobytes written:                               0    ▼


                              Open Files

     SYS:PUBLIC/NLS/ENGLISH/RCONJ.HEP
     SYS:PUBLIC/TEXTUTIL.IDX
     SYS:PUBLIC/NLS/ENGLISH/TEXTUTIL.MSG
     SYS:PUBLIC/NLS/ENGLISH/RCONJ.MSG




 Tab=Next window   Enter=Select file   Ins=Refresh list          F8=More
```

Figure 14-11   Connection Information window

Use the Storage Devices option to check the status of a disk drive. The size of the disk drive, the disk driver, the number of partitions, mirroring, and hot fix status are indicated. In the Storage Devices screen, a piece of information that is important to monitor is the number of blocks that appear in the Hot Fix redirected blocks field. This number tells you how many times a block of the disk failed to work properly, causing data to be redirected to the redirection area of the disk partition.

Typically, the number of used Hot Fix redirection blocks should be zero. Anytime it increases, you should closely monitor the situation. If only a few blocks are used, and then the count remains stable, your hard disk has a bad spot in it, but the system will continue to perform. However, you are on notice that there are problems with that disk.

If the number of redirected blocks starts to grow, it is a clear sign that the disk drive is wearing out. You should plan to replace it before all the redirection blocks are used up, at which point you will start losing data as a result of disk write errors (or you will suffer a catastrophic drive failure).

Selecting the LAN/WAN information option displays a window showing all LAN drivers currently loaded on the server. If you are experiencing sluggish network performance and the server utilization is low, use the LAN information option to view the error summary for the network card. In addition to recording the total packets sent and received, the LAN information option keeps track of a number of error statistics.

VREPAIR The VREPAIR module can often be used to repair the FAT of a volume that cannot be mounted. If your server crashes due to a hardware problem, power failure, or software bug, the server may not mount the SYS volume (or other volume) because of errors in the FAT of the volume. (You will see the dreaded "Unable to mount Vol SYS" error message.) In this situation, VREPAIR is your first recourse. Because VREPAIR is so important for fixing volume errors and checking for volume problems, as a CNA you must be familiar with the VREPAIR utility.

If you encounter a problem with your SYS volume, and the SYS volume won't mount, then you will need access to VREPAIR to fix it. Verify that there's a working copy of this NLM on the DOS partition of the server's hard disk (such as in C:\NWSERVER). You also might want to keep a copy on a floppy disk for emergency use.

If a volume other than SYS cannot be mounted, VREPAIR automatically loads.

14

As happens with any repair tool, sometimes valuable data files are corrupted when VREPAIR writes its fixes to the disk. Any time FAT entries are modified, there is a risk that data in the files being fixed can actually be lost due to incorrect reconnection of FAT chains. In a worst-case scenario, the loss or corruption of records in an important database file might not be discovered until several weeks or months later, losing time and money for a company. To help prevent this problem, VREPAIR reports each file in which it finds FAT or directory problems. You can make a note of each file and then thoroughly test or restore the data from any important database or document files.

To use the VREPAIR command to check or fix problems on an existing volume, follow these steps:

1. Dismount the volume you want to test if it is still mounted. VREPAIR cannot run on a mounted volume. (Use DISMOUNT *volumename* to do this.)

2. Type LOAD VREPAIR at the server console. This displays the Volume Repair Utility menu shown in Figure 14-12.

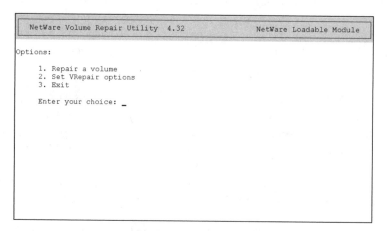

```
NetWare Volume Repair Utility   4.32              NetWare Loadable Module

Options:

      1. Repair a volume
      2. Set VRepair options
      3. Exit

      Enter your choice: _
```

Figure 14-12   VREPAIR main menu

3. Press the number 2 on your keyboard and then press [Enter] (Set VRepair options) to view and set the VREPAIR options shown in Figure 14-13. Notice the currently active settings displayed at the top of the screen. More options, preceded by numbers, are listed on the lower half of the screen. Generally it is best to choose the item "Keep changes in memory for later update." This choice gives you the option of writing the changes to disk after you have noted all files that are being fixed. (The default is to immediately write changes to disk.) To return to the VREPAIR main menu after you have finished setting options on the VREPAIR configuration screen, enter Option 5.

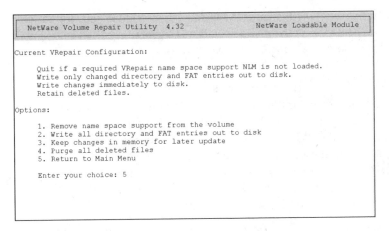

```
 ┌──────────────────────────────────────────────────────────────────────┐
 │  NetWare Volume Repair Utility  4.32          NetWare Loadable Module  │
 ├──────────────────────────────────────────────────────────────────────┤
 Current VRepair Configuration:

      Quit if a required VRepair name space support NLM is not loaded.
      Write only changed directory and FAT entries out to disk.
      Write changes immediately to disk.
      Retain deleted files.

 Options:

      1. Remove name space support from the volume
      2. Write all directory and FAT entries out to disk
      3. Keep changes in memory for later update
      4. Purge all deleted files
      5. Return to Main Menu

      Enter your choice: 5

 │                                                                        │
 └──────────────────────────────────────────────────────────────────────┘
```

Figure 14-13   VREPAIR options

4. To start the volume repairs, select 1 (Repair a Volume) from the main menu. If more than one volume is currently dismounted, VREPAIR displays a list to choose the volume you want to repair. If only one volume is currently dismounted, VREPAIR immediately begins scanning that volume. If no volumes have been dismounted, you will see the error message "There are no unmounted volumes."

5. To record filenames and error messages automatically in a text file for later analysis, press [F1] to display the additional VREPAIR options. Use option 2 (Log errors to a file) to write each message to the text file you specify. Use option 1 (Do not pause after errors) to keep VREPAIR from pausing after each error message. Use Option 3 to stop the volume repair. Use Option 4 to continue the volume repair process.

6. During the repair process, VREPAIR will stop whenever it encounters a FAT or directory error and will report onscreen the error message along with the filename onscreen. To verify that VREPAIR has correctly restored the files, record the error messages and filename. You can then have the appropriate users verify the repaired files to see if they were corrected properly. This maintains the integrity of the data.

7. After the volume has been restored, VREPAIR pauses and asks whether you want to write the repairs to disk. Normally you should enter Y and press [Enter] to write the new FAT and directory table to the disk. If you have written any changes to disk, run the VREPAIR program again to scan the volume and check for any additional volume problems. In some cases, it will take several passes to fix all problems.

8. When you receive a clean report showing that there are no corrections to write to disk, you can exit the VREPAIR program and mount the volume.

14

> ⚠️ **Caution**
> At this point, you will immediately pledge to do faithful network backups every day. This is something you should do. At some point, even VREPAIR won't help and only a good backup will save you.

DSREPAIR   As stated earlier, the NDS directory tree is a distributed and replicated database that is stored on several different servers. Because of this distribution, the NDS directory tree can occasionally develop problems with consistency between the servers. The NLM module DSREPAIR lets you correct those problems. Although the theory and practice of NDS operations and maintenance is beyond our scope (it is covered in much more detail in the CNE program), you may be asked to run a repair using DSRE-PAIR. To run the program, enter the command LOAD DSREPAIR or simply DSRE-PAIR. The main menu has the following options:

- *Unattended full repair.* This option comprehensively checks the tree for any inconsistencies and repairs any problems it finds. This check does close the NDS database, so running this repair essentially closes down this server while it runs.

- *Time synchronization.* This option checks and then displays the version of NDS and the time synchronization status of each server.

- *Report synchronization status.* This option displays a report of the synchronization status from all servers containing a replica of this server's NDS partition.

- *View repair log file.* DSREPAIR keeps a log file (SYS:SYSTEM\DSREPAIR_LOG) of all actions taken by the utility. This option lets you view that file.

- *Advanced options menu.* This option displays a submenu of options that let you perform individual repair tasks. These include listing servers known to this NDS database, repairing replicas and replica rings, checking volume objects and trustees, and repairing this server's local NDS database.

REMOTE CONSOLE MANAGEMENT

At times it is difficult or time consuming to go to the server console to check server status, make changes, or fix problems with the NetWare operating system. Sometimes you would have to spend valuable time walking to the server's location just to spend a few minutes at the console. (At other times, the server itself is locked away, so physical access is restricted.) To get around this problem, NetWare lets you perform console operations from a workstation located on the network.

With NetWare 5.0, Novell has completely revised its remote access capability. In the past, access to the server depended on the IPX/SPX protocols to establish and maintain the connection. With the conversion to native IP support in NetWare 5.0 if the network is pure IP the older tools such as RCONSOLE that use IPX/SPX can no longer be used with NetWare 5.0. Instead, Novell has introduced RCONSOLEJ to provide remote access and control. (The J stands for **Java**, a programming language often used to develop applications for the Internet that run on multiple platforms.)

RCONSOLEJ is available to users with appropriate rights and who can make a valid connection to the network via IP. Like the older remote software, RCONSOLEJ requires that you load two NLMs on the server—one to provide the remote access, and one to provide the interactive session. These are REMOTE.NLM and RCONAG6.NLM, respectively. When you load the NLMs, you will have to specify the user name and password required for remote access.

Unlike the older RCONSOLE, which ran in a DOS window under Windows, the newer utility requires the workstation to have installed a **Java Virtual Machine (JVM)**, an interpreter and run-time environment for Java applications. This makes using the remote utility a little more difficult, because a setup step is required; however, the JVM software installs easily and quickly from the Novell Client CD-ROM for NetWare 5.0. Choose the Java option in the main menu shown in Figure 14-14.

Don't confuse RCONSOLEJ with ConsoleOne. ConsoleOne is a Java GUI tool for performing functions similar to NetWare Administrator. It can be run on the server or on a workstation with the JVM software installed. RCONSOLEJ is a workstation-based tool for viewing the server console remotely. It cannot display the GUI screens of the server.

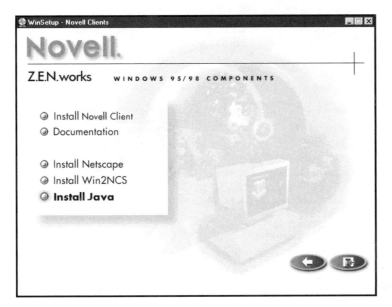

Figure 14-14   Client Install Java option required to run RConsoleJ

14

Once the JVM software loads on the workstation, you can run the RCONJ.EXE program from the SYS:PUBLIC directory. RCONSOLEJ will ask you to provide the IP address of the server and your remote administrator password, as Figure 14-15 shows.

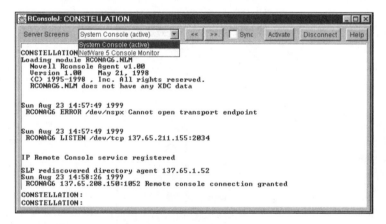

Figure 14-15 Logging in with RConsoleJ

Once you have authenticated to NetWare, NetWare will display a menu along with the server screen. Figure 14-16 shows a sample session.

```
RConsoleJ: CONSTELLATION                                              _ □ X
Server Screens   System Console (active)   ▼   <<   >>   □ Sync  Activate  Disconnect  Help
                 System Console (active)
CONSTELLATION NetWare 5 Console Monitor
Loading module RCONAG6.NLM
   Novell Rconsole Agent v1.00
   Version 1.00    May 21, 1998
   (C) 1995-1998 , Inc. All rights reserved.
   RCONAG6.NLM does not have any XDC data

Sun Aug 23 14:57:49 1999
  RCONAG6 ERROR /dev/nspx Cannot open transport endpoint

Sun Aug 23 14:57:49 1999
  RCONAG6 LISTEN /dev/tcp 137.65.211.155:2034

IP Remote Console service registered

SLP rediscovered directory agent 137.65.1.52
Sun Aug 23 14:58:26 1999
  RCONAG6 137.65.208.150:1052 Remote console connection granted
CONSTELLATION:
CONSTELLATION:
```

Figure 14-16 Sample RConsoleJ session

RCONSOLEJ and RCONSOLE do not display the graphical interfaces for ConsoleOne or for the Additional Products installation section of NWConfig on the remote workstation. However, text-based tools such as MONITOR and the main part of NWConfig do display.

If you installed NetWare 5.0 with IPX as well as IP, or only IPX, then you will also want to enable RCONSOLE support. At the server, load two NLMs: REMOTE and RSPX. The REMOTE NLM will ask you for a password. Users running RCONSOLE will need to type in this password to make a connection to this server. (They do not authenticate through NDS.) It only asks for the password once, so if you type it in wrong, you'll need to unload REMOTE, then load it again to enter a new password.

At the workstation, run a DOS session, then locate the RCONSOLE program from the SYS:PUBLIC directory (or you can click it in Windows Explorer). It will display a text-based tool. It will also display a message stating that Windows may cause problems with running RCONSOLE (although such problems don't happen often). Press [Enter] to continue.

The program then asks you which type of connection to make, asynchronous (modem) or LAN (over the network). Choose LAN. The program asks you to select the server you want to link up with. Highlight the server name and press [Enter]. The system asks you for the RCONSOLE password. Type that in, and the session is established.

Pressing the [Alt] + [F1] key combination will display the RCONSOLE menu. If you forget this, nothing onscreen can help you remember it.

The RCONSOLE menu includes a couple of unique options (compared with the Java console utility) to copy files from the DOS partition to the NetWare partition of the server. Use Directory Scan to copy a file from the DOS partition of the server's hard disk to the NetWare volume. If the files you want are on your local workstation (where you are running RCONSOLE) then use Invoke Operating System Shell to access the workstation's DOS prompt.

14

MANAGING WITH CONSOLEONE

Both RCONSOLE and RCONSOLEJ let you perform server operations while at any workstation logged into the network. This frees you from always having to use the server to run an NLM or view a log file. However, sometimes you may find yourself at the server console wanting to perform some NetWare Administrator functions. For example, let's say you add a User or container object to the NDS tree. Rather than having you return to a workstation to run the NetWare Administrator, NetWare 5.0 includes a Java GUI tool called ConsoleOne, which you can run on the server.

Novell recommends a minimum of a 200 MHz processor and 128 MB of RAM in the server to run ConsoleOne. Otherwise, it will seem quite slow.

ConsoleOne is in its first iteration. For this reason, it lacks many functions of the NetWare Administrator, so don't run it anticipating the same usefulness. However, in many ways it is adequate for common tasks at the server.

To run ConsoleOne on the server, type LOAD SYS:JAVA\BIN\JAVA.NLM and press [Enter], then press STARTX [Enter] at the server console. NetWare loads the GUI tool. Click the Novell menu in the lower left corner of the tool. Doing this displays a short menu. Choose ConsoleOne on the menu.

Although the tasks you perform with ConsoleOne are similar to those of the NetWare Administrator, ConsoleOne's main screen is much closer to Windows 95/98's Network Neighborhood, as Figure 14-17 shows.

Figure 14-17 ConsoleOne main screen with NDS tree expanded

In ConsoleOne you'll see My World, similar to the Windows Network Neighborhood. It lists My Server, The Network, and Shortcuts. As you might guess, My Server displays a list of the volumes on the particular server on which you're running ConsoleOne. The Network will display a list of the NDS trees available for management. The Shortcuts item displays a list of available folders with some demonstration software and directory shortcuts.

Although the ConsoleOne screen appears similar to the Windows Network Neighborhood, it doesn't always work like a Windows dialog screen. In Windows, you can simply click anywhere on the name of a container object in a list to get it to open. In ConsoleOne, you must click the dot to the left of the object's name. (You can, however, right-click the name to display an Options menu, as described later in this section.)

When using Java-based tools such as ConsoleOne, note that the dialog boxes work somewhat differently from Windows 95/98 dialog boxes. The Close button (with the X icon) is in the upper *left* corner of the dialog box, rather than the upper *right*. The Shrink and Expand buttons are in the usual place in the upper right, however.

The My Server List

My Server offers you a display of this server's Volumes, Configuration Files, and a Tools submenu to choose from a set of remote management tools. Like Network Neighborhood, the display of the server's volumes lets you list the contents of the volume, drill down into those folders on the volume, and view and edit files. You can also delete files and folders or add folders as needed on the server.

Unfortunately, the local floppy drive is not a device available in ConsoleOne. (RCONSOLE did have that capability.) You therefore can't use ConsoleOne to access the contents of the floppy and load them onto the server, for example.

The Configuration Files listing gives you access to the AUTOEXEC.NCF, Console Log, and the TCP/IP configuration files. ConsoleOne includes a text editor called JEditor, so you can modify text files as required. (You can do the same thing with the EDIT NLM at the server console as well.) For example, to modify your AUTOEXEC.NCF file you would:

1. Click the dot before My Server in the ConsoleOne display. The tool displays the three options under My Server.

2. Right-click Configuration Files. ConsoleOne displays a list of the configuration files in the right panel.

3. Double-click the AUTOEXEC.NCF file in the right panel. ConsoleOne opens the file in the Jeditor program so you can edit it.

4. Once you have finished editing your file, click File, Exit to save the file and exit JEditor.

The Tools menu offers a choice for local and remote server management: RCONSOLEJ and Console Manager. The two offer similar console access, but in a first for a native NetWare tool this access extends to other servers besides the current one you are running on. (The key difference between the two tools is that Console Manager requires NDS authentication while RCONSOLEJ only requires the Remote password to gain access to the server console.)

This function is particularly useful for troubleshooting where you want to know the status or results of some change on one server as seen from the other. It is also useful if a tool or NLM needs to be loaded at the second console. Before this innovation, you would have had to return to a workstation, run RCONSOLE, and access each server in turn to perform these functions.

14

One drawback to these tools, however, is that none support reading and copying files from a local drive (such as a floppy or CD-ROM drive) across the network to the other server. Local drive access is handy when you want to update some file from one server to another. However, you can also see that this restriction does close a possible door to a malicious server attack by transferring files from one system to another if access is gained to one server's console.

The Network List

The Network object is probably the most useful one for management tasks in ConsoleOne. When you right-click The Network object, ConsoleOne displays a list of the available trees you can log in to and then manage. Once the list of trees displays, when you right-click a tree, NDS asks you to authenticate to this tree.

ConsoleOne is different from the C-Worthy character-based screens when it comes to authentication. Typically, when you authenticate using those tools at the server, you must use a fully distinguished name (for example, cn=admin.o=cbe_labs), otherwise the login attempt fails. Here, you type only the appropriate names:

TREE	CBELABS
CONTEXT	CBE_Labs
Username	Admin
Password	*****

where the CONTEXT is the name of the container that holds the User object you want to log in as. Notice how you only have to type the actual user name. If you attempt to include a fully distinguished name, the login attempt fails.

Once you are authenticated, ConsoleOne displays an NDS tree similar to that of the NetWare Administrator as shown earlier in Figure 14-17.

 ConsoleOne can also run on a workstation. In that case, only the Network object appears in the left list. My Server and Shortcuts don't appear. To run it from a workstation, install the JVM using the Novell Client CD-ROM. (Look under the Windows 95/98 Client option.) Then use Windows Explorer to run the SYS:PUBLIC\MGMT\CONSOLE1.EXE program.

Viewing Object Information

You can do a variety of operations using the Network tree display. If you right-click a leaf object, such as a User object, you can view this object's Details (Properties) dialog box. This dialog is similar to that of the NetWare Administrator, but offers only a few pages of details.

For users, it displays options for:

- General Information (such as full name or address)
- Password Restrictions (length, duration, and grace logins)
- Group Membership (add or delete)
- Login Script
- Trustees of this Object (display and add or delete)

For container objects, such as an organization or organizational unit, it displays four pages:

- General Identification (location, description)
- Security Equal to Me
- Login Script
- Trustees of this Object

Each of these general pages also may contain one or more additional subpages, such as the Inherited Rights Filter under the Trustees of this Object page or the Security Equal to (security equivalent to) page under the Memberships page.

Adding Objects

You can also add objects to your NDS tree using ConsoleOne. If you select a container object, you can add an organizational unit, a group, or a user. For example, if you want to add a user to a container:

1. Right-click the container object in which you want to place the User object.

2. Select New, User. ConsoleOne displays an Add User dialog box quite similar to that of the NetWare Administrator.

3. Type the first name of the new user, then his or her last name.

4. Choose to Define Additional Properties by checking that box if you want to edit the user's login script, add a group membership, or add a trustee to this user. Click Create.

5. ConsoleOne then displays the Create Authentication Secrets dialog box in which you can define this new user's initial password. Type it, then click OK.

6. If you chose to define additional properties, ConsoleOne displays the User object's Details dialog box described earlier. You can select the Login Script page to create the user's login script or choose Memberships to add this user to a particular group, and most importantly, set the trustee rights of this user.

7. Click the Close icon in the upper-left corner of the dialog box to close it. NDS now displays the new User object in the tree in the right panel.

14

To delete objects from the NDS tree, right-click the object in the NDS tree and choose the Delete menu option.

The Shortcuts List

The Shortcuts list displays two items: Applets and Folders. The Applets listing has one folder—JDK Demos—which includes four demonstration applets. These are very simple demos, and simply serve to illustrate the possibilities of the Java interface.

The Folders listing offers shortcuts to the contents of SYS:PUBLIC, SYS:SYSTEM, and SYS:ETC. These are primary repositories of server utilities and configuration files, and being able to access them (or simply view their presence and location on the server) is a benefit previously unavailable at the console.

SERVER LICENSING

An ongoing concern of every network administrator is having the necessary number of licenses to support users and applications. With NetWare 5.0, Novell provides network administrators and software vendors with **Novell Licensing Services (NLS)** to help monitor and control the use of licensed software on your network. NLS consists of the License Service Provider (LSP) software that loads on NetWare servers, license certificates that the LSP software uses for each software package it licenses, and NLS client software for each workstation that will run the licensed software.

When NLS-enabled software requests a license, the License Service Provider (LSP) searches the NDS database for a license container object with available licenses. The LSP then checks out a license from the license container object for the requesting software to use. If no licenses are available, an error message is sent to the workstation requesting to run the software. You can use NetWare Administrator, NLS Manager, or the NWConfig NLM to install and create license certificates. NetWare Administrator or NLS Manager can also be used to monitor and manage license usage. In addition, with NLS Manager you can create a report to show license usage over a selected time period.

Viewing Licensing Information

Suppose at a recent staff meeting the senior manager asked if you could verify that the number of users currently running on NetWare was close to the maximum of the company's license agreement. To find this information, you could use NetWare Administrator to view the license certificate for your NetWare server as follows.

1. Launch NetWare Administrator.

2. Open a browse window showing the CBE_Labs tree and locate the CONSTELLATION server object. Along with the server object are two licensing objects, including the Novell+NetWare 5 Conn license object.

3. Double-click the Novell+NetWare 5 Conn license object. This displays the Certificate object. Double-click the Certificate object to display the General window. (Your license object will have an extension appropriate to the type of license you have, based on the number of users.)

4. Click the Policy Information button to view detailed information about the license agreement.

5. Click Cancel to return to the NetWare Administrator browse window.

6. Exit NetWare Administrator.

Installing Additional Licenses

Suppose, after reviewing your licensing information in the NetWare Administrator, you discover you need to install additional user licenses. NetWare 5 offers the option of increasing the numbers of users with what are called **additive licenses**. You can purchase these licenses in packs of 5, 10, 25, 50 and on up to 500 users depending on your requirements.

When you do purchase an additive license, you'll receive a floppy disk with the user authorization information on it in a file that has the filename extension .NLF. To install and thus upgrade your server to this higher number of users:

1. At the server console, load NWConfig.

2. Select the License Options menu option on the main menu.

3. Select the Install Licenses option.

4. Specify the path to your floppy disk (such as A:) where the .NLF file is with the license. The default path is A:\License.

5. NetWare now asks you to log in to NDS. Type the administrator's complete name and password; for example, .admin.cbe_labs, not just ADMIN.

6. NetWare now displays the Installable Licenses screen. Select the envelope file from the floppy disk (the one with the .NLF extension).

7. Choose Install. NetWare now installs this new license into the server's existing licensing services.

8. Exit NWConfig.

9. Run NetWare Administrator and repeat the preceding steps for viewing licensing information. You will now see this expanded number of licenses available on your server.

You can also add licenses in NetWare Administrator using these steps:

1. Select Tools.

2. Select Install License.

14

3. Select Install License Certificate.

4. Select the path to the NLF file and NetWare will install the certificate.

Although this example illustrates adding licenses for NetWare, NLS works for any application that supports the NLS specification.

PROTECTING NETWORK DATA

An organization's data plays a critical role in today's highly competitive and rapidly changing world of business and industry. A company robbed of its information would certainly suffer major losses and could even be forced out of business. As a network administrator in an organization that relies on the network for data storage and retrieval, you therefore become the "keeper of the flame." You are responsible for many, if not all, of your organization's critical data files. Management counts on your knowledge to provide a reliable storage system that is secure from unauthorized access and protected from accidental loss caused by equipment failure, operator error, or natural disaster.

In previous chapters you learned how to use the NetWare network to establish a secure directory structure that protects the organization's data from unauthorized access. Now we will look at how NetWare can provide a centralized backup-and-restore procedure that can protect valuable data from being lost to equipment or operator error. With NetWare, you can also implement a disaster recovery procedure so that your organization can continue operating despite the loss of the server or even an entire building.

The Storage Management System

Backing up data on a network is far more complex than backing up a single PC. A network may contain client workstations running different operating systems—such as Windows 95/98, Unix, Macintosh, and DOS—that each contain different file types. In addition, these files have special attributes (such as compression and migration) and rights information that must be retained. Network users also will need to use the data stored on the server as well as have their local computers backed up regularly.

To tackle these complex backup issues, Novell developed the **Storage Management System (SMS)**. SMS lets you back up even complex networks consisting of data that resides on multiple servers as well as data on workstations running different operating systems. The server that runs the backup program and has the tape or other backup medium attached to it is called the **host** server. The servers and client workstations that are being backed up are called **target** machines. A **Target Service Agent (TSA)** is a program that helps handle data transfers between the host and target. SMS uses NLMs on the host server to communicate with modules on target devices, reading the information from the target devices and sending it to the backup medium, as Figure 14-18 shows.

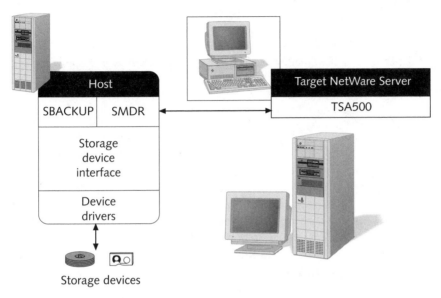

Figure 14-18   SMS backup process

 SMS can work with an entire range of archiving hardware, from single-tape backup systems to CD-ROM jukeboxes that hold several hundred gigabytes of data.

The NetWare SMS consists of the following software components. They can be run on NetWare servers as well as on client workstations.

- Storage device drivers that are loaded on the host server. They control the mechanical operation of various storage devices and media, such as tape drives.

- TSAs that are loaded on the target servers. The purpose of TSAs is to get information from the target server's volumes and send it to SBCON (SBackup Console program) running on the host server. A server can act as both host and target by running both the backup and TSA software.

- The Store Management Data Requester (SMDR) that passes commands and information between the backup program and the storage devices and media.

- Workstation TSAs that are run on the local clients. They back up data located on the local drives across the network through the SMDR. (They include versions for Windows 95, Windows NT, and DOS/Windows 3.x.)

14

- SBackup backup software (on the server this is run using the SBackup console command SBCON). This NLM provided with NetWare is the principal module that works with the SMS architecture to control the backup process on the host server. It makes requests for data to the SMDR device and then routes the returned data to the storage device.

 Past versions of NetWare also included SBackup. The new version is officially the Enhanced SBACKUP utility for NetWare 5.0. Not only is this an improved version of the tool, it is also IP-based to eliminate the dependence on SPX that characterized previous versions. However, it is fully compatible with SPX and can be used on mixed NetWare 4.11 and 5.0 networks.

Establishing a Backup System

The first step in establishing a backup system for your network is to calculate how much data needs to be copied to the backup tape on a daily basis. Decide which volumes and directories to back up. Then, if possible, get an SMS-compatible tape backup system that has enough capacity to store one day's records on one tape cartridge. In a single-file-server environment, the server acts as both the host and target devices, requiring you to load both the SBCON and TSA modules on the same server. An advantage of having one server function as both host and target device is that a server backing up its own data runs almost four times faster than a host server backing up data across the network from a target server. When you implement SMS in a multiple-file-server environment, make the host system the server that has the most data.

Installing SMS on the Server

To back up data, you need to install a backup tape device along with its software drivers on the host server. The host server will need 3 MB of RAM above the minimum required to run NetWare and will need at least 2 MB of free disk space on the SYS volume for temporary file storage. In addition to storing temporary files on the host server, the SMS also stores temporary files on the target servers. It is important to monitor the size of these files regularly (by using the command NDIR SYS:SYSTEM\TSA$TMP.* on a client workstation logged into the network), because they can become quite large. Erase them as necessary.

SMS is an optional component of NetWare 5.0 and is included on the Installation CD-ROM. If you did not install it initially, you can add it later as follows:

1. Verify that you have loaded the NetWare 5.0 Installation CD-ROM in the server's CD-ROM drive. Then verify that it is mounted by entering CDROM at the server console. If the volume is not mounted, NetWare will then mount a volume called NETWARE5.

2. Run NWConfig.

3. Choose Product Options, then Install a Product Not Listed. You are asked for the path to the NISETUP.IPS file at the root of the Installation CD-ROM volume.

4. Press [F3] to insert the path to your mounted NetWare 5.0 installation CD-ROM volume. Typically, this is NETWARE5. Then press [Enter]. This starts the GUI configuration utility. (If the installation CD-ROM is not mounted, then insert that CD-ROM into the server's CD-ROM drive, then type CD-ROM at the server console. NetWare will display the name of the volume as it mounts it.)

5. Check the box to the left of Storage Management Services in the list that appears.

6. Choose Install, then Finish. NetWare installs the SMS service, extends the NDS schema for this, and runs two additional configuration utilities at the server.

7. Accept the defaults for the SMDR services as shown onscreen.

8. Type QMAN NEW at the server console to set up the SMS queuing mechanism.

9. SMS proposes to place the job queue in the same container as the server you are now installing on. Press [Enter] to accept this default.

10. SMS then proposes to name the queue "Backup Job Queue". Press [Enter] to accept this name.

11. Log in as a user with the managing rights for SMS. Most often this is the administrator. Remember to type the full name, not just ADMIN (ie: Admin.cbe_labs). NetWare loads the queuing mechanism.

To load the SMS modules and run SBackup, follow these steps:

1. Load the device drivers for the backup device. For example, to load Novell's generic driver, type LOAD TAPEDAI.DSK.

2. Register the storage device with the operating system by entering the command SCAN FOR NEW DEVICES.

At this point, NetWare may ask you to load the NWTAPE.CDM driver for the tape drive. You can locate this (if it isn't already on your server) on the NetWare 5.0 Installation CD-ROM in the DRIVERS\STORAGE directory.

3. Load the appropriate TSA modules for the type of backup. For example, to back up a NetWare 5.0 server, type LOAD TSA500. If you want to back up the NDS database, load TSANDS.

4. Load the queue manager and location specification by typing LOAD QMAN (or just QMAN) if you didn't do so in the previous steps for installing SMS.

5. Load the backup utility by typing LOAD SBCON or just SBCON.

6. If you want to back up workstations, you need to run TSA software on each one. For example, for Windows 95, run WIN95TSA.EXE, which is on the Client CD-ROM in the PRODUCTS\WIN95\IBM_ENU directory. For DOS and Windows 3.x clients, run TSASMS.COM, which is in the PRODUCTS\DOSWIN32\TSA directory.

Running SBCON

When you load the SBCON utility at the server, you will see the main menu, as Figure 14-19 shows.

Figure 14-19 SBCON main menu

To back up a target device, follow these steps:

1. Highlight the Job Administration option, and press [Enter].

2. Select the Backup option on the menu, and press [Enter].

3. Choose the server or workstation running the TSA you want to use for the backup.

4. Choose what you want to back up. For servers, you can select the entire server or one or more mounted volumes on that server. For workstations, you can select which local drive you want to back up.

5. Type a descriptive name for your backup session, such as Constellation Full Back 9/99 for a full server backup or ACCT Workstations 9/99 for a backup of local drives in the accounting area.

6. Choose the mounted tape drive device by highlighting the Device field and pressing [Enter]. NetWare will then display the list of available devices. Highlight one and press [Enter] to select it.

7. Use the Advanced Options submenu to select between a full or incremental backup as well as to specify the date and time to run this backup session.

8. Choose whether you want to append this session to your existing backup tape or to overwrite what is on there already. (For example, when you do a full backup you could overwrite the contents of the backup tape.) If you are only going to do an incremental backup and save only changed files to the backup tape, you would choose to append this session to the tape. That way, you can do a full restore using both sessions on the tape.

9. Press [Esc] to save your session information. NetWare asks you to confirm this session and submit the job to the job queue. Press [Enter] to select Yes, schedule this session.

10. NetWare will now run this backup session when you have it scheduled.

 Any time you edit or save a file, NetWare sets the Archive Needed [A] attribute to Y. When you perform a backup, SMS resets this bit back to N until the file is modified again.

After SMS completes a successful backup, you should test your backup system by restoring selected files from the backup medium. Doing a complete restore is often not feasible, because of time constraints as well as possible data loss if the restore process fails. To restore selected files:

1. Select the Job Administration option on the main SBCON menu.

2. Select Restore on the submenu.

3. Select the server or workstation running your TSA to which you want to restore the files.

4. Select the job you want to restore using the name you gave it as a descriptor (in our example, Constellation Full Back 9/99).

5. Select the backup device to which you backed up this session.

6. Select the specific session you want by pressing [Enter] to view the list of available sessions.

7. Finally, you can use the Advanced Options submenu to schedule the restoration, rather than run it immediately.

8. Press [Esc] to accept this restoration session, then choose Yes. NetWare will perform the restoration when you have it scheduled.

Developing a Backup Procedure

Once the backup system has been tested, you need to implement a reliable disaster recovery plan. This entails developing a tape rotation procedure and backup schedule. A procedure that rotates multiple tapes means that backups can be saved for long time periods. This is an important part of a disaster recovery plan because it provides a way to restore an earlier backup. It also provides a way to store backup tapes in a separate

14

building, to protect them in case of catastrophic damage at your location. It is sometimes important to be able to recover a file from an earlier backup if that file becomes corrupted by a software virus, operator error, or software bug and the damage is not discovered for several days or weeks. If you are rotating your backups on a limited number of tapes, by the time such an error is discovered, the original backup containing the valid file may have been overwritten by a backup copy of the corrupted file. To help prevent this loss, a good tape rotation system should consist of 20 tapes, as Figure 14-20 shows.

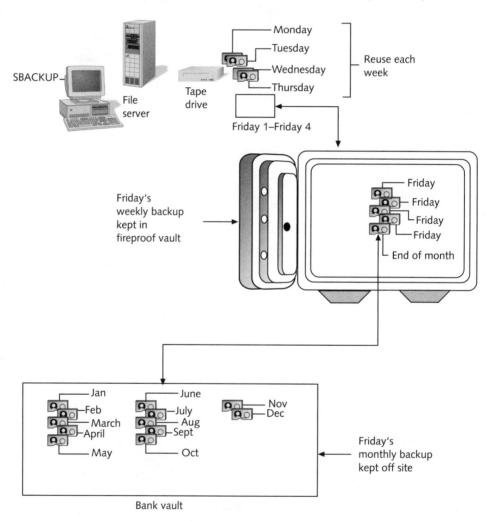

Figure 14-20   Tape rotation procedure

Label four tapes Monday through Thursday and rotate them each week. Label four tapes Friday 1 through Friday 4. Use Friday 1 on the first Friday of the month, Friday 2 on the second, Friday 3 on the third, and Friday 4 on the fourth. In addition, label 12 tapes

January through December. Rotate these tapes each year and use them on the last (fifth) Friday of each month. On months with only four Fridays, substitute the following month's Friday 1 tape with the monthly backup tape. Another alternative, if someone is available to change the tape, is to make the monthly backup on the last Saturday of each month. Storage of backup tapes is also important in the event of a fire or damage to the building. As a precaution, many administrators store weekly backups in an onsite fire-proof vault and keep monthly backup tapes offsite in a secure location, such as a bank safety deposit vault.

The final step in implementing the backup system is to establish a time for the backup to be performed and to make sure no users are logged in during the backup process. To prevent interference with user work schedules, many network administrators start the backup each night at about midnight. To restrict night owls from working late and to prevent users from leaving their workstations logged in during the backup, all user accounts, except the user name used to back up the system, should have a time restriction to prevent users from accessing the network between midnight and 5 a.m. This provides a 5-hour time interval that should be enough to create the backup. If extra time is needed, the backup can be set to begin at 11 p.m. and/or extend to 6 a.m., provided user time restrictions are also set for the longer backup period.

A time restriction prevents users from logging in during a specified time interval. It does not log them out if they logged in before that interval. This is a problem for users who go home without logging out, which may leave files open and unavailable for backup. To meet this need, there are third-party tools that perform auto-logoff for users who have been inactive for a specified period of time.

You need to develop a procedure to deal with the files in the working directory, because the size of these files grows with each backup made. The session files in the working directory play an important role in the restore process by enabling you to select quickly the files and directories you want to restore. One way to deal with the restore files is to copy them to a floppy disk each day and to store the floppy disk with the corresponding backup tape. If you need to restore a backup tape, you can then copy the corresponding floppy disk into the working directory prior to restoring the files with the SBCON program. Using this procedure, each morning you can first check the status of the backup to be sure all files were successfully copied. Next copy the files from the working directory specified in the SBCON program to a floppy disk and delete the session files in the working directory. Finally, store the backup tape and corresponding disk in a secure location. Once the disaster recovery procedure is in place and operating, you can rest easier knowing you have done all you can to provide a secure environment for your organization's precious data and software.

14

OTHER MANAGEMENT TOOLS

We covered the basics for distributing an application using Z.E.N.works in Chapter 11. We'll now explore the range of capabilities in Z.E.N.works to do a number of configuration tasks.

As we discussed in Chapter 11, one of the best reasons for using NetWare is its management capabilities using NDS. The Z.E.N.works enhancement to NetWare Administrator leverages NDS to help you manage workstations and applications more easily. It eliminates the need to manually configure each desktop. Z.E.N.works automates this configuration by distributing applications and configurations to desktops at login time.

Because you manage your network using Z.E.N.works in the NetWare Administrator, you can now have central control over workstation configuration and application distribution. You can create policy packages for each kind of workstation and for each application so you can apply a common policy across several systems, rather than duplicate this effort at each station. In fact, Z.E.N.works also supports workstation groups that work like user groups. This again gives you the ability to maintain a set of workstations that are very different but that require a similar setup or configuration.

To make this happen, we will discuss how to register workstations with NDS and import them into your tree. We will also review how to create and apply policies on your network. Finally, we will discuss two features of the optional full Z.E.N.works package—remote control access to your users' workstations and the Help Requester application for Help Desk support in NetWare.

The Z.E.N.works Maintenance Schedule

The key to using Z.E.N.works to facilitate management of Windows workstations is maintaining a current registry of the workstations in NDS. As time goes on, workstations are added, removed, or moved to another location within the network. If the information on these workstations in NDS becomes stale, Z.E.N.works won't be able to update the software on those workstations or distribute applications to them.

There are four steps in the Z.E.N.works maintenance schedule:

1. Register new workstations on the network.

2. Update information on all existing workstations on the network.

3. Remove any workstations that are no longer on the network.

4. Import the new workstations into NDS.

Fortunately, you only have to perform step 4, because NetWare performs the first three steps automatically.

It is important that you reregister workstations that have had new interface cards installed. Z.E.N.works uses address information from the card to identify the individual workstation.

This schedule will take some time, because registration takes place when a user logs in from that workstation. Some systems will be immediately registered, whereas registering others (less frequently used) might take several days or even weeks.

You can speed up the process by removing any workstation that is no longer on the network. You can do so in NetWare Administrator by locating that workstation object in the tree and deleting it.

Creating Policy Package Objects

A new object class added to NDS by Z.E.N.works is the Policy or Policy Package object. This object defines various properties of individual users, groups, organizational units, or workstations, which you determine as a policy for the network. In effect, however, there are three types of policy objects: Container, User, and Workstation policy packages. (Users and workstations also have subvariants for Windows 3.x, 95/98, and NT.) Table 14-8 shows these policy objects.

Table 14-8   Policy Package Objects

Policy Package	Applies to
Container Policy Package	Container objects

User Policy Packages
    Windows 3.1 User Package
    Windows 95/98 User Package
    Windows NT User Package
	Containers, groups, or users
	    Windows 3.1 workstations
	    Windows 95/98 workstations
	    Windows NT workstations

Workstation Policy Packages
    Windows 3.1
    Windows 95/98 Workstation Package
    Windows NT Workstation Package
	Containers, workstation groups, workstations
	    Windows 3.1 workstations
	    Windows 95/98 workstations
	    Windows NT workstations

14

The Policy objects differ depending on the focus of the package:

- Container packages apply only to searches for other policies within that container.
- User packages apply to properties on users themselves.
- Workstation packages apply to properties of workstations.

Container policy packages do only one thing: They locate existing policies within that container. This lets you canvas your tree more rapidly than if you had to search all containers for policies. Ultimately, you can use this package to determine exactly what policies are in place for the objects within the container. If a policy has been applied in error, you can fix that. The search order goes from the object to any group the object is a member of (remember, NDS supports both user and workstation groups), up to the current container, then to parent containers on up to [ROOT]. (You can change this order with an option in the Policy package object.)

User policy packages allow the administrator to limit what users can do, based on their login platforms.

 You can use more policies with users on Windows 95/98 and NT than with Windows 3.x because Microsoft included more capabilities in the Registry than in the WIN.INI and other configuration files of 3.x.

Z.E.N.works supports more than one Policy object per container and per platform. How-ever, only one user policy and one workstation policy can apply to a single user. If you try to set up a user with more than one such association, NDS will beep and display a warning alert.

Users will also find that the policy restrictions apply no matter which workstation they log in to. These can include:

- *Desktop Preferences*—Defines the user's default desktop as laid out using the functions within the Windows Control Panel (such as Wallpaper, Monitor, Network, etc.).

- *User System Policies*—Limits what Windows applications a user can run.

- *Help Desk*—Provides access to the optional NetWare Help Requester program. (This policy sets rules for the interaction between the Help Desk and users. As a minimum, it requires the help desk phone number and user name or an e-mail address.)

- *Dynamic Local User* (NT only)—Manages user access to the workstation.

- *Remote Control*—Limits the use of the Z.E.N.works optional Remote Control module when a specific user logs in from a workstation. (If you want to limit the use on a specific workstation, use the Remote Control Workstation policy instead.)

- *User Printer* (NT only)—Sets up one or more printers along with the appropriate drivers when a specific user logs in from a workstation.

- *Workstation Import*—Specifies how NDS will name the registered workstations in the tree and where they should appear.

Workstation policies apply, as expected, to workstations themselves. This also means that no matter who logs in from that class of workstation (whether it is Win3.x, Win95/98, or WinNT) these same rules will always apply. They include:

- *Workstation Inventory*—Catalogs the hardware configuration of the workstation using the optional Z.E.N.works inventory module.

- *Login Restriction*—Limit when and how logins occur from this workstation.

- *Novell Client Configuration*—Allows for varying settings such as default protocols, login targets, and services to load on the workstation (SNMP, TSA agents).

- *Remote Control*—Limits access to a workstation via a remote communications and control program such as the optional Z.E.N.works module. (If you want to limit such access based on who logs in from the workstation, use the Remote Control User policy instead.)

- *Computer System* (Available on all three Windows platforms)—Defines applications you want to automatically deliver to the workstation no matter who logs in from the system (as opposed to using a User policy that would specify a download only when a specific user logs in on that system).

- *Computer Printer*—Sets up one or more network printers on the workstation as well as installs appropriate drivers.

- *RAS (Remote Access Services) Configuration*—Configures the workstation to use a dialup connection.

You can also be quite specific with policies such as with the Win95/98 class where you can set a 95 Computer Printer policy. The 95 Computer Printer policy can assign both printers and identify (and deliver) appropriate drivers for that workstation. The user need only log in to NDS, and Z.E.N.works will add the printer or printers to the Printer Control Panel and install the driver or drivers.

Before you use policies, you definitely need to think through the various types and the impact they will have on users. Policies work best where you have many users to configure. Your network may be small enough that policies won't be as applicable or at best an extra difficulty compared with visiting a half-dozen or so desktops to set up printers and the like. For a larger site, however, a policy will make configuration standardization easy. Some additional rules of thumb include:

- Don't cross containers with policies. Keep the user or workstation policy objects within the containers where the affected user or workstation objects are. (This is another reason not to use so-called single-purpose containers for workstations, users, printers, servers, etc.)

- Individual policies apply to a User or Workstation object over those created for the container or group to which the object belongs. (This is similar to file system rights—if you are granted specific rights to a file, then you have rights to that file even if the container has a restriction against those rights.)

- Apply policies at the highest level possible and let them flow down the tree, rather than apply them on an individual basis.

14

- Keep an eye on your partition limits. Adding an automatic Workstation Import policy creates a new object for every workstation to which the policy applies. This can cause you to exceed the 1500-object limit for effective partitions in NDS, because you will want the Workstation objects and their User objects to be in the same container.

We mentioned earlier the advantages of having Workstation objects in your tree, to apply policies and maintain the network. Creating a large number of such objects in the tree would again be a tedious job, so NDS automates this via a Workstation Registration agent. Once the user logs in from that workstation, Z.E.N.works will create an entry about this workstation. Later these entries will be imported into NDS.

Using Application Launcher and the user container's Applications dialog box's Forced Run option (as described in Chapter 11), the administrator can set up Z.E.N.works to gather the registration information. Z.E.N.works does this by distributing the appropriate Workstation Registration software, based on platform, to users at login time. (A container login script entry could also run this utility.) Once the workstation information is gathered, the administrator can then import the data into the NDS tree. (Of course, this importation is done after creating an appropriate policy object for each workstation platform the administrator wants to support in the NDS tree.) NDS stores the information gathered by the registration software under the relevant container object's Registered Workstations page, shown in the object's Details dialog box.)

 Use WSREG32.EXE for Windows 95/98 or Windows NT workstation registration. Use WSREG16.EXE for Windows 3.x or DOS registrations. If you upgrade your workstations to the Novell Client for Z.E.N.works, you will also install the Scheduler on the system. The Scheduler shows up after you log in to NetWare as an icon in System Tray of Windows 95/98 and Windows NT workstations. The Scheduler automatically registers your workstations in the user's container, so you don't need to do anything else to register the workstation. As the name suggests, the Scheduler also lets you specify a time for this registration to occur if it can't be done immediately.

If you prefer, you can add a few commands to the container login script to run the registration software. If you are on a Windows 95/98 workstation, include the following commands in the container script:

```
If "%platform" = "W95" THEN begin
#wsreg32.exe
end
```

For Windows NT workstations, change the "W95" in the first line to "WNT". For Windows 3.x workstations, change the "W95" to "WIN". Also, change the executable name to WSREG16.EXE. Z.E.N.works stores the executable file in the Windows\System directory.

Before you register and import the workstations into the NDS tree, first follow these steps to create an import policy for your workstation platform:

1. Run NetWare Administrator.

2. Highlight the container object in which you want the workstations to appear.

3. Right-click the object and choose Create.

4. Select the Policy Package object type and click OK.

5. Open the drop-down menu for the Select Package Type field and choose the one that matches the workstation platform you want to import. For our example, we will choose Win95 User Package.

6. Give your Policy object a name, such as User_platform, in which you substitute Win95/98 or WINNT for the platform type.

7. Check the box marked Define Additional Properties so you can configure the import policy.

8. Choose Create. The NetWare Administrator now creates the workstation import Policy object, then displays the object's Details dialog box.

9. In the Policies window, check the box labeled Workstation Import Policy.

10. To configure the location, click Details.

11. The default page is Workstation Location. If this page is not displayed, click the Workstation Location button on the right side of the dialog box.

12. Click the drop-down menu for the "Create Workstation objects in" field. Choose the Selected Container option.

Verify that the Path field in the dialog box shows the correct path for the container in which you want to place the imported workstation objects.

14

13. Click OK. You are now ready to associate your policy package with your selected container.

14. In the container object's Policies window, click Associations.

15. Click Add.

16. In the Browse context field, select your container.

17. In the Available Objects field, double-click your selected container.

18. To save your configuration information, click OK.

You can now begin importing all the currently registered workstations and creating the workstation objects in the tree. To do this:

1. Right-click the container object to which you registered the workstations.

2. Select Details to display that dialog box.

3. Click Workstation Registration. This now displays all the currently registered workstations in that container. The field may be blank if no workstations are registered. If you see an error message stating that you do not have rights to register workstations, click OK to continue.

4. Exit from the Details dialog box and go back to the NDS tree.

5. Click your workstation container. Then choose Tools, Import Workstations on the menu bar. If this doesn't work, check to make sure you still have the correct container highlighted.

6. The NetWare Administrator will ask you from where you want to import the workstations. This should be the current container.

7. Choose OK. NDS will now import the new workstation objects into the container. You will need to refresh the view in NetWare Administrator to see them.

If you prefer a higher degree of control over importing workstations into NDS, you can configure and perform the import manually. To do this:

1. Select the container in which you want to place the workstation objects, then the Workstation or User policy package you created.

2. Check the Workstation Import Policy in the list of policies. Then click Details.

   You can now specify where you want to place the workstation objects and how NDS should name them as it creates each one.

3. When you have finished configuring the import, click OK to save it.

Once you have imported the workstation objects into the NDS tree, any policies and policy packages you have configured that apply to those workstations will now become effective.

Using Policies in Desktop Environments

You can also manage your users' desktop environments with both user and workstation policies. These allow you to tailor the available applications and the desktop to exactly what you want users to view or run. With more than a dozen different policies, we cannot explore every way that Z.E.N.works can be used. However, by way of example, let's highlight just two such policies—one in the user package and the other in the workstation package—which are the User System Policies and the Computer System Policies.

The first, User System Policies, limits what specific users can access on their desktops. For example, suppose we want to restrict users from seeing the Start menu's Find or Run options as a way of reducing the threat of outside software introducing viruses to the network. You could check the User System Policies box, then click Details. You can then click Shell, Restrictions, the Remove Find command, and the Remove Run command. The next time users log in, these two command options will disappear from the Start menu.

There is also a Desktop Preferences policy for including a specific wallpaper or screensaver on the workstation. This gives you a way to install, for all workstations, a corporate background that you can periodically update without going to each workstation. To do this, highlight your User Policy Package object in the NDS tree. Enable the Desktop Preferences. Then highlight this policy and choose Details. You can now perform a typical configuration using the Windows Control Panel as you would for a standalone workstation, only now the changes you make will apply to multiple workstations. Once you save this configuration, the next time an appropriate user logs in that user will receive the new desktop configuration.

The second, Computer System Policies, runs an application on specific platforms no matter who logs in from them. By choosing the Run option under Computer System Policies, you can list those programs that must run each time a login occurs from that workstation platform. This can include simply the Application Launcher (NAL.EXE). In effect, the Launcher becomes the only "group" of applications the user can interact with on the NetWare desktop—all others vanish from the desktop.

Remember to use the UNC path to the program's executable files. (For example, \\SARATOGA\SYS:APPS\WP\WP.EXE rather than G:\APPS\WP\WP.EXE.) Otherwise you will have to ensure all users have a drive G mapped to the SYS volume so the application can run.

14

The combination of the two policies, User System Policies and the Computer System Policies, gives users their final desktop. (That is, if both policies are implemented.)

Using Z.E.N.works Remote Control

We mentioned in Chapter 11 that the Z.E.N.works shipped with NetWare 5.0 is only a starter pack. The full version includes Remote Control, Help Desk, and Workstation Inventory modules. Should your site choose to purchase this extra cost option, you will find these modules useful.

Z.E.N.works includes software that enables you to take control of another user's workstation across the network. This Remote Control software allows you to view, diagnose, and rectify network and workstation problems from the NetWare Administrator. As part of this, Z.E.N.works also includes a Remote Control policy in both the User and the Workstation policy packages. You can use either one, depending on your network needs.

The actual Remote Control software installs as part of the Novell Client for Z.E.N.works as part of the full version of the product. The workstation on which you install it must be registered and logged into the network, and there must be a workstation object in your tree for the Remote Control software to run.

 Remote Control only works using IPX/SPX. If your network is pure IP, the tool will not work.

If you want to assign a user or group of users for your help desk, the minimum rights they will need are in the workstation objects—Read rights to all attributes of the workstation objects and the Write right to the DM Remote Verification attribute.

If you plan on only a few such users, then you can configure them individually. If you plan on a more extensive assignment, then you can use the Remote Control Policy of the User or Workstation Policy packages to establish the security criteria you want.

 The default is to have Remote Control enabled for workstations.

Because remote control is a serious tool that requires careful use, the workstation will do an equally careful check to ensure that only properly authorized users perform this function. It checks the security parameters of the Workstation object itself, then the Remote Control Policy configuration. If each of these permit remote control, then NetWare checks the User object itself (the one requesting the remote access and control). If that object passes the authentication check, then NetWare checks for any user policy packages and verifies the remote control policies in that package.

If all these permit remote control of the workstation, then NetWare grants the access.

There are four parameters that can be set in the various Remote Control policy locations:

- Enable/disable Remote Control
- Prompt user to okay Remote Control
- Provide audio alert during remote session
- Provide visual alert during remote session

The last three are checkbox parameters (check to enable them, uncheck to disable). They effectively eliminate the possibility that the user could be unaware of someone taking control of his or her workstation.

By default, NetWare requests that the user okay the remote session. It also defaults to providing a visual indicator of the active remote session. However, no audio alert is the default.

All these parameters appear in the User or Workstation object's Details screen on the Remote Control page that appears when you install the full Z.E.N.works package. They also appear as part of a General User policy or Workstation Policy Package object, again on the Remote Control page.

To launch a remote session, follow these steps:

1. Start NetWare Administrator.

2. Highlight the Workstation object you want to control (called the target).

3. Select Tools, Remote Control Workstation. NetWare will then ask the remote user at the target workstation to okay the remote session. If the user okays the session, then a window opens to display the contents of the screen of the remote workstation. You can then read any error messages, or run programs that have caused problems for the user.

 The keyboard and mouse remain active on the target workstation, so you may want to ask the user not to use them during your session, to prevent a conflict.

Windows includes a multitude of similar menus on both the target and your administrative workstation; the Z.E.N.works Remote Control software provides some additional buttons on the View window to take the place of some of these menus. Table 14-9 lists these buttons.

Table 14-9   Remote Control buttons

Button	Function on the Target Workstation
Start	Activates the Start menu.
Application Switcher	Toggles between open applications.
System Key Pass-Through	Toggles on/off to send a [Ctrl] or [Alt] keystroke to the target rather than local workstation. For example, for [Alt-Esc] to work the System Key Pass-Through would need to be on.
Navigation	Displays a minimized view of the target's desktop.

14

In addition, the Remote Control software has a selection of hot keys, as shown in Table 14-10. These hot keys can be defined by the user with the menu option for Hot Keys on the View window menu bar.

Table 14-10 The Remote Control hot keys

Hot Keys	Function
Ctrl-Alt-M	Toggles the View window to full screen and back.
Ctrl-Alt-R	Refreshes the screen.
Ctrl-Alt-T	Reconnects to the target and refreshes the screen.
Ctrl-Alt-S	Works like the System Key Pass-through button. Sends all [Ctrl] and [Alt] keystrokes to the target.
Ctrl-Alt-H	Enables the hot keys on the target workstation.
Ctrl-Alt-A	Increases the refresh rate of the screen display on the host but not the target workstation.
Left Shift-Esc	Ends the session.

Using Help Requester

Another part of the full Z.E.N.works package is Help Requester. This module provides an automated way for users to report network and workstation problems to you or to your help desk via e-mail. You can distribute the actual Help Requester application to workstations using the Application Launcher (as discussed in Chapter 11).

Z.E.N.works includes two versions of Help Requester—HELPREQ16 for Windows 3.x workstations and HELPREQ32 for Windows 95/98 and NT.

Before that happens, you need to make sure that your users have the package on their workstations and that you have configured the Help Desk policy in NetWare Administrator. (You also need administrative rights to the Root of your NDS tree.) To run Help Requester, you also need a MAPI-compliant e-mail package (such as Novell's GroupWise).

MAPI is the Message Application Program Interface, a set of object-oriented functions that produce messaging capabilities between two pieces of software.

The user must be logged into NDS, and the workstation must be registered and have a Workstation object in the tree.

To configure a Help Desk policy in NetWare Administrator:

1. Right-click the User_Win95/98 User Policies Package object in your tree (use the name you have given this object.) Select a user package, because the Help Desk program is oriented toward the user's needs.

2. Select Details.

3. Click Help Desk Policies. You can now specify if Help Requester will integrate with e-mail.

4. Click Yes, and then fill in the e-mail package you wish to use. If you choose not to integrate with e-mail, then you can continue to fill out the Help Desk contact name, e-mail address, and phone number in the fields provided.

5. Click OK to save the configuration.

You can also use the Help Requester Configuration page to specify whether users can run Help Requester, any preconfigured subject lines, or set the delivery mode of the e-mail requests for help.

When users run Help Requester, they can choose to send e-mail, with a blank form to fill out appearing onscreen. If they choose to call, then the Help Requester shows the name and phone number of the person they should contact. If they click Info, then an additional contact name appears whom they can call.

CREATING ADMINISTRATIVE ASSISTANTS

You probably now realize that being a network administrator covers a lot of territory. To make your life easier, you may want to assign various duties to specific users. In Chapter 12 we discussed how to add print services managers and operators as one way to assign duties to others. There are other tasks that you can assign as well.

However, you don't want to create a legion of ADMINs with access rights to the whole network. (In the old days of NetWare, this status was called being supervisor-equivalent.) You can, of course, grant a user Supervisor rights only to objects within a container, but too often other objects need management access that are outside a container. (We'll look at some of these in the next section, on multiple contexts.)

Table 14-11 lists the minimum requirements to grant and use specific NDS objects.

14

Table 14-11   Minimum requirements for NDS access

Desired User Action for Object Type	Assistant Administrator Only Needs	User Needs
Use Alias objects	The right to assign rights to the object the Alias refers to.	Access rights to the object the Alias refers to.
Run application objects	Supervisor or Access Control rights to the application's directory or file.	File system rights (Read/File Scan as a minimum) to the application referenced by the object.
Associate with application objects	Write right in the ACL property of the Application object. Write right in the ACL property of the user.	To be declared associated with the Application object.

Table 14-11   Minimum requirements for NDS access (continued)

Desired User Action for Object Type	Assistant Administrator Only Needs	User Needs
Use Directory Map objects	Supervisor or Access Control rights to the Directory Map object's referenced path. Write right to the ACL property of the directory map object.	File system rights to the referenced directory. Read right to the Path property of the Directory Map object.
Add users to Group objects	Write right to the Member and Object Trustees (ACL) properties of the specific Group object.	To be added to the specific Group object.
Add users to Organizational Role objects	Write right to the Occupant and Object Trustees (ACL) properties of the specific organizational role object.	To be added to the specific organizational role object.
Access to an NDPS printer object	Write right to the Users and Object Trustees (ACL) properties of the specific NDPS Printer object.	To be added to the user role list of the specific NDSP Printer object.
Add users to a Profile object	Write right to the Object Trustees (ACL) property of the specific Profile object.	To have the specific Profile object added to the user's Profile property. The Read right to the Login Script property of the specific Profile object.
Access to a Volume or Directory object	Supervisor or Access Control rights to the directory or volume.	File system rights to the directory or volume. (*Note*: NetWare automatically gives all users Read and File Scan rights

MANAGING YOUR MULTIPLE-CONTEXT NETWORK

As the network administrator, you have some advantages over your users, because you have unlimited access to the entire NDS tree. Users will typically be restricted to one or more containers within that tree for security reasons as well as for ease of management. You will need to be familiar with procedures for enabling users to traverse a multiple-context NDS tree so they can access the resources they need on the network.

Helping users understand the nature of contexts can be frustrating at first. When they try to access a known network resource, only to get an error message "does not exist in the specified context," they will call you for help. The idea that a network service can exist in the office, yet remain apparently unavailable, is counter-intuitive.

You can make this process easier by reviewing your NDS tree. As discussed in Chapter 4, the NDS tree structure affects users and network performance. Plan your tree with the multiple-context, multiple-container idea in mind, and try to simplify access. Consider where you place resources and how you set up those resources. As we said in Chapter 4, taking the simplest way out may prove a disaster for security and network performance. Placing all users in one container, all workstations in another, and all servers and volumes in a third may be easy to view onscreen, but will be a nightmare to maintain.

An efficient NDS tree should include:

- Logical and intuitive locations for objects in the tree
- Effective use of containers to provide rights and access
- Fault tolerance using partitions and multiple application locations
- Focus on reducing network traffic

A logical tree makes finding resources in the tree easier for users. By granting containers rights to services, the administrator can make certain all appropriate users in that container receive those rights. By creating partitions, administrators can ensure continuous network access even when one server in the tree goes down. The fault tolerance option with applications distributed through Z.E.N.works provides a simple solution to a server failure as well. Finally, by careful analysis the administrator can review the flow of data across the network for logging in, application access, printing, and data storage. The aim is to avoid long-distance communications and to use more localized resources.

The CNE or network administrator will have addressed most of these issues while creating the network. However, often the CNA can help analyze the existing tree and network to find bottlenecks and improve efficiency.

Here are some suggestions to help when you have multiple contexts and users logging in from various contexts. To keep appropriate users in and inappropriate users out of certain containers:

- Set up intruder detection in each container to keep out inappropriate users.
- Use an Alias for users who may wander from site to site (and hence from one login context to another) rather than granting users extended rights in every context.
- Create and maintain a template object in each user container rather than one central template for all users.
- When adding an additional network administrator, consider not making this person simply security equivalent to ADMIN, but something less. Grant less than the Supervisor right, to prevent these assistants from performing more than their assigned tasks.
- Keep default assignments for rights and access unless you need to increase them for a specific reason.

To make management easier for you:

- Grant access rights through containers or groups rather than to individual users.

- When granting rights to a volume, use the trustee rights to this object to cite the recipient of those rights.

- Use Directory Map objects, Alias objects, or distinguished names to reference objects in the tree in login scripts, to avoid problems with the current user context.

- Assign a print manager and operator in each context to handle routine maintenance and print job duties. This eliminates having to give an additional outside person access to the container.

- If a printer is used by everyone, and it supports NDPS, then you may want to designate it as a public access printer rather than a controlled access printer. This again removes a reason for users to have rights and access outside their own container.

- Assign users to the User role for each controlled access printer, rather than granting them explicit rights to the printer.

Understanding Contexts

We have used the analogy of a filing cabinet to describe a server and its volumes. We can also use the analogy to describe how contexts work. Suppose you have a cabinet with drawers marked A–F and G–M. If you open the A–F drawer but want to see the Gardner file, you won't be able to. If you then close the A–F drawer and open the G–M drawer, you can now view the Gardner file. Each of these drawers could be likened to a context; in a particular context, you may not be able to access all available network resources.

Another way to look at it is to compare using contexts to locating a file on your local hard disk. Suppose you want to locate a particular WAV sound file on your disk. There are several ways you could do this. If you open a DOS session and type DIR, you will only see a list of the files in the current directory. If you want to search in another directory, you have to type CD and some parameter to move to another directory. For example, you would enter CD \My Documents to go to the My Documents directory. You could then type DIR again to view the contents of the My Documents directory. You could then search for the WAV file there.

In the same way, if you are in a particular context in the NDS tree, you may or may not be able to view certain network resources. For example, you may attempt to log in, or map a drive, or set up a printer. If you aren't using the correct context, you won't be able to see this resource or access the network.

Contexts are not related to drive mappings. You may need the correct context to create the drive mapping, but they are not the same thing. You can keep a drive mapping, but change your context.

To illustrate the difference between context and drive mapping, try the following:

1. Run a DOS session from the Windows desktop.

2. Type MAP to display your drive mappings. Notice that they relate to a specific server volume.

3. Now type CX to display your current context. Notice what your current context is.

Don't worry that we haven't covered the CX command before. It isn't a required skill for CNAs. CX stands for ConteXt and is the command line tool for viewing or changing your current NDS context. This is different from using the Windows Explorer to view the tree. Viewing doesn't change your current context. The CX command does. (Think of CX as similar to the DOS DIR command, only it is used for NDS.)

4. Now type CX .TEST&EVAL.CBE_Labs.CBELABS to change your context to the Test&Eval container. (If your tree is named something other than CBELABS, for example, TESTLAB, substitute that name for CBELABS.)

5. Type CX again to verify that you have changed context.

6. Now type MAP H:=CONSTELLATION_SYS:. Notice the error message you receive. The MAP command failed because the current context you are in, Test&Eval, does not contain CONSTELLATION_SYS—the volume you tried to map to.

7. Now type CX /R to change your context to the Root of your NDS tree.

8. Type MAP H:=CONSTELLATION_SYS: and press [Enter] again. The command was successful this time because the volume you requested, CONSTELLATION _SYS, exists in the Root context. Note, too, that this whole time your current drive mapping stayed exactly the same. Changing context has no effect on current drive mappings. (Your SYS volume may have a different context. In this case, use the context supplied by your instructor to complete this step.)

9. Type MAP DEL H: and press [Enter] to remove your drive mapping, then exit the DOS session.

As you can see, changing contexts can open or close access to network resources. To eliminate some of this confusion, you can set a default context for logins, set contexts using login scripts, and use Windows utilities to access NDS objects in any context you have rights to. Finally, you need to ensure that mappings in the login scripts are in the proper format to work without regard to the user's current context.

Automating Login Contexts

You can set a default context for the login process at the workstation. Use the following steps:

1. Right-click the N icon in the System Tray.

14

2. Select the Novell Client32 Properties option.

3. Select the Client tab from the dialog box as Figure 14-21 shows.

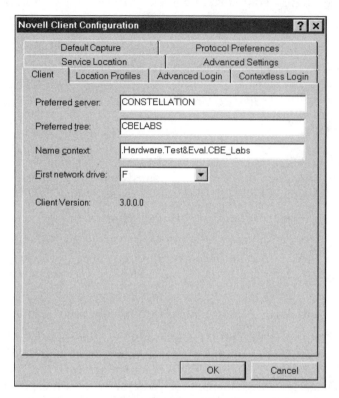

Figure 14-21 Novell Client Configuration dialog box

4. In the field labeled Name Context, type the context for the User object that represents this workstation's primary user. For example, if this was John Cunningham's workstation, then his context would be .Pubs.CBE_Labs_Admin.CBE_Labs. If it were Bert Simpson's, then his context would be .Software.Test&Eval.CBE_Labs.

The Novell Client does not care whether you include the leading period in the context or not. So Pubs.CBE_Labs_Admin.CBE_Labs is the same to the Novell Client as .Pubs.CBE_Labs_Admin.CBE_Labs.

5. After you type the context, click OK to save the configuration.

After logging in, you may, however, want to access files, directories, or even your home directory from a different context from where you log in. You can also set a context in the login scripts of containers, profiles, or users. To do this, add the command

```
CONTEXT distinguished_name
```

in your login script. For example, if we wanted to set the context to be CBE_Labs, then you would include the command

```
CONTEXT .CBE_Labs
```

in the container, profile, or user login script.

The most effective context to use is the one in which the user's most commonly accessed resources are located. Note, however, that you can use Alias objects to "locate" resources closer to users rather than move the users closer to the resources. In this way, users can simply think of resources using their common names, rather than their distinguished names.

For example, they can refer to an HP printer using the common name HP4Si rather than the .HP4SI.CBE_Labs_Admin.CBE_Labs distinguished name.

Working with Windows Utilities

Once your users have logged in, they still must keep their context in mind when using DOS. With Windows utilities such as Windows Explorer, however, they will encounter fewer problems with contexts. In DOS you must change contexts manually to map a drive to a volume. In Windows, you change context using the "drill down" method:

1. Open Windows Explorer.

2. Open Network Neighborhood.

3. Double-click your lab tree.

4. Double-click the CBE_Labs organization object.

5. Right-click the CONSTELLATION_SYS object.

6. Select Novell Map Network Drive.

7. Choose drive H: from the drop-down list.

8. Click MAP.

You have now drilled down through the NDS tree, changed contexts, and mapped to the SYS volume. (There are several ways to do this besides using Explorer and drilling down. The purpose in this example is to show how changing contexts works in Windows.)

You can do the same thing with Directory Map objects, Printer objects, and the like. For example, if you wanted to configure a workstation to use an additional network printer (as outlined in Chapter 12), you would use the Windows NWPMW32.EXE program

14

(otherwise known as the Novell Printer Manager). When you select Printer, New, then click Add, you will see (in the NDS tree) a list of printers to which you have rights.

If you tried this in a DOS session, you would have to locate the correct context for the printer (using the printer's full distinguished name), or change to that context to locate and reference the printer.

Remember our analogy earlier about using the DOS DIR command; this can help explain how Windows makes things easier. If we were still looking for that WAV file, we could use the Windows Find function. In the Windows Startup Menu's Find Files or Folders option, you could type in a wildcard name to limit the search. For example, if you know it was a WAV sound file, you could type *.wav, or simply wav, in the search field. Windows would then search through all the existing directories on the drive until it had found all files that matched the wildcard name. You don't have to tell it to search all directories, because it already knows to do that.

You can use the N icon in the System Tray to choose the Novell Map Network Drive option. You can use the Browse button in the Map dialog to browse through your NDS tree to locate the appropriate Directory Map object or Server Volume object to map to. Again, you are changing context as you do this.

Object Names in Login Scripts

In the past, drive mappings were simple—MAP H:=CONSTELLATION_SYS worked every time. Now, with contexts, you cannot simply write that out in a login script and have it work, because the MAP command, like all DOS commands, depends on the current context. If the referenced object isn't in the current context, the command fails.

To avoid this, you can use two techniques in login scripts. One is to reference a Directory Map object in the user's current context during login. Another is to use the distinguished name of the directory and volume so MAP can find it even if the object is in another context.

 It doesn't hurt to use a distinguished name for objects if there is any question about what context a user is in after login. If you use container and/or profile login scripts only, then this task is simpler than spelling out a distinguished name time after time in multiple-user login scripts.

For example, the command

```
MAP H:=CONSTELLATION_SYS
```

would only work if the user's context were CBE_Labs. However, the command

```
MAP H:=.CONSTELLATION_SYS.CBE_Labs
```

will work every time.

Another trick is to use a Directory Map object that is in the user's current context once the user logs in. For example, if you create a SYS Directory Map object (or, for that matter, an Alias object called SYS), you can then reference this object in the login scripts:

```
MAP H:= SYS
```

where SYS is the Directory Map object in the user's current context.

Easing Management with Shortcut Objects

We mentioned earlier three types of objects that provide an in-context shortcut to out-of-context resources: Aliases, Application and Directory Map objects, and Groups. Each of these can reduce the hassle of managing a network while improving performance.

You would use an Alias to represent most NDS except a Directory Map object. Directory maps reference specific NetWare volumes, directories, and files. Groups, in contrast, gather together users who need a common set of tools, access rights, or other identity. These users can come from anywhere in the NDS tree.

Aliases provide an easier way to locate specific network resources that appear as NDS objects in the tree. (This makes the Alias object different from the Directory Map or Application objects that can reference non-NDS resources.) Users can use common names rather than distinguished names for resources that have aliases in the users' current context (their container or organizational unit). However, users still need access rights to the original object that the Alias object references.

 You should be acquainted with Alias objects, having used them from Chapter 7 on to represent the CBE Labs multiple-server environment with the single server in your lab.

You create Alias objects using NetWare Administrator. Right-click the container in which you want to place the object, then choose Create, then Alias. You can then specify a name for the Alias object and locate the referenced object in the NDS tree using the Browse button in the Create Alias dialog box.

Application and Directory Map objects differ in purpose, although they could perform the same task of granting access to an application. Application objects represent software that users will run, whereas Directory Map objects typically represent destinations for data produced by users' applications.

You create Application and Directory Map objects using the NetWare Administrator. Right-click the container where you want the object, choose Create, then Application. You could also choose Directory Map at that point to create a Directory Map object. With Application objects, you will have to select the program's main executable file. With Directory Map objects, you must specify the server volume and the directory path to the specific directory.

14

Again, you'll need to grant users (through the container object) access rights to the application and directories you specify. Otherwise the shortcut reference with the Application and Directory Map objects will be useless.

Groups provide you with a quick way to grant rights to network resources to users. Often you can place these rights in the users' container object to grant them access to resources. However, sometimes a certain type of user needs specific access but is not in the same container (or it does not make sense to put this type of user into the same container.)

Instead, NetWare provides the Group object type to gather these users together into a global container, so to speak. For example, suppose CBE Labs wants to provide each departmental manager with access to the spreadsheet files on projected annual earnings versus costs for the current year. This group would normally exist within their own containers for most of the time. By creating a group called Managers, with Read rights to these crucial files, these users' needs could be taken care of.

Another use of groups would be to fill a transitory staffing need. For example, suppose the CBE Labs shipping department required temporary help during certain times of the year to meet deadlines. By creating a group called TEMPS, the administrator could grant all required rights (printing, file access, mail access) to the group TEMPS for anyone who serves as a temp in the shipping department. When a temp is hired, the administrator need only create the User object in the shipping department's container, then make the user a member of the group TEMPS to have all the required rights.

Most important for security, only the Group object has rights across containers, rather than individual users. This again reduces the number of points to check for intruders.

Groups, like other objects, are created using the NetWare Administrator. Users can come from any part of the NDS tree to be a member of a group. The Group object alone needs to be referenced as a trustee in other objects for all members to have rights to the other objects.

CHAPTER SUMMARY

- ❑ Managing a network involves mastering the NetWare console commands and using several NetWare Loadable Modules (NLMs) to perform various tasks on the server computer. Console commands are built into the NetWare operating system and can be divided into four categories based on their use: installation commands, configuration commands, maintenance commands, and security commands.

❏ NLMs are external programs that are loaded into the server to control devices and add more functionality to the server. NLMs can also be divided into five categories based on their three-letter filename extensions. Host adapter cards use the extension .HAM, whereas specific disk drivers have the filename extension .CDM and enable NetWare, for example, to control an attached hard disk drive. LAN drivers have the extension .LAN and are used to attach the server to a network topology. Name space modules have the extension .NAM and provide NetWare with the additional logic needed to translate filenaming conventions from other workstation operating systems to NetWare's directory system. General-purpose modules have the extension .NLM and provide services to the network such as the MONITOR utility, which enables you to view server performance and status, or the NWConfig module, which is used for installation.

❏ It is often more convenient for a network administrator to operate the server console from a workstation in his or her office than to go to the server itself. The RCONSOLEJ program provides access to the console from a remote workstation. This requires upgrading a workstation to support the Java Virtual Machine or JVM.

❏ Protecting critical network data is one of the most important functions of a network administrator. Novell provides the Storage Management System (SMS) for this purpose. It lets the network administrator establish a backup-and-restore system that is capable of backing up all servers as well as data contained on local drives of the client workstations running a variety of operating systems.

❏ The importance of managing workstations on the network can never be over-looked. Novell provides Z.E.N.works to automate many of the time-consuming tasks of configuring and updating workstations. Using the Application Launcher, Z.E.N.works can deliver applications, system updates, service packs, or new clients to user desktops. It can also set policies for users, workstations, or containers that allow the administrator to manage the network to whatever degree of control is required. In effect, the network workstation can display exactly what the administrator specifies. Finally, Novell offers a full version of Z.E.N.works that includes both remote control and help desk software. These provide other ways to leverage NDS and ease the difficulty in managing large networks.

❏ NDS trees include multiple contexts. To ease management tasks and to preserve security, NDS includes shortcut objects to reduce or eliminate the need to grant individual users rights outside their containers. These objects include Group, Application, Directory Map, and Alias objects. Windows utilities provide an easy method for moving around in contexts to locate network resources. Administrators can also automate the setting of contexts using the Novell Client configuration and login scripts.

14

COMMAND SUMMARY

Command	Syntax	Definition
ADD NAME SPACE	*ADD NAME SPACE NAME volume_name*	Adds space to a volume's directory entry table to support other operating system file-naming conventions. Replace *name* with MAC or LONG. Replace *volume_name* with the volume to which the specified name space is to be added.
BIND	*BIND protocol TO driver | board_name [driver_parameters]*	Attaches a protocol to a LAN card. Replace *[driver_parameters]* with protocol name (e.g., IPX or IP). Replace *driver | board_name* with either the name of the card drive program or an optional name assigned to the network board. You can optionally replace *driver_parameters* with the hardware settings that identify the network interface card (e.g., I/O port and interrupt).
CLEAR STATION	*CLEAR STATION number*	Terminates the specified connection number.
CLS/OFF	*CLS/OFF*	Clears the server console screen.
CONFIG	*CONFIG*	Displays the current server's internal network number and information about each network card.
DISABLE LOGIN	*DISABLE LOGIN*	Prevents additional users from logging on.
DISMOUNT	*DISMOUNT volume_name [ALL]*	Closes a volume and removes it from the network.
DISPLAY [IPX] NETWORKS	*DISPLAY (IPX) NETWORKS*	Displays all network addresses and internal network numbers currently in the server's router table for servers. (The IPX parameter is optional.)

DISPLAY [IPX] SERVERS	*DISPLAY (IPX) SERVERS*	Displays the name of each network server currently in the server's router table. (The IPX parameter is optional.)
DOWN	*DOWN*	Removes all attachments to the server, dismounts the volumes, and takes the server off line.
DSREPAIR	*DSREPAIR*	Lets you repair the NDS directory tree.
ENABLE LOGIN	*ENABLE LOGIN*	Allows users to log in to the network.
LIST DEVICES	*LIST DEVICES*	Displays a list containing information about all device drivers attached to the network server.
LOAD	*LOAD [path] module_name [parameters]*	Loads an NLM in the file server's RAM. An optional path can be entered, depending on the module being loaded. Optionally replace *[path]* with the DOS or NetWare path leading to the directory containing the module to be loaded. Replace *module_name* with the name of the NLM you want to load. Optional parameters can be entered, depending on the module being loaded.
MEMORY	*MEMORY*	Displays the total amount of memory in the server computer.
MODULES	*MODULES*	Lists all currently loaded modules.
MOUNT	*MOUNT volume_name [ALL]*	Opens a volume for use on the network.
NAME	*NAME*	Displays on the console the name of the server computer.
PROTOCOL	*PROTOCOL*	Displays all protocols currently in use.

14

SCAN FOR NEW DEVICES	*SCAN FOR NEW DEVICES*	Causes the server to search for any additional devices that have been activated since the server was started.
SEARCH	*SEARCH [ADD path]* *SEARCH [DEL number]*	Adds or removes a directory path from the search path used by the LOAD command when NLMs are being loaded. When no parameters are specified, the current server search paths are displayed. To add a search path, replace *path* with the DOS or NetWare path leading to the directory from which you want to load NLMs. To delete an existing search path, replace *number* with the number of the search path to be deleted.
SECURE CONSOLE	SECURE CONSOLE	Increases the server's console security.
SEND	*SEND 'message' [TO] username	connection_number*	Transmits a message to a specific user or connection number.
SET	*SET*	Displays a menu of options that let you view or change network configuration parameters in the server.
SET TIME	*SET TIME [month/day/year] [hour:minute:second]*	Used by itself to display the current server time. Used with the date and time settings to change the server date and time.
TRACK	*TRACK ON/OFF*	Lets you see all service advertising packets that the server sends or receives.
UNBIND	*UNBIND protocol [FROM] LAN_driver	board_name*	Removes a protocol stack from a network card.
UNLOAD	*UNLOAD module_name*	Removes a NetWare Loadable Module from memory.

KEY TERMS

additive licenses

console commands

hop

host

Java

Java Virtual Machine (JVM)

Novell Licensing Services (NLS)

Storage Management System (SMS)

target

Target Service Agent (TSA)

tick

REVIEW QUESTIONS

1. _____ are external programs that are loaded into the memory of the server computer to add functionality to the NetWare operating system.

2. Console commands are built into the core server operating system program _____.

3. The _____ command is used to provide space on a volume for non-DOS filenames such as Macintosh or long names used in Windows 95/98.

4. The _____ command assigns a network address to a LAN driver.

5. Reading an NLM into memory and executing it is done by using the _____ command.

6. The _____ command shows total file memory available on the server computer.

7. The _____ command will cause the server to load NLMs from the SYS:SYSTEM\NLM directory when it does not find the requested module in the SYS:SYSTEM directory.

8. The _____ console command displays the network addresses assigned to each LAN in the server.

9. The _____ console command lets you know whether your newly installed server can "see" other servers on the network.

10. Suppose your server is up and running and you have just switched on an external CD-ROM drive but it does not show up in the CD-ROM device list. What would you do next?

11. Write a console command that changes the server's clock to 11:59 p.m. on December 31, 1999.

14

12. Write the sequence of commands a network administrator should enter before turning off the server computer in the middle of the day.

13. After starting the server, you notice that the TEXT volume did not mount because of errors in the file allocation table. Identify which NLM can be used to fix the volume and then the command necessary to bring the TEXT volume back online.

14. After you load the NE2000 Ethernet card driver and bind the IPX protocol with the network address 1EEE8023, your server begins reporting router configuration errors that indicate that other servers on the network are using the network address 10Base2 for the Ethernet LAN. Write the commands you can use to correct the problem.

15. The _____ console command prevents NetWare from loading NLMs from the SYS:PUBLIC\NLM directory.

16. NetWare disk drivers all have the _____ file extension.

17. If the number in the Total cache buffers field on the MONITOR screen is less than _____ of the amount in the Original cache buffers field, you need to add more memory to your server.

18. Your server has just crashed, and now the SYS volume will not load. The _____ utility can be used to repair that volume.

19. Enter the correct sequence of commands to provide a redundant remote console link on your server.

20. List the software modules that must be installed on the host server so that the SMS backup facility can be used.

21. The _____ program checks the date of the current programs on each workstation and then automatically updates a program having a date prior to the version stored on the server.

HANDS-ON PROJECTS

Project 14-1: Downing the Server

In this project, you use NetWare console commands to perform the specified console operations and obtain requested information. So that you can perform this exercise, your instructor will provide you with access to a specified NetWare server console.

1. Use the CONFIG command to obtain the following information about a network board:

Driver: _____

I/O port: _____

Network address: _____

Frame type: _____

Protocol: _____

2. Use the DISPLAY NETWORKS command to document the different networks currently in use at your location. On the following lines, identify each network address along with the number of hops and ticks required to reach that network.

Network address   Number of hops   Number of ticks

_____   _____   _____

_____   _____   _____

_____   _____   _____

3. Use the DISPLAY SERVERS command to identify up to three servers available from your network. On the following lines, identify each server's name along with the number of hops needed to reach that server.

NetWare server name   Number of hops

_____   _____

_____   _____

_____   _____

4. Set the date and time on the server to 8:30 a.m. on December 28, 1999. Record here the command or command you would use: _____

5. Explain how to by perform the following procedures to down a server. In the spaces provided, record each command or commands you would use.

   a. Load MONITOR to determine the number of connections. _____

   b. Prevent any new logins. _____

   c. Send a message to all users that the server is going down. _____

   d. Take the SYS volume off line. _____

   e. Use the VREPAIR utility from the DOS partition of your server (drive C), and check the volume for any errors. _____

   f. Use the DSREPAIR utility to check directory services for errors.

   g. Bring the volume back on line. _____

   h. Remove DOS. _____

   i. Try to load the VREPAIR utility from the C disk drive, and record the message displayed. _____

   j. Clear any existing connections. _____

   k. Down the server. _____

14

6. Because DOS has been removed from the server, exiting the server should cause the server computer to restart. What would happen on your server computer when you exited to the DOS prompt? _____

If you had actually downed the server in Step 5, you would follow these steps to bring the server back on line.

a. Use the **TRACK ON** command to view the router tracking screen. Record an OUT packet message, and identify it as either a SAP or RIP packet.

b. Press [**Ctrl**] + [**Esc**] to change from the TRACK screen to the console prompt.

c. Enter the **RESET ROUTER** command to rebuild the router table. Then press [**Alt**] + [**Esc**] to rotate to the TRACK screen. What effect does the RESET ROUTER command have on the TRACK screen?

d. Use the **TRACK OFF** command to exit the tracking function.

e. Use the **UNBIND** and **BIND** commands to change the network address assigned to the network card from its current address to **BEEBEE**. What command do you use?

f. Change the address back to its original number. What command do you use?

g. Enter the **SECURE CONSOLE** command. Attempt to change the date back one year. What was the result?

h. Record the modules that are currently loaded in the server.

Project 14-2: Working with NLMs

In this project, you will use NLMs to obtain information but you do not modify the existing server environment. It can therefore be done on any server to which the instructor has provided you access.

1. Use the MONITOR NLM to obtain the following information about your server:

Version and release date of server: _____

Original cache buffers: _____

Total cache buffers: _____

Packet receive buffers: _____

Number of connections: _____

Number of Hot Fix redirection blocks: _____

Number of Hot Fix redirected blocks: _____

Total packets received: _____

Number of packets received that were too large: _____

2. Load the SCRSAVER screen saver NLM to lock the console with a password obtained from your instructor.

3. Use the **SCRSAVER HELP** command to obtain information on how to perform the console locking procedure.

4. Load the CDROM module.

5. Use the HELP utility to identify the command to view installed devices on this server.

6. Use the appropriate command to list any existing devices. Record the fields of information available in the onscreen display.

7. Use the NWConfig module to determine the following:

The size of the SYS volume in megabytes. _____

Whether any free space is available to be assigned to an existing volume.

Record the number of free space: _____

The size of the DOS and NetWare partitions.

DOS: _____

NetWare: _____

Project 14-3: Managing a Remote Console

In this project you configure and load the appropriate remote access tool on the server designated by your instructor and perform the following procedure from the server:

1. Load support for remote console management on the designated server. Modify the startup files to load this support automatically each time the server is started. Record the commands you place in the startup file.

Name of startup file containing remote console commands:

Commands included:

2. Create a remote console operator. If you do not have supervisory rights on the server, your instructor will provide you with rights to the RCONSOLEJ programs.

3. Log in as a remote console operator from a workstation.

4. Access the server console. Record the console message received as a result of accessing the remote console.

5. Scan the files in the server's DOS drive.

6. Copy a file from the workstation to the C drive of the server.

7. Print the screen and highlight the new file.

14

Project 14-4: Defining a User with Multiple Context Resources

In this project you create and configure a user with the appropriate access to resources. These resources exist in another container besides the one in which the user resides.

1. Create a new user in your CBE Labs tree in the Software container of the Test&Eval Organizational Unit. Use your own name—first initial and your last name—as the user name.

2. Grant this user rights to manage records in the CONSTELLATION_SYS:MAIL directory.

3. Grant this user rights to read the contents of the ETC directory.

4. Discuss why or why not to give the new user access to the CONSTELLA-TION_SYS: volume object.

5. Grant this user access to the lab printer object.

6. Create a Directory Map object called DATA in the CBE_Labs_Admin container. Have this point to the CONSTELLATION_DATA: volume object.

7. Grant your new user only READ and FILE SCAN rights to this directory.

8. Grant your user the Read right to the Path property of the Directory Map object.

9. Discuss which login script—user or container—you will use for setting drive mappings for this user. These mappings will be for drive F, which will point to the DATA volume on CONSTELLATION, and for drive G, which will point to the MAIL directory on the SYS volume of CONSTELLATION.

10. Specify these mappings so that they will work regardless of the user's current context.

11. Log in as your new user, and verify your configuration.

12. Record your steps in creating and configuring your environment. Deliver this report to your instructor.

Project 14-5: Performing Workstation Registration Using Application Launcher

When you installed Z.E.N.works, it also created two Application objects in your NDS tree called WREG32 and WREG16. As administrator for CBE Labs, you will need to register the workstations in the tree, starting with the Test&Eval container. In this project you will configure Application Launcher to distribute and run the appropriate platform workstation registration software. You will then verify that the workstation correctly ran the software.

1. Right-click the **Test&Eval** container object in your CBELABS tree.

2. Select the **Details** option, then choose the **Applications** tab. The NetWare Administrator displays the container's current list of applications to run using Application Launcher. (It may be blank if you haven't defined it before.)

3. Click **Add**. Select the **WREG32** Application object from the tree. Browse if necessary to locate this object. Click **OK**. WREG32 now will appear in the list.

4. Check the left-most box on the WREG32 application. This is the Forced Run box, which means the software will run as soon as the user logs in.

5. Click the **Login Script** tab. Verify that the container login script includes the line:

       @\\CONSTELLATION\SYS\PUBLIC\NAL

    If it isn't there, add it.

6. Click **OK** to save your container configuration.

7. Test this configuration by logging in as GBurns.

8. Verify that your workstation ran the software correctly. Run the Windows Explorer program.

9. Locate the WSREG32.LOG file, which will be stored at the root of your local C drive.

10. Double-click **WSREG32.LOG** to open it into Notepad.

11. Review the information shown there, then close Notepad.

12. Copy the WSREG32.LOG file onto a floppy disk, and turn it in to your instructor after completing this project.

CASE PROJECTS

Case
Project

Case 14-1: Restarting a Remote Server

14

Nashville Net and Twine (NN&T), a leading distributor of commercial and recreational nets and accessories, has a long history of working with local area schools in a co-op program. One area in which NN&T has just started using students is in the Information Systems support group. You have been asked to participate in the co-op and help NN&T with networking. First you are asked to help NN&T develop the steps to restart a remote server located at the warehouse. These steps will take the form of a document that will be available for the third-shift Information Systems employees who only occasionally may need to perform this function, yet need written documentation to help remind them of the steps.

To do this project, you need access to a server that is not currently being used by other students. Your instructor will provide you with a time when—or a NetWare server on which—this project can be performed.

For each of the following steps, record the actions you took.

1. Disable new logins.
2. Broadcast a message indicating that employees of NN&T cannot log in until further notice.
3. Use the **LOAD EDIT C:\AUTOEXEC.BAT** command to be sure the server will automatically load when the computer is restarted.
4. Use the **EDIT** command to create an NCF file using your name and the extension .NCF. In the NCF file, include the commands necessary to restart the server. Record the commands.
5. Execute the NCF file to restart the server.
6. Wait for the server to come back on line and then attempt to access it through the RCONSOLE utility. If necessary, restart your workstation and log back in. Record what actions you need to take to reattach to the server once it is back on line.
7. Create a document that outlines the steps just listed.

Case 14-2: Backing Up the NetWare Server

Nashville Net and Twine (NN&T) has now requested that you document the steps involved in backing up the server. Although the company has an employee who performs this function each evening, it still wants to have this document on file in the event she is out sick or on vacation. In this project you use the SBCON program along with the device driver provided by your instructor to back up the SYS:PUBLIC directory on the "installation" server.

Create a document that outlines the steps to back up the server.

Case 14-3: Updating Workstation Software

In the process of helping NN&T, you have become aware that its Novell Client software is not the most recent version available from Novell. Some of the minor problems that the company has been having may be caused by these outdated files. You have taken it on yourself to update Novell Client.

Through the Internet, access a NetWare site and find the latest Novell Client versions. Download these files and place them on the server. Use Z.E.N.works to update the Novell Client at each workstation and put the procedure in the profile login script.

A

NetWare 5.1 CNA Objectives

This book originally was written to meet the NetWare 5.0 CNA objectives as of January 1999. With the release of NetWare 5.1, the CNA objectives have been updated to include some of the new features found in NetWare 5.1. Because the NetWare 5.0 CNA test is constantly being revised and updated, you should obtain the latest CNA objectives by checking the Novell Education Web site at http://education.novell.com for details. Table A-1 is intended to help you study for the CNA test by relating each of the August 2000 objectives to one or more chapters in this textbook.

Table A-1   NetWare 5.1 CNA Objective Update

Number	CNA Objective	Chapter(s)/Appendix
1	Describe what a network is, and list its components.	1
2	Describe what NetWare is, and list the types of workstations you can use to access it.	1
3	List the responsibilities of a network administrator.	1
4	List the NetWare resources and services you will learn to administer.	1
5	Describe Novell Directory Services (NDS), including the NDS Directory and NDS objects.	1, 2
6	Describe how a workstation communicates with the network.	1
7	Install the Novell Client software.	2
8	Explain and perform the login procedure.	1
9	Install and configure a browser client.	9
10	Create and modify a user account using NetWare Administrator.	2, 4
11	Create a User object with the Java-based Console One utility.	10, B
12	Use the DOS utility UIMPORT to create User objects.	4

Table A-1 NetWare 5.1 CNA Objective Update (continued)

Number	CNA Objective	Chapter(s)/Appendix
13	Describe and establish login security, including login restrictions for users.	4
14	Describe NetWare printing using NDPS.	7
15	Explain the four NDPS components and their functions.	7
16	List the NDPS printer types, and explain the difference between public access printers and controlled access printers.	7
17	Configure the network for NDPS.	7
18	Configure a workstation to print to NDPS printers.	7
19	Manage printer access and print jobs.	7
20	Use utilities to perform file system management tasks	3, 5
21	Access the file system by configuring drive mappings.	3
22	Select the correct utilities for managing the directory structure.	3
23	Select the correct utilities for managing files.	3
24	Manage the use of volume space using NetWare Administrator.	3
25	Explain how file system security works.	5
26	Plan and implement file system security for your organization.	5
27	Plan and implement file and directory attribute security.	5
28	Describe the types of login scripts, and explain how they coordinate at login.	8
29	Design login scripts for containers, user groups, and users.	8
30	Use the MAP command to map network drives from a login script.	3, 8
31	Create, execute, and debug a login script.	8
32	Define NDS security and how it differs from file system security.	6
33	Control access to an object in the NDS tree.	6
34	Determine rights granted to NDS objects.	6
35	Block an object's inherited rights to other NDS objects.	6
36	Determine effective rights.	6
37	Explain guidelines and considerations for implementing NDS security.	6
38	Troubleshoot NDS security problems using NetWare Administrator.	6
39	Explain the benefits of using Application Launcher.	9

Table A-1   NetWare 5.1 CNA Objective Update (continued)

Number	CNA Objective	Chapter(s)/Appendix
40	Explain the components of Application Launcher.	9
41	Distribute applications using Application Launcher and snAppShot.	9
42	Manage applications with Application Launcher.	9
43	Describe the available Z.E.N.works products and their purposes.	9
44	Describe Z.E.N.works policy packages and policies.	9
45	Identify NDS design considerations for Z.E.N.works.	B
46	Register workstations in NDS, and import them into the NDS tree using NetWare Administrator.	9
47	Use policies to configure desktop environment.	9
48	Establish remote control access to workstations on the network.	9, B
49	Set up and use the Help Requester application.	9, B
50	Identify NDS planning guidelines to follow in sample directory structures.	6
51	Provide users with access to resources.	2, 6
52	Create shortcuts to access and manage network resources.	6
53	Identify the actions to take and the rights needed to grant a user access to NDS resources.	6
54	Create login scripts that identify resources in other contexts.	8
55	Describe the function of a NetWare server and its interface, and identify the server components.	1
56	Perform a basic NetWare 5.0 server installation.	B
57	Install the Novell Licensing Service (NLS).	10, C
58	Managing licensing through NLS.	10, B

B

UPGRADING TO AND INSTALLING NETWARE 5.1

Your primary responsibility as a network administrator is to set up and maintain the NetWare network environment after NetWare has been installed on the server(s). The tasks of installing NetWare and configuring the server's computer hardware are often performed by technical support specialists. In addition to providing the Certified Novell Administrator (CNA) program, Novell provides a separate Certified Novell Engineer (CNE) program to certify technical support specialists in planning, installing, and troubleshooting NetWare. Because network administrators do not usually need to install NetWare on the server computer, installing or upgrading NetWare is not a task required to become a CNA. However, a CNA needs to understand the basic installation process and options to be successful in planning and maintaining the network system.

NetWare 5.1 provides several major enhancements to NetWare 5.0 that strengthen its capabilities as an e-commerce platform and Internet server. Although many of these enhancements are directed toward Internet applications and e-commerce, NetWare 5.1 also includes additional management tools and an improved version of NDS, called eDirectory. In this appendix, you will learn about the new NetWare 5.1 enhancements as well as how to upgrade an existing NetWare server or install NetWare 5.1 on a new server.

To better understand how the NetWare 5.1 enhancements can be applied to a business environment, you will be placed in the role of a network administrator for the Universal Aerospace (UAS) company and help it as it upgrades to NetWare 5.1. Universal Aerospace is a fictitious aerospace company that specializes in designing and manufacturing high-tech aerospace components. After obtaining a NASA contract to design and manufacture components for both the International Space Station and Mars Rover projects, Universal Aerospace installed a NetWare 5.0 server with a Novell Directory Services (NDS) tree structure. The tree structure includes separate containers for the users and resources of the Business, Engineering, and Manufacturing Departments, as shown in Figure B-1.

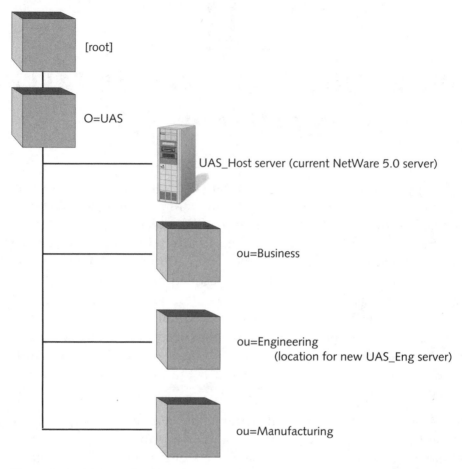

Figure B-1   Universal Aerospace tree containers

In the last year, Universal Aerospace expanded its organization to support the NASA contracts. As part of the expansion project, management would like to add a new server in the Engineering Department. Placing a new server in Engineering will allow the large engineering files and applications to be removed from the UAS_HOST server, thereby providing additional space and capacity on UAS_HOST to accommodate the growth of the Business and Manufacturing Departments. Future expansion plans call for adding another server to support the projected growth of the business and manufacturing applications.

Because the new servers will be installed with NetWare 5.1, the consultant has recommended upgrading the existing UAS_HOST server from NetWare 5.0 to 5.1 to take full advantage of the NetWare 5.1 enhancements. To start, management has asked you to work with the network consultant to develop a proposal listing the benefits of converting to NetWare 5.1, along with a conversion plan and schedule for the next weekly meeting.

After discussing with you the expansion of the Universal Aerospace network, your consultant has recommended that you include the following six advantages of upgrading to NetWare 5.1 in your proposal to management:

- The new NDS version 8 eDirectory system will provide for an almost unlimited number of objects in the NDS tree, along with better performance for reads, writes, and searches. A major advantage gained by Universal Aerospace will be eDirectory's ability to support improved management tasks using ConsoleOne and the new NetWare Management Portal. EDirectory also contains an improved version of the DSREPAIR utility that is important in managing and troubleshooting problems that may occur periodically in NDS networks. In addition, eDirectory's support of a variety of operating systems through an improved version of the Lightweight Directory Access Protocol (LDAP) will be important in helping to integrate the Linux and Windows 2000 applications we discussed. The new BULKLOAD utility improves on the original NetWare 5.0 UIMPORT utility by allowing a variety of NDS objects to be added, modified, or deleted through a batch process.

- The new NetWare Management Portal provides a browser-based tool that can be used from either Netscape or Internet Explorer to remotely access and manage the company's NetWare volumes, servers, applications, NDS objects, and schemas, as well as monitor server health and hardware, while working from home or traveling to other internet-connected sites.

- NetWare 5.1 includes a Deployment Manager tool (NWDEPLOY.EXE) that runs on a client and can be used to prepare the existing network before upgrading to NetWare 5.1. In addition, Deployment Manager can be used to update an existing NetWare 5.1 server with products that were not installed during the initial server installation.

- An important part of the Universal Aerospace network expansion plan is to replace existing dial-up network access with a router to allow users higher-speed access the Internet. Because registered IP addresses are difficult to obtain, assigning each client a registered IP address may not be feasible. In addition, having "live" Internet addresses can allow an intruder to gain access to a client computer through an open Internet connection port. NetWare 5.1 provides a solution to these needs through Network Address Translation or NAT. NAT will allow you to use your NetWare 5.1 server as a router between the company's intranet using privately assigned IP addresses and the Internet. Only one registered IP address will need to be assigned to the NetWare 5.1 server's Internet connection. Whenever a client needs to access a service on the Internet, its default gateway setting will direct the packet to the NetWare 5.1 server. NAT running on the NetWare 5.1 server will then replace the client's IP address with its registered IP address and send the packet out to the Internet host. NAT assigns a port number to the connection with the outside host to save connection information. When the Internet host responds, NAT uses the port number assigned to that connection to retrieve the client's information and then send the Internet host's response back to the requesting client. The NetWare 5.1 NAT system eliminates the cost of a dedicated router and effectively isolates the clients from unwanted Internet access, while still providing access to outside services.

■ Although Universal Aerospace currently is not soliciting business on the Internet, NetWare 5.1 contains the following enhancements intended to help businesses develop and manage e-commerce applications. The Netware 5.1 enhanced Internet and e-commerce capabilities will be important should Universal Aerospace want to develop any of the following Internet services in the future.

- A fully integrated **enterprise web server** that is specifically adapted for maximum performance in the NetWare 5.1 eDirectory environment

- A **NetWare FTP Server** to provide for transfer of files to and from NetWare volumes

- **A NetWare News Server** you can use to host group discussions and forums; the NetWare News Server uses the Network News Transport Protocol (NNTP) to provide compatibility with other NNTP news servers.

- A **NetWare MultiMedia Server**, which provides multimedia streaming capabilities on a NetWare server platform; the NetWare MultiMedia Server supports the WAV, MP3, MPEG-1, and RM file formats.

- A **NetWare Web Search** engine that provides a powerful and customizable search and print solution to let you index information located on a NetWare or web server; the NetWare Web Search engine runs from a super-thin Java client that downloads quickly and yet is powerful enough to perform searches in alternative languages.

- The **IBM WebSphere Application Server** provides a robust and portable environment to deploy and manage Java Applications running under NetWare. Novell is working to integrate NDS and other services and products with IBM WebSphere to ensure an open application server model that leverages the best tools and services available.

■ The **Novell Certificate Authority** service allows your organization to issue digital certificates to clients to provide secure, encrypted transmission for users of your network. The Novell Certificate Server uses Public Key Cryptography consisting of public and private keys to secure e-mail, web servers, and network applications, such as LDAP.

Upgrading an existing network to NetWare 5.1 requires planning and experience. The networking consultant has recommended that your proposal to management include the following four phase approach to upgrading the existing Universal Aerospace network from NetWare 5.0 to 5.1.

1. Prepare for the network upgrade and installation. You will need sufficient time to evaluate server hardware requirements, identify drivers, plan protocol usage, and determine NDS context locations for the new server.

2. Use Deployment Manager to upgrade your existing NetWare 5.0 tree structure to NDS 8 eDirectory and install the NetWare 5.1 Licensing Service (NLS).

3. Install the new NetWare 5.1 server in the Engineering Department.

4. Upgrade existing NetWare 5.0 UAS_HOST server to NetWare 5.1.

After reviewing your recommendation, Universal Aerospace management has given its approval to install a new NetWare 5.1 server in the Engineering Department and upgrade the existing network from NetWare 5.0 to 5.1. Because of your busy schedule and the need to do this quickly, management has agreed to have Eric Kenton from Computer Technology Services upgrade the existing UAS_HOST server to NetWare 5.1 and install NetWare 5.1 on the new Engineering server. In this appendix you will learn the NetWare 5.1 upgrade and installation process by following Eric Kenton as he uses Deployment Manager to upgrade the Universal Aerospace network, installs NetWare 5.1 on the new Engineering server, and then upgrades the existing NetWare 5.0 server to NetWare 5.1.

PREPARING FOR NETWARE INSTALLATION

Just as in other activities, preparation is important to the success of your NetWare server installation. Preparing for NetWare installation involves determining the hardware configuration of the server computer as well as identifying the physical and logical network environment in which the server is to be installed. A NetWare server's hardware environment can become quite complex with two or more disk drives and controllers, multiple volumes, network card configurations, and protocols. To help identify and manage all this information, the Universal Aerospace consultant has prepared a NetWare Server Worksheet as shown in Figure B-2. In this section you will refer to this Worksheet to help you learn how to prepare for a NetWare server installation by identifying the hardware configuration and network information you will need to install NetWare 5.1 successfully.

NetWare Server Worksheet

Page 1 of 2

File Server Name: ENG-HOST _____ **Internal Network #**:   random __X__
                                                                        assigned _____

System Information

Computer make/model: _____
CPU: _Intel Celeron_   **Clock Speed**: _566 MHz_   **BUS**: _PCI_
Memory Capacity: 19_6 MB_

Disk Information
Disk Controller 1
    Type: _SCSI_   Manufacture\model: _Adaptec 2940_
    Interrupt: _5_____   I/O Address: _340-343_   DMA channel: _3_
    Memory address:_____ - _____
    Disk Driver name: _AHA2940_

Drive Address	Type	Manufacturer	Speed\ Capacity	Partition Size DOS	NetWare	Mirrored with Controller	Drive
0	SCSI	Western Digital	12 ms/20GB	100 MB	19 GB	2	

Disk Controller 2
    Type: _SCSI_   Manufacture\model: _Adaptec 2940_
    Interrupt: _11_____   I/O Address: _350-353_   DMA channel: _3_
    Memory address:_____ - _____
    Disk Driver name: _AHA2940_

Drive Address	Type	Manufacturer	Speed\ Capacity	Partition Size DOS	NetWare	Mirrored with Controller	Drive
0	SCSI	Western Digital	12 ms/20GB	100 MB	19 GB	1	

Volume Information

Volume Name	Capacity	Partition (Controller number/Drive)
SYS	2 GB	Controller 1 drive 0
Eng-data	16 GB	Controller 1 drive 0
Free	2 GB	Controller 1 drive 0

Network Card Information

Card Number	Network Type	Manu- id	Driver	LAN Bus	I/O Port	Memory Address	IRQ/DMA
1	100BASET	Microdyne	NE2000	PCI	300	0D000	10/None

Figure B-2   NetWare 5.1 Server Worksheet

B

NetWare Server Worksheet

TCP/IP Protocol Information

Network Card: 3COM3C90X
Frame type: Ethernet II
    IP Address: 192.168.1.51
      IP Mask: 255.255.255.0
      Gateway: 192.168.1.1

IPX Protocol Information

Network Card: 3COM3C90X
Frame type: 802.2
Network Address: 1EEE8022

Server NDS Context

Tree name: *UA_Tree*   Organization: *UAS*   Organizational Unit: *Engineering*

Figure B-2   NetWare 5.1 Server Worksheet (continued)

Determining Server Hardware Requirements

NetWare is a network operating system (NOS) that is designed to perform server functions. Essentially, both NetWare 5.0 and 5.1 consist of an operating system kernel (SERVER.EXE) that provides core NetWare server services to the network along with a software bus that allows other modules containing specialized services and control functions to be loaded and unloaded, as shown in Figure B-2. In addition to providing file and print services, both NetWare 5.0 and 5.1 servers can run Java-based applications as well as communicate directly using the TCP/IP (Transport Control Protocol/Internet Protocol) protocol.

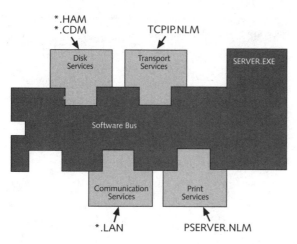

Figure B-3   NetWare software bus

In order to support the Kernel, NLM services, and enhanced Java based console and applications, NetWare 5.1 requires considerably more memory and CPU speed than previous versions. The minimum hardware environment specifications for a NetWare 5.1 server are shown in Table B-1.

Table B-1   NetWare 5.1 minimum hardware requirements

Processor	Pentium 166 MHz or Higher
Disk space	Minimum 50 MB free on DOS partition
	750 MB free space on volume SYS for standard NetWare products and an additional 750 MB for the WebSphere Application Server for NetWare
Memory	128 MB RAM for standard NetWare products and an additional 128 MB (512 MB total recommended) for WebSphere Application Server for NetWare
Network	A NetWare 5.1-compatible Network board
CD drive	A CD drive that can read ISO 9660-formatted CDs
Monitor	VGA or better

The Server Name and Internal Number

Each NetWare server on the network must have a unique name and internal number assigned to it. The internal number is used to create a logical network that is used to send packets of data between modules attached to the software bus. The server name can consist of up to 45 characters, including special characters such as $, &, and *.

The internal network number can consist of up to eight hexadecimal digits, and it can be either a random number assigned by the installation program or a specific number identified by the organization. If your server is to be attached to a wide area network with other servers of which you do not have control, you may wish to register your internal number with Novell to ensure that it is unique. If you do not need a registered number, the best alternative is to allow the NetWare installation program to assign a random number and then record the assigned internal network number on the NetWare Server Worksheet shown in Figure B-3.

Disk Information

Because NetWare 5.1 is a complete operating system that is independent from DOS, it requires its own disk drivers to access the computer's disk system. As a result, one of the first steps you need to perform in preparing for NetWare 5.1 installation is to obtain information regarding the disk controller card and drives used on the server computer. This information is important because during installation you will need to select and configure the correct disk driver for your server's disk hardware. For example, before installing NetWare 5.1 on the new Engineering server, Eric identified the type, make, and model of the disk controller and drives on the NetWare Server Worksheet shown in Figure B-2.

Selecting The Disk Drivers

Most server computers use either IDE (Intelligent Drive Electronics) or SCSI (Small Computer System Interface) disk controller cards. Larger servers that support more storage devices, such as large hard drives, CD-ROMs, and tape back-up systems, often use SCSI controllers because they provide higher speeds and support a wider range of devices than IDE controllers. On the other hand, for the same cost, IDE controllers often provide higher storage capacity at acceptable speeds. Universal Aerospace selected a SCSI disk controller because the corporation is planning to expand its storage devices in the future to support additional disk drives along with a planned optical disk system for archiving engineering designs.

In addition to the type of controller, the make and model are important to select the correct driver during installation. NetWare 5.1 comes with drivers for many popular SCSI disk controllers, such as the Adaptec 2940 being used by Universal Aerospace. In previous versions of NetWare, most disk drivers consisted of a single driver file with the extension .DSK. The .DSK drivers included in previous NetWare versions were used to manage the server's disk controller card along with all storage devices attached to it. To support more sophisticated SCSI controllers with a wider range of storage devices, Novell introduced a new driver system with NetWare 4.11. The new driver system provides for a wider range of storage devices by using Host Bus Adapter (HBA) drivers with the extension .HBA to manage the controller cards and Custom Device Modules (CDM) with the extension .CDM to control the individual storage devices attached to the controller card. Starting with NetWare 5.0, the older DSK modules are no longer supported, and you will need to be sure that the disk controller you select for the server has the necessary HBA and CDM modules available for NetWare 5.1. Disk controllers that do not have HBA and CDM modules included with NetWare will need to have their NetWare drivers loaded from a floppy disk supplied by the manufacturer before they can be used with NetWare. Therefore, to make installation simpler, when selecting a SCSI disk controller for a server, check to see that the disk controller you select is included with NetWare. In most cases, you can best ensure that this is the case by purchasing controller cards that are NetWare 5 certified.

In addition to the SCSI controllers, NetWare includes HBA and CDM modules for IDE controllers that will handle most IDE and Enhanced IDE (EIDE) type controllers with drives ranging from 500 MB to over 2 GB. As with SCSI controllers, it is best to select an IDE controller that has been Novell certified.

Planning Disk Partitions

Once the disk controller has been selected and the driver has been identified, the next step in preparing for server installation is to define the amount of disk storage to be allocated to DOS and NetWare. On a NetWare server, disk storage space is divided into two separate areas called **partitions**—one partition for use by DOS in booting the server computer and the other partition for use by the NetWare operating system. The DOS partition is quite small; usually 50 MB is recommended to start the computer initially and then start the NetWare SERVER.EXE program. The remainder of the disk space on the drive is then reserved for the NetWare partition as shown on the NetWare Server Worksheet in Figure B-3. Once the SERVER program is running, the correct disk driver for the controller card will be loaded to provide access to the NetWare partition.

Another consideration in planning NetWare volumes is disk mirroring or duplexing. **Disk mirroring** is the process of duplicating data on two different NetWare partitions. **Duplexing** occurs when the partitions are on drives attached to different controller cards. To do mirroring or duplexing, the NetWare partitions on the drives to be mirrored must be the same size. The NetWare Server Worksheet shown in Figure B-2 contains a section to identify the NetWare partition size for each disk drive attached to a controller, along with a Mirrored column that may be used to specify any mirrored partitions.

Identifying the NetWare Volume Requirements

After the size of the DOS and NetWare partitions have been defined, the next step is to identify the NetWare volumes to be created. Each NetWare server must have a SYS volume to contain operating system files. At a minimum, the SYS volume for a NetWare 5.1 server should be at least 750 MB, but in most cases you will want an additional 750 MB to contain space for additional services such as the Web server. In the NetWare Server Specification Worksheet shown in Figure B-2, Eric identified two volumes: a 2 GB SYS volume and 16 GB Eng-data volume, leaving at least 2 GB of free space on the NetWare partition. It is a good idea to leave some free space in the NetWare partition. The NetWare partition's free space can later be used to expand an existing volume or to create a new volume.

The Network Environment

To communicate with other devices on the network, a server computer needs at least one network interface card. Additional network interface cards, up to eight, may be installed to allow access to the server from multiple network cable systems. When multiple network cards are installed in a server, the server will act as a router, passing packets of data among network cable systems. Figure B-4 illustrates how a NetWare 5.1 server with multiple network interface cards (NICs) could be used to connect both the Engineering and Business department networks to the Internet. A packet from a workstation in the Business network destined for the Engineering server would first be sent from the workstation to the UAS_HOST server. After receiving the packet, the UAS_HOST server would compare the network address of the receiver to network address assigned to each NIC and then re-transmit the packet on the NIC attached to the engineering network.

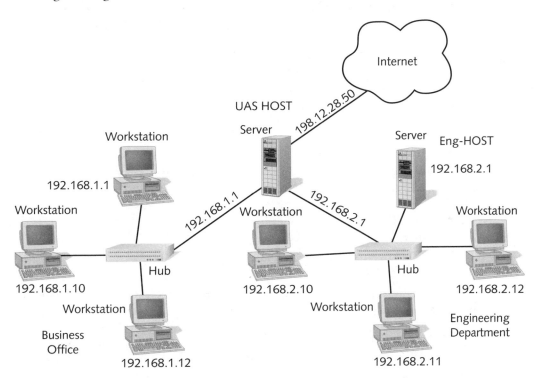

Figure B-4   Universal Aerospace intranet layout

To access network interface cards, NetWare requires a driver to be identified for each NIC during installation. As a result, before installing NetWare 5.1 on the server computer, you will need to identify the make, model, and configuration for each network interface card in your server. To make installation easier, NetWare contains drivers for many popular network interface cards. As with disk controllers, one of the best ways to be sure a driver for your network card is included with NetWare is to purchase a card that has been Novell certified. Along with identifying the make and model of each network card, during installation you will also need to supply the hardware configuration for the card. The card's hardware configuration can consist of an interrupt, Direct Memory Access (DMA) channel, input/output port, and memory address. You can configure the card by using special software or by placing jumpers or setting switches on the card itself. The NetWare Server Worksheet shown in Figure B-2 shows the network card and configuration used with the Universal Aerospace server.

Defining Network Protocol Usage

After you have identified the network interface cards to be installed in the server computer, the other major consideration in configuring the network environment is identifying the network protocol(s) the server will need to support. The network protocol environment consists of network protocols along with the network address and frame type to be used for each network card in the server. In addition to providing the legacy IPX (Internet Packet eXchange) protocol, Novell enables NetWare 5.1 to communicate directly using the TCP/IP protocol. The IPX protocol has the advantage of being simpler to set up as well as providing compatibility with older NetWare servers. Although more complex to implement, the TCP/IP protocol is a more universal protocol and enables you to connect the server to the Internet through an Internet service provider (ISP) or provide services directly to a company intranet. Because of the existing NetWare 3 server and applications, Universal Aerospace has decided initially to install support for both IPX and TCP/IP on the server. After converting all servers, workstations, and applications to TCP/IP, the corporation can remove support for IPX from the NetWare 5.0 and 5.1 servers. In this section, you will learn about the factors that affect the IPX and TCP/IP protocols along with how they apply to the Universal Aerospace server installation.

The IPX Protocol

When installing the IPX protocol, you must assign each network cable system a unique network address and frame type. The frame type specifies the format of the data packets to be sent across the network cable. To communicate, all computers need to use a common frame type. Because the default Ethernet frame type used with IPX packets is 802.2, Eric has entered 802.2 in the frame type field of the NetWare Server Worksheet.

The network address works much like a zip code in that it allows packets to be efficiently delivered to the correct network cable of the recipient. If you are installing the first server on the network cable, you can use any network address consisting of up to eight hexadecimal digits. Additional servers attached to the same network cable will then also need to use the same network address of the existing server. As the NetWare Server Worksheet in Figure B-2 shows, Eric has selected a network address of 1EEE8022 for the 10BaseT network card. He selected this number because it stands for the IEEE 802.2 standard used by the 10BaseT Ethernet card.

B

The TCP/IP Protocol

As described earlier, in addition to the IPX protocol, NetWare also supports TCP/IP. The TCP/IP protocol column of the NetWare Server Worksheet, shown in Figure B-2, may be used to identify information regarding the TCP/IP protocol that will be configured during installation. To install support for the TCP/IP protocol during installation, you will need to supply the server with an IP address and mask. An IP address consists of a 32-bit (4-byte) number that is divided into a network address and a host or node address. The network part of the address must be the same for all computers on the same network cable segment. The host or node address must be unique for each computer on that network segment. The network mask identifies what bytes in an IP address are part of the network address. The number 255 in the network mask identifies the entire byte as part of the network address. Zeros in the network mask identify bits that are part of the host or node address.

IP addresses are divided into three classes. A Class A address has a default network mask of 255.0.0.0, indicating that only the first byte represents the network address. A Class B address has a default network mask of 255.255.0.0, indicating that the first two bytes represent the network portion of the address, and the last two bytes represent the host or node. A Class C address has a default mask of 255.255.255.0, indicating that the first three bytes are the network address, and only the last byte may be used to represent the node. Because 0 and 255 are not valid node values, a Class C address provides for up to 254 devices to access the network at the same time. If your company will be attaching its network or server to the Internet, you need to obtain an IP address range for your company to use. You can obtain a registered Internet address by contacting your local Internet Service Provider (ISP). For example, assume that Universal Aerospace is planning to attach its server to the network in the near future, and that Universal Aerospace President David Heise has obtained a class C address of 198.12.28.50 for the Universal Aerospace server. Rather than obtain a unique Internet address for each workstation attached to the Universal Aerospace intranet, David has decided to establish a private address scheme for internal use. The Network Address Translation feature of NetWare 5.1 will be used to attach the Universal Aerospace networks to the Internet using only the class C address as shown previously in Figure B-4. While you could assign computers any IP addresses you want for internal use on a private intranet, Table B-2 lists certain address ranges that have been reserved for this purpose. Because these address ranges are considered non-routable by Internet routers, using the 192.168.1.1 – 192.168.1.255 and 192.168.2.1 – 192.168.2.254 address schemes on the Universal Aerospace internal networks will increase security by preventing Internet computers from sending packets directly to any computers attached to the Universal Aerospace internal networks. The only way for packets to get from the Universal Aerospace internal networks to and from the Internet will be through the Network Address Translation (NAT) feature of the NetWare 5.1 server.

Table B-2 Reserved Private Network Addresses

Class	Reserved network addresses
Class A	One reserved network address: 10.0.0.0
Class B	16 reserved network addresses: 172.16.0.0 through 172.31.0.0
Class C	254 reserved network addresses: 192.168.1.0 through 192.168.254.0

Using the Compatibility Mode Driver

As mentioned earlier, Universal Aerospace is currently using both the TCP/IP and IPX protocols on the network clients. The IPX protocol is used to access the NetWare servers, and IP is used to access the Internet. Using both IPX and IP protocols on your network clients increases network traffic and can cause performance bottlenecks. To provide better network performance in the future, Universal Aerospace wants to convert the clients to use only the TCP/IP protocol to access both the NetWare servers and the Internet. Whereas NetWare 5.1 can use only the TCP/IP protocol to communicate with clients, some application software still requires the IPX protocol stack to access NetWare server. When using only the TCP/IP protocol, NetWare 5.1 servers can still support IPX applications by loading a compatibility mode driver named SCMD on both the client and server. The compatibility mode driver is loaded on the client when you select the **IP with IPX compatibility** option during client installation. The NetWare 5.1 server will automatically load a compatibility driver named SCMD.NLM when you bind only the TCP/IP protocol to the network card. The compatibility mode driver on the client encapsulates an IPX-formatted request from an application into a TCP/IP packet and sends it to the server. The SCMD.NLM software running on the NetWare 5.1 server then removes the IPX-formatted data from the TCP/IP packet and processes the request on the server. In this way, the compatibility mode driver will allow Universal Aerospace to gain network performance while gradually migrating their IPX applications to TCP/IP.

The NDS Context

During NetWare installation, you will have a choice of either placing the new server in an existing tree or creating a new tree. To place the server in an existing tree, you will need to be able to log in as the Admin user of the existing tree and then enter the context of the container where the server will be created. To create a new tree, you will need to determine the name of the tree as well as the context of the container where the new server object and Admin user will be placed. As a result, an important step in preparing for NetWare installation is to identify where the server will be placed in the NDS database.

When you are installing the first server in a new tree structure, the default approach is to place the server within the main Organization container. If necessary, you can later move the server and volumes objects or rename the Organization container as the tree structure is fully developed. In the sample NetWare Server Worksheet shown in Figure B-2, Eric has identified the NDS Context for the new NetWare 5.1 and its SYS volume as being the Engineering Organizational Unit of the UAS Organization within the existing UAS_Tree.

USING DEPLOYMENT MANAGER TO UPGRADE THE EXISTING NETWORK

NetWare 5.1 includes a new utility called Deployment Manager (NWDEPLOY.EXE) that runs from a client computer and is used primarily to prepare your existing network for upgrading to NetWare 5.1. In addition to performing network preparation tasks, Deployment Manager also provides Help information on installation and upgrading options and post-installation tasks. Because Universal Aerospace will be installing the new NetWare 5.1 server into an existing NetWare 5.0 environment, there are two preparation tasks that need to be performed. These tasks are to prepare the existing NetWare 5.0-based NDS tree for the new NetWare 5.1 eDirectory system, and install the new NetWare Licensing Service.

Upgrading the Existing UAS_Tree

To prepare the existing UAS_Tree for the new NetWare 5.1 server installation, Eric performs the following tasks on the existing UAS_HOST server during a time when no users are attached to the network:

1. Eric makes sure the current server is backed up.

2. After the back-up is complete, Eric makes sure the existing server's volumes are problem free by dismounting the volumes and running the VREPAIR utility.

3. Eric uses the DSREPAIR utility to check the existing NDS tree structure and correct any problems that are encountered.

4. After the volumes and NDS tree are checked out, Eric downloads the latest support pack for NetWare 5.0 from *http://support.novell.com/products/nw5/patches.htm* and installs it.

5. To use the Deployment Manager to update the existing UAS_Tree, Eric goes to a client workstation and logs in to the NetWare 5.0 network as Admin. He then inserts the NetWare 5.1 CD into the client, which automatically starts Deployment Manager.

6. After accepting the license agreement, Eric selects the **Step 3: Prepare for NDS 8** option, and follows the prompts to update the existing NetWare 5.0 tree to the new NDS eDirectory.

7. After the NDS 8 upgrade is complete, Eric selects the **Step 4: Novell Licensing Services** option to install NLS on the existing NetWare 5.0 network.

8. After all upgrades are complete, Eric exits Deployment Manager, logs off, and restarts the NetWare 5.0 server.

INSTALLING NETWARE 5.1

Once the preliminary planning has been done, the existing network has been updated, and the new server's hardware has been installed, Eric is ready to start the installation of NetWare 5.1 on the new server. The installation process consists of two major tasks:

1. Creating the DOS boot partition.

2. Installing the NetWare 5.1 operating system.

In this section, you will learn how to perform these two tasks by following Eric as he installs NetWare 5.1 on the Universal Aerospace server.

Creating the DOS Boot Partition

After completing the installation of the server hardware according to the NetWare Server Worksheet, Eric prepares for installation by first obtaining a copy of a DOS boot disk that contains the FDISK and FORMAT programs along with the drivers necessary for DOS to access the CD-ROM drive.

1. To configure a bootable DOS partition initially, Eric starts the server computer with the DOS disk and then enters the FDISK command to obtain the FDISK menu.

2. Next he uses the Create DOS partition option to create a small 100 MB DOS partition.

3. After creating the DOS partition, Eric uses the Set active partition option to make the newly created DOS partition the active partition (the partition from which the computer will start). This is necessary to start from the hard drive after creating a DOS partition that does not use the entire hard disk space.

4. When all the partion changes have been completed, Eric exits the FDISK program and restarts the computer from the DOS diskette. Restarting the computer is necessary in order to assess the newly created partition.

5. After the computer restarts, Eric uses the FORMAT C: /S command to format the DOS partition with a copy of the operating system to make it bootable.

6. Once the DOS partition has been formatted, Eric enabled the CMOS to boot from the CD-ROM drive.

Installing the NetWare 5.1 Operating System

Now that a formatted DOS partition has been created and the CMOS configured to boot from the CD-ROM, Eric is ready to install NetWare by booting the computer from the NetWare 5.1 CD-ROM. [Note: If the server computer is not able to boot from its CD-ROM drive, you can still install NetWare 5.1 by first installing the necessary CD-ROM drivers in the DOS partition and then running the INSTALL batch file, located on root of the NetWare 5.1 CD-ROM, from the DOS prompt.]

1. To automatically boot the installation program, Eric simply inserts the NetWare 5.1 Operating System CD-ROM and restarts the computer. If your system does not boot from a CD-ROM, you can manually start the installation software by installing the necessary CD-ROM drivers on the DOS partition and then running the INSTALL program from the root of the NetWare 5.1 CD.

2. When the installation program starts it displays the license agreement screen containing options to read the agreement, accept the agreement, or cancel the installation. Eric selects the option to accept the license agreement.

3. After pressing Enter, the installation program checks for a DOS partition and displays the message "Valid boot partition detected, use it or create a new one? Eric selects the option to use the existing boot partition and then presses Enter to display the Installation Type screen shown in Figure B-5.

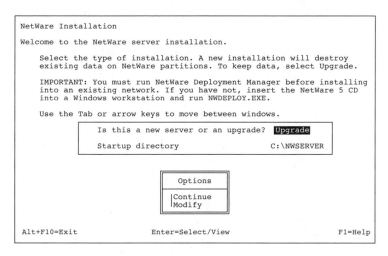

Figure B-5 NetWare Installation window

4. To start the installation process, Eric selects the **New server** option along with the default **C:\NWSERVER** directory as the location for the startup files on the DOS partition. He then highlights the **Continue** option and presses **Enter** to display the Server Settings screen.

5. The Server Settings screen contains NDS version, Server Id, and server boot options. NetWare 5.1 needs NDS version 8 to provide the enhanced NDS functionality required by many new Web networking products, such as WebSphere. However, because the Universal Aerospace tree has not already been updated for NDS 8, Eric will need Supervisor rights at the root of the existing UAS_Tree for the installation program to update that existing tree to

NDS version 8. If Eric did not have supervisor rights to the root of the existing tree, he could install NDS version 7 and then the network administrator could update the tree to NDS version 8 at a later time. The Server ID number contains a randomly generated 8-digit hexadecimal number that must be unique for each NetWare server on the network. The Load Server at Reboot option allows Eric to select whether or not the server will automatically load when the computer is started. As described in the main text, the NetWare 5.1 server reads setup commands from the STARTUP.NCF and AUTOEXEC.NCF file during startup. Some device drivers for network boards and disk storage devices may require customized settings to be made to the server's environment during startup. You can customize many server settings by using the Server SET Parameters option to place commands in the server's STARTUP.NCF file. Information regarding any required SET parameters should be provided in the documentation that comes with the network board or storage device driver. Since no special SET parameters are required for the Engineering server, Eric presses Enter to continue the installation using the randomly supplied Server ID number along with the defaults of NDS 8 and automatic server startup.

6. Eric clicks the **Continue** button on the Regional Settings screen to accept the default Country, Keyboard, and Code page settings.

7. Eric clicks the **Continue** button again to accept the default display and mouse settings.

8. After copying some initial files to the DOS partition, the installation program attempts to detect the disk storage devices and then displays the Device types screen, as shown in Figure B-6. Since the storage adapter type matches the driver identified on the NetWare Server Worksheet shown in Figure B-2, Eric clicks the **Continue** button to accept the detected storage adapter.

9. The installation program next attempts to automatically detect the network card driver and displays the updated Device Types screen shown in Figure B-7. If the network card was not correctly detected, Eric could use the Modify option to manually select a driver for the network card. After verifying that the detected network driver matches the one specified on the NetWare Server Worksheet, Eric clicks the **Continue** button.

B

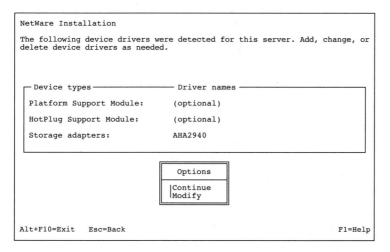

```
NetWare Installation

The following device drivers were detected for this server. Add, change, or
delete device drivers as needed.


 ┌ Device types ─────────────── Driver names ───────────────
 │ Platform Support Module:      (optional)
 │
 │ HotPlug Support Module:       (optional)
 │
 │ Storage adapters:            AHA2940
 │

                    ┌─────────────────┐
                    │    Options      │
                    ├─────────────────┤
                    │ │Continue       │
                    │ │Modify         │
                    └─────────────────┘

Alt+F10=Exit   Esc=Back                              F1=Help
```

Figure B-6   Device Types window

Figures B-7 through B-11 contain sample entries, not those entered by Eric.

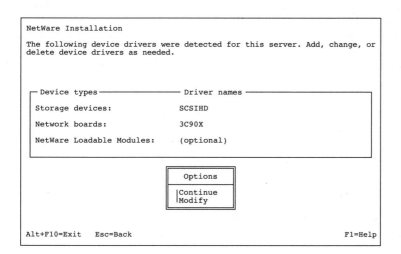

```
NetWare Installation

The following device drivers were detected for this server. Add, change, or
delete device drivers as needed.


 ┌ Device types ─────────────── Driver names ───────────────
 │ Storage devices:             SCSIHD
 │
 │ Network boards:              3C90X
 │
 │ NetWare Loadable Modules:    (optional)
 │

                    ┌─────────────────┐
                    │    Options      │
                    ├─────────────────┤
                    │ │Continue       │
                    │ │Modify         │
                    └─────────────────┘

Alt+F10=Exit   Esc=Back                              F1=Help
```

Figure B-7   Updated device Types window

10. The installation program goes out to the disk controller, checks for free space on the boot drive, and then displays the Create a NetWare partition and volume SYS screen as shown in Figure B-8. By default, all free space on the NetWare partition has been assigned to the SYS volume. Because Eric wants to create another volume on this drive, he uses the Modify option to change the size of the SYS volume to match the size specified on the NetWare Server Worksheet and then presses F10 to save his changes.

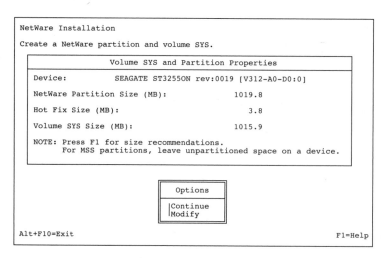

Figure B-8   Create a NetWare partition

11. When the NetWare partition and volume sizes match those specified on the NetWare Server Worksheet, Eric highlights **Continue** and presses **Enter** to start copying files to the SYS volume.

12. After the initial file copy is complete, the installation program launches the Java X-Windows environment and displays a Server Properties window similar to the one shown in Figure B-9. Eric enters the name **ENG_HOST** for the server name and then clicks the **Next** button to display a Configure File System window similar to the one shown in Figure B-10.

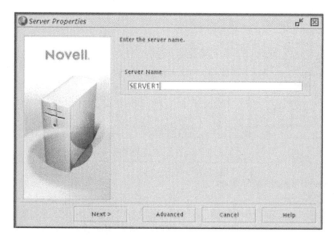

Figure B-9   Server Properties

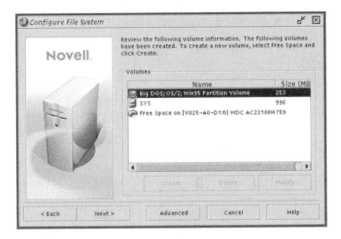

Figure B-10   Configure File System

13. To create a new volume named Eng-data, Eric clicks on the free space and then clicks the **Create** button to display a New Volume window similar to the one shown in Figure B-11.

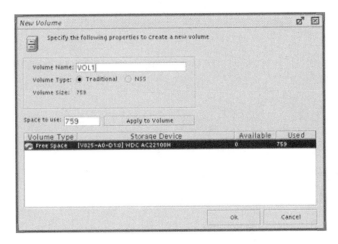

Figure B-11   New Volume window

14. By default, the system assigns all free space to the new volume. To keep space free for future use, Eric next enters the size for the Eng_Data volume along with the volume name. He then clicks the **Apply to Volume** and **OK** buttons to return to the Configure File System window.

15. After verifying that the volume information is correct, Eric clicks the **Next** button to save the volume information and display the Mount Volumes window. He then clicks the **No, Mount volumes now** option and clicks the **Next** button to display the Protocols window shown in Figure B-12.

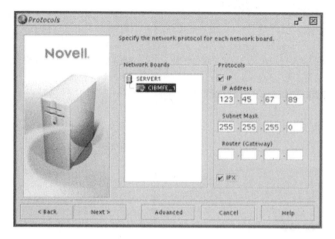

Figure B-12   Protocols

16. Eric highlights the server's network card and checks both the IP and IPX boxes. After clicking the **IP** check box, Eric enters the IP address and Mask values defined on the NetWare Server Worksheet and clicks the **Next** button to display a Domain Name Service window, as shown in Figure B-13.

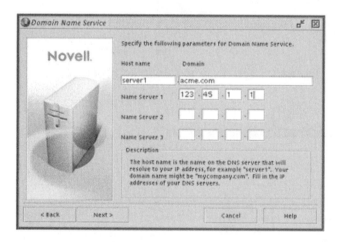

Figure B-13   Domain Name Service

17. The Domain Name Service window is used to identify the DNS host name and domain of the new server along with the IP address of the DNS server containing this NetWare server's host name and IP address. Since Universal Aerospace does not yet have a DNS server or registered host name, Eric leaves this window blank and clicks Next to continue.

18. When a warning message is displayed indicating that no host name or DNS server has been specified, Eric clicks OK to continue.

B

19. He next selects the correct time zone for the server and clicks the **Next** button to continue.

20. When the Install NDS window shown in Figure B-14 is displayed, Eric clicks the Existing NDS Tree option. He is next presented with a window asking him to enter the Tree name and context where the new server will be installed. He enters "UAS_Tree" in the Tree Name field and .OU=Engineering.O=UAS in the Context for Server field. After clicking Next the Login to NDS window is displayed.

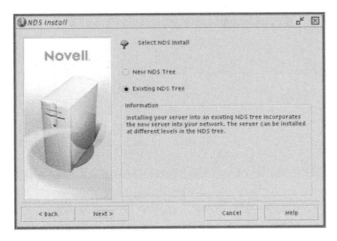

Figure B-14   NDS Install

21. Eric enters the distinguished name and password of the UAS_Tree administrator and then clicks Next to continue.

22. After clicking the **Next** button the server displays an NDS summary window containing the NDS context information. Eric records this information for later reference and then clicks the Next button to continue.

23. When the license window is displayed, Eric inserts the NetWare 5.1 license diskette into the drive and then uses the Browse button to select the NLF license file contained in the A:\license folder. After the license file(s) are installed, Eric clicks Next to display the Installation Options windows shown in Figure B-15.

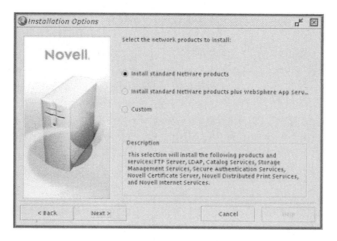

Figure B-15   Installation Options

24. Eric clicks the Custom option and then clicks Next to display the Components window shown in Figure B-16. Eric clicks to remove the check marks from both the NetWare Enterprise Web Server and FTP servers leaving only the Novell Distributed Print Services (NDPS) selected at this time. Eric then clicks Next to continue the NetWare 5.1 installation. [Note: Additional products such as the NetWare Enterprise Web Server and FTP Server can be added later using NetWare 5.1 graphical console.]

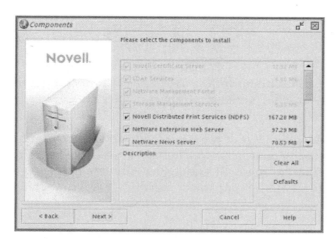

Figure B-16   Components

25. Eric clicks the **Next** button to accept the default components. Because this is the first NetWare 5.1 server in the tree, the installation program next displays the Novell Certificate Server Objects window shown in Figure B-17. The purpose of the Novell Certificate Server is to enable secure data transmissions

B

for Web-enabled products by issuing digital certificates. The *first* NetWare 5.1 server will automatically create and physically store the Security container object and Organizational CA object for the entire NDS tree. Both objects are created at, and must remain at the [Root] of, the NDS tree.

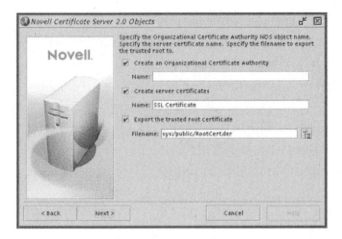

Figure B-17   Certificate Server Objects

26. Eric clicks Next to accept the default certificate settings. He then clicks OK to accept the Certificate warning message. After completing the certificate server installation, a Summary window showing all products along with their space requirements is displayed.

27. After verifying that all components are selected, Eric clicks the **Finish** button to begin the main file copy process.

28. After all files are copied to the server's SYS volume, the completion is displayed. Eric clicks the **Yes** button to complete the installation and reboot the server.

Once the server is up and running, Eric tests the server's operation from a client computer by changing context to the UAS container and logging in as the Admin user. Once the installation of the server is confirmed, the process of setting up the file system for the Eng-data volume can be performed from the NetWare Administrator program.

UPGRADING NETWARE 5.0 TO NETWARE 5.1

Novell provides three major methods that can be used to upgrade an existing server to NetWare 5.1—In-Place Upgrade, Across-the-Wire Upgrade, or Accelerated Upgrade. If the current server meets the NetWare 5.1 upgrade requirements listed below, the simplest method is to use the In-Place upgrade. The In-Place upgrade works much like the new server installation process described previously except that it uses the existing server's configuration and NDS tree information.

- A NetWare 3, NetWare 4, IntraNetWare, or NetWare 5.0 operating system installed on the server

- A 200 MHz Pentium or compatible processor

- A VGA or better resolution display adapter (SVGA recommended)

- At least 35 MB free in the DOS partition

- At least 750 MB free on the SYS volume

- At least 128 MB RAM for standard NetWare products and an additional 128 MB RAM for WebSphere Application Server for NetWare

- A NetWare 5.1-compatible network board

- A NetWare 5.1-compatible disk controller

- A CD drive that can read ISO 9660-formatted CD disks

If you are upgrading an existing NetWare 3.x or NetWare 4.x server that does not meet the NetWare 5.1 requirements, you will need to use the Across-the-Wire method. When using the Across-the-Wire upgrade, you first need to do a new install of NetWare 5.1 on the target server using a temporary tree name and then create NetWare volumes on the target server with the same names as the existing (source) server. The Across-the-Wire upgrade is then run from a workstation logged in to both servers. All NDS tree information, users, and data are then transferred from the source server to the NetWare 5.1 server. An advantage of the Across-the-Wire method is the ability to recover from upgrade problems (such as a power outage in the middle of the upgrade) without losing or damaging data on the original server.

The new NetWare 5.1 Accelerated Upgrade procedure involves copying the NetWare 5.1 files from the Installation CD to an existing NetWare 5.1 server referred to as the Staging server, as shown in Figure B-18.

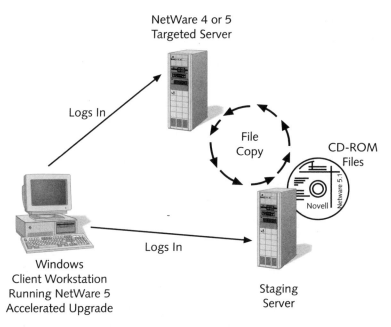

Figure B-18   Using the Accelerated Upgrade Method

The NetWare Accelerated Upgrade program (ACCUPG.EXE), located on the root of the NetWare 5.1 CD-ROM, is run from an existing workstation. When the NetWare Accelerated Upgrade launches, you log in to the target and staging servers using the Admin name and password. After a server-to-server connection is established, the Accelerated Upgrade program compares the existing target server properties with the staging server. Based on the results of the comparison, the upgrade software copies the necessary NetWare 5.1 files from the staging server to the target server. After the files are copied, the target server reboots to complete the upgrade process. Although the NetWare Accelerated Upgrade method is faster than the In-place upgrade when upgrading multiple servers, a disadvantage of this method is that it does not install additional network products, licensing services, or license certificates on the new server.

Because the UAS_HOST server meets the minimum NetWare 5.1 requirements, Eric can upgrade it using either the In-Place Upgrade or the new NetWare Accelerated Upgrade method. Because NetWare 5.1 has been installed on the engineering server, the engineering server could be used as a staging server to perform an Accelerated Upgrade on UAS_HOST. However, given that you only have one server to upgrade, the extra time and trouble it would take to copy all the NetWare 5.1 installation files to the staging server and then install the NetWare 5.1 license certificate after the upgrade do not seem worth the effort when there is only one server to upgrade.

Performing the In-Place Upgrade

Performing an In-Place Upgrade on the UAS_HOST server is similar to doing a new server installation except that the installation process preserves the existing server's data and NDS configuration. Following is an outline of the steps necessary to upgrade the UAS_HOST server from NetWare 5.0 to NetWare 5.1.

1. Back up the existing server and document any hardware settings for network and disk controller cards.

2. Use VREPAIR and DSREPAIR to verify that your volume and NDS tree are in good condition.

3. Be sure all users are logged out until the upgrade is complete.

4. Down the existing server and return it to the DOS prompt.

5. Because the UAS_HOST server can boot off a CD, you can simply insert the NetWare 5.1 CD and use the Ctrl+Alt+Del key combination to restart the computer from the NetWare 5.1 CD. An alternate method is to change the default DOS prompt to the root of the CD drive letter and enter the command **INSTALL**.

6. In the NetWare Installation window, be sure you select the **Upgrade** option and then press **Enter** to continue.

7. You will next be asked to confirm the server settings, including mouse and video drivers. Although at this point you can choose not to install NDS eDirectory, to use all the NetWare 5.1 enhancements, you should be sure **NDS 8** is selected.

8. If needed, modify the automatically detected storage, network, and platform support drivers. Because the UAS_HOST network and disk controller are supported by NetWare 5.1, you should be able to verify the settings and continue.

9. The Installation process will now mount the existing SYS volume and then starts the graphical portion of the upgrade by loading the Java-based virtual machine.

10. Because UAS_HOST will continue to use its IPX and IP protocol settings, you should not need to make any changes to the Protocols window. Verify that the settings match those that you recorded for UAS_HOST and then click the **Next** button to continue.

11. If necessary, select the option to upgrade NDS to version 8 and click the **Next** button to continue.

12. Install the NetWare 5.1 NLF license files from the diskettes provided with your server software. In addition to the NLF license files, your server will also need to install the Novell International Cryptographic Infrastructure (NICI) license. This license is called the encryption foundation key and is contained in a file having a .NFK extension.

13. Given that additional products can be added later, at this time it is easiest to take the default products and complete the upgrade without any customization.

14. After the Installation program has completed copying all files to the server, select the option to reboot the computer.

15. UAS_HOST should now be upgraded to NetWare 5.1

C

WORKING WITH NETWARE 5.1

NetWare 5.1 provides some new and enhanced utilities to help you manage your network system. Novell's ConsoleOne utility is becoming the cornerstone of NetWare system management. While you will still need to use NetWare Administrator to perform certain network functions, some of the new features of NetWare 5.1, such as the Certificate service and schema extensions, can only be performed using ConsoleOne. In this appendix, you will learn to use ConsoleOne to perform the tasks required by the NetWare 5.1 CNA objectives.

Managing user desktops and providing support for client problems is an important part of a network administrator's job. In this appendix, you will also learn how the Z.E.N.works version 2.0 product can help you provide user support through the use of its Remote Control and Help features.

One of the other new utilities you will learn about in this appendix is the NetWare Management Portal. NetWare Management Portal uses the HTTP protocol to allow you to view and manage NetWare servers and network configurations using a standard Web browser such as Netscape or Internet Explorer.

In order to do the projects in this appendix you will need an environment that simulates the Universal Aerospace network on your server. To keep your work separate from other students, you will be assigned an organization named ##UAS and a directory named ##Corp, where ## represents your assigned student number. During the activities you will occasionally be asked to reference certain network objects such as the UAS_Tree, UAS_HOST server or Corp volume. Since your network's tree, server, and volume names may be different, your instructor will provide you with the names of the objects you will be using. Record the names of the network objects you will be using below:

Tree name: _____

Server name: _____

Physical volume name: _____

Server context: _____

(This is the volume that contains your ##Corp directory.)

USING THE NEW CONSOLEONE

One of the new features included with NetWare 5.1 is the upgraded version of the Java-based ConsoleOne utility. The new ConsoleOne utility included with NetWare 5.1 extends the NDS management capabilities that can be performed from either a workstation or the server console. ConsoleOne can now be used to perform many NDS management tasks such as modifying the NDS schema and object properties, creating and searching for NDS objects, defining user templates, and managing the NetWare file system. Novell is in the process of making ConsoleOne the main Network management utility. Already, certain new NetWare 5.1 features, such as Certificate services, need to be managed from ConsoleOne rather than NetWare Administrator. In addition, if you need to browse huge NDS containers or create and configure LDAP containers and services, you will need to use ConsoleOne because neither NetWare Administrator nor NDS Manager provides these capabilities. Just as snap-ins are used to add capability to NetWare Administrator, ConsoleOne also requires snap-ins to manage certain NetWare products and features.

Novell is in the process of expanding ConsoleOne capabilities and snap-ins. However, until the necessary ConsoleOne snap-ins are available, ConsoleOne is not yet able to perform certain tasks, such as setting up accounting charges on NetWare servers, working with DNS and DHCP services, or managing certain additional Novell products such as Z.E.N.works version 2, GroupWise, BorderManager, and NDS for NT. Future upgrades and releases will add these capabilities as well as allow ConsoleOne to perform NDS partition management tasks, such as checking a server's NDS version, creating partitions and replicas, or deleting server objects. Z.E.N. works version 3 requires the use of ConsoleOne to perform administrative tasks.

In this section, you will learn how to install ConsoleOne on your workstation and then use ConsoleOne from either a workstation or the server console to create NDS objects, extend the NDS schema, and manage the NetWare file system.

ConsoleOne Requirements

To install and run the ConsoleOne on a client computer, the Novell documentation states that you need a Windows 9x or NT workstation using the latest Novell client software with at least a 200 MHz processor and a minimum of 64 MB RAM. In order to run ConsoleOne on the server, the server computer needs to have a display with 800 × 600 screen resolution and at least a 200 MHz processor with 128 MB of RAM and 25 MB free disk space. As is the case with most software, you may experience marginal performance using the minimum hardware requirements. The more memory and processor speed, the better the performance.

Keeping with the theme in Appendix B, Universal Aerospace has again turned to Eric Kenton. (Remember that Eric was hired to upgrade the existing UAS_HOST server.)

Although you do not need to use the LDAP capabilities of ConsoleOne at this time, Eric has recommended taking time to get familiar with the product because Novell will be developing more capability and snap-ins for it in the future. In addition, being able to manage the NDS tree and NetWare file system from a server console can save you from running out to a client workstation to perform certain NDS or file system tasks when you are working in the server room.

In this hands-on activity you will create a desktop shortcut to the ConsoleOne utility, and then use ConsoleOne to browse the network tree.

1. Log in to the network using your ##Admin user name.

2. To start ConsoleOne, you need to run the ConsoleOne.exe program from the PUBLIC\MGMT\CONSOLEONE\1.2\BIN folder. To make starting ConsoleOne easier, in this step you will add a shortcut to ConsoleOne on your desktop.

   a. Use My Computer or Windows Explorer to navigate to the F:\ PUBLIC\MGMT\CONSOLEONE\1.2\BIN folder.

   b. Drag and drop the **ConsoleOne.exe** program on your desktop and create a shortcut.

   c. Close all windows.

3. Double-click **ConsoleOne** and notice how long it takes to start. Does ConsoleOne take longer to start than NetWare Administrator? Why or why not?

4. Expand your tree by clicking the "**+**" icon, as shown in Figure C-1.

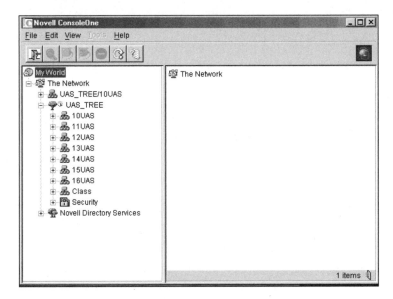

Figure C-1 ConsoleOne tree

5. Expand the Class container by clicking on the "+" icon. Click on the Class container and record the names of any group objects you see in the right-hand results pane. _____

6. Browse to the container where your server is located and highlight it. Identify the two NetWare 5.1 license container objects.

7. Double-click each of the license objects and, in the space below, record each license container and what objects are in it.

   License container: _____

   Contents: _____

   License container: _____

   Contents: _____

8. Double-click the **Students** group object.

9. Click the **Members** tab to display all members of the student group.

10. Click the **NDS Rights** tab and record below the rights assigned to the [Root] object: _____

11. Click **Cancel** to return to the ConsoleOne window.

12. Exit ConsoleOne.

Assume that as part of the expansion of their engineering and manufacturing facility Universal Aerospace has recently purchased and equipped another building to house engineering and manufacturing staff dedicated to the NASA contracts. Because the users in the new facility have their own network resources that need to be secured from use by other departments, you have decided to create a separate container and disk storage area for the NASA engineering division.

In this hands-on activity, you will learn how to use ConsoleOne to create a new organizational unit that contains a volume object for the new NetWare 5.1 server.

1. If necessary, log in using your assigned Admin account.

2. Double-click the **ConsoleOne** icon on your desktop.

3. Click the "+" icon next to your tree to view all containers.

4. Click the ##UAS organization container object assigned to you.

5. With your organization container highlighted, click **File**, **New**, **Object** and then double-click **Organizational Unit** from the New Object window.

6. In the Name field type **NASA_Eng** and click **OK**.

7. Create a volume object in the new NASA_Eng organizational unit.

   a. If necessary, expand your ##UAS organization by clicking the "+" icon.

   b. Click on your **NASA_Eng** organizational unit to highlight it.

   c. Click **File**, **New**, **Object** and then scroll down and double-click **Volume** in the New Object Class window.

   d. Enter **EngData** in the Name field.

   e. Click the **Browse** button to the right of the Host Server field and then use the up arrow icon to the right of the "Look in" field to navigate to the container holding your server object.

   f. Double-click your server.

   g. In the Physical Volume field, select the volume name assigned to you and then click **OK** to create the volume object.

Once the container and volume objects are created, your next step will be to create a directory structure for the user home directories and shared NASA engineering project data.

In this hands-on activity, you will use ConsoleOne to create the directory structure shown in Figure C-2.

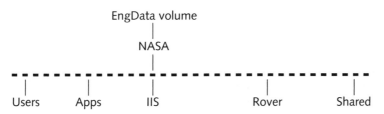

Figure C-2   Universal Aerospace NASA division directory structure

1. If necessary, click the "+" icon to expand the **NASA_Eng** organizational unit object you created.

2. Click the **"+"** icon next to your EngData volume object to display your assigned directory.

3. Right click your assigned ##Corp directory and then click **New**, **Object** to display the New Object window.

4. Select **Directory** and click **OK** to display the New Directory window.

5. Enter **NASA** in the Name field and then click **OK** to create the NASA directory.

6. Right-click the newly created **NASA** directory then click **New**, **Object**, select **Directory**, and click **OK** to display the New Directory window.

7. Enter **Users** in the Name field and click the **Create another Directory** check box.

8. Click **OK** to create the directory and return to the New Directory window.

9. Repeat steps 7 and 8 to create the **Apps**, **IIS**, **Rover**, and **Shared** subdirectories.

10. Click **Cancel** to return to ConsoleOne.

In addition to the two existing engineers assigned to the NASA contract projects, Universal Aerospace has recently hired three additional engineers along with an administrative assistant for the NASA engineering division.

 In this hands-on activity, you will use ConsoleOne to create a user account and home directory for Cleo Stowe, the new administrative assistant for the NASA engineering division.

1. If necessary, highlight your **NASA_Eng** organizational unit by clicking on it.

2. Create two groups named **Engineers** and **AdmAsst**.

   a. With your NASA_Eng organizational unit highlighted, click **File**, **New**, **Group**.

   b. In the Name field, enter **Engineers** and then click **Create another Group**.

   c. Click **OK** to create the Engineers group and return to the New Group window.

   d. In the Name field, enter **AdmAsst** and then click to remove the check from the **Create another Group** check box.

   e. Click **OK** to create the AdmAsst group and return to ConsoleOne.

3. With your NASA_Eng organizational unit highlighted, click **File**, **New**, **User**, or click the **New User** button on the toolbar.

4. Enter **Cleo** in the Name/Unique ID property field and enter **Stowe** in the Surname property field.

5. Click the **Create Home Directory** check box.

6. Click the **Browse** button to the right of the Path field and navigate to your **NASA\Users** directory.

7. Click the **Define Additional Properties** check box and then click **OK**.

8. Enter *password* for the password and click **OK** to create the user account for Cleo and display the Properties of Cleo window.

9. Click the **General** tab and enter the following values:

   - Given name: **Cleo**

   - Title: **Administrative Assistant**

   - E-Mail Address: **Cleo@uas.com**

10. Click the **Memberships** tab and then click **Add**.

11. Double-click the **AdmAsst** group to add it to the Group Memberships.

12. Click **OK** to save the changes and return to ConsoleOne.

As you have learned in previous chapters, templates are a great way to standardize and simplify the creation of user accounts. Like NetWare Administrator, ConsoleOne also allows you to create and configure template objects that you can use when creating new users.

 In this hands-on activity, you will use ConsoleOne to create a template for the new engineering users that contains the specifications shown in Table C-1.

Table C-1   Engineer template specifications

Template Property	Value
Department	NASA Engineering
Home directory volume	Your assigned volume name (CORP:)
Home directory path	NASA\USERS
Login times	Monday through Saturday 5:00am–11:30pm
Groups	Engineers
Require password	Yes
Password duration	120 days
Require unique passwords	Yes
Grace logins	5

1. If necessary, highlight your **NASA_Eng** container by clicking on it.

2. Click **File**, **New**, **Object**, and then scroll down the Class list box and double-click **Template**.

3. In the name field, enter **_Engineer**. (Starting template names with an underline symbol makes it easier to find templates objects in the container.)

4. Click **Define additional properties** and then click **OK** to create the template object and display the Properties of _Engineer window.

5. Enter **NASA Engineering** in the Department field.

6. Click the **arrow** next to the General table, then click **Environment** from the pull down menu.

7. Click the **Browse** button next to the Home Directory field and navigate to your NASA\Users directory and click **OK**.

8. Click **Memberships**, then click the **Add** button and add the Engineers group.

9. Click the **Restrictions** tab and enter the password restrictions shown in Table C-1.

10. Click the **arrow** next to Restrictions, then click **Time Restrictions** from the pull-down menu.

11. Enter the time restrictions specified in Table B-1.

12. Click **OK** to save your template properties and return to ConsoleOne.

Table C-2 contains the names of the three new engineers recently hired to work in Universal Aerospace's new NASA engineering facility.

Table C-2 Engineering users for NASA division

User Name	Login Name	Group Membership	Template
Travis Scott	TScott	Engineers	_Engineer
Lucas Teague	LTeague	Engineers	_Engineer
Lindsey Barton	LBarton	Engineers	_Engineer

In this hands-on activity, you will use your new engineering template to create the three engineering users.

1. If necessary, highlight your **NASA_Eng** container by clicking on it.

2. Click the **New User** button on the toolbar.

3. Create a user account for Travis Scott.

   a. Enter **TScott** in the Name property and **Scott** in the Surname property.

   b. Click **Use Template** and then use the **Browse** button next to the Use template box to double-click your **_Engineer** template.

   c. Click **Create Another User** and then click **OK**.

   d. Enter an initial password of **password** and then click **OK** to create the first engineering user account.

4. Create a user account for Lucas Teague.

   a. Enter **Lteague** in the Name property and **Teague** in the Surname property.

   b. Click **Use Template** and then use the **Browse** button next to the Use template box to double-click your **_Engineer** template.

   c. Click **OK**.

   d. Enter an initial password of **password** and then click **OK** to create the second engineering user account.

5. Create a user account for Lindsey Barton.

   a. Enter **LBarton** in the Name property and **Barton** in the Surname property.

   b. Click **Use Template** and then use the **Browse** button next to the Use template box to double-click your **_Engineer** template.

   c. Click to remove the check from the **Create Another User** check box and click **OK**.

   d. Enter an initial password of **password** and then click **OK** to create the third engineering user account and return to ConsoleOne.

6. Enter an initial password of *password* and then click **OK**.

7. Enter the name and Surname of the second engineer, use the **Browse** button to select the _Engineer template, and click **OK**.

8. Enter an initial password of *password* and then click **OK**.

9. Enter the name and Surname of the third engineer, click to remove the check from **Create another User**, use the **Browse** button to select the _Engineer template, and click **OK**.

10. Enter an initial password of *password* and then click **OK** to create the third user and return to ConsoleOne

To work with the file system, the new engineering users will need rights to the system.

In this hands-on activity, you will use ConsoleOne to assign the rights specified in Table C-3.

Table C-3   File system rights

Path	AdmAsst	Engineering	All UAS Users
NASA\Shared	RWCEMF	RWCEMF	RF
NASA\IIS	RF	RWCEMF	None
NASA\Rover	RF	RWCEMF	None
NASA\Users	RF	None	None

1. If necessary, expand your EngData volume object to display all folders in the NASA directory.

2. Grant the rights specified in Table C-3 for the Shared folder.

   a. Right-click the **Shared** folder and click Properties, then click the **Trustees** tab.

   b. Click the **Add Trustee** button and then click the up-arrow to display all objects in your NASA_Eng container.

    c. Double-click **AdmAsst** group and then click the **Write**, **Create**, **Erase**, and **Modify** rights.

    d. Click the **Add Trustee** button and click the up arrow to display all objects in your NASA_Eng container.

    e. Double-click the **Engineers** group and then click the **Write**, **Create**, **Erase**, and **Modify** rights.

    f. Click the **Add Trustee** button and then click the up arrow three times.

    g. To give all your UAS users Read and File Scan rights, click your **##UAS** container and then click **OK**.

    h. Click **OK** to return to ConsoleOne.

3. Grant the rights specified in Table C-3 for the Rover folder.

    a. Right-click the **Rover** folder and click Properties, then click the **Trustees** tab.

    b. Click the **Add Trustee** button and then click the up arrow to display all objects in your NASA_Eng container.

    c. Double-click **AdmAsst** group to assign the default Read and File Scan rights.

    d. Click the **Add Trustee** button and click the up arrow to display all objects in your NASA_Eng container.

    e. Double-click the **Engineers** group and then click the **Write**, **Create**, **Erase**, and **Modify** rights.

    f. Click **OK** to return to ConsoleOne.

4. Grant the rights specified in Table C-3 for the IIS folder.

    a. Right-click the **IIS** folder and click Properties, then click the **Trustees** tab.

    b. Click the **Add Trustee** button and then click the up arrow to display all objects in your NASA_Eng container.

    c. Double-click **AdmAsst** group to assign the default Read and File Scan rights.

    d. Click the **Add Trustee** button and click the up-arrow to display all objects in your NASA_Eng container.

    e. Double-click the **Engineers** group and then click the **Write**, **Create**, **Erase**, and **Modify** rights.

    f. Click **OK** to return to ConsoleOne.

5. Grant the rights specified in Table C-3 for the Users folder. Because of inheritance, providing the AdmAsst organizational role object with Read and File Scan rights to the Users folder will allow the administrative assistant user to retrieve files from individual user's home folders when they are away from the office.

    a. Right-click the **Users** folder and click Properties, then click the **Trustees** tab.

    b. Click the **Add Trustee** button and then click the up scroll arrow to display all objects in your NASA_Eng container.

      c. Double-click **AdmAsst** group to assign the default Read and File Scan rights.

      d. Click **OK** to return to ConsoleOne.

  6. Exit ConsoleOne

After setting up the users and file system for the NASA Engineering department, the last activity you should perform is to test the user accounts and access rights by performing the following steps for each user:

  1. Log in as Travis Scott.

  2. Use Network Neighborhood to map the N: drive letter to your NASA folder.

  3. Launch Wordpad.

  4. Create a document containing the user's name and title.

  5. Save the document in the user's home directory with the name Test.doc.

  6. Save the document in the shared directory using the user's name as the document name.

  7. Save the document in the NASA/IIS folder and then exit Wordpad.

  8. Use My Computer or Windows Explorer to browse the N: drive and view the files in each directory.

  9. Log out.

 10. Log in as Cleo, the administrative assistant, and repeat steps 2–8. Are you able to save the document in the NASA\IIS folder? _____

     Can you see files in Travis Scott's home folder? _____

Using Z.E.N.works Version 2

The Z.E.N.works starter pack is included with NetWare 5.0 and 5.1. However, to use certain Z.E.N.works features, such as workstation inventory, remote control, and Help information, you will need to purchase the full version of Z.E.N.works from Novell. To install Z.E.N.works, you will need a minimum of NetWare 4.11 with Support pack 6 (NetWare 5.0 or 5.1 recommended), NDS version 6.x or higher, and 175 MB of additional disk space if client software is copied to the server. In this section, you will learn how to upgrade the Starter pack to Z.E.N.works version 2 and then use Z.E.N.works to set up the Help requester and implement remote control of a workstation.

Assume that Universal Aerospace management has approved the request you made to purchase the full version of Novell's Z.E.N.works through Computer Technology

Services. In this section, you will follow Eric Kenton as he upgrades the Z.E.N.works starter pack installed on the UAS server to the full version.

1. Before installing Z.E.N.works, Eric selects the UAS_HOST server to act as the main Z.E.N.works host and prepares the UAS_HOST by exiting the graphical console and unloading the JAVA module.

2. To install Z.E.N.works, Eric needs to log in to the network as an administrator with Supervisor rights to the root of the tree. After logging in as the system administrator, Eric inserts the new Z.E.N.Works 2 CD into the workstation, which automatically launches the Z.E.N.works installation wizard.

3. He clicks **English**, **ZENworks**, **Install ZENworks**, and then clicks **Next** to display the license screen.

4. After clicking **Yes** to accept the license agreement, Eric clicks the **Custom** option and then clicks **Next** to display the product options.

5. In addition to the Application Management, Remote Management, Workstation Management, and NWAdmin32 options, Eric clicks the **Copy Clients to Network** option and then clicks **Next** to display the Part Selection window.

6. Eric clicks **Next** to select the default Files, Schema extensions, Application Objects, and Workstation Registry components.

7. The installation needs to identify the Tree on which Z.E.N.works will be installed. Eric selects the **UAS_Tree** and clicks **Next**.

8. In addition to the Tree, the installation program also needs to know the names of the server or servers to contain the Z.E.N.works software. He selects **UAS_Host** and clicks **Next**.

9. Z.E.N.works needs a volume in which to store the workstation inventory information. If using the SYS volume, you need to be sure there is sufficient space reserved to prevent filling up the SYS volume and halting the server. When the installation displays the Inventory Database Server Selection window, Eric clicks **Next** to select the default UAS_Host server. He then selects the SYS volume from the Inventory Database Volume Selection windows and clicks **Next**. A warning message is displayed indicating that the inventory database may use large amounts of disk space and that placing it on the SYS volume is not recommended. Since Eric has verified that approximately .5 MB of space is reserved on the UAS_Host server's SYS volume for each workstation, he clicks **OK** to acknowledge the warning message.

10. Eric then clicks **OK** again to acknowledge the message informing him that some components will be automatically loaded on the server running the inventory database.

11. The installation program next displays the language. Eric confirms that **English** is selected and clicks **Next**.

12. Finally, he verifies the summary list of installation options and then clicks **Next** to begin the installation. During installation the files are copied to the server and then the NDS tree's schema is extended to include the new Z.E.N.works NDS objects.

13. Z.E.N.works 2 requires workstations to be registered before they can be imported into the NDS tree. Workstation registration is usually done automatically by Z.E.N.works when a user first logs in. To provide users with the rights necessary to register their workstations in the tree, the installation program next displays a dialog box prompting Eric to enter the context in which to grant users auto-registration rights. To provide users the auto-registration rights throughout the entire tree, Eric clicks **OK** to select the default [root] container and all subcontainers. When a message box then appears stating that workstation auto-registration rights were successfully set up, Eric clicks **OK** to continue.

14. When the Setup Complete dialog box is displayed, giving Eric options to Launch Read Me and Setup Log files. Eric clicks to remove the check from the Launch Read Me check box and then clicks **Finish** to read the Setup Log using Notepad. After verifying that that there are no errors in the setup log Eric prints the log and exits Notepad. A Congratulations on installing Z.E.N.works message is displayed suggesting that you distribute and install the new client software on all workstations. Eric exits the Congratulations message and then logs out.

15. To complete the installation, Eric issues the RESTART SERVER command on the server console to reload NetWare 5.1. Z.E.N.works is now ready to configure and use.

In addition to installing the Z.E.N.works components, implementing Z.E.N.works requires creating objects for users, applications, workstations, and policies within the NDS tree structure. Because proper placement of these objects affects setting up and managing Z.E.N.works capabilities, there are several NDS design considerations you should be aware of when setting up and managing Z.E.N.works. Table C-4 lists some of the NDS objects and how Novell recommends implementing them in your NDS tree structure.

Table C-4   NDS objects

NDS Object	Implementation
Application objects	Placing application objects in the same container as the majority of users that run the application reduces search times when Application Launcher starts, as well as makes it easier to associate users with the application object.
Application folders	Application folder objects are a method of grouping application objects for administrative purposes. Information in each application folder object is linked to any applications that are associated with it. Linking information from application folder objects to applications reduces NDS traffic and provides for centralized administration. Because application folder objects are used by administrators and do not need to be accessed by the users, you should consider placing all application folder objects in a container that is convenient for you. For example, you may wish to place application folder objects in the same container as your Admin user name.
Group objects	To reduce the number of user associations you need to make, whenever possible you should associate applications objects with group objects and then make the users that need to use the application members of the associated group. When creating groups, try to place group objects in the same container as the application and avoid having members in the group that are separated by a WAN.
Workstation objects	To use workstation policies, inventories, or the new remote control feature, you will need to register and import workstations into the NDS tree. When workstation objects are imported into the tree, they are created in the container you specify in a user policy package. If workstations are normally used by a specific user, you should set the import policy to create the workstation object in the same container as the user object. Because workstation objects can double the number of objects in a container, be careful that the number of objects in any one partition does not exceed 1500.
Policy packages	Container policy packages govern how the policies in the container and its subcontainers are managed. Novell recommends placing container policy packages at the beginning of a location or site container to control the search policy for that location. For example, in the Universal Aerospace structure, a container policy package could be created for the NASA organizational unit because it is located in a different building. When workstations are used by multiple users located in different containers, consider creating a separate container for the workstations and placing the corresponding workstation objects in that container. User policy packages should be created in the same container as the user accounts.

Establishing Remote Control of a Workstation

Because the new engineering users will be located in a different building, you would like to implement the new Z.E.N.works remote control feature to help engineering users who have technical problems accessing the network resources. In the past, Universal

Aerospace has been reluctant to implement other third party remote control software because of the possibility of unauthorized access to the systems. The Z.E.N.works remote control feature provides security by allowing you to use NDS to authorize which users can remotely control a system as well as providing the user with notification when remote control is being used. The management at Universal Aerospace would like you to configure security for the remote control feature by limiting remote control to only the Admin user and requesting the user to authorize the remote control session.

Before you can use the remote control feature of Z.E.N.works, you need to perform four preparatory steps, each of which is detailed in the following sections. First you need to import the workstations into the NDS tree. Once the workstation objects are imported into the tree, you need to create a workstation policy package and configure it for remote control of the workstations associated with the package. Then use Application Launcher to run the Z.E.N.works Remote Management utility on each workstation that could be remotely controlled. The final step is to test the remote control feature to ensure it is configured correctly.

In the following hands-on activities, you will implement remote control by performing the preparatory steps and then testing remote control by working with a lab partner to remotely control their workstation. As mentioned previously, one of the remote control preparatory activities involves importing your workstation into a container of the NDS tree. If your workstation already exists in another NDS tree or container, you can either perform the optional activity to remove it from that location or skip to activity 2 and enable the remote control policy on the workstation in its current location.

To practice importing your workstation for remote control purposes, you may wish to perform the optional step in this hands-on activity and remove your workstation from the tree. If your workstation has not been imported into a tree, you can skip the optional step and continue with importing your workstation in step 1.

Optional Activity: Removing Your Workstation from the Tree

The process of removing a workstation from a tree involves two steps. First you will need to delete the workstation object from the tree using either NetWare Administrator or ConsoleOne. After the workstation's object is deleted, you next need to modify the workstation's client so that it will re-register itself in a different tree or container. The most reliable method to reset the workstation's client is to un-install and then re-install the client software. An alternate method is to manually modify the workstation's registry and then delete the remote id files.

Follow these steps to remove the workstation from the tree by uninstalling and reinstalling the Novell client.

1. If necessary, log in as your Admin account and start NetWare Administrator.

2. Browse to the container where your workstation object is located, click on your workstation object to highlight it, and then use the Delete key to delete your workstation object.

3. Exit NetWare Administrator and log out.

4. Insert the Novell Z.E.N.works Client CD-ROM.

5. If the autostart launches the install wizard, click the **Exit** button to exit the wizard.

6. Click **Start**, **Run**, then click the **Browse** button and navigate to the Products\Win95\ibm_enu\Admin folder of the Z.E.N. works client CD-ROM.

7. Double-click the **Unc32.exe** program and click **Continue** to start the uninstall process.

8. Reboot your computer.

9. Install the Novell Z.E.N.works client by inserting the CD-ROM and following the installation guidelines presented in the textbook.

The alternate method of removing the workstation from the tree and resetting the client by modifying the workstation's registry is described in the following steps.

1. If necessary, log in as Admin and start NetWare Administrator.

2. Browse to the container where your workstation object is located, click on your workstation object to highlight it and then use the Delete key to delete your workstateion object.

3. Exit NetWare Administrator and start RegEdit.

4. Highlight **HKEY_LOCAL_MACHINE** and then click **Edit**, **Find**, enter **Workstation Object**, then click **Find Next**.

5. Delete the following values in the Identification key: **Registered In**, **Registration Object**, **Tree**, **Workstation Object**.

6. Exit RegEdit.

7. Delete the following files from the root of the C: drive: **Wsreg32.log**, **Wsremote.id**.

8. Restart your workstation.

Activity 1: Importing Your Workstation into the NDS Tree

Assume that you have decided to test the Z.E.N.works remote control feature on Cleo's computer. To import Cleo's workstation into the NASA_Eng container, you first need to create a User Policy package in that container and enable the workstation import policy by performing the following steps:

1. If necessary, log in as the Admin user and launch NetWare Administrator.

2. Highlight your **NASA_Eng** container and click the **Create a new object** button.

3. Double-click the **Policy Package** object type, then double-click the **Win95–98 User Package** option.

4. Click **Next** to accept the default name and location.

5. Click to place a check mark in the **Workstation Import Policy** option and click **Next**.

6. Click **Next** to associate the policy with all objects in the NASA_Eng container.

7. Verify your results in the selections windows, then click **Finish** to create the policy package.

8. To configure the workstation import policy, double-click the newly created policy package, click **Workstation Import Policy** and then click **Details**.

9. Verify that the workstation objects will be created in the User Container, then click the **Workstation Naming** tab.

10. Notice that by default a workstation name will consist of Computer name and network address. To use the IP address of the workstation, click **Network Address** and then use the scroll down arrow next to the Preferred network address to select **IP Address**.

11. Click the **Add** button under the Add name fields pane and record the possible name fields below:

_____

12. Click **Cancel** and then click **OK** to use the default name fields.

13. Click **Cancel** to return to NetWare Administrator.

14. Exit NetWare Administrator and log out.

15. Log in to the NASA_Eng container as Cleo. (Logging in registers the workstation in that container.) Use My Computer to open a window to the root of your C: drive and then use Notepad to open the **Wsreg32.log**. Did the workstation successfully register? _____ If not, perform the **Remove workstation from the tree** procedure and try again.

If the message in the Wsreg32.log indicates that users do not have rights to register workstations in the NASA_Eng container, perform the following process:

Log in using your ##Admin username and start NetWare Administrator. Highlight your ##UAS container and then click **Tools**, **Workstation utilities**, **Prepare workstation registration**. Click the **Include subcontainers** check box and then click **OK**. After workstation registration rights are granted, close NetWare Administrator and repeat step 15.

16. Log out, then log back in as the Admin user.

17. Start NetWare Administrator.

18. Right-click the **NASA_Eng** container and click **Details**.

19. Click **Workstation Registration**. Your workstation should appear in the Workstations that are registered to be imported pane.

20. Click your workstation, then click **Import** to import your workstation into the NASA_Eng container.

21. Click **Close**, then click **OK** to return to the NetWare Administrator window.

22. Expand your NASA_Eng container and verify that your workstation object is not listed in the container.

23. Exit NetWare Administrator and log off.

Activity 2: Creating and Configuring the Remote Control Policy

In order to be remotely controlled, a workstation must have its remote control property enabled. This can be done by enabling the remote control property on each workstation object individually, or by associating the workstation object, a group it belongs to, or its parent container, with a policy that has remote control enabled. When multiple workstations in a container need to the same remote control settings, you should associate the workstations' parent container with a policy that has the remote control policy settings you want. In this activity you will create a workstation policy object with remote control enabled and then associate that object with the container that your workstation object is located in.

1. Log in as the Admin user and start NetWare Administrator.

2. Highlight the **NASA_Eng** container and click **Create a new object** button.

3. Double-click **Policy Package**, click **Win95-98 Workstation Package**, then click **Next**.

4. Click **Next** to accept the default name and location.

5. Click to place a check in the **Remote Management Policy** check box and then click **Next** twice to display the summary window.

6. Click **Finish** to create the workstation policy package.

7. Double-click the newly created **Win95-98 Workstation Package**.

8. Click to highlight the **Remote Management Policy** and then click **Details**.

9. Click the **Control** tab and verify that **Enable Remote Control** is selected along with **Prompt user for permission to remote control**.

10. Click the **View** tab and verify that the settings are the same as in step 9.

C

11. Click the **Execute** tab and remove the check from the **Enable Remote Execute** check box.

12. Click **OK** to return to the Policy Package.

13. Click the **Associations** button and record the associations below:

_____

14. Click **Cancel** to return to NetWare Administrator.

15. Exit NetWare Administrator.

Activity 3: Running the Remote Management Software

In order to control a remote workstation, the workstation needs to run the Z.E.N.works remote control software named "zenrc32.exe". This program is located in the SYS:PUBLIC\ ZENWORKS directory and can be run manually, placed in a login script, or added to the Novell Desktop Management scheduler. In this activity you will run the zenrec32 program manually to test your remote control setup.

1. Click Start, Run, and then browse to your SYS:PUBLIC\ZENWORKS directory.

2. Double-click the zenrc32.exe program and then click **OK**.

After the remote control program is loaded, a small remote management computer icon will appear in your system tray.

Activity 4: Testing the Remote Control of the Workstation

Now you will test the remote control of your workstation by working with a lab partner. Wait until your lab partner has completed Activities 1–3 and then take turns performing the steps below with one person playing the role of Cleo while the other plays the role of the Administrator.

1. The Cleo user should log into their NASA_Eng container as Cleo.

2. Double-click the **Remote Management** icon located in the lower–right task bar of Windows to display the Remote Management window.

3. To remote control Cleo's station, the person playing the Admin user should perform the following steps:

   a. Log in as the ##Admin user for Cleo's ##UAS organization.

   b. Start NetWare Administrator and **Browse** to Cleo's workstation and highlight it.

   c. Click **Tools**, **Workstation Remote Management**, **Remote Control**.

4. On Cleo's workstation click **Yes** to allow the remote control of the workstation.

5. Perform the following steps from the Admin's workstation:

a. The upper right of the remote computer's windows contains control icons that perform the functions listed below. Place your cursor on each of the icons and sequence the following functions from left to right:

_____ **System Key Passthrough**. This icon allows control keys such as Alt+Esc to pass through to the remote computer.

_____ **App Switcher**. This icon allows you to rotate the remote computer's screen between currently running applications.

_____ **Start**. This icon can be used to open the Start menu on the remote computer.

_____ **Navigate**. The complete screen of the target computer may not fit in the window on the controlling workstation. You can use this icon to view other areas of the controlled computer's screen.

_____ **Reboot**. This icon allows you to reboot the remote computer.

b. Use the **Start** button to start **NotePad**, **Paint**, and **Calculator** on the remote computer.

c. Use the **App Switcher** to switch between the applications.

d. Close all applications.

e. Use the **Navigate** button to view other areas of the remote computer's screen.

f. Click the **System Key Passthrough** button. Table C-5 contains a list of hot-key sequences.

g. Try various hot-key sequences so that you become familiar with their function.

h. Click the **System Key Passthrough** button and then use the appropriate hot-key sequence to release control of the target workstation.

6. Log out both the Admin and Cleo users.

Table C-5   Remote control hot-key sequences

Option	Hot Key Sequence	Description
Full screen toggle	Ctrl+Alt+M	Sizes the viewing window to use the full screen
Refresh screen	Ctrl+Alt+R	Refreshes the target workstation's screen
Restart viewer	Ctrl+Alt+T	Reconnects your workstation to the target and refreshes the viewing window
System key routing toggle	Ctrl+Alt+S	Switches between passing Windows-reserved keystrokes to the target workstation and using them locally
Hot key enable	Ctlr+Alt+H	Enables the Control Options hot keys on the target workstation
Accelerated mode	Ctrl+Alt+A	Increases screen refresh rate of the viewing window without changing the refresh rate on the target workstations's monitor
Stop viewing	Left-Shift+Esc	Releases control of the target workstation

Configuring the Help Requester

To help users with problems or questions, Z.E.N.works includes a Help Desk feature that can be configured to allow users to send messages to an administrator or obtain the phone number and e-mail address of their assigned support person. A Help Desk message when combined with remote control can sometimes allow you to quickly solve certain types of problems by accessing the user's desktop and then working through the problem.

To help speed up the user support at Universal Aerospace, in this hands-on activity you will configure the Help Desk feature to include a desktop icon that users in the Engineering Department can use to send you a message briefly describing their problem or question.

1. Log in as the Admin user and start NetWare Administrator.

2. Double-click the **Win95-98 User Package** in your NASA_Eng container.

3. Click to place a check mark in the **Help Desk Policy** check box.

4. With the Help Desk Policy highlighted, click **Details**.

5. Enter the Contact name, E-mail address, and Telephone number that you want displayed to the user in the Help Requester application.

6. Click the **Help Requester** button.

7. Click to place a check mark in the **Allow user to launch the Help Requester** check box.

8. To allow users to e-mail trouble tickets, click to place a check mark in the **Allow user to send trouble tickets from the Help Requester** check box and then select the delivery mode. Since Universal Aerospace is not yet

using Novell's Groupwise system, click **MAPI** to enable delivery of trouble tickets using a standard Internet e-mail format.

9. Click the **ellipsis** button to the right of the Trouble ticket subject lines text box and use the **Add** button to add the following subjects:

   ■ Network problem

   ■ Workstation problem

   ■ Application problem

10. Click **OK** to return to the Help Desk Policy window.

11. Click the **Trouble Tickets** tab and select the following items to be sent with each trouble ticket: **User Context**, **User Location**, and **Workstation ID**.

12. Click **OK** to save your Help Desk Policy configuration.

13. Click **Associations** and verify that all users in the NASA_Eng container will be able to use the Help Requester.

14. Click **OK** to save the Help Requester configuration.

15. Create a Help Requester application in the NASA_Eng container.

   a. Highlight your **NASA_Eng** container and click the **Create a new object** button.

   b. Double-click **Application** and click **Next** to accept the default of creating a simple Application object.

   c. In the Object name text box type **Help**.

   d. Click the **Browse** button to the right of the Path field to navigate to the Z:\Public folder.

   e. Double-click the **Hlpreq32.exe** program and click **Open**.

   f. Click **Finish** to create the Help application object.

   g. Double-click the **Help** application and verify the settings in the System Requirement and Environment tabs.

   h. Click the **Associations** tab and use the **Add** button to select the **NASA_Eng** container as shown in Figure C-3. When the "Add Container Association" dialog box appears, verify that the "users within this container" option is selected and then click OK to continue.

   i. Click the **System Tray** and **Desktop** check boxes to have the Help icon easily available.

   j. Click **OK** to save your Help configuration.

16. Exit NetWare Administrator and log out.

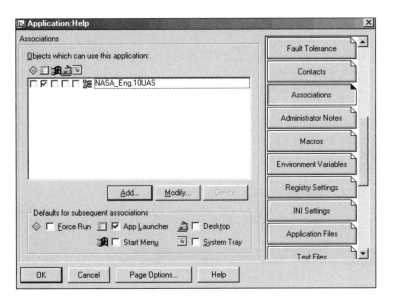

Figure C-3   Associations tab for Help Application

17. Test the Help Requester by performing the following steps:

a. Log in to your NASA_Eng container as Cleo.

b. Click **Start**, **Run**, enter **NALEXPD**, and press **Enter** to place the help application icon on the desktop and system tray.

c. Double-click the **Help** icon from the desktop or system tray.

d. Click the **Mail** tab, select **Workstation problem** for the subject and enter a message.

e. Click the **User** and **Workstation** tabs to determine user name, context, and workstation Id.

f. If you have e-mail software such as Outlook Express on your computer, click **Send**. Your computer e-mail software should be started. Exit the e-mail software and return to the Help Requester.

g. Click the **Call** tab to display the help number you configured. Notice that the user's context, tree, and workstation information is available.

h. Exit the Help Requester and log off.

USING THE NETWARE MANAGEMENT PORTAL

NetWare 5.1 includes a new feature called NetWare Management Portal. NetWare Management Portal provides for remote management of server and network environments using a browser such as Netscape Navigator or Internet Explorer. NetWare Management Portal allows many management tasks to be performed without additional software needed on either the server or workstation. To implement NetWare Management Portal, all you need is TCP/IP installed on your server and a 32-bit Windows client running either Netscape version 4.5 or later, or Internet Explorer version 4 or later. The TCP/IP protocol uses port numbers to route packets to applications. For example, the standard port number used by web servers is port number 80. When you install NetWare 5.1, as described in Appendix B, port number 8009 is reserved for NetWare Management Portal use. When accessing the NetWare Management Portal, you need to supply the IP address or URL of the server followed by a colon and the port number as shown in Figure C-4.

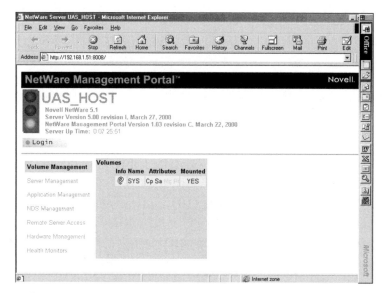

Figure C-4   NetWare Management Portal

Notice that the NetWare Management Portal window contains a stop and go light for showing the server's health, along with management options for volumes, servers, applications, NDS, remote access services, hardware, and health.

Part 1: Accessing NetWare Management Portal

In this hands-on activity, you are to assume that you are attending the Comdex convention in Las Vegas and, being bored one evening, you decide to check on the status of the Universal Aerospace server using your hotel room's Internet connection.

1. If you are currently logged in to the server, log out.

2. Click **Cancel** to exit the Login window.

3. From your Windows desktop, start either Netscape or Internet Explorer.

4. In the Address or Location field, enter **http://*IPaddress*:8009** (where *IPaddress* is the IP address of your server) and press **Enter**.

5. If necessary, click **OK** to view information over a secure connection.

6. The NetWare Management Portal main window should be displayed.

Part 2: Server Health

The traffic light indicator that appears on the main NetWare Management Portal window allows you to quickly view the server's health. A green light means that all server components are in good health, yellow indicates a potential problem with at least one of the components, and red indicates the failure of a component or service. You can view the status of an individual component by clicking on the traffic light indicator or clicking the Health Monitor tab and then selecting the component you want to view.

 In this part of the activity, you will use the Health Monitor tab to check the status of several components on your server.

1. Click **Login** and then enter the distinguished name of your admin use (.##admin.##UAS). Enter your password and click **OK**.

2. Click on the **traffic light** icon to display the Server Health Monitor window similar to the one shown in Figure C-5.

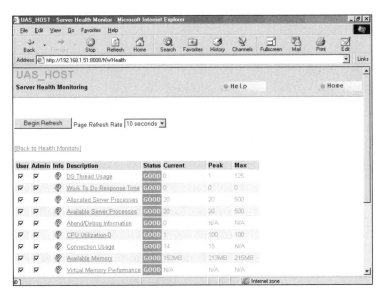

Figure C-5 Server health components

3. The check marks in the check boxes under the User and Admin columns are used to control which users can view these fields. To prevent users other than Admin from accessing one of the server components, remove the check mark from that monitor's User box.

4. Scroll through your server's health monitors and check their status. Is the status of all your health monitors good? _____

5. Looking at the server health monitors shown in Figure C-5, what two health monitors should we be most concerned about? _____
_____

6. Click the **Info** icon next to the CPU utilization and record the criteria for Green, Yellow, and Red below:

   Green:

   Yellow:

   Red:

7. Click the browser's "Back" button to return to the Volume Management window.

8. In the left-hand pane, scroll up and click **Logout**. If necessary, click **Yes** to close the browser window.

In order to perform server management tasks you will need to log in as an administrator who has supervisor rights to the server. If you do not have access to a user that has supervisor rights to the server object, skip this part of the activity.

Part 3: Server Management

Server management includes the ability to manage user connections, view and set parameters, view system statistics, manage memory, and access current console screens. Being able to access the server console screens remotely is a powerful management feature when troubleshooting or repairing NetWare server problems.

In this activity, you will access your server's console and check the status of virtual memory.

1. If necessary, use your browser to connect to the NetWare Management Portal. Click **Login** and then enter the distinguished name of the admin user that has supervisor rights to the server object. Enter the password and click **OK**.

2. Scroll down the left-hand pane and view the options under Server Management.

3. To display the current console screens, click on the **Screens** option.

4. Click **System_Console** to display a replica of the server console screen.

C

5. Enter **Swap** in the command line box located at the bottom of the window.

6. Click **Execute Command Line** button or press **Enter** to display the Swap information screen.

7. After viewing the virtual memory settings, close the system console screen by clicking the **Close** button.

8. In the left-hand pane, scroll down and view the options under Application Management.

9. To view the NLMs currently loaded on the server, click **Module List**.

10. To view the modules in descending order by allocated memory, click the **Alloc Memory** button. Record below the two modules that use the most Alloc memory: _____ , _____

11. To sort modules by name, click the **Name** button.

12. Click **Home** from the NetWare Management Portal web page to return to the main menu.

13. In the left-hand pane, scroll up and click **Logout**. If necessary, click **Yes** to close the browser window.

Part 4: Volume Management

In addition to working with server information, NetWare Management Portal allows you to view volume information, mount or dismount volumes, and perform many file management tasks, such as uploading, downloading, and renaming or deleting files. Assume that while at Comdex you discover that you need to replace a .DLL file for one of the engineering applications.

In this activity, you will use NetWare Management Portal to simulate accessing volume information and then uploading and renaming a file.

1. If necessary, use your browser to connect to the NetWare Management Portal. Click **Login** and then enter the distinguished name of your admin user (.##admin.##UAS). Enter your password and click **OK**.

2. In the left-hand pane, if necessary, scroll up and click the **Volume Management** option.

3. Click the **Info** button next to the **SYS** volume and record the volume statistics requested below:

Name: _____

% Free: _____

Sub-Allocation size: _____

Salvageable blocks: _____

Name: _____

% Free: _____

Sub-Allocation size: _____

Salvageable blocks: _____

4. Click on the name of the volume object containing your NASA directory structure.

5. Navigate down to your NASA\Apps folder.

6. Click the **Upload** button.

7. Use the **Browse** button to navigate to the Windows directory on your local workstation.

8. Select a .DLL file by double-clicking it.

9. Click the **Upload** button. The file will be copied to your NASA\Apps folder.

10. Click the **Home** button to return to the NetWare Management Portal main window.

In order to perform NDS tasks you will need to log in as an administrator that has supervisor rights to the root of the tree. If you do not have access to a user that has supervisor rights to the root of the tree, skip this part of the activity.

Part 5: NDS Management

NetWare Management Portal also provides the administrator with the ability to view and delete NDS objects.

In this activity, you will use NetWare Management Portal to walk the tree and view your NDS objects.

1. If necessary, use your browser to connect to the NetWare Management Portal. Click **Login** and then enter the distinguished name of the admin user that has supervisor rights to the root of the tree. Enter the password and click **OK**.

2. In the left-hand pane, scroll down to view the NDS Management options.

3. Click on the **Tree Walker** option and then browse your ##UAS organization and view the details on each user. Notice that the only NDS function you can perform is to delete an NDS object, so be careful.

4. Click on the **NDS Partitions** option and record the number of partitions in your tree: _____ .

5. In the left-hand pane, scroll up and click **Logout**. If necessary, click **Yes** to close the browser window.

Part 6: Hardware Management

The hardware management option allows you to view the current hardware configuration settings. This information can be useful in helping you to diagnose problems or plan for new equipment. For example, assume that while at Comdex you find a 1 GB network card that you would like to install in the engineering server.

 In this activity, you will use NetWare Management Portal to determine the feasibility of installing the new network adapter by viewing the slots and interrupts currently available on your server.

1. If necessary, use your browser to connect to the NetWare Management Portal. Click **Login** and then enter the distinguished name of your admin user (.##admin.##UAS). Enter your password and click **OK**.

2. In the left-hand pane, scroll down to view the Hardware Management options.

3. From the Hardware Management pane, click the **Hardware Resources** option.

4. Click the **Interrupts** option and record the interrupt assigned to your server's network adapter: _____

5. List two available interrupts: _____ , _____

6. Click the **Back to Hardware Resources** option.

7. Click on **Slots**.

8. List any Non-ISA slots and modules used by your server: _____

9. Click the **Back to Hardware Resources** option.

10. View information for the Ports, DMA, and Shared Memory resources.

11. In the left-hand pane click on the **Processor Information** option and record the following processor statistics:
Speed: _____ Family: _____ Model: _____

12. In the left-hand pane, scroll up and click the **Logout**. If necessary, click **Yes** to close the browser window.

D

FORMS AND WORKSHEETS

Computer Worksheet

Specification developed by: _____

SYSTEM INFORMATION

Computer make/model: _____

CPU: _____ **Clock speed (MHz):** _____

Bus type/speed: _____ **Memory (RAM):** _____

DISK INFORMATION

Disk controller

Type: _____ Vendor: _____

Model: _____

Drive address	Type	Mfg	Cyl/Hd/Sec	Speed/capacity	DOS partition size
_____	____	_____	__ /__ /__	_____	_____

DEVICE INFORMATION

Device name	IRQ	I/O port
_____	_____	_____
_____	_____	_____
_____	_____	_____

Bid Specification Form

Specification developed by: _____

SYSTEM INFORMATION

Computer make/model: _____

CPU: _____ **Clock speed (MHz):** _____

Bus type/speed: _____ **Memory (RAM):** _____

Estimated cost: _____

DISK INFORMATION

Disk controller

Type: _____ Vendor: _____

Model: _____

Drive address	Type	Mfg	Cyl/Hd/Sec	Speed/capacity	DOS partition size
_____	_____	_____	__ / __ / __	_____	_____

NETWORK CARD INFORMATION

Network type	Manufacturer ID	I/O port	Interrupt
_____	_____	_____	_____

NONNETWORK DEVICE INFORMATION

Device name	IRQ	I/O port
_____	_____	_____
_____	_____	_____
_____	_____	_____

NetWare Server Worksheet

Installed by:	Date:
NetWare server name:	Internal IPX network number:
NDS Tree name:	Organization name:
Container where server object was placed:	

SYSTEM INFORMATION

Computer manufacturer:		Model:	
CPU type:	Clock speed:	Bus:	Memory:

DISK INFORMATION

Disk Controller 1:

Type:	Manufacturer:	Model:
Interrupt:	I/O address:	DMA channel:

Memory address:

Disk driver name:

Drive address	Type	Mfg	Cyl/Hd/Sec	Speed/ capacity	DOS partition size	NetWare partition size	Mirrored with drive

Disk Controller 2:

Type:	Manufacturer:	Model:
Interrupt:	I/O address:	DMA channel:

Memory address:

Disk driver name:

Drive address	Type	Mfg	Cyl/Hd/Sec	Speed/ capacity	DOS partition size	NetWare partition size	Mirrored with drive

NETWORK CARD INFORMATION

Network type	Manufacturer	LAN driver	I/O port	Memory address	IRQ/ DMA	Frame type	Network address

IP INFORMATION

IP address:	Subnet address:	Gateway:

NONNETWORK DEVICE INFORMATION

Device name	IRQ	I/O port	DMA	Memory address

D

NetWare Server Planning Form	
Created by:	**Date:**
Organization:	
NetWare Servers	
NetWare server name:	
NetWare operating system version:	
Volumes:	SYS
Purpose:	
NetWare server name:	
NetWare operating system version:	
Volumes:	SYS
Purpose:	
NetWare server name:	
NetWare operating system version:	
Volumes:	SYS
Purpose:	

Directory Planning Form

Created by:	Date:
Organization:	

Workgroups:

Workgroup name	Members	Space requirement

Directories:

Directory description	Type	Users	Capacity

D

Volume Design Form

Designed by:		Date:
Volume name:		Maximum capacity:
NetWare version:		

Block size:		4 KB	
		8 KB	
		16 KB	
		32 KB	

Volume name

Directory Design Form	
Designed by:	**Date:**
Volume name:	**Directory name:**
Estimated size:	**NetWare version:**
Directory name	

D

Drive Mapping Planning Form

Organization:		Date:	
Planned by:			

GROUP:

Drive letter	Description of use	Path

GROUP:

Drive letter	Description of use	Path

GROUP:

Drive letter	Description of use	Path

Group Planning Form			
Designer:		**Date:**	
Group name	**Members**	**Context**	**Description**

D

User Planning Form						
Company:				Date:		
Created by:						
User name	Login name	Context	Template name	Home directory	Groups	Additional properties

User Template Planning Form	
Designer:	**Date:**

Template name	
Context	
Home directory path	
Minimum password length	
Require unique passwords	
Days before password changes	
Grace logins	
Valid login times	
Maximum connections	
Groups	
Users	

Template name	
Context	
Home directory path	
Minimum password length	
Require unique passwords	
Days before password changes	
Grace logins	
Valid login times	
Maximum connections	
Groups	
Users	

D

Print Services Definition Form

Prepared by: _____   Date: _____

NDS tree: _____   Organization: _____

Organizational unit: _____   Server host: _____

Manager name: _____

Printer name	Printer type	Make/Model	Attachment type	Location	Users/applications	Public or controlled access?	Printer agent

Notes:

Container Login Script Form

Designed by:	Date:

Container context:

REM Preliminary Commands

REM Common Application Search Drive Mappings

REM Common Regular Drive Mappings

REM Mapping for _____ Workgroup

REM Mapping for _____ Workgroup

REM Mapping for _____ Workgroup

REM End of Login Script Commands

D

Profile Login Script Form

Created by:	Date:

Container context:

Profile script name:

Login script for: _____ **Profile object**

Users: _____   _____   _____

_____   _____   _____

Profile script name:

Login script for: _____ **Profile object**

Users: _____   _____   _____

_____   _____   _____

Glossary

10Base2 — A 10 Mbps linear bus implementation of CSMA/CD Ethernet using coaxial cable with T-connectors to attach networked computers. A terminator is used at each of the coaxial cable wire segments.

10Base5 — A 10Mbps linear bus implementation of CSMA/CD Ethernet using a heavy coaxial cable but otherwise similar to 10Base2.

10BaseT — A 10 Mbps star implementation of CSMA/CD Ethernet using twisted-pair wires to connect all stations to a central concentrator.

100BaseFX — A 100 Mbps star implementation of CSMA/CD Ethernet using fiber-optic cables to connect all stations to a central concentrator.

100BaseT — A 100 Mbps star implementation of CSMA/CD Ethernet using twisted-pair wires to connect all stations to a central concentrator.

AARP — *See* Apple Address Resolution Protocol.

absolute directory path — Another name for a complete directory path, which identifies the location of a file or directory by specifying the path: NetWare Server/Volume:Directory\Subdirectory [\Subdirectory].

access arm — A device used on disk drives to position the recording heads over the desired disk track.

access control list (ACL) — A property of an NDS object that stores the trustee list for that object.

Access Control right (A) — A NetWare trustee right that allows a user to assign rights to other users.

access rights — When referring to NDS, access rights control which NDS objects and properties a user can work with. Object access rights, also called Object rights, include Supervisor, Browse, Create, Delete, and Rename. Property access rights, also called Property rights, include Supervisor, Compare, Read, Write, and Add or Delete Self. When referring to the network file system, access rights control what disk functions a user can perform in a directory or on a file. Directory and file access rights, also called Directory rights and File rights, include Read, File Scan, Write, Create, Erase, Modify, Access Control, and Supervisor.

access time — The time required for a storage device to locate and transfer a block of data into RAM.

adapter — When referring to Windows 95/98, a network interface card (NIC).

ADD NAME SPACE utility — NetWare utility that adds support on a volume for Macintosh or Unix filenames. NetWare 5.0 automatically provides Windows 95/98 long filename support on each volume.

Add or Delete Self right (A) — An NDS Property right that lets users add themselves to or remove themselves from the object's access control list (ACL).

address — When referring to a workstation's memory, a number used to identify the location of data within the computer system.

address bus — The number of bits that are sent from the CPU to the memory indicating the memory byte to be accessed. The size of the address bus determines the amount of memory that can be directly accessed. The 20-bit address bus on the 8088 computer limited it to 1 MB. The 24-bit address bus on 80286 and 80386SX computers provides for up to 16 MB. The 32-bit address bus used on 80386DX and above computers can access up to 2 GB of memory.

AFP Server object — An NDS informational leaf object that represents a network AppleTalk File Protocol server in the Directory tree.

agent — When referring to Windows 95/98, client software that allows the workstation to use network resources provided by server software on an applications server.

AGP (Accelerated or **Advanced Graphics Port)** — A new type of connector on system-boards for attaching high-performance screen adapter cards.

Alias object — An NDS leaf object that represents an NDS leaf object located in another part of the Directory tree.

American National Standards Institute (ANSI) — The U.S. organization that creates standards for telecommunications, networking, and programming languages. It also represents the United States in the International Standardization Organization (ISO).

analog signals — The signals carried by a broadband system such as radio or television.

Apple Address Resolution Protocol (AARP) — One component of the AppleTalk protocol, the AARP works at the physical and data link layers.

AppleTalk — Apple's network protocol developed to enable Macintosh computers to work in peer-to-peer networks.

AppleTalk File Protocol (AFP) server — A NetWare 5.0 server running NetWare's AppleTalk File Protocol (AFP) so that Apple workstations can connect to the network.

Application Launcher (formerly the **Novell Application Launcher** or **NAL**) — A NetWare feature that helps network administrators configure and manage applications from within the NDS Directory tree. The Application Launcher software resides on the user's workstation, whereas NetWare Application Manager (NAM) software resides on the NetWare server.

application layer — The top software layer of the OSI model that interacts with the user to perform a communication process on a network.

Application Object Template (AOT) — A template used by Z.E.N.works in configuring workstations to run a specific application.

Application Object Text Template (AXT) — A template similar to the AOT except that it is modifiable by the administrator.

application-oriented structure — A directory structure that groups directories and subdirectories according to application or use rather than by department or owner.

application server — A network server that stores software applications for use by network users.

Archive Needed — A file attribute set by the computer whenever the contents of a file have changed.

assign — The act of giving rights to a trustee. *See* grant.

assigned rights — The set of rights granted or assigned to a trustee.

asynchronous communication — A form of communication in which each byte is encapsulated with start and stop bits and then sent separately across the transmission media.

ATOTAL — A DOS-based utility used to extract auditing information from NetWare.

attribute — A flag that is used by NetWare to determine the type of processing that can be performed on files and directories. Directory attributes include Delete Inhibit, Don't Compress, Don't Migrate, Hidden, Immediate Compress, Normal, Purge, Rename Inhibit, and System. File attributes include Archive Needed, Can't Compress, Compressed, Copy Inhibit, Delete Inhibit, Don't Compress, Execute Only, Hidden, Immediate Compress, Migrated, Normal, Purge, Read Only, Read Write, Rename Inhibit, Sharable, System, and Transactional.

authenticating — The process of sending a user name and password to the NDS Directory or a NetWare server and having them checked and validated.

AUTOEXEC.NCF — A NetWare Command File (NCF) that is run when the server is starting (booting) up after SERVER.EXE is started.

backbone network — A network cable system used to connect network servers and host computer systems. Each network server or host may then contain a separate network card that attaches it to client computers.

bandwidth — A measurement of the range of signals that can be sent across a communications system.

baseband — A digital signaling system that consists of only two signals representing one and zero.

baud rate — A measurement of the number of signal changes per second.

bidirectional communications — The ability of newer printers to communicate status information to users as well as be managed remotely.

bindery — The NetWare 3.1x files that contain security information such as usernames, passwords, and account restrictions. The bindery files are stored on NetWare 3.1x servers in the SYS:SYSTEM directory and consist of NET$OBJ.SYS, NET$PROP.SYS, and NET$VAL.SYS.

bindery emulation mode — A mode of operation on a NetWare 5.0 server that mimics the NetWare 3.1x bindery for devices that can't work with NDS.

Bindery object — An NDS miscellaneous leaf object that represents NetWare 3.1x bindery data in the Directory tree.

Bindery Queue object — An NDS miscellaneous leaf object that represents a NetWare 3.1x bindery queue in the Directory tree.

bits per second (bps) — Number of bits transmitted per second in a data transfer; standard measure of transmission speed in digital communications.

block — When referring to a database, a collection of data records that can be read or written from the computer RAM to a storage device at one time. When referring to a hard disk, a storage location on the physical disk volume consisting of 4 KB, 8 KB, 16 KB, 32 KB, or 64 KB.

block suballocation — A method that allows data from more than one file to be placed in a single data block.

blocks read charge — In NetWare accounting, a charge to a user account for reading data from disk drives.

blocks written charge — In NetWare accounting, a charge to a user account for writing data to disk drives.

bounded media — Media that confines a signal within a cable.

bridge — A device used to connect networks of similar topology. Operates at the data link layer.

broadband — A signaling system that uses analog signals to carry data across the media.

Browse right (B) — An NDS object right that enables a trustee to see the object in the Directory tree and have the object's name appear in search results.

buffer — A storage location in memory used to hold blocks of data from disk to reduce the number of disk accesses needed to process a request.

bundled pair — Fifty or more pairs of twisted wire put together in one large cable.

bus — An electronic pathway that connects computer components.

bus mastering — A technique used by certain high-speed adapter cards to transfer data directly into a computer's RAM.

cable system — The physical wire system used to connect computers in a local area network.

cache memory — The memory area used to temporarily hold data from lower-speed storage devices to provide better access time.

Can't Compress (Cc) — A NetWare file attribute used to flag files that can't be compressed.

Carrier Sense Multiple Access with Collision Detection (CSMA/CD) — A channel access control method used on Ethernet networks in which a computer waits for the media to have an open carrier signal before attempting to transmit. Collisions occur when two or more devices sense an open carrier and attempt to transmit at the same instant.

Category 5 cable — A network cable specification most commonly used today with 10BaseT and 100BaseT.

centralized processing — A processing method in which program execution takes place on a central host computer rather than at a user workstation.

Certified Novell Administrator (CNA) — A network administrator who has taken and passed the Novell CNA exam.

Certified Novell Engineer (CNE) — A network administrator who has taken and passed the Novell CNE exam.

channel access method — A method of controlling when a device can transmit data over a local area network. Common access methods include token ring and CSMA/CD.

child partition — When referring to NDS, a partition that is below (farther away from the [Root]) a parent partition, in the Directory tree structure. The child partition is subordinate to the parent partition.

children — When referring to NDS, container levels that are subordinate (farther away from the [Root]) to another container. The superior (closer to the [Root]) container level is called the *parent*.

client — When referring to Windows 95/98, a client is the software that provides network connectivity for the workstation, which is called a network interface card (NIC) driver in NetWare.

client-server — *See* client-server network operating system.

client-server applications — A type of application in which part of the application runs on the network server and part of the application runs on the client workstations.

client-server network operating system — A type of network operating system in which certain computers are dedicated to performing server functions, while other computers called *clients* run application software for users.

client workstation — A networked computer that runs user application software and is able to request data from a file server.

clock — A device in the system unit of a computer that sends out a fixed number of pulses or signals per second. The clock pulses are used to synchronize actions in the system unit. The clock speed is measured in millions of cycles per second called *megahertz* or MHz. The faster the clock speed, the more work a given system unit can do per second.

coaxial cable — A thick plastic cable containing a center conductor and shield.

collision — An event that occurs when two or more nodes attempt to transmit on the network at the same time. After the collision, the nodes wait a random time interval before retrying.

command line utility (CLU) — A NetWare utility that performs a specific function from the DOS prompt given specific command line parameters. Examples are NDIR, NCOPY, and MAP.

command queuing — A method of storing commands for future processing.

common name (CN) — The name type associated with an NDS leaf object.

compact disc read-only memory (CD-ROM) — A data storage device that uses the compact disc format and can store about 680 MB of data. The data is recorded by the manufacturer and cannot be altered by the user.

Compare right (C) — An NDS Property right that enables a trustee to compare a value to the value of the property, but not to see the value itself (the Read [R] right is needed to see the value).

compiler — A program that converts source commands to a form that is executable by the computer system.

complementary metal oxide semiconductor (CMOS) memory — A type of memory that is capable of holding data with very little power requirements. This type of memory is used to store configuration data that is backed up by a battery on the systemboard. The battery prevents CMOS from being erased when power is turned off.

complete directory path — Identifies the location of a file or directory by specifying the path: NetWare Server/Volume:Directory\Subdirectory [\Subdirectory].

complex instruction set computer (CISC) — A computer with a microprocessor that uses instructions in a wide range of formats that can require more that one clock cycle to complete.

Compressed (Co) — A NetWare file attribute used to flag files that are compressed.

Computer object — An NDS informational leaf object that represents a user's workstation in the Directory tree.

concentrator — A central hub device used to connect 10BaseT computers together to form a network.

conditional variables — Login script variables that have a value of "True" or "False."

connect time charge — In NetWare accounting, a charge to a user account for the length of time a user workstation has been logged into a NetWare server.

consistent — The same throughout. When referring to NDS, all the replicas of a partition must be updated so that they are consistent. Because the updating process takes time, the Directory database is said to be loosely consistent at any moment in time.

console command — A command that affects the NetWare server and is issued from the NetWare server console. Examples include CONFIG, LOAD, and DOWN.

console operator — A user name that has been assigned the privilege of running the FCONSOLE program. Console operators are assigned using the supervisor options of SYSCON.

container login script — A login script that is stored in a container object and that is used by all users within the container unless the user is assigned a profile login script or has a user login script.

container object — An NDS object that contains other NDS objects. The NDS container objects are the [Root], Country, Organization, and Organizational Unit objects.

contention access method — A channel access method in which computer nodes are allowed to talk whenever they detect that the channel is not in use. This often results in collisions between packets. In Ethernet, this becomes the Carrier Sense Multiple Access with Collision Detection (CSMA/CD) method.

context — The location of an NDS object in the Directory tree.

contextless login — A NetWare login during which the user does not have to specify a context. Instead, NetWare is either configured to understand the User object's context or the user selects it from a dropdown list of valid users.

controller card — An adapter card used to control storage devices such as disk drives.

conventional memory — The first 640 KB of memory used by DOS to run application programs.

Copy Inhibit (Ci) — A NetWare file attribute that prevents Macintosh computers from accessing certain PC file types.

Country object — An NDS container object that represents a country in the Directory tree.

Create right (C) — When referring to NDS Object rights, lets a user create new objects in a container (applies to container objects only). When referring to the network file system, a NetWare Directory right and File right that allows a user to create new files and subdirectories.

current context — The user's current location in the NDS Directory tree.

Custom Device Module (CDM) — One of the components of the Novell Peripheral Architecture (NPA) introduced in NetWare 4.1. Using NPA, drivers are broken into two parts—the Host Adapter Module (HAM) and the Custom Device Module (CDM).

cycle — The time it takes a signal to return to its starting state.

cyclic redundancy check (CRC) — An error-checking system that allows a receiving computer to determine if a block of data was received correctly, by applying a formula to the data and checking the results against the value supplied by the sending computer.

cylinder — The number of disk tracks that can be accessed without moving the access arm of the hard drive mechanism.

data bus — The "highway" that leads from a device to the CPU. Computers based on 80286 and 80386SX have 16-bit data bus architecture compared to 32 bits on the 80386DX and 80486 computer models and 64 bits on Pentium-based computers.

data communications equipment (DCE) — The type of a connector used on a computer that connects to the computer modem cable.

data compression algorithm — The algorithm used by NetWare's file compression system to compress the file size.

data file — Used with the NetWare UIMPORT command line utility, the data file contains the specific data for each user account to be created.

data frame packet — The packet created at the data link layer based on the datagram received from the network layer.

data link layer — The OSI software layer that controls access to the network card.

data migration — A NetWare feature that moves files that have not been used for a long time to another type of storage medium such as an optical disk. The filename is retained on the volume, and if the file is needed, it is retrieved.

data terminal equipment (DTE) — The type of connector used on a modem that connects to the computer modem cable.

Datagram Delivery Protocol (DDP) — One component of the AppleTalk protocol, the DDP works at the network layer.

datagram packet — The name of an information packet at the network layer.

date variables — Login script variables that contain date information such as month, name, day of week, and year.

default directory — The directory from which data will be accessed when no path is supplied.

default drive — The drive from which data will be accessed when no path is supplied.

default login script — The login script that is used if no other login script exists for a user.

default volume name — The name automatically assigned to a volume by NetWare if no other name is specified. The first volume is named SYS, the next is named VOL1, the next is named VOL2, and so on.

Delete Inhibit (Di) — A NetWare attribute that prevents a file or directory from being removed.

Delete right (D) — An NDS Object right that enables users to delete the object from the Directory tree.

departmental structure — A directory structure that groups directories and subdirectories according to the workgroup or department that uses or controls them.

depth — When referring to the NDS Directory tree, the number of levels in the tree. *See* width. A Directory tree should be planned with only as much depth as necessary because each level adds another term to the distinguished name of objects at that level.

device driver — A software program that controls physical access to an external device such as a network card or storage drive.

digital signals — Signals that can have a value of only zero or one.

Digital Versatile Disc (DVD) — An upgraded version of CD-ROM, often called DVD-ROM, which holds up to 4.7 GB of data in the current versions.

direct memory access (DMA) channel — A device used to transfer data between RAM and an external device without taking time from the processor.

direct printer or **directly attached printer** — A printer that is connected to the network by its own network interface card.

directory — When referring to the network file system, a logical storage unit on a volume. Called a *folder* in Windows 95/98.

directory caching — A method of improving hard disk access time by keeping the directory entry table (DET) and file allocation table (FAT) in memory.

Directory database — The NetWare database that stores NDS data.

directory entry table (DET) — A table on a storage device that contains the names and locations of all files.

directory hashing — A method of improving access time by indexing entries in the directory entry table.

Directory Map object — An NDS server-related leaf object that is used in the Directory tree to reference a drive mapping

directory path — A list of network file system components, such as the names of directories and subdirectories, identifying the location of data on a storage device.

Directory rights — The set of rights to directories in the network file system that can be granted to a trustee. Directory rights also generally apply to files in the directory, although they can be blocked with individual File rights. Directory rights include Supervisor (S), Read (R), Write (W), Create (C), Erase (E), Modify (M), File Scan (F), and Access Control (A).

Directory tree — The hierarchical tree structure created to visualize the organization of the NDS Directory database.

Directory tree name — The name of the NDS Directory tree.

disk storage charge — In NetWare accounting, a charge to a user account for storing data on a disk.

dismounting a volume — A method of taking a disk volume off line to perform system functions.

distinguished name — When referring to an NDS object, an object's distinguished name is its complete name, which is the object's common name plus the object's context. A distinguished name always shows the path to the object from the [Root]. An example of a distinguished name is .EFranklin.FDR_Admin.FDR.

distributed database — A database that is split into parts, with each part residing on a different server.

distributed processing — A processing method in which application software is executed on the client workstations.

Don't Compress (Dc) — A NetWare file attribute used to flag files that you do not want compressed.

Don't Migrate (Dm) — A NetWare file attribute used to flag files that you do not want migrated.

Don't Suballocate (Ds) — A NetWare file attribute used to flag files that you do not want suballocated.

dot pitch — A measurement of the spacing between color spots on video monitors. A smaller dot pitch provides sharper images.

DOWN command — The console command used to take a NetWare server off line.

drive mapping — The assignment of a drive pointer to a storage area on a hard disk.

drive pointer — A letter of the alphabet that is used to reference storage areas in the file system.

driver software — When referring to a network interface card (NIC), the software needed to control the NIC and interface between the data link layer and the network layer software.

DSMERGE.NLM — A NetWare NLM that allows you to merge two Directory trees.

duplexing — A method of synchronizing data on storage devices attached to different controller cards.

dynamic execution — A feature of the Intel Pentium Pro CPU. It consists of three processing techniques: multiple branch prediction, dataflow analysis, and speculative execution.

dynamic RAM (DRAM) — A common form of dynamic memory chip, used in computer RAM, that requires a refresh cycle to retain data contents.

effective rights — A subset of the access rights that control which disk processing a user can perform on a specific directory or file. Effective rights consist of a combination of rights the user has as a user and as a member of groups, container objects, and so on.

El Torito — A specification for CD-ROM drives that allows the drive to serve as the boot drive.

electromagnetic interference (EMI) — An undesirable electronic noise created on a wire cable when it runs close to a strong power source or magnetic field.

electronic mail (e-mail) applications — Software applications that allow network users to send messages to each other.

elevator seeking — A technique used in NetWare file servers to increase disk access performance by smoothly moving an access arm across a hard disk surface to read and write the requested data blocks in the sequence they are encountered rather than in the sequence received.

end user — The person who uses the computer to directly accomplish his or her job tasks.

Enhanced IDE — A disk drive system that improves on the standard IDE system by supporting up to four disk drives with higher-drive capacities (above the 528 MB limitation of IDE), and faster performance.

entry-level PC — The PC configuration typically purchased by a company as its standard configuration.

Erase right (E) — When referring to a network file system, a NetWare Directory and File right that allows the user to delete files and remove subdirectories when assigned to a directory.

Error-checking and -correcting (ECC) memory — A type of RAM that can automatically recognize and correct memory errors.

Ethernet — A network system that uses the Carrier Sense Multiple Access with Collision Detection (CSMA/CD) access method to connect networked computers. Originally, the term also meant only the 10BASE2 system, but now refers to the entire Ethernet family, also including 10BASET, 100BASETX, and 100BASEFX.

Execute Only (X) — A NetWare file attribute that may be used with executable (.COM and .EXE) program files to prevent the files from being copied while still allowing users to run them.

expansion bus — The system board bus that allows expansion cards plugged into expansion slots on a computer's system board that connects the adapter cards to the rest of the computer.

expansion card — A circuit board that plugs into an expansion slot and extends the computer's capabilities, such as a network interface card or modem.

expansion slot — An electrical connection on the system board into which expansion cards plug.

Extended Data Output (EDO) RAM — A faster version of RAM now standard in Pentium, Pentium MMX, and Pentium Pro computers.

Extended Industry Standard Architecture (EISA) bus — A system board expansion bus that supports both ISA cards along with high-speed 32-bit cards for increased performance.

extended memory — Memory above 1 MB. This memory requires special software to access it.

fault tolerance — A measurement of how well a system can continue to operate despite the failure of certain hardware components.

fiber-optic cable — A cable made of light-conducting glass fibers that allows high-speed communications.

Fields section — Used with the NetWare UIMPORT command line utility, the Fields section of the import control file contains a list of the NDS object fields that correspond to the data contained in the data file.

file allocation table (FAT) — A table stored on a disk that is used to link together the storage blocks belonging to each file.

file attribute — A flag used by NetWare to determine what type of processing can be performed on the file.

file caching — A method used by a NetWare file server to increase performance by storing the most frequently accessed file blocks in RAM.

file compression — A method of coding the data in a file to reduce the file size.

File rights — The set of rights to files in the network file system that can be granted to a trustee. File rights include Supervisor (S), Read (R), Write (W), Create (C), Erase (E), Modify (M), File Scan (F) and Access Control (A).

File Scan right (F) — When referring to the network file system, a NetWare Directory and File right that allows the user to view file and directory names.

file system security — A security system that prevents unauthorized users from accessing or modifying file data.

file trustee — A user or group that has been granted access rights to a file.

folder — When referring to the network file system or a user's workstation, the Windows 95/98 term for a directory or subdirectory.

frame — The name of an information packet at the data link layer.

general-purpose application — An application package, such as a word processor or a spreadsheet, that is used to perform many different functions.

global shared directory — A directory in which all users in an organization may store and retrieve files.

grace login — An extra login given to a user after the user's password has expired to allow the user a chance to change his or her password.

grant — To give to someone. When referring to NetWare trustee rights, to assign rights to a user, group or other NDS object. *See* assign.

graphical utility — A NetWare utility run on a workstation that uses a graphical user interface such as Windows 95/98 or OS/2. An example is NetWare Administrator.

graphics accelerator — A video adapter with a microprocessor preprogrammed to speed up graphics operations.

Group object — An NDS user-related leaf object that is used in the Directory tree to manage groups of users.

Hidden (H) — A NetWare file or directory attribute used to prevent a file or directory from appearing on directory listings.

hierarchical structure — An logical organizational structure that starts at one point, called the [Root], and branches out from the starting point. Points in the structure are logically above or below other points on the same branch.

home directory — A private directory in which a user typically stores personal files and works on projects that are not shared with other users.

Host Adapter Module (HAM) — One of the components of the Novell Peripheral Architecture (NPA) introduced in NetWare 4.1. Using NPA, drivers are broken into two parts—the Host Adapter Module (HAM) and the Custom Device Module (CDM).

host server — When using SMS, the host file server is the server that contains the backup tape drive and backs up data from other computers called "target" devices.

hot fix — A NetWare feature whereby data on bad and unreliable disk storage sectors is copied to a reserved redirection area located in a different area on the hard disk.

hot-swapping — A fault-tolerant system that allows a disk drive to be replaced without shutting down the computer system.

hub — A central connection device in which each cable of a star topology network is connected together.

identifier variables — Login script variables that may be used in login script commands to represent such information as the user login name, date, time, and DOS version.

IEEE 802.3 — Standard issued by the Institute of Electrical and Electronic Engineers specifying an Ethernet protocol.

IEEE 802.5 — Similar to 802.3 except that this specifies a token ring standard.

Immediate Compress (Ic) — A NetWare file attribute used to flag files that should be compressed immediately instead of waiting for the standard waiting period to elapse.

Import Control file — Used with the NetWare UIMPORT command line utility, the Import Control file controls the creation of user accounts by specifying general information that applies to all user accounts being created. It has two sections: the Import Control section and the Fields section.

Import Control section — Used with the NetWare UIMPORT command line utility, the Import Control section of the Import Control file contains control parameters that specify UIMPORT options.

Industry Standard Architecture (ISA) bus — A system board bus structure that supports 16-bit data and 24-bit address buses at 8 MHz clock speed. This bus was developed for the IBM AT computer in 1984, and is still popular. However, used with high-speed processors it greatly reduces the performance of expansion cards.

informational leaf objects — A group of NDS objects, including the Computer object and the AFP Server object, that store data that would otherwise be unrepresented in the NDS Directory tree.

infrared — An unbounded media system that uses infrared light to transmit information. Commonly used on television remote control devices and small wireless LANs.

inherited rights — Rights that flow down into a container object, directory, or file from a higher level. For example, if a user is granted the RFW rights to the DATA:SALES directory, the user will also inherit the RFW rights into the DATA:SALES\ORDERS and DATA:SALES\USERS subdirectories.

Inherited Rights Filter (IRF) — Each container object, directory, and file contains an Inherited Rights Filter that controls what access rights can flow down to the container object, directory, or file from a higher level.

input/output (I/O) port — An interface used to transfer data and commands to and from external devices.

Institute of Electrical and Electronic Engineers (IEEE) — A U.S. professional organization that has established network standards, including those for LAN topologies.

instruction set — The set of binary command codes a CPU chip can recognize and execute.

Integrated Drive Electronics (IDE) — A type of hard disk controller that can control up to two hard drives with capacities up to 528 megabytes.

internal network number — A network address used internally by NetWare to communicate with its software components.

International Standards Organization (ISO) — The group responsible for administering the OSI model.

Internet — An information highway that is not controlled by any single organization and is used worldwide to connect business, government, education, and private users.

internetwork — One or more network cable systems connected together by bridges or routers.

Internetwork Packet Exchange (IPX) — The NetWare protocol that manages packet routing and formatting at the network layer.

interoperability — The ability of computers on different networks to communicate.

interrupt request (IRQ) — A signal that is sent from an external device to notify the CPU that it needs attention.

intranet — A computer network based on Internet technology (TCP/IP), but designed to meet the needs of a single organization.

IntraNetWare — A shortlived renaming of NetWare 4.11.

Java — A programming language providing multiple-platform support without the need to recompile software for each platform.

Java Virtual Machine (JVM) — A utility in NetWare and on workstations for running a Java application (also called an applet).

KB — Kilobyte or 1024 bytes.

LDAP (Lightweight Directory Access Protocol) — A protocol specification for locating, extracting, and updating information from a directory service such as NDS.

leading period — When referring to an NDS object, a period that appears at the beginning of the object's context or the object's common name in its distinguished name. The leading period indicates that the path to the object is beginning at the [Root]. In the context *.Admin_FDR.FDR*, the period before *Admin_FDR* is the leading period.

leaf object — An NDS Directory tree object that cannot contain other objects. Leaf objects are used to store data about network resources, such as NetWare servers, volumes, users, groups, and printers.

linear bus topology — A LAN topology that consists of a coaxial cable segment that connects computers by running from one machine to the next with a terminating resistor on each end of the cable segment.

link support layer (LSL) — A software component of Novell's ODI specification, it connects the data link layer of the protocol stack and the network interface card (NIC) driver.

local area network (LAN) — A high-speed, limited-distance communication system designed to support distributed processing.

local bus — The internal address, data, and instruction buses of the system board, often used to refer to a high-speed expansion bus structure that allows adapter cards to operate close to the speed of the internal system board.

local drive pointer — A drive pointer (normally A: through F:) that is used to reference a local device on the workstation such as a floppy or hard disk drive.

local printer — In the context of network printing, a network printer attached directly to a port of the print server computer. In the context of a workstation, the printer attached directly to a port on the workstation.

local shared directory — A directory in which all users of a department or workgroup may store and retrieve files.

logical block address (LBA) — A feature of the Enhanced Integrated Drive Electronics (EIDE) interface that allows EIDE drives to provide up to 8.4 GB of storage.

logical entity — When referring to NDS, a network resource that exists as a logical or mental creation, such as an organizational entity that models the structure of an organization. *See* physical entity.

logical link control (LLC) layer — A sublayer of the data link layer of the OSI model, in interfaces with the physical layer.

login name — The name a user enters at the login prompt or in the Novell Client Login dialog box when logging into the network. The login name is also the name displayed for the user's User object in the NDS Directory tree.

login script — A set of NetWare commands performed each time a user logs into the file server.

login script variable — A reserved word that may be used to substitute values into login script statements to modify processing.

login security — A security system that employs user names, passwords, and account restrictions to prevent unauthorized users from accessing the network.

loosely consistent — The same throughout, more or less. When referring to NDS, all the replicas of a partition need to be updated so that they are consistent. Because the updating process takes time, the Directory database is said to be loosely consistent at any moment in time.

machine language — A program consisting of binary codes that the CPU can directly interpret and execute.

mainframe computers — Large computers in which the processing power is in the computer and users access it via terminals.

master replica — When referring to NDS, the main copy of a partition. There is only one master replica for each partition. A master replica can be read from and written to, and can be used for login purposes.

math coprocessor — An extension of the CPU that lets it directly perform mathematical functions and floating-point arithmetic.

media — The device or material used to record and retrieve data.

media access control (MAC) layer — A sublayer of the data link layer of the OSI model, in interfaces with the network layer.

megahertz (MHz) — Millions of cycles per second.

message packet — A packet containing data that is being sent via the network from one user to another.

Micro Channel bus — A system board design patented by IBM that allows for 32-bit expansion cards along with automatic card configuration.

microprocessor — The central processing unit (CPU) of a microcomputer system.

Migrated (M) — A NetWare file attribute used to flag files that have been migrated.

millions of instructions per second (MIPS) — A measure of speed for computer CPUs.

minimum compression percentage gain — The minimum file size reduction that must be possible before NetWare will compress the file. The default is 2 percent.

mirroring — A disk fault tolerance system that synchronizes data on two drives attached to a single controller card.

miscellaneous leaf objects — A group of NDS Directory tree objects, including the Alias object, the Bindery object, the Bindery Queue object, and the Unknown object, that are not classified as other types of leaf objects.

mission-critical application — An application that is necessary to perform the day-to-day operations of a business or an organization.

Modify right (M) — When referring to the network file system, a NetWare Directory and File right that allows a user to change file and directory attributes as well as rename files and subdirectories.

MONITOR utility — A NetWare console utility that displays essential information about NetWare server performance.

motherboard — Another name for the system board, the main circuit board in a computer that ties together the CPU, memory, and expansion slots.

mounting a volume — The process of loading the File Allocation Table and Directory Entry Table of a volume into memory. A volume must be mounted before it can be accessed on a network.

Multiple Link Interface Driver (MLID) — The term used by Novell's ODI specification for a network interface card (NIC) driver.

multiple NetWare server network — A network with more than one NetWare server attached.

Multiple Station Access Unit (MSAU) — A central hub device used to connect IBM token ring network systems.

multiple-user application — An application that is either NetWare-aware (and designed to support multiple users) or is designed with enough flexibility so that the application can be set up to keep each user's work files separated.

multiplexing — Placing multiple message packets into one segment.

multiuser — application — A special type of multiple-user application that allows more than one user to access the same file simultaneously.

name context — When referring to the Novell Client, the context of the user's User object.

name space — A NetWare module that provides support for Macintosh, OS/2, or Windows 95/98 long filenames.

name type — A NetWare NDS descriptor of object types. There are four name types: Country name type (abbreviated as C), Organization name type (abbreviated as O), Organizational Unit name type

(abbreviated as OU), and Common Name type (which refers to all leaf objects and is abbreviated as CN). There is no name type for the [Root] object.

NCP Server object — Another name for the NetWare Server object, which is an NDS Server-related leaf object used in the Directory tree to manage NetWare servers. NCP is an abbreviation for NetWare Core Protocol.

NDS Directory tree — A visual structure used to organize NDS objects.

NDS security — A security system that prevents unauthorized users from accessing or modifying the NDS database and the NDS Directory tree.

nesting — A programming technique involving placing one IF statement inside another so that the second IF statement is executed only when the first IF statement is true.

NET.CFG — A network shell configuration file used with the old NETX shell and the NetWare DOS Requester shell.

NETADMIN utility — An older DOS-based NetWare menu utility used to manage NDS objects.

NetBEUI — Microsoft's network protocol stack, integrated into Windows for Workgroups, Windows 95/98, and Windows NT. It consists of NetBIOS and service message blocks (SMBs) at the session layer and NetBIOS frames (NBFs) at the transport layer. NBF can be replaced with NetBIOS over TCP/IP (NBT) for direct communication over TCP/IP-based networks.

NetBIOS — The Network Basic Input/Output System (NetBIOS) was developed by IBM and is now used in Microsoft's NetBEUI protocol.

NetBIOS frames (NBF) — One component of Microsoft's NetBEUI protocol.

NetBIOS over TCP/IP (NBT) — An alternate component of Microsoft's NetBEUI protocol that enables its use with TCP/IP networks.

NetWare Accounting — An optional service provided in NetWare for tracking usage charges to individual users for storage space or other criteria.

NetWare Administrator utility (NWAdmin) — The primary tool for administering NetWare 5.0.

It is a Windows-based graphical utility used to manage NDS objects.

NetWare Application Manager (NAM) — A NetWare feature that helps network administrators configure and manage applications from within the NDS Directory tree. The NAM software resides on the NetWare server, whereas the Application Launcher software resides on the user's workstation.

NetWare Application Manager-related objects — A group of NDS Directory tree objects, including the DOS Application object, the Windows 3.x Application object, the Windows 95/98 Application object, and the Windows NT Application object, that are used to manage applications as part of the NetWare Applications Manager and Application Launcher software.

NetWare-aware — Software designed to take advantage of the features found in NetWare, such as printing or separate work and configuration files for each user.

NetWare Command File (NCF) — A NetWare Command File is similar to a DOS batch file in that it contains console commands and program startup commands that will be executed by the operating system. STARTUP.NCF and AUTOEX-EC.NCF are two examples.

NetWare-compatible — Software that can be installed in the NetWare file system and will run properly from any workstation.

NetWare Core Protocol (NCP) — The NetWare protocol that provides session- and presentation-layer services.

NetWare DOS Requester — An older requester type of network shell for workstations. It was introduced after NETX, and before Novell Client 32. The NetWare DOS requester is based on Virtual Loadable Modules (VLMs).

NetWare file servers — Network servers in a NetWare LAN for NetWare versions 3.1x and earlier. After NetWare 4.x, the term *NetWare server* is used.

NetWare Loadable Module (NLM) — A program that may be loaded and run on the NetWare server. There are four types of NLMs, identified by their three-letter extension. The filename extension NLM is used for general-purpose programs, DSK for disk drivers, LAN for network card drivers, and NAM for name space support modules.

NetWare Provider for Windows 95/98 — A component of the Novell Client network shell that extends the capabilities of Windows 95/98 programs (such as Explorer) to provide access to NetWare features.

NetWare server — A term first used to refer to network servers in a NetWare LAN for NetWare version 4.x.

NetWare server name — The name that a NetWare server broadcasts over the network. When referring to NDS, the name of the NetWare Server object.

NetWare Server object — An NDS Server-related leaf object used in the Directory tree to manage NetWare servers.

network address — An address used by the network layer to identify computers on the network.

network administrator — The network user in charge of the network and all its resources, who is responsible for maintaining, allocating, and protecting the network.

network-centric — A network in which a user logs in only once to the network itself, and not to each network server, as is done in a server-centric network.

network drive pointer — A network drive pointer is a letter that is assigned to a location on a NetWare server and controlled by NetWare, normally G: through Z:.

Network Driver Interface Specifications (NDIS) — A set of standard specifications developed by Microsoft to allow network card suppliers to interface their network cards with the Microsoft Windows operating system.

network file system — The logical organizational structure of file storage on network volumes.

network interface card (NIC) — An adapter card that attaches a computer system to the physical network cable system.

network interface card (NIC) driver — The software that controls a network interface card (NIC) and access to the network.

network layer — An OSI software layer that is responsible for routing packets between different networks.

network layout — The physical topology of the network cable system.

network media — The method used to carry electronic signals from one computer to another.

network operating system (NOS) — The software used to provide services to client workstations.

network shell — The workstation software component that carries out session- and presentation-layer functions on the workstation.

network standards — Agreements about how to operate the network.

network topology — The physical geometry or layout of the network cable system. Common topologies include ring, bus, and star.

network variables — Login script variables that contain the workstation's network and node address information.

NETX — An early redirector type of network shell for workstations.

Normal (N) — A NetWare file attribute used to identify files that have no attributes set.

Novell Client — Novell's current network shell, in versions for DOS/Windows 3.1, Windows 95/98, and Windows NT. The Novell Client for Windows 95/98 is written as a requester and uses 32-bit code to speed up its performance.

Novell Directory Services (NDS) — The main administrative architecture for NetWare 5.0, NDS is a database to store information about network resources combined with tools to use the data. The database is called the Directory database or just the Directory. NDS was formerly called NetWare Directory Services, but the name was changed to reflect a use of NDS on systems besides NetWare.

Novell Distributed Print Services (NDPS) — The native architecture for managing printers and print jobs in NetWare 5.0.

Novell Peripheral Architecture (NPA) — A driver architecture introduced in NetWare 4.1. Using NPA, drivers are broken into two parts—the Host

Adapter Module (HAM) and the Custom Device Module (CDM).

Novell Storage Services (NSS) — An optional storage architecture (and NLM) that better supports extremely large (up to terabytes) volumes than previously practical with NetWare.

NuBus — An expansion slot used on Macintosh computers to allow adapter cards to be plugged into the system board.

null modem cable — A special type of RS232 cable used to connect two DTE computers without using a modem.

object — When referring to NDS, a representation of a network resource in the Directory database, that appears as an icon in the Directory tree. NDS objects can be associated with physical entities and logical entities.

object dialog box — A dialog box that displays data about an NDS object, and allows you to manage that data.

Object rights — The set of rights to NDS objects that can be granted to a trustee. Object rights include Supervisor (S), Browse (B), Create (C), Delete (D), and Rename (R).

Open Data Interface (ODI) — A set of standard specifications developed by Novell to allow network card suppliers to interface their network cards with multiple protocols including the IPX protocol used with the NetWare operating system.

Open Systems Interconnect (OSI) model — A model for developing network systems consisting of the following seven layers: application, presentation, session, transport, network, data link, and physical.

optical disk — A type of high-capacity storage medium used for long-term storage in data migration systems.

Organization object — An NDS container object used to organize the structure of the Directory tree, the Organization object can contain Organizational Unit objects and leaf objects.

organizational entity — When referring to NDS, a logical entity that models the structure of an organization.

Organizational Role object — An NDS User-related leaf object used in the Directory tree to manage users' privileges by associating them with specific positions, such as president, vice president, and so on, in an organizational structure. The privileges are assigned to the Organizational Role object, and the users assigned to that role inherit those privileges.

Organizational Unit object — An NDS container object used to organize the structure of the Directory tree, the Organizational Unit object can contain other Organizational Unit objects and leaf objects.

packet — A group of consecutive bits sent from one computer to another over a network.

packet burst mode — A packet transmission technique used by NetWare workstation clients to provide faster communication by acknowledging a group of packets from the server rather than acknowledging each packet separately.

packet signature — A security technique used by NetWare workstation clients that places a unique packet signature on each packet, making it possible for NetWare to be sure the packet came from an authorized workstation.

page — Any screen in an object dialog box that displays data about an NDS object.

parallel port — A communications interface that transfers eight or more bits of information at one time.

parent — When referring to NDS, a designated container level that has other container levels subordinate to it (farther away from the [Root]). The subordinate container levels are called the *children*. When referring to the network file system, a data set such as a directory or subdirectory.

parent partition — When referring to NDS, a partition that is above (closest to the [Root]) another partition called a *child partition*, in the Directory tree structure.

parity bit — A ninth bit added to a byte for error-checking purposes.

partial directory path — Identifies the location of a file or directory by specifying all directories and subdirectories starting from the user's current default directory location. Also called a *relative directory path*.

partition — When referring to NDS, a logical division of the Directory database based on the Directory tree structure.

partitioning — When referring to hard drives in NetWare server or user workstation, a method of allocating storage space on a disk drive to an operating system.

patch — A supplementary program written to correct a problem discovered in NetWare. Also known as a Service Pack.

patch cable — A cable segment used to connect a network card to the main cable system.

patch panel — A panel that consists of a connector for each cable segment that is used to connect the desired cable segments together using a central hub.

PC workstation — A personal computer (PC) used by an end user.

PCI bus — A high-speed expansion bus developed by Intel for use in Pentium-based computer systems.

peer-to-peer — A network system in which each computer can act as both a server and client.

Peripheral Component Interconnect — or **Interface (PCI) bus** — The current expansion bus design by Intel that is used in older 80486, Pentium, Pentium MMX, and Pentium Pro computers. It is a local bus design that moves data at 60 to 66 MHz.

peripherals — External devices such as printers, monitors, and disk drives.

physical address — A unique hexadecimal network interface card (NIC) address coded into the NICs electronics. This first part of the address identifies the manufacturer, and the second part is a unique number for that manufacturer.

physical entity — When referring to NDS, a network resource that has a physical existence, such as a NetWare server (*see* logical entity).

physical layer — The lowest layer of the OSI model consisting of the cable system and connectors.

pixel — A picture element, the smallest point on a monitor screen that can be addressed individually for color changes, etc.

presentation layer — The OSI layer that is responsible for the translation and encoding of data to be transferred over a network system.

PowerPC processor — A microprocessor built by Motorola, IBM, and Apple for use in Apple and other vendors' PCs as an alternative to Intel microprocessors.

primary time server (PTS) — When designated a primary time server (PTS), a NetWare server synchronizes the official network time by working with all other primary time servers and any reference time server (RTS) on the network.

print data — The material to be printed.

print job — Print jobs are items in a print queue just as files are items in a directory. Print jobs contain data and printing parameters in a format that can be sent by a print server to a printer.

print queue — A holding area in which print jobs are kept until the printer is available to print them. In NetWare, a print queue is a subdirectory on an assigned volume.

print server — The software component of the network printing environment that makes printing happen by taking jobs from a print queue and sending them to a printer. In NetWare a print server can support up to 16 printers.

Printer Agent object — An NDS object representing the software that manages a particular printer. There is a one-to-one correspondence with a printer agent and a printer.

printer function — A specific escape code sequence that causes the printer to perform one specific operation such as setting landscape mode.

printer mode — A printer mode is a configuration setting for a printer that consists of one or more functions.

Printer object — An NDS Printer-related leaf object used in the Directory tree to manage printers.

printer-related leaf objects — A group of NDS Directory tree objects, including the Printer object, the Print Queue object, and the Print Server object, that are used to managed the NetWare print services.

profile login script — A login script stored in a Profile object, and used by all users assigned that script.

Profile object — An NDS User-related leaf object used in the Directory tree to manage users' login scripts. The login script is stored in the Profile object, and the users assigned to that profile use the login script.

property — When referring to NDS, an aspect of an NDS object, such as the user's last name for the User object. An actual user's last name—for example, Burns—is the property value.

Property rights — The set of rights to the properties of an NDS object that can be granted to a trustee. Object rights include Supervisor (S), Compare (C), Read (R), Write (W), and Add or Delete Self (A).

property value — When referring to NDS, an actual value of an NDS object property. For example, the user's last name is a property of the User object, and an actual user's last name—for example, Burns—is the property value.

protected mode — The mode used by 80286 and above processor chips that allows access to up to 16 MB of memory and the ability to run multiple programs in memory without one program conflicting with another.

protocol stack — The software used to send and receive packets among networked computers.

[Public] — A special trustee, [Public] is similar to a group. When [Public] is made a trustee of an object, every object in the NDS Directory tree inherits the [Public] rights. In addition, [Public] rights are available to users who are not even logged into the Directory tree, as long as they have a Novell Client running on their computer.

Purge (P) — A NetWare file or directory attribute that specifies the storage space of a file that is to be immediately made available for reuse by the server.

QMS (Queue Management Services) — An older NetWare print architecture now replaced by NDPS in NetWare 5.0.

RAM shadowing — A method of increasing computer system performance by copying instructions from slower ROM to high-speed RAM.

random-access memory (RAM) — The main work memory of the computer that is used to store program instructions and data currently being processed. The contents of RAM are erased when a computer's power is interrupted or switched off.

Read Only (Ro) — A NetWare file attribute that prevents data in a file from being erased or changed.

read-only memory (ROM) — Memory that is set at the computer factory and cannot be erased. ROM is used to store startup and hardware control instructions for your computer.

read-only replica — When referring to NDS, a copy of the master replica that can only be read from, not written to, and cannot be used for login purposes.

Read right (R) — When referring to NDS, the Property right that enables a trustee to see the property values of an object. When referring to the network file system, a Directory and File right that allows a user to open and read data from a file or run programs.

Read Write (Rw) — A NetWare file attribute that allows data in a file to be modified or appended to.

read/write replica — When referring to NDS, a copy of the master replica that can only be read from and written to, and can be used for login purposes.

Real mode — The processing mode used by 8088 computers.

record locking — A NetWare feature that allows a multiuser application program to prevent network users from accessing a specific database record in a file while it is being updated.

recording tracks — The concentric circular areas on a disk where data is stored.

redirector — A type of network shell that checks workstation operations to see if the operation requires workstation or network resources. *See* requester.

reduced instruction set computer (RISC) — A computer with a microprocessor that uses instructions in a uniform format that require only one clock cycle to complete. A RISC workstation provides high performance for CAD workstations and scientific applications by using a simplified and highly efficient set of instructions that lends itself to parallel processing.

redundant array of inexpensive disks (RAID) — A method of writing data across several disks that provides fault tolerance.

reference time server (RTS) — A NetWare server that is connected to an "official" time source, such as an atomic clock. Reference time servers synchronize with every primary time server (PTS), but don't change their time, which forces the PTSs to change theirs.

register — A storage location inside the microprocessor unit.

regular drive pointer — A network drive pointer that is normally assigned to a file storage directory on the NetWare server.

relative directory path — Identifies the location of a file or directory by specifying all directories and subdirectories starting from the user's current default directory location. Also called a *partial directory path*.

relative distinguished name — When referring to an NDS object, an object's distinguished name is its complete name, which is the object's common name plus the object's context. A distinguished name always shows the path to the object from the [Root]. An example of a distinguished name is *.EFranklin.FDR_Admin.FDR*. An object's relative distinguished name specifies the path to the object from an object other than the [Root]. An example of a relative distinguished name is *EFranklin.FDR_Admin*. Note that there is no leading period, because the path is not from the [Root].

remote printer — A printer attached to a port of a networked workstation and controlled by the print server. In NetWare, remote printing is done by running the RPRINTER software on each workstation that supports a network printer.

Rename Inhibit (Ri) — A NetWare file or directory attribute that prevents changing the name of the file or directory.

Rename right (R) — When referring to NDS, the Object right that enables a user to change the object's name.

repeater — A network device that allows multiple network cable segments to be connected.

replica — When referring to NDS, a copy of a partition. There are four types of replicas: master, read/write, read-only, and subordinate reference.

replica synchronization — When referring to NDS, the process of updating all replicas of a partition so that they are consistent.

requester — A type of network shell that is called by the workstation's operating systems when network resources are needed. *See* redirector.

resolution — A measurement of the number of bits on a display screen. Higher resolution provides better screen images.

rights — When referring to NDS or the network file system, the type of access that has been granted or assigned to a user, who is called a *trustee*. In NDS there are Object rights and Property rights, while the network file system has Directory rights and File rights.

ring topology — A topology in which the cable runs to each computer and then back to the first, forming a circle.

[Root] — The starting point of a hierarchical structure, such as a tree, that starts at one point (the [Root]) and branches out from the starting point. When referring to NDS, [Root] is the [Root] object.

root drive pointer — A regular drive pointer that appears to DOS and application software as if it were the beginning or "root" of a drive or volume.

[Root] object — When referring to NDS, the starting point of the Directory tree.

[Root] partition — When referring to NDS, the partition of the Directory tree that contains the [Root] object.

rotational delay — The time required for a disk sector to make a complete circle and arrive at the disk drive's read/write head.

router — A device used to connect more complex networks consisting of different topologies. Routers operate at the network layer.

RS232 — A serial communication standard developed by the Electronics Industry Association that specifies which voltage levels and functions are to be used with the 24-pin interface.

scaleability — The capability to work with systems of different sizes.

scheduling applications — Software applications used to create and maintain personal and workgroup time schedules.

SCSI-2 — An advanced version of the SCSI controller specification that allows for higher speed and more device types.

search drive pointer — A network drive pointer that has been added to the DOS path. Search drives are usually assigned to directories containing software to make the software available to run from any other location.

secondary time server (STS) — A NetWare server that gets network time from other time servers, and then sends the time to workstations.

sector — A physical recording area on a disk recording track. Each recording track is divided into multiple recording sectors in order to provide direct access to data blocks.

security equivalence — An NDS object assignment that grants one object the same set of rights as another object.

seek time — A measurement of the amount of time required to move the recording head to the specified disk track or cylinder.

segment — When referring to packets on a network, the name of an information packet at the transport layer. When referring to the physical network structure, a single cable run.

Sequenced Packet eXchange (SPX) — The NetWare protocol that operates at the transport layer.

serial port — A communication port that sends one bit of data per time interval.

server — A network computer used for a special purpose such as storing files, controlling printing, or running network application software.

server-centric — A network in which a user logs into each network server in the network that he or she needs access to, rather than logging in only once to the network itself in a network-centric network.

server duplexing — A fault tolerance technique that uses two identical servers so that if one goes down, the other is still available.

server-related leaf objects — A group of NDS Directory tree objects, including the NetWare Server object, the Volume object and the Directory Map object, that are used to manage NetWare servers, the network file system, and drive mappings.

SERVER.EXE — The core of the NetWare network operating system. When SERVER.EXE is started, the NetWare NOS replaces DOS as the NetWare server's operating system.

Service Advertising Packet (SAP) — SAPs are broadcast from each NetWare server on the network and identify the server's name and network location. SAPs are used to create and maintain entries in the router tables.

service message block (SMB) — One component of Microsoft's NetBEUI protocol.

service request charge — In NetWare accounting, a charge to a user account for using NetWare server services.

session layer — The OSI software layer that establishes and maintains a communication session with the host computer.

SET commands — NetWare console commands used to control NetWare performance parameters.

Sharable (S) — A NetWare file attribute that allows multiple users to access or update data in a file at the same time.

shielded twisted-pair (STP) cable — A type of twisted-pair cable that has electromagnetic shielding, and is thus less susceptible to external electrical interference.

single in-line memory module (SIMM) — A memory circuit that consists of multiple chips and provides the system board with memory expansion capabilities.

single reference time server (SRTS) — A NetWare server that provides the only time source on the network. The time on an SRTS is set by the network administrator.

single-user application — A software package that is designed to operate from the user's workstation, and is limited to being used by only one user at a time.

small computer system interface (SCSI) — A general-purpose controller card bus that can be used to attach disk drives, CD-ROMs, tape drives, and other external devices to a computer system.

snAppShot — A Z.E.N.works utility that captures the installation configuration for a given application so that this install can be replicated to workstations automatically.

source tree — When two Directory trees are being merged, the source tree is the tree that is merged into the combined Directory tree, and thus loses its original name.

spanning — A technique available with NetWare that allows a volume to be expanded by adding space from up to 32 disk drives.

star topology — A cable system in which the cables radiate out from central hubs.

STARTUP.NCF — A NetWare Command File (NCF) that is run when the server is booting up but before SERVER.EXE is started. It is limited to commands that can be run with the resources on the DOS partition of the NetWare server.

static RAM (SRAM) — Static RAM provides high-speed memory that can operate at CPU speeds without the use of wait states. SRAM chips are often used on high-speed computers in order to increase system performance by storing the most frequently used memory bytes.

Storage Management System (SMS) — The SMS consists of several NLMs along with workstation software that enables the host computer to back up data from one or more target devices by using the SBACKUP NLM.

subdirectory — When referring to the network file system, a division of a directory.

subnetwork — A separate logical network based on a specific frame type. For example, if the network is using both the 802.3 and 802.3 frame types, there are two subnetworks.

subordinate — Below or under. When referring to NDS, a child partition is a partition that is below (farther away from the [Root]) another partition, called a *parent partition*, in the Directory tree structure. The child partition is subordinate to the parent partition.

subordinate reference replica — When referring to NDS, a copy of the master replica that is automatically generated by NetWare 5.0 to make sure that a child partition has a replica on a NetWare server that has a replica of the child's parent partition. The subordinate reference replica is not-modifiable. Subordinate reference replicas are used to ensure that there are sufficient replicas of all partitions.

subtree — An NDS container object that contains leaf objects.

SuperVGA (SVGA) — Video systems that provide higher resolutions (800 × 600 pixels and greater) and additional color combinations (up to 16.7 million colors) than the VGA systems.

Supervisor right (S) — A NetWare access right that provides a user with all rights to an NDS object and its properties and the entire directory structure. Once assigned, the supervisory right cannot be restricted on the network file systems (Directory and File rights), but it can be restricted for NDS rights (Object and Property rights).

Supervisor utility — A command line or menu utility that is normally stored in the SYS:SYSTEM directory and requires supervisor privileges to run.

switching power supply — A power supply used with most computers that will cut off power in the event of an electrical problem.

synchronous communication — A serial communication system that sends data in blocks or packets where each packet includes necessary control and error checking bits.

synchronous dynamic random access memory (SDRAM) — High-speed random access memory (RAM) technology that can synchronize itself with the clock speed of the CPU's data bus. Used on high-end systems.

syntax — The rules of a programming language and of NetWare login scripts.

System (S) — A NetWare file attribute used to flag system files.

system board — The main circuit board of a computer system that contains the CPU, memory, and expansion bus (also called the *motherboard*).

system console — The monitor and keyboard on a network server.

system console security — A security system that prevents unauthorized users from accessing the system console.

target — A workstation or NetWare server that has data that is being backed up by a host server.

Target Service Agent (TSA) — NetWare software that helps handle data transfers between a target and host server during backups.

target tree — When two Directory trees are being merged, the target tree is the tree that maintains its identity in the combined Directory tree, and thus keeps its original name.

terminals — User workstations that connect to a mainframe computer or minicomputer without a CPU of their own so that the mainframe computer or minicomputer must do all processing.

ThickNet — Also called 10Base5, an Ethernet network system that uses a heavier coaxial cable than ThinNet.

ThinNet — An Ethernet network system that uses T-connectors to attach networked computers to the RG-58 coaxial cable system.

tick — A time measurement representing $\frac{1}{18}$ of a second.

time variables — Login script variables that contain system time information such as hour, minute, and a.m./p.m.

token — A special packet that is sent from one computer to the next in order to control which computer can transmit when using a token passing channel access method.

token passing method — A channel access method that requires a computer to obtain the token packet before transmitting data on the network cable system.

topology — The geometry of a network cable system.

tracks — Circular recording areas on a disk surface.

trailing period — When referring to an NDS object, a period that appears after an object's common name or other object name in the object's distinguished name or context. The trailing period indicates a shift up one level in the Directory tree. In the context *.Admin_FDR.FDR*, the period after *Admin_FDR* is a trailing period.

Transaction Tracking System (TTS) — A NetWare fault tolerance system that returns database records to their original value if a client computer system fails while processing a transaction.

Transactional (T) — A NetWare file attribute that enables Transaction Tracking on a database file.

transfer time — The time required to transfer a block of data to or from a disk sector.

Transmission Control Protocol/Internet Protocol (TCP/IP) — TCP/IP is the most common communication protocol used to connect heterogeneous computers over both local and wide area networks. In addition to being used on the Internet, the Unix operating system uses TCP/IP to communicate between host computers and file servers. Today, NetWare 5.0 uses TCP/IP as its native protocol, with IPX/SPX an option.

transport layer — The OSI layer responsible for reliable delivery of a packet to the receiving computer by requiring some sort of acknowledgment.

trustee — A user given access to NDS object and network file system directories and files. Access is given when rights are assigned or granted to the user or another NDS object that the user is associated with.

trustee assignments — The set of NDS or file system rights granted to user.

trustee list — The set of trustee assignments for an NDS object or network file system directory or file.

trustee rights — The set of NDS or file system privileges that can be assigned to users.

twisted-pair wire — Cable consisting of pairs of wires twisted together to reduce errors.

typeful name — When referring to an NDS object, when an object's distinguished name is written with name type abbreviations, it's referred to as a typeful name. An example of a typeful name is .CN=*EFranklin*.OU=*FDR_Admin*.O=*FDR*.

typeless name — When referring to an NDS object, when an object's distinguished name is written without name type abbreviations, it's referred to as a typeless name. An example of a typeless name is .*EFranklin*.*FDR_Admin*.*FDR*.

UIMPORT — A DOS-based utility that can import large numbers of users into NDS rather than having to key each user in individually.

unbounded media — Signals that are sent through the air or space.

uninterruptible power system (UPS) — A battery backup power system that can continue to supply power to a computer for a limited time in the event of a commercial power failure.

Universal Data Format (UDF) — A specification for how data is stored on storage media. Originally intended for all storage devices, it is most commonly used on CD-ROM and DVD-ROM discs.

Universal Naming Convention (UNC) — A systematic specification of a location in the file system in the form: \\ServerName\Volume\Directory\Subdirectory

Universal Serial Bus (USB) — An upgraded specification for the venerable serial port providing for multiple devices to be attached on the same port and at higher speeds than before.

Unknown object — An NDS Miscellaneous object used in the Directory tree to identify corrupted objects that cannot be recognized by NDS.

unshielded twisted-pair (UTP) cable — A type of twisted-pair cable that has no electromagnetic shielding, and is thus susceptible to external electrical interference.

upper memory — The memory above 640 KB used by controller cards as well as by DOS when loading device drivers into high memory.

user account manager — A user account name that has been assigned one or more user accounts or groups to manage.

user login script — A login script stored in a User object, and executed for only a single user.

User object — An NDS User-related leaf object used in the Directory tree to manage network users.

user-related leaf objects — A group of NDS Directory tree objects, including the User object, the Group object, the Organizational Role object, and the Profile object, that are used to manage network users.

USER_TEMPLATE User object — An NDS object that allows you to specify property values that will be used whenever a User object is created.

user variables — Login script variables that contain information about the currently logged in user, such as the user's login name, full name, or the hexadecimal ID given to the user.

users — The people who use PC workstations to do their jobs.

vertical application — A software application that is designed for a specific type of processing. Vertical applications are often unique to a certain type of business such as a dental billing system or an auto parts inventory system.

VESA bus — An older fast local bus expansion bus designed by the Video Electronics Standards Association, now largely replaced by PCI.

video graphics array (VGA) — A standard video circuit used in many conventional PCs that provides up to 640 × 320 resolution and up to 256 different colors.

virtual file allocation table (VFAT) — A 32-bit extension to the standard FAT introduced in Windows 95/98 and MS-DOS 7.0.

Virtual Loadable Module (VLM) — A NetWare software component used in the NetWare DOS Requester network shell. VLMs can be loaded as necessary to provide exactly the needed network capabilities for each workstation.

virtual memory — Allows the computer system to use its disk drive as if it were RAM, by swapping between disk and memory.

virtual real mode — An instruction mode available in 80386 and above microprocessors that allows access to 2 GB of memory and concurrent DOS programs running at the same time.

volume — The major division of the NetWare file system consisting of the physical storage space on one or more hard drives or CD-ROMs of a file server. A volume can span up to 32 disk segments with a maximum capacity of 32 terabytes. Up to 64 volumes can exist on a file server.

Volume object — An NDS Server-related leaf object used in the Directory tree to manage volumes on NetWare servers.

wait state — A clock cycle in which the CPU does no processing. This allows the slower DRAM memory chips to respond to requests from the CPU.

wide area network (WAN) — Two or more local area networks in geographically separated locations connected by telephone lines.

width — When referring to the NDS Directory tree, the number of branches at any level of the tree—particularly the first (*see* depth).

word size — The number of bits in the microprocessor's registers.

workgroup manager — A user account that has the privilege to create new users and groups and to be an account manager to the users created.

workstation — Generally used as a term for PC workstation; also refers to RISC workstations that run the Unix operating system and are sold for graphics-intensive uses such as CAD.

workstation variables — Login script variables that contain information about the workstation's environment such as machine type, operating system, operating system version, and station node address.

Write right (W) — When referring to NDS, a Property right that enables a trustee to change, add, or delete the value of the property. When referring to the network file system, the NetWare Directory or File right that allows a user to change or add data to a file.

XGA (eXtended Graphics Array) — A new specification for monitors, chiefly used on portable and notebook computers.

Z.E.N.works — A NetWare tool that leverages the NDS database to provide automated distribution of software titles to desktops as well as the ability to manage those desktops remotely.

Index